Commercial Design Using AutoCAD 2027

Daniel John Stine

SDC PUBLICATIONS

SDC Publications
P.O. Box 1334
Mission, KS 66222
913-262-2664
www.SDCpublications.com
Publisher: Stephen Schroff

Examination Copies
Books received as examination copies are for review purposes only and may not be made available for student use. Resale of examination copies is prohibited.

Electronic Files
Any electronic files associated with this book are licensed to the original user only. These files may not be transferred to any other party.

Trademarks
AutoCAD is a registered trademark of Autodesk, Inc. Autodesk screen shots reprinted with the permission of Autodesk, Inc. All other trademarks are trademarks of their respective holders.

Disclaimer
The author and publisher of this book have used their best efforts in preparing this book. These efforts include the development, research and testing of the material presented. The author and publisher shall not be liable in any event for incidental or consequential damages with, or arising out of, the furnishing, performance, or use of the material.

ISBN-13: 978-1-63057-839-8
ISBN-10: 1-63057-839-8

Printed and bound in the United States of America.

Foreword

To the Student:
The intent of this book is to provide the student with a solid knowledge of Computer Aided Drafting (CAD) tools and techniques for use in both school and industry. The student is not expected to have any prior knowledge of AutoCAD or Architectural Drafting to successfully complete this textbook.

It is strongly recommended that this book is completed in lesson order. Many (pretty much all) exercises utilize drawings created in previous lessons.

To the Instructor:
This textbook is an introductory level tutorial which uses commercial design exercises as the means to teach AutoCAD 2027. The student begins a campus library floor plan. Using step-by-step tutorial lessons, the library project is followed through to create FFE plans, interior elevations, schedules, and details. Throughout the project, new AutoCAD commands and design concepts are covered at the appropriate time. Focus is placed on the most essential parts of a command rather than an exhaustive review of every sub-feature of a particular command.

An Instructor's Resource Guide is available with this book. It contains:

- Answers to the questions at the end of each chapter
- Outline of tools & topics to be covered in each lesson's lecture
- Suggestions for additional student work (for each lesson)

Errata:
Please check the publisher's website from time to time for any errors or typos found in this book after it went to the printer. Simply browse to www.SDCpublications.com, and then navigate to the page for this book. Click the **View/Submit errata** link in the upper right corner of the page. If you find an error, please submit it so we can correct it in the next edition.

About the Author:
Dan Stine is a registered Architect (WI) with over twenty years of experience in the architectural field. He is the Director of Design Technology at the top-ranked architecture firm Lake Flato in San Antonio, Texas. Dan has worked in a total of five firms. While at these firms, he has participated in collaborative projects with several other firms on various projects (including the late Cesar Pelli, Weber Music Hall – University of Minnesota - Duluth). Dan is a member of the *American Institute of Architects* (AIA), *Construction Specification Institute* (CSI). He taught *AutoCAD* and *Revit Architecture* classes for 12 years at Lake Superior College and currently teaches Revit to graduate Architecture students at North Dakota State University (NDSU); additionally, he is a Certified Construction Document Technician (CDT). He has presented at *Autodesk University* in Las Vegas (http://au.autodesk.com) and internationally via the *Revit Technology Conference* (http://www.dbeinstitute.org).

Mr. Stine has written the following textbooks (published by SDC Publications):

- *Residential Design Using Autodesk Revit 2027*
- *Commercial Design Using Autodesk Revit 2027*
- *Design Integration Using Autodesk Revit 2027 (Architecture, Structure and MEP)*
- *Interior Design Using Autodesk Revit 2027*
- *Residential Design Using AutoCAD 2027*
- *Chapters in Architectural Drawing*
- *Interior Design Using Hand Sketching, SketchUp and Photoshop*
- *SketchUp 2024 for Interior Designers*
- *Microsoft Office Specialist, Excel Associate 365/2019, Exam Preparation*
- *Microsoft Office Specialist, Word Associate 365/2019, Introduction & Exam Preparation*
- *Microsoft Office Specialist, PowerPoint Associate 365/2019, Introduction & Exam Preparation*

You may contact the publisher with comments or suggestions at service@SDCpublications.com.

Table of Contents

Online Content

Lesson 1
Getting Started with AutoCAD 2027:

This chapter will introduce you to AutoCAD 2027. You will study the User Interface (UI); you will also learn how to open and exit a drawing and adjust the view of the drawing on the screen. It is recommended that the student spend an ample amount of time learning this material, as it will greatly enhance your ability to progress smoothly through subsequent lessons.

Exercise 1-1:
What is AutoCAD 2027?

What is AutoCAD 2027?

AutoCAD 2027 is the world's standard 2D Computer Aided Design (CAD) software. AutoCAD 2027 is a product of Autodesk, which also makes Revit, AutoCAD Architecture and 3DS Max to name a few. The Autodesk company web site (www.autodesk.com) claims more than 8 million users in over 100 countries. Autodesk's thousands of employees create products available in many languages.

What is AutoCAD 2027 used for?

AutoCAD 2027 is used by virtually every industry that creates technical drawings.

Just a small sampling of AutoCAD users includes industries like these:

Construction
(Architects, Manufacturers and Contractors)
Aviation
Management
Automotive
Ship Design
Facilities
Media and Entertainment

Why use AutoCAD 2027?

Many people ask the question, why use AutoCAD 2027 versus other programs? The answer can certainly vary depending on the situation and particular needs of an individual/organization.

Generally speaking, this is why most companies use AutoCAD:

- Many designers and drafters are using AutoCAD to create highly accurate drawings that can be easily modified.
- As the "standard" CAD software among many industries, transferring drawings (i.e., sharing) is very simple.
- AutoCAD's large set of features and ability to handle very large, complex drawing projects.
- Many people are trained to use AutoCAD, whether at a previous job or in school. An employer is more likely to find an employee trained in the use of AutoCAD than any other CAD program.

Many universities and colleges teach AutoCAD. Many companies require potential employees to know how to use AutoCAD.

Architecture and AutoCAD:

The Architectural profession heavily uses AutoCAD, or AutoCAD Architecture, to create drawings, schedules and presentation materials. A seasoned AutoCAD user can quickly generate several design options for a reception area, for example, and then even create a photo-realistic 3D rendering to show the client.

What about the Architectural Software Programs?

Many architectural firms still use AutoCAD even though there are several software packages that are specifically designed for architecture. The general reason has to do with design tools needed, cost, and staff knowledge of the software.

The architectural programs, like Autodesk Revit and AutoCAD Architecture (ACA), cost quite a bit more than AutoCAD, and for good reason. For example, ACA is built on top of AutoCAD. That means that ACA has everything AutoCAD has plus many additional features geared specifically towards architecture; it stands to reason that ACA would be equal to the cost of AutoCAD plus something for the additional features.

In any case, students are typically first trained using AutoCAD and then they are exposed to the more advanced programs (either in school or industry). This is similar to other programs such as Computer Science, where the student first learns a popular/industry standard program (to focus on the basics) and then, later in the program, tackles advanced languages such as Microsoft .Net.

Installation:

This book is not intended to cover installing AutoCAD on your computer. All the steps and screenshots in this book are based on the default installation, with no modifications unless noted. If needed, in the Windows **Start menu**, under AutoCAD 2027, you can use the **Reset Settings to Default** tool, which will make the program look like it would if just installed from scratch.

New features:

Every version of AutoCAD is usually packed with new features. The goal of this text is to teach you the basics, and if those fundamental tools have changed you will then be learning something unique to this version of the software. But this book is not going to cover a new feature just because it is new – many new features are often intermediate to advanced tools such as the recently added "organic" 3D modeling tools. A new user needs to focus on the basics before jumping in the deep end!

Exercise 1-2:
Overview of AutoCAD 2027 User Interface

AutoCAD is a powerful and sophisticated program. Because of its powerful feature set, it has a measurable learning curve. However, when broken down into smaller pieces, you can easily learn to harness the power of AutoCAD; that is the goal of this book.

This exercise will walk through the different sections of the User Interface (UI). Understanding the user interface is the key to using any program's features.

> ***NOTE:** Make sure the Workspace feature is set to* ***Drafting & Annotation*** *(see pg. 1-10); this will help ensure your screen matches the book images.*

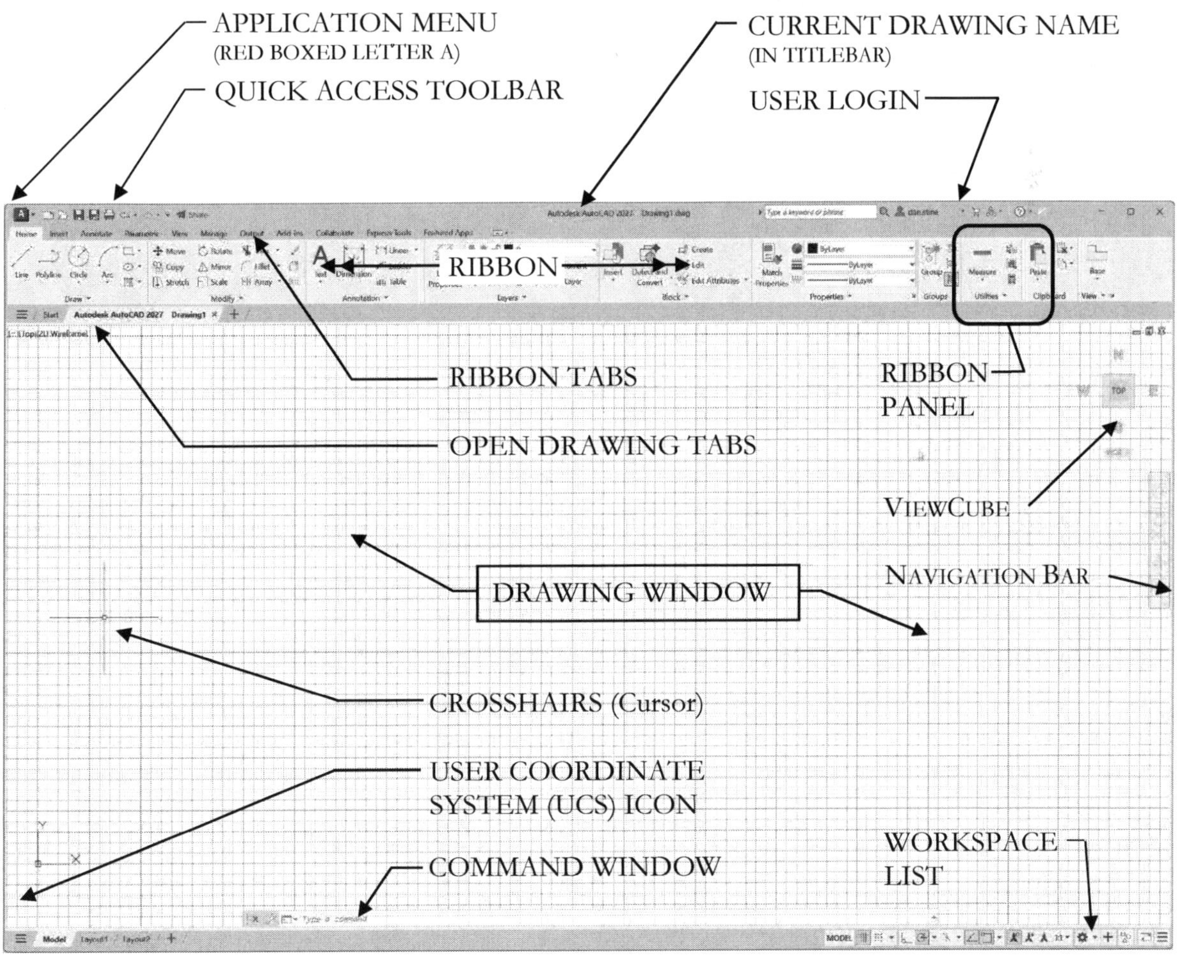

FIGURE 1-2.1
AutoCAD User Interface

The AutoCAD User Interface (the details):

To follow along in this section, you will need to open a drawing from the **Start Tab**—for now, simply click on the **New** button on the left (see image to right). Also note that all the images in this book are based on AutoCAD's **Light** *Color Scheme*, which will be discussed at the end of this section. By default, AutoCAD uses the **Dark** *Color Scheme*; use whichever you prefer.

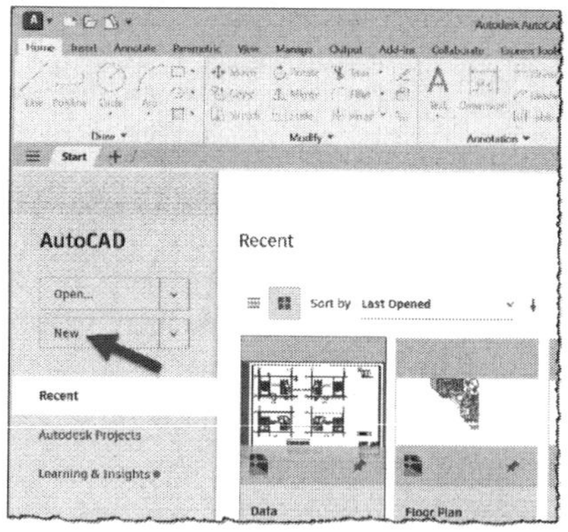

Application Menu: Clicking the red "A" in the upper left reveals several menus and tools. AutoCAD has a series of menus on the left. Click on each of the menus (with an arrow to the right) to explore their contents. The options shown vary depending on whether a drawing or the home screen is active.

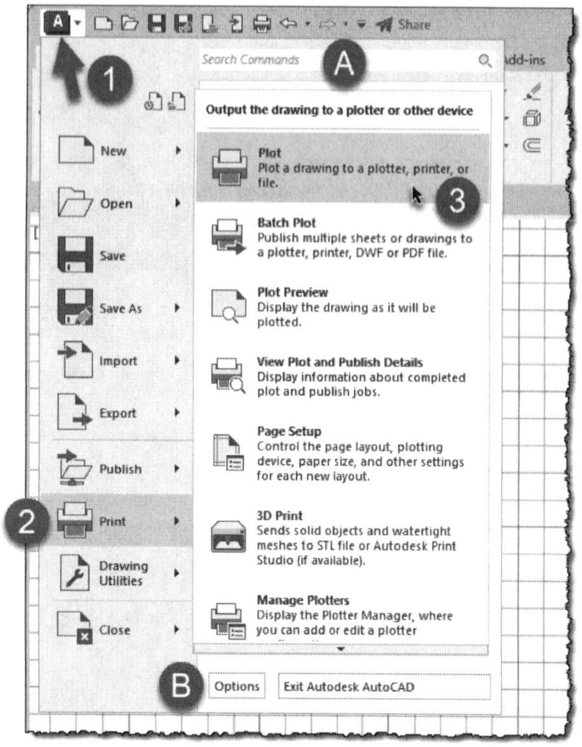

The *Open, Save and Close* commands will be covered in the next exercise.

The numbered clicks, 1-3 in the image, show how to start the **Plot** (aka Print) command – you do not need to click Plot at this time.

Item A:
The *Search* box, highlighted by the letter A, allows you to type in a word to find related commands. For example, try typing "arc" (no need to press Enter) and you will see several items appear. Click the "X" to the right of the search box to clear the search.

Item B:
The *Options* button opens a dialog with a plethora of settings; the new user would do well to avoid changing settings here.

Next, you will explore the *Ribbon* and how the various *Tabs* control the tools displayed there. Again, if your screen does not display these graphics, make sure the "Workspace" is set to **Drafting & Annotation** (see pg. 1-10 for more information).

> ***FYI:*** *You should know that some of the graphics you see in this textbook for the User Interface are new to this version of AutoCAD, so if you are using an older version of the program, you will not have access to the same graphics. (You should use the version of this textbook that matches the version of your software.)*

Now, you will just look at a few of the *Panels* on the **Home** tab.

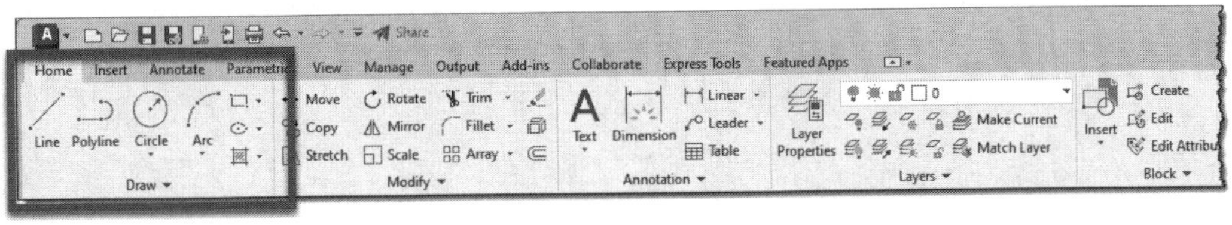

Home → **Draw:**

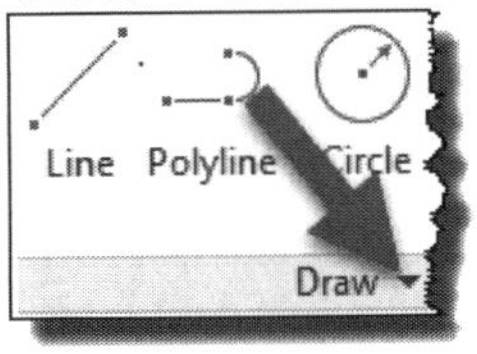

The *Draw* panel, on the *Home* tab, contains commands that allow you to draw basic 2D lines and shapes as well as hatching (hatching is a type of object that fills an area with a pattern).

Expanding panels

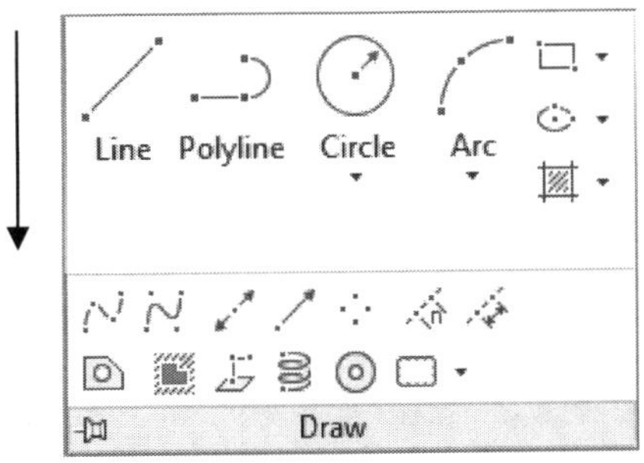

Many *Panels* have additional, but less-used tools, available in a fly-out portion of the *Panel*; you can tell if a *Panel* can be expanded by the little down-arrow (triangle) next to the panel name (see upper example to the left). Clicking anywhere in the bottom "title bar" will expand the *Panel* as shown to the left. Once you click away from the *Panel,* the extended portion will close – unless you click the "pin" icon in the lower left, which will keep the *Panel* expanded until you un-pin it. The remaining example images in this section will only be shown expanded (if available) to save space in this book.

Home → **Modify:**

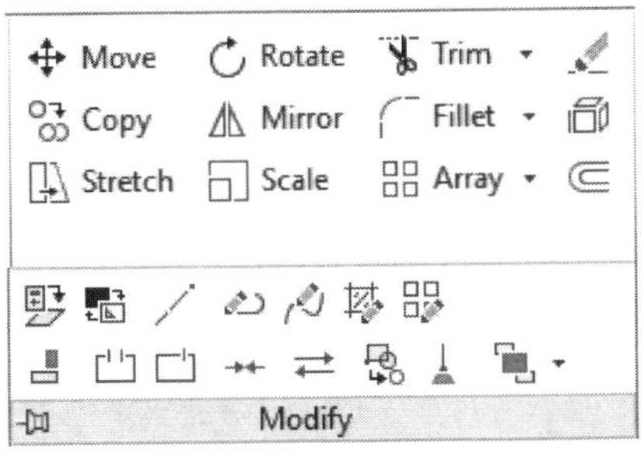

This *Panel* contains commands that modify objects in your drawings: Move, Mirror, Array, Stretch, Copy, Offset, Rotate and Erase.

This book spends a significant amount of time helping you develop a solid understanding of how these tools work; you use these commands throughout the book – practice makes perfect!

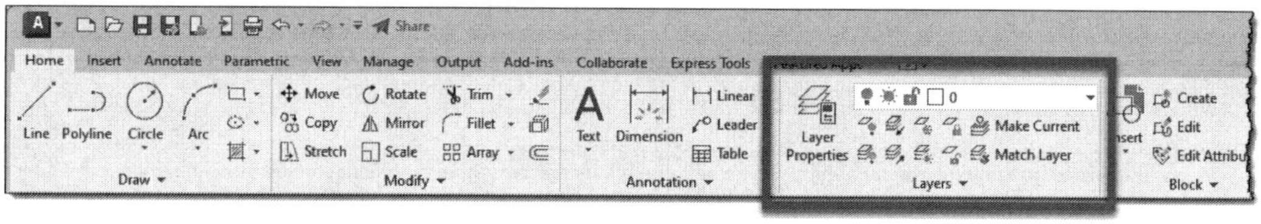

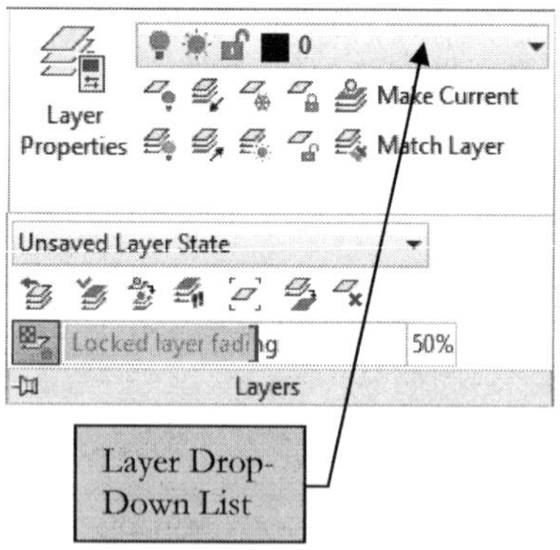

Home → **Layers**:
This *Panel* contains tools for creating and managing drawing *Layers.*

FYI: *Layers allow you to manage the display and the organization of drawing entities; more on this later.*

TIP: *When nothing is selected, the Layer drop-down list displays the current layer; when something is selected, it displays which layer the selected entity is on. (If objects on multiple layers are selected, the display is blank.)*

Drawing Tabs:

Each open drawing file is represented by a tab just below the *Ribbon* (see image below). This allows you to quickly switch between drawings. You can click the "X" to the right of the drawing name to close the file; if the drawing has unsaved changes (indicated by an asterisk next to the name), you will be prompted to save. The plus icon to the right of the last tab allows you to quickly start a new drawing. A right-click presents several options. The Start tab is always visible by default. Finally, hovering your cursor over a tab shows a model/paper space thumbnail preview.

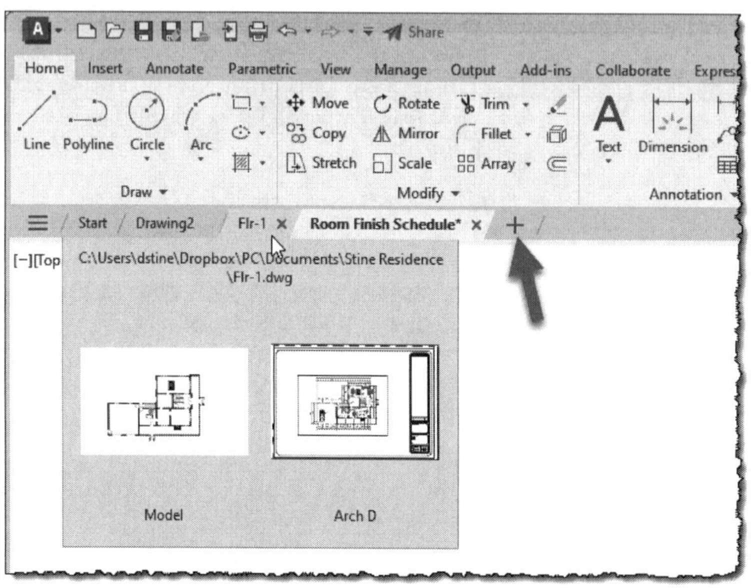

Command Window:

The *Command Window* allows you to type in commands; suggested commands will be listed as you type (Auto Complete). AutoCAD displays options and prompts for specific input for a command. When the main line says, "*Type a command,*" as in the image below, you know there are not any commands active or running. Command history is displayed above the *Command Window*.

TIP: If you accidentally close the Command Window, you can restore it by pressing **Ctrl + 9** *(i.e., press both keys at the same time) on the keyboard.*

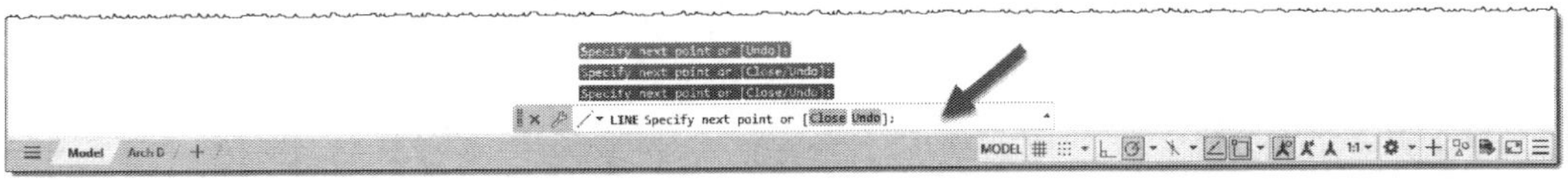

Status Bar:

This area indicates the status of various settings plus the current drawing scale. The icons are buttons which toggle whether that feature is on or not; a blue fill means the tool/feature is active. You can also right click on the buttons to adjust some settings associated with that tool. You may wish to click the **Display Drawing Grid** icon to toggle it off as it is not needed now. The last icon, to the far right, gives you several options related to what tools are displayed on the *Status Bar*.

TIP: When you hover over an icon, a tooltip will appear telling you the name of the icon; this is handy until you learn what the icon for each tool looks like.

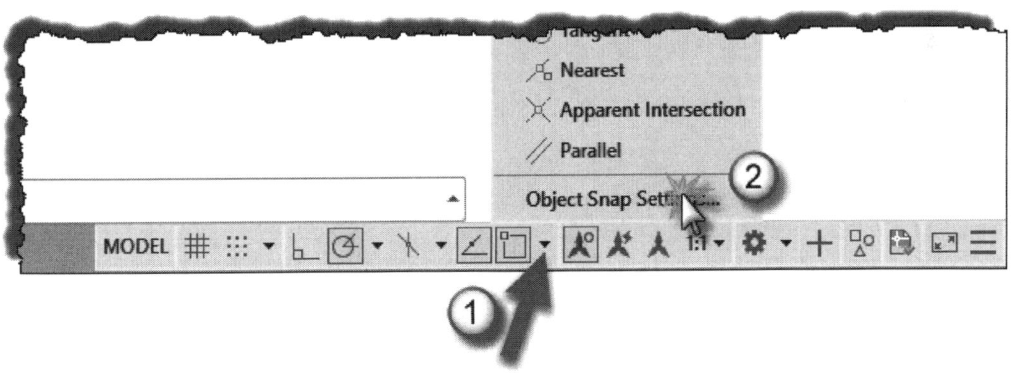

Title Bar: The *Title Bar* lists the program name, when space permits, and then the name of the drawing that is active. The *Quick Access Toolbar*, on the left, gives you convenient access to often-used commands: New, Open, and Save drawing, plus Print, Undo, Redo, & Share (for external collaboration). The area on the right provides quick access to search the *Help System* and App login.

UCS Icon: This symbol helps to keep track of your drawing's orientation relative to the X, Y, Z coordinate system. It also serves as a visual indicator of the current display mode: 2D view, 3D view, perspective, or shade mode, for example.

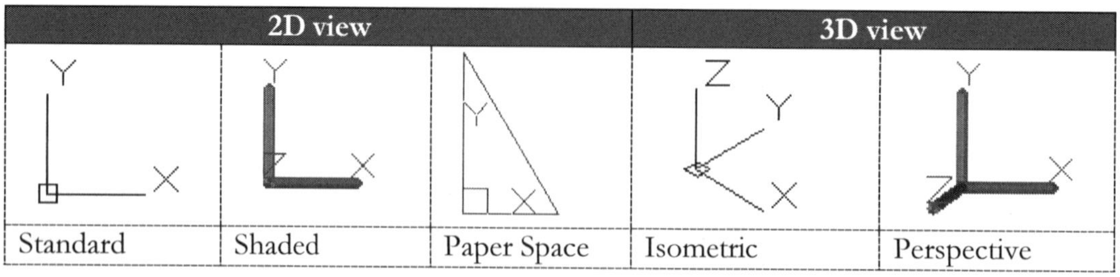

Start Tab: The Start Tab, always available, provides access to relevant information from Autodesk and easy access to recently opened documents. Clicking the large "New" button will open a new drawing based on the default template. Autodesk *Connect* is listed on the right. Finally, helpful links are located in the lower-left corner.

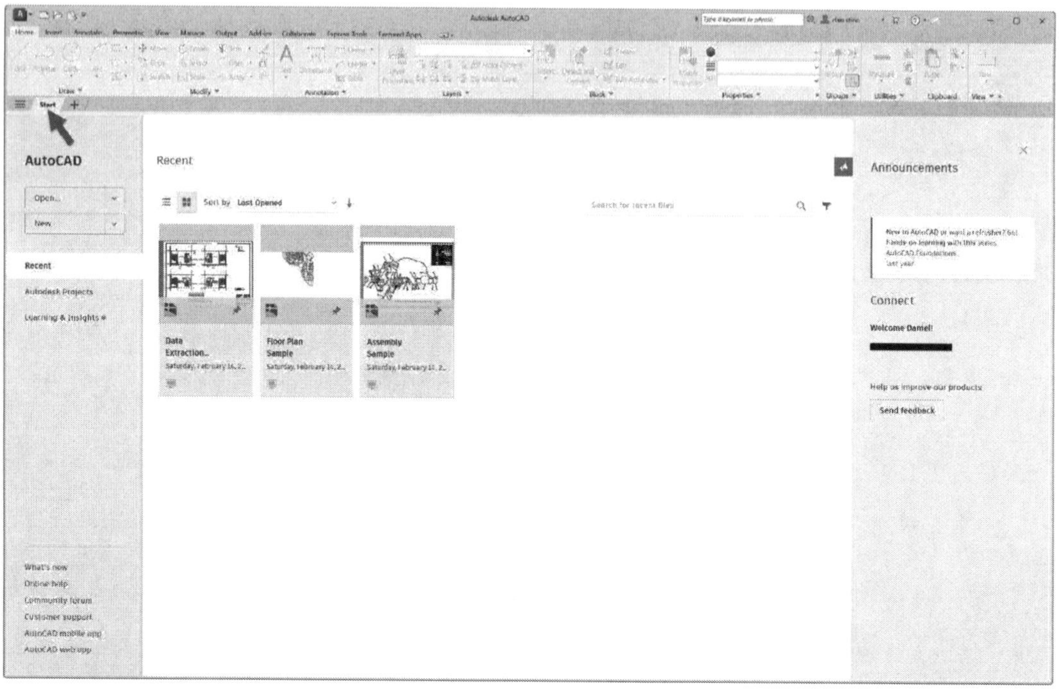

Color Scheme: By default, AutoCAD will start with a "dark" color scheme (see second image below). The author has chosen to use the "light" color theme for the images in this textbook. You are encouraged to use whichever color theme you prefer. If you wish to change it, go to **Application Menu → Options (button) → Display (tab) → Color Scheme** (see image below). Note: the title bar is controlled by the operating system (i.e., Windows); you can right-click on your desktop and select *Personalize* to change it.

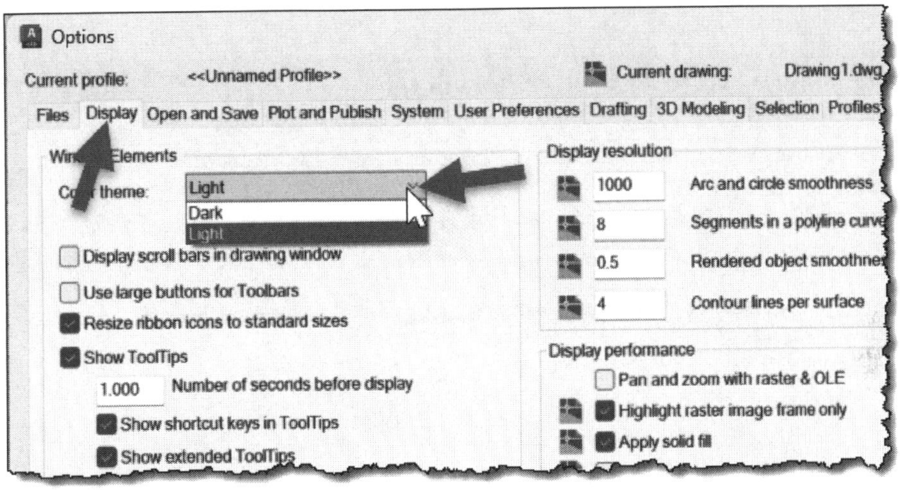

Adjusting the color theme via Options

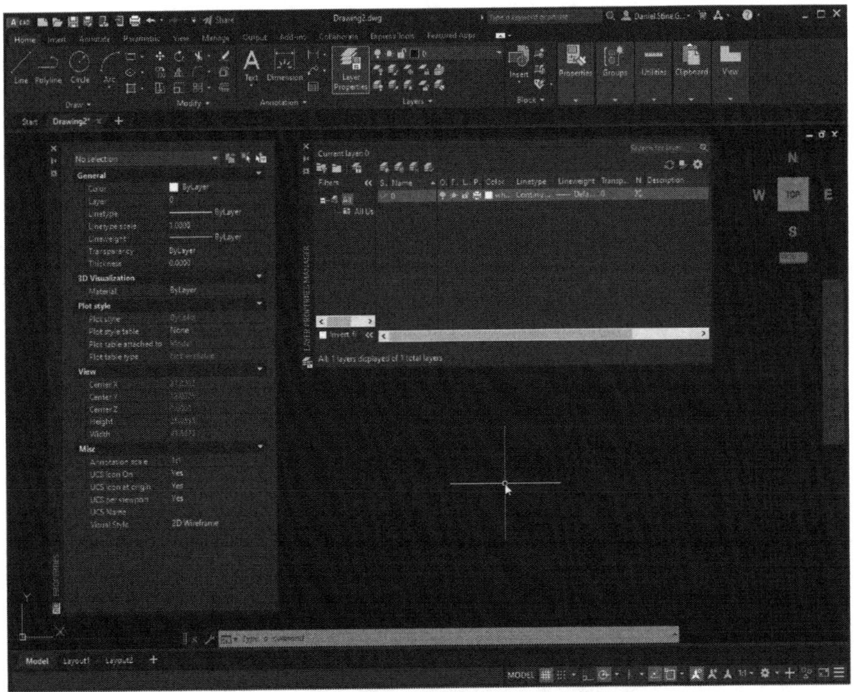

Example of the default dark color theme

Resetting the User Interface:

If the *User Interface* shown in Figure 1-2.1 does not match your computer's display, you can reset it. You, or someone who uses your workstation, may have customized some settings (although settings should be saved by user login). The next steps will describe how to reset the screen configuration.

> **NOTE:** *This step is not necessary to work through this book. It is simply offered for individuals who may have an extremely customized display and want to reset it to make comparing the images in the textbook easier.*

1. **Open AutoCAD** (see Exercise 1-3 for instructions on this).

2. Locate the **Workspace Switching** icon, as shown in Figure 1-2.2.

> **NOTE:** *The* Workspace Switching *icon is located on the* Status Bar *in the lower-right corner of the screen.*

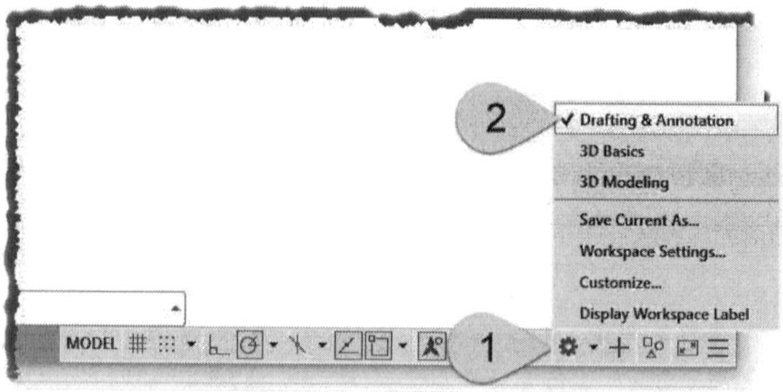

FIGURE 1-2.2 Workspace switching menu – menu shows after clicking down-arrow

3. Click the down arrow and select **Drafting & Annotation** from the pop-up menu.

> **FYI:** *Another option is* **3D Modeling**, *which reorganizes the screen to make the 3D commands readily available (not used in this book). You can try switching to another Workspace to see what it does, just switch back to Drafting & Annotation before moving on.*

Your screen should look similar to Figure 1-2.1. You can reset this at any time to return to a clean slate.

If you are still having problems, you can try resetting the program to its default settings. This will remove any customization applied to the user interface. The tool to reset AutoCAD is found in the *Windows* **Start** menu, not in AutoCAD. With AutoCAD closed, click Start → All → Autodesk → AutoCAD 2027 – English →**Reset Settings to Defaults**. This command is shown in the image on the next page.

This concludes our brief overview of the AutoCAD user interface.

Exercise 1-3:
Open, Save and Close an Existing Drawing

Open AutoCAD 2027:

Start → All Apps → AutoCAD 2027 - English → **AutoCAD 2027 - English** (Figure 1-3.1) – see notes below. Or double-click the AutoCAD icon on your desktop.

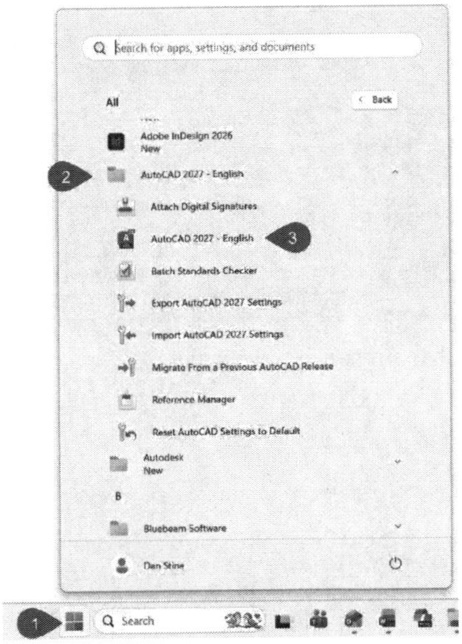

FIGURE 1-3.1 Start Menu

Notes on starting AutoCAD:

- Steps shown are for Windows 11.
- Click the items in the order shown.
- You may also simply type "autocad" in the search box. A link to start AutoCAD 2027 will appear at the top of the list.
- You can also start the program by double-clicking on a DWG file via your file browser (i.e., My Computer, File Explorer, Computer).
- Right-click on the AutoCAD icon and select one of the "Pin" options for quick access from the task bar or the start menu.

Open an AutoCAD Drawing:

By default, AutoCAD will open to the *Start* tab.

1. Open AutoCAD as described previously.
2. On the *Start* tab, click the **Open…** button (Figure 1-3.2).

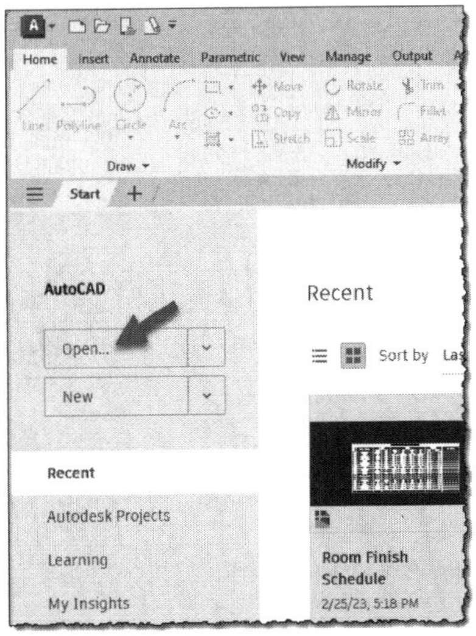

FIGURE 1-3.2 Click Open…

TIP: You can also open drawings via the Open icon on the Quick Access Toolbar (Figure 1-3.3). *Many users prefer using keyboard shortcuts; you can select a drawing to open by pressing Ctrl + O on the keyboard (hold down the Ctrl key and then press the letter O).*

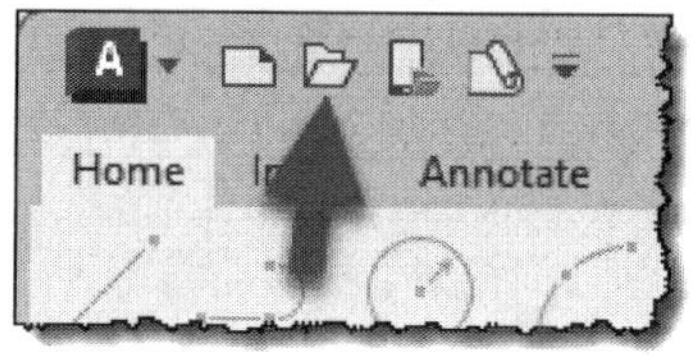

FIGURE 1-3.3 Open icon on the QAT

The icon to the right of open, is **Open from Web & Mobile** for files which might be saved in the cloud.

3. Browse to the following folder: **C:\Program Files\Autodesk\AutoCAD 2027\Sample\Sheet Sets\Architectural\Res** (see Figure 1-3.4A).

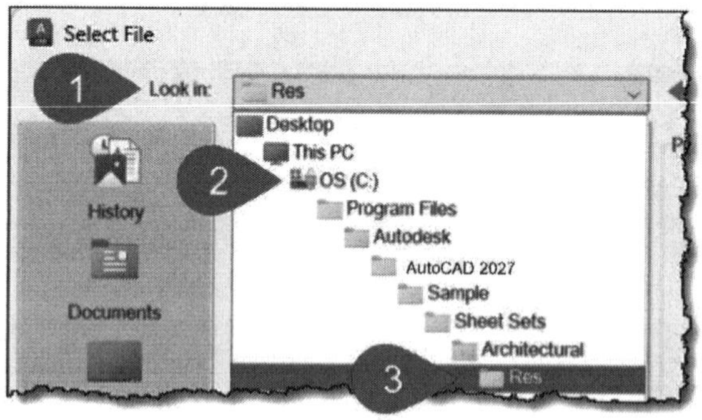

FIGURE 1-3.4A Browse to sample files

4. Select the file named **Exterior Elevations.dwg** and click **Open** (Figure 1-3.4B).
   a. Click **Yes** for any prompts about the file being "read only."

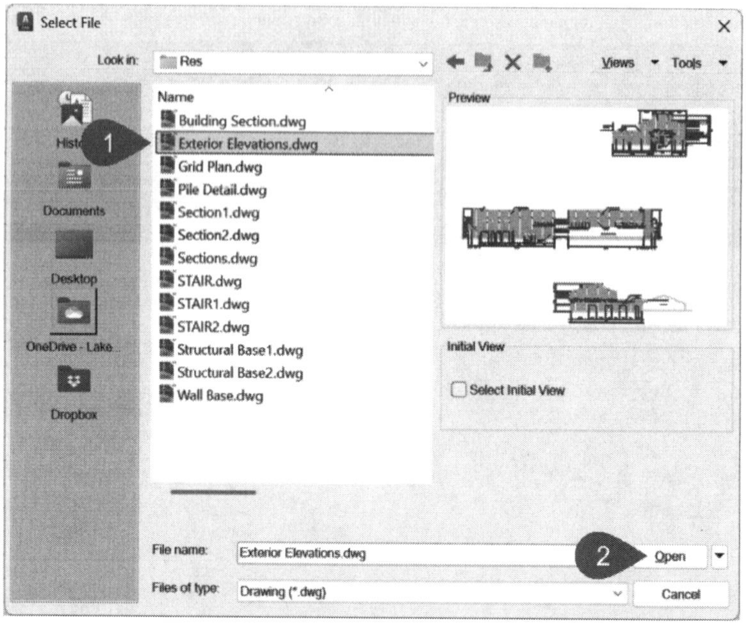

FIGURE 1-3.4B Selecting a file to open

The *Exterior Elevations.dwg* file is now open, and the last saved view is displayed in the *Drawing* window.

The *Open Documents* list, via the ***Application* Menu**, are the drawings currently open on your computer.

5. Click the *Application* menu and then select the **Open Documents** icon (Figure 1-3.5).

Notice that *Exterior Elevations.dwg* is listed. You can toggle between opened drawings from this menu; however, it is more convenient to do so via the document tabs below the Ribbon.

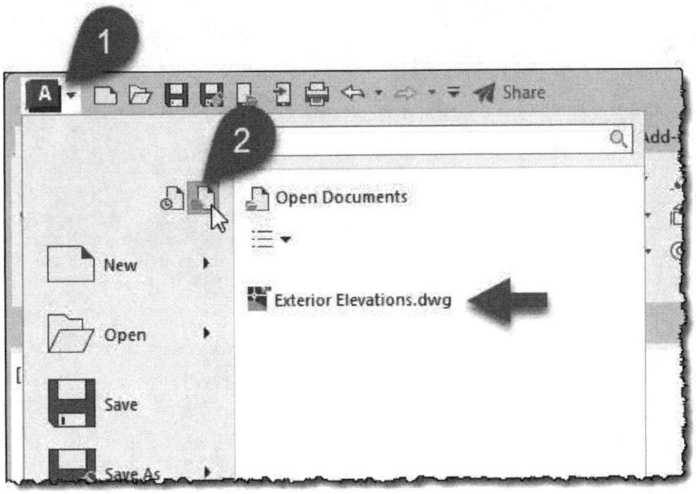

FIGURE 1-3.5 Open Documents list – one file shown to be open

Open Another Sample AutoCAD Drawing:

AutoCAD lets you open more than one drawing at a time.

6. Using the steps just described, open the following file: **C:\Program Files\AutoCAD 2027\Sample\Sheet Sets\Architectural\A-03.dwg**.
    a. If the **Sheet Set Manager** palette opens, click the "X" to close it.

Notice that the *A-03* tab is now shown (see Figure 1-3.6). Try toggling between drawings by clicking on *Exterior Elevations* tab. This is similar to switching websites in a web browser such as *Chrome* or *Edge*.

TIP: Press ***Ctrl + Tab*** *to cycle through open drawings quickly.*

FIGURE 1-3.6 Document tabs

Close an AutoCAD Drawing:

7. Click the **X** next to **A-03** in the *Drawing Tab*. Do <u>not</u> save if asked (see image to right).

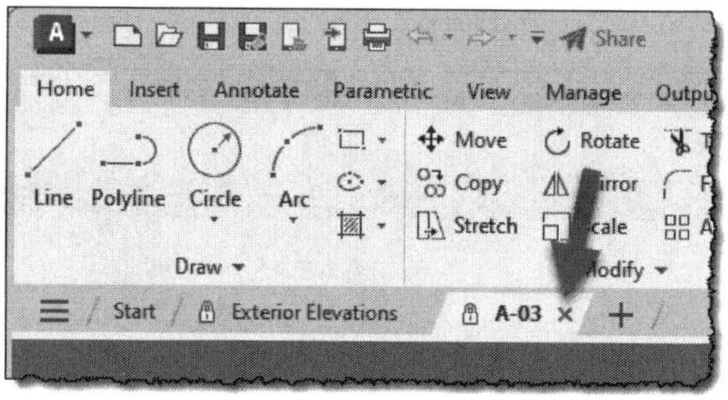

Only the specific drawing will close unless you right-click and select *Close All*. Another option via the right-click is **Close All Except This Tab**.

8. Repeat the previous step to close the other open drawing file – **Exterior Elevations**.

Whenever you try to close a drawing, if you have not saved your drawing, you will be prompted to do so before AutoCAD closes the drawing. **Do not save at this time.**

Saving an AutoCAD Drawing:

At this time you will <u>not</u> actually save a drawing.

To save a drawing, click the **Save** icon - looks like an old floppy disk - from the *Quick Access* toolbar (see image to right). The next exercise shows you how to save your files to the *Cloud*; this is a safe and secure way to back up your files and access them from anywhere. TIP: **Ctrl+S** will save as well.

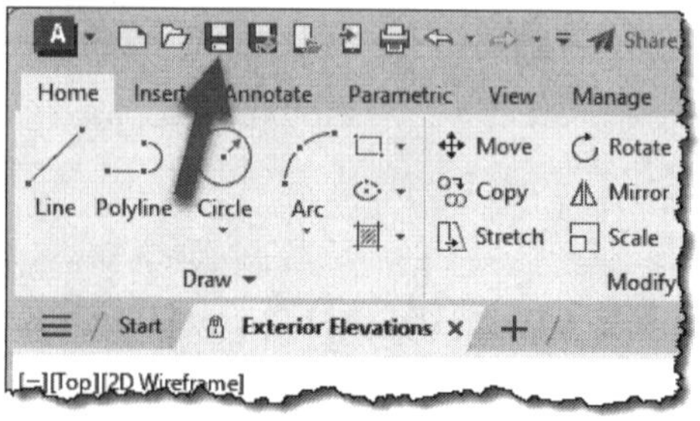

FIGURE 1-3.7 Save icon

You should get in the habit of saving often to avoid losing work due to a power outage or program crash.

> ***FYI:*** *The program does perform automatic saves that are available only if AutoCAD closes abnormally – that is, it crashes. See HELP for more information on this (type 'savetime' to set auto-save time interval).*

Closing the AutoCAD Program:

Finally, from the *Application Menu*, select **Exit AutoCAD**. This will close any open drawings and shut AutoCAD down. Again, you will be prompted to save (if needed) before AutoCAD closes any open drawings. Do not save at this time.

> ***TIP:*** *To close AutoCAD, you can also click the* ***X*** *in the <u>upper</u> right corner of the AutoCAD window (see image to the right); clicking the <u>lower</u> "X" closes the current drawing file.*

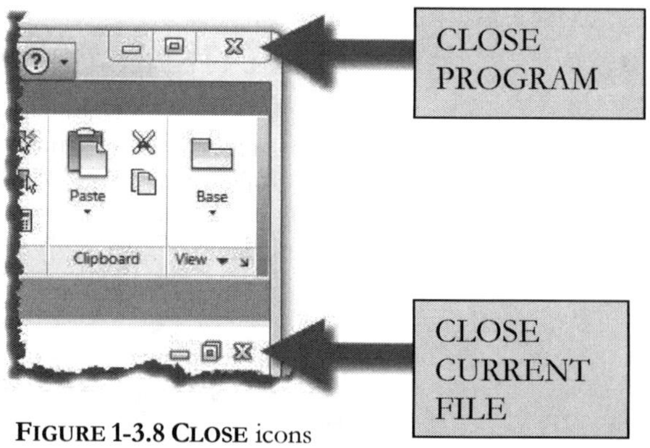

FIGURE 1-3.8 CLOSE icons

Exercise 1-4:
Creating a New Drawing

Creating a New Drawing File:

The steps required to set up a new AutoCAD drawing file are very simple. The important thing to remember is to start with the correct template file, as this will save you lots of work!

To manually create a new drawing (maybe you just finished working on a previous assignment and want to start the next one):

1. Click the **Start** tab (Figure 1-4.1. – Step #1).

2. Click the **New** down-arrow (Step #2) and then select **Browse templates** (Step #3).

3. Select **Architectural Imperial.dwt** from the SheetSets folder and then click **Open**.

IMPORTANT: This is the file you will use to start all drawings created in this book. The Sheet Sets *feature will be covered later in this book.*

FYI: The word "Imperial" simply refers to a drawing based on ***feet and inches*** *rather than metric unit of measure.*

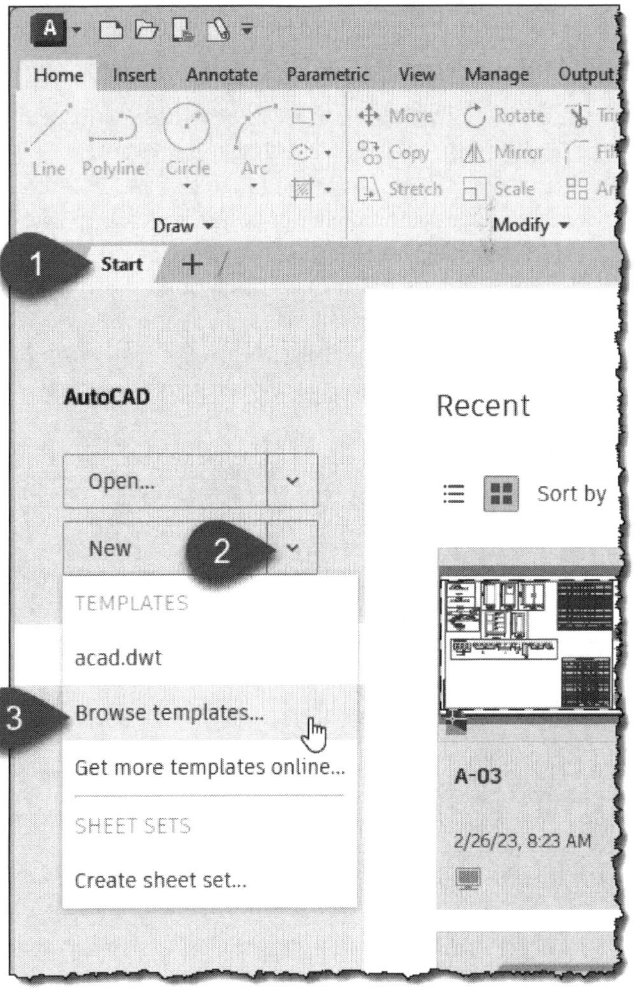

FIGURE 1-4.1 Creating new drawing

To name an unnamed drawing file, you simply save it. The first time an unnamed drawing file is saved, you will be prompted to specify the **name** and **location** for the drawing file.

4. Select the **Save** icon from the *Quick Access Toolbar*; you do not have to actually save your drawing at this time.

5. Specify a **name** and **location** for your new drawing file. *Your instructor may specify a location or folder for your files if you are in a classroom setting.*

   TIP: You can also select the New Drawing icons on the Quick Access Toolbar or Drawings tab (Figure 1-4.2).

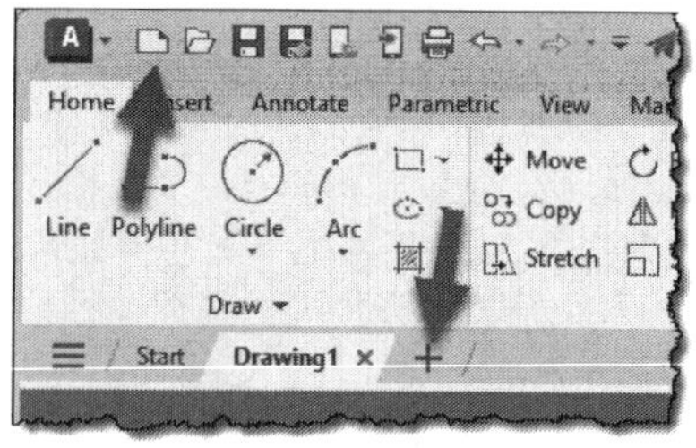

FIGURE 1-4.2 New drawing icon (QAT)

What is a Template File?

A template file allows you to start your drawing with certain settings preset the way you like or need them.

For example, you can have the units set to Imperial (i.e. feet and inches) or Metric. You can have things like dimension and text styles preloaded, etc. You can also have your company's title block and standard *Layers* preloaded.

A custom template is a must for design firms using AutoCAD and will prove useful to the student as he or she becomes more proficient with the program.

> ***BE AWARE:*** *It will be assumed from this point forward that the reader understands how to create, open and save drawing files. Please refer to this section as needed. If you still need further assistance, ask your instructor for help or search the AutoCAD Help system (more on how to do this at the end of the chapter).*

Exercise 1-5:
Using Zoom & Pan to View Your Drawings

Learning to *Pan* and *Zoom* in and out of a drawing is essential to accurate and efficient drafting and visualization. You will review these commands now, so you are ready to use them with the first drawing exercise.

Open AutoCAD 2027:

You will select a sample file included with the files that came with the book.

1. Select **Open** on the *Quick Access* toolbar.

2. Open a file provided with this book: Browse to the following folder: **Sample Files\Residence**. See the inside front cover of this book for instructions on accessing the required custom sample files.

3. Select the file named **A1 - First Floor Plan.dwg** and click **Open**; your *Drawing* window should look similar to Figure 1-5.1.

   FYI: If they are open, you can close the Tool Palette, Properties and Sheet Set Manager for now; just click the "X" in that palette's titlebar. These are like dialog boxes floating within the drawing area, which can remain open while you work.

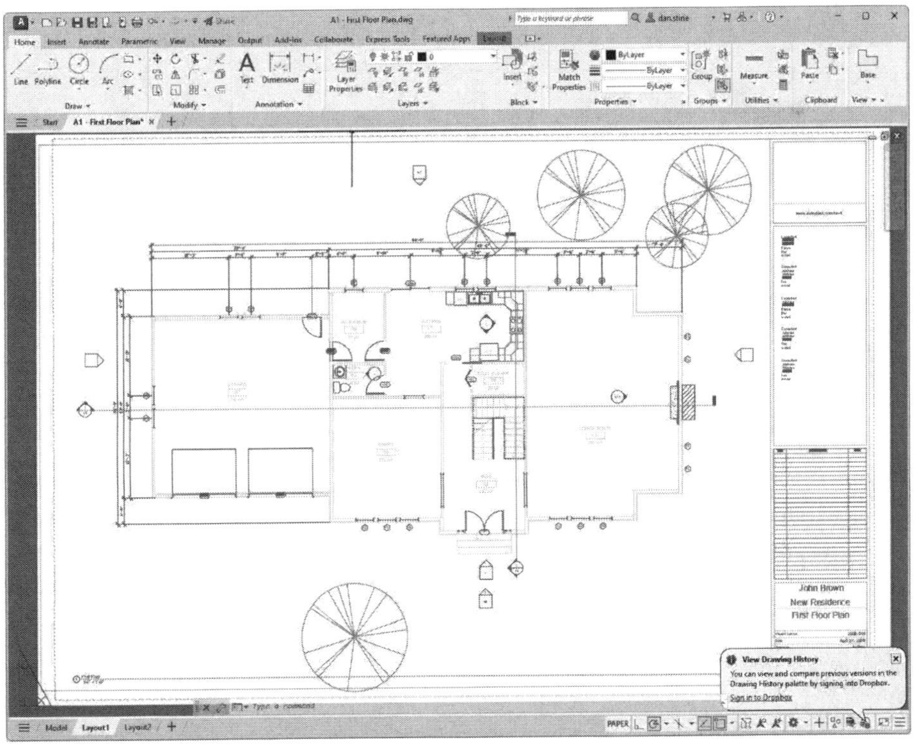

FIGURE 1-5.1 A1 - First Floor Plan.dwg drawing

Switching to Model Space:

The ***Layout*** **tab**(s) to the right of the ***Model*** **tab** is primarily used for printing sheets with drawings, details and title blocks composed on them.

> The *Model* tab (i.e., *Model Space*) is really where all the drawing is done. Then the drawings are arranged in *Layout Views* on sheets (e.g., 8 ½″ x 11″ or 24″ x 36″) for printing.

The *A1 - First Floor Plan* drawing should have opened with the ***Layout1*** tab current.

NOTE: Layout Views *can be named (or renamed) to anything you want; simply right-click on the tab and select* Rename.
(Exception: *You cannot rename the* Model *tab.)*

Next you will switch to the *Model Space* where you will learn to *Zoom* and *Pan* in a drawing.

4. Click on the ***Model*** tab directly below the *Drawing Window* (Figure 1-5.2); you are now in *Model Space*.

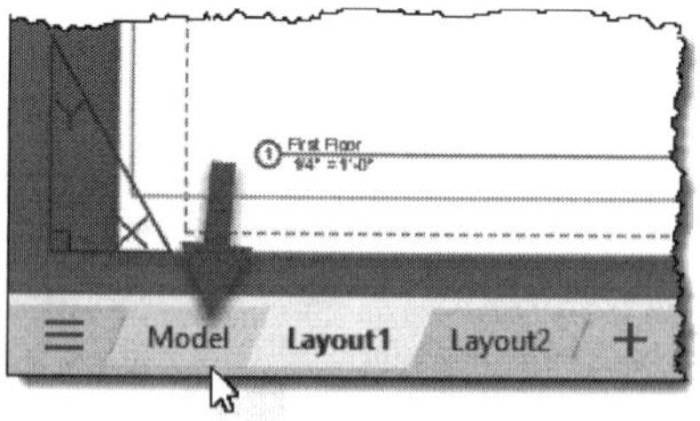

FIGURE 1-5.2 *Model* and *Layout* tabs below the *Drawing Window*

Using Zoom and Pan Tools:

You can access the zoom tools from the *Navigation Bar* or the *scroll wheel* on your mouse (the latter being the most used).

Click the down-arrow to see all of the options (Figure 1-5.3). The text label aptly describes what each zoom tool is programmed to do. The most used tools are **Zoom Window**, **Zoom Previous** and **Zoom Extents**. You will look at each of these plus the **Pan** tool located just above the **Zoom** icon.

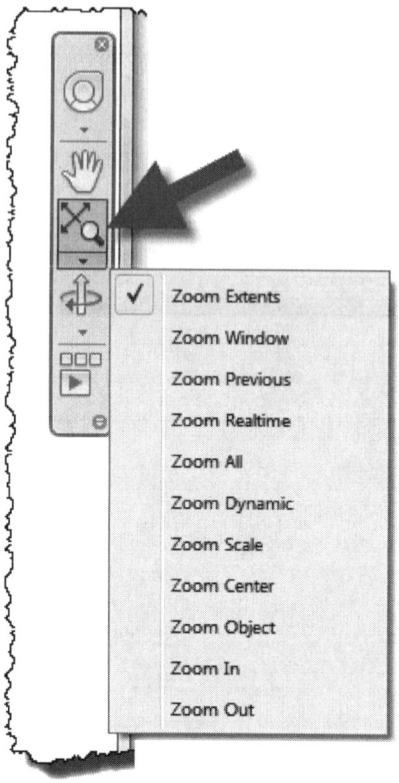

FIGURE 1-5.3 *Zoom* tools on the Navigation Bar

Zoom In:

5. Select the Zoom **Window** tool by clicking on its icon (Figure 1-5.3).

6. Select a window over your floor plan. The dashed-line rectangle has been added to Figure 1-5.4 to describe where you should click.

   TIP: Click and release the mouse button; do not "drag."

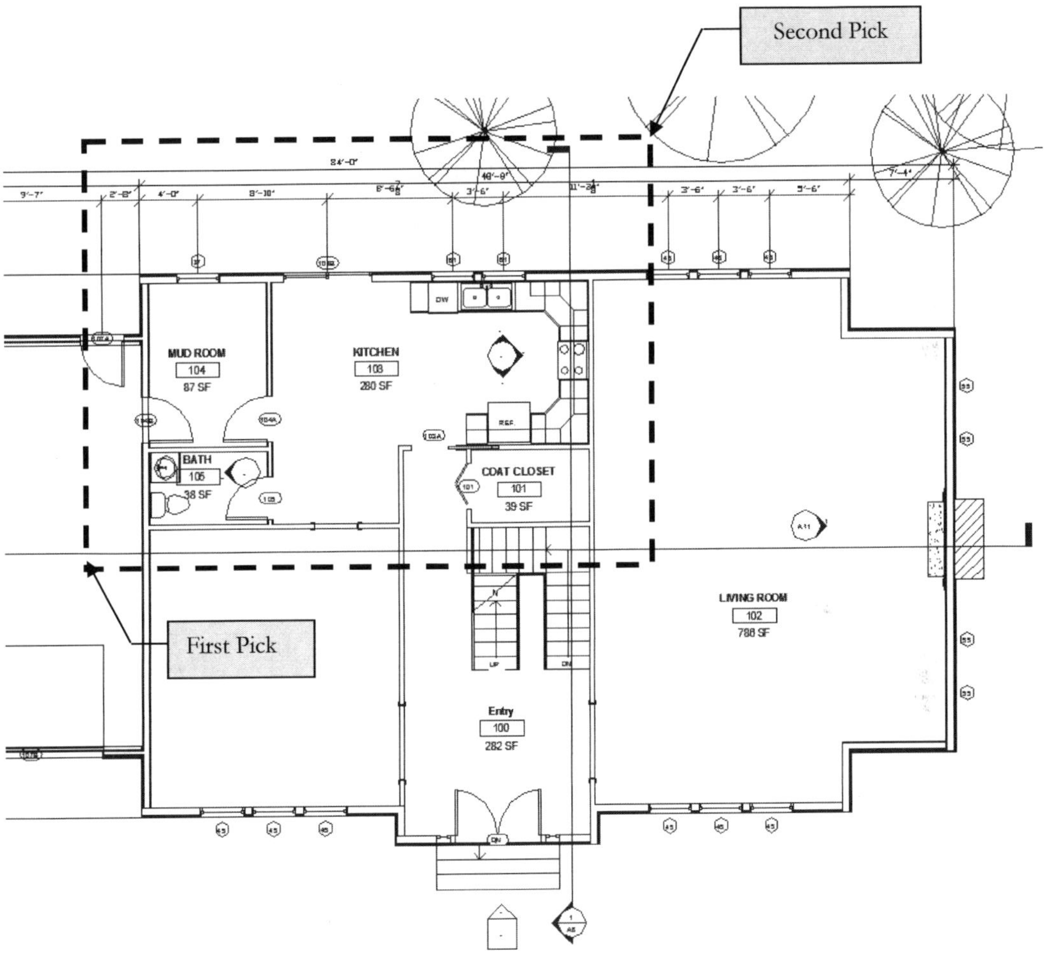

FIGURE 1-5.4 Zoom Window area

You should now be zoomed in to the specified area (Figure 1-5.5). Depending on the proportions of the rectangular area selected (and compared to the proportions of your monitor), the "zoomed in" area may be slightly larger in one direction.

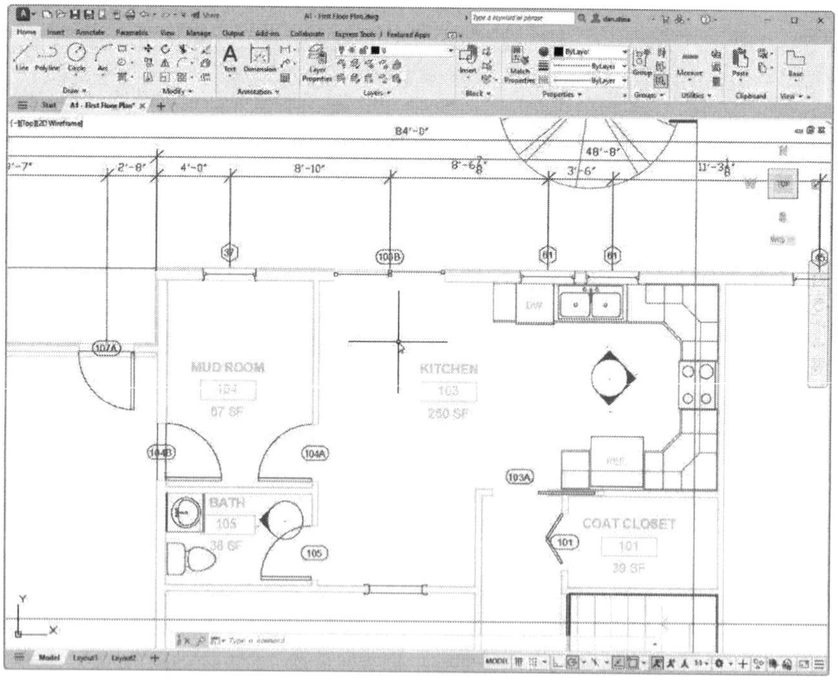

FIGURE 1-5.5 Zoom Window results

Zoom Previous:

7. Select the **Zoom Previous** tool by clicking on its icon in the *Navigation Bar* under the *Zoom* fly-out (Figure 1-5.3).

You should now be back where you started.

> ***FYI:** AutoCAD generates a smooth transition between zoom operations. This helps you keep track of where you are in the current drawing.*

Zoom Extents:

This tool allows you to quickly get to a view where you see everything in the current drawing; this is more useful if you are in a floor plan drawing rather than a drawing of all the utilities for an entire city (as you may essentially be zoomed too far out). If you have "garbage" lines way off to one side of your drawing, the main drawing area will not fill the screen (keep it clean!)

8. Select the **Zoom Extents** tool by clicking on its icon (Figure 1-5.3).

9. Take a minute and try the other zoom tools to see how they work. When finished, click **Zoom Extents** before moving on.

> ***FYI:** Whenever this book refers to clicking the mouse button, it is always referring to the left button. Any other variation will be specifically instructed. <u>For example</u>: Right-click on the OSNAP icon on the Status Bar.*

Pan:

The **Pan** tool allows you to slide the viewing area, in real-time, to a different part of a "zoomed in" drawing (floor plan, elevation, detail, etc.).

Panning is similar to using the horizontal and vertical scroll bars next to the drawing window (these are turned off by default), except you drag the mouse on the screen and are able to go in both directions at the same time (i.e., at an angle).

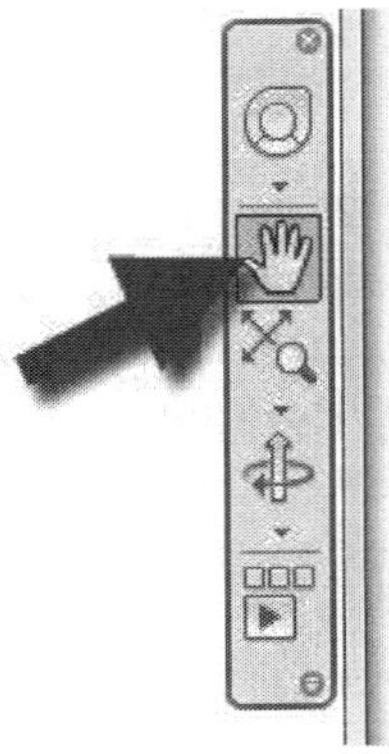

Real-time means that you see the drawing "smoothly" slide across the screen as you move the mouse. On older versions you would pick two points and then AutoCAD would move the drawing instantly from point A to point B with no "smooth" transition between.

10. Click the **Pan** icon; this icon is located in the *Navigation Bar* (see image to right).

You should now notice a **Hand Symbol** in place of the typical Arrow Pointer (or cursor). You can think of this hand as grabbing *Model Space* (when you hold down the mouse button) and "moving" it within the *Drawing* window.

11. Try panning around in the *A1 - First Floor Plan* drawing currently open on your computer; hold the mouse button down, drag the mouse, release the mouse button; drag again if you wish.

BE AWARE: You are not moving the drawing. You are just changing what part of the drawing you see in the drawing window.

12. When you are done *Panning*, with the *Pan* tool still active, right-click anywhere in the *Drawing* window, and then select **Exit** from the pop-up menu (Figure 1-5.6), or press the *Esc* key.

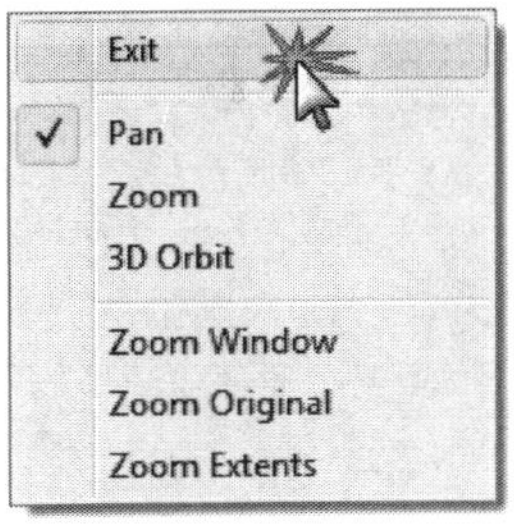

FIGURE 1-5.6 Pan right-click pop-up menu

Notice the other options you have in the pop-up menu shown in Figure 1-5.6. You can quickly toggle from **Pan** to **Zoom**, or **Zoom Window**, **Original** or **Extents**.

13. **Close** the *A1 - First Floor Plan* drawing without saving.

Using the Scroll Wheel on the Mouse:

Using a mouse with a scroll wheel is highly recommended for AutoCAD users. You can seamlessly perform most of the commands covered in this exercise without typing a command or clicking on any icons. Learning to use the wheel is so straightforward and intuitive that the following paragraph should be all that is required for you to start using the wheel productively!

The scroll wheel on the mouse is essential for CAD users. In AutoCAD you can Pan and Zoom without even clicking a zoom icon. You simply **scroll the wheel to Zoom** and **hold the wheel button down to Pan**. This can be done while in another command (e.g., while drawing lines). Another nice feature is that the drawing zooms into the area near your cursor, rather than zooming only at the center of the drawing window like the **Zoom In** tool does. Finally, if you double-click on the wheel, AutoCAD zooms the extents of the drawing.

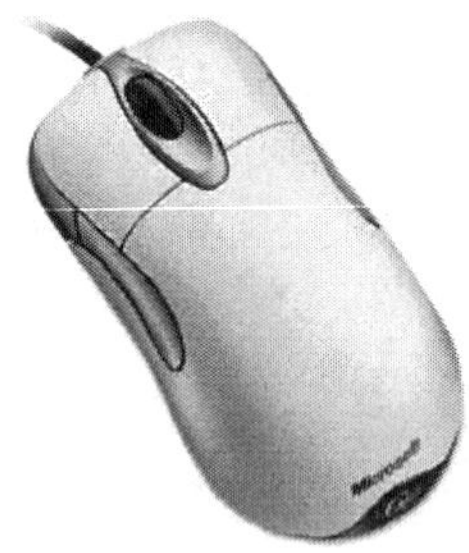

FIGURE 1-5.7 Microsoft's Optical IntelliMouse shown

The sample floor plan drawing used in this exercise is based on the residential project used in the author's textbook *Residential Design Using Autodesk Revit 2027*. The image below shows a rendering of the exterior of the building, similar to one created in that book.

RENDERING OF RESIDENTIAL PROJECT;
RESIDENTIAL DESIGN USING AUTODESK REVIT 2027

Exercise 1-6:
Using the AutoCAD Help System

The AutoCAD Help system can be very useful when you understand how it works. This exercise will walk you through the Help system user interface and the new AI-powered Autodesk Assistant.

Open AutoCAD 2027:

1. Select the **Help** icon (question mark) from the upper right corner of the program window (Figure 1-6.1).

TIP: Click directly on the question mark; the small down-arrow reveals additional Help related items.

FIGURE 1-6.1 Help access icon

You should now be in AutoCAD's *Help* system window (Figure 1-6.2). The next section walks you through its various features. Note that the *Help* window is a local website that you may leave open while you return to AutoCAD. However, when you close AutoCAD the *Help* window will be closed as well. Finally, you may close the *Help* window at any time by clicking the "X" at the upper right.

Keyboard Shortcuts:

Many commands in AutoCAD have a keyboard shortcut, which means you can press a key(s) on the keyboard instead of clicking an icon or the application menu. **For example**: to start the **Line** command (and you are not currently in another command), you can type the letter **L** and then *Enter*. The Help system can be accessed by pressing **F1** on the keyboard.

Most advanced users employ a combination of keyboard and icon use. For a list of keyboard shortcuts, go to **Express Tools** (tab) → **Command Aliases**.

Exploring the Help System User Interface:

AutoCAD contains an extensive set of documentation on your computer's hard drive. This is basically your owner's manual; from this window you can research the "ins" and "outs" of the program.

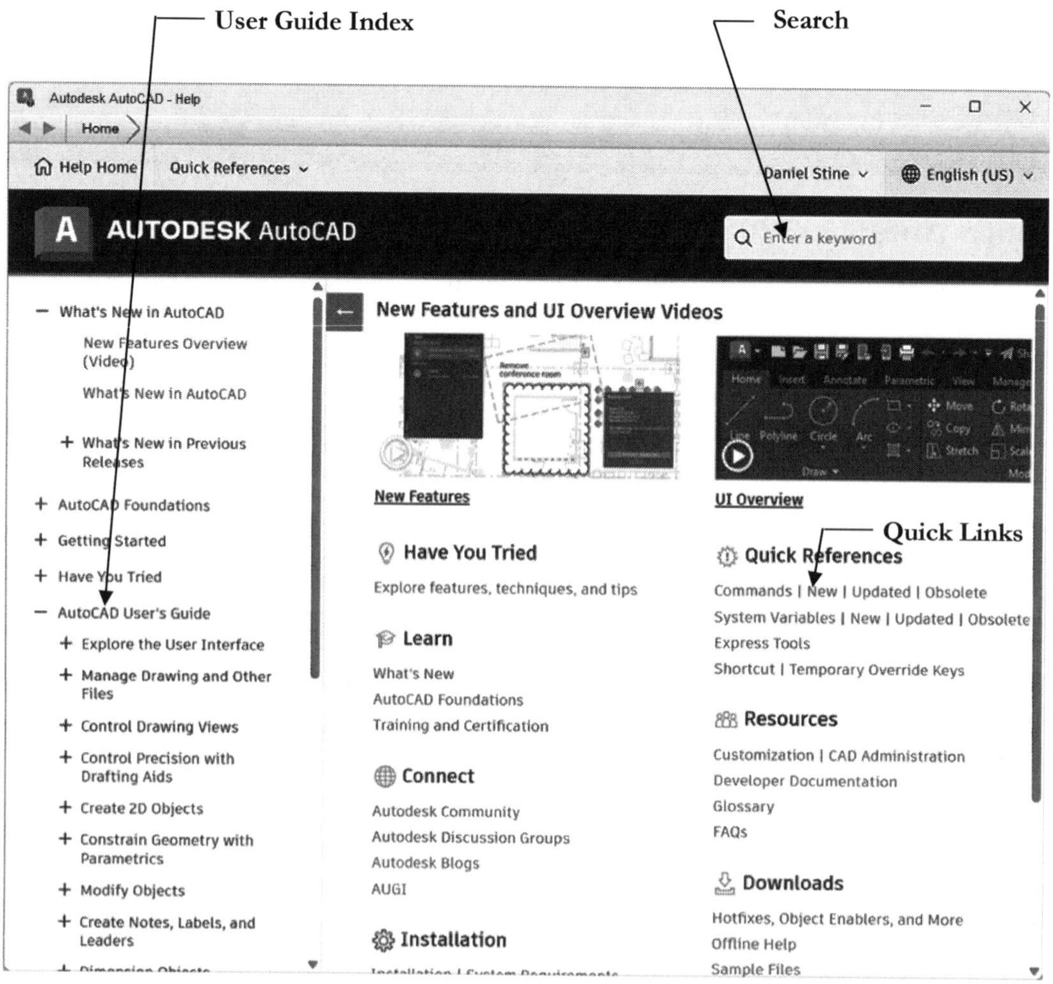

FIGURE 1-6.2 AutoCAD's Help system window

Help System in Action:

You will learn how to find information in the *Help System* on drawing *Circles*.

2. Click in the *Search* text box and enter **draw circle** (Figure 1-6.3).

3. Press **Enter**.

You should see the results shown in Figure 1-6.3. The results can be filtered using the red filter menu pointed out on the left (but, not now).

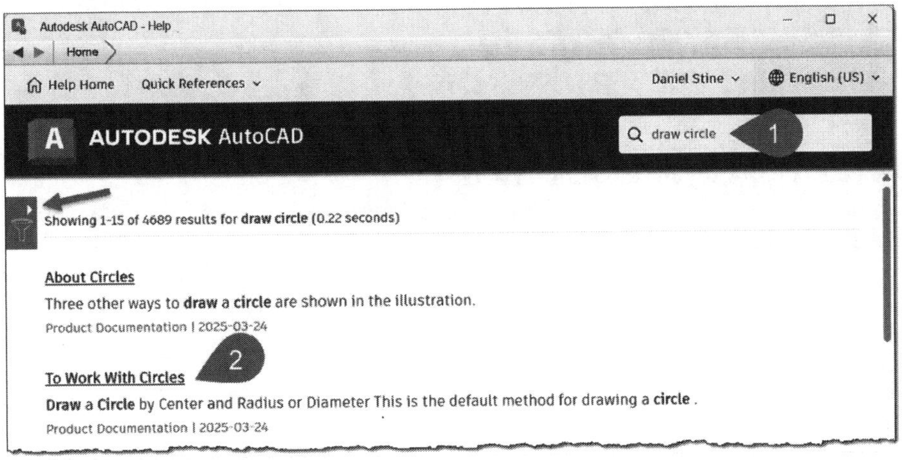

FIGURE 1-6.3 Search results

4. Click the link **To Work With Circles** (see Figure 1-6.3).

You will see specific instructions on drawing a circle in AutoCAD. Notice the various links near the bottom of the view contents window: Related Tasks, Related References, Related Concepts. These are all bits of information closely related to the main topic.

5. Click the **Home** link at the very top of the *Autodesk Help* screen to get back to the main *Help* interface (Figure 1-6.4).

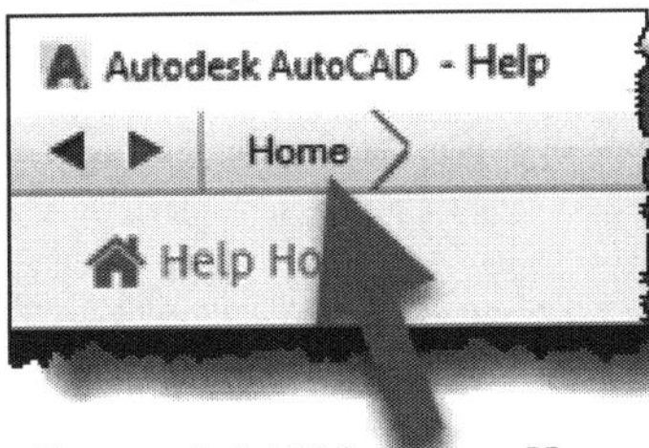

FIGURE 1-6.4 Help system: Home option

In some dialog boxes, like the **Plot** dialog shown in Figure 1-6.5, a Help button provides a direct link to related material in the AutoCAD Help system.

FIGURE 1-6.5 Help system: direct link

While in a command, pressing F1 will open Help with information about the current command selected.

While in Help, if you are not sure how to access a command in AutoCAD, click the **Find** icon when available (Figure 1-6.6). The command will be revealed in the AutoCAD UI with a red arrow pointing at it – this may involve a menu expanding.

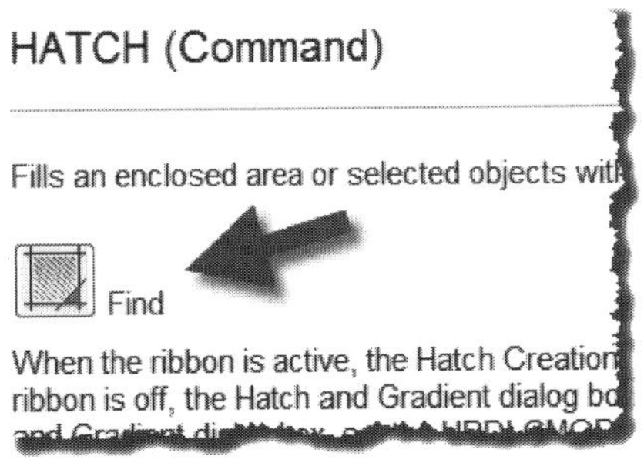

FIGURE 1-6.6 Find command in UI

Discussion Groups:

You can also post questions in a user-to-user forum at Autodesk's website: http://forums.autodesk.com/. Here, other users can respond to your question. Sometimes you will get three ways to do the same thing. You choose which is best for you. However, beware, as not all replies will help, and some may create more problems.

Autodesk Assistant, Powered by AI:

The Autodesk Assistant is an AI-powered chatbot designed to answer questions within, and specific to, AutoCAD.

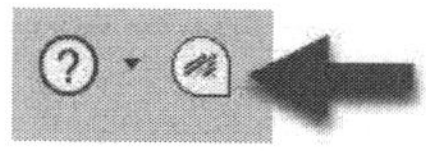

Here you are asked to describe your question in detail using complete sentences and then AutoCAD will use AI to get you to the right solution.

Here are some example questions:

- "Unhandled exception has occurred in a component"
- "Display file tabs was turned off"
- "How to create a Torus?"

When you type a question, such as "How do I draw a circle?", you will get a detailed response like the one shown in Figure 1-6.7. Below the response, it also lists the sources that can be used to verify the answers.

The box below the prompt input box says "Powered by AI. Mistakes are possible. Please double-check the responses."

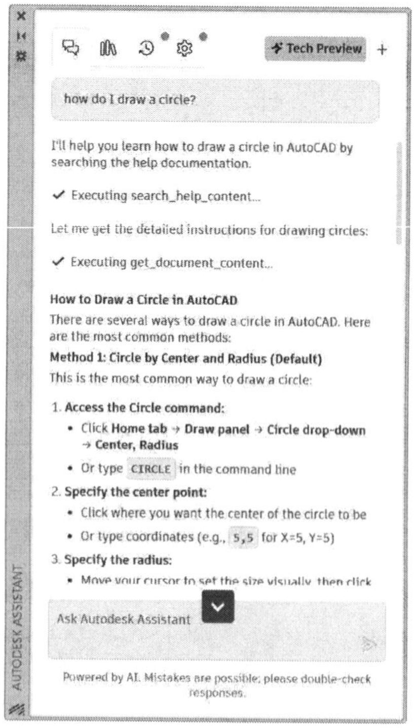

FIGURE 1-6.7 Autodesk Assistance

The example below shows how the Tech Preview, when enabled, can interact with your current drawing.

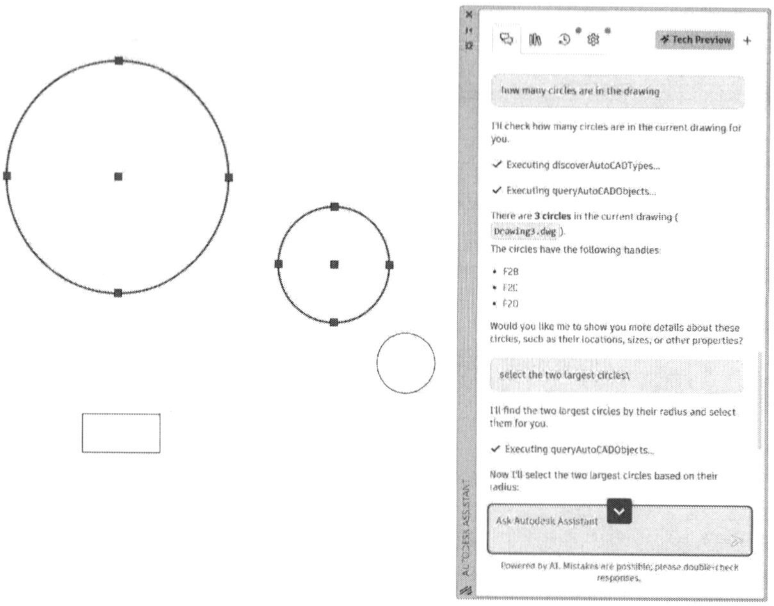

The feature will continue to develop and become more robust, so it is worth monitoring it.

Exercise 1-7:
Introduction to Autodesk Drive

We will finish this chapter with a look at Autodesk Drive, which is an integral foundation for much of Autodesk's **Cloud Services**. You do not necessarily need to use Autodesk's cloud services to complete this book successfully.

Here is how Autodesk describes *Autodesk Drive* on their website:

Autodesk Drive is a cloud storage solution that allows individuals and small teams to organize, preview, and share any type of design or model data.

You can use Autodesk Drive to:

- Upload data to a personal cloud drive.
- Organize and manage your data into folders.
- View 2D and 3D designs and models within the browser on any device.
- Share files & folders with others for viewing, editing, uploading, and managing data.
- You can also access, view, and edit data that others have shared with you.
- With Desktop Connector installed, you can also view and organize files stored in Drive from your desktop and desktop applications.

The Cloud, Defined

Before we discuss *Autodesk Drive* with more specificity, let's define what the *Cloud* is. **The Cloud is a service, or collection of services, which exists partially or completely online.** This is different from the *Internet*, which mostly involves downloading static information, in that you are creating and manipulating data. Most of this happens outside of your laptop or desktop computer.

The cloud gives the average user access to massive amounts of storage space, computing power and software they could not otherwise afford if they had to actually own, install and maintain these resources in their office, school or home. In one sense, this is similar to a *Tool Rental Center*, in that the average person could not afford, nor would it be cost-effective to own, a jackhammer. However, for a fraction of the cost of ownership and maintenance, we can rent it for a few hours. In this case, everyone wins!

Creating an Autodesk Account

The first thing an individual needs to do in order to gain access to *Autodesk Drive* is create a free Autodesk account at drive.autodesk.com. If you are already using an Autodesk product, you likely already have an Autodesk account.

This account is for an individual person, not a computer, not an installation of Revit or AutoCAD, nor does it come from your employer or school. Each person who wishes to access *Autodesk Drive* services must create an account, which will give them a unique username and password.

Generally speaking, there are two ways you can access *Autodesk Drive* cloud services:

- Autodesk Drive website
- Within Revit or AutoCAD; local computer

Autodesk Drive Website

When you have documents stored in the *Cloud* you can access them via your web browser. Here you can manage your files, view them without the full application (some file formats are not supported) and share them. These features use some advanced browser technology, so you need to make sure your browser is up to date; Chrome works well.

Using the website, you can upload files from your computer to store in the *Cloud*. To do this, you create or open a **Folder** and click the **Upload** option (Fig. 1-7.1).

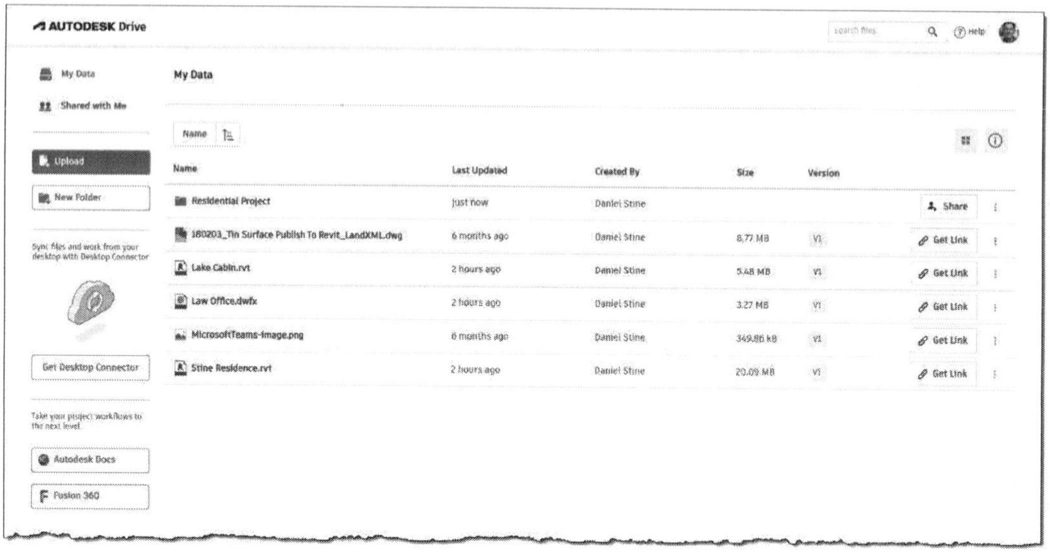

FIGURE 1-7.1 Viewing files stored in the cloud

Tip: If using a modern browser, you can drag and drop documents onto the window. This is a great way to create a secure backup of your documents.

You can share files stored in the *Cloud* with others. Simply hover over a file within *Autodesk DRIVE* and click the **Get Link** icon to see the Share dialog (Figure 1-7.2). Anyone who has this link can view and download (if Allow Downloads is toggled on) the files shared.

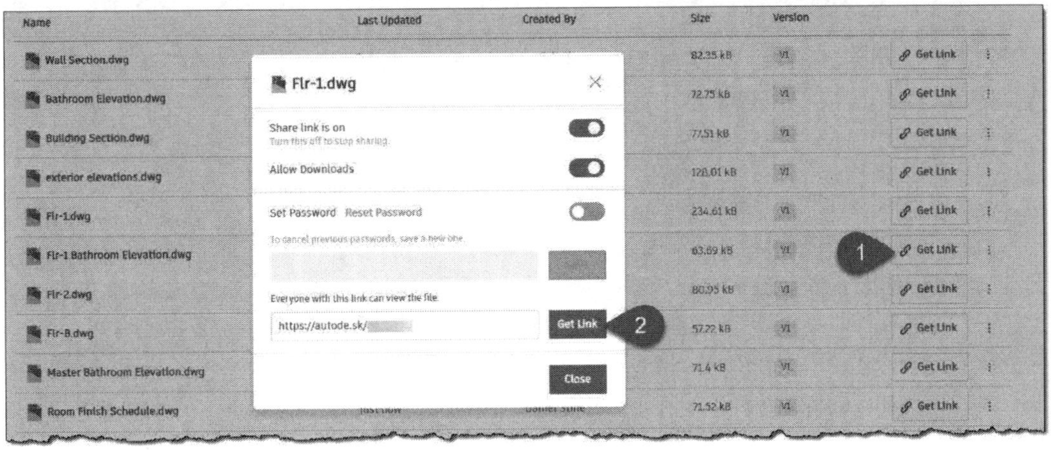

FIGURE 1-7.2 Sharing files stored in the cloud

Installing Autodesk Desktop Connector

To sync the Autodesk Drive files with your local computer and work directly on the files, you must first download Autodesk Desktop Connector. This tool creates an environment similar to OneDrive or Dropbox but with enhanced features supporting Autodesk-specific CAD and BIM workflows.

To install Desktop Connector, first close any open Autodesk products, such as AutoCAD. Then click the **Get Desktop Connector** button (Fig. 1-7.1) to access the download page. Download the latest version and install it.

Files are now synced locally and found via **This PC** within Windows Explorer (Fig. 1-7.3).

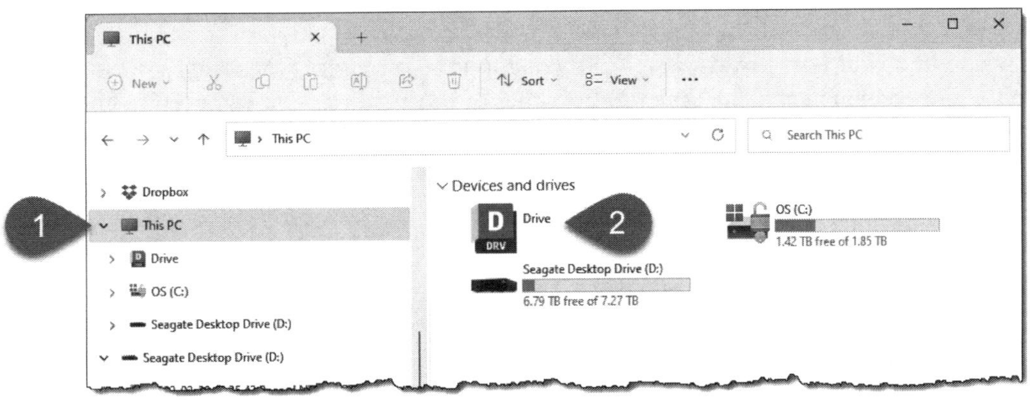

FIGURE 1-7.3 Accessing Drive files via Desktop Connector

The same cloud-based files appear locally, as shown below (Fig. 1-7.4).

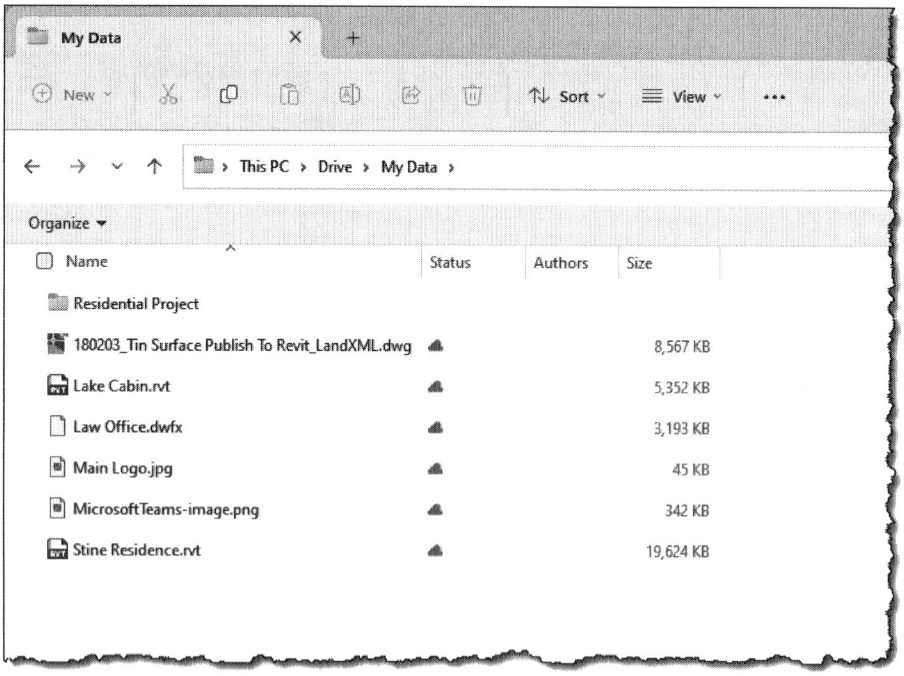

FIGURE 1-7.4 Accessing Drive files via Desktop Connector

Accessing Autodesk DRIVE within your CAD/BIM application

Another way in which you can access your data, stored in the cloud, is from within your Autodesk application, for example, Revit or AutoCAD. This is typically the most convenient, as you can open, view and modify your drawings. Once logged in, you will also have access to any *Cloud Services* available to you from within the application, such as rendering services or *Green Building Studio.*

To sign into your *Autodesk Account* within your application, simply click the **Sign In** option in the notification area in the upper right corner of the window. You will need to enter your student email address and password, or work/personal email if you are not a student. When properly logged in, you will see your username or email address listed, as shown in Figure 1-7.5 below. Note: most likely, you are already signed in, as this is required to use most Autodesk products.

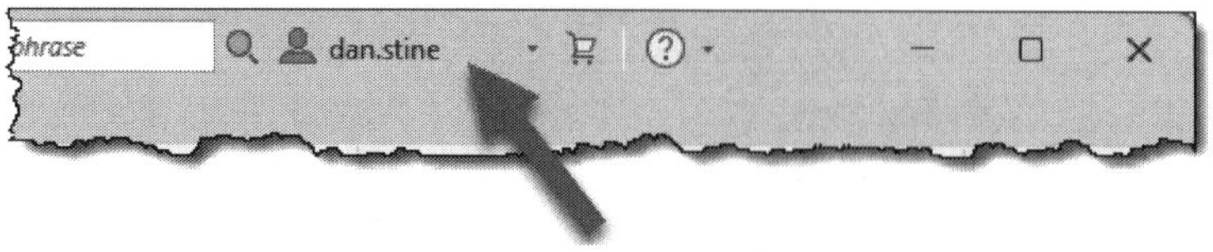

FIGURE 1-7.5 Example of user logged into their Autodesk account

The files within Autodesk Drive may be accessed via the **Open** dialog, as shown in Figure 1-7.6 below. Working on the files in this location ensures they are automatically backed up every time you save your work.

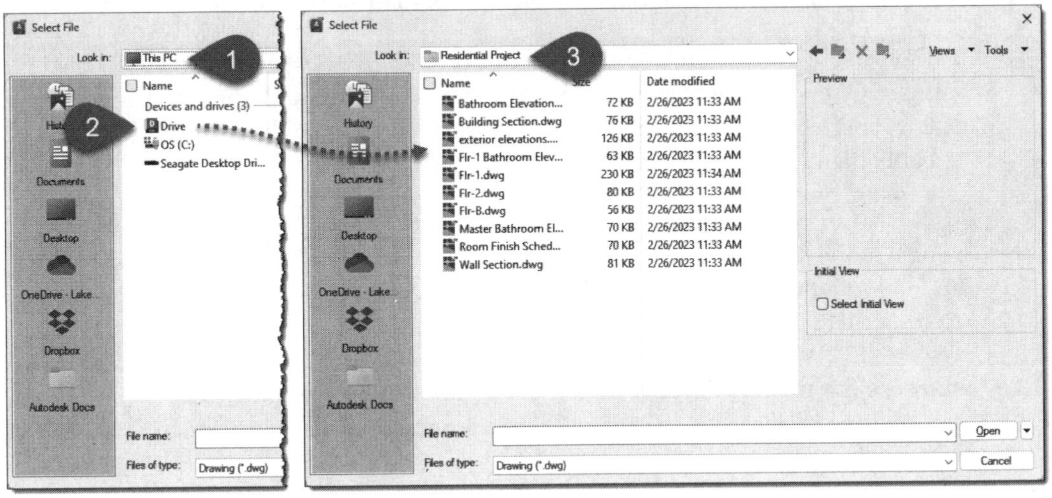

FIGURE 1-7.6 Accessing Autodesk Drive within AutoCAD or Revit

Notice that once a file has been modified, you can tell by the **Version** being incremented in Autodesk Drive when viewed in your browser, as shown below (Fig. 1-7.7).

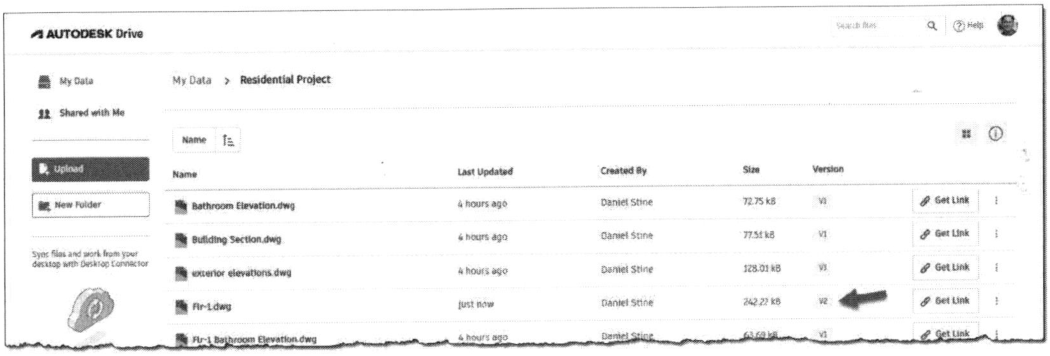

FIGURE 1-7.7 Accessing Autodesk Drive within AutoCAD or Revit

When using AutoCAD, and when sharing files with others via Drive, only one person may modify a DWG file at a time. Similarly, when working with Revit models, an additional paid service called BIM Collaborate Pro is required for multiple users to work within the same BIM.

It is recommended, as you work though this book, that you save all of your work in the *Cloud*, via Autodesk Drive, so you will have a safe and secure location for your files. These files can then be accessed from several locations via the two methods discussed here. It is still important to maintain a separate copy of your files on a flash drive, portable hard drive or in another *Cloud*-type location such as *Dropbox*. This will be important if your main files ever become corrupt. You should manually back up your files to your backup location, so a corrupt file does not automatically corrupt your backup files.

TIP: If you have a file that will not open try one of the following:

- In AutoCAD: Open AutoCAD and then, from the *Application Menu*, select Drawing Utilities → Recover → Recover. Then browse to your file and open it. AutoCAD will try and recover the drawing file. This may require some things to be deleted but is better than losing the entire file.

- In Revit: Open Revit and then, from the *Application Menu*, select Open, browse to your file, and select it. Click the Audit check box, and then click Open. Revit will attempt to repair any problems with the project database. Some elements may need to be deleted, but this is better than losing the entire file.

Be sure to check out the Autodesk website to learn more about Autodesk BIM Collaborate Pro and the growing number of cloud services Autodesk is offering.

Self-Exam:

The following questions can be used as a way to check your knowledge of this lesson. The answers can be found at the bottom of the next page.

1. The *Modify* panel allows you to save your drawing file. (T/F)
2. You can zoom in and out using the wheel on a wheel mouse. (T/F)
3. AutoCAD is made specifically for architectural design. (T/F)
4. A ______________ file allows you to start your drawing with certain settings preset the way you like or need them.
5. In the AutoCAD user interface, the ________________________ displays prompts for specific user input.

Review Questions:

The following questions may be assigned by your instructor as a way to assess your knowledge of this section. Your instructor has the answers to the review questions.

1. Many commands have a keyboard shortcut. (T/F)
2. AutoCAD does not provide much in the way of online documentation. (T/F)
3. The drawings listed in the *Open Documents* menu allow you to see which drawings are currently open. (T/F)
4. When you use the **Pan** tool you are actually moving the drawing, not just changing what part of the drawing you can see on the screen. (T/F)
5. To *close* AutoCAD you simply click the X in the upper right. (T/F)
6. The icon with the floppy disk image ( ) allows you to _____________________ a drawing file.
7. A *Ribbon* "panel" with a small black down-arrow to the right of the label has additional tools in an extended panel fly-out. (T/F)
8. Use the ___________________________ tool to switch the view back to the one just prior to your last zoom command.
9. Holding the Scroll Wheel down initiates the _____________ command.
10. The **Model** tab (aka Model Space) is where most of the actual drafting and design is done. (T/F)

SELF-EXAM ANSWERS:
1 – F, **2** – T, **3** – F, **4** – Template, **5** – Command Window

Notes:

Lesson 2
Introduction: The Must Know Commands

Introduction

It may surprise you that at the end of this chapter, you will have a basic understanding of approximately 80% of the CAD drafting tools used on a daily basis; the remainder of this book provides architectural exercises to apply and hone your skills, as well as learning several other tools.

In this chapter, you will pragmatically look at several tools designed to get you off to a good start within the AutoCAD environment. You can refer back to this chapter throughout the semester if you need a refresher on a specific command.

You should spend ample time on these fundamental tools to help ensure success as you progress through the rest of this text.

See the inside front cover of the textbook for instruction on accessing the required files and bonus content.

The website has several files that you will use to complete the exercises in this chapter. You should follow the instructions below, or those given by your instructor, to successfully complete the required tasks in this chapter:

- Copy the files from the **website** to your hard drive (usually the C: drive); for example, **C:\Cad Training** (or similar).

- Each exercise has a corresponding AutoCAD drawing file located in the folder you just copied. You can open these files at the beginning of each exercise and do a **Save-As**, adding your initials to the file name.

Exercise 2-1:
Drafting and Display Tools

Introduction

Object Snap is a tool that allows you to accurately pick a point on an object. For example, when drawing a line, you can use *Object Snap* (*OSNAP*) to select the start-point, the endpoint, or the midpoint of another line.

This feature is absolutely critical to drawing accurate technical drawings. Using this feature allows you to be confident you are creating perfect intersections, corners, etc. (Figure 2-1.1).

Object Snaps Options:

You can use *Object Snaps* in one of two ways:

- Using the *Running OSNAP* mode
- On an individual pick-point basis

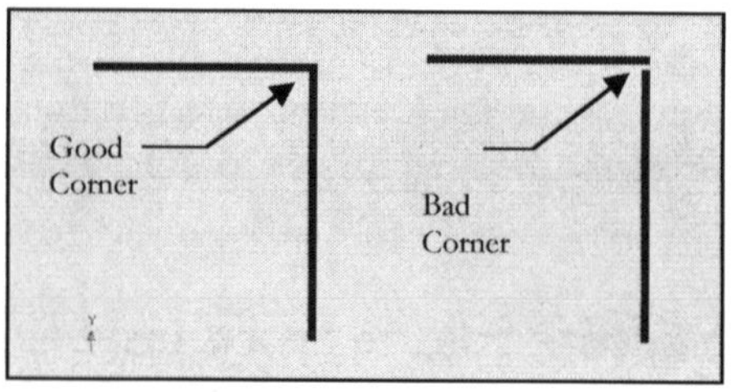

FIGURE 2-1.1 Typical problem when Object Snap is not

Running OSNAP mode is a feature that, when turned on, constantly scans the area near your cursor when AutoCAD is looking for user input. You can configure which types of points to look for.

Using an *Object Snap* for individual pick-points allows you to quickly select a particular point on an object. This option will also override the *Running OSNAP* setting, which means you tell AutoCAD to just look for the endpoint on an object (for the next pick-point only) rather than the three or four types being scanned for by the *Running OSNAP* feature.

Enabling Running Object Snaps:

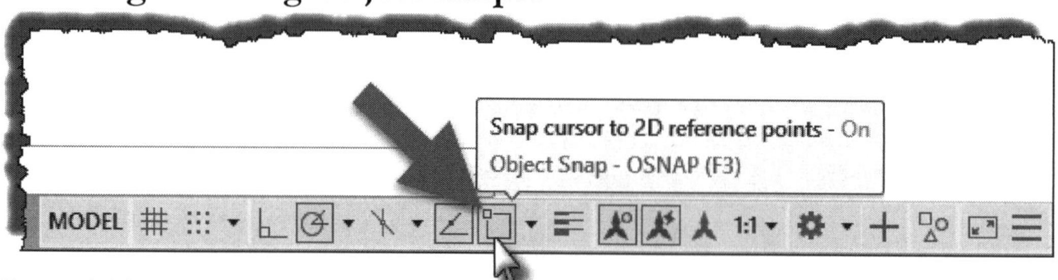

FIGURE 2-1.2 Status Bar – shown with OSNAP (Object Snap) turned on

To toggle *Running Object Snap* on and off you click the **Object Snap** button on the *Status Bar.*

Snap Symbols:

When *Object Snap* is turned on, AutoCAD displays symbols as you move your cursor about the *Drawing* window (while you are in a command like **Line** and AutoCAD is awaiting your input or pick-point).

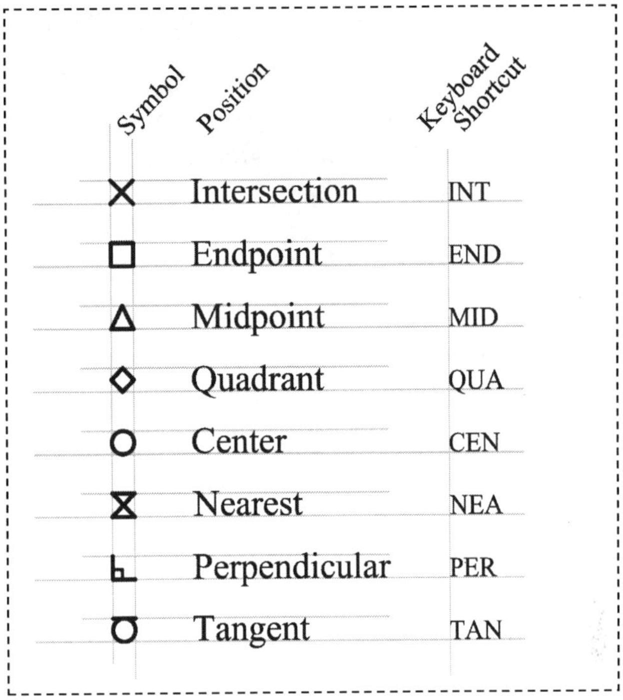

FIGURE 2-1.3 OSNAP symbols that are displayed on the screen when selecting a point.

If you hold your cursor still for a moment, while a snap symbol is displayed, a tooltip will appear on the screen. However, when you become familiar with the snap symbols you can pick sooner, rather than waiting for the tooltip to display.

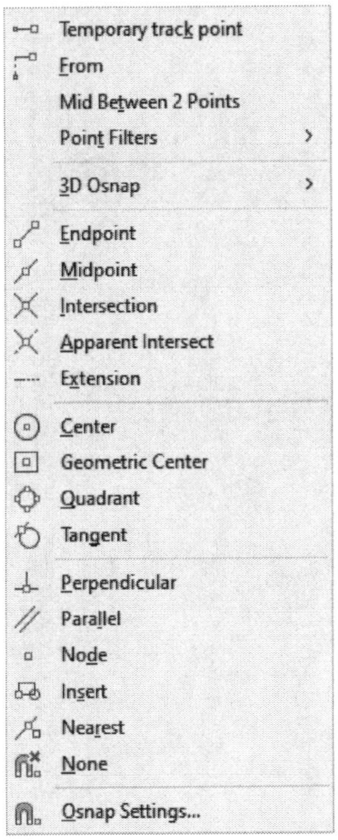

The TAB key cycles through the available snaps near your cursor.

The keyboard shortcut turns off the other snaps for one pick. For example, if you type *END* on the keyboard while in the **Line** command, AutoCAD will only look for an *Endpoint* for the next pick.

Finally, if you need a particular snap for just one pick, you can hold the ***Shift*** **key and right-click** for the *OSNAP* context menu (see image to left). If you pick **Center**, AutoCAD will only look for a Center to snap to for the next pick and then revert back to the previous settings.

Setting Object Snaps:

You can set AutoCAD to have just one or all *Object Snaps* running at the same time. Let's say you have *Endpoint* and *Midpoint* set to be running. While using the **Line** command, move your cursor near an existing line. When the cursor is near the end of the line, you will see the *Endpoint* symbol show up. When you move the cursor towards the middle of the line, you will see the *Midpoint* symbol show up.

The next step shows you how to tell AutoCAD which *Object Snaps* you want it to look for.

First you need to **Open** the drawing from the online files.

1. **Open** drawing **ex2-1 Osnap.dwg** from the online library.

2. Next, do a **Save-As** and save to your hard drive.

3. Click the down-arrow next to the *OSNAP* button on the *Status Bar* and select **Object Snap Settings** from the pop-up menu (Figure 2-1.4).

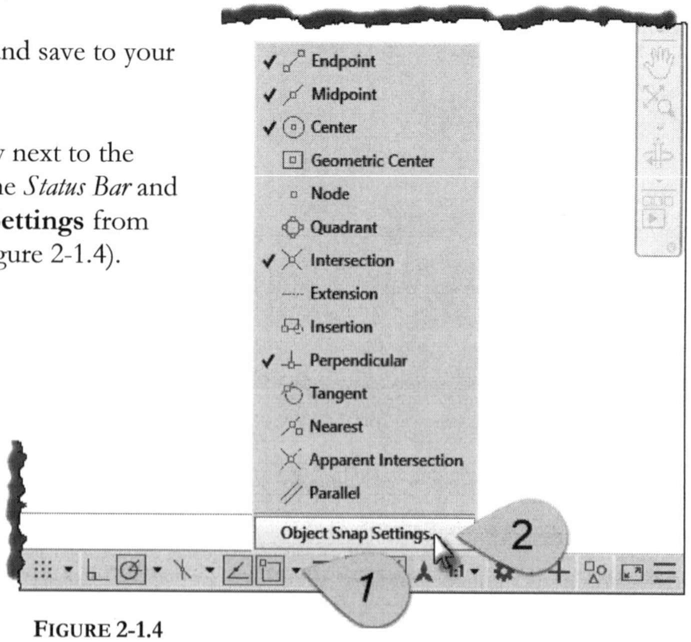

FIGURE 2-1.4
Right-click on the OSNAP button located on the *Status Bar*

You are now in the **Drafting Settings** dialog box on the *Object Snaps* tab; compare to **Figure 2-1.5**.

4. Make sure only the following *Object Snaps* are checked:
   a. Endpoint
   b. Midpoint
   c. Center
   d. Intersection
   e. Perpendicular

5. Click **OK** to close the *Drafting Settings* dialog box.

***FOR MORE INFORMATION:** For more on using Object Snaps, search AutoCAD's Help system for **Drafting Settings**. Then click the **Drafting Settings Dialog Box** and select the **Object Snap** link within the article.*

FYI: The Running Object Snaps shown in Figure 2-1.5 are for AutoCAD in general, not just the current drawing. This is convenient; you don't have to adjust to your favorite settings for each drawing (existing or new).

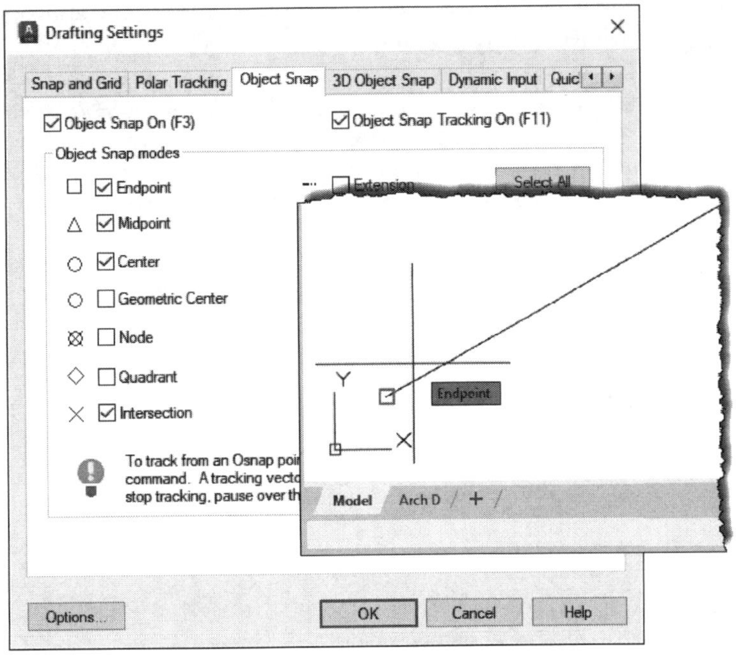

FIGURE 2-1.5 Object Snap tab on Drafting Settings dialog

Now that you have the *Running Object Snaps* set, you will give this feature a try.

6. On the *Home* tab, in the *Draw* panel, pick the **Line** command, move your cursor to the lower-left portion of the diagonal line (Figure 2-1.6).

7. Hover the cursor over the line's endpoint (without picking), when you see the *Endpoint* symbol you can click to select that point.

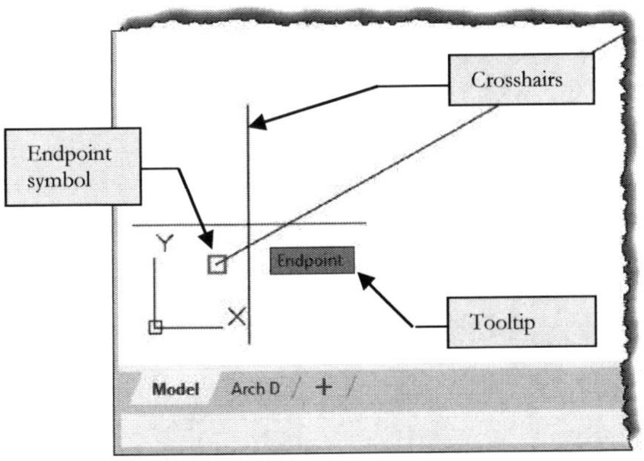

FIGURE 2-1.6 Endpoint OSNAP symbol visible

JUST SO YOU KNOW…

It is important that you see the *OSNAP* symbol before clicking. Also, once you see the symbol you should be careful not to move the mouse too much.

These steps will help to ensure accurate corners.

While still in the Line command, you will draw additional lines using *OSNAP* to accurately select the line's *start point* and *endpoint.*

8. Draw the additional lines shown in **Figure 2-1.7** using the appropriate *Object Snap* (changing the *Running Snap* as required to select the required point).

   TIP #1: *When using the Line command you can draw several line segments without the need to terminate the Line command and then restart it for the next line segment. After picking the start and end points for a line, the end point automatically becomes the first point for the next line segment; this continues until you finish the Line command (i.e., right-click and select Enter).*

   TIP #2: *At any point, while the Line command is active, you can right-click on the OSNAP button (on the Status Bar) and adjust its settings, or press Shift+Right-click; the Line command will not cancel.*

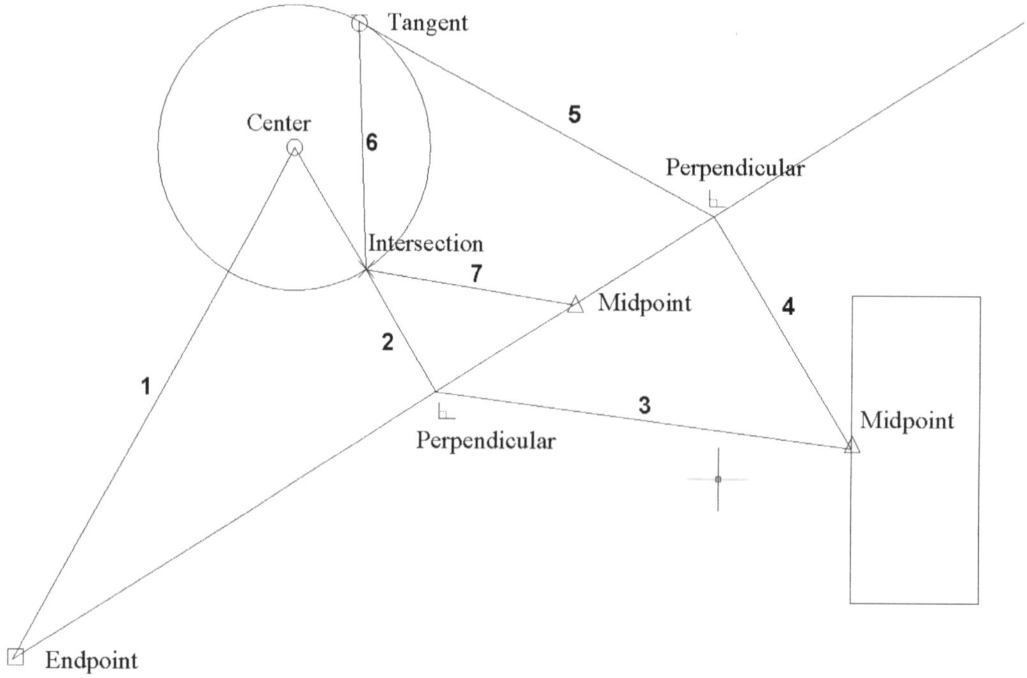

FIGURE 2-1.7 Several lines added using running OSNAPs.
The numbers indicate the order the lines are to be drawn in.

9. **Save** your drawing as Ex2-1.dwg.

This is an Architectural Example?

OK, this is not really an architectural example yet. However, the point here is to focus on the fundamental concepts and not architecture just yet.

Selecting Entities:

At this time we will digress and take a quick look at the various techniques for selecting entities in AutoCAD. Most commands work the same when it comes to selecting entities. As mentioned before, you need to keep your eye on the *prompts* so you know when AutoCAD is ready for you to select entities or provide other user input.

When selecting entities, you have two primary ways to select them:

- Individually select entities one at a time
- Select several entities at a time with a Window

You can use one, or a combination of both, methods to select entities (when using the Copy command for example).

Individual Selections:
When prompted to select entities (to copy or erase, for example), simply move the cursor over the object and click. With most commands you repeat this process until you have selected all the entities you need. Then you typically press Enter or right-click to tell AutoCAD you are finished selecting.

Window Selections:
Similarly, when prompted to select entities, you can pick a Window around several entities to select them all at once. To select a Window, rather than selecting an object as previously described, you select one corner of the Window you wish to select (that is, you pick a point in "space"). Now as you move the mouse you will see a rectangle on the screen that represents the Window you are selecting. When the Window encompasses the entities you wish to select, click the mouse.

You actually have two types of Windows you can select. One is called a **Window** and the other is called a **Crossing Window**.

Window:
This option allows you to select only the entities that are completely within the Window. Any lines that extend out of the Window are not selected.

Crossing Window:
This option allows you to select all the entities that are completely within the Window and any that extend outside the Window.

Using Window versus Crossing Window:
To select a *Window* you simply pick your two points from left to right (Figure 2-1.8a).

Conversely, to select a Crossing Window, you pick the two diagonal points of the window from right to left (Figure 2-1.8b).

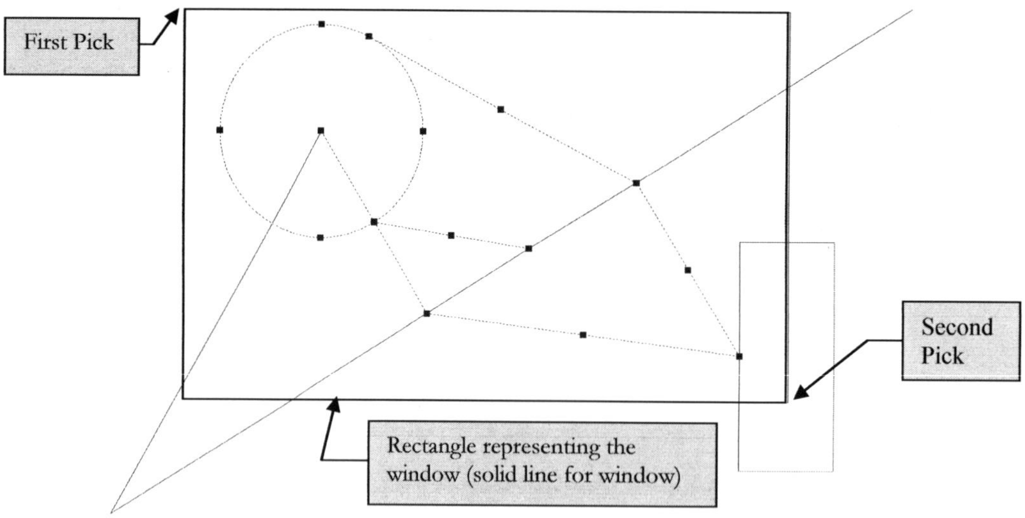

FIGURE 2-1.8A Lines selected using *Window;* only the lines within the window are selected.

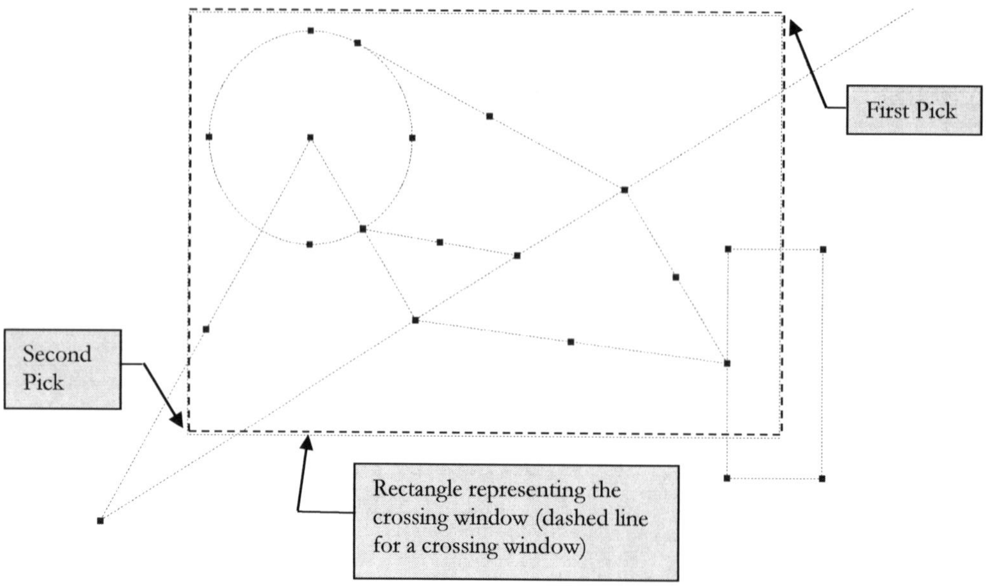

FIGURE 2-1.8B Lines selected using a *Crossing Window;* all lines are selected.

Exercise 2-2:
Draw Commands

Getting Started

It should not surprise you that the world's most used 2D drafting program has several tools which allow you to draw! Several tools exist that allow you to draw lines, squares, rectangles, circles, ellipses, hexagons, etc. These tools have been refined over the years and made available as new releases in the software.

On a side note, new versions of AutoCAD come out every year (this has been the trend over the last few years). The version number is meant to be the year; however, this is slightly out of sync with the actual year. For example, the version you are using, AutoCAD 2027, actually was released in the second quarter of 2026. Once a company buys the software, they only have to pay a small fee (small relative to the initial price) to get an upgrade. Another option is to buy into the subscription program, which includes additional perks and any upgrades. This allows companies to budget for their design software as it's a fixed yearly fee.

Draw → Line

The *Line* command is the most fundamental command within AutoCAD. A line, in AutoCAD, can represent pretty much anything (walls, furniture, doors, cars, beams, etc.). Lines are usually distinguished from each other by color and layer (you will learn about *Layers* later).

The next few pages will walk you through the various ways in which to draw lines. You can draw lines by picking points in "space," which usually does not create very accurate geometry because the points are arbitrary. You can also create lines by typing coordinates relative to the drawing's origin. Another option is to pick points, like the endpoint of another line or the midpoint of a rectangle; this will create lines that are only accurate if the lines you are snapping to were accurately placed. Finally, you can create lines by entering the specific length and angle to create an accurate line with no other reference material required (i.e., coordinates or existing geometry to snap to).

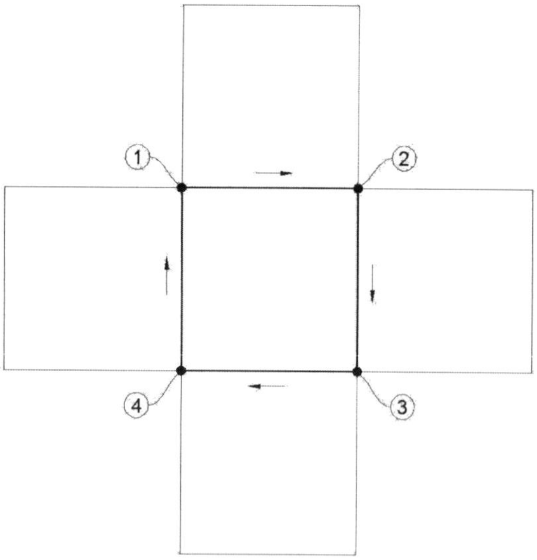

A Draw: Line

1. Open **Ex2-2a Draw Commands – Line.dwg** from the online files.

2. From the **Home** tab (in the **Draw** panel) select the **Line** command.

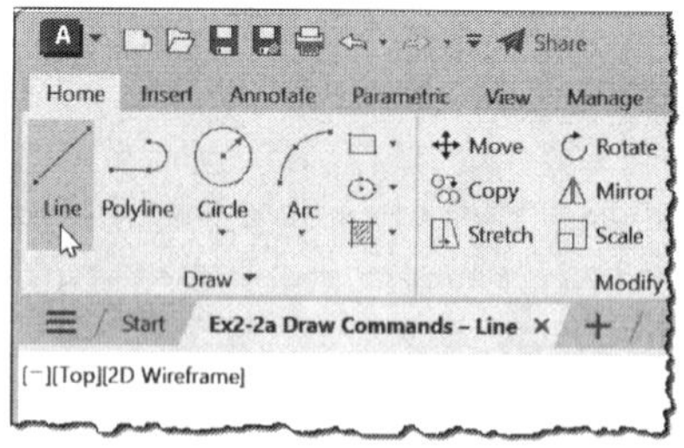

3. Using ***Object Snaps***, pick the (4) points identified (with a number in a circle).

4. At this point you only have three lines; to create the last segment quickly and accurately, right-click and select **Close** from the pop-up menu.

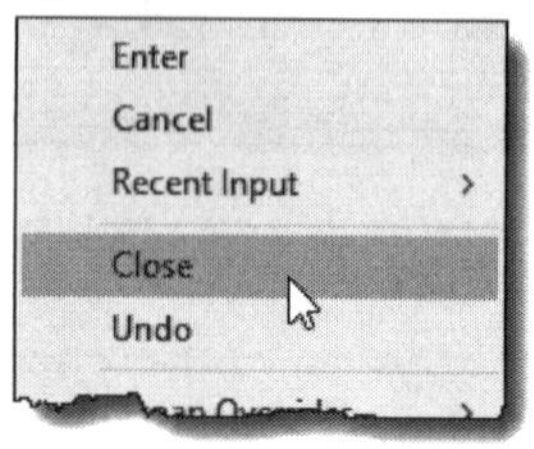

Task Objective:

Draw four contiguous lines by snapping to previously drawn objects. Use the "Close" feature of the Line command to create a closed area.

TIP: If you accidentally pick or snap to an incorrect point while using the Line command, you do not have to cancel and start over. After picking the wrong point, simply right-click and select Undo from the pop-up menu; this will only undo the previous pick point. Be careful not to mistake this for the Undo icon up on the Quick Access toolbar, as this will completely cancel the current command.

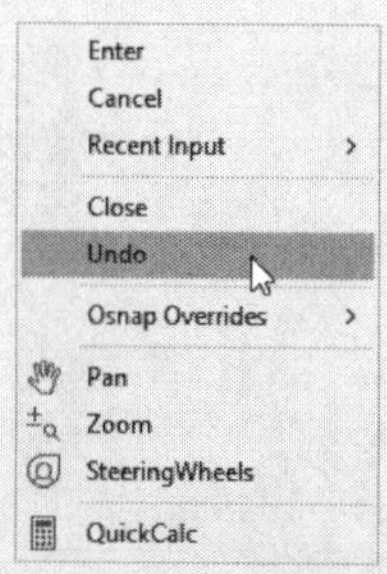

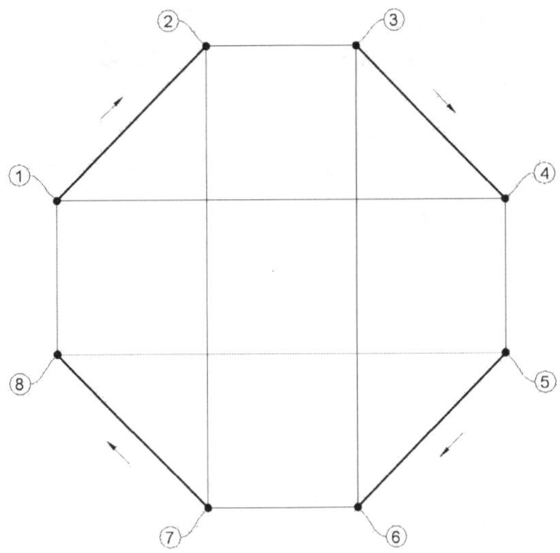

Task Objective:

Draw four individual angled line segments by snapping to previously drawn objects; this requires the Line command to be finished and restarted.

B Draw: Line

1. From the **Home** tab (in the **Draw** panel) select the **Line** command.
2. Using ***Object Snaps***, pick points (**1**) and (**2**).
3. At this point you need to finish the *Line* command (see *TIP* below); **right-click** and select **Enter**.

   TIP: You can also press the ***Esc*** *key to cancel the current command. (This is the preferred method as it is faster.)*

4. Repeat the previous steps to create the remaining three angled lines.

Because of the symmetry of the existing geometry, the lines you just drew are 45 degree lines. The existing "t" shaped line work is 15′-0″ x 15′-0″ overall and each individual square is 5′-0″ x 5′-0″. (This drawing is used for most of the tasks in this chapter to help you think about each task in a similar way. If you did not know the existing dimensions of the line work, you would need to verify them before you could rely on them as valid "pick points" for creating accurate new geometry.)

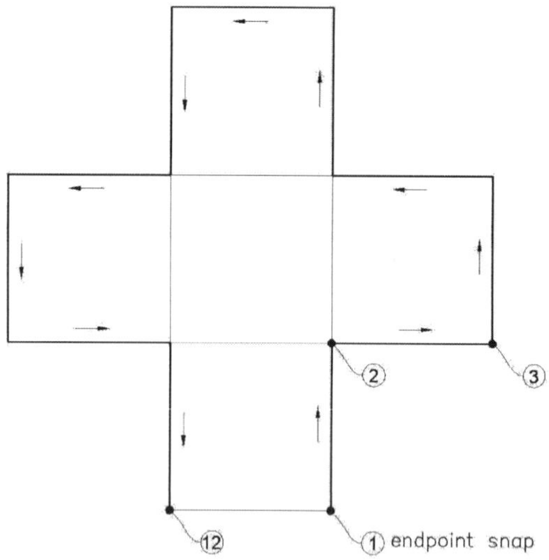

C Draw: Line

When you do not have points to pick you must tell AutoCAD the desired length and direction of a line; here you start with the 5′x5′ square in the middle and a 5′ horizontal line at the bottom.

1. Select the **Line** icon.
   (NOTICE: You will get less detailed instructions once a topic has been previously covered in the book.)

2. Using ***Object Snaps***, pick points (**1**) and (**2**).

3. Make sure **Polar Tracking** is turned on (icon toggle on the Application Status Bar Menu located at the bottom of the screen; see image below). This will allow you to easily create horizontal and vertical lines.

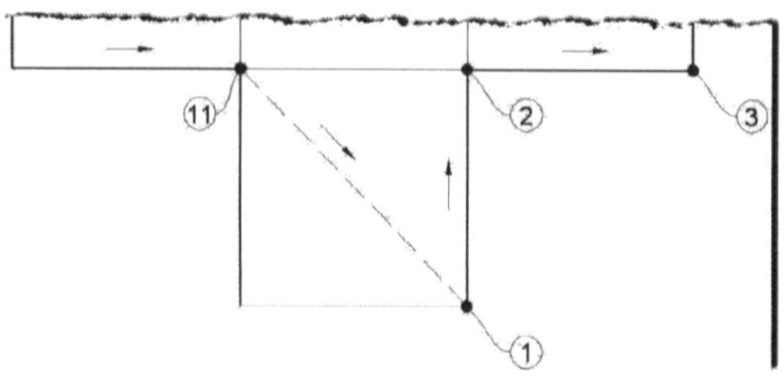

WARNING…
You cannot use the "Close" feature after point "11" as you will get the results shown in the image above (dashed line).

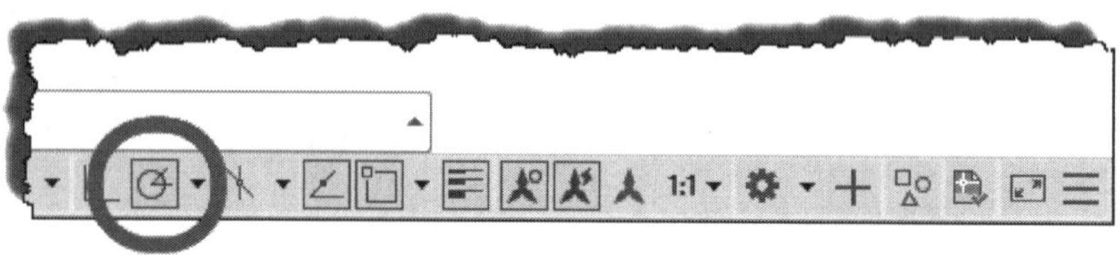

4. While still in the *Line* command, start moving your cursor to the right until you see the cursor snap to the horizontal and then type **5′** and then press **Enter**. See image and comments below.

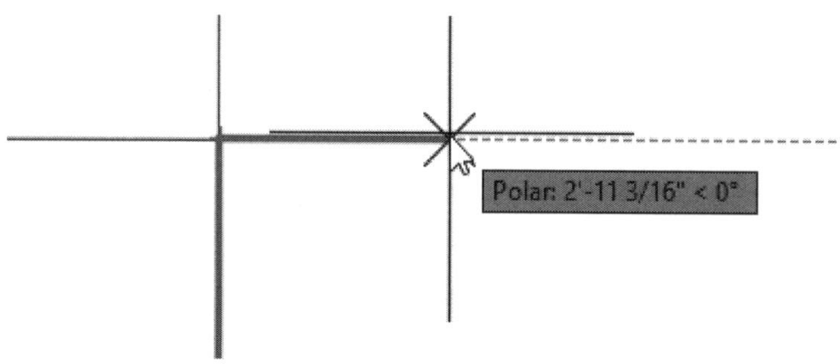

You can tell you have "snapped" to the horizontal when you see the dashed line between the start point and your cursor. Make sure you TYPE the distance and do not try to pick it based on the dimensions shown on the screen, which should only be used for reference. It is very difficult to click the correct point without moving the mouse and making the line off by a fraction of an inch.

5. Move your cursor straight up (i.e., vertical), and while "snapped" to the vertical type **5′** and then **Enter**.

   TIP: Make sure you add the foot symbol when entering your length. AutoCAD assumes inches when you do not specify via a foot or inch symbol. Thus, simply typing 5 and Enter would yield a 5 inch line, which may be hard to see and leave you to think you did not actually draw a line. Also, in this step you did not have to enter zero inches; you only have to enter inches when it is non-zero.

6. Continue the prescribed steps to complete the shape shown above.

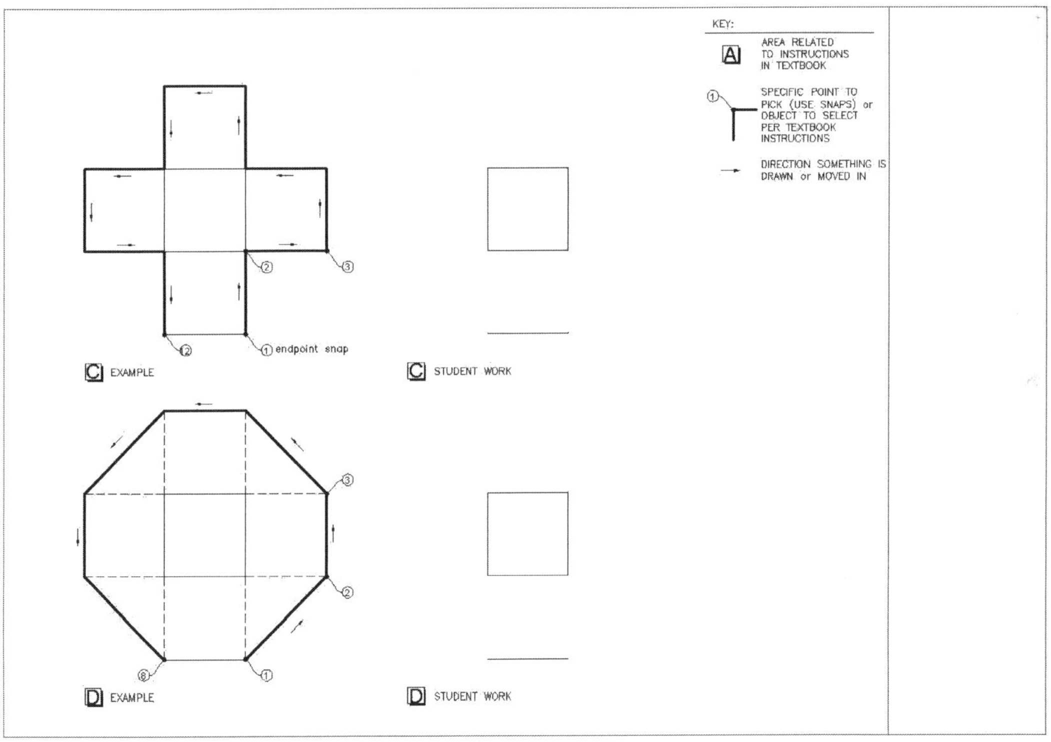

WORKING WITH THE ONLINE FILES…

This image shows you what you can expect to see when working with the online files which come with your textbook. The drawings on the left are examples of what you will be drawing and the area just to the right is where you are to do your work. Later in this chapter you will learn how to print these drawings so they can be turned in for grading.

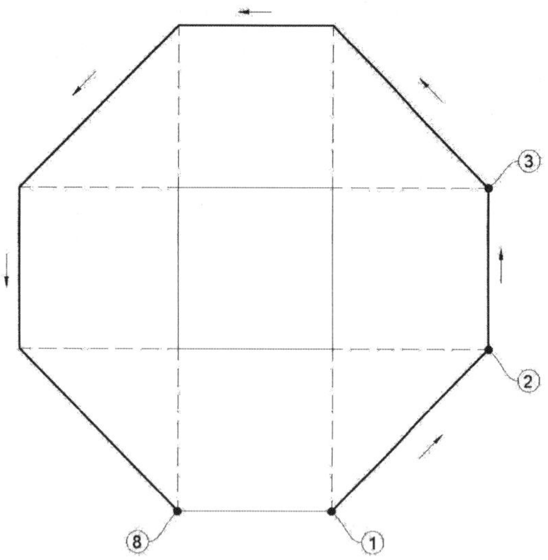

D **Draw: Line**

In this exercise you will learn to specify an angle and how to enter lengths with fractions.

You will be drawing 45 degree, horizontal and vertical line segments (7 lines total); you will be hitting the same relative points as in the previous example (example "B" above).

1. Use the **Line** command to begin a line at the right endpoint of the existing horizontal line (at the bottom).

AutoCAD, by default, is looking for the length of the line first. You will be entering it next, but consider the following warning first:

After typing the length, do not press *Enter*. If you do, you will get the correct length, but in an arbitrary angle/direction. You will need to press the *Tab* key to toggle over to the angle value before pressing *Enter*.

2. Type the following length with no spaces: **7'0-7/8** and then press **Tab**.
   a. Notice you did not have to add the inch symbol. (You can if you want to, but it is not required; less typing is better.)
   b. You should take note that the "dash" is between the whole inch and the fractional inch, rather than how you would write it (between the foot and the inch); AutoCAD needs to know where one part starts and the other stops; the "foot" and "dash" symbols do that (e.g., 7'0-7/8).
   c. Here are other ways to enter the same value in AutoCAD:
      i. 7'0.875 (decimal inch)
      ii. 84.875 (all inches)

3. Enter the desired angle; type **45** and then press **Enter**.

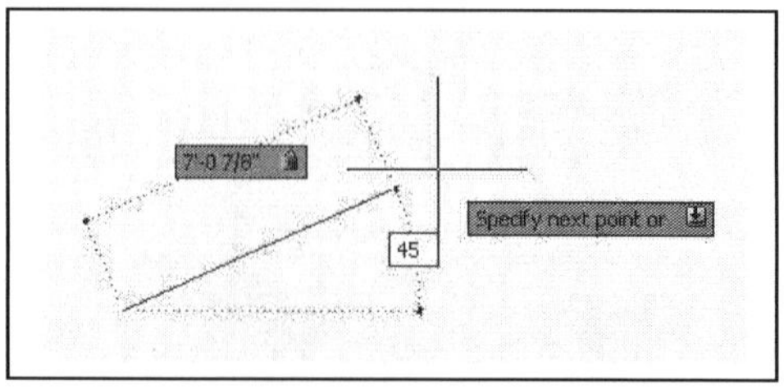

The image to the right shows the length "locked" in and the angle being entered. Once the angle is entered you can press *Tab* again to toggle back to edit the length.

You have now drawn your first line with a specific length and angle! Before drawing the remaining lines you need to understand how AutoCAD deals with angles.

- Angles are measured off a horizontal plane in a counterclockwise direction as shown in the image below.
- Therefore, wherever you want to draw an angled line you can imagine a horizontal line passing through the start point and determine the proper angle to enter.

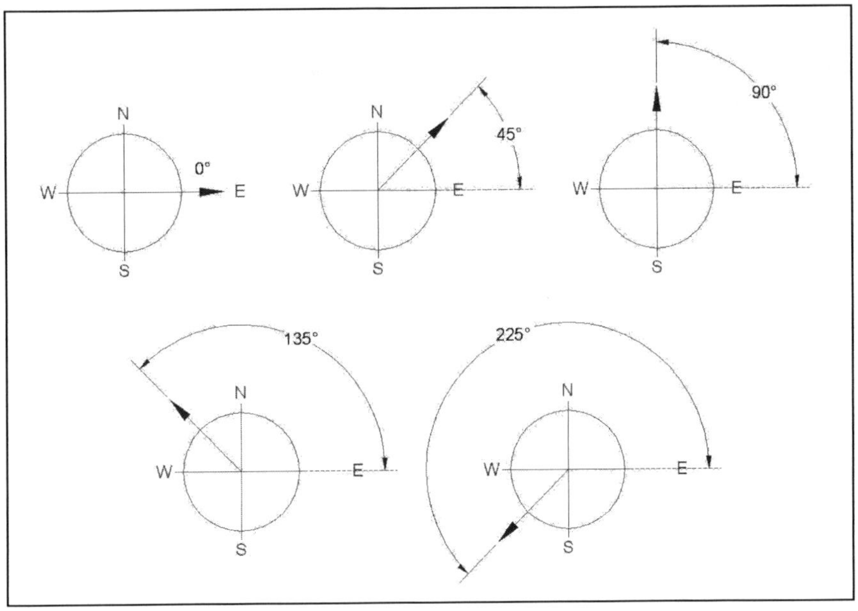

4. Finish drawing the remaining lines (5′-0″ and 7′-0 7/8″ long lines) at the proper angle. Remember to use the Tab key to toggle between entering the length and the angle.

   ***FYI:** The length of the angled line (i.e., hypotenuse) is determined via the Pythagorean Theorem (see image to the right).*

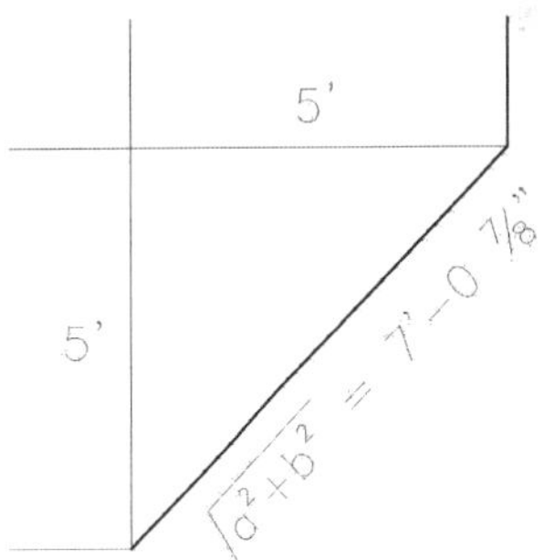

When finished, the last point should coincide with the left endpoint of the existing horizontal line from which you started.

Draw → Arc

Now that you have explored the basics of the *Line* command you will take a look at drawing curved lines, Arcs to be specific. You will soon see that AutoCAD offers several predefined ways in which you may create Arcs.

You will only look at four variations here, but you are encouraged to try the others if you have time. **Open file Ex2-2b Draw Commands – Arc.dwg from the online files.**

> *FYI: A number of the following exercise graphics have been condensed onto one "t" reference background to save a little paper. Notice in the image below that the four letters correspond to the written instructions on the right. Also, the number pick/ select items should be visually grouped together and related to the lettered keys.*

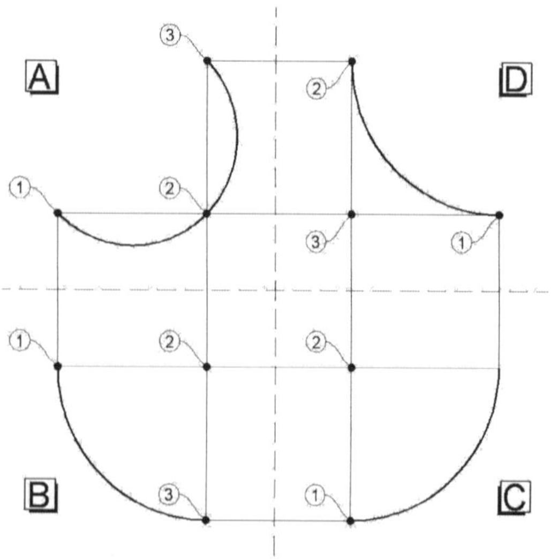

A Draw: Arc

3-Point… This version of the *Arc* command draws an arc through three points picked on-screen.

1. On the **Home** tab (in the **Draw** panel) select the **Arc** icon (not the down-arrow, just the icon). This icon is located directly to the right of the *Line* command.

Notice the prompt near your cursor: "Specify start point of arc" (see image below). It is important to pay close attention to these prompts when learning AutoCAD so you know what information is required and in what order.

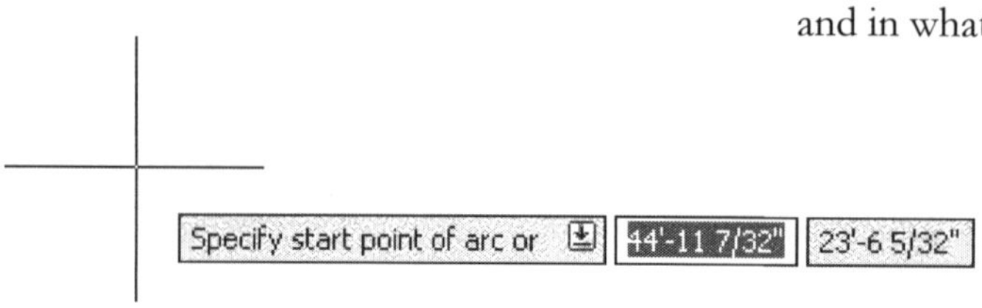

ON-SCREEN PROMPT
This image shows the on-screen prompt (aka, the Dynamic Input feature) just after selecting the Arc icon – the user is instructed to pick or type the coordinates of the first point of the Arc.

2. Pick the three points shown in area "A" per the following comments:
   a. Be sure to use *Object Snaps.*
   b. Pick points in order shown.
   c. Actually, the first and last picks can be reversed; the second pick cannot change in order to get the desired results.

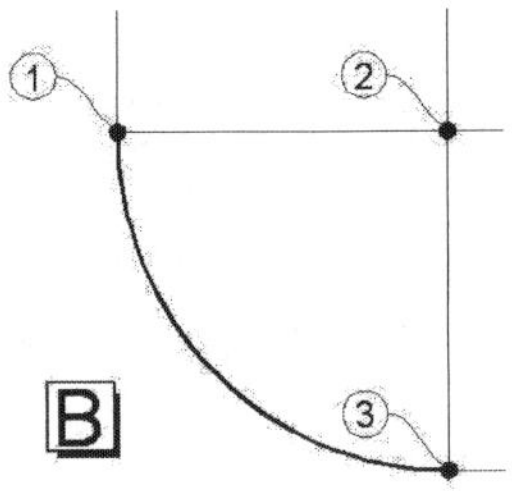

B Draw: Arc

Start, Center, End… This version of the *Arc* command draws an arc based on three points picked, similarly to the previous command, but the second pick represents the Center of the arc rather than its Midpoint.

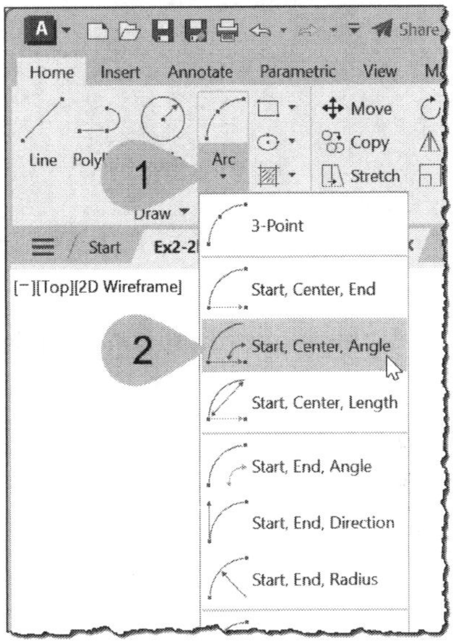

Arc icon options…
This image shows the additional Arc options revealed by the down-arrow.

1. Click the "down-arrow" attached to the Arc icon (see image to the right) and then select the Arc command named: **Start, Center, End.**
2. Pick the three points shown in area "B" per the following comments:
   a. Be sure to use *Object Snaps.*
   b. Pick points in order shown.
   c. Actually, the first and last picks can be reversed; the second pick cannot change in order to get the desired results.
3. Notice the Start, Center, End icon has moved to the top of the *Arc* "icon stack"; this is done in anticipation that you use this command again. When you close AutoCAD and re-open it all icon "stacks" will be reset.

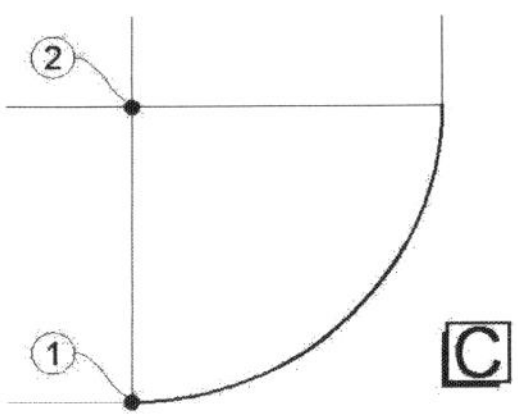

C Draw: Arc

Start, Center, Angle… This version of the *Arc* command lets you pick two points and then type an angle. This is handy if you only have two points you can snap to in the current drawing.

1. Select the **Start, Center, Angle** icon.
2. Pick the two points shown in area "C" per the following comments:
   a. Pick points in the order shown and use *Object Snaps.*
3. Type **90** and then press **Enter.**

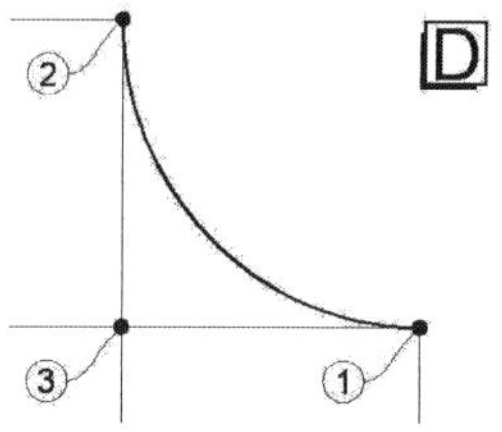

Draw: Arc

Start, End, Direction… With this version of the *Arc* command, you pick the start and end points followed by the direction in which the Arc should be drawn.

1. Select the **Start, End, Direction** icon.

2. Pick the three points shown in area "D" per the following comments:
   a. Pick points in the order shown and use *Object Snaps.*

At this point you should be able to draw an Arc when needed. You are encouraged to try the other *Arc* commands to learn how they work.

TIP: When you hover your cursor over an icon, you will get an informative tooltip about that command. For more information, press the F1 *key as suggested to read more on that subject in the AutoCAD Help system. The image below shows an example of a tooltip for an Arc icon and the Help location you are automatically taken to when you press* F1.

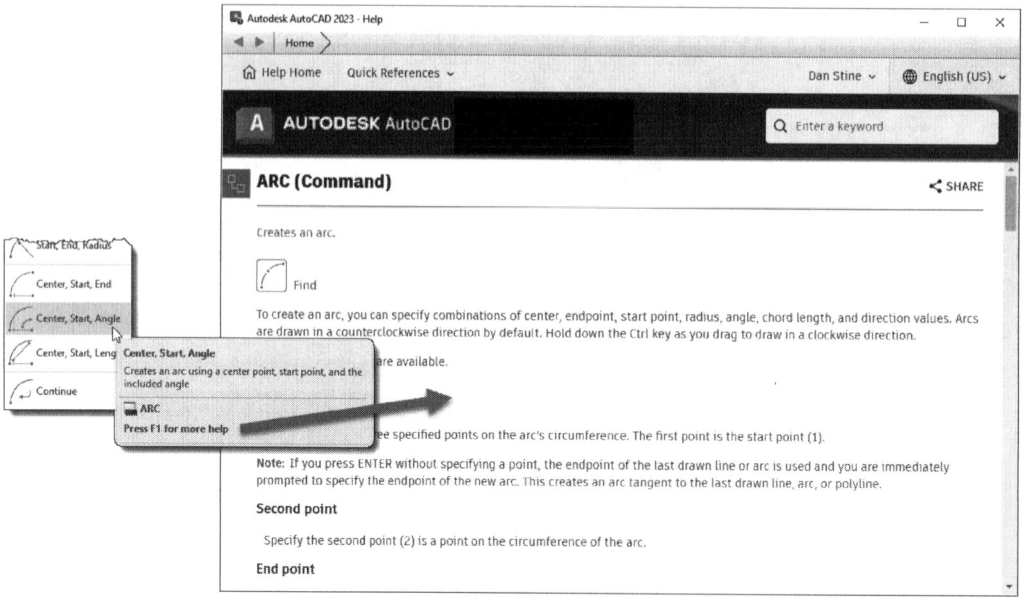

Draw → Circle, Rectangle, Ellipse and Hatch

The *Circle* command is used to draw many things in an architectural drawing, for example, columns, tables, etc. Sometimes an entire building is round when viewed from the sky; in this case the large circle would have been drawn in AutoCAD as the starting point for everything else. Modify commands like *Break* and *Trim* (covered later in this book) can remove a portion of a previously drawn circle, thus converting it to an Arc object.

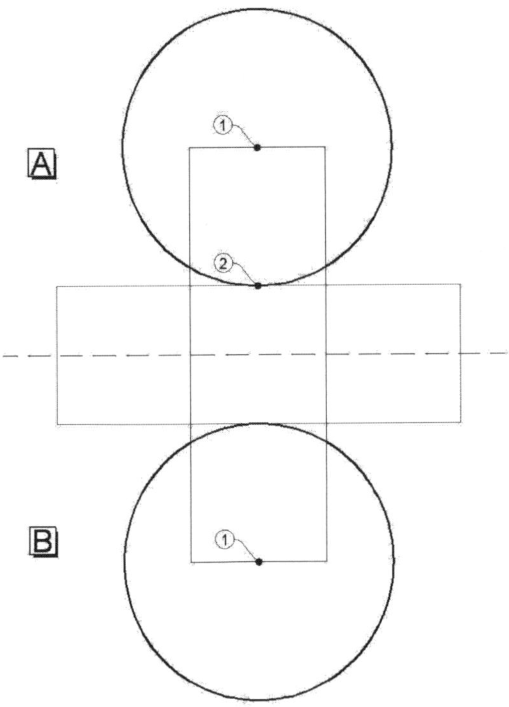

A Draw: Circle

Center, Radius… This [default] version of the *Circle* command draws a circle by picking the circle's center point and then picking or typing a radius. When picking a point for the radius, the radius is determined by the distance between your two picks.

1. Open **Ex2-2c Draw Commands – Circle.dwg**.

2. On the **Home** tab (in the **Draw** panel) select the **Circle** icon (not the down-arrow, just the icon). This icon is located directly to the right of the *Line* command.

Remember to look at the prompt near your cursor if you have Dynamic Input turned on (toggle located in the Drafting and Display Tools area below the Drawing Window).

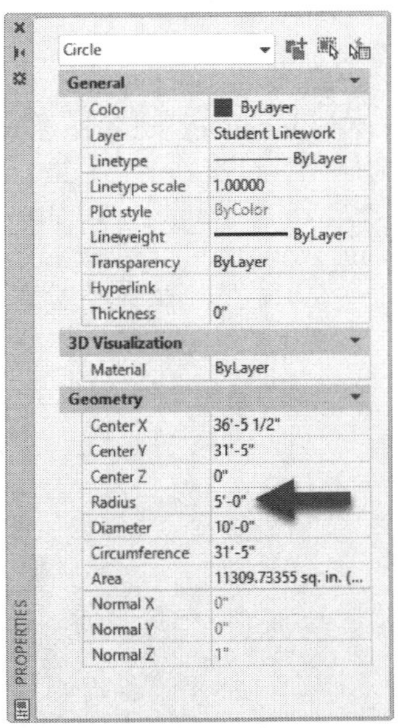

3. **Specify center point for Circle:** Use the *Midpoint* snap for the first pick shown in the image above (area "A").

4. **Specify radius of circle:** Use either the *Midpoint* or the *Perpendicular* snap for the second pick point (area "A").

5. Select the circle, right-click, and then pick **Properties** from the pop-up menu (see image to the right). Notice the radius is 5′-0″ and the circumference and area are also listed!

B Draw: Circle

Center, Radius… This time you will type the radius rather than picking a second point on-screen.

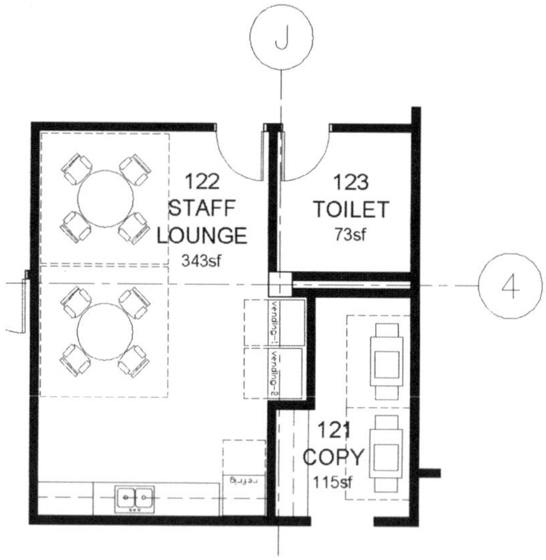

ARCHITECTURAL EXAMPLE…
Here you can see circles drawn to represent two tables and two grid bubbles. Arcs are used to show door swings as well.

1. Select the **Circle** icon; you may also close the *Properties* palette if you wish.

   TIP: Selecting a "draw" command will automatically cancel any active command and/or deselect objects.

2. **Specify center point for Circle:** Use the *Midpoint* snap for the first pick shown in the image above (area "B" – see previous page).

3. **Specify radius of circle:** Rather than picking a point you will type the radius; type: **5′0** and then press **Enter**.

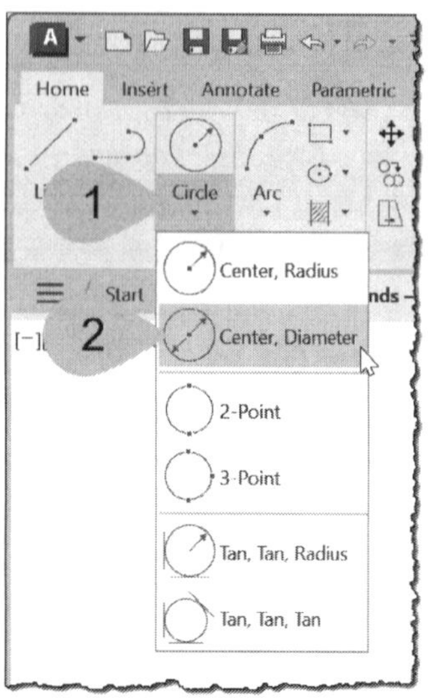

You have just drawn two circles that are the same size. For one you picked two points and for the other you picked one point and typed a radius to define the circle. It is possible to draw a circle without picking any points; this would require typing an X,Y,Z coordinate for the first (i.e., center) point. If you leave off the Z value, AutoCAD will assume 0 (well, actually it will assume you want the current elevation, which is usually zero but can be changed with the *Elevation* command).

The image to the left shows the various predefined *Circle* creation tools. This list is revealed by clicking the down-arrow located next to the *Circle* icon. Similar to the *Arc* icon stack, when you select one from the list, that command will move to the top (until AutoCAD is restarted).

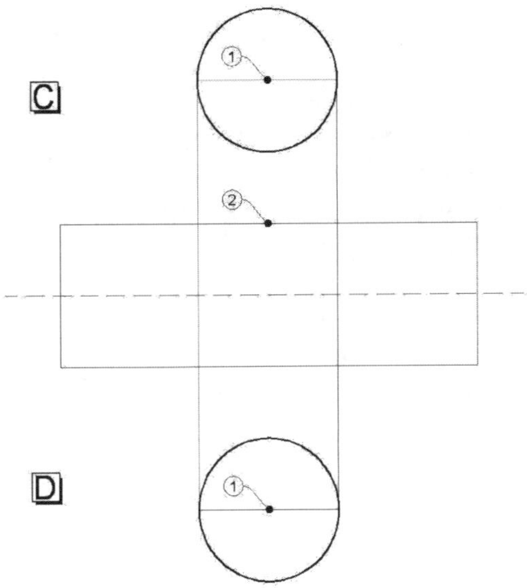

SMALLER CIRCLES...
These circles are exactly half the size of the circles in the previous example because the circle's radius is exactly half its diameter.

C Draw: Circle

Center, Diameter... This version of the *Circle* command allows you to enter the diameter rather than the radius.

1. On the **Home** tab (in the **Draw** panel) select the down-arrow next to the *Circle* icon, and then select **Center, Diameter** (see icon stack expanded on the previous page).

2. **Specify center point for Circle:** Use the *Midpoint* snap for the first pick shown in the image above (area "C").

3. **Specify radius of circle:** Use either the *Midpoint* or the *Perpendicular* snap for the second pick point (area "C").

D Draw: Circle

Center, Diameter... This time you will pick one point and type a length value for the diameter.

1. Select the **Center, Diameter** icon, which should be accessible without clicking the down-arrow (assuming you are doing this exercise immediately after the previous one).

2. **Specify center point for Circle:** Use the *Midpoint* snap for the first pick shown in the image above (area "D").

3. **Specify radius of circle:** Rather than picking a point you will type the radius; type **5'0** and then press **Enter**.

As you can see, by picking the same points and entering the same values in examples A-B and C-D, you get different results because one *Circle* icon requires the radius and the other expects the diameter.

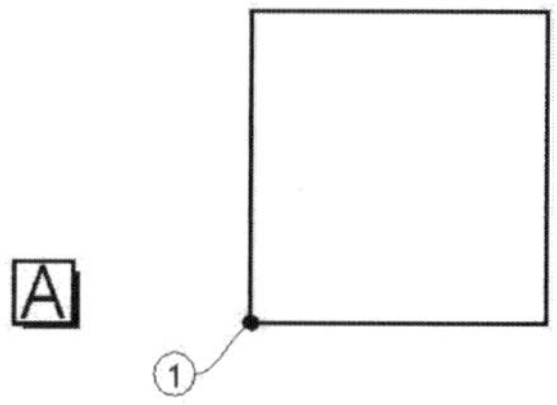

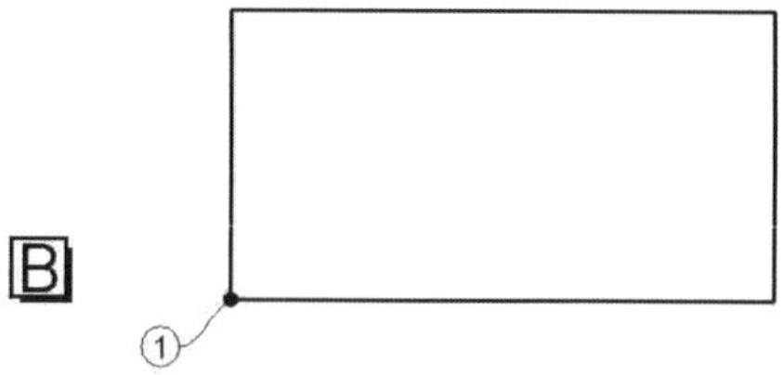

A Draw: Rectangle

Drawing a square… there is no “rectangle” object in AutoCAD (like there is a *Circle* object as viewed in the *Properties* palette); the Rectangle command creates what is called a *Polyline*. The *Rectangle* tool simply automates the creation process – the manual method would be to use the *Polyline* command and individually draw the four sides of the rectangle desired.

Open file: **Ex2-2d Draw Commands - Rectangle**

1. On the **Home** tab, in the **Draw** panel, select the **Rectangle** icon.

   You use the *Rectangle* command to draw squares.

2. **Specify first corner point:** Pick approximately as shown.

3. **Specify other corner point:** type: **5′** and then **Tab** (not Enter).

4. Type **5′** and then press **Enter**.

B Draw: Rectangle

Rectangle… Next you will draw a rectangle.

1. Select the **Rectangle** icon.

2. **Specify first corner point:** Pick the first point (the lower left corner of the rectangle).

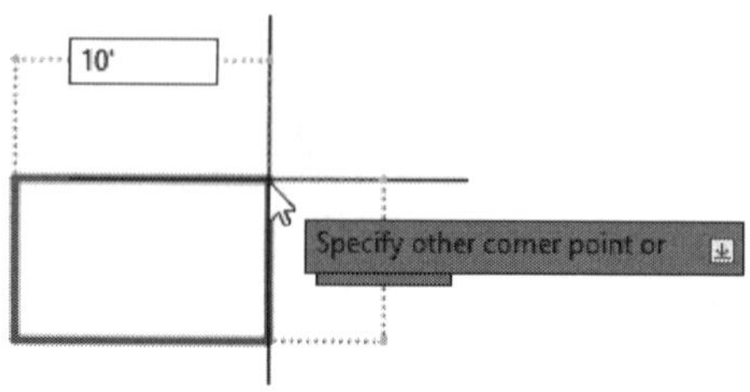

When manually entering the dimensions of a rectangle, you enter the width and then the height, pressing *Tab* to toggle back and forth between these two values. Press *Enter* to finish.

3. **Specify other corner point:** type **10′** and then press **Tab** (not Enter).

4. Type **5′** and then press **Enter**.

As you can see, drawing a rectangle is not difficult. Next you will look at two ways in which you can “embellish” the rectangle as you draw it.

C

D

C Draw: Rectangle

Filleted rectangle… The *Rectangle* command has a sub-command that lets you fillet, or round, the corners of the rectangle. This can be done with the *Fillet* command (a Modify command covered later) after the rectangle has been drawn as well; there is no need to erase and redraw.

1. Select the **Rectangle** icon.
2. The prompt near your cursor should say "Specify First Corner or", which is followed by a down-arrow icon. You cannot click this icon as it moves with your cursor; this icon is telling you to press the down-arrow on your keyboard for more options relative to the current command. **Press the down-arrow on your keyboard** (see image below).

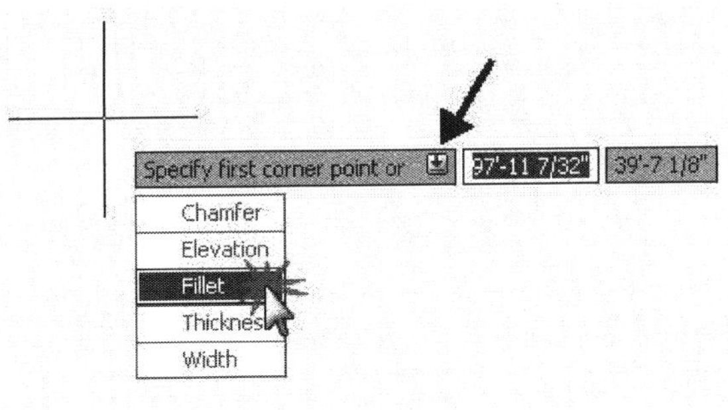

3. With your cursor, click the **Fillet** option.
4. Type **6** and **Enter** to specify a 6″ radius for all corners.
5. Now draw a **10′-0″ x 5′-0″** (width x height) rectangle to finish the command.

Notice the rectangle is the same overall size as the one drawn in the previous exercise, except this one has corners rounded with a 6″ radius.

D Draw: Rectangle

Heavy rectangle… Another sub-command of the *Rectangle* tool is the *Width* option. This allows you to create thick (or heavy) lines. Normally you use another method to deal with line weights; however, this option lets you create lines that are heavier than the commonly used drafting lines.

1. Select the **Rectangle** icon.
2. Press the **Down-Arrow** on the keyboard.
3. Select **Width** from the on-screen drop-down list (see image below).

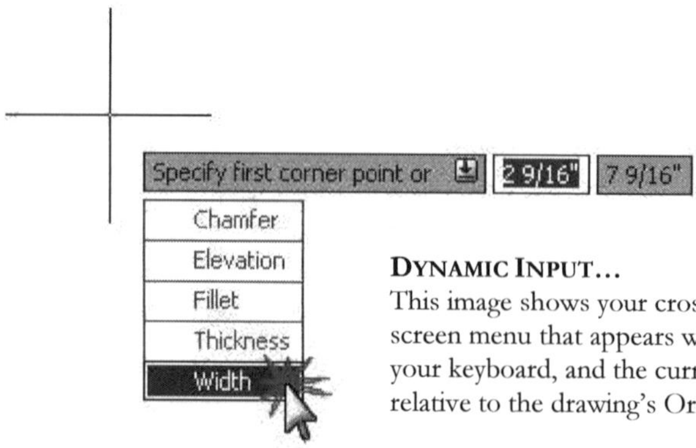

DYNAMIC INPUT…
This image shows your crosshairs in the upper left, the on-screen menu that appears when you press the down-arrow on your keyboard, and the current coordinates of your crosshairs relative to the drawing's Origin (for your reference).

4. Type **2** and then press **Enter**. ***REMEMBER:*** *2 by itself equals inches.*
5. Set the *Fillet Radius* back to **0** (*see the steps on the previous page*).
6. Now draw a **10'-0" x 5'-0"** (width x height) rectangle to finish the command.

TIP: *When you press the down-arrow on your keyboard to see the menu of options, you can continue pressing the down-arrow to highlight one of the options, and then pressing Enter selects it. This is a little faster than using the mouse.*

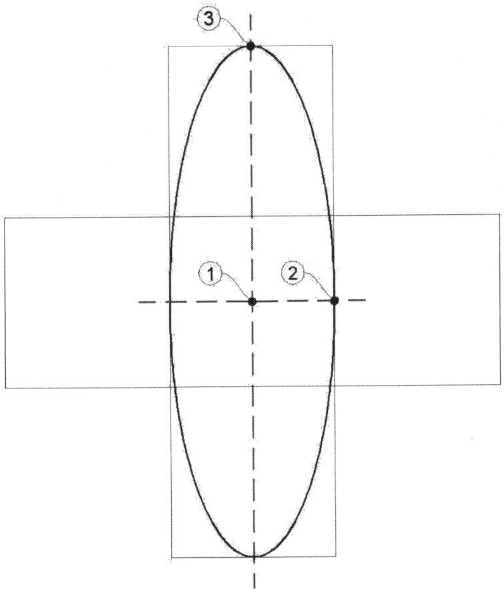

A Draw: Ellipse

Center… The ellipse is a special shape in AutoCAD; that is, when selected, the *Properties* palette identifies it as an ellipse, not a polyline. AutoCAD provides three ways (i.e., icons) to create an ellipse, each of which are simply different ways to derive the major and minor axes, the main ingredients of an ellipse! The first one you will try requires you to pick the *Center* and then two edges of the ellipse.

1. On the **Home** tab, in the **Draw** panel, select the **Ellipse** icon.

You will use ***Object Snap Tracking*** to accurately pick the center point of the ellipse, which will be a point centered on the "t" shaped background. The center point is not directly "pickable" as no lines exist in that area. To pick the center point you could draw temporary lines before using the *Ellipse* command and then erase the temporary lines. A better option is to use *Object Snap Tracking*, which allows you to pick a point based on other nearby points. You will try this now…

2. Make sure that ***Object Snap Tracking*** is turned on (see image below) on the *Status Bar*. If it is not, you can turn it on while the *Ellipse* command is still active; a bluish highlight means enabled.

For the next few commands, see the image on the next page.

3. Referring to the image on the next page, **hover** your cursor at **point A**. You will see a *Midpoint* snap icon appear (*Midpoint OSNAP* must be active). Also note the following comments:
   a. <u>Do not click</u> the mouse button.
   b. You must hover for about 2-3 seconds for the *Object Snap Tracking* to kick in. You will see a small "plus" symbol when you move the cursor away to signify it worked.

4. **Hover** your cursor over **point B** (see image below).
    a. Do not click the mouse button.
    b. You will also see a *Midpoint* snap icon here.

5. Now move your cursor to the middle/center of the "t" shaped background drawing. When your cursor snaps and you see vertical and horizontal reference lines appear, you can **click** the mouse button.

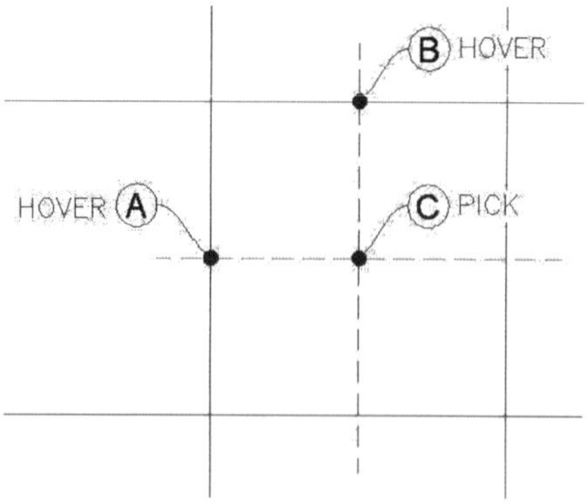

▲ OBJECT SNAP TRACKING...
This image shows how you can snap to the midpoint of the square even though no point exists to snap to. While in a command, with *Object Snap Tracking* enabled, you hover your cursor over points A & B (you never actually pick these points), then move the cursor to where those two points intersect, and then click the mouse button (point C).

The previous three steps must be done in consecutive order as *Object Snap Tracking* only "remembers" reference points until a command is canceled or another one is activated.

You can learn more about this feature by typing "object snap tracking" (including the quotation marks) in the search box as shown below.

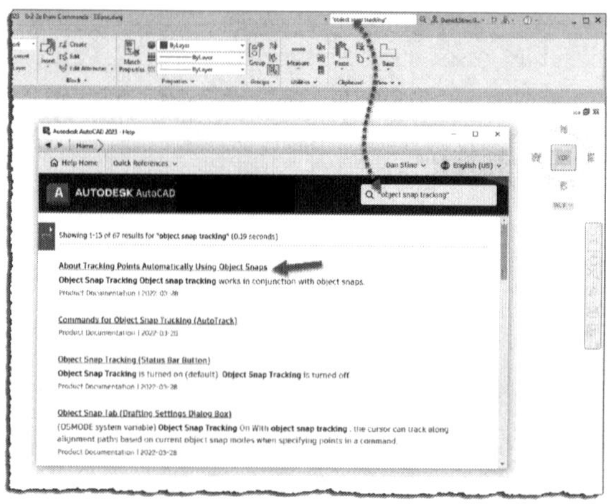

6. Now finish the command by picking points 2 and 3 (see image on previous page); these are both *Midpoint* snaps.

You have now drawn an ellipse whose minor axis is 5′-0″ and major axis is 15′-0″. (Remember the background image consists of 5′ x 5′ squares.) You can type values rather than picking points 2 and 3 if you know them. For example, you could pick the centerpoint, start moving the cursor to the right, type **2′6**, and then *Enter*; next, start moving the cursor up from center, type **7′6**, and then *Enter* (never actually picking points 2 and 3). If you have points to snap to, that is easier, but when you don't you usually have to type the values.

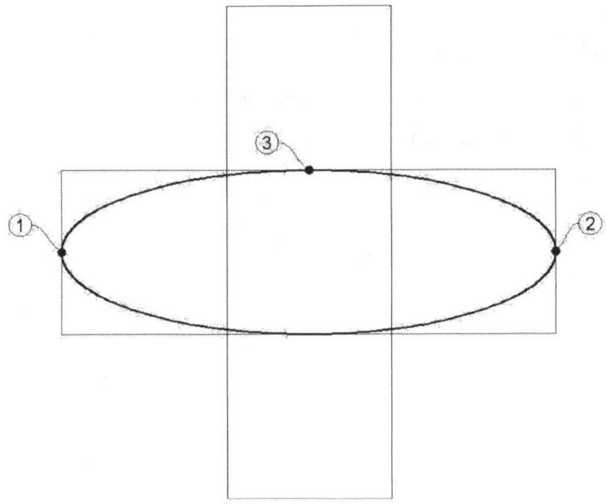

B Draw: Ellipse

Axis, End… This variation on the *Ellipse* command allows you to pick two points (or type a value) that define one axis and then pick a third point (or type a value) that defines half the length of the opposite axis.

1. Click the down-arrow next to the *Ellipse* icon, and select **Axis, End**.

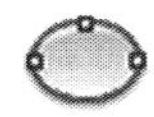

You will draw an ellipse by picking three points…

2. Using your *Midpoint* snap, pick the three points in the order shown.

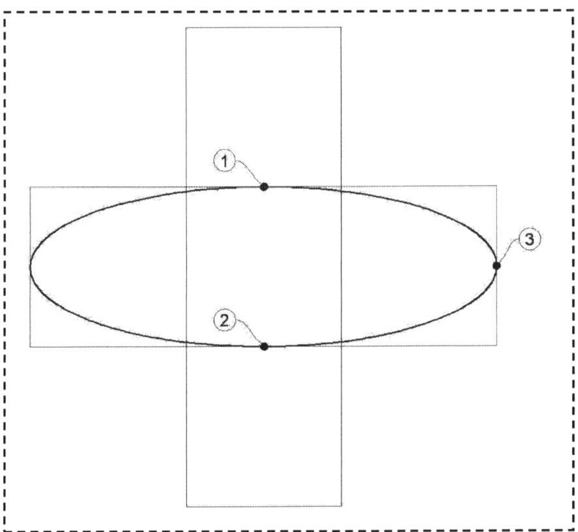

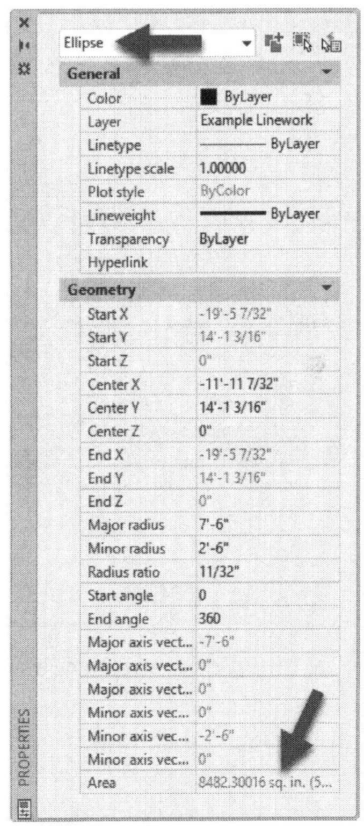

The image above shows how the same ellipse could be produced by picking three different points.

In both images on this page, points 1 and 2 can be selected in either order; AutoCAD is only looking for the total distance between the two pick points.

Note the various types of information available via the *Properties* palette for the ellipse just drawn. The object type, *Ellipse* in this case, is identified at the top of the palette. The area is given in square inches and square feet.

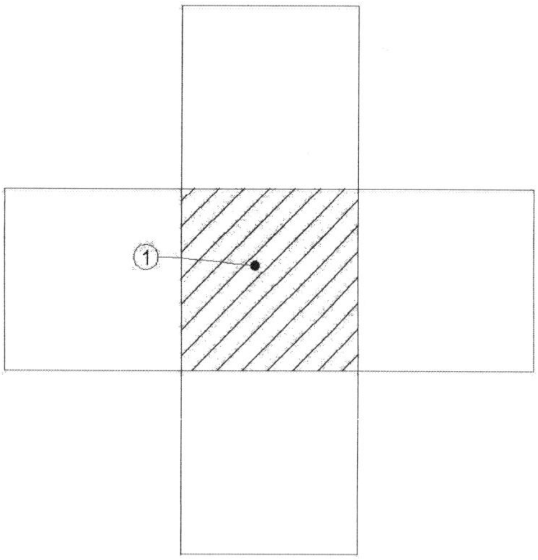

Draw: Hatch

Add: Pick points… The *Hatch* command allows you to fill an enclosed area with a pattern or solid fill. While using the command, you can pick the lines that define the perimeter or, more conveniently, you can pick within the perimeter and AutoCAD will automatically find the extents; this is called *Pick points*. The *Hatch* can be set to adjust as the perimeter is modified; this is called *Associative*. Here you will just learn the basics…

Open file: **Ex2-2f Draw Commands – Hatch.dwg**

1. On the **Home** tab, in the **Draw** panel, select the **Hatch** icon.

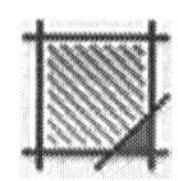

Next you will create a hatch pattern by picking a point within the middle of the center square area. Once the *Hatch* command is initiated, you will see the contextual tab shown below.

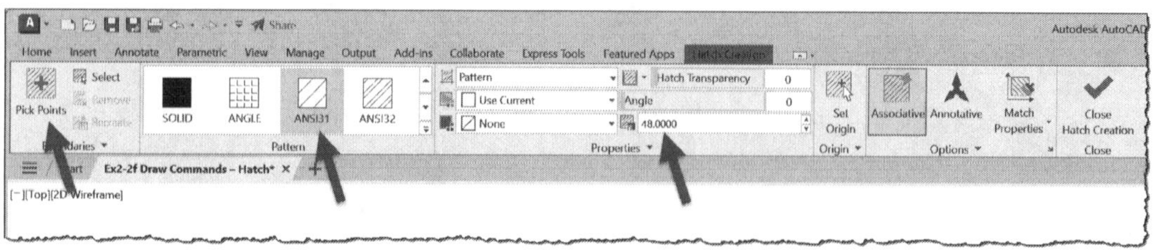

2. Set the *Scale* to **48** (click in the box and type the number).

3. Click the **Pick points** icon (this is the default).

4. Make sure the Pattern panel is set to **ANSI31** (this is a specific pattern).

5. Click anywhere in the center square (you will see the found perimeter highlight).

   FYI: *Just hovering your cursor in an enclosed area, AutoCAD will show a preview of what the pattern would look like if you click.*

6. Click **Close Hatch Creation** to finish the *Hatch* command.

Those are the basics; next you will learn how to change the pattern…

B Draw: Hatch

Pick points… Next you will simply change the pattern used to hatch an area, plus you will *Hatch* more than one area.

1. On the **Home** tab, in the **Draw** panel, select the **Hatch** icon.

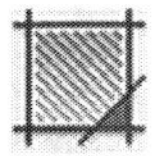

FYI: When you Hatch multiple areas at one time, AutoCAD creates one Hatch object (by default). This example is done this way; thus, if you delete the Hatch, all four areas are deleted.

2. Change the pattern to **Gravel**:
   a. Click to expand the Pattern panel (see image to the left).
   b. Select pattern as shown below.

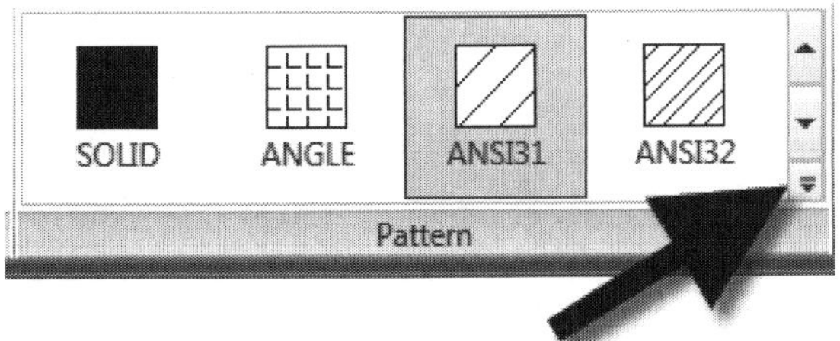

HATCH PATTERN PANEL…
When selecting a pattern you can either click the up and down arrows to scroll through the patterns or click the expand icon to see more patterns at once.

3. Set the *Scale* to **24**.

4. Use **Pick Points** to pick the four outer squares.

5. Click **Close Hatch Creation** to finish the *Hatch* command.

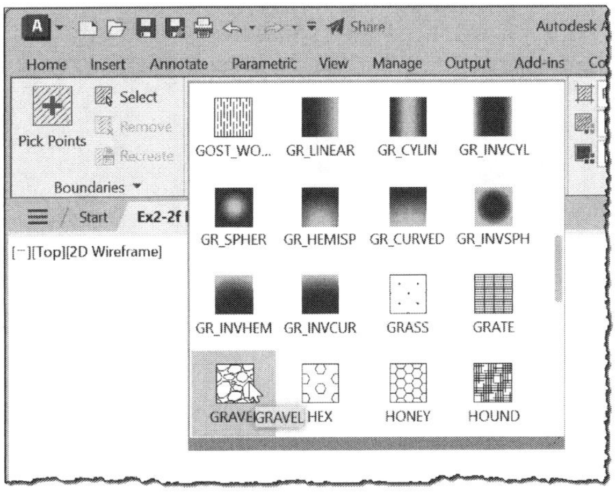

PATTERN PALETTE EXPANDED ➤
This image shows the preview swatches you can use to visually see what each Hatch pattern looks like

Exercise 2-3:
Modify – Part 1

Introduction

Now that you have a few *Draw* tools under your belt you will take a look at some of the *Modify* tools that allow you to manipulate the things created with the *Draw* tools. It is much faster, usually, to edit the existing line work than to erase it and redraw.

Modify → Move

The *Move* command works exactly like the *Line* command in that you specify a length and direction (i.e., angle). The difference is that something(s) is relocated rather than a line being drawn. The example below shows the comparison between drawing a line (on the left) and moving a line (on the right).

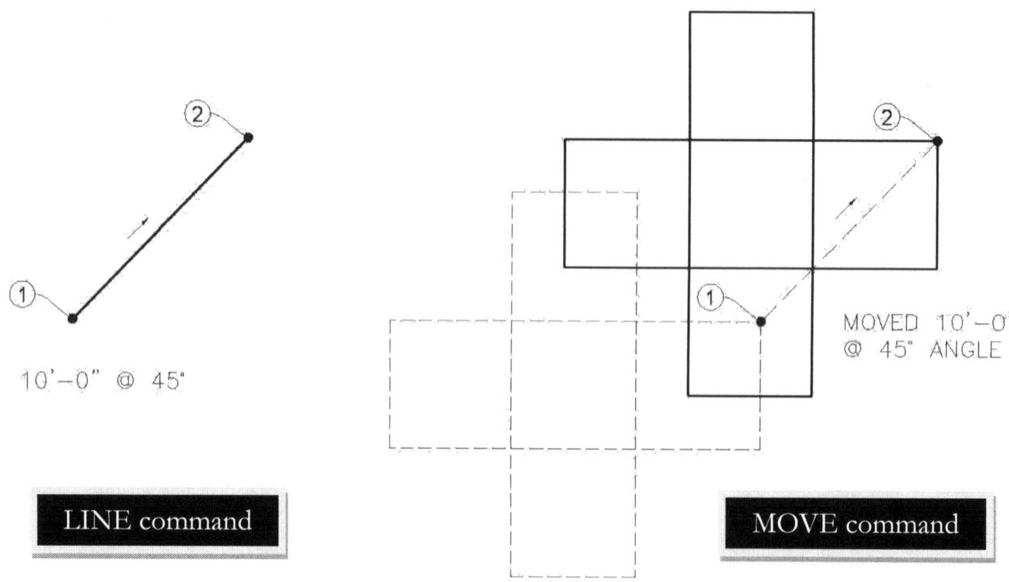

If you know the exact distance and angle you want to move something, you do not have to snap to any points.

The points picked in the example to the right are close to the object to be moved but are not on it. Actually, the second point is not really "picked" when you are typing the values.

NOTE: The imaginary vector accurately represents the displacement.

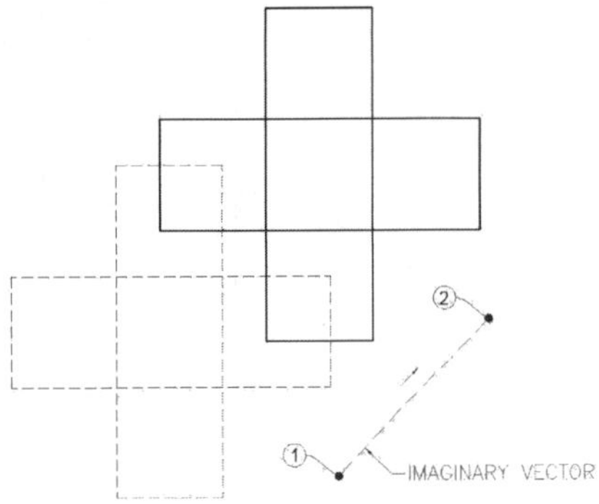

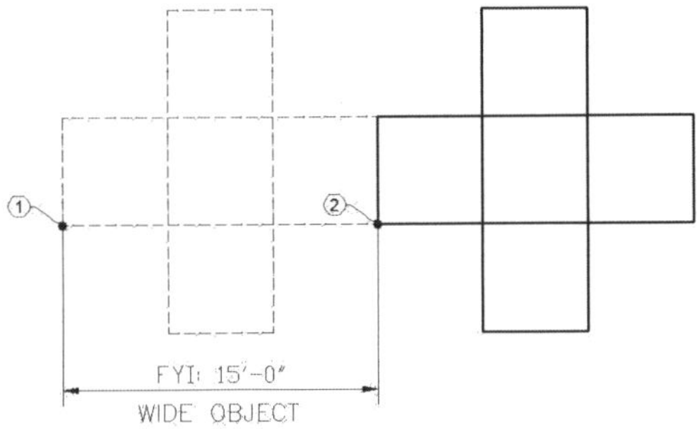

If you have points to pick, that is easier than typing the values. The example to the left shows how you can move the "t" exactly 15′-0″ to the right.

Move command outline:

- **Select the *Move* icon**
- **Select objects to move**
  - You can pick one or more items; you can select items individually or by windowing (or both).
  - Right-click or press Enter to tell AutoCAD you are done selecting objects to move.
- **Specify the distance and angle**
  - You can pick/snap to two points if available.
  - Or, you can pick one point and then type the length and angle (a.k.a., displacement).

That's it; next you will give it a try…

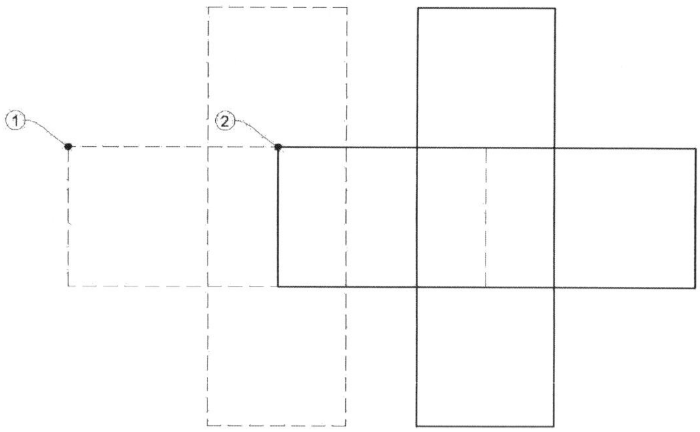

A **Modify: Move**

Picking points… In this exercise you will be picking points to define the object's displacement. You should note the concept that you can pick both points from the object you are moving, which are based on its original location (i.e., before it was moved) all while the object is being moved.

Open file: **Ex2-3a Modify Commands - Move.dwg**

1. On the **Home** tab, in the **Modify** panel, select the **Move** icon.

Next you will select the entire "t" shaped object by window selection, and then move it 7′-6″ to the right.

2. **Select** all the lines that represent the "t" shaped object (use a window to quickly select them all).

3. **Right-click** (to tell AutoCAD you are done selecting items to move).

Both points you are about to pick are on the object in its original location, represented by the dashed lines in the example above.

4. **Pick point #1** (*Endpoint* snap).

5. **Pick point #2** (*Midpoint* snap because we know the overall length is 15′-0″ thus ½ or mid-way is 7′-6″).

Everything has now been moved 7′-6″ to the right and the *Move* command is no longer active.

As long as your original drawing is accurate and you know what its dimensions are, you can use its snap points to accurately draw and modify line work. If the original line work is not perfectly orthogonal (i.e., horizontal or vertical), you would not have moved the lines exactly to the right. (You would have to type the values, or better, fit the drawing and then move it.)

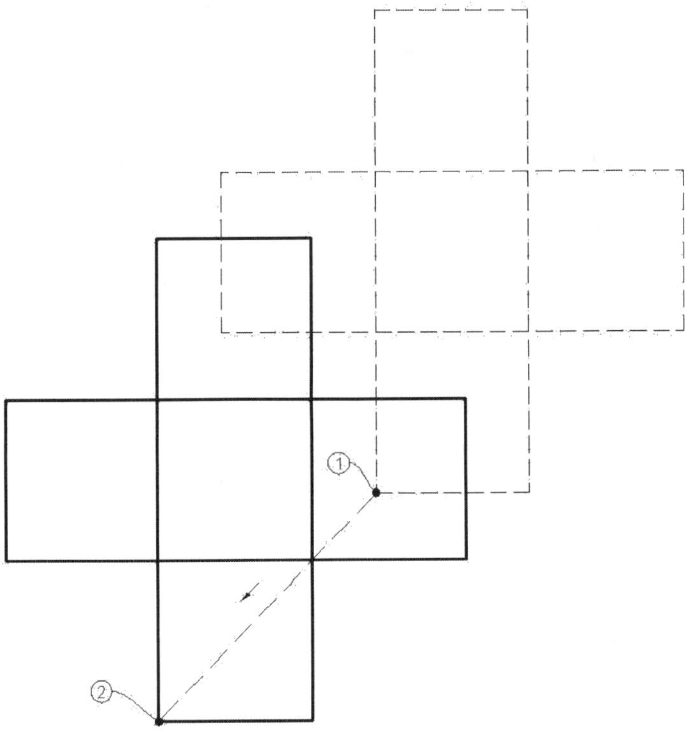

B Modify: Move

Typing values… In this exercise you will be typing the length and angle because you have nothing to snap to for the second point.

TIP: On complex drawings it may be easier to reduce the number of running snaps. Otherwise, AutoCAD has to think about more options, and you might click thinking you are snapping to an endpoint but a center point of a nearby circle was accidently selected instead. You can also hold the Shift key and then right-click your mouse button for snap overrides – good for one pick!

1. Select the **Move** icon.

Next you will select the entire "t" shaped object by window selection and then move it 10′-0″ at a 45 degree angle (down and to the left).

2. **Select** all the lines.

3. **Pick point #1** (*Endpoint* snap).

4. Start typing **10′** and then press **Tab** (not Enter).

   TIP: Make sure Ortho is not active.

5. Type **225**. (Remember the angle is off the horizontal from the right.)

6. Press **Enter**.

The lines are now relocated 10′-0″ away at a 45 degree angle. (AutoCAD needed to know the angle relative to the first pick point.)

A Modify: Copy

The *Copy* command works exactly like the *Move* command, except the original linework is retained. If you look closely, you will see the only difference between the command outline for *Copy* (below) and *Move* (a few pages back) is that the word Move has been replaced with Copy.

Copy command outline:

- **Select the *Copy* icon**
- **Select objects to copy**
  - You can pick one or more items; you can select items individually or by windowing (or both).
  - Right-click or press Enter to tell AutoCAD you are done selecting objects to copy.
- **Specify the distance and angle**
  - You can pick/snap to two points if available.
  - Or, you can pick one point and then type the length and angle (a.k.a., displacement).

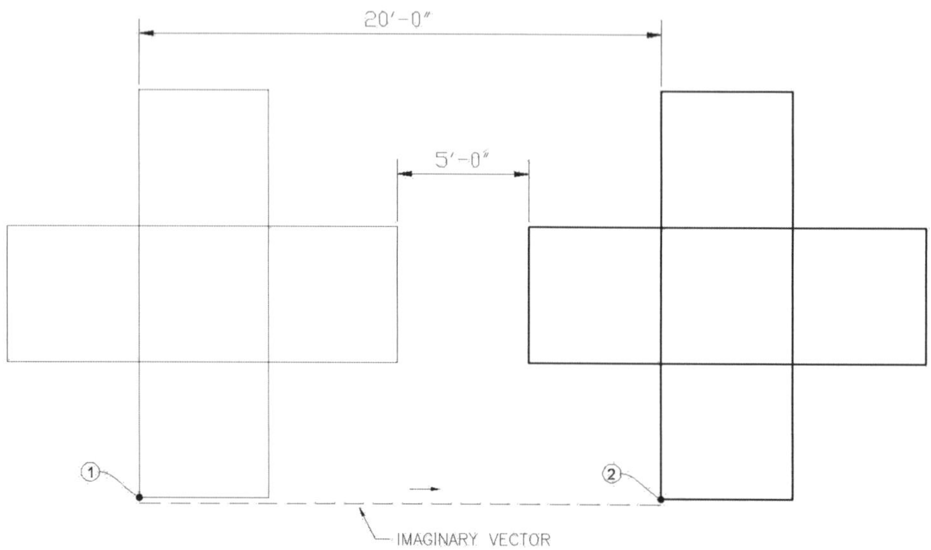

Open file: **Ex2-3b Modify Commands - Copy.dwg**

1. On the **Home** tab, in the **Modify** panel, select the **Copy** icon.
2. Select all the lines.
3. Pick **point #1** – *Endpoint* snap. (See image on previous page.)
4. Move the mouse toward the right (east), until you see the *Horizontal Polar Tracking* reference line: type **20′** and then **Enter**.

You now have two "objects" with 5′-0″ of space between them.

> ***FYI:*** *The overall object is 15′-0″, so 20′ (move) minus 15′-0″ (object) = 5′-0″ (space).*

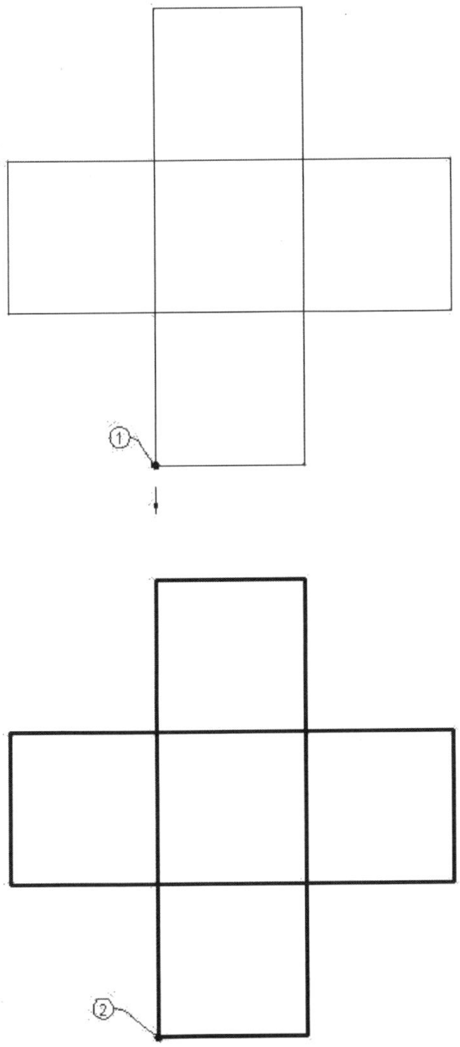

B Modify: Copy

1. On the **Home** tab, in the **Modify** panel, select the **Copy** icon.
2. Select all the lines (example B).
3. Pick **point #1** – *Endpoint* snap. (See image on previous page.)
4. Move the mouse downward (south) until you see the *Vertical Polar Tracking* reference line: type **18′8-7/8** and then **Enter**.

Refer back to the *Line* and *Move* commands for more information and examples on how to enter the length plus an angle.

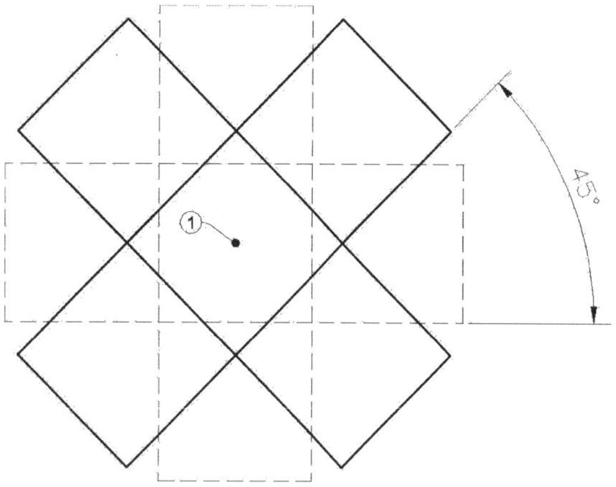

A Modify: Rotate

The *Rotate* command allows you to rotate one or more elements about a specific point and at a specific angle (or a somewhat arbitrary angle if you just pick on the screen rather than typing an angle).

Open file: **Ex2-3c Modify Commands - Rotate.dwg**

1. On the **Home** tab, in the **Modify** panel, select the **Rotate** icon.

Rotate command outline:

- **Select the *Rotate* icon**
- **Select objects to Rotate**
  - You can pick one or more items; you can select items individually or by windowing (or both).
  - Right-click or press Enter to tell AutoCAD you are done selecting objects to rotate.
- **Specify the base point**
  - This is the point about which the selected elements will rotate.
- **Specify the angle**
  - You can pick a point on the screen to visually select the rotation angle (this is not very accurate).
  - You can also type an angle (this is very accurate).
  - Typing **-45** will rotate clockwise and typing **45** will rotate counterclockwise.

2. **Select** all the lines.

3. **Right-click** to finish selection process.

4. **Pick the Base Point** (point #1); this point is dead center. Use *Object Snap Tracking* as previously covered. (See the *Ellipse* section for more.)

5. Specify the angle you want selected items to be rotated: type **45** and then press **Enter**.

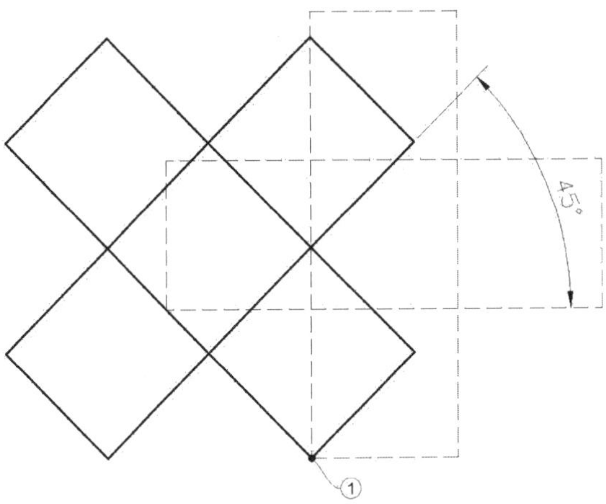

B Modify: Rotate

The *Rotate* command allows you to rotate one or more elements about a specific point and at a specific angle (or a somewhat arbitrary angle if you just pick on the screen rather than typing an angle).

1. On the **Home** tab, in the **Modify** pane, select the **Rotate** icon.

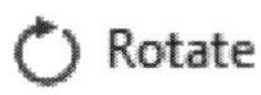

2. **Select** all the lines.

3. **Pick** the **Base Point** shown in the image above.

4. Type **45** and then press **Enter**.

Notice that both *"Rotate"* exercises had you enter 45 for the rotation angle, but about different *base points*, which affected the outcome.

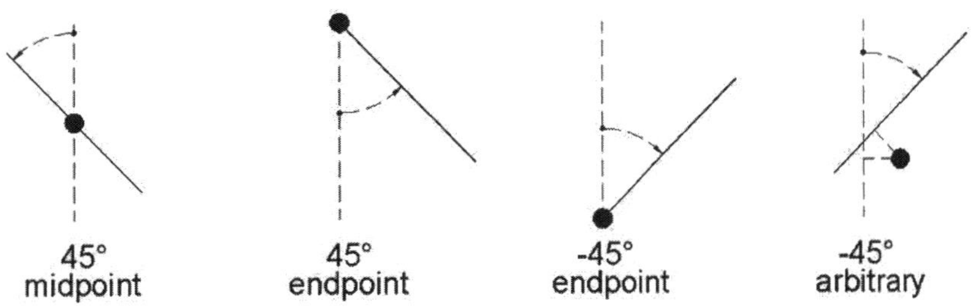

Base Point Options: Rotate Command

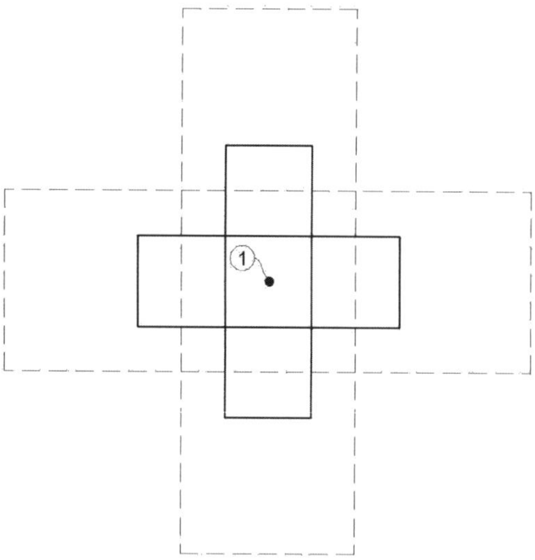

A Modify: Scale

The steps for the *Scale* command are very similar to the steps for the *Rotate* command in that you select objects, pick a base point and then, instead of entering an angle, you enter a scale factor.

Ex2-3d Modify Commands - Scale.dwg

1. On the **Home** tab, in the **Modify** panel, select the **Scale** icon.

 Scale

Scale command outline:

- **Select the *Scale* icon**
- **Select objects to Scale**
  - You can pick one or more items; you can select items individually or by windowing (or both).
  - Right-click or press Enter to tell AutoCAD you are done selecting objects to scale.
- **Specify the base point**
  - This is the point about which the selected elements will be scaled.
- **Specify the scale factor**
  - You can pick a point on the screen to visually select the scale factor (this is not very accurate).
  - You can also type a value (this is very accurate).
  - Typing **2** will make the items twice their original size (i.e., 200%) and **.5** becomes half (50%).

2. **Select** all the lines.

3. **Pick** the **Base Point**; dead center (using *Object Snap Tracking*).

4. Type **.5** (be sure to add the decimal point).

5. Press **Enter** to complete the command.

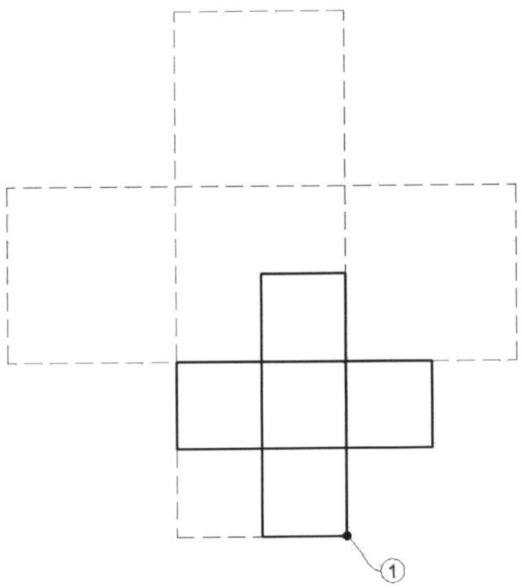

B Modify: Scale

The same *Scale Factor* will be used, but with a different *base point* so you can compare the results.

1. Select the **Scale** icon. 

2. **Select** all the lines.

3. **Pick** the **Base Point** as shown (lower right corner).

4. Type **.5** (i.e., 50%).

5. Press **Enter** to complete the command.

Notice that both "*Scale*" exercises had you enter .5 for the scale factor, but about different *Base Points*, which affected the outcome.

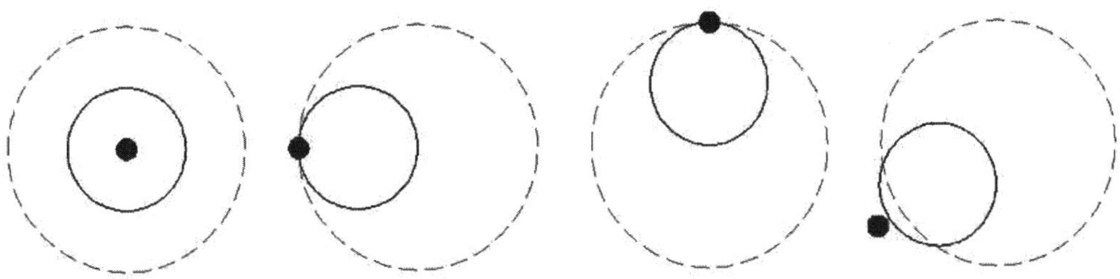

Base Point Options: Scale Command

Modify → Offset

You can think of the *Offset* command as a specilized *Copy* command where you only have to provide the distance and not the angle. The *Offset* command makes a parallel copy of a selected element, thus the angle is figured out automatically.

You will only practice on a few straight lines at the moment, but be aware that you can also offset *Arcs*, *Circles* and *Polylines*. The last example in the image below is a *Polyline*, which is one entity and therefore offsets as one entity. The new line (the darker one) is also a single *Polyline*.

Open file: **Ex2-3e Modify Commands - Offset.dwg**

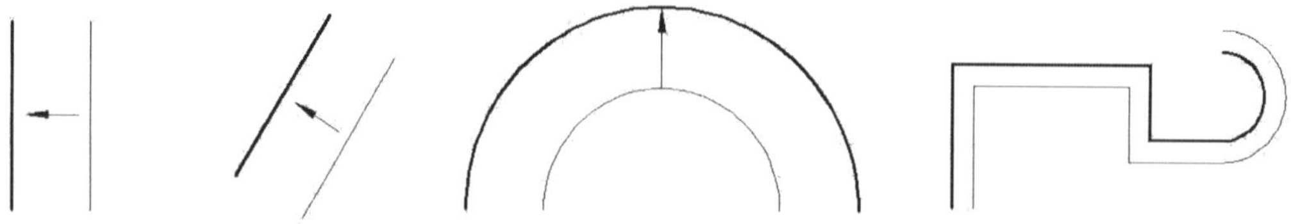

Offset command outline:

- **Select the *Offset* icon**
- **Specify offset distance**
    - This is the perpendicular distance between the original linework and the new linework.
- **Select object to Offset**
    - You can only pick one item at a time.
    - Because you can only pick one item, you do NOT have to right-click or press Enter to tell AutoCAD you are done selecting objects.
- **Specify the direction in which to offset**
    - You must pick in the direction you wish the line to be offset.
    - It is better to pick away from the original line so as not to confuse AutoCAD. It does not matter how far away you pick as you have previously entered the desired distance.

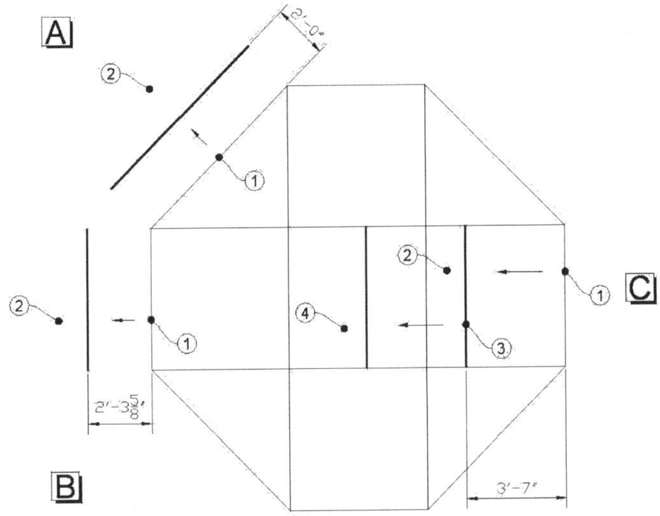

A Modify: Offset

Angled lines… In this exercise you will *Offset* an angled line.

1. On the **Home** tab, in the **Modify** panel, select the **Offset** icon.

2. Type **2'** and then press **Enter**.

3. Select the angled line: pick point #1 (area "A").

4. Click up, and to the left, of the angled line to indicate the direction you wish to offset the line. Press the ***Esc*** key to end the command.

B Modify: Offset

Vertical lines… In this exercise you will *Offset* a vertical line.

1. Select the **Offset** icon.

2. Type **2'3-5/8** and then press **Enter**.

   FYI: The dafult value <2'-0"> is from the previous use of this command. If this is the value you wanted you could just press Enter.

3. Select the vertical line: pick point #1 (area "B").

4. Click to the left of the vertical line to indicate the direction you wish to offset the line.

5. Press the ***Esc*** key to end the command.

C Modify: Offset

Multiple offsets… in one command.

1. Select the **Offset** icon and type **3'7**; press ***Enter***.

2. Select the vertical line: pick point #1 (area "C").

3. Click to the left of the vertical line to indicate the direction you wish to offset the line (pick point #2).

4. Select the vertical line just created (pick point #3).

5. Click to the left (point #4).

6. Press the ***Esc*** key to end the command.

Modify → Mirror

The *Mirror* command allows you to make a mirror image of one or more items. The last step in the command gives you the option to erase the original items or retain them.

The three examples below show you, conceptually, how you might use the *Mirror* command. This example is a floor plan, and after a daylighting/solar angle study you determine the building needs to be mirrored to create a more sustainable design. The mirror lines (ML), shown in the examples below, are defined by picking two points on the screen (the two points define an imaginary vector which represents the mirror line). You can snap to existing linework to define the mirror line or you can pick points in "space" in conjunction with *Polar Tracking*.

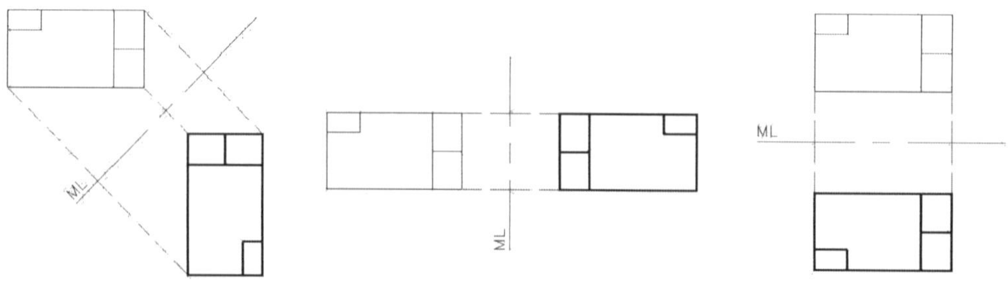

Diagonal Mirror Line   Vertical Mirror Line   Horizontal Mirror Line

In the examples above, either floor plan could be the "original." That is, the *Mirror* command works in either direction. If you select the option to retain the original, you end up with both floor plans.

Open file: **Ex2-3f Modify Commands - Mirror.dwg**

Mirror command outline:

- **Select the *Mirror* icon**
- **Select objects to Scale**
    - You can pick one or more items; you can select items individually or by windowing (or both).
    - Right-click or press Enter to tell AutoCAD you are done selecting objects to mirror.
- **Define the mirror line**
    - By picking two points.
    - You see a preview of the end result before picking the second point.
- **Erase original items?**
    - Press Y or N

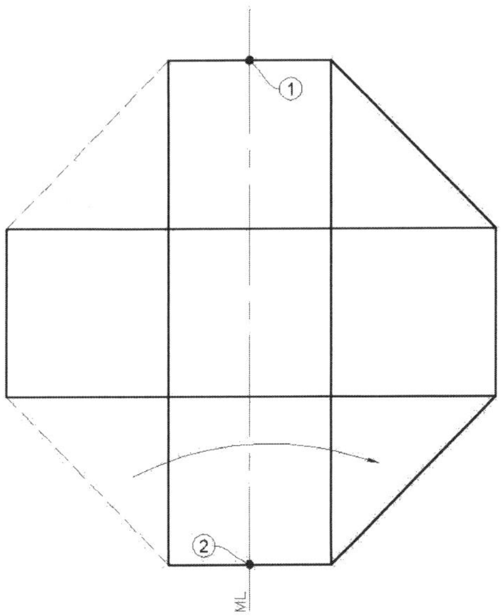

A **Modify: Mirror**

In-place, vertical… In this exercise you will *Mirror* the entities about themselves (i.e., in-place).

1. On the **Home** tab, in the **Modify** panel, select the **Mirror** icon.
2. **Select** all the linework.
3. **Pick point #1** (*Midpoint*).
4. **Pick point #2** (*Midpoint*).
5. Type **Y** and press *Enter.*

The dashed lines in the image above show the location of the angled lines prior to mirroring the geometry.

WARNING: In the example above, if you were to have typed "N" to retain original linework you would be left with two sets of lines everywhere (except the angled lines). This is typically bad as you do not want overlapping lines; this is referred to as "sloppy CAD".

B Modify: Mirror

About an angle… In this exercise you will *Mirror* the entities about an angled mirror line.

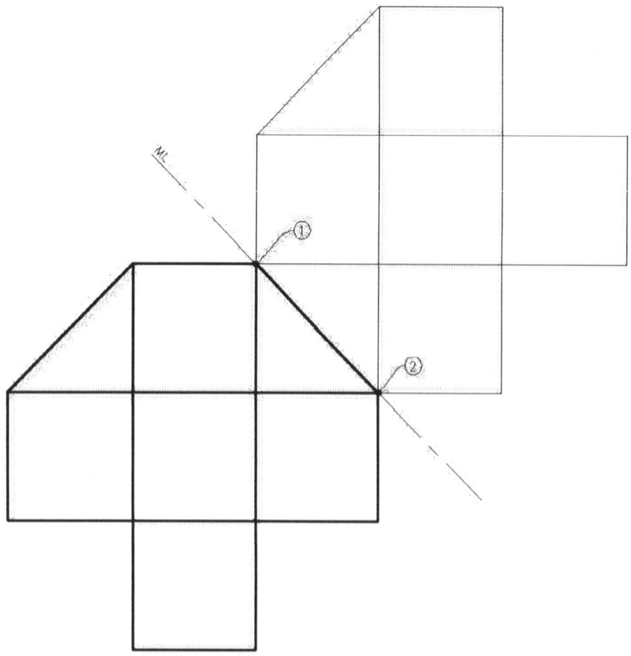

1. Select the **Mirror** icon.

2. **Select** all the linework.

3. **Pick point #1** (*Endpoint*).

4. **Pick point #2** (*Endpoint*).

5. Type **Y** and press Enter.

You now have two lines overlapping directly on the mirror line, but that is it. You could use the *Erase* command and click to select one of the lines to erase it. You would not want to select using a *Crossing Window* as that would select both overlapping lines, and both would be deleted.

Modify → Erase

This command requires little explanation: Once anything is erased, you have limited options for retrieving it. If you need to restore something that has been erased, you may use the *Undo* command as long as the drawing remains open; once closed, you cannot use *Undo*. Another option is to access the backup file, but this only contains the information for the second-to-the-last *Save* preformed, so if you erase something and then save three or more times, the item cannot be restored. If you think you might need something in the future, you should save a copy of the drawing file before deleting the items.

Erase command outline:

- **Select the *Erase* icon**
- **Select objects to Erase**
  - You can pick one or more items; you can select items individually or by windowing (or both).
  - Right-click or press *Enter* to tell AutoCAD you are done selecting objects to erase.
- **Press Enter**

- **Alternatively**, you can simply select the items you wish to erase and then press the ***Delete*** key on the keyboard (no *Erase* icon required).

Exercise 2-4:
Modify – Part 2

Once lines, arcs, circles, text and dimensions have been added they inevitably need to be changed to varying degrees. Sometimes mistakes are found, while other times the project needs to grow or shrink to better align with the budget. The designer may also just be interested in probing for a more functional and aesthetically pleasing design solution.

Whatever the reason, drawings do need to be modified, and of course AutoCAD has a whole host of tools which aid the designer in this area. From completely erasing items in an area to copying those items off to one side and modifying the "copy" to explore another design idea, the *Modify* tools are well developed and at your fingertips.

In this section you will explore the most used *Modify* tools. You are encouraged to play with the other tools not covered and read about them in the **Help** menu.

Just for fun… Steam rising off Lake Superior on a chilly Duluth, Minnesota, morning. Near the center of the picture are two piers with lighthouses which provide safe harbor access to international cargo ships and the Great Lake's "1000 footers." Lake Superior is the largest freshwater lake by surface area. Duluth (the most inland port in the world) is located on a rather steep hillside which provides great views of the lake and makes things interesting when the roads are covered with snow and ice!

Modify → Trim

The *tooltip* for the *Trim* command describes this tool well: "Shortens objects to meet the edges of other objects." ***FYI:*** *The dashed lines in the example images below represent portions of a line deleted by the* Trim *command.*

Open file: **Ex2-4a Modify Commands - Trim.dwg**

You can trim to one or more lines (i.e., cutting edges) as you will see in the examples below. You can also trim several lines back to a common cutting edge all at once, rather than having to pick each line, one at a time.

Trim command outline:

- **Select the *Trim* icon**
- **Select the Cutting Edge**
  - Select the line, or lines, you want another line trimmed to.
  - Right-click or press Enter to tell AutoCAD you are done selecting cutting edges.
- **Select Lines to Trim**
  - You can pick one or more items; you can select items individually or by windowing (or both).
- **Press Enter to conclude the command**

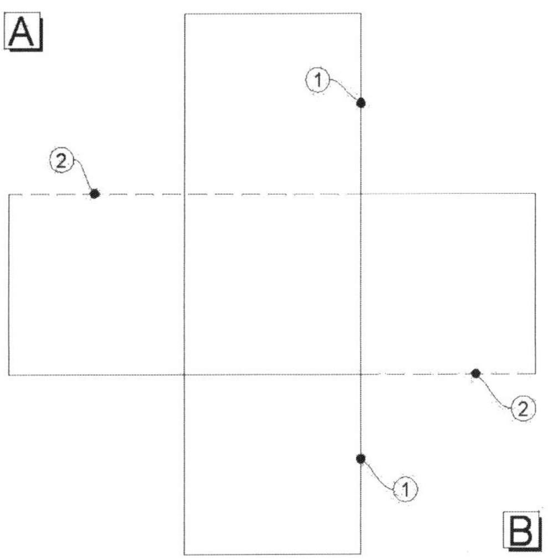

A Modify: Trim

One cutting edge… You will *Trim* one line up to another.

1. On the *Home* tab, in the **Modify** panel, select the **Trim** icon.
2. **Select** the vertical line (at point #1), then **right-click** to finish selecting.
3. **Pick** the portion of the horizontal line on the left side of the vertical line just selected.
4. Press **Esc** to finish.

B Modify: Trim

One cutting edge… Use the process learned in example A to trim the line shown in the image on the previous page.

C Modify: Trim

Two cutting edges… A center portion of a line is removed between two selected cutting edges.

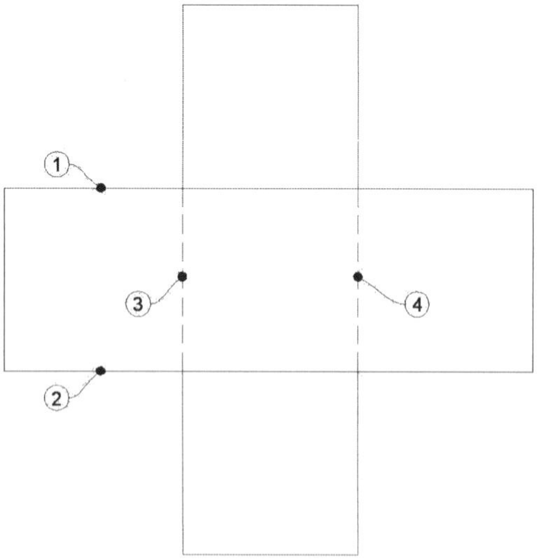

1. Select the **Trim** icon.

2. **Select** the two horizontal lines shown (points #1 and #2), and then **right-click** to finish selecting.

3. **Click** on a portion of the two vertical lines that fall between the two selected cutting edges (near points #3 and #4).

4. Press ***Esc*** to finish.

D Modify: Trim

Multiple lines at once…

1. **Select** the vertical line shown (point #1), and then **right-click** to finish the selection process.

2. **Pick points 2 and 3** in "space" to specify a selection-window, selecting the lines you want to trim (picking from right-to-left).

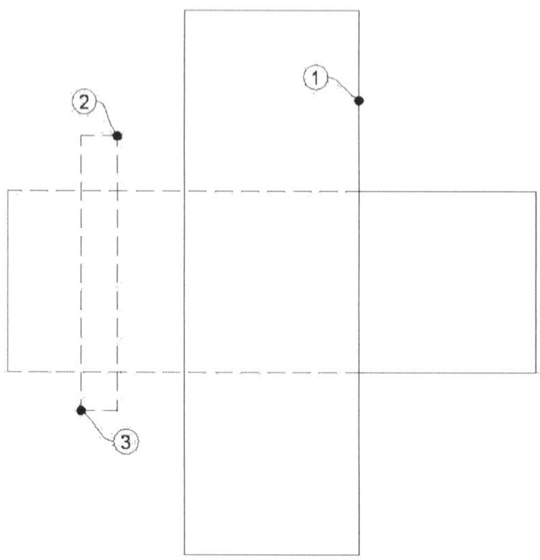

Modify → Extend

With the *Extend* command, you can extend (or lengthen) one or more lines over to another line. Similarly to *Trim*, you can *Extend* several lines at one time.

Open file: **Ex2-4b Modify Commands - Extend.dwg**

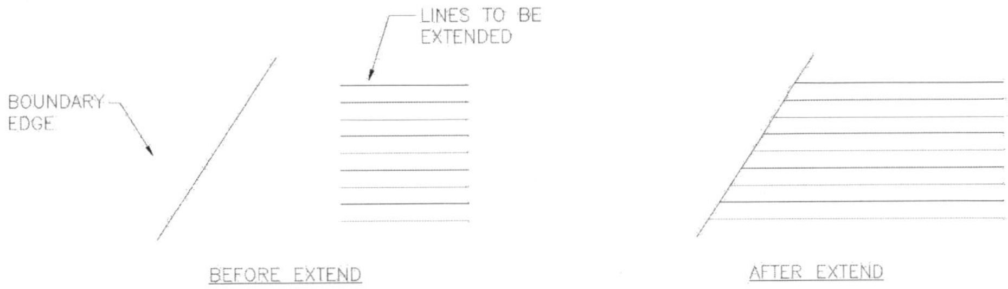

Extend command outline:

- **Select the *Extend* icon**
- **Select the Boundary Edge**
  - Select the line, or lines, you want another line to extend to.
  - Right-click or press Enter to tell AutoCAD you are done selecting boundary edges.
- **Select Lines to Extend**
  - You can pick one or more items; you can select items individually or by windowing (or both)
- **Press Enter to conclude the command**

A **Modify: Extend**

One boundary edge… You will *Extend* three lines over to another line.

1. On the **Home** tab, in the **Modify** panel, select the down-arrow next to the Trim icon, and then click the **Extend** icon. 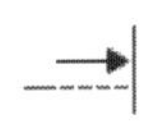

2. **Select** the vertical line (at point #1, area "A"), then **right-click** to finish selecting (see image on next page).

3. **Pick** the three horizontal lines (#2-4) in any order. ***TIP:** You must pick the half of the line closest to the boundary edge (i.e., the right half).*

Notice the command stays active until you end it by pressing ***Esc*** or right-clicking and picking ***Enter***.

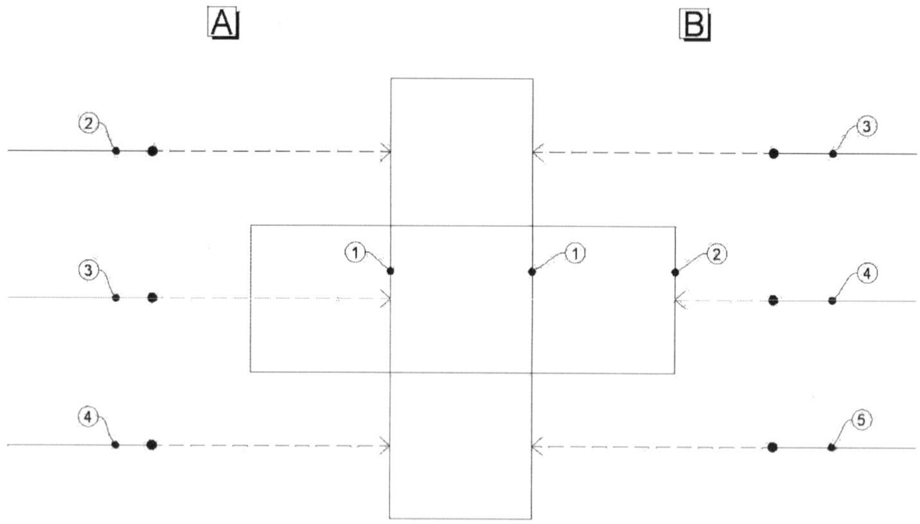

B Modify: Extend

Multiple boundary edges… You will *Extend* three lines over to two lines.

1. Select the **Extend** icon.

2. **Select** the two vertical lines (at points #1 and #2, area "B"), then **right-click** to finish selecting (see image above).

3. **Pick** the three horizontal lines (#3-5) in any order.

   TIP: You must pick the half of the line closest to the boundary edge (the left half in this case).

   FYI: If you selected the middle horizontal line (#5) again it would extend to the next active boundary edge – the result would then be similar to the previous example (area "A").

4. Press ***Esc*** to end the command.

   TIP: When you are using the Extend command, you can hold down the **Shift** *key to toggle into the Trim command, in which case the Boundary Edge becomes the Cutting Edge. As soon as you release the* **Shift** *key, the Extend command returns. The opposite is true while using the Trim command (i.e., holding the Shift key toggles into Extend mode).*

Modify → Fillet

The *Fillet* command (pronounced *Fill*-it) provides a way to round off a corner between two lines. This command works on two lines that already form a corner, or not. See the three examples below:

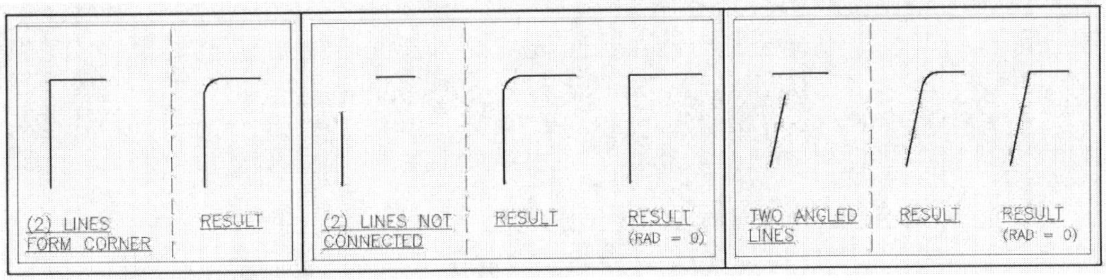

Open file: **Ex2-4c Modify Commands - Fillet.dwg**

As you can see in the examples above, the result is the same. The example on the left actually shortens the two orthogonal lines and adds an arc. The example in the middle lengthens the two lines and also adds an arc. The user specifies the radius of the arc while using the command. The last example, on the right, shows that the command also works on angled linework.

Notice in the examples above that when the radius within the *Fillet* command is set to 0", AutoCAD will create a corner.

There are a few subtleties about the *Fillet* command you should know. First, when selecting two lines to fillet, you need to select the portion of the line you wish to retain; a preview of the arc appears when hovering over your second selection. (This applies to lines that cross each other and will have a portion of the line removed as a result of the trim, similar to the example on the right, above.) Secondly, you should understand that the end result is two lines and an arc (unless the radius is set to zero, in which case you still only have two lines), thus the radius cannot be so large that one of the line segments cannot still exist; see the example below.

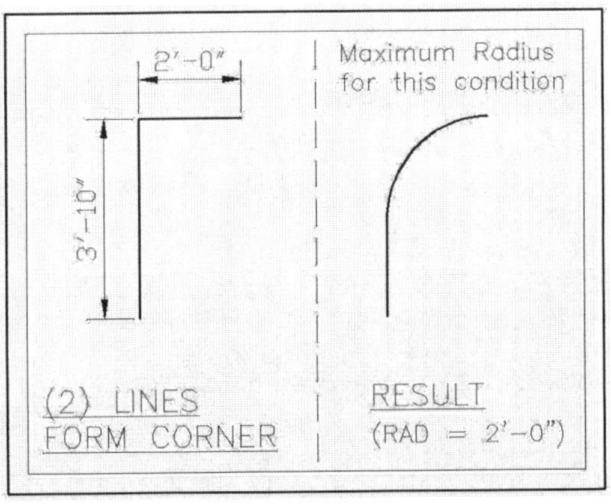

Fillet command outline:

- **Select the *Fillet* icon**
- **Enter Radius**
  - Or accept the default.
  - Holding the Shift key while selecting lines ignores the current radius and uses 0.
- **Select Two Lines to Fillet**
  - If two lines are parallel and the radius is set to zero, you will get a half-round arc at the end, connecting the two lines.

A Modify: Fillet

1. On **Home** tab, in the **Modify** panel, select the **Fillet** command.

2. Type **R** for *Radius*; press ***Enter***.

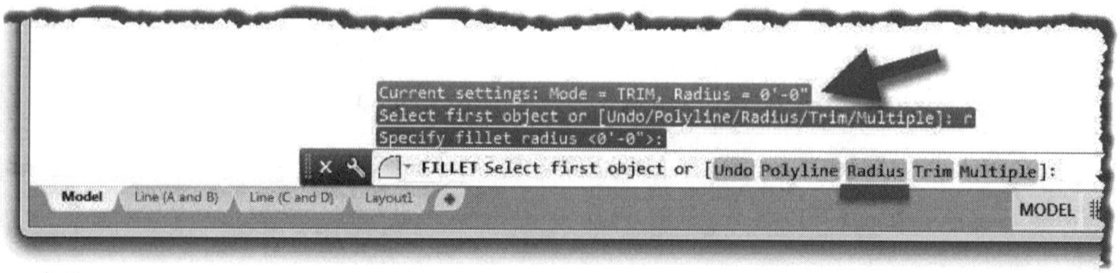

SUB-COMMANDS (R FOR RADIUS)...
Many commands have sub-commands which allow you to refine how a tool will work or what its outcome will be. In the case of the *Fillet* command, once started—as shown in the partial screen shot of the Command Prompt above, you can see several sub-command options (*Undo/Polyline/Radius/Trim/Multiple*). By typing the capitalized letter, such as "R" in Radius, you will activate that sub-feature, being able to set the radius in this case. ***NOTE:*** *The default radius only appears when you type the command.* Try typing "R" and then Enter in the *Command Window*.

3. Type **6**; press ***Enter*** (i.e., 6"). *This changes the radius from 0" to 6".*

4. **Select** the two lines shown in the image on the next page.

The corner now has a 6" radius, which is an AutoCAD *Arc* element.

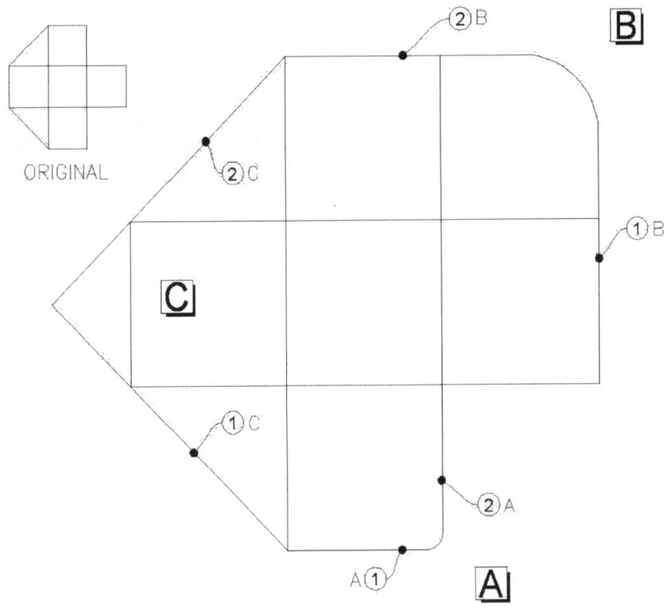

B **Modify: Fillet**

1. Select the **Fillet** icon.

2. Type **R** for *Radius*; press ***Enter***.
   a. Notice the current detault is 6″, which is based on the last time you used the command.

3. Type **2′4–5/8**; press ***Enter*** (i.e., 2′-4 5/8″).

4. **Select** the two lines shown (area "B" in the image above).

C **Modify: Fillet**

1. Select the **Fillet** icon.

2. Type **R** and ***Enter***.

3. Type **0** (i.e., zero); press ***Enter***.

4. **Pick** two lines shown (area "C" in the image above).

   TIP: Try to keep exercise "C" in your mind; this is a great way to clean up a corner quickly.

Modify → Chamfer

The *Chamfer* command is very similar to the *Fillet* command previously covered; the only difference is an "eased" corner rather than a "rounded" corner. As you can see, the examples below are based on the same "original" linework as the *Fillet* exercise just covered on the previous pages:

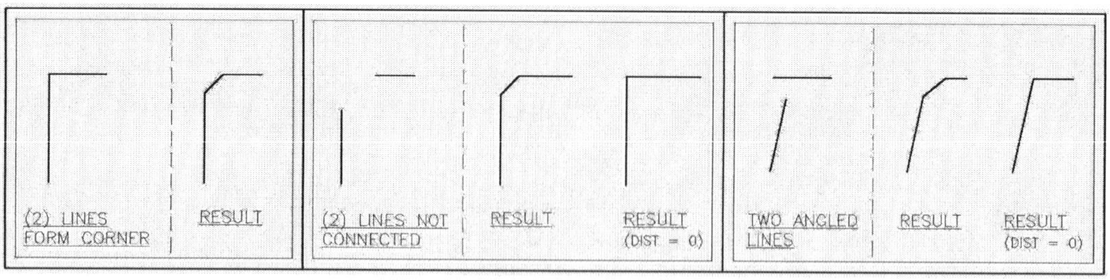

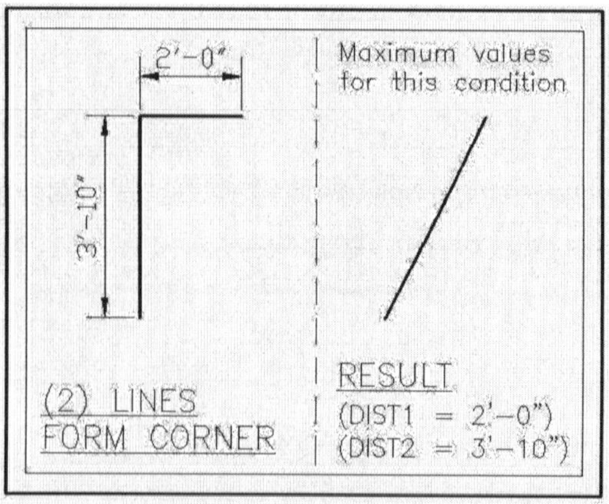

← Similar to the *Fillet* command, the *Chamfer* command will not allow distances to be entered that cause the original linework to become "reversed". In the example to the left, the two original lines still exist, but have a 0" length. It may seem strange that AutoCAD will let you even go this far, but in fact it does.

Open file:**Ex2-4d Modify Commands - Chamfer.dwg**

Chamfer command outline:

- **Select the *Chamfer* icon**
- **Enter DIST1 and DIST2 values**
  - Or accept the default.
  - Holding the Shift key while selecting lines ignores the current radius and uses 0.
  - DIST1 corresponds to your first line picked, not horizontal or vertical.
- **Select two non-parallel Lines to Chamfer**
  - If the two lines cross each other, you must pick the portion of the line you wish to keep for each line.

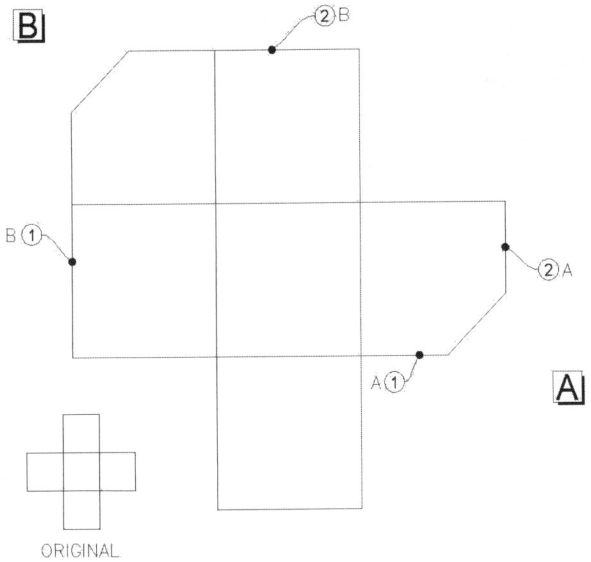

A **Modify: Chamfer**

1. On **Home** tab, in the **Modify** panel, select the down-arrow next to the *Fillet* command and then select the **Chamfer** icon (see image below). 

2. Type **D** for *Distance*; press ***Enter***.

3. Type **2'**, then ***Enter*** (the foot symbol is needed).

4. **Select** the two lines shown (area "A").

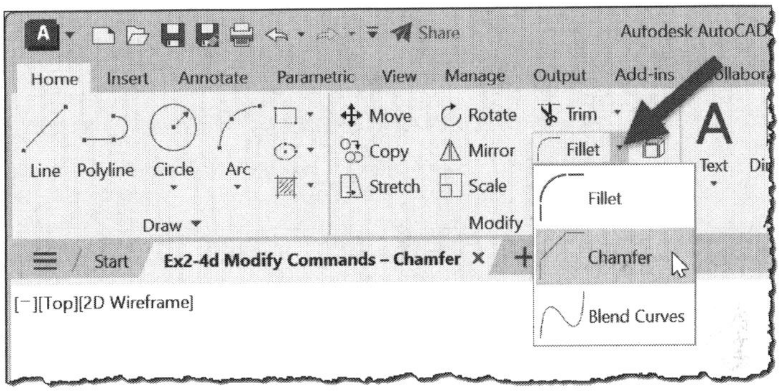

In the previous example of the *Chamfer* command, you modified a corner condition (i.e., two lines that formed a corner – 90 degrees in this case). In the next example, you will use the exact same steps but pick to lines that do not form a corner. The result will be two lines that are lengthened to create the desired chamfered corner (in the previous example, the two lines actually got shorter when the chamfer was added).

B **Modify: Chamfer**

1. Repeat the same steps for area "B"; notice the distance will be the defaults.

Modify → Break

Open file: **Ex2-4e Modify Commands - Break.dwg**

The *Break* command allows you to "break" a line into two lines. The two resultant lines can have a space between them if you wish; that is, a portion of the original line is omitted, as shown in the example below:

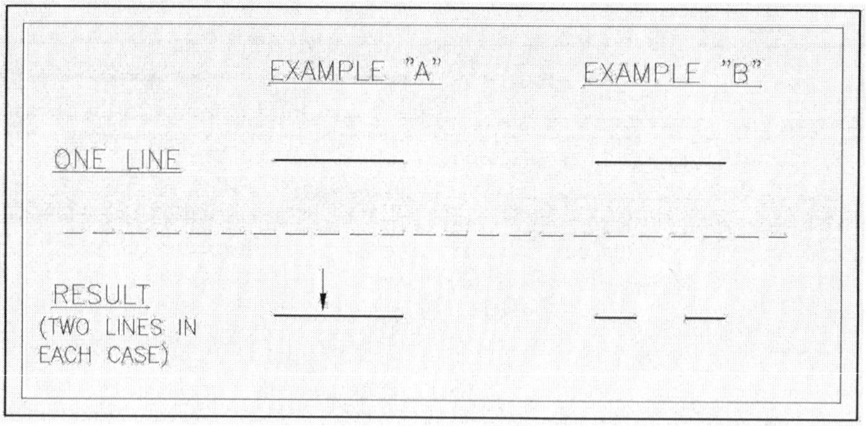

In example "A" the result (i.e., after using the *Break* command) looks the same visually, but it is now two lines. The break is at the arrow, which coincides with the selected point while using the *Break* command. The gap shown in example "B" is the space between the two points selected while using the *Break* command.

Break command outline:

- **Select the desired *"Break"* icon**
  - *Break* or *Break at Point*
- **Select the line (or Arc, Polyline, etc.) to be broken**
- **Break the line based on which *Break* command you selected:**
  - Break
    - Pick another point on the line and the space between the point at which you selected the line and the second point is deleted.
    - Or type F and then press Enter to more accurately pick the first point and then pick the second point (this is often the preferred method).
  - Break at Point
    - Pick a point on the line and you instantly have two contiguous lines (i.e., they do not have a space between them).

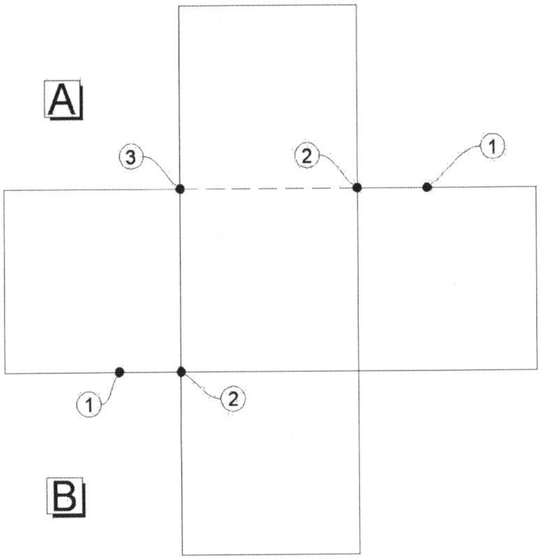

A Modify: Break

1. On **Home** tab, in the **Modify** panel, select the **Break** icon in the extended panel.

2. Select the horizontal line shown; **pick point #1** (Area "A").

3. Type **F** and then ***Enter***.

Typing **F** (for First point) allows you to more accurately select the first point from which to break the line. The point at which you selected the line in step #2 is the first point by default.

4. Pick point #2 using the ***Intersection*** snap.

5. Pick point #3 using ***Intersection*** snap.

The command is now finished and the result is two new lines with a gap between points #2 and #3. The gap is represented by the dashed line in the image above (the dashed line will not show up in AutoCAD).

B Modify: Break at Point

1. On the **Home** tab, in the **Modify** panel, click anywhere on the bar that contains the word "Modify"; this expands the *Modify* options. Now select the **Break at Point** icon (see image to the right).

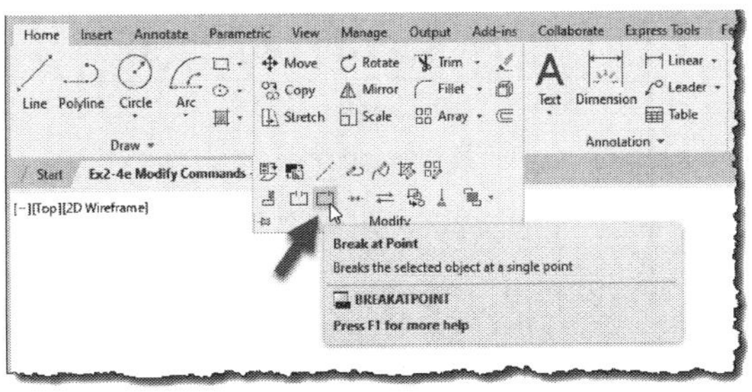

2. **Select** the line (point #1) shown (area "B").

3. Pick the point (point #2) using the ***Intersection*** snap.

Modify → Array

Open file: **Ex2-4f Modify Commands - Array.dwg**

The *Array* command allows you to create several copies of something with the same spacing. You can create rectangular, polar (i.e., circular) or path arrays using the *Array* command. With a rectangular array you can create an array in one or two directions.

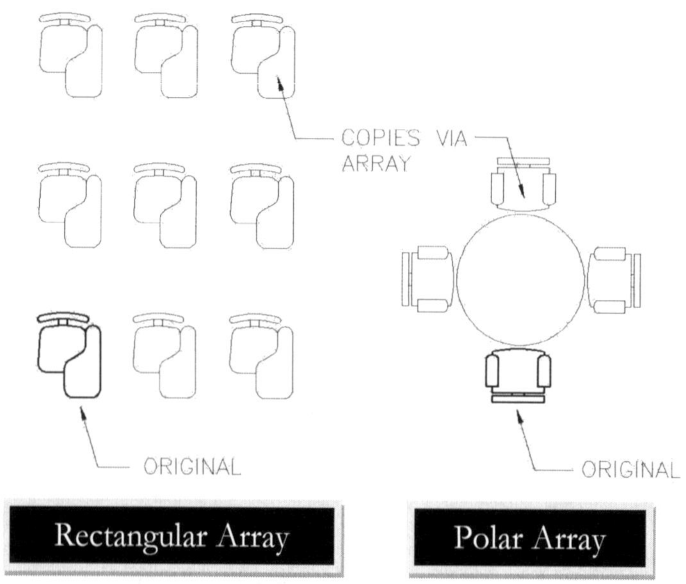

Array command outline:

- **Select the *Array* type**
- **Select the object(s):**

  \- **Rectangular Array**:
  - Specify # of Rows/Columns on *Ribbon*
  - Specify Row/Column spacing on *Ribbon*

  \- **Polar Array**:
  - Pick base point (i.e., center of rotation)
  - Specify number of objects desired
  - Specify angle for array to fill

- Select **Close Array** on *Ribbon*

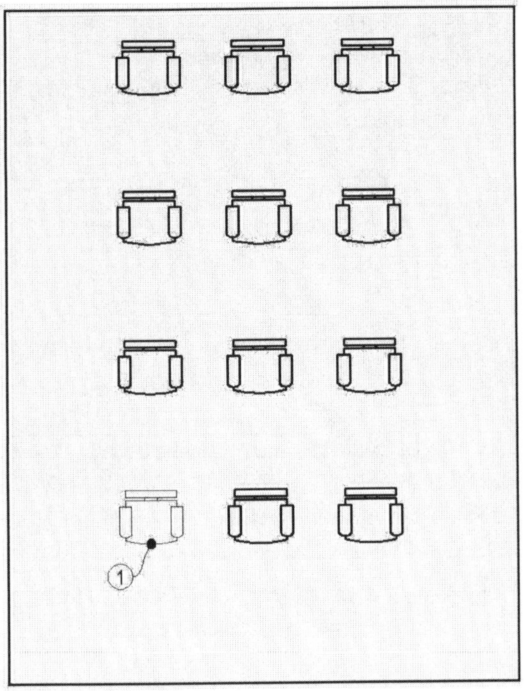

A Modify: Array

Rectangular… You will *Array* a chair to quickly fill a small theater. The chair is a *Block*, meaning it acts as one object that consists of several lines. You will learn about *Blocks* later in this book.

1. On **Home** tab, in the **Modify** panel, select the **Rectangular Array** icon.

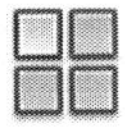

You are now in the *Array* command (notice the prompts in the *Command Window*).

2. **Select** the chair (point #1) per image above.

3. Press **Enter** to finish select.

4. Enter the following on the *Ribbon* (see image below):

   a. *Rows:* **4**
   b. *Columns:* **3**
   c. *Row spacing (between):* **4′-0″**
   d. *Column spacing (between):* **3′-0″**

5. Click the **Close Array** button on the *Ribbon* to finish the command.

Anytime you select one of the objects in the array, the **Array** contectual tab appears on the *Ribbon* (see image below). This allows you to change the row/columns/spacing and other information at any time.

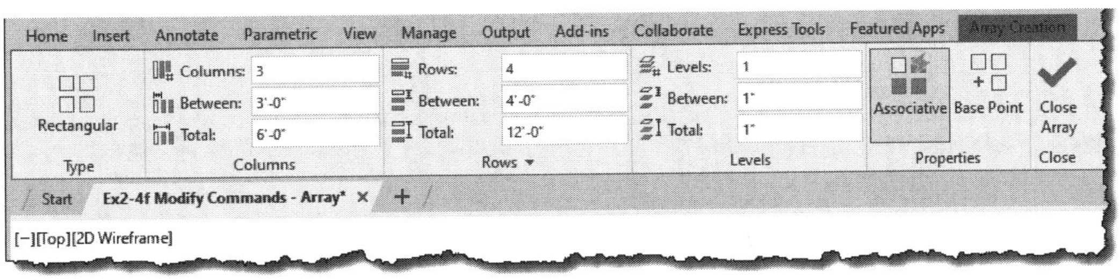

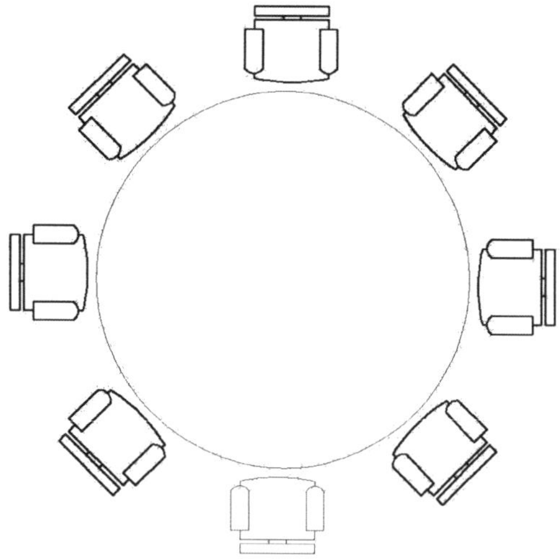

B Modify: Array

Polar… You will *Array* a chair around a round table.

1. Click the down-arrow next to *Rectangular Array* and select the **Polar Array** icon.

2. **Select** the chair at the round table (area "B"); press **Enter**.

Next you will define the point about which the chair will be rotated and copied, which will be the center of the table.

3. At the *Specify center point of array* prompt, click and snap to the *Centerpoint* of the table.

4. Enter **8** for number of items on the *Ribbon.*

5. Click into another text-box to see the drawing update.

6. Click the **Close Array** button to finish the command.

The image below shows the contextual tab for polar arrays; this only appears when a polar array item is selected.

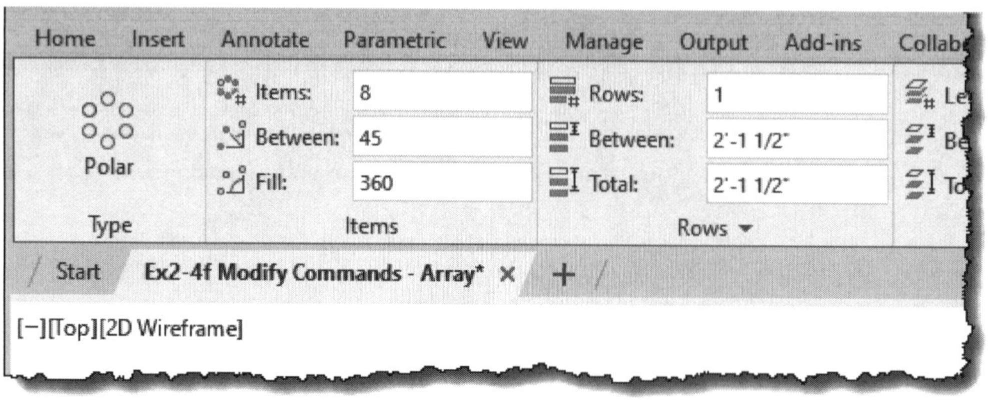

TIP: The row/column offset should be equal to the width/height of the object to be arrayed plus the desired space between the arrayed objects. For example, a 1'-9" wide chair with a 3" space desired would require a 2'-0" column spacing.

Modify → Stretch

Open file: **Ex2-4g Modify Commands - Stretch.dwg**

The *Stretch* command allows you to increase or decrease the size of one or more objects. For example, you can stretch a rectangular conference room table two feet longer to accommodate more people or stretch a wall to decrease the size of a room to reduce cost. These concepts are conveyed in the examples shown below. ***NOTE:*** *The extra chairs are not automatically added by the* Stretch *command.*

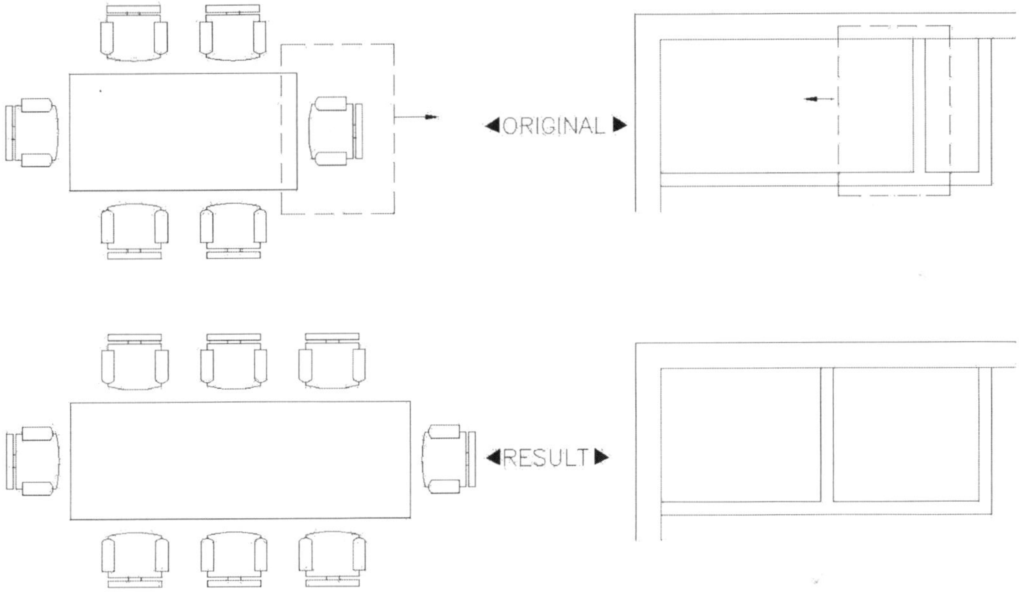

Stretch command outline:

- **Select the *Stretch* icon**
- **Select window to define area to stretch**

  TIP: See examples above.

  - Window must be selected from right to left.
- **Right-click to finish selection process**
- **Pick a point (base point) on screen**
- **Start moving the mouse in the desired direction** (*Snap* to horizontal or vertical if needed)
- **Type the desired stretch length**
  - Otherwise you can pick a point rather than enter length.

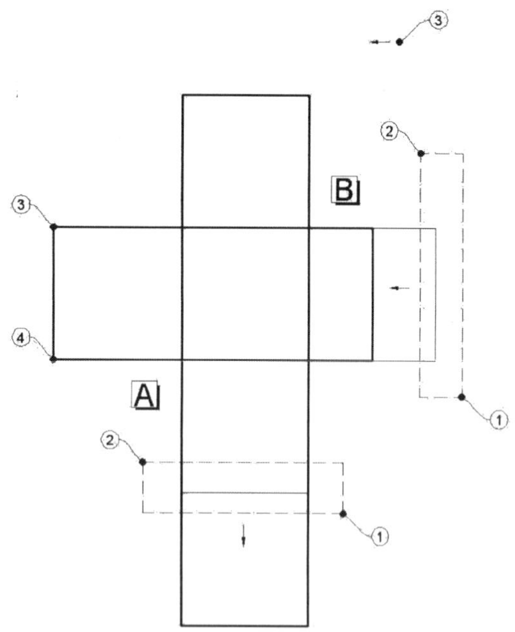

A Modify: Stretch

Picking Points… You will *Stretch* lines based on the distance between two picked points.

1. On the **Home** tab, in the **Modify** panel, select the **Stretch** icon.

2. **Pick** two diagonal points to define a selection window (#1 and #2 - Area "A").

3. **Snap** to *Endpoints* as shown (#3 and #4).

4. This stretched the object exactly 5′-0″ because that is the distance between points #3 and #4.

B Modify: Stretch

Enter a distance… You will *Stretch* lines based on the distance you type rather than picked points.

1. Select the **Stretch** command.

2. **Select** window (points 1 and 2 – Area "B").

3. **Pick** a point in "space" (point 3). Note, in space just means away from any lines so as not to *Snap* to them. This shows that you do not always have to snap to somthing.

4. Move the cursor to the right while snapping to the horizontal (via *Polar Tracking* or *Ortho*).

5. Type **2′6** and ***Enter***.

Notice that the linework that exists completely within the stretch selection window is actually just moved and not really stretched.

Exercise 2-5:
Annotation and Layers

Text is an essential part of any set of architectural drawings. Text fills in the gaps where a drawing cannot adequately describe what is happening. This may be something like the strength of concrete walls or steel bolts, or the gauge of a steel door frame. AutoCAD is not a word processor, but it does contain many of the same features, such as font styles, height, bold, italics, columns, spell checking and more.

Layers do not relate to text in any extra special way, but this is one additional thing about AutoCAD that you must know before proceeding. In a nutshell, *Layers* provide a way to manage and organize graphical data, mainly controlling the viability and printed thickness of line work.

Annotate → Text

More will be covered on text later in the book. This section will give you a quick peek at the basics, which will allow you to add your name and a date to drawings to be turned in for grading.

Open file: **Ex2-5a Annotate Commands - Mtext.dwg**

A Annotation: Setting Up a Drawing for Text

Setting up a drawing for text

1. The ideal way to work with text in AutoCAD requires a few settings be adjusted first. This will have to be done in each new drawing, but could be set up in an office template file in the workplace.

2. Once things are set up properly, any text added will automatically be the correct height based on the intended plot scale. If the plot scale (i.e., annotation scale) is changed, all the text in the drawing will be updated to the correct height.

3. Specific steps to perform:
   - On the *Application Menu*, *Drawing Utilities* fly-out, select the **Units** command.
   - Set the precision to **0'-0 1/32"**.
   - Click **OK** to save the change.

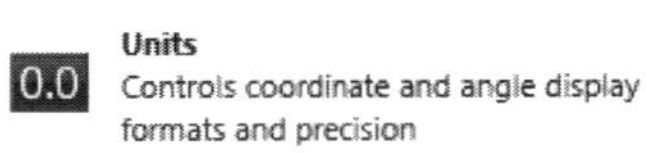

Additional steps to perform:

4. On the **Annotate** tab, in the **Text** panel, click the **Text Style** link (small arrow, lower right). You are now in the dialog box shown below.

   - In the *Text Style* dialog, select **Roman** under Styles. (It should already be selected.)

   - In the *Size* area, check **Annotative** and set the *Paper Text Height* to **3/32″**. (This is the size the text will be on paper regardless of the drawing scale.)

   - Click **Set Current**. ***FYI:*** *This will make this the default text style.*

   - Click **Apply** and then **Close**.

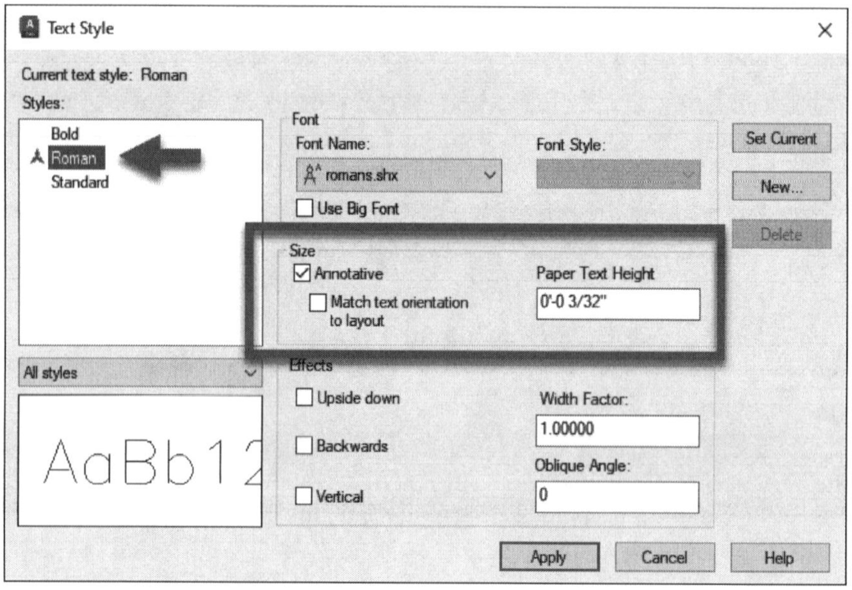

5. At the bottom of the screen, on the *Application Status Bar* menu, right-click on the "*Automatically Add Scales…*" icon and select the **Automatically Add Scale to Annotative Objects** option.

6. Just to the right of the previous item, click the *Annotation Scale* listed (it should be 1:1) and select **1/8″=1′-0″** from list. (See image on next page.)

Now when you add text to this drawing, the height will automatically be set based on the scale selected at the bottom of the screen. This scale can be changed on-the-fly, instantly updating the height of all text in the drawing. You will try this next.

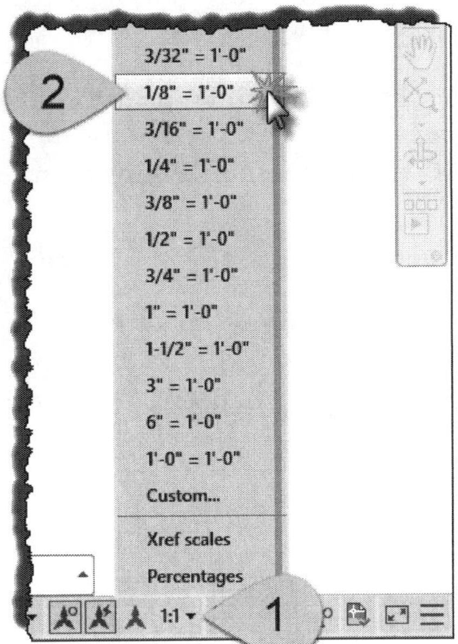

7. On the **Annotate** tab, in the **Text** panel, select **Multiline Text** from the options there.

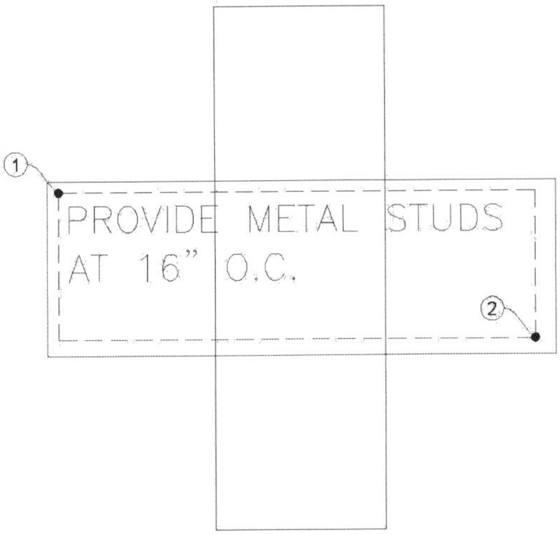

8. **Pick two points** in the drawing window, forming a rectangle in which the text will be contained, as shown below.

9. Type the following: **PROVIDE METAL STUDS AT 16" O.C.** (Notice the *Ribbon* has temporarily changed.) *Do <u>not</u> press* **Enter** *at all.*

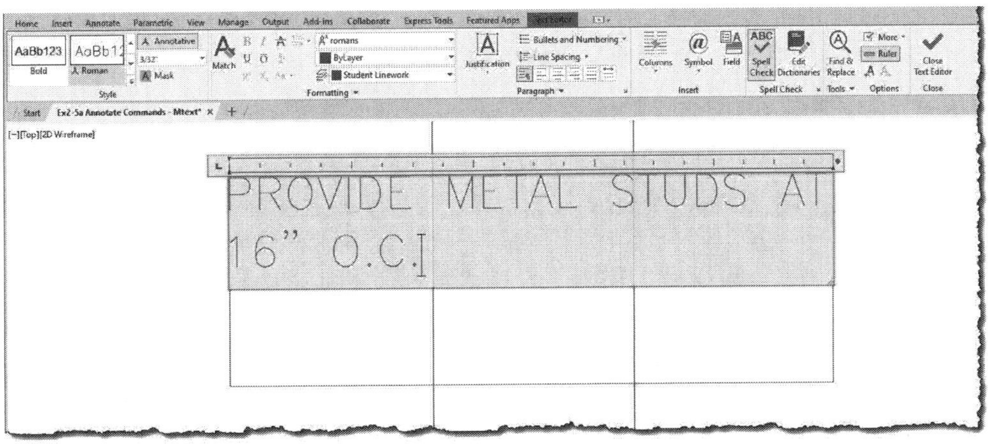

Take a moment to review some of the text editing options available on the *Ribbon* while in the *Text* command. Also, notice that the text automatically "returned" to the next line when text could no longer fit within the windowed area you selected.

10. Click **Close Text Editor** on the *Ribbon*.

    ***FYI:** All achitectural text is typically uppercase.*

11. Click the **Close** icon from the *Ribbon*.

12. Change the *Annotation Scale* to ¼"=1'-0". The text should shrink 50%.

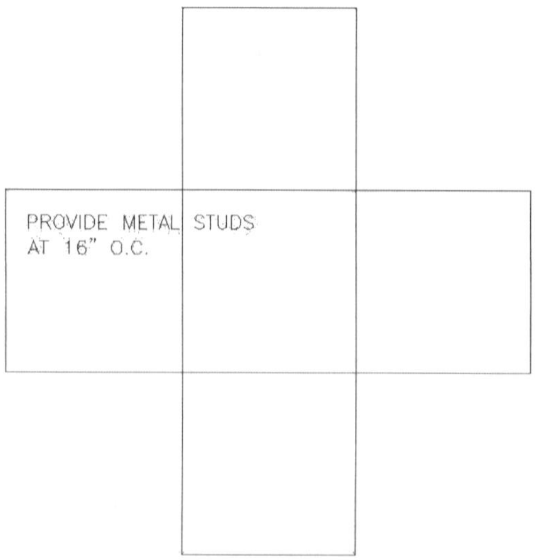

← Changing the *Annotation Scale* on the *Application Status Bar* menu to ¼" = 1'-0" caused the text in the drawing to change to half its original size. This scale change means the drawing will be twice as large on the sheet of paper, but regardless of the drawing scale the text is always the same height. Thus, to maintain the proper size, the text got 50% smaller to account for the drawing getting 200% larger. Getting this concept takes a little practice and experience.

The Roman text style is meant for most notes within a set of drawings. You can set up additional text styles for Titles, Labels, Borders, etc., as needed.

***FYI:** This book will specifically tell you if you need to do this.*

Text can be edited by selecting it and then double-clicking directly on the text.

Annotate → Dimensions

Dimensions in AutoCAD seemingly have an infinite number of variables to accommodate the needs of the design world as a whole. The software does not cater to just one industry, such as Architecture. In this exercise you will just get an introduction to the basics so you know what dimensions are in the software. Later in the book, when you need to add dimensions, you will be instructed to look at an appendix that will give you specific instructions on how to make the dimensions look appropriate for architectural drawings. (It should be pointed out that there is no standard within the architectural community; several "office standards" exist across the United States.)

Dimensions can be used to check the size or length of something in your drawing, but AutoCAD provides a specific tool for this. With the *Dimension* command you have to draw the dimension, look at the distance listed, and then delete the dimension object. With the *Distance* command, you pick two points and note the distance in the Command Prompt area (you also get the X and Y distances for angled lines), and you are not required to delete anything. You will also take a quick look at the *Distance* tool.

Similar to text, you have to make a few adjustments to get the dimensions to automatically scale based on the intended plot scale (specifically, the Annotative Scale). You will also adjust a Dimension Style setting, so the dimensions have a "feet & inches" value displayed; most default templates display inches only. Again, all this would be preset in an office template if you were working in an architectural office. You are not given such a template with the online files, nor are you instructed to create a template; this is so you will thoroughly understand these concepts (via repetition) and that will help you troubleshoot problems when they arise.

Open file: **Ex2-5b Annotate Commands - Dimension.dwg**

Setting Up the Drawing for Dimensions:

1. On the *Application Status Bar* menu, make sure **Automatically Add Scales to Annotative Objects…** is turned on and **¼" = 1'-0"** is selected for the *Annotative Scale.* (See the previous exercise/section on *Text* for more information on this.)

2. On the **Annotate** tab, in the **Dimensions** panel, select the **Dimension Style** link (see image to the right).

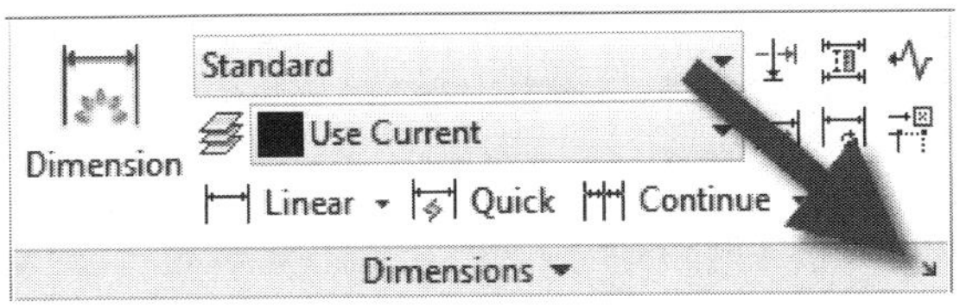

3. With the **Standard** style selected (on the left in the image below), click the **Modify** button.

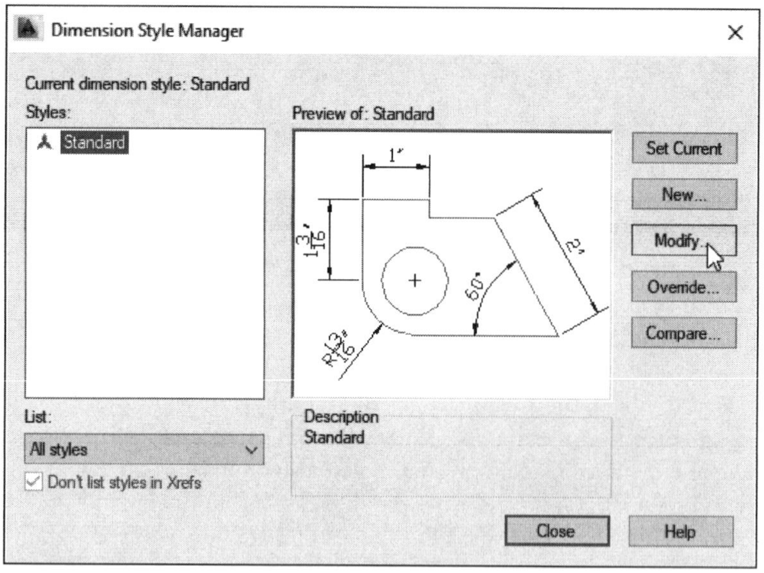

4. On the **Fit** tab, check **Annotative**.

   FYI: This sets all the dimension values, which are "printed on paper" values, to automatically scale based on the Annotative Scale setting.

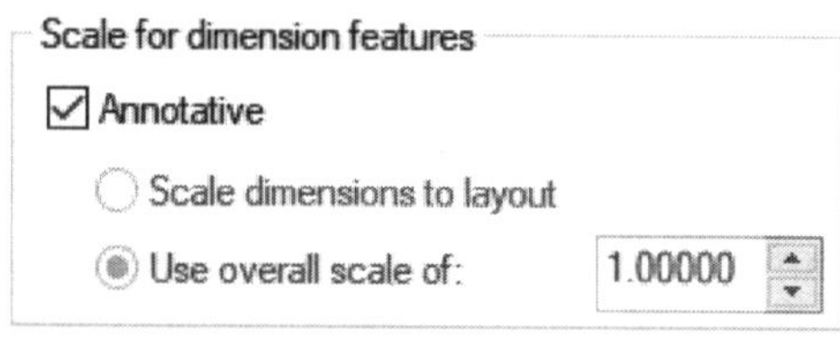

5. On the **Primary Units** tab, change the *Unit Format* from *Decimal* to *Architectural.*

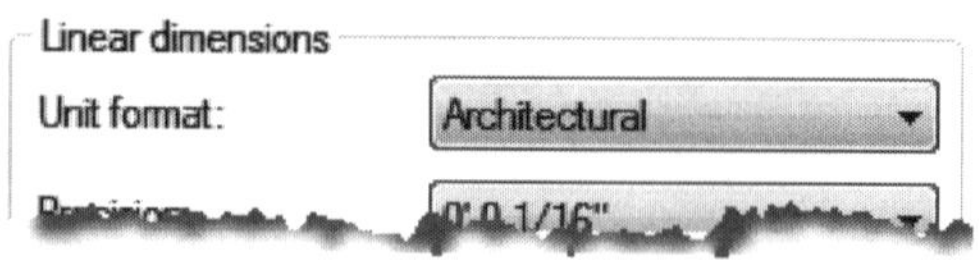

6. Also, on the **Primary Units** tab, uncheck the option to **suppress 0 inches**.

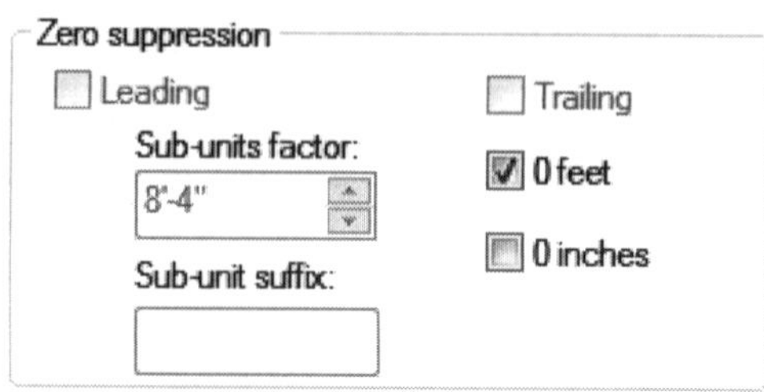

7. Finally, on the **Text** tab, adjust the **Vertical Text Placement** and **Text Alignment** as shown.

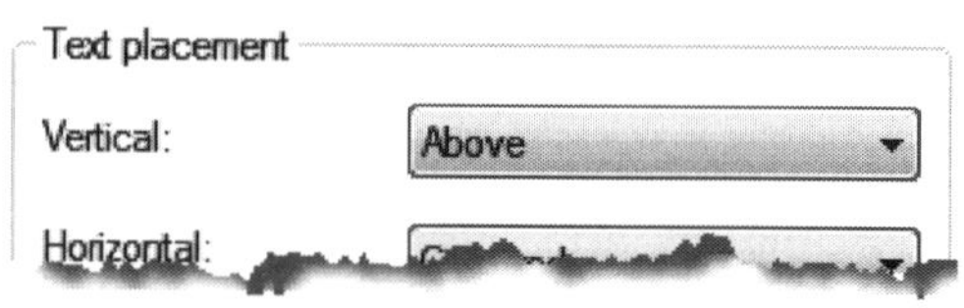

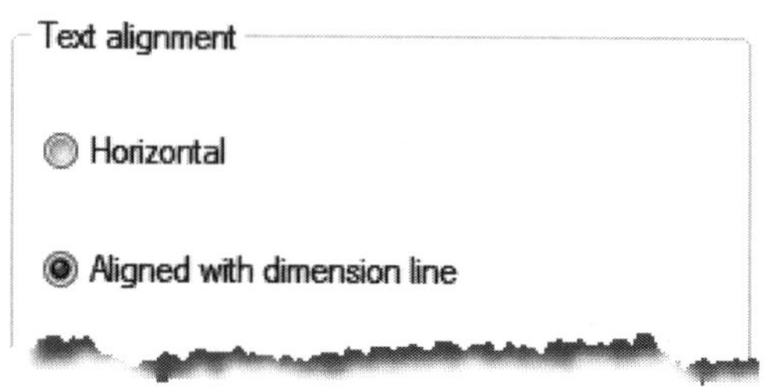

8. Click **OK** and then **Close**.

You are now ready to try the *Dimension* command. There are still several settings that need to be adjusted (see *Appendix A*) to make the dimension conform to general industry standards, but this will get you started.

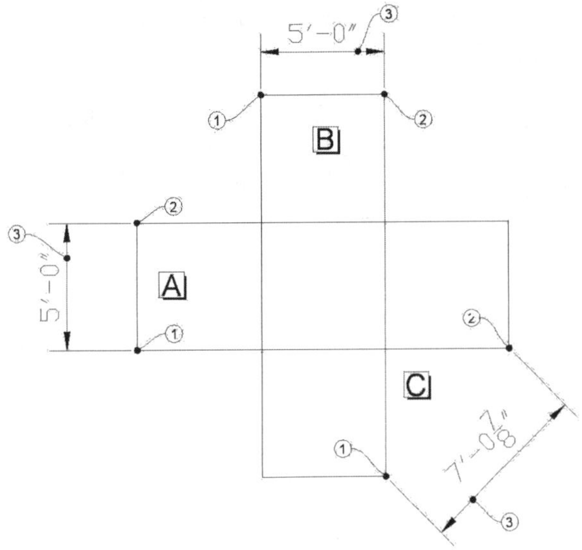

A Annotation: Dimensions

Linear (vertical)… First you will draw a vertical dimension. You use the same command to draw vertical or horizontal dimensions; the end result is based on how you pick your points.

1. On the **Annotate** tab (in the **Dimensions** panel) click the **Dimension** icon.

2. **Pick** the first two points shown in area "A".

These two points represent the distance you wish to dimension. Make sure you have *OSNAP* turned on and are using it!

3. Now move your cursor to the left and notice the preview image of the dimension that will be drawn based on your next pick. **Click** the third point approximately as shown.

That's it – one icon and three picks in the drawing and you have your first dimension.

B Annotation: Dimensions

Linear (horizontal)… Now you will draw a horizontal dimension.

1. Select the **Dimension** icon again.
2. **Select** the first two points shown in area "B".
3. Start moving your cursor straight up from your first two points; **pick** point #3 to create the horizontal dimension.

FYI: If you pick two points that are at an angle from each other, you can create a horizontal or vertical dimension based on your third pick (see image below).

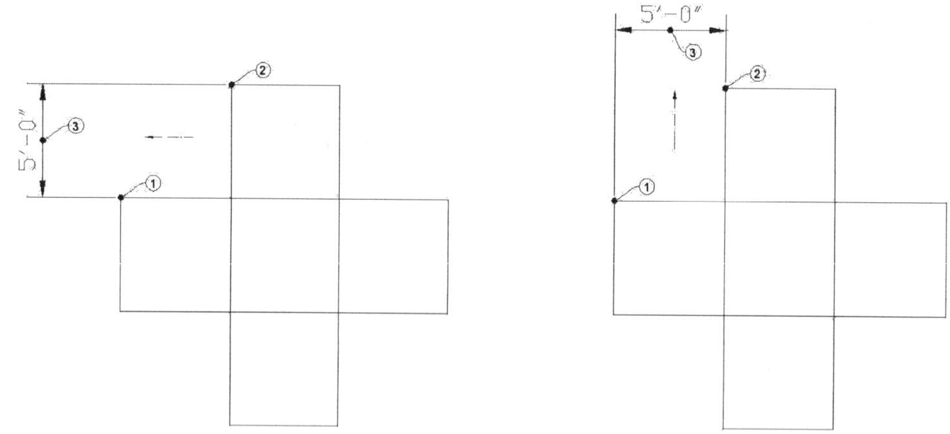

C Annotation: Dimensions

These steps allow you to draw an angled dimension.

1. Select the **Dimension** icon again.

2. **Select** the first two points shown in area "C".

3. Start moving your cursor down and to the right, from your first two points; **pick** (point #3) to create the angled (or aligned) dimension.

Note that the dimension value is the same as the **hypotenuse** you had to calculate previously in the *Line* exercise; AutoCAD can do a lot of the math for you!

D Annotation: Dimensions

Adjusting the Annotative Scale… If the scale of the drawing needs to change, AutoCAD will adjust the text and arrow sizes automatically.

1. On the *Application Status Bar* menu, change the **Annotative Scale** to **½" = 1'-0"** (see image to the right).

2. Notice the arrows and text for all the dimensions change size!

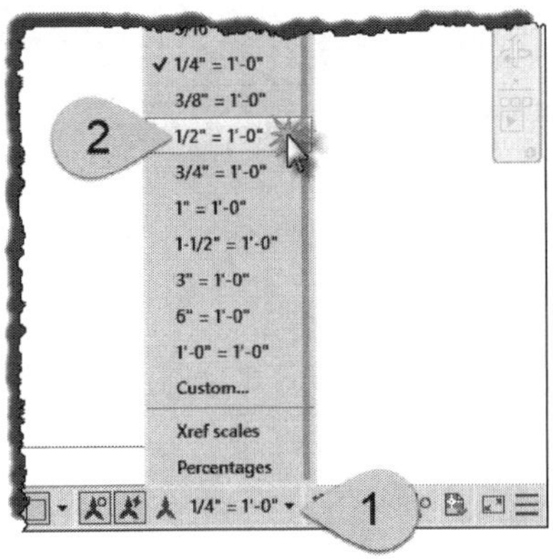

Annotative Scaling helps to ensure that all the text and dimensions are the same size for all scales on all plotted sheets. Before this feature came along, drafters had to manually set the text and dimension heights; this was challenging as each drawing scale had a different height. If a drawing scale was changed, the text and dimensions would not automatically update.

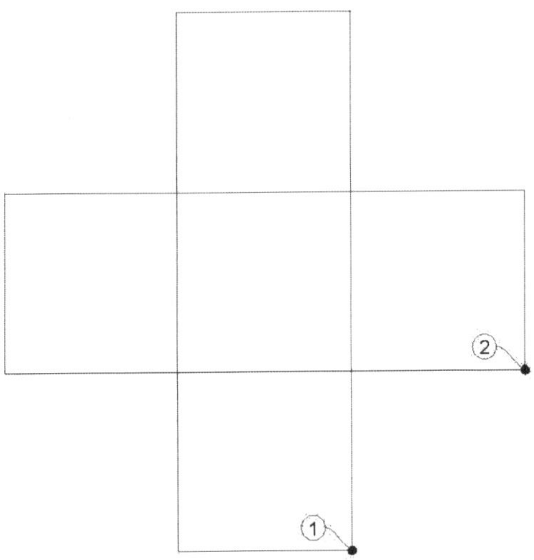

E Home: Distance

Information without drawing anything… As mentioned at the beginning of this exercise, you can use the *Distance* command if you simply want to know the distance between two points or to verify something you just drew.

1. On the **Home** tab (in the **Utilities** panel under *Measure*) select the **Distance** tool.

2. **Pick** the two points shown; be sure to use *Endpoint* snaps, type **X** to finish.

Notice the results displayed in the **Command Window** (see image below). The second image below is a graphical representation of the results.

> ***FYI:*** *This is not provided by the program.*

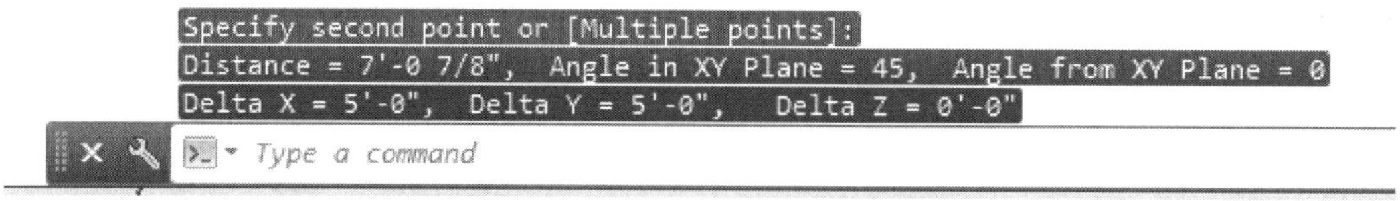

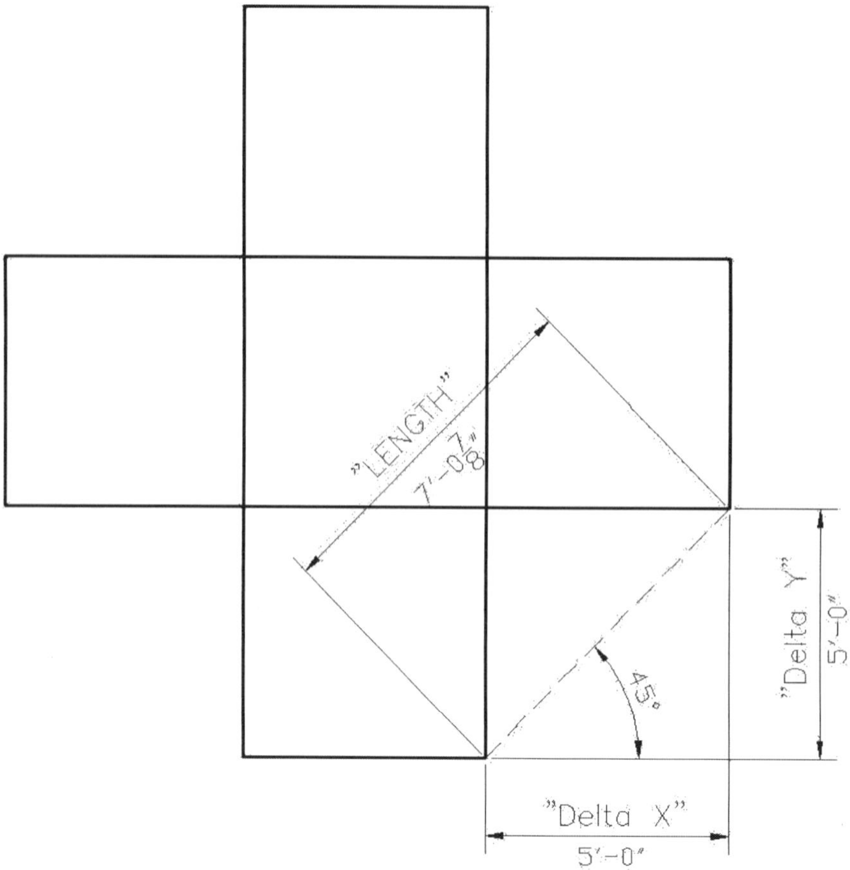

As you can see, you get a lot more information with the *Distance* tool than you do with the *Dimension* command, and you don't have to delete anything at the end!

> ***TIP:*** *Typing **DI** and then **Enter** is a quick way to start the Distance command without having to open the **Measure** fly-out and then click on the icon.*

Using Layers:

Using *Layers* in AutoCAD helps to separate different types of data. Mostly, you will use *Layers* to make things visible or invisible, and to control lineweights.

In a Floor Plan, for example, you will draw all the walls on one *Layer* and the doors on another *Layer*. You will also draw items such as windows, stairs, furniture, appliances, etc. each on its own *Layer*.

Many architectural firms have an Office Standard when it comes to *Layers*. This means that everyone in the firm uses the same *Layer* name (e.g., A-WALL) to draw walls on, for example. This helps make sharing drawings between projects more efficient; if you Copy/Paste from one drawing to another, and each project used a different *Layer* name for the walls, then you would have both *Layer* names in the drawing you pasted into (e.g., *A-Wall* and *AR-Wall*).

Example:
To see a quick example of how layers work you will open the *A1 First Floor Plan* drawing again and adjust some of the layer settings and then notice the effect those changes have on the drawing.

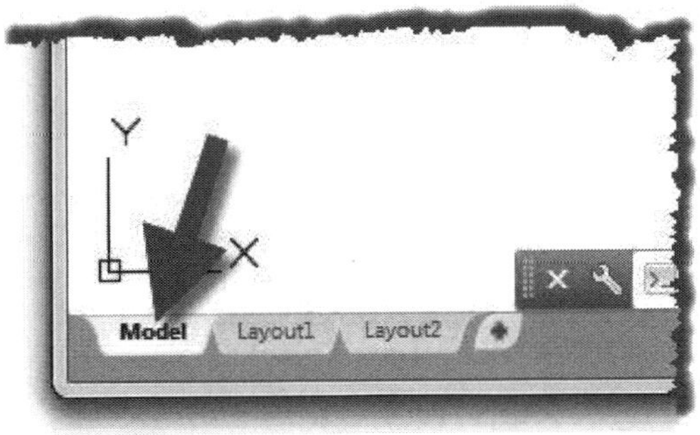

1. **Open** the *A1 First Floor Plan.dwg* from the online files (*Residence* folder).

2. Switch to ***Model Space*** by clicking the 'Model tab' at the bottom of the screen; see the image below.

3. Select the **Layer Properties** icon from the *Layers* panel on the *Home* tab.

You are now in the *Layer Properties Manager* where you can adjust the visibility and properties, such as lineweight, color and linetype, of the entities on a particular layer.

All drawings have a *Layer* named 0 (i.e., zero). You can add as many layers as you wish in a drawing file. Notice in **Figure 2-5.1** that the *current* drawing has several *Layers* (34 to be exact). Many of the layer *names* are descriptive enough for you to tell what information is drawn on each layer.

Next you will *Freeze* (i.e., turn off the visibility of) three *Layers*.

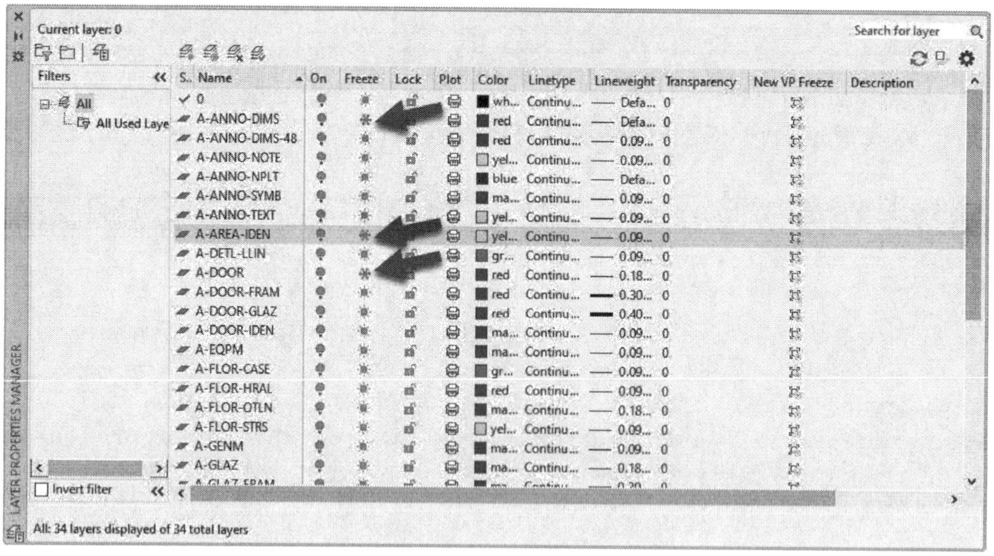

FIGURE 2-5.1 Layer Properties Manager

4. In the column labeled "**Freeze**" click the *Sun* symbol (which will change the symbol to a B&W *Sun*) for the following *Layers (See Figure 2-5.1)*:
   - A-Anno-Dims
   - A-Area-Iden
   - A-Door

*TIP: The "Freeze" column may not display the full label; instead, you will see a portion of the label (e.g. Fre…) as in the image above, which means the column is not wide enough to display the full label. You can, if you wish, stretch the column(s) wider with your mouse. You simply place the cursor between two labels and drag the mouse. This is helpful when the **Layer** names are long as well.*

5. Click the "X" in the upper corner of the *Layer Properties Manager* to close the palette; there is no "OK" or "Apply" button as changes are made instantly.

Notice the changes to the *A1 First Floor Plan* drawing. Compare the "before" on the left to the "after" on the right in the image on the next page (Figure 2-5.2). The dimensions, doors and room names are no longer visible. However, it is important to realize that they still exist in the drawing file.

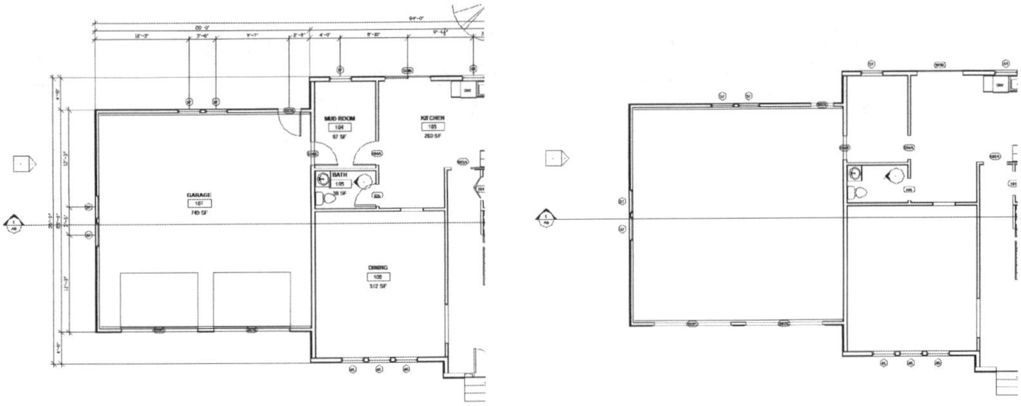

FIGURE 2-5.2
Sample drawing with layers frozen – original on left; notice doors, text and dimensions are hidden on the right

You should be able to see how this functionality is useful. If the electrical designer links the architectural designer's floor plan drawing into their drawing, they will want to turn off a few of the architectural *Layers* to "clean up" their drawing. For example, the electrical drawings might not need to see the dimensions, window tags and trees. When drawings are set up correctly this task is easy!

Next you will change the color of a *Layer* to see the effect it has on the current drawing.

6. **Open** the **Layer Properties Manager** again.

7. Locate the *Layer* named **A-Wall**, and then in its *Color* column, **select the color swatch** listed for this *Layer* (which should be yellow).

You are now in the *Select Color* dialog box (Figure 2-5.3).

8. Select color ***Blue*** (color #5) shown selected in **Figure 2-5.3**.

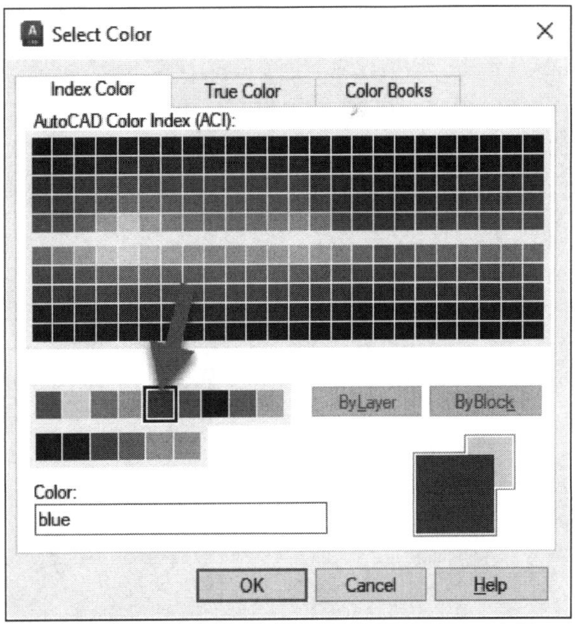

FIGURE 2-5.3
Select Color dialog *(part of the Layer Properties Manager)*

9. Click **OK** to exit the *Color Selector* and then click **X** (in the upper left or upper right corner – shown in the upper left in the image below) to close the *Layer Properties Manager.*

Notice the walls are now blue.

10. **Close** the *Sample* drawing without saving any changes.

Now you will open a new drawing and walk through the basics steps of creating and using *Layers* in a drawing.

Creating Layers:

11. **Open** a new drawing and switch to *Model Space.*

    TIP: Remember to start with the correct template: SheetSets\Architectural Imperial.dwt.

12. **Open** the *Layer Properties Manager.*

    TIP: Notice some Layers already exist; they came from the template file you started with.

13. Click the **New** Layer icon.

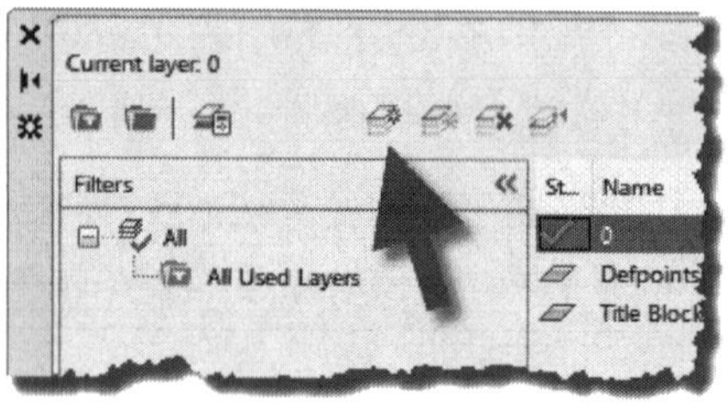

A new row has been added to the list; by default you are immediately positioned to enter the *Layer* name.

14. Type the word **Circles** and then press ***Enter.***

15. Repeat steps 13 and 14 to create the following layers:
    a. **Lines**
    b. **Rectangles**
    c. **Text**

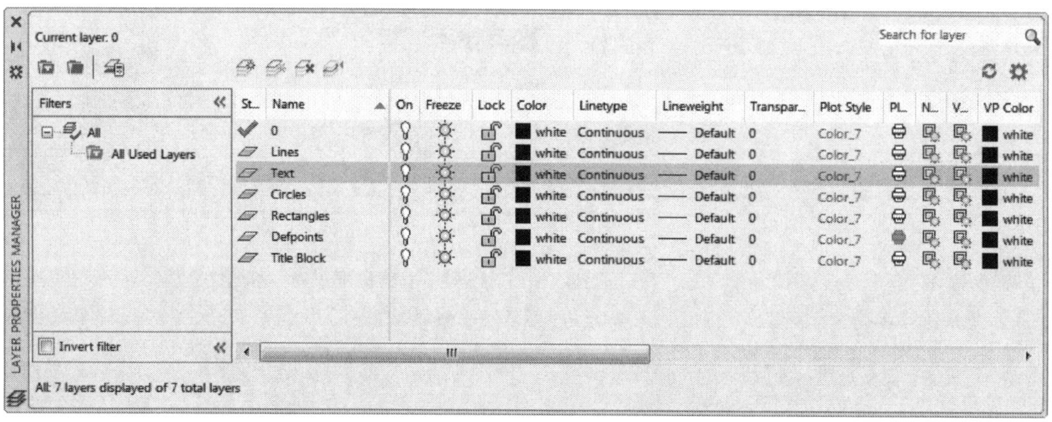

FIGURE 2-5.4 Layer Properties Manager; with 4 new layers created

Next you will assign a new color to three of the new *Layers*.

16. Set the *Layer* colors as follows:
    a. **Circles** Green *(color #3)*
    b. **Rectangles** Red *(color #1)*
    c. **Text** Cyan *(color #4)*

17. Click the **X** to close the *Layer Properties Manager*.

You now have four new *Layers*, each with a different color.

> ***FYI:*** *The Layer named Title Block is from your template file. Additional Layers can be added to template files to reduce new drawing setup steps.*

Drawing on Layers:

Now that you have *Layers* you will learn how to draw on different *Layers*. The easiest method is to set a *Layer* Current, and then all entities drawn after that will automatically be placed on that *Layer* (i.e., the current layer). Looking at Figure 2-5.4, notice in the upper left is the drawing's *Current Layer* (which is set to 0).

AutoCAD provides a few different ways to change the *Current Layer*. One is in *the Layer Properties Manager* (Figure 2-5.4). You simply click on the *layer name* you want to set to current and then click the **Current** icon (a green check mark). Another method is described next.

You can quickly set the *Current Layer* via the *Layers* panel (Figure 2-5.5); this is a dynamic toolbar. The toolbar will change its display per the following three scenarios:

- No entities in the current drawing are selected (no grips visible).
    - The *Current Layer* is displayed.
- One or more entities selected which are on the same *Layer*.
    - Displays which layer the selected entities are on.
- A group of entities selected which are on two or more *Layers*.
    - Display is blank to indicate multiple layers.

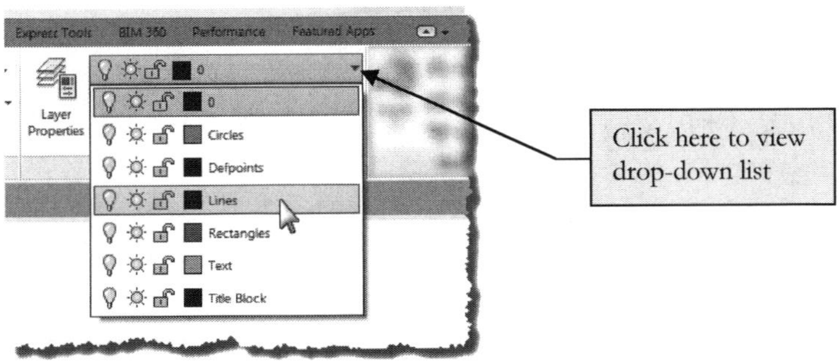

FIGURE 2-5.5
Layers panel; figure shows layer drop-down list in the dropped-down position

So, to change the *Current Layer*, you click the down arrow to the right of the display in the *Layers* panel (on the Home tab of the Ribbon) to view the drop-down list (which lists all the layers in the current drawing). Next, you click on the name of the layer you want to be current and that's it! *This only works if nothing is selected; otherwise, you are changing which Layer the selected entities are on.*

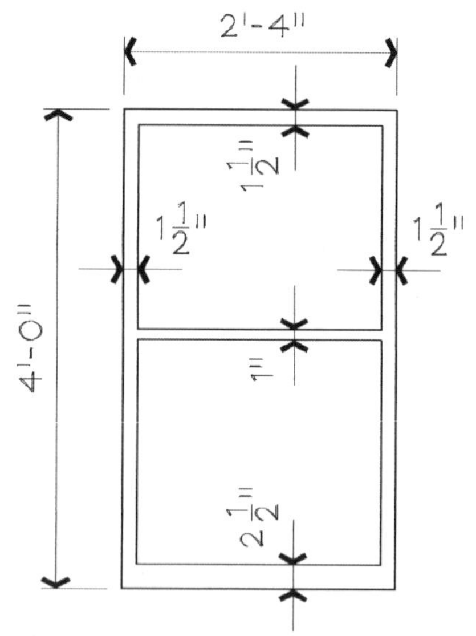

FIGURE 2-5.6 Three Rectangles drawn

Next you will change the *Current Layer* to *Rectangle* so when you draw rectangles, they will automatically be drawn on the Rectangle layer.

18. Press the ***Esc*** key twice on the keyboard. This ensures that no entities are selected.

19. Click the **Down-Arrow** on the *Layers* panel (Figure 2-5.5).

20. Move the cursor over the *Layer* named *Rectangle* and click.

The *Rectangle* layer is now set current which means that anything drawn from now on (until the current layer is changed again) will be drawn on the *Rectangle* layer.

Be aware that the layer name in no way implies that only rectangles can be drawn on the *Rectangle* layer. That is the intention and the drafter's responsibility to make sure only rectangles go on the *Rectangle* layer. *Note that we could rename the* Circle *layer to* Ellipse *and it would have no effect on the circles previously drawn on that layer.*

21. **Draw a Rectangle** that is **28"** wide and **48"** tall (*with the lower left corner at the Origin*).

22. **Draw** two more rectangles per the dimensions provided in **Figure 2-5.6**. *(This can be accomplished using a combination of the following commands: Offset, Stretch and Move.)*

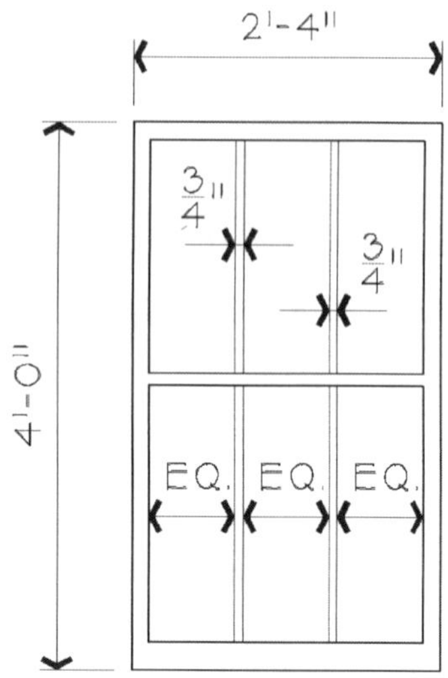

FIGURE 2-5.7 Three Rectangles drawn

Next you will draw several lines, so you will need to change the *Current Layer.*

23. Making sure no entities are selected, use the *Layers* toolbar to make ***Lines*** the *Current Layer.*

24. Using the dimensions provided in **Figure 2-5.7**, draw the vertical lines shown. (*This can be achieved using either the Move or Offset commands.*)

You may have already figured out what you are drawing; it is a double-hung window in elevation view.

You have two more lines to draw.

25. **Draw** the two short horizontal lines shown in Figure 2-5.8. *(The lines are near each side towards the middle; compare with Figure 2-5.7.)*

26. Use the **Mtext** command to enter the text: "**Double-Hung Window**" directly below the window. Make the text 2¼″ high (Figure 2-5.9).

FIGURE 2-5.8
Two short horizontal lines drawn (cf. Figure 2-5.7)

Oops:

If you were following the directions step by step, you missed a step. You forgot to change the *Current Layer* to *Text.*

You should notice one visual clue that the text is on the wrong layer: it's the same color as the lines previously drawn (*White*). If the text were on the correct layer it would be *Cyan* (the color you assigned to the text layer).

Next you will take a quick look at how to change which layer an entity is on without the need to erase and redraw.

FIGURE 2-5.9 Text added

Moving Entities From One Layer to Another:

Remember, when nothing is selected the *Layers* toolbar shows the *Current Layer* and when something is selected it shows which *Layer* the selected entity is on.

27. **Select the text,** make sure nothing else is selected (*press Esc key*) and click on the text. *(Notice the* Layer *panel is indicating that the text is on the* Lines *layer.)*

28. From the *drop-down* list, on the *Layer* panel, select **Text**.

Notice now, with the text still selected, the *Layer* pane indicates that the text is on the *Text* layer (Figure 2-5.10). The text should also now be the proper color: cyan.

29. Now press the ***Esc*** key to unselect the text.

Notice the *Layer* panel is now showing the *Current Layer* again. Try selecting and unselecting the various entities in your drawing to see the *Layers* panel change.

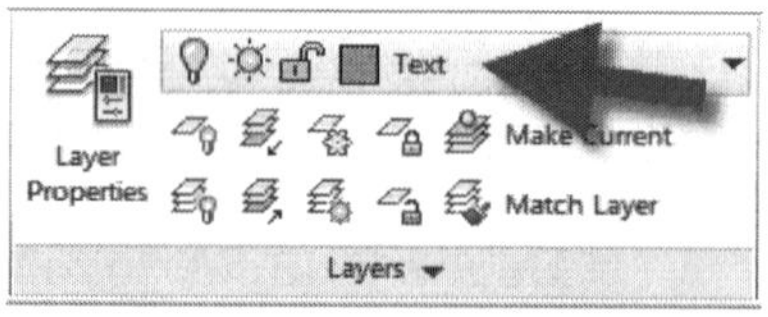

FIGURE 2-5.10 Text currently selected

30. Make the *Circle* layer current and then draw a large circle around the window/text, similar to Figure 2-5.11.

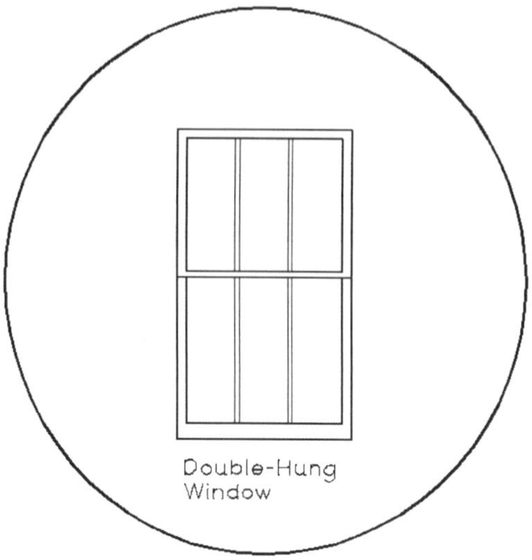

FIGURE 2-5.11 Circle added

One More Look at Controlling Layer Visibility:

Before concluding this chapter, you will take one more look at *Freezing* and *Thawing* layers, this time using your own drawing.

31. **Freeze** the *Lines* layer *(via the Layer Properties Manager).*

Notice the lines all disappear from the screen.

32. **Thaw** the *Lines* layer.

33. **Freeze** the *Circle* layer.

You should have received a message stating that AutoCAD "cannot freeze the current layer" (Figure 2-5.12). To freeze the *Circle* layer, you would have to set another layer as current first.

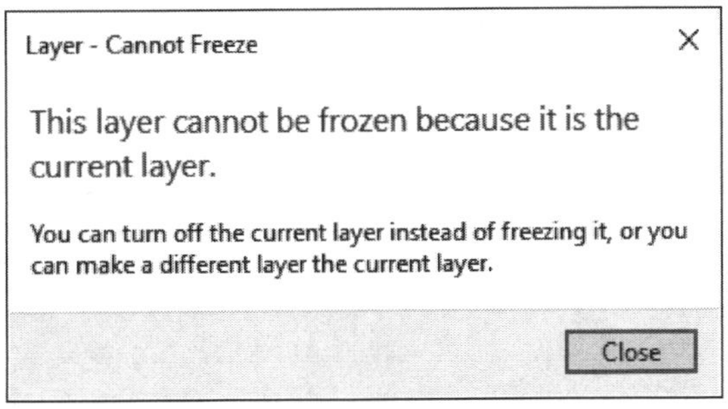

FIGURE 2-5.12 AutoCAD message

34. Set the *Rectangle* layer as *Current.*

35. Now *Freeze* the *Circle* layer.

Try a few more variations on the Freeze/Thaw scenarios before proceeding to the next step.

36. Make sure all *Layers* are turned **On** and **Thawed**.

37. **Print** the drawing showing all entities (including the circle).

38. **Save** the drawing as **Ex3-3 Layers.dwg**.

What's the Difference between Freeze and Off?

On the surface there is no difference between Freeze and Off when it comes to controlling layer visibility. If you Freeze a layer, its contents are not displayed; the same is true when you turn a layer Off.

The difference has to do with display memory. When a layer is Frozen the information required to display it onscreen is not loaded into your graphics card's memory. On the other hand, when a layer is only turned Off, all the information required to display the entities on that layer is loaded into your graphics card's memory.

The Pro's and Con's:
The main benefit to turning a layer Off rather than Freezing it is:

> When you turn a layer back on, it will instantly display (without a regeneration).
> [*Negative:* slower panning and zooming on large / complex drawings]

The benefit to Freezing a layer rather than turning it Off:

> Faster Panning and Zooming without the extra baggage required in the graphics card
> [*Negative*: requires a time-consuming Regen whenever a layer is Thawed]

Recommended use:
Freeze the following layers in your drawing if:

> The layer will typically "never" be on in the current drawing (e.g., doors and furniture in a reflected ceiling plan)

Turn a layer Off in your drawing if:

> The layer is generally always on, but you want to make it invisible for a short period of time (e.g., hiding the *Text* and *Dimension* layers to print a "clean" floor plan).
>
> When using this method, you can confidently select all the layers in the *Layer Properties Manager* and turn them all On without worrying about making a layer show up that shouldn't.

Exercise 2-6:
Plotting

You have learned a significant amount of information about AutoCAD in this chapter. You may be wondering how you will remember it all (especially if you never used AutoCAD prior to this study/class). Fear not; the remainder of this book is dedicated to providing architectural exercises that will refine and hone those skills covered in this chapter. Also, along the way you will be exposed to new commands and techniques that will make your job easier.

One last thing you need to have a basic understanding of before moving on is plotting (a.k.a., printing) your drawings out on paper. This will likely be required by your instructor for grading. This short introduction will just cover the very basics; you will learn more about plotting towards the end of this textbook.

Model Space versus Layout Views

Everything you have drawn and modified so far has been in what is known as *Model Space*. This is where you will almost always do all of your drafting and design. Another space exists known as *Layout View* (or *Paper Space*); which is an area dedicated to printing your drawings.

In *Model Space* you draw everything to full scale, with no exceptions. (Let this sink in as it is very important). If you are drawing a building that has a 350′-0″ wall along one side, you draw the line in AutoCAD 350′-0″ long. If, in another drawing, you are drawing a roof detail which has a 2 x 8 nailer strip at the edge, you will draw the lines for the wood at its actual size (1 ½″ x 7 ¼″ – this is the actual size of a 2 x 8).

A *Layout View* is where you can set up a drawing to be printed. For example, you can specify the paper size (e.g. 22″x34″, 11″x17″, etc.) as well as locate the drawing (from *Model Space*) on the sheet at a specific scale and even cropped if you wish. Once this is set up, you can continue to work on the drawing in *Model Space* and quickly switch to a *Layout View* and plot the drawing without having to re-specify all the settings desired.

You may still print from *Model Space* if you simply wish to print a small area of the plan that might never be printed again; maybe you need to review this area with a colleague. When you print from *Model Space*, you need to specify what scale you want the drawing to fit on the paper. Typically, you will want to print the drawing as large as possible within the normal architectural scales. It is usually a bad idea to print a drawing "Fit to paper", as this could mislead someone, such as a contractor, and estimates or timelines could be way off.

Each drawing only has one *Model Space* but may have several *Layout Views*.

Accessing Layout Views

The drawings you have been using in this chapter already have *Layout Views* set up and ready to use; you will explore this now.

1. **Open** the drawing file associated with the *Move* command; this should be the file with your finished work.

2. Hover your cursor over the drawing tab (see image below)

As you can see on your screen, and in the image below, small thumbnail images appear below the tab. The one on the left will always be *Model Space*, and the *Layout View(s)* will be to the right. Clicking on one of these images switches you to that space. The one with the blue border is the active view.

> *TIP: You can also right-click on an image to get additional options.*

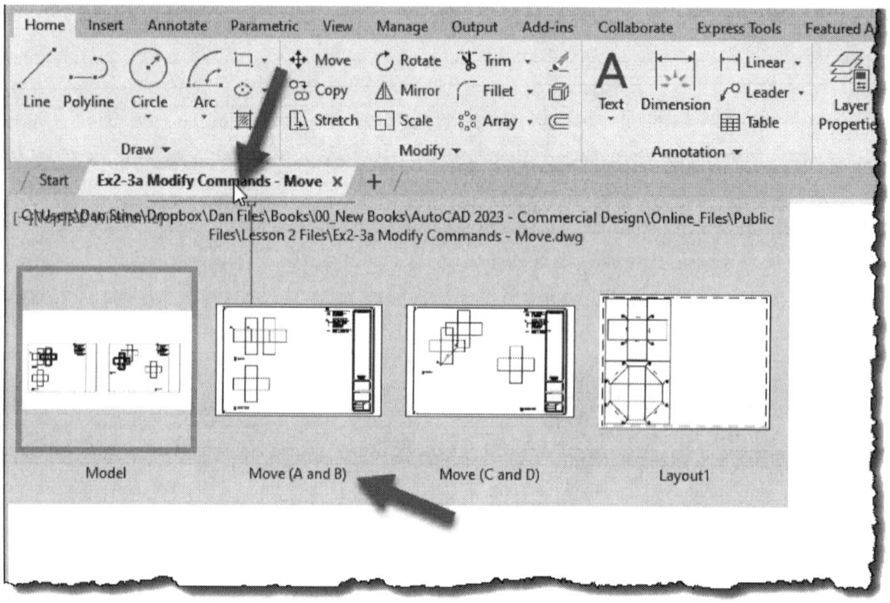

3. **Click** directly on the second thumbnail/image labeled **Move (A and B)** as shown in the image above.

You are now in the selected *Layout View* Line (A and B); see the image on the next page. This gives you a clear picture of the paper and how things are laid out on it. For the most part, things will print exactly as they appear here.

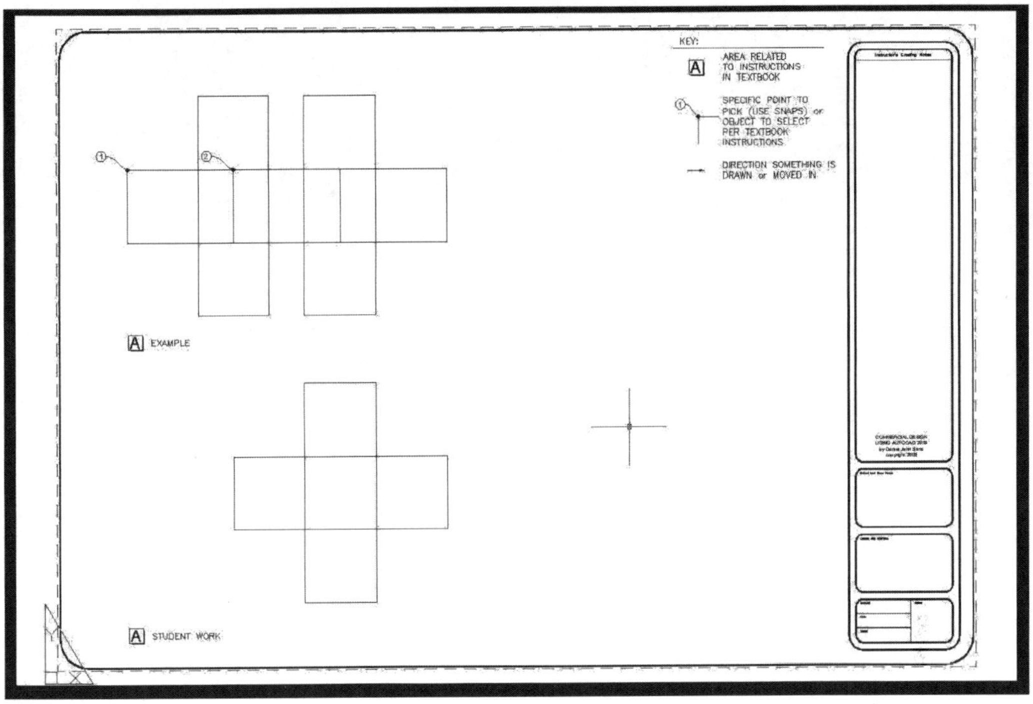

Next you will take a quick look at the area, called **Page Setup**, where the various settings have been selected for this view.

4. On the **Output** tab, select the **Page Setup Manager** icon (shown below with arrow).

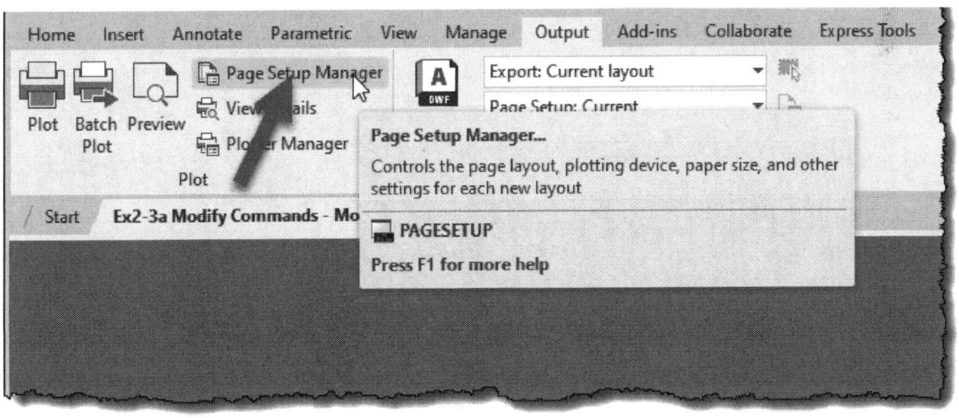

5. With ***Move (A and B)*** selected, click the **Modify** button.

Take a minute to look at the various settings available; the main ones are *Plotter*, *Paper Size*, *Scale*, *What to plot* and *Plot style table*.

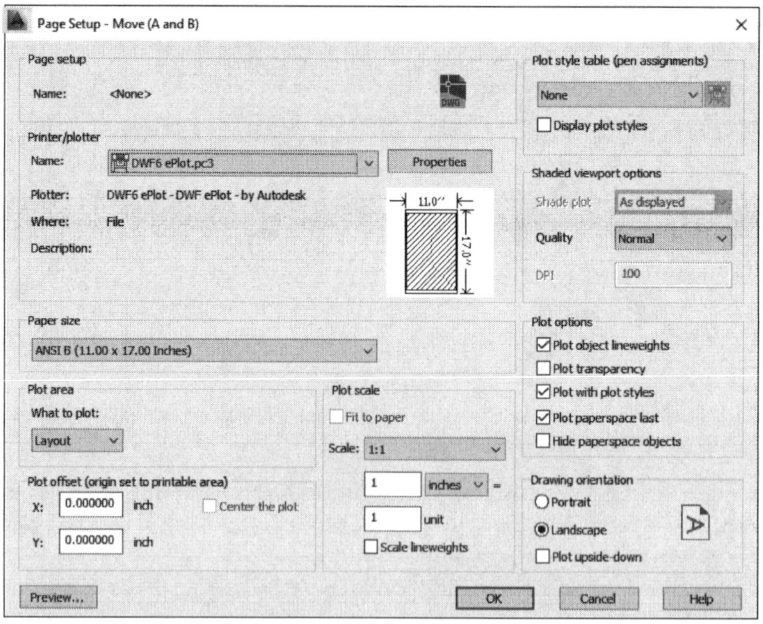

PAGE SETUP...
This is the area where you can pre-specify the various plot settings. When you go to plot this *Layout View*, all the settings here will be the default in the *Plot* dialog box.

6. Click **OK** to close the *Page Setup* dialog box, and then **Close**.

7. Now select the **Plot** icon on the **Output** tab (or click *Plot* on the *Quick Access Toolbar). Click Continue to Plot Single Sheet, if prompted.*

Notice that the settings all match those shown in the previous *Page Setup* dialog box; also note:

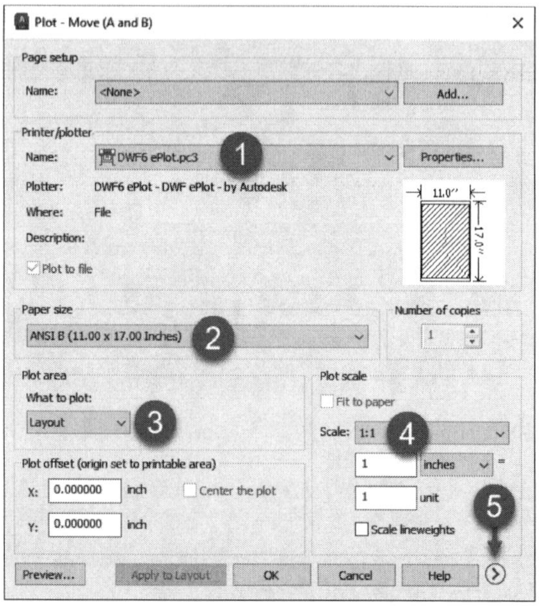

(1) Select a plotter in the drop-down list (these are the ones installed on your computer).

(2) The paper size is set to 11″x17″; if your printer cannot print this size, you can change it to 8 ½″x11″ (a.k.a., Letter).

(3) Here you are saying you want to plot the paper. You can also choose Window or Extents. (You need to select Extents when printing to Letter size.)

(4) The paper is actual size and the drawing has already been scaled to the paper, thus the scale is 1:1.

(5) Reveals more options.

8. If you are able, go ahead and Plot the drawing; click **OK**.

The *Plot* dialog box goes away and your drawing should have printed to the selected output device.

9. Similar to steps 2 and 3 above, you can switch to the other *Layout View* "**Move (C and D)**" and plot it.

Returning to Model Space

10. A quick way to return to *Model Space* is by clicking the tab to the far bottom-left; see image below.

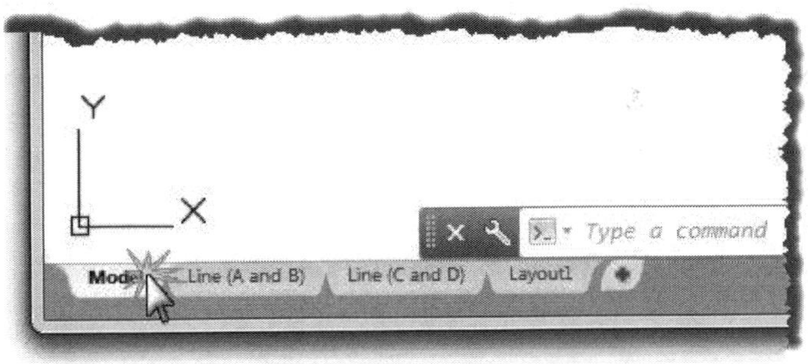

Any changes in *Model Space* automatically show up in each *Layout View*, as the drawings on each sheet are essentially set up as "windows" that look into *Model Space*; they are not copies.

11. If required for your class, you can follow the steps learned to plot the rest of the drawings from this chapter (i.e., their layout views).

12. Seeing as you did not actually change the current drawing, you only plotted it, you can **Close** the drawing **without saving**.

Plotting from *Model Space* is similar to that just covered. In this case you usually select "*Window*" for *What to plot* and a specific scale (i.e., 1/8″ = 1′-0″) as the drawing is "real-world scale" in *Model Space*.

The only other "big" thing you will need to start thinking about when it comes to printing is something called *Plot Style Tables* which control line weights. For now, just know that the *Plot Style Table* controls the various line weights based on the color of an item in the drawing. You will be reviewing this next, in *Appendix A*, before moving on in the next chapter.

Self-Exam:

The following questions can be used as a way to check your knowledge of this lesson. The answers can be found at the bottom of this page.

1. There is no difference between Freeze and Off. (T/F)
2. A drawing's Origin is 0,0. (T/F)
3. All drawings have a 0 (i.e., zero) *Layer.* (T/F)
4. Use the ______________ command to create an oval shape.
5. When you want to make a previously drawn rectangle wider you would use the _______________ command.

Review Questions:

The following questions may be assigned by your instructor as a way to assess your knowledge of this section. Your instructor has the answers to the review questions.

1. Use the *Offset* command to quickly create a parallel line(s). (T/F)
2. AutoCAD provides several ways in which to draw an arc. (T/F)
3. With the *Stretch* command, lines completely within the crossing-window are actually only moved, not stretched. (T/F)
4. You have to select entities and a center point when using *Polar Array.* (T/F)
5. The *Linear Dimension* command can create either a horizontal or a vertical dimension depending on where you pick your three points. (T/F)
6. Selecting this icon () allows you to ____________ two intersecting lines.
7. You cannot *Extend* several lines at once to a common boundary edge. (T/F)
8. Use the _______________ command to create a reverse image.
9. You can use either ___________ or _____________ in the *Layer Properties Manager* to control the visibility of a *Layer.*
10. When no entities are selected, the **Layers** panel displays the ________ layer.

SELF-EXAM ANSWERS:
1 – F, **2** – T, **3** – T, **4** – Ellipse, **5** – Stretch

Lesson 3
Library Project: FLOOR PLANS – Part 1

In this lesson you will jump right in and get started drawing your floor plan for the Campus Library project. Throughout the lesson you will be introduced to a few new commands, and you will study common methods used to draw floor plans.

Exercise 3-1:
Project Overview and Standards

Introduction

Throughout this book you will be drawing a library building for a medium-sized state university's local campus. The building consists of several floors. However, you will only be working with the first floor (the floor is complex enough and large enough to achieve the goals of this book).

Subsequent to drawing the floor plans (i.e., walls, doors and windows) you will develop several spaces; a few examples: Classrooms, Offices, Stacks, Break Room and Toilet Rooms.

Interior elevations and details will also be drawn for this project. Throughout these drawing exercises several new AutoCAD commands and techniques will be introduced.

The project in this book is not intended to meet any particular building code. Several general aspects of the building code will be discussed.

It is recommended (and, if in a class setting, likely required by your instructor) that you draw everything as instructed. This will allow the instructor to grade for accuracy and one's ability to follow directions. Furthermore, the exercises are designed to create certain situations that will be covered or resolved in a later lesson.

Project Standards

In an attempt to simulate the real-world situation of conforming to an office standard, you will be required to follow the standards stated in the lessons and the information contained in Appendix A.

The bulk of the "Office Standards" have been located in an appendix to make them more accessible throughout the book as you will need to refer to them several times.

Read Appendix A Now!!!

You should take the time to read Appendix A at this time. That information might have just as well been placed here, but as previously mentioned it has been located at the end of the book to make it more accessible. An understanding of this information is required before you can proceed with this lesson.

Overview of the Plan You Will Be Drawing

The following (Figure 3-1.1) will give you an idea of the floor plan you will draw in this book – *this represents more than one chapter's worth of work.*

The following components of this floor plan will be used to present several AutoCAD commands and techniques: *Exterior walls with veneer lines; *Various types of interior walls; *Windows and Doors; *Columns and Structural Grid; *Casework; *Stairs; *Furniture; and *Toilet rooms.

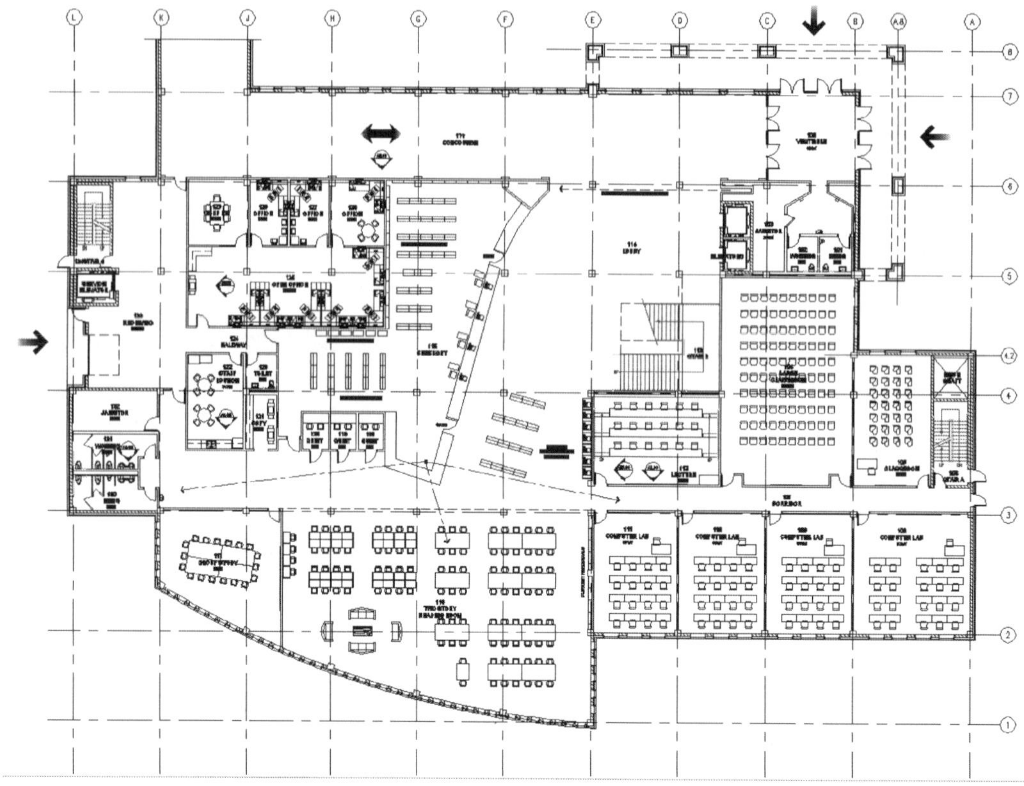

FIGURE 3-1.1 Example of what will be drawn in this book - First Floor Plan

Exercise 3-2:
Structural Grid Layout and Columns

Getting Started

In this exercise you will draw the structural grid layout and the columns. Although you would not necessarily start with a formal grid like this one, you typically design to a general grid (e.g., 5′ x 5′) to accommodate a practical column and beam system; this helps avoid columns ending up in undesirable locations further into the design process.

You will be creating the grid and columns in a separate drawing file from the floor plan. This will help to simulate how a floor plan of this magnitude is typically set up; the reasoning for this methodology is described next.

Many design firms have the structural engineers draw the structural grid layout in a separate drawing file, which is then "linked" (i.e., an external reference) into all the floor plan files. This forces the architects to communicate all changes affecting the building structure to the structural engineers who, in turn, are responsible for making changes to the structural grid drawing. You can think of it like a labor union – dividing the work (i.e., the drafting) by the designers responsible for their respective portions of the building. Similar situations occur elsewhere in your typical project; for example, light fixtures and mechanical diffusers in the reflected ceiling plan.

Whenever possible, things should only be drawn once and referenced as needed. Architects and Interior Designers should avoid redrawing or simply "pasting" content into their drawings. "Constant Change" is a good description of the design process. Duplicating content rather than "linking" the source is unsophisticated and inefficient to say the least.

A common mistake might be this: You want to create a Floor Finish Plan which will be a separate plan on its own sheet. You open the floor plan drawing; copy everything to the "clipboard" and then "paste" it into the new drawing file. Next, you begin designing and noting the various floor finishes throughout the building. Then, even after the client said they will never change the plan again, revisions are required (they are even willing to pay for additional services). Now you have to update the base plan (moving walls, adding notes, etc.) and every other floor plan file into which you "copied" the floor plan; a significant amount of redundant work that could have been avoided if the project files were set up correctly!

At this point, as previously mentioned, you should be familiar with the "Office Standards" described in Appendix A, which is to be adhered to throughout this book in an attempt to better simulate a real-world environment.

File Name and Location:

All the drawings for this book should be placed in the same folder on your computer (this may be specified by your instructor). Naming files is very important in identifying and managing them – especially on large projects that can have hundreds of files and extend over one or more years. Many firms add the office Project Number (or commission number) to the beginning of the file – which helps in identifying and locating files when they are misplaced. For this book, the file name spelled out in the next step consists of the following information (which should be modified with your information):

- *Your Initials (e.g., DJS)* *FYI: "e.g." means "for example"*
- *Your Zip Code (e.g., 55803)*
- *Discipline (e.g., A = Architectural)*
- *Description* of what the file contains *(e.g., GD = Grid).*

The other files created in this book will have a similar format. You will now start drawing the grid layout in a new drawing file.

1. Start a new drawing named **DJS55803AGD01.dwg**.
   Don't forget to use the correct template: click Application Menu → New → Drawing and then "SheetSets\Architectural Imperial.dwt".

2. Switch to *Model Space* if necessary.

Setting the Drawing Limits:

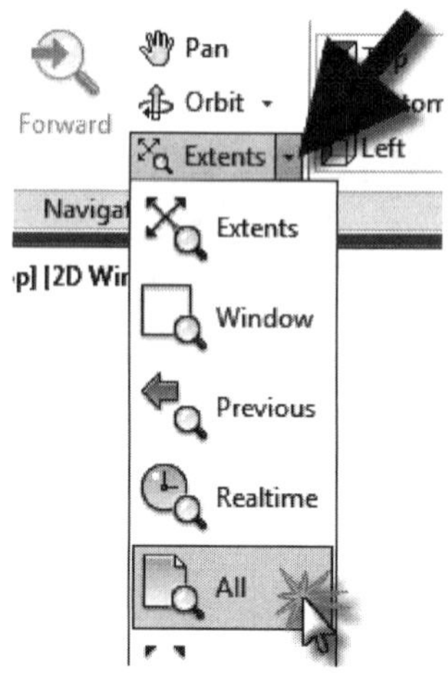

Next you will set the Model Space drawing limits. The drawing space does not actually have limits; this setting relates more to zooming and drawing regenerations.

3. Type **Limits** and then ***Enter***. *(You should see the typed text near your cursor.)*

4. Type -**100'**, press the ***Tab*** key *(or type a comma if you are typing in the Command Window)* and then type -**200'** and then ***Enter***. ***FYI:*** don't miss the minus symbol for each entry.

5. Type **300'**; press the ***Tab*** key *(or type a comma if you are typing in the Command Window)* and then type **100'** and then ***Enter***.

6. Select **Zoom All** from the *Navigate 2D* panel on the *View* tab.

   FYI: The Zoom All command will zoom to the drawing's extents or the drawing's Limits (whichever is greater). In this case nothing has been drawn so you have no drawing extents; thus, the drawing Limits are used. You are now viewing a drawing area 400' wide and 300' tall (based on the Limits just set), with the drawing's origin (i.e., 0,0) somewhat centered in the view. This will allow you to start drawing the floor plan without having to stop and zoom (and regenerate the drawing).

Setting the Line Type Scale:

Setting the LTscale variable will help you to see how the dashed lines will look when the plan is plotted at ⅛″ = 1′-0″ (in this example). See Appendix A, page A-14, for more information on this.

7. Type **LTscale** (in the *Command Window*), type **96** and then ***Enter***.

8. If you have not already done so, create the two layers required to draw the structural grid on (see Appendix A).

   TIP: *Make sure the layer color and linetype are set properly as well.*

9. Draw the structural grid using the following guidelines (Figure 3-2.1):
   a. Do not draw the dimensions; the "boxed" dimensions indicate how far the grid line ends are to extend out.
   b. The drawing origin is given; do not add the text or the dot.
   c. The grid bubbles shall have a 4′-0″ diameter; use object snaps to accurately place them at the end of the grid lines. ***TIP:*** *Draw circle and Move into place.*
   d. The text in the bubble shall be **Single Line Text** (not Multi-Line):
      i. Style: Roman
      ii. Height: 1′-6″
      iii. Justification: Middle
      iv. Snap the middle grip to the center of the circle (See Figure 3-2.2).
      v. Use letters across the top with letter "A" on the right.
      vi. Use numbers vertically with number "1" on the bottom.

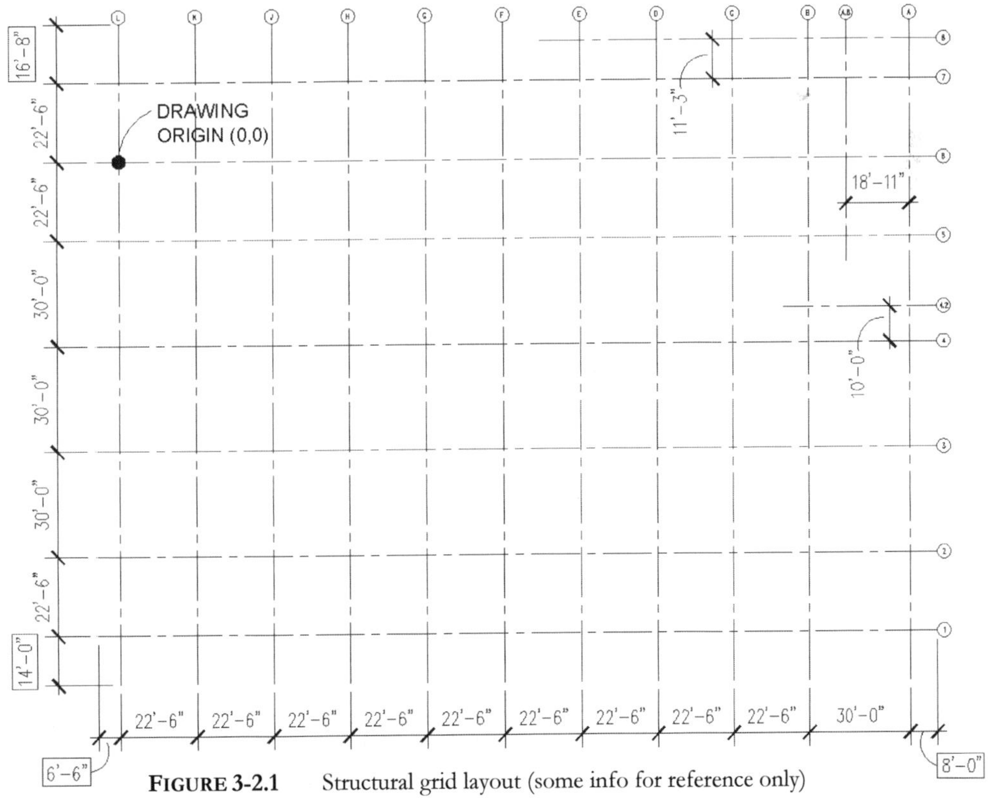

FIGURE 3-2.1 Structural grid layout (some info for reference only)

The image below shows the upper right portion of the structural grid; just a few comments about the grid before proceeding.

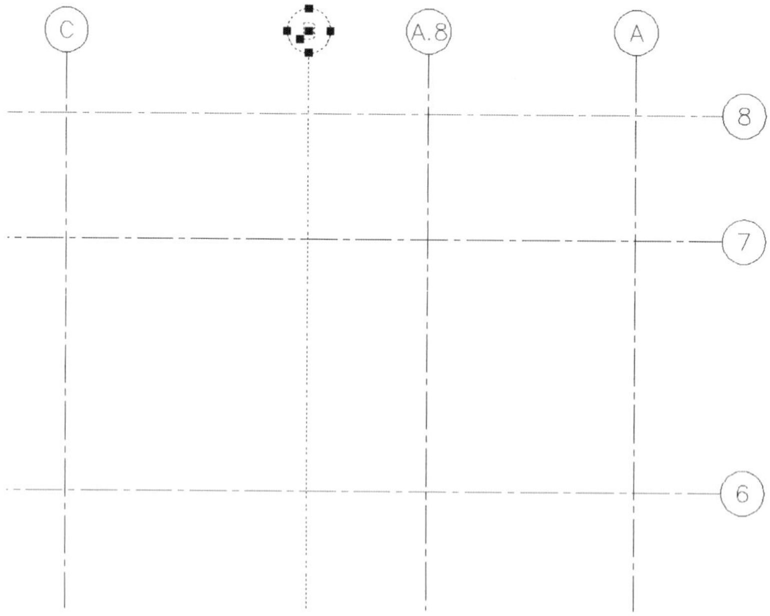

FIGURE 3-2.2 Structural grid; with one grid line, bubble and text selected

When the various elements are properly laid out, the GRIPS will perfectly overlap. In the example above the grip for the bottom quadrant of the circle and the endpoint of the line overlap; also, the GRIP for the center of the circle and the text's "middle" GRIP overlap.

> ***NOTE:*** *The text also has a GRIP in the lower-left corner.*

The text JUSTIFICATION being set to MIDDLE is different than CENTER. Setting the text justification to CENTER places the control grip at the center (horizontally), but at the bottom. The MIDDLE option also places the control grip in the center (horizontally), but also centers it vertically. The Middle justification allows you to edit the text string (e.g., change the text from A to AA) and even change the text height and it will always stay centered on the circle (see Figure 3-2.3). When you click on the text you can select the MIDDLE grip and then SNAP to the center of the circle – effectively moving the text to its proper location relative to the circle. Once you have one bubble/text item set up, you can copy it to the other locations.

FIGURE 3-2.3 Text Justification Example
Two bubbles on left are CENTER justified; two bubbles on right are MIDDLE justified. The right-hand bubble in each group shows how the same text modification (i.e., adding a letter and changing the height) has a different result.

A grid is a very critical part of laying out a building – many components of the building rely on its accuracy. Therefore, the grid should be drawn very accurately and when dimensioned, the dimension text should never be manually overridden (which is sometimes done in a project at the last minute where someone wants to avoid a lot of "extra" work).

If the grid layout were drawn in the same drawing as the floor plan (which it will not be in this tutorial), you would LOCK the two grid LAYERS so that you would not accidentally move, trim or erase the grid lines while working on the floor plans. In this tutorial the grid and columns will be in a separate drawing file and Xref'ed (external referenced) into the floor plan, which also prohibits one from making changes *without opening the grid drawing file.*

Placing the Columns:

At this point you will add the structural columns to the grid drawing. You will create a Block for each column size, with its insertion point at the center point of the column, to facilitate inserting the columns at grid intersections.

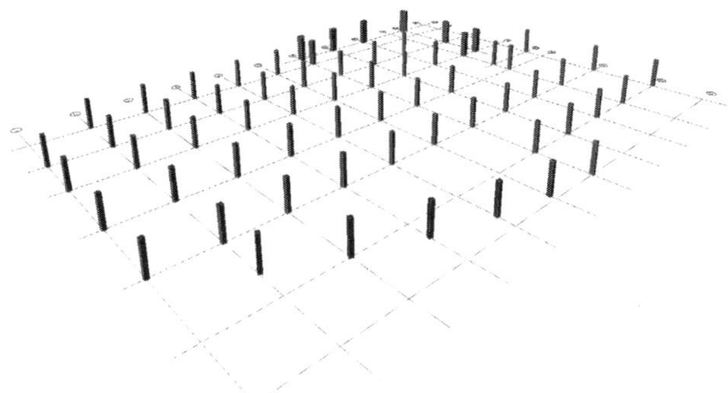

Isometric: Structural grid with Columns

When drawing anything in AutoCAD, line work that represents one item (e.g., table, marker board, column) should, at the very least, be drawn using a POLYLINE rather than individual lines; this makes selecting and moving the item easier. If the item will be used many times in a drawing, you should consider making a BLOCK. Search for "*Polylines, Drawing*" in Help to learn more about what this means; you will learn more later in this book.

A BLOCK is like clipart; it is composed of several individual lines, arcs and circles. When you select any part of a BLOCK, the entire thing highlights (i.e., is selected). In this example (creating columns), the BLOCK can have a convenient insertion point, as previously mentioned. Also, if all the 12″x12″ concrete columns need to change to 14″x14″ concrete columns, you can simply redefine the BLOCK and they will all change at once.

Creating a Block:

You have two primary ways to create a BLOCK: one is to create a new drawing file that has the column in it; the other option is to define the BLOCK right in the drawing you are in.

Creating a separate drawing file to be used as a BLOCK:
With this option you would create the linework in a new (i.e., empty) drawing file – with the *Drawing Origin* (0,0) positioned at the desired insertion point for that symbol. In this example you would draw a 12″x12″ square with the *Drawing Origin* in the center of the square. Then you would open the drawing you want the BLOCK in and use the *Insert* command, then *Browse* for the external file (the one you just created) and place it in your current drawing. This is the preferred method if you need to use the symbol in several drawings (or on other projects in the future); the files can be organized in folders for quick access.

Defining a BLOCK within the current drawing file:
With this option you would use the BLOCK command to specify a name, select linework (already drawn in the current drawing) and an insertion point. Then the BLOCK would be available for insertion in the current drawing only; no external file would exist. This option is preferred if you only need the symbol in one drawing and are unlikely to use it in the future. This is the option you will use in this exercise.

The last thing you need to understand, regarding BLOCKS, before proceeding has to do with LAYERS. Typically, all the linework for a BLOCK should be created on LAYER zero. When a BLOCK is inserted, any lines within the BLOCK on LAYER zero take on the properties of the LAYER the BLOCK is inserted on. For example, if a door has been defined properly (i.e., lines on LAYER zero), when the door BLOCK is inserted on the demo LAYER the door will be red and the lines will be dashed. If the linework in the door was drawn on LAYER *A-DOOR* (rather than zero), the door would be yellow and the lines continuous, no matter what LAYER the door BLOCK is inserted on.

10. Anywhere in your grid drawing, create a **12″x12″** square using the **Rectangle** tool (which will ultimately create a closed polyline).

11. Make sure the square is on LAYER **zero.**

12. Type **Block** to open the *Block Definition* dialog box (Figure 3-2.4).
    a. *Name:* **12x12_Column**

    FYI: *The BLOCK name cannot have the inch symbol in it.*

    b. *Base point:* Click the button and pick center of square.

    TIP: *Draw a temporary diagonal line and select its mid-point.*

    c. *Objects:* Click the button to the left of *Select objects* and **select the square.** (Do not select the temporary diagonal line.) Press **Enter**.
    d. *Objects:* Select **Delete**; this will erase the rectangle once the block has been defined in the drawing.
    e. *Description:* **Structural Column: 12"x12" Column.**
    f. Click **OK** to create the *BLOCK*.

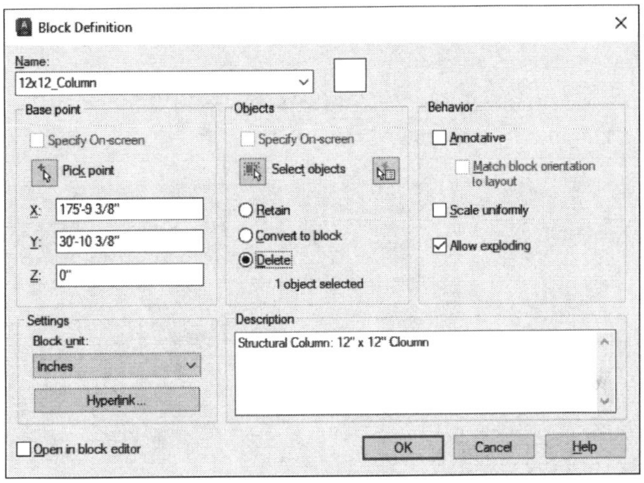

FIGURE 3-2.4 Block Definition dialog box
NOTE: X and Y values will vary in your drawing based on where you drew the square.

A few additional comments about the Block Definition dialog box:
The Settings area allows you to specify the units of the Block (Inches, Feet, Miles, Millimeters, etc.). Architectural drawings are always "inches," and the other options are for engineers and scientists. When used correctly, this allows the symbol to be inserted correctly in any drawing (architectural or engineering drawing). You will learn about the Hyperlink feature in Lesson 5.

The Objects area allows you to select the objects to include in the Block you are about to create and what happens to those objects after the Block is created. *Retain* leaves the original linework as-is; *Convert to block* replaces the original linework with a copy of the newly created Block (nothing will be visually different until you try selecting it); *Delete* will erase the original linework and leave you with a new Block definition that exists in the drawing but has not been inserted anywhere yet.

The Behavior area controls things about the Block once it's placed in the drawing. Things like whether the *Block* can be *Exploded* (i.e., reduced back down to individual elements), if the symbol can be scaled disproportionately via its properties, and if its size changes based on the scale the drawing will be plotted at (this is what Annotative means). You would never want your column to change size; this feature is for notes and tags.

13. Referring to **Appendix A** (Office Standards), create the appropriate layer for the columns (i.e., proper name and color).

Your drawing now contains a *Block* definition called "12x12_Column" which can be inserted anywhere in the current drawing and on the proper *Layer*.

Next you will insert the *Block* you just created. This involves using the *Insert* [Block] command, selecting which *Block* to place (from a drop-down list) and then *Snapping* to the intersection of two grids.

14. From the **Home** tab, select the **Insert** icon.

15. Select the newly created **12x12_Column** (Figure 3-2.5):

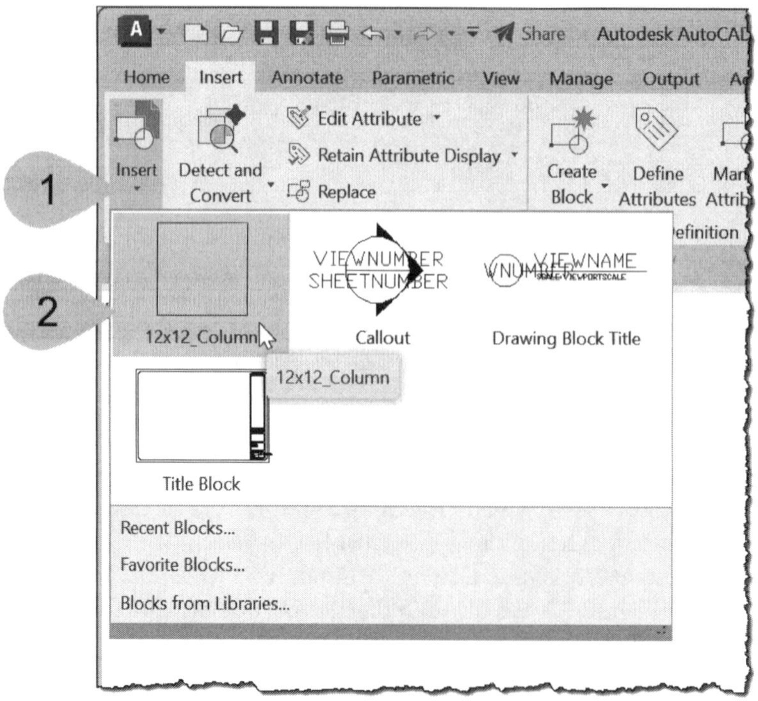

FIGURE 3-2.5 Insert [Block] Dialog Box

16. Follow the steps on the next page to insert the column block in your drawing.

The *Block* which you are about to insert is attached to your cursor. The insertion point of the *Block* will correspond to the *Base Point* you selected when creating the *Block (if not at your cursor, retry the last few steps).*

17. Make sure **Intersection** is set as one of your Running OSNAPs.

    TIP: *Right-click OSNAP on the Status Bar and select Intersection.*

18. Using the following tips, insert the column as shown in Figure 3-2.6.
    a. Use the **Insert** command to accurately place one column.
    b. Then use the **Copy** command to quickly locate the remaining columns; make sure you *Snap* to the intersection of grids.
    c. A larger circle has been added at each column to help you more easily identify where each column is on the image in this book; do <u>not</u> draw the circles in your drawing.

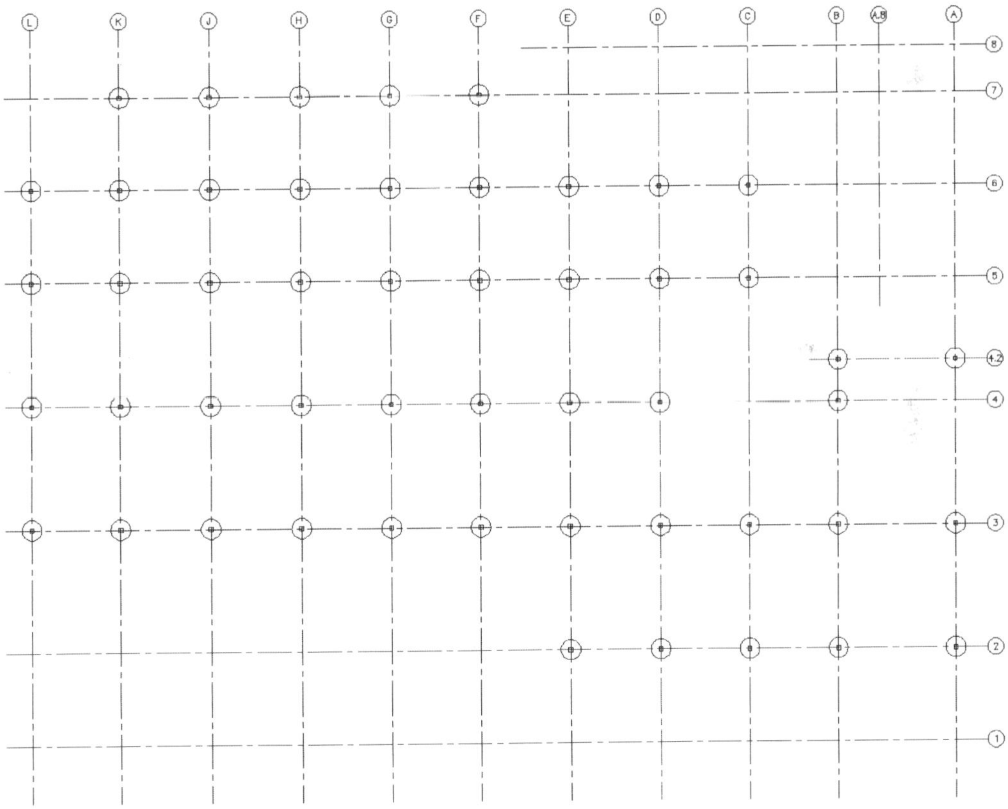

FIGURE 3-2.6 Step 18 Column Locations
NOTE: *The circles are for reference only and should not be drawn.*

Placing Columns in the Curved Exterior Wall:

You now have most of the columns in their proper position. Next you will place the columns along the large curved wall at the bottom of the plan (Figure 3-1.1).

The columns along the curved wall do not fall on the intersection of any grids. Additionally, the columns are rotated along the curve. The grids do align with vertical grids, but not the horizontal grids. Where several "odd" columns fall between two typical grids, it would be messy to add several horizontal grids.

Typically, these "odd" columns are simply dimensioned off the major grid lines. In our example we have several and they are rotated so a table will be used. This example will be similar to a real-world example of documenting this condition for the contractor to understand exactly how to build it.

So even though this book gives you a lot of step-by-step instructions, you are also learning what documentation information is required by the contractor to accurately construct the building. Even if a floor plan has been accurately drawn in a CAD program, if it is not accurately dimensioned and noted the building cannot be built (or, in this case, drawn by you).

19. Insert the **12x12_Column** column *Block* per the following:
    a. See Figure 3-2.7 for locations.
    b. Each column is labeled with a letter (do not add the letters).
    c. Refer to Table 3-2.A to determine the vertical offset distance from grid 1 and the column rotation angle.
    d. One at a time, create a temporary insertion point for each column per the following steps:
        i. Offset grid line 1 upward to required distance.
        ii. Insert the column Block (at the temp grind intersection).
        iii. Erase the temporary grid line.
    e. Enter the proper rotation angle in the Insert [Block] dialog.
    f. The center of Column F is 4 ½" to the right of grid K.

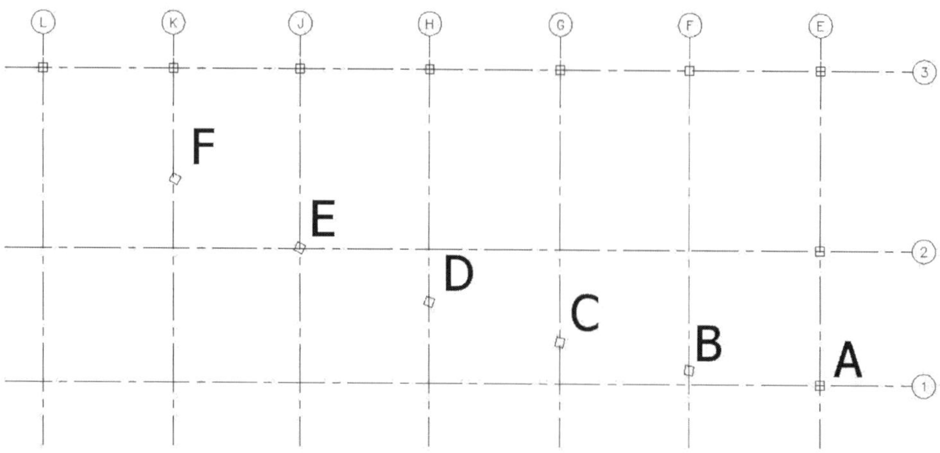

FIGURE 3-2.7 Step 19 Column Locations

Column →	A	B	C	D	E	F
Grid 1 Offset	0″	2′-5 5/16″	6′-11 9/16″	13′-7 7/16″	22′-7 1/4″	33′-11 5/8″
Rotation	0	351	346	341	336	330

TABLE 3-2.A Column location table for columns in curved wall

Architecture vs. Interior Design – where is the line?

If you are studying Interior Design specifically you may be thinking this is more information than you personally need. However, this could just as easily be false columns along a curved interior wall that you have designed.

Currently, drawing the "structural" portion of the floor plan is a means to an end (e.g., to draw architectural floor plans, interior elevations, etc.). These techniques are still very useful to learn and can be applied to many other situations. This author works with five Certified Interior Designers, and they often have a hand in drafting/designing much more than just the interior portions of a building.

There is no clear line between "architecture" and "interior design." The two elements are (and should be) very much interrelated. For example, the location of the exterior windows in a space should be considered by the interior designer when arranging systems furniture. If a conflict exists, the exterior windows may need to move which affects the aesthetics of the exterior façade of the building.

LEED projects

Additionally, many Interior Designers are leading the charge on managing and implementing program requirements to comply with LEED® (Leadership in Energy and Environmental Design). Another example here, again with windows, has to do with the LEED credits involving daylighting – if a space does not have the proper amount of exterior windows the floor plan and exterior elevation designs need to be modified to comply to get the credits. If the interior designer is the one that knows the LEED requirements, they are often in the best position to offer a design solution. This author has recently worked on two projects that will be LEED certified. To learn more about LEED, visit the U.S. Green Building Council's website at www.usgbc.org.

Next you will create columns for the NE entry area and place them.

20. Using steps previously discussed, create the *Blocks* shown in Figure 3-2.8. (Do not draw the black dot or the dimensions.) Use the label below each column for the *Block* name.

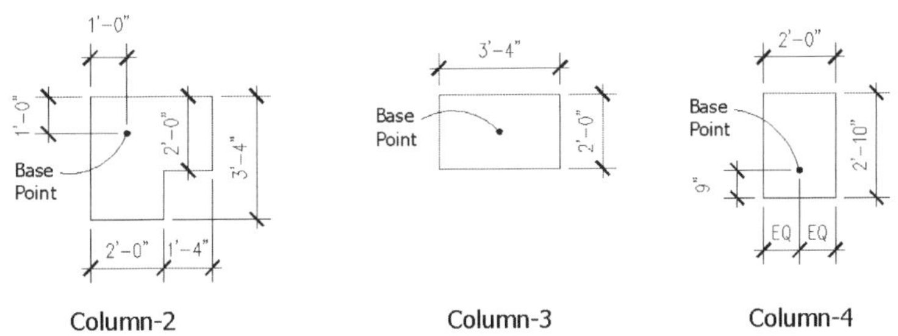

FIGURE 3-2.8 Create Blocks: Near Building Entry

21. Place the three column *Blocks* as shown in Figure 3-2.9. The insertion point will be the intersection of the grids in each case; rotate and mirror the *Blocks* as required.
    a. (3) **Column-2** Blocks *(i.e., corner columns)*
    b. (3) **Column-3** Blocks
    c. (2) **Column-4** Blocks *(called Col-4 in image below)*

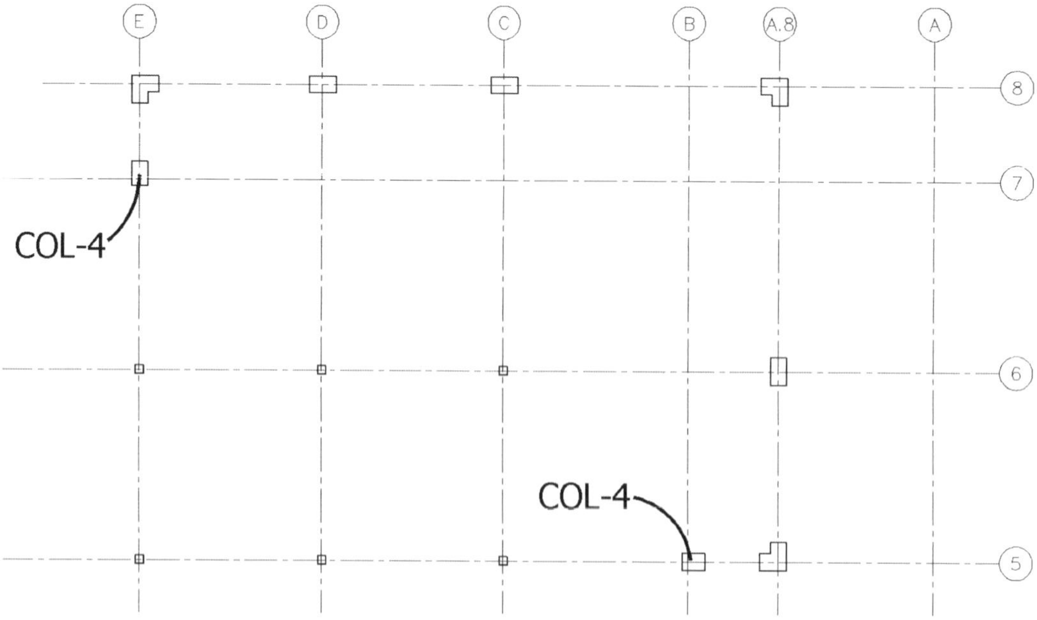

FIGURE 3-2.9 Place Remaining Blocks: Near Building Entry

TIP: Problems Picking the Intersection?
You may have trouble snapping to the intersection of two grids when the dashes in the grid lines do not create a visual intersection (i.e., a dash from each line occurs at the intersection). You have two options to achieve an intersection snap: 1) use the OTRACK feature on the Status Bar or 2) temporarily change the linetype setting to continuous for the grid layer.

Redefining a Block via the Block Editor:

Earlier in this exercise it was stated that *Blocks* can be redefined and all instances of that *Block* would be updated throughout the current drawing.

Well, the structural engineer has done her preliminary analysis and determined the typical column size; it will need to be 1′-6″x1′-6″. You have made all the typical columns 1′-0″x1′-0″ in your Schematic Design.

Next you will see how powerful *Blocks* can be. You simply double-click on the *Block* to open it in the *Block Editor*, make any changes required and then save and close the *Block Editor* – that's it! All the 12″x12″ *Blocks* in the drawing are now 18″x18″ (even the rotated ones!).

This can save a tremendous amount of time and reduce the chance for errors (i.e., missing one or two if changing them manually).

You will try this next…

22. **Zoom In** near one of the *12x12_Column* Blocks and **Double-Click** directly on one of the lines "within" the *Block*.

You are now in the *Edit Block Definition* dialog box. This gives you the opportunity to either Cancel or select a different Block to edit.

So, if you accidentally double-clicked on a Block you can select Cancel.

23. Click **OK** to edit *12x12_Column*.

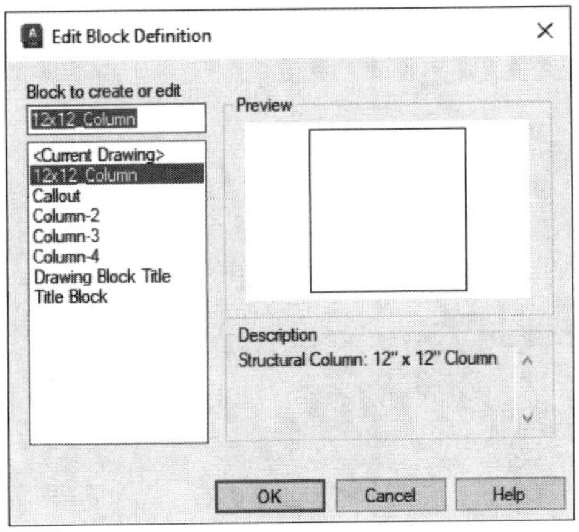

FIGURE 3-2.10 Edit Block Definition Dialog

You are now in the *Block Editor* which is very similar to the normal AutoCAD environment, with the following exceptions:

- The *Block Authoring* palette is visible.
- Special tools are available in the *Ribbon*.

Before you make any changes, you need to understand one thing: the *Drawing Origin* (i.e., 0,0) is located at the Block's *Base Point*. In order for your columns to stay centered on the grid intersections, the *Origin* must remain in the center of the column. What this means is that you will need to stretch the square 3″ in all four directions (as opposed to 6″ in only two directions). See Figure 3-2.11 for a graphic explanation of this topic.

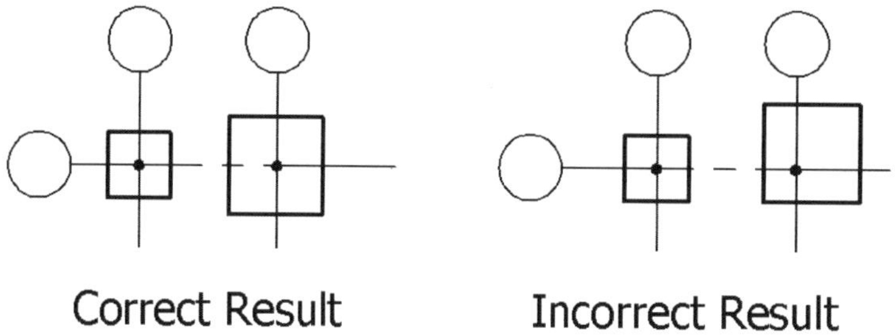

FIGURE 3-2.11 Redefined block results:
Left: Origin remained centered on column when redefined
Right: Block modified without regard for Origin (i.e., Base Point)

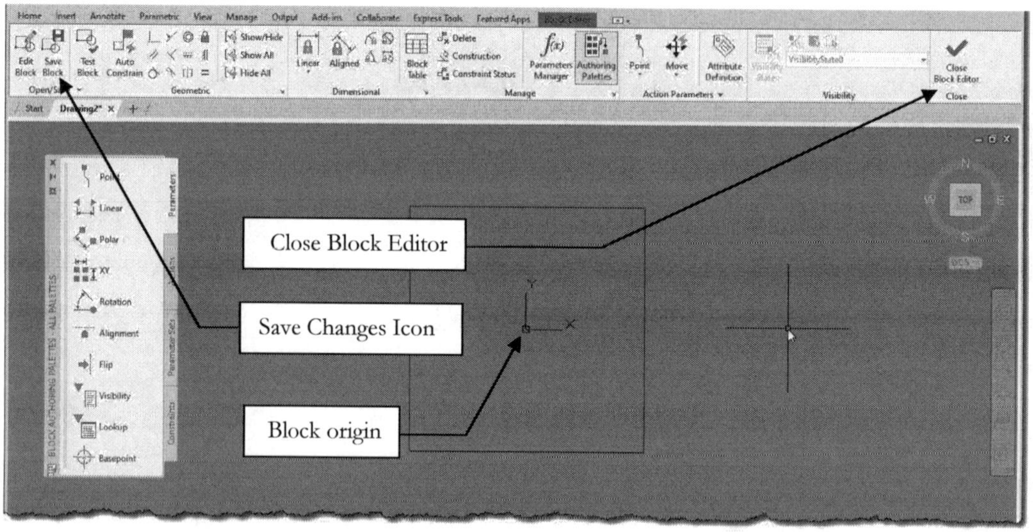

FIGURE 3-2.12 Block Editor: 12x12_Column block opened for editing (0,0 is centered on column)

24. Using the **Stretch** command, stretch the square **3″** in each direction (see *TIP* below).

    TIP: *Do not use the "Stretch" tool shown on the Block Authoring palette as seen in the image above (on the Actions tab). This is a tool for advanced Block creation, not the normal Stretch tool.*

25. Click the **Save Block** icon (Figure 3-2.12).

26. Click the **Close Block Editor** button (Figure 3-2.12).

That's it; all the 12″x12″ Blocks in your drawing are now 18″x18″!

Renaming a Block:

The next thing you will do in this exercise is learn how to rename a *Block*. In this example you now have a *Block* named 12x12_Cloumn that is really an 18x18 column. Next you will rename the 12x12_Cloumn *Block* to Column-1.

27. At the *Command Prompt* type **Rename** and press ***Enter***.

You are now in the *Rename* dialog box (Figure 3-2.13). Notice the other types of objects you can rename (not just blocks).

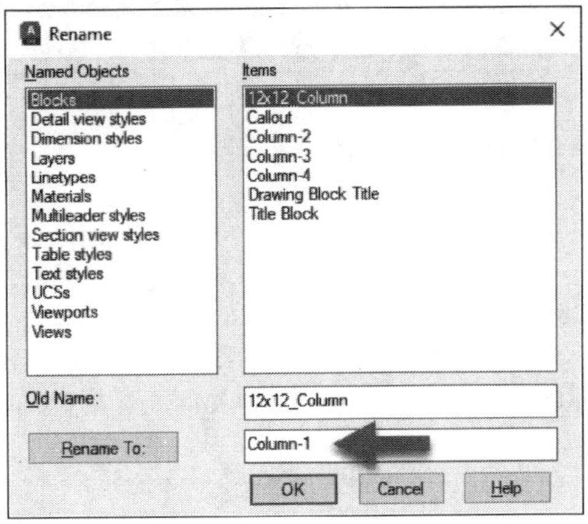

FIGURE 3-2.13 Rename dialog box

28. Make the following adjustments to the *Rename* dialog:
    a. *Named Objects:* **Blocks**
    b. *Items:* **12x12_Column**
    c. *Old Name:* automatically filled by previous step
    d. *Rename to:* type **Column-1**

29. Click **OK** to commit to the changes.

The *Block* definition is now renamed. Next time you insert a *Block* you will only see the new name (the 12x12_Column will not exist).

Block Properties:

The last thing you will do in this exercise is learn how to view the properties for a selected *Block*; this should be something you already know how to do.

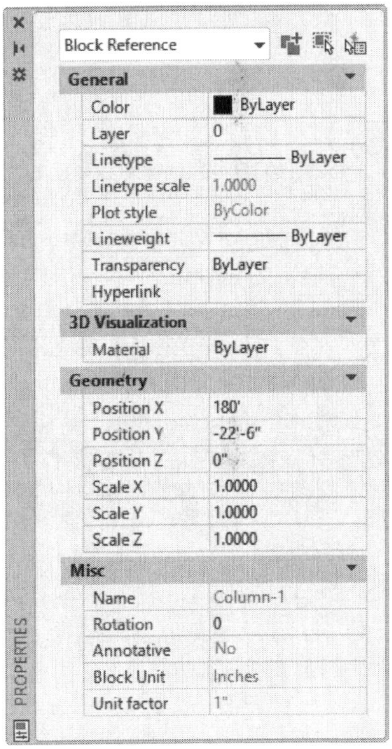

FIGURE 3-2.14
Properties dialog

30. **Click** on one of your 18x18_Column *Blocks* (in the drawing) to select it.

31. **Right-click** and select *Properties*.

The *Properties* palette opens, where you can verify its rotation angle, the name of the block and if it is on the correct *Layer* (Figure 3-2.14).

32. **Save** your drawing.

Exercise 3-3:
Drawing the Exterior Walls

Introduction

Two lines, a certain distance apart, represent the walls in a floor plan. In AutoCAD these walls are drawn on a layer named A-WALL; additionally, the exterior walls often have "cavity" lines which represent the various individual components of the wall – these lines go on a layer named A-Wall-Cvty (as per Appendix A). The distance between the two lines is the same as the actual thickness of the wall (use nominal dimensions for masonry).

You will now start drawing the first floor plan.

1. Start a new drawing named **DJS55803APL01.dwg**.
   Don't forget to use the correct template: click the New icon on the Quick access Toolbar and then "SheetSets\Architectural Imperial.dwt".

2. Switch to *Model Space* if necessary.

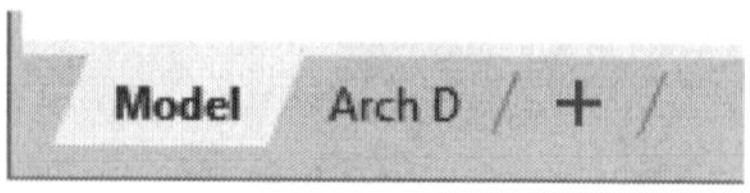

Setting the Drawing Limits:

The overall area required to draw the floor plan is the same as that required for the previous grid assignment.

3. Type **Limits** (in the *Command Window*) and then **Enter** (see *TIP* below).

4. Type -**100′**, press the *Tab* key and then type -**200′** *Enter.*

5. Type **300′**, press the *Tab* key and then type **100′** *Enter.*

6. Select **Zoom All.**

TIP: Make sure the Dynamic Input icon, on the Status Bar, is turned on (bluish background) so things work per the instructions in this textbook. This can also be toggled on and off using the F12 key.

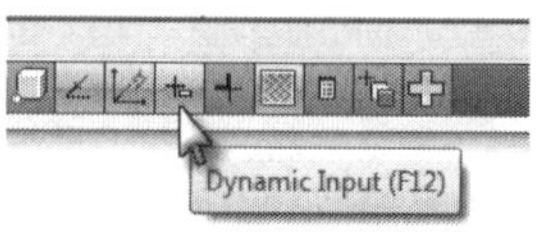

Setting the LineType Scale

Setting the LTscale (LT means Line Type) variable will help you to see how the dashed lines will look when the plan is plotted at ⅛″ = 1′-0″ (in this example). See Appendix A, page A-14 for more information on this.

7. Type **LTscale**, Enter **96** and then **Enter**.

Xref the Grid Drawing:

The first order of business will be to "link" in the grid drawing into your floor plan drawing. An Xref (i.e., external reference) acts just like a *Block* with the exception that it is defined in a separate drawing (rather than within the current drawing). So, just like a *Block*, you need to make sure an Xref gets placed on the proper *Layer*; if you placed the Xref on the A-DOOR *Layer*, the Xref would disappear whenever the A-DOOR *Layer* was turned off.

The Xref'ed drawing (i.e., the grid file in this case) is never actually saved in the drawing it is being inserted into (lets call it the "host" file). Each time the "host" file is opened all Xref's are reloaded. This also means that the "host" file is smaller in size, which saves disk space on your hard drive.

AutoCAD only needs to remember the file name, file location and X,Y,Z insertion point in the "host" drawing. You should be able to draw a logical conclusion from the previous statement; that is, do not change the file name or location. If either the file name or location changes, AutoCAD will not be able to find the file and the Xref will not be visible.

Xref's can be manually reloaded when you know one has changes. You can also update the name and location information via the *External References* palette if necessary.

In addition to the benefits discussed in a previous lesson, another useful aspect of using Xref's is that someone else can be working on the grid drawing while you are working on the floor plan drawing.

8. Create the *Layer* **G-Xref** and set this *Layer* current. (This is the *Layer* you will insert the Xref on.)

9. From the **Insert** tab, select the **External References** link – see image to the right (small arrow in lower right).

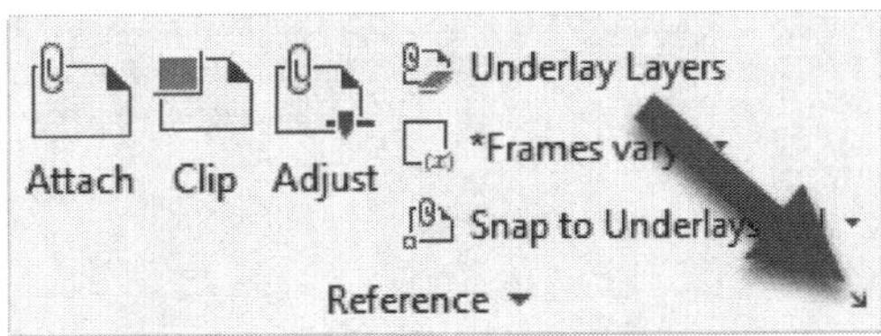

The *External References* palette is now displayed (see Figure 3-3.1), which allows you to do the following (via right-clicking on xref names):

- Attach: Select a file to "link" into the current drawing
- Detach: Remove an Xref from the drawing/sever the "link"
- Reload: Force AutoCAD to update the Xref (if it changed)
- Unload: Turn off Xref visibility (can also be done via layers)
- Bind: Copies the Xref into the current drawing
- Open: Opens the drawing being Xref'ed for editing

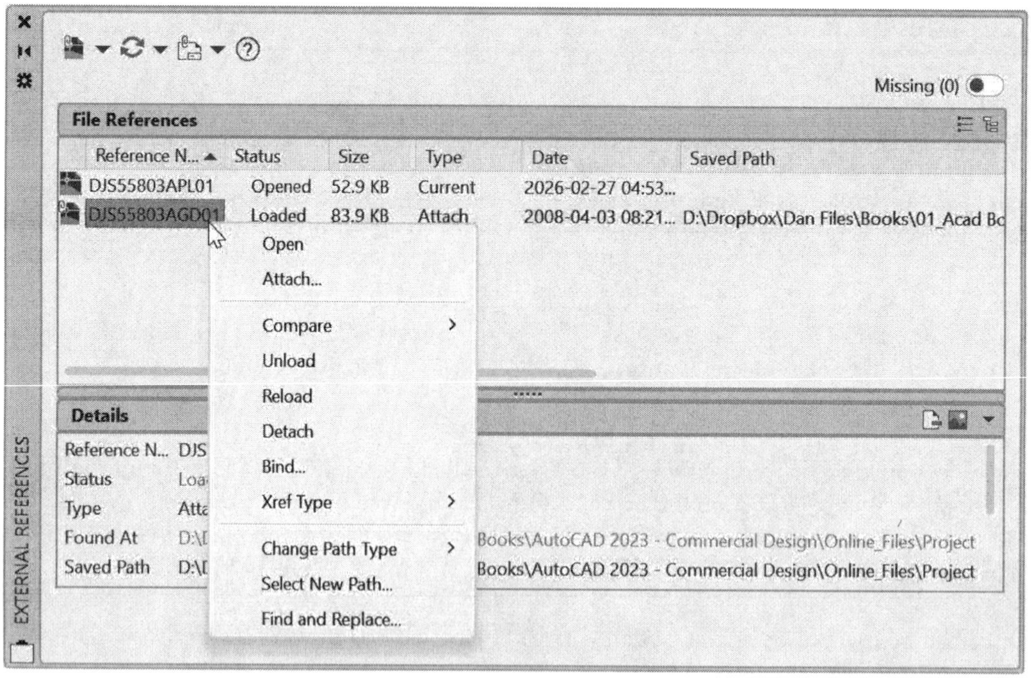

FIGURE 3-3.1 External References Palette – Initial view *FYI: The grid drawing will not be listed yet.*

10. **Close** the *References* palette and then click the **Attach** button (on the *Insert* tab, *References* panel – see image on previous page).

11. **Browse** to the location where your grid drawing (DJS55803AGD01.dwg) is located on your hard drive, change the File of Type to Drawing (*.dwg), select your file, and then click the **Open** button to proceed to the next step (don't click **OK** yet).

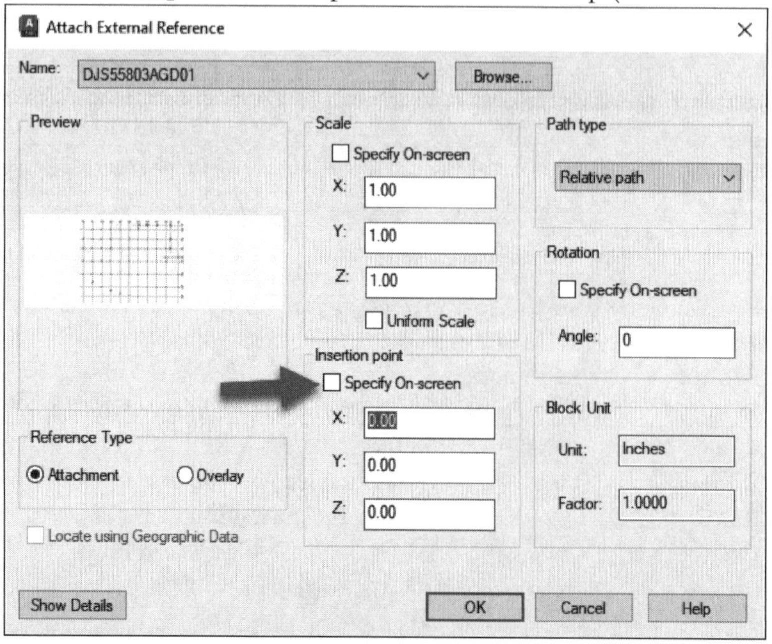

FIGURE 3-3.2 External Reference dialog; file selected and ready to be placed

You are now in the *External Reference* dialog (Figure 3-3.2), which allows you to control how the drawing is placed in the current drawing.

Many of the controls are straight forward and identical to the *Insert Block* dialog. In this exercise you will leave all the "Specify On-screen" checkboxes unchecked because you do not need to manually change the *Insertion Point*, the *Scale* or the *Rotation.*

One setting that is often confusing to many users is the *Reference Type* setting – the two options are *Attach* and *Overlay.* When an Xref is *Attached* it will follow the "host" drawing if it is Xref'ed into another drawing. Conversely, when an Xref is *Overlaid* it will not follow the "host" drawing if it is called on to be "linked" into another drawing. See the following image for a graphical explanation (Figure 3-3.3):

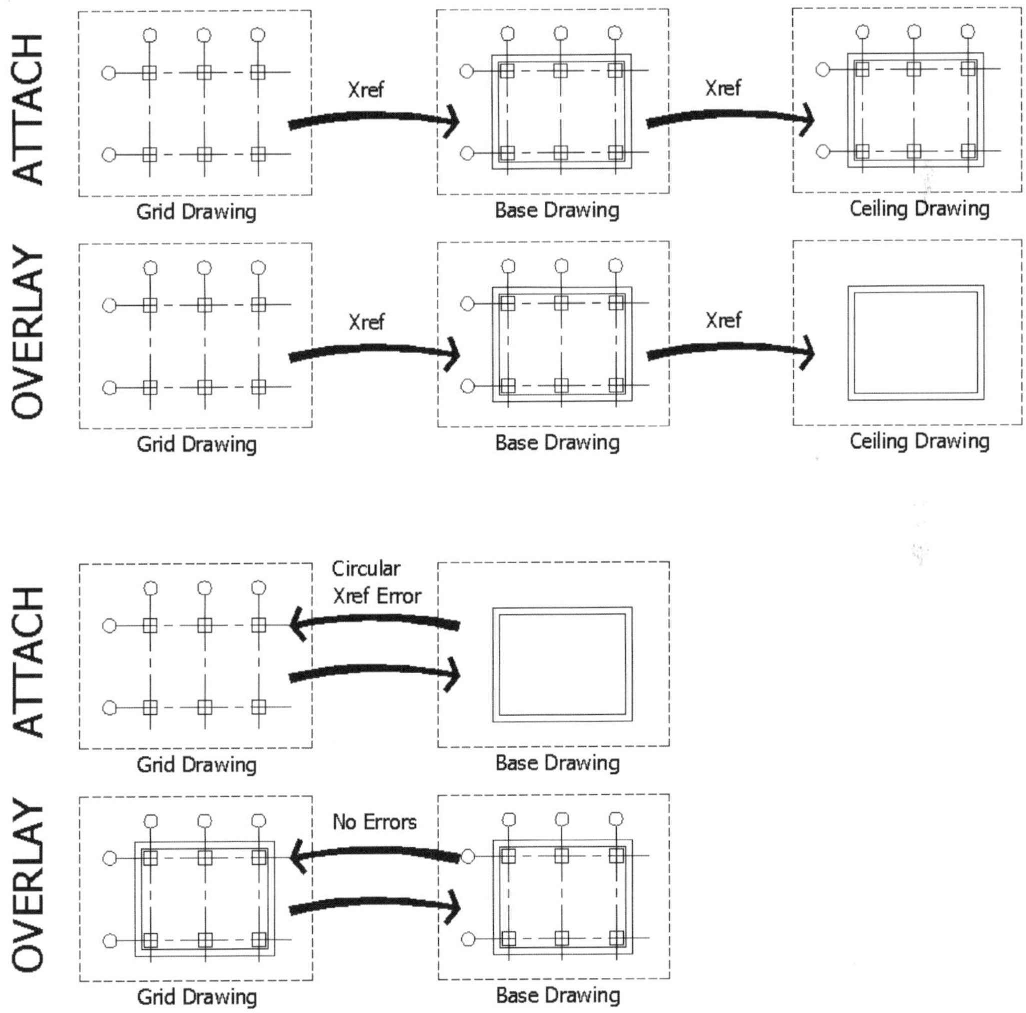

FIGURE 3-3.3 External Reference Type Example – Attach vs. Overlay

The last two examples in the previous illustration are the main reason most design firms use *Overlay* instead of *Attach* for most, if not all, Xrefs. The Architect or Interior Designer wants to Xref the Structural Engineer's Grid/Column drawing, and the Structural Engineer wants to Xref the Designer's floor plan. For this to work without errors or complications you need to use the *Overlay* option when Xrefing drawings.

12. With your settings adjusted to look similar to Figure 3-3.2, click the **OK** button to place the Xref.

13. Open the *Layer Properties Manager* and **Lock** the G-Xref layer (Figure 3-3.4); do not close this dialog yet.

While the *Layer Properties Manager* is open you should take a moment to understand how the *Layers* from the grid drawing are represented in the "host" drawing; refer to **Figure 3-3.4**.

All the *Layers* that exist in the grid drawing are listed in the *Layer Properties Manager* with the *Drawing File Name* as a prefix. For example, the A-Grid layer is listed as **DJS55803AGD01 | A-Grid** in the "host" drawing. This allows the "A-Grid" layer to be controlled separately from a *Layer* with the same name in the "host" drawing (should one exist).

Whenever possible you should limit the number of *Layers* in Xref'ed drawings (i.e., delete or purge any unused layers). This will reduce the overall Layer list in the "host" drawing.

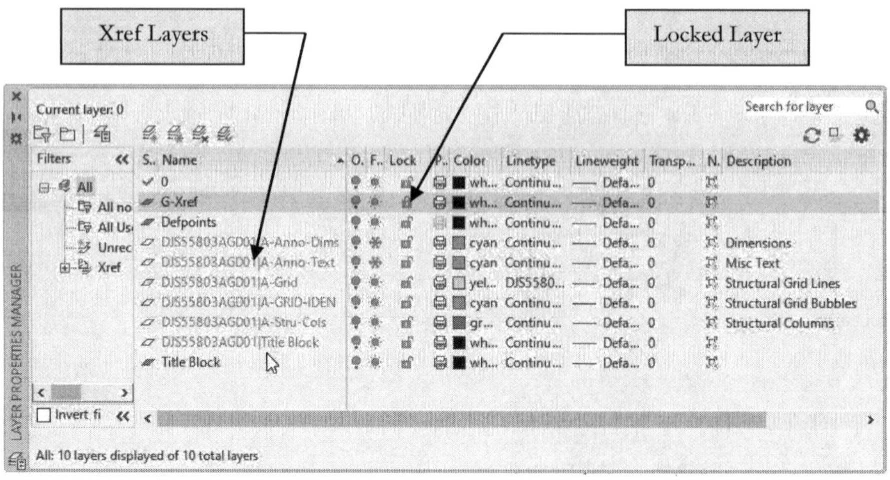

FIGURE 3-3.4 Layer Properties Manager; Xref'ed layers have the file name as a prefix

Drawing the Exterior Walls:

14. Create the *Layers* **A-WALL** and **A-Wall-Cvty**.
(See appendix A for layer details, i.e., layer color and linetype).

15. With A-WALL *Layer* current, draw the lines shown in **Figure 3-3.5** using the following information:

    a. All lines shown are 8″ away from the face of column.

    b. This includes all the columns in the upper right (as shown).

    FYI: You can look ahead to Figure 3-3.10 for a better image of the columns.

    c. Draw the four lines that arbitrarily end approximately as shown.

    TIP: Draw a line at the exterior face of the column, Offset it out 8″, and then use Fillet to clean up the corners.

16. Use the **Distance** command to double check your dimensions before moving on. Now is the time to make corrections *(located on the Utilities panel, under the Home tab).*

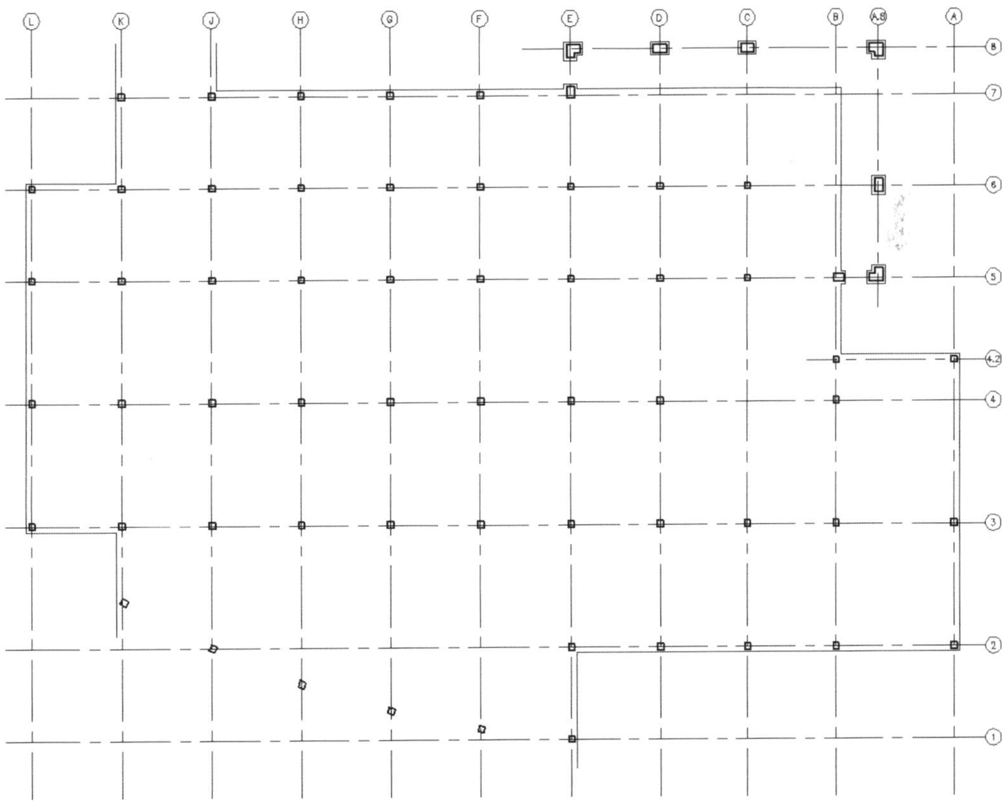

FIGURE 3-3.5 Exterior wall perimeter - the Origin (i.e., 0,0) is at grid 6/L

Next, you will draw the curved wall line. Normally you would draw this line in a "freehand" fashion early in the design process and then firm up the dimensions as the design progressed. In this exercise you will be given specific instructions on how to draw the arc; you will be given coordinates (relative to the origin) for the center of the arc; you will then draw a large circle and trim it with the orthogonal lines drawn in the previous step.

17. *Temporary line:* Enter the **Line** command (Figure 3-3.6).
    - Type **0,0** and then Enter for the first point
    - Type **152'3.125,123'7.5** *(or 152'3-1/8,123'7-1/2)*.

18. Draw a **Circle** (radius = 260'-8") from the upper endpoint of the line just drawn and then **Erase** the Temporary line.

19. Select the **Trim** command, pick the two vertical wall lines, and then pick the part of the circle to be omitted.

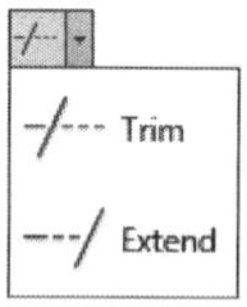

20. Use **Trim** or **Fillet** to finish cleaning up the corners.

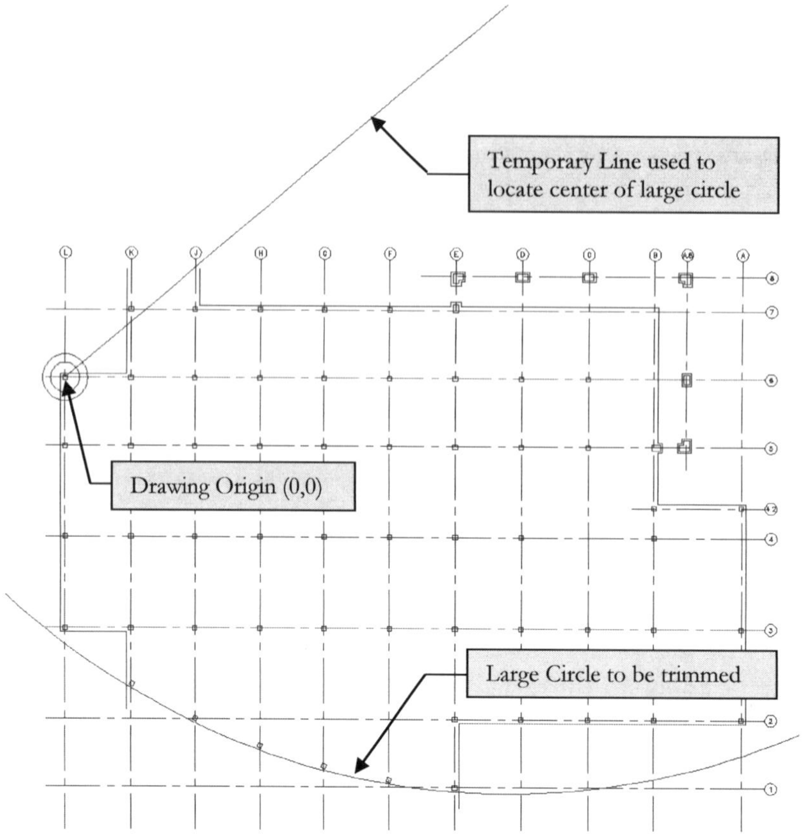

FIGURE 3-3.6 Drawing curved wall

Now you will develop the exterior wall such that the major components are identified. The image below (Figure 3-3.7) details the exterior wall construction. The portion of the wall you are concerned with is the 1′-4″ portion of the wall. (The studs and gypsum board will be added later.)

At this point you have already established the exterior face of the brick.

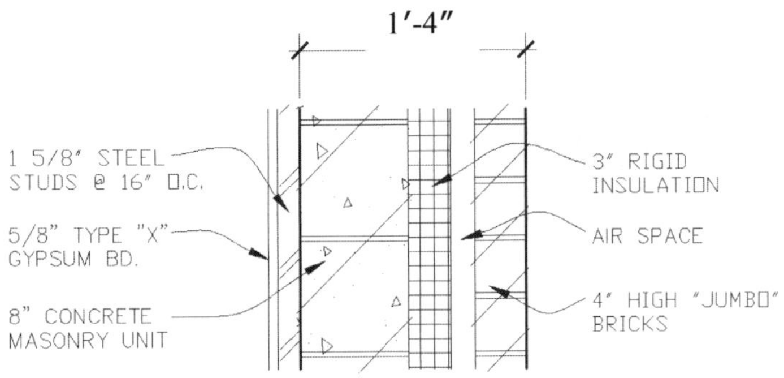

FIGURE 3-3.7 Exterior Wall Type

As discussed previously, the two outermost lines will be on *Layer* A-Wall and the two inner lines will be on *Layer* A-Wall-Cvty.

21. Draw the remaining exterior wall lines per the following info:
    - Refer to Figure 3-3.8.
    - No lines are to extend through the columns (use Trim or Break).
    - Make sure all lines are on the correct *Layers*.

    TIP: *Offset the perimeter line previously drawn.*

    - All the columns in the upper right have a 4″ cavity line.
    - The "air space" and "insulation" are shown as one 4″ space.

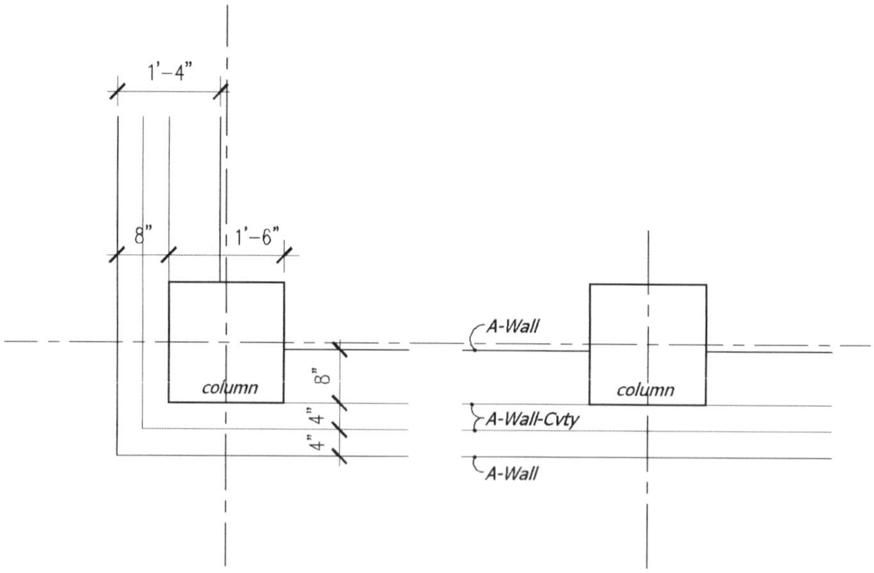

FIGURE 3-3.8 Exterior Wall information relative to columns and grids

Your base plan should now look like Figure 3-3.9 and 10. Later, after you add the doors and windows you will poche (i.e., hatch) the concrete block to future delineate the wall construction in the floor plan view.

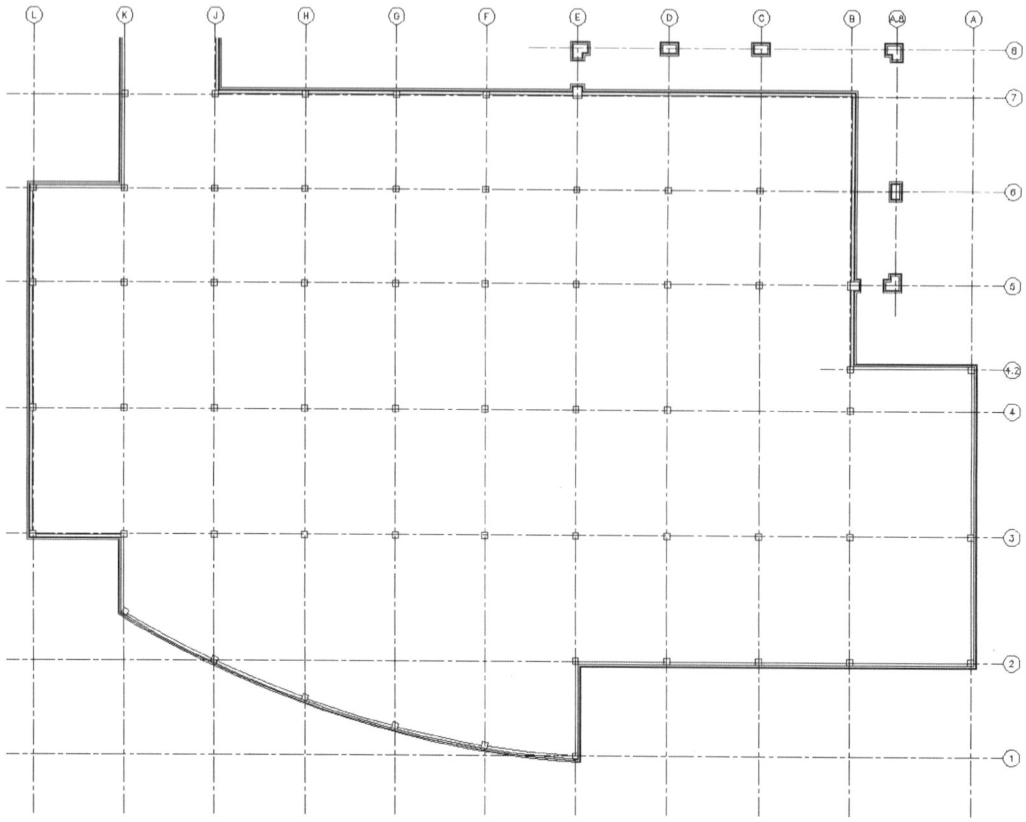

FIGURE 3-3.9 Exterior Walls completed

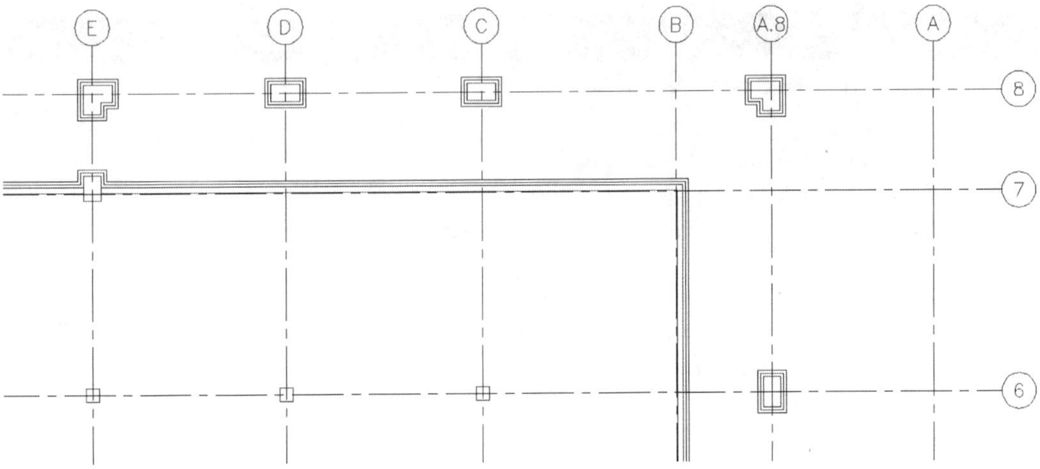

FIGURE 3-3.10 Exterior Walls completed – enlarged view to show detail

Exercise 3-4:
Drawing the Interior Walls

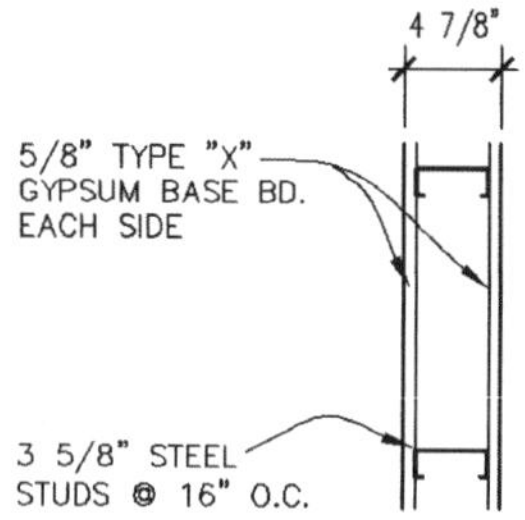

One of the most typical walls on a commercial project consists of 3 ⅝″ metal studs (at 16″ O.C.) with one layer of gypsum board on each side; making a wall system that is 4 ⅞″ thick.

This composition can vary greatly. For example, you may need to add resilient channels to one side of the wall to enhance sound control; they are ⅞″ thick and are installed on the noisy side of the wall.

Finishes: Gypsum board walls can be finished in a variety of ways. The most economical finish is usually paint (one or more colors). Other options include wall fabrics (i.e., high-end wallpaper) which are used in executive offices and conference rooms; fiberglass liner panels which are used in janitor rooms and food service areas; veneer plaster which is used for durability (high-impact gypsum board can also be used); and tile which is used in toilet rooms, showers to name a few. These finishes are nominal and are not included in the thickness used to draw the wall.

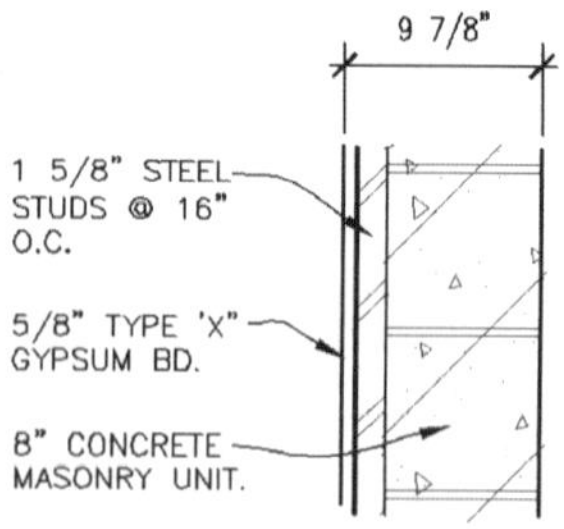

Concrete block (often referred to as CMU) walls are often used to construct stair and elevator shafts, high traffic/high abuse areas, and for security; filling the cores with concrete or sand can increase strength, sound control and even stop bullets. The most used size is 8″ wide CMU; 6″, 10″ and 12″ are also commonly used (typically, 6″ for aesthetics and 10″ and 12″ CMU for structural reasons).

Finishes: Concrete block can just be painted or it can have special finishes such as Glazed Block or Burnished Concrete Block, which cost more but are durable and are available in many colors. In offices, conference rooms and other more refined areas concrete block walls are not desirable so they are covered with metal furring channels and gypsum board, especially in rooms where three walls are metal studs and only one would be CMU. The sooner this is taken into consideration the better as this can significantly affect space for furniture in a room (another major furniture obstacle is fin-tube radiation at the exterior walls).

Walls often have several Life Safety issues related to them. Finishes applied to walls must have a certain flame spread rating (per local building code). Several walls are usually required to be fire rated (protecting one space from another in the event of a fire); these walls have restrictions on the amount of glass (windows + doors), type of door and window frames (wood vs. steel) and the need to extend the wall to the floor/roof deck above.

This represents a quick overview of the most common interior walls used in commercial construction and in this book project.

Now you will begin drawing the interior walls. At this time you will draw the stud walls 6″ thick; if they are not dimensioned, they are centered on a grid line or align with the face of a column.

1. Zoom into the south-east corner of the building (lower right).

2. Draw all the **6″ stud walls** shown in Figure 3-4.1 (on layer A-Wall) – all walls are centered on the grid or aligned with column faces as shown.

FIGURE 3-4.1 Drawing interior walls; south-east corner (4 classrooms)

You will add doors later.

Next you will draw 8″ CMU (Concrete Masonry Units *or* concrete block) walls around a stair shaft and a shaft for duct work.

3. **Pan** up a little to the intersection of grid line **4** and **A**.

4. Draw the **8″ CMU walls** (on the A-Wall *Layer*); see Figure 3-4.2.
   - Trim the "T" intersections where the interior/exterior CMU meet.
   - The two CMU wall lines, right next to each other, along grid line **A** shall both be on *Layer* A-Wall-Cvty.

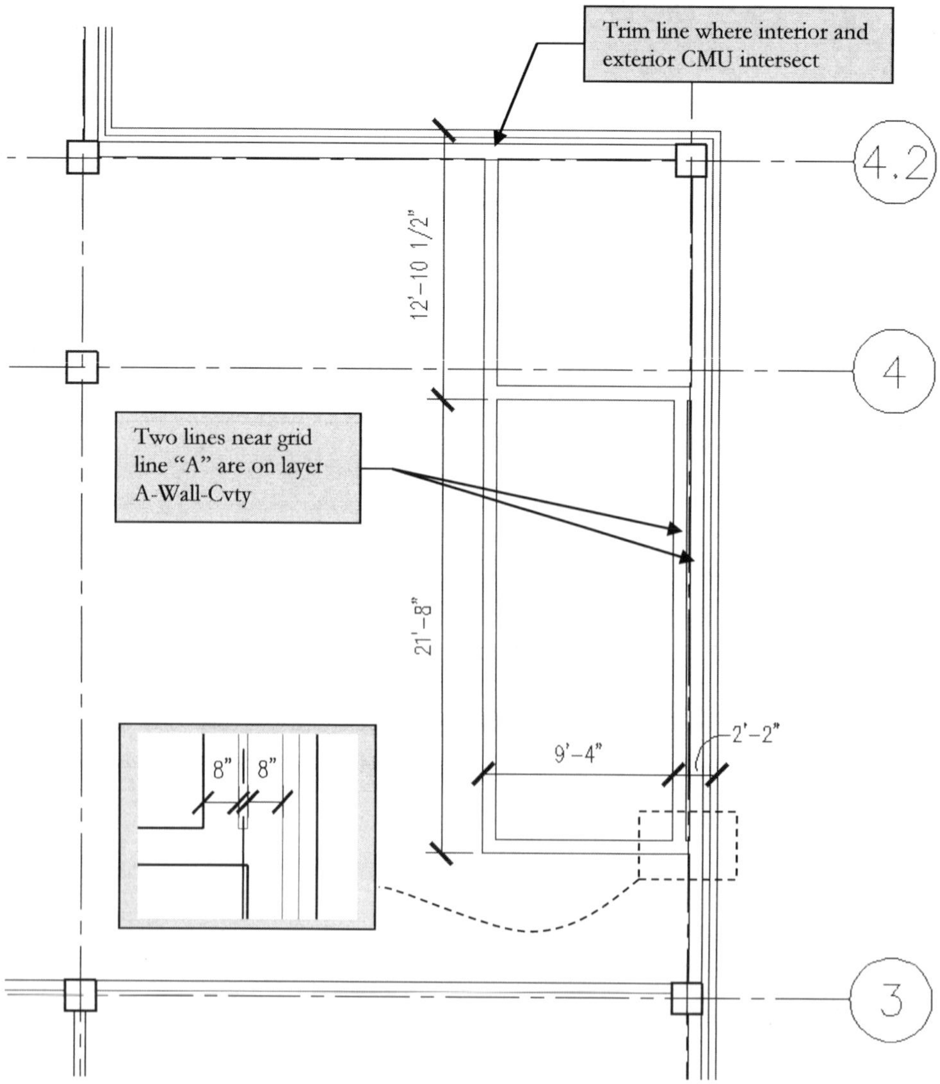

Designing Walls to Masonry Coursing:

There are many reasons a designer should keep masonry coursing in mind when laying out a floor plan. When walls are laid out with coursing in mind, concrete blocks and bricks do not have to be cut as they are installed, saving time, materials and waste. Aesthetically you may end up with slivers of block (vertically or horizontally) if coursing is not implemented (Figure 3-4.3). The guidelines for coursing are simple; see "Masonry Coursing Dimension Rules" on the next page.

In Figure 3-4.2 above, which dimensions are coursing and which are not? If you were asked to adjust this preliminary plan to comply with coursing, what would the closest coursing dimension be?

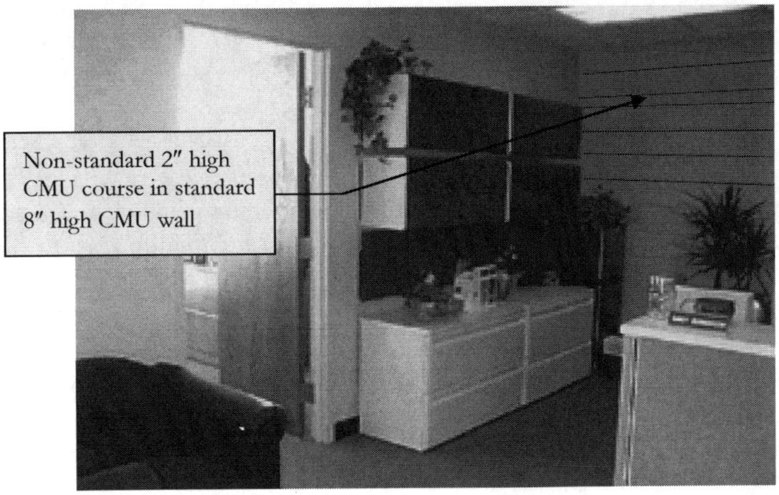

FIGURE 3-4.3 Vertical wall coursing non-standard

Before moving on, notice that one wall is painted gypsum board and the other is CMU in the picture above. Having two walls of different materials is usually avoided when possible (or affordable). Also notice the small personal refrigerator in the back corner; things like these are often missed while programming a space, making furniture layouts tighter and creating excess power requirements on the building.

MASONRY COURSING DIMENSION RULES:

Concrete blocks (i.e., CMU) come in various widths, and most are 16″ long and 8″ high. When drawing plans there is a simple rule to keep in mind to make sure you are designing walls to coursing. This applies to wall lengths and openings within CMU walls.

Dimension rules for CMU coursing in floor plans:

- *e*′-0″ or *e*′-8″ — where ***e*** is any even number (e.g., **6**′-0″ or **24**′-8″)
- *o*′-4″ — where ***o*** is any odd number (e.g., **5**′-4″)

Furring-Out Walls:

Next you will draw a classroom adjacent to the stair shaft. The south wall of the classroom and of the stair shaft starts to create a corridor. In the corridor you want the wall to be all painted gypsum board; not gypsum board and CMU (i.e., two materials). Since the CMU wall is required around the stair for fire rating and as a structural shear wall you will have to cover the CMU with metal furring channels and gypsum board. Therefore, rather than aligning the wall with the CMU, you will offset the wall so the gypsum board "skims" past the CMU. The offset amount is based on the size of the furring channels and the thickness of the gypsum board. Here are a few options:

- On rare occasion, the gypsum board can be glued directly to the CMU wall; this saves the most space but requires the masonry wall to be built plumb and true (which is hard to assure).

- Metal furring strips (sometimes wood, depending on the occupancy type) are typically used; they use minimal space while allowing the furring to be shimmed plumb and true apart from the CMU construction quality (within reason). The gypsum board is then screwed to the furring the same as one would with metal studs.

- Sometimes full-blown metal studs are used in conjunction with covering masonry walls. When walls will have electrical outlets, full-size studs allow most of the electrical work to be done after the CMU wall is built and does not require cutting the block to recess the outlet into (this is done often in existing construction). The stud space also allows for insulation in exterior walls.

You will use the second option: gypsum board over metal furring channels. The following plan detail graphically describes the situation (Figure 3-4.4):

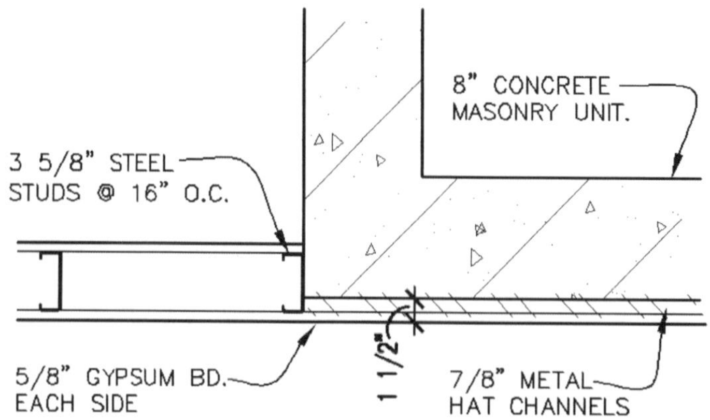

FIGURE 3-4.4 Plan detail showing furring over CMU wall

Drawing the wall in the correct location impacts finishes, ceiling grid layouts, floor finishes and many other unforeseen conditions. As you can see in the drawing above, the 6" stud wall ***(REMEMBER:*** *The stud walls are being drawn 6" wide at the moment)* will be offset 1 ½" from the CMU wall.

5. Draw the **6″ stud walls** shown in Figure 3-4.5, plus:
   - Center the vertical walls on the grid;
   - Align the south wall with the furring condition shown in Figure 3-4.5.

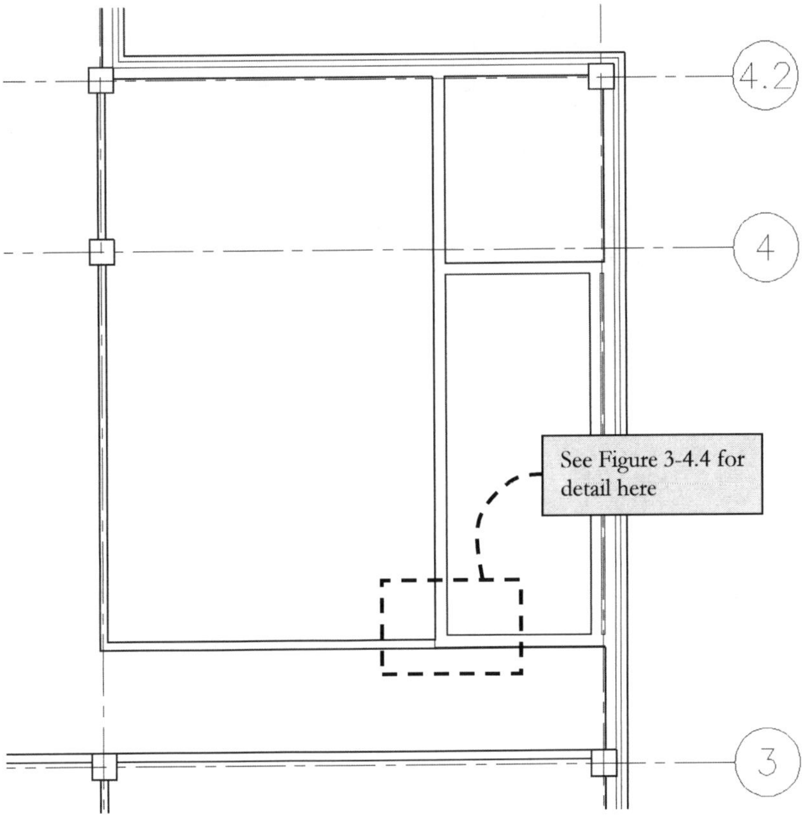

FIGURE 3-4.5 Stud walls added to form classroom and corridor

Next you will draw two more classrooms.

6. Draw the **6″ stud walls** shown in Figure 3-4.6, plus:
   - All walls not dimensioned are to be flush with adjacent interior columns.
   - Trim the intersection of all stud walls.
   - Create column-like form using wall lines as noted.
   - Add two walls along grid 4 (as shown); one wall is to be flush with the north side of the column, and the other wall is to be flush with the south side of the same column.

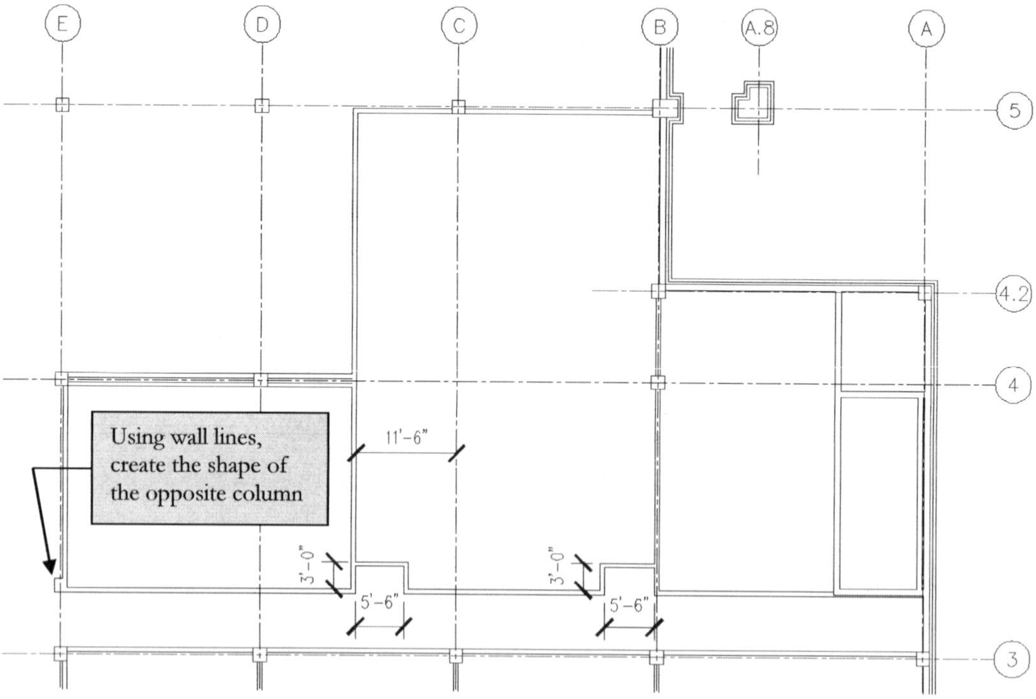

FIGURE 3-4.6 Stud walls added to form additional classroom and the corridor

7. Draw the **8" CMU walls** shown in Figure 3-4.7, plus:
   - The size is determined by the elevator; more on this later.

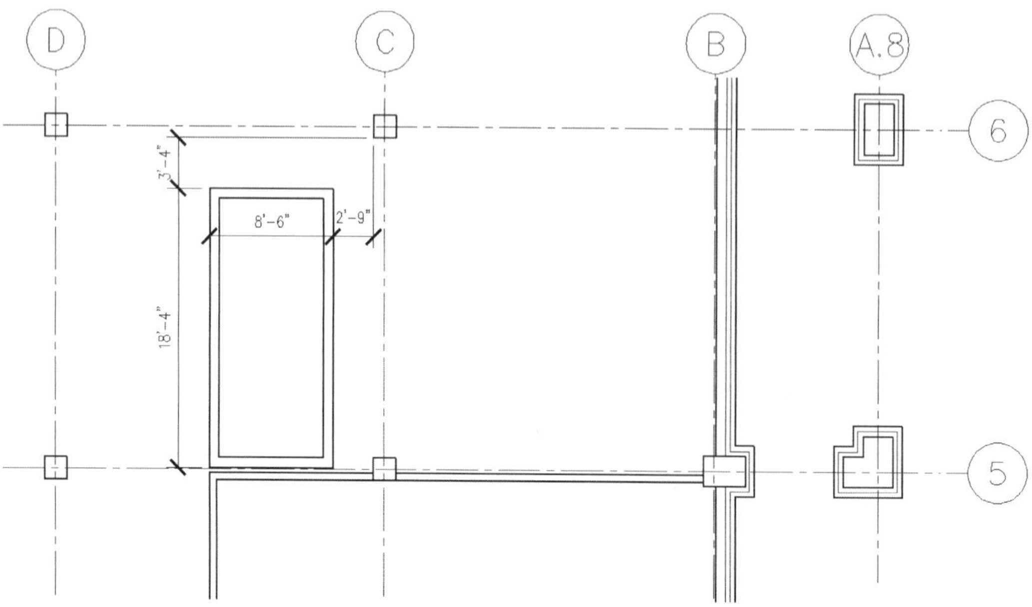

FIGURE 3-4.7 Adding the elevator shaft (this shaft is for two elevators)

Next you will draw the building's main entry vestibule and toilet rooms. All these walls are stud construction and will be drawn at the usual 6″ dimension.

8. Draw the **6″ stud walls** shown in Figure 3-4.8, plus:
   - All walls not dimensioned are to be flush with adjacent interior columns; except the horizontal wall just north of grid line 6 shall touch the column as the 6″ wall passes the column.
   - Add the wall centered on grid line C.
   - The 4′-0″ dimension is centered on the 16′-6″ dimension.

TIP: Draw one side of the wall and offset it 6″.

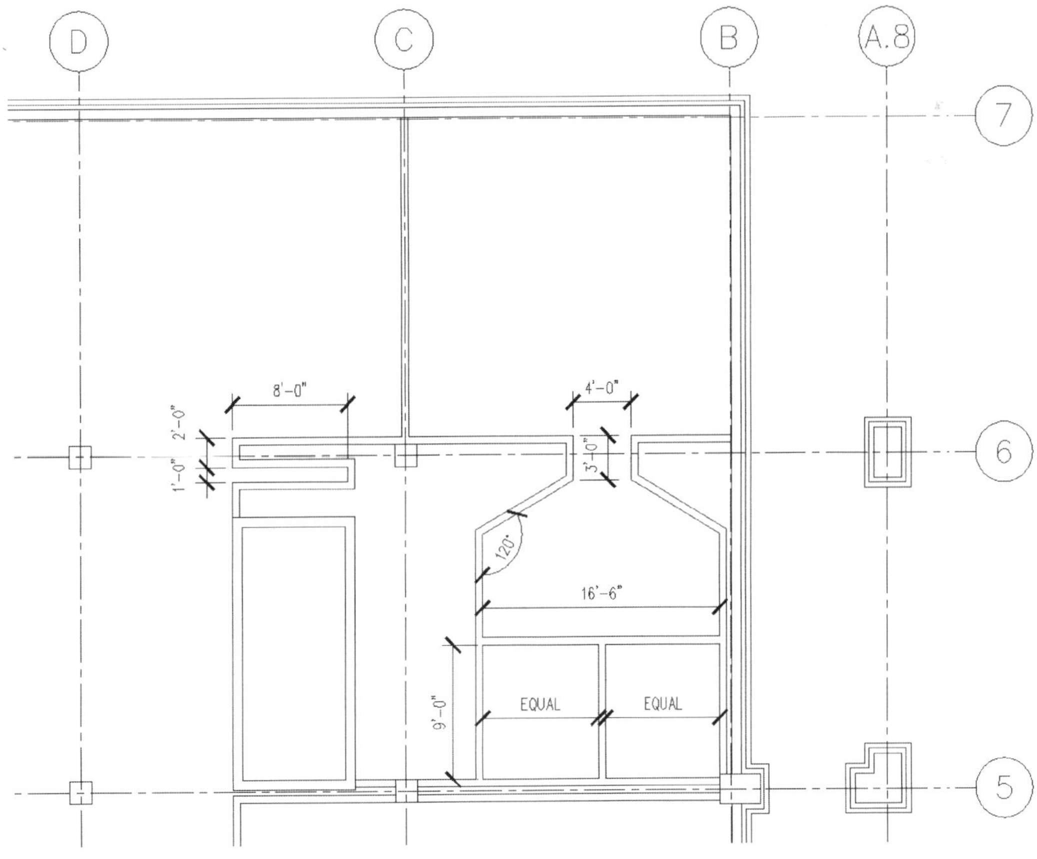

FIGURE 3-4.8 Adding walls near the building's main entry

The large irregular shaped space between the toilet rooms and the elevator shaft will be a janitor's closet/storage room. The 1′-0″ wide by 8′-0″ deep pocket will be for a horizontal-type rolling fire-rated door that will secure the library at night but still allow students thru-access to the public concourse.

Now you will draw another stair shaft – this one and the previous one are both "utilitarian" stair shafts, meaning they are primarily for emergency egress and as such are built with simple/durable finishes because they are rarely seen (e.g., painted CMU walls and steel pipe railings). Later in the book you will be adding an open stair near the public elevators that will have higher quality finishes and is intended for day-to-day vertical circulation (in conjunction with the public elevators).

> ***FYI:*** *Circulation in conjunction with egress can be a significant design challenge in buildings like this (i.e., a library). The student/public needs to be restricted in where they can go and where they can exit the building to ensure all inventory (i.e., the books) are accounted for. Sometimes an exit door will sound an alarm if it is opened; in other situations the door will be held shut by a magnetic lock and only open during an emergency.*

9. Draw the **8" CMU walls** shown in Figure 3-4.9, plus:
    - All walls not dimensioned are to be flush with adjacent columns.
    - Make sure you add the second 8" CMU (flush with the interior column face) at the exterior walls.

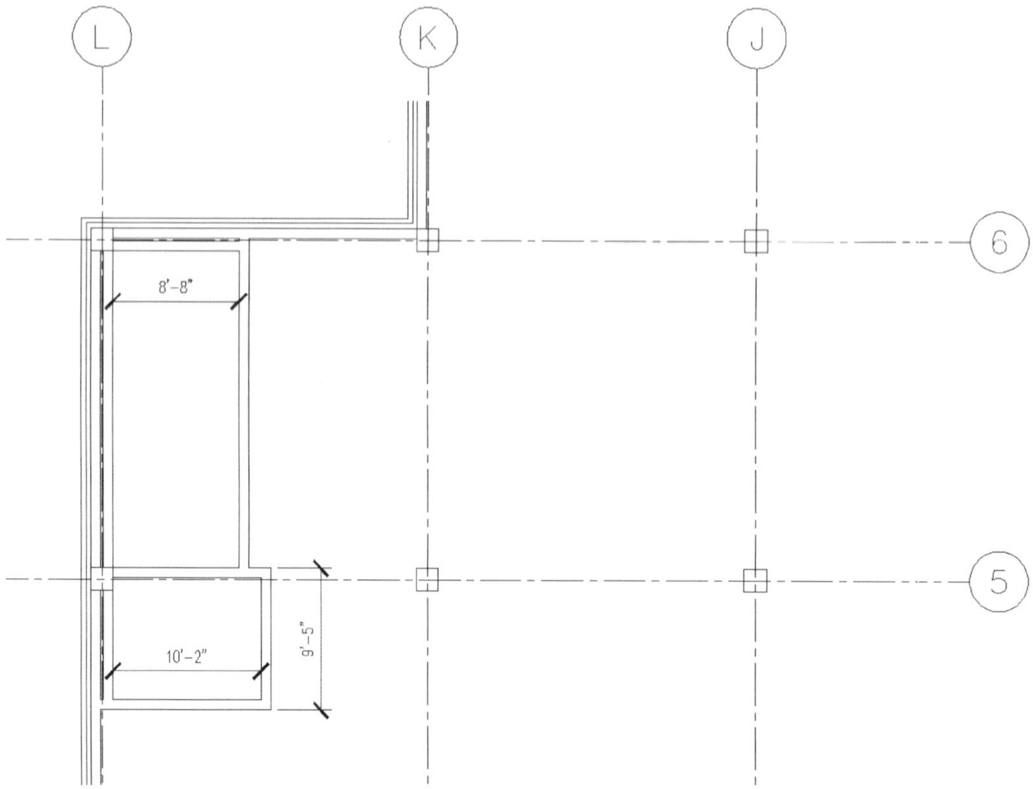

FIGURE 3-4.9 Adding the rear stair shaft and service elevator

The exterior wall will now undergo a slight modification to accommodate a recessed loading dock. This is where books and supplies will be delivered to the building. The loading dock is placed conveniently near the service elevator.

10. Modify the exterior wall as shown and Draw the **8″ CMU wall** along grid line 4 as shown in Figure 3-4.10, plus:
    - The outermost line at the loading dock shall be on *Layer* **A-Flor-Levl**, this is the edge of concrete below.
    - Remember that all "inner" lines in a wall should be on *Layer* **A-Wall-Cvty**; these lines will print lighter (via their color).
    - The 19′-3″ dimension is given so you can double-check your accuracy; because you are "land-locked" between the service elevator and grid line 4 you do not really need this dimension.

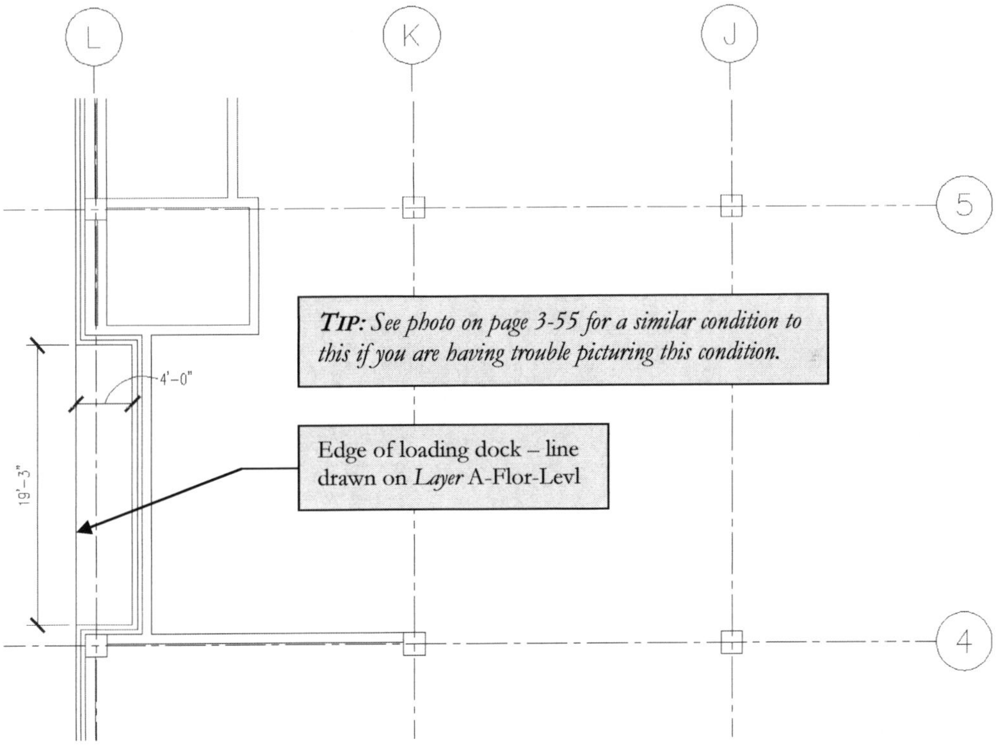

FIGURE 3-4.10 Modify exterior walls; loading dock area near service elevator

FYI: *The preceding images have been printed from a Layout View using Viewports. One Viewport was used to crop the floor plan and two other Viewports have been used to view the grid bubbles and bring them in close to the floor plan. You will do this later when setting up an enlarged plan on a plot sheet.*

Efficient Drafting Practices

Practice makes perfect – although this plan is large, it is a good exercise in becoming an efficient CAD drafter/designer. This plan will be the basis for many future lessons in this book, so make sure you take the time to accurately draw this floor plan. Otherwise, you will need to come back later and make changes to get your future assignments to work out.

The *Ribbon* and menus are really helpful when learning a program like AutoCAD; however, most experienced users rarely use them! The process of moving the mouse to the edge of the screen to select a command and then back to where you were is very inefficient, especially for those who do this all day long, five days a week. Here are a few ways experienced CAD operators work:

- Use the wheel on the mouse to Zoom (spin the wheel), Pan (press and hold the wheel button while moving the mouse) and Zoom Extents (double-clicking the wheel button). All this can be done while in another command; so, if you are in the middle of drawing walls and need to zoom in to see which point you are about to Snap to, you can do it without canceling the line command and without losing focus on the area you are designing by having to click an icon near the edge of the screen.

- AutoCAD conforms to many of the MS Windows operating system standards. Many programs, including AutoCAD, have several standard commands that can be accessed via keyboard shortcuts. Here are a few examples (pressing both keys at the same time):
    - Ctrl + S	Save	*(saves the current drawing)*
    - Ctrl + Q	Quit AutoCAD	*(prompts to save drawings)*
    - Ctrl + A	Select All	*(selects everything in the drawing)*
    - Ctrl + Z	Undo	*(undoes the previous action)*
    - Ctrl + X	Cut	*(Cut to Windows clipboard)*
    - Ctrl + C	Copy	*(does not replace AutoCAD Copy)*
    - Ctrl + V	Paste	*(used to copy between drawings)*
    - Ctrl + R	VP Toggle	*(switch between view ports)*
    - Ctrl + 1	Properties	*(opens the properties palette)*
    - Ctrl + 2	DC Palette	*(opens DesignCenter palette)*
    - Ctrl + 3	Tool Palette	*(Opens the Tool Palette)*
    - Ctrl + 8	QuickCacl	*(AutoCAD calculator palette)*

- If you recall from Chapter 1, the *Open Documents* area in the *Menu Browser* lists all the drawings that are currently open on your computer. By clicking one of the names in the list you "switch" to that drawing. A short-cut is to press **Ctrl + Tab** to quickly cycle through the open drawings.

- Many AutoCAD commands also have keyboard shortcuts – also, the space bar acts like an *Enter* key when you are not editing text. So, with your right hand on the mouse (and not moving from the "design" area), your left hand can press **L** and then **Space Bar** (Space Bar is usually pressed with your thumb) when you want to draw a

Line for example. You can see all the preloaded shortcuts and add new ones by clicking *Express Tools (tab)* → *Tools (panel)* → *Command Aliases* (Figure 3-4.11).

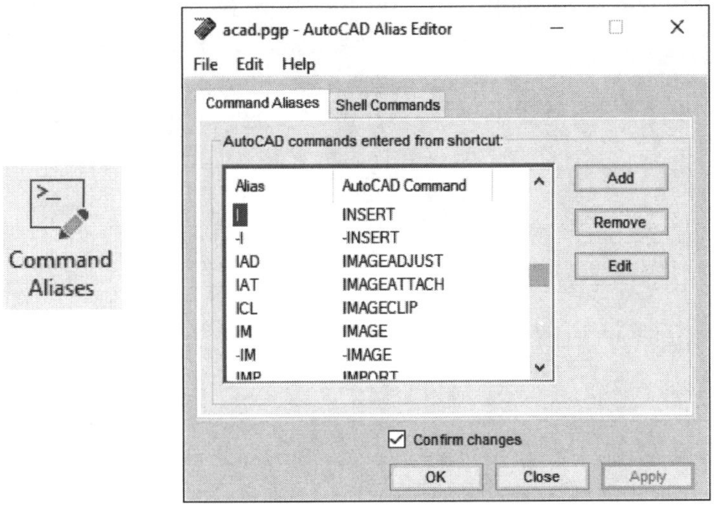

FIGURE 3-4.11 AutoCAD Alias Editor dialog

Now you will draw the main toilet rooms for this floor of the building.

> ***FYI:*** *The two walls 1'-7" apart are required for wall-hung toilets, which are often used in commercial projects because they are easy to clean under.*

11. Draw the **6" stud walls** as shown in Figure 3-4.12.

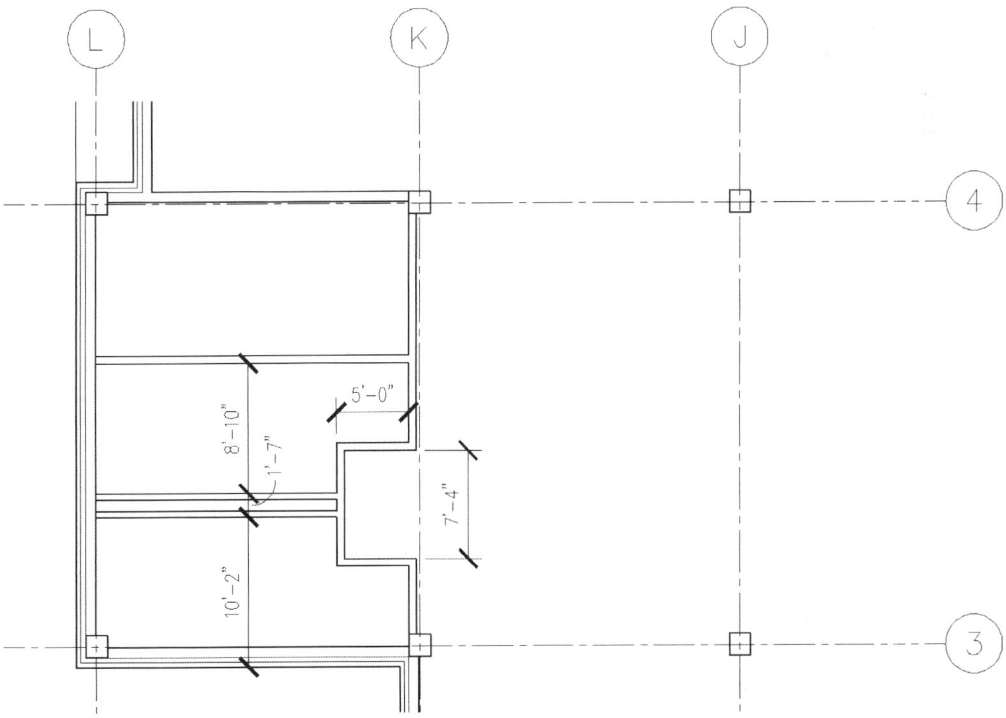

FIGURE 3-4.12 Adding stud walls at toilet rooms and janitor's closet/storage room

Just south of the toilet rooms and east of grid K you will draw a group study room. There are many ways to establish the 9′-3⅝″ wall location. You can draw temporary lines, snapping to the grid and deleting when you are done. You can also use *Object Tracking* and not have to draw temporary lines.

12. Draw the **6″ stud walls** as shown in Figure 3-4.13.

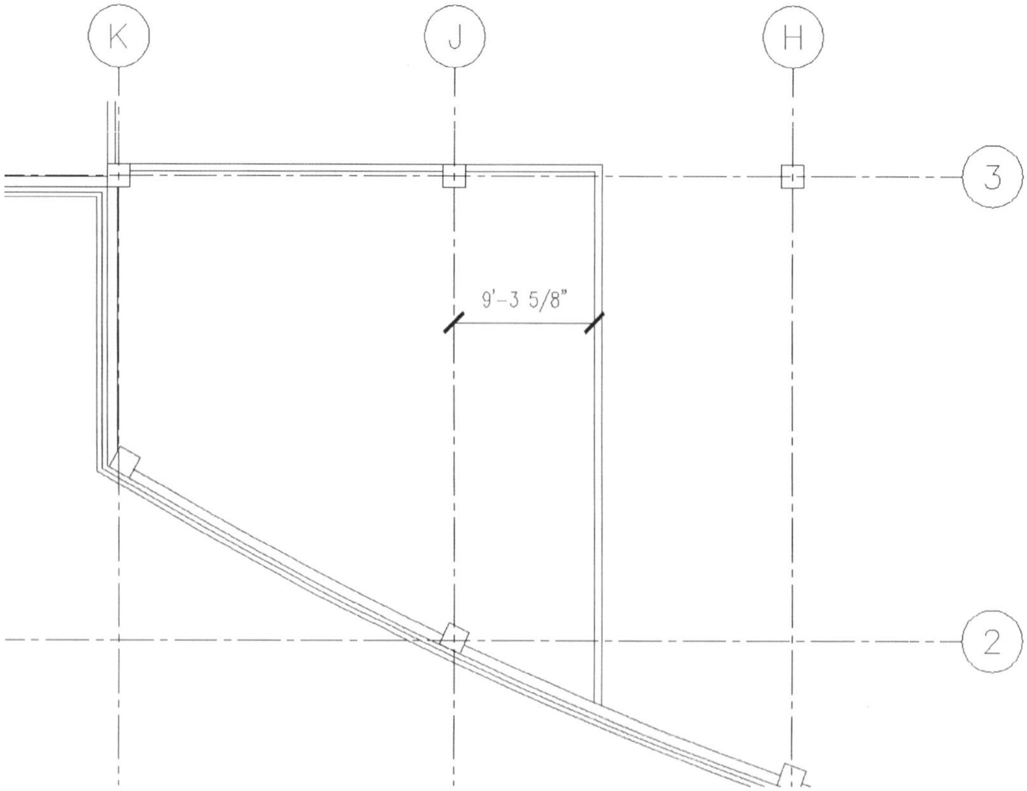

FIGURE 3-4.13 Adding stud walls for a group study room

Grids as a Communication Tool:

Next you will add walls near the north end of the floor plan. By now you should be aware of how useful grid lines are in helping locate areas within the floor plan. It would be very difficult to show the entire plan for each step in this lesson as it would take up lots of space in this book and the area you are working on would be hard to read. Grids are used just like this to document changes after construction has begun (Proposal Requests and Change Orders). The grids are also used verbally while talking to a contractor or manufacturer on the telephone (while both are looking at the same drawing). So, as you can see, the grids not only play an important role in delineating the building's structural system, they also help the designers and builders communicate better!

13. Draw the **6" stud walls** as shown in Figure 3-4.14, plus:
    - Notice the wall along grid line 6 "skims" past the columns.
    - All other walls should be drawn as shown/dimensioned.

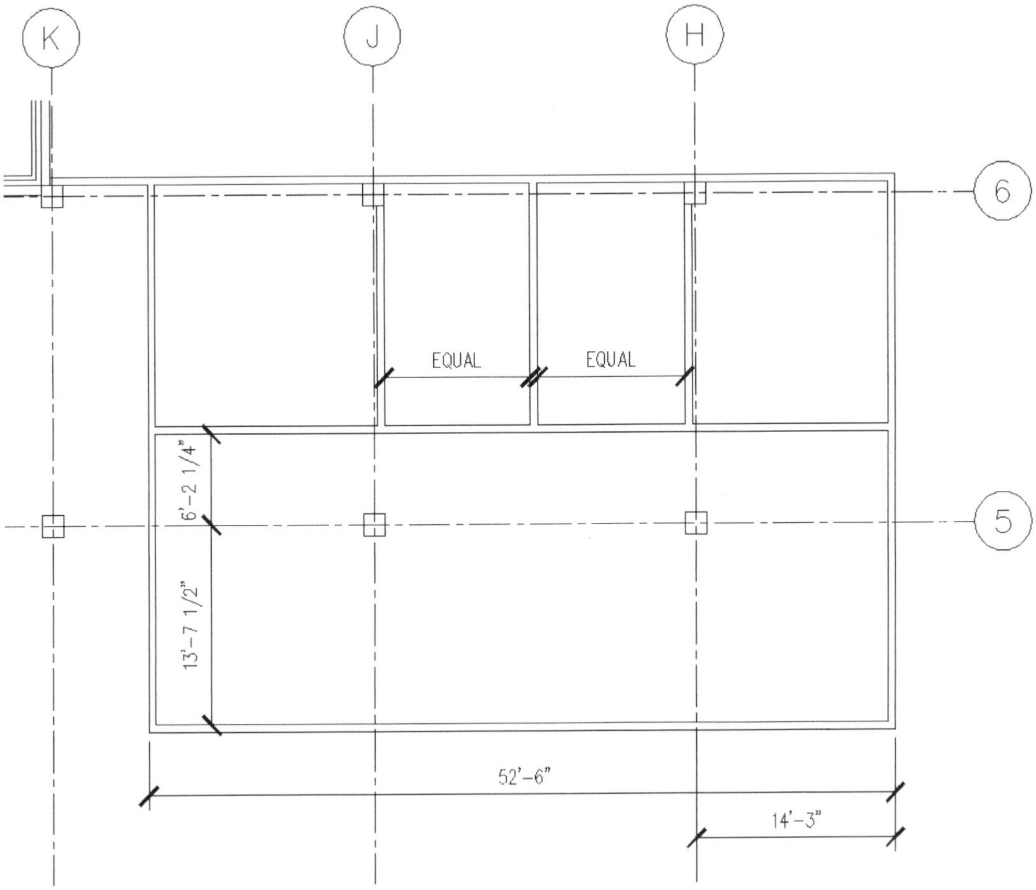

FIGURE 3-4.14 Adding stud walls for the office area

Indicating Design Intent:

In the next step you will once again be adding stud walls. The image for this step (Figure 3-4.15) introduces you to a new technique in dimensioning walls, which is often used in construction documents. Notice the centerline with the word "align" above it; this indicates that the two walls are to align with each other. One of the two walls must be located (by a dimension or a grid line); in this case two walls have been drawn in the previous step and in the third case, one wall is dimensioned. This technique is a way of indicating "design intent" without having to add additional dimensions that may, at some point, be in conflict with the other dimension.

14. Draw the **6" stud walls** as shown in Figure 3-4.15, plus:
    - See the "Design Intent" discussion on the previous page to understand the "align" labels in the image.
    - All other walls should be drawn as shown/dimensioned.
    - Don't miss the new stud wall near grids K/4.

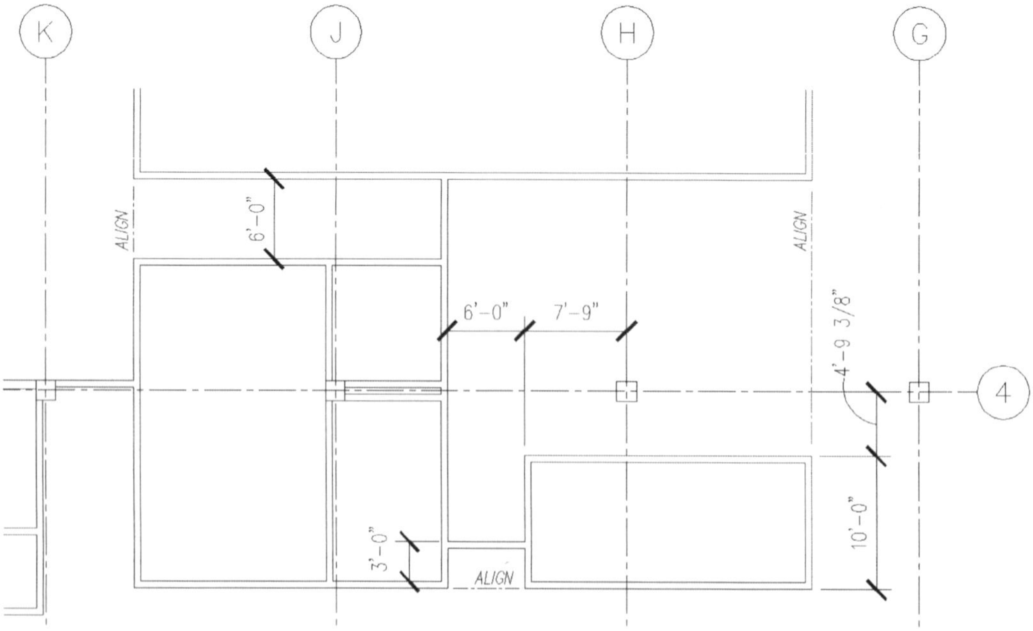

FIGURE 3-4.15 Adding stud walls for the office area

Drawing Equally Spaced Rooms:

It is often required and/or desired to draw several adjacent rooms with the same dimension (i.e., width). For example, rooms that have the same function or offices for people with the same job title will typically want to have the same dimensions (whenever possible).

As designers, working with the building users, you will quickly learn about the typical "human nature" which forcefully indicates that "Mary" better not have a bigger office than "Me" (or more windows, etc.)! This is common in government and large corporation-type projects where building users can sometimes have a large influence on the design process.

The next steps will show you one technique to quickly draw several equally spaced rooms in a row. This involves the use of the *Divide* command, which does not actually divide a line but places *Points* equally spaced along the selected line (which can be *Snapped* to via the *Nodes* snap).

Here is a brief overview of how you will divide a larger space into three smaller and equally sized spaces:

- First you will draw a line from the right-hand side of the west wall to the right-hand side of the east wall (this is the same length as a line drawn from center to center of the same two walls).
- Next you will use the *Divide* command which will place two *Points* equally spaced along the line (based on you entering 3 to the prompt asking for number of equal spaces to divide).
- Next you delete the line so you can see the *Points* just created.
- Using the *Node Snap* you draw a line from each point.
- The lines just drawn are the right-hand side of the wall (because your temporary line was based on the right-hand side of the walls), so you offset the two new lines 6″ towards the west (i.e., the left).
- Finally, to clean house you delete the *Points* using Erase and a Window Selection (i.e., picking from left to right) so as not to select the new lines.

15. Using the information just outlined above draw two **6″ stud walls** as shown in Figures 3-4.16 through 3-4.18.

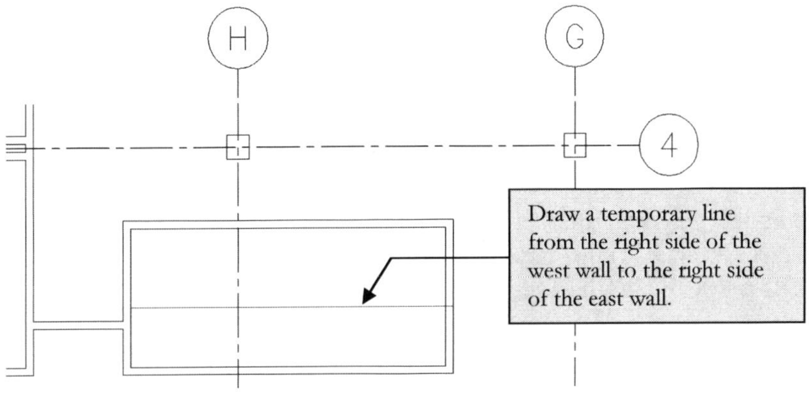

FIGURE 3-4.16 Draw a temporary line (from right to right)

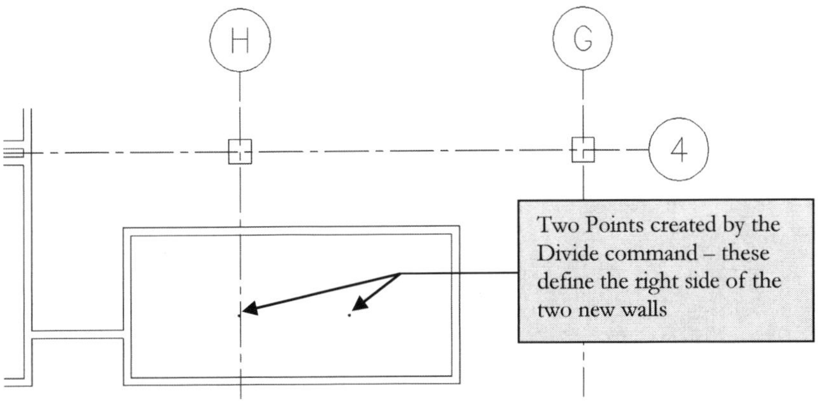

FIGURE 3-4.17 Use Divide on temp. line and then erase the line

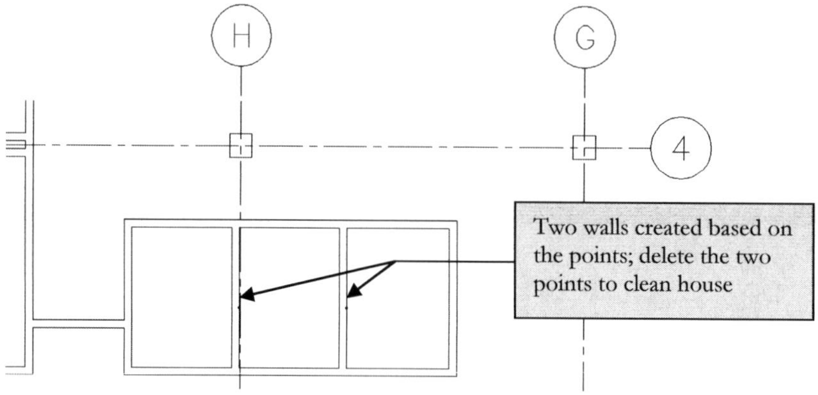

FIGURE 3-4.18 Draw a vertical line from the Points using Node Snap

16. Use the **Distance** command to verify that each room is **6′-8″** wide.

TIP: Search the help system for PDMODE and PDSIZE for information on how to adjust the appearance and size of the Points created by the Divide command. You can also type Point to manually draw them.

A common mistake is to draw the temporary line from the right-hand side of the west wall to the left-hand side of the east wall. This creates three equal spaces within the larger space but neglects the thickness of the two new walls that need to be added.

All this could have been done mathematically and then the adjacent linework could have been offset. For example, you could use the **QuickCalc** palette (accessible from the calculator icon on the *View* tab → *Palettes* panel or pressing Ctrl + 8).

→ Enter the overall space:
 (**21′-0″**)

→ Subtract the two new wall thicknesses:
 (21′-0″ – (2x6″) = **20′-0″**)

→ Divide the available space by 3
 (20′/3 = **6′-8″**)

See the image to the right (see Figure 3-4.19) for an example of how this can all be entered as on mathematical equation.

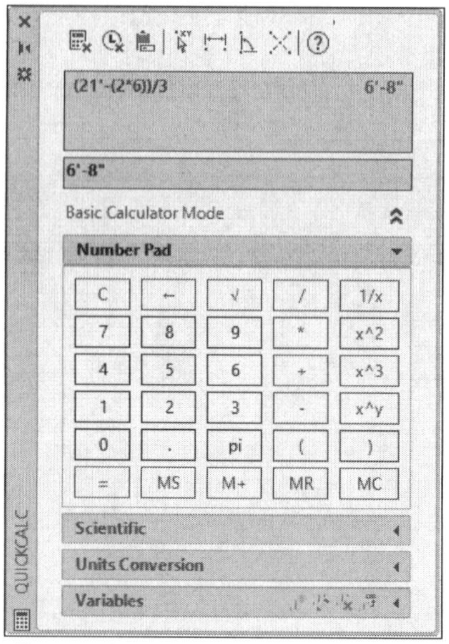

FIGURE 3-4.19 AutoCAD Calculator

FYI: The icons at the top of the calculator can be used to get values directly by picking points within your drawing.

17. Draw the **6″ stud walls** as shown in Figure 3-4.20, plus:
    - Notice the wall along grid 6 is a continuation of a wall previously drawn; make sure to clean up the intersection.
    - Draw all the "straight" lines via the information given and then draw the curved lines (arc or trimmed circle).
    - There are several ways to draw the angled line. The most basic way would be to draw a long vertical line straight down from the corner of the column (F/6), then offset it to the east 7′-3 ¾″, and then rotate the first line 51 degrees. Next you would trim the angled line back to the offset line and then delete the offset line. (Clear as mud?) Give it a try!

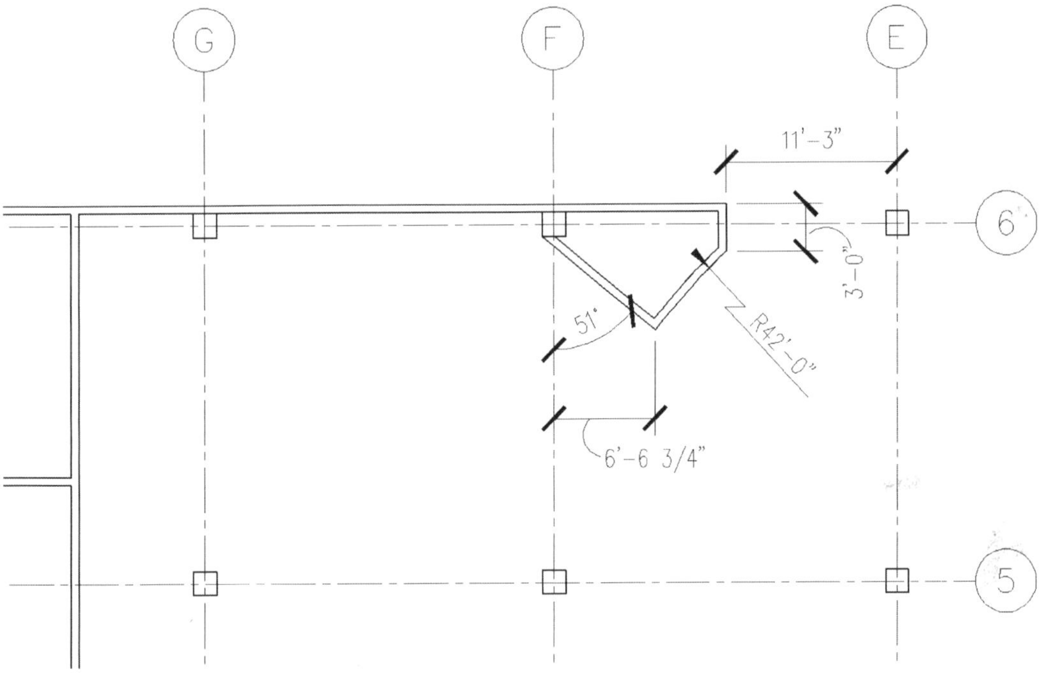

FIGURE 3-4.20 Adding the final interior stud walls

This concludes the placement of the interior CMU and stud walls for the first floor plan of the campus library project. Your drawing should look like the overall image in Figure 3-4.21.

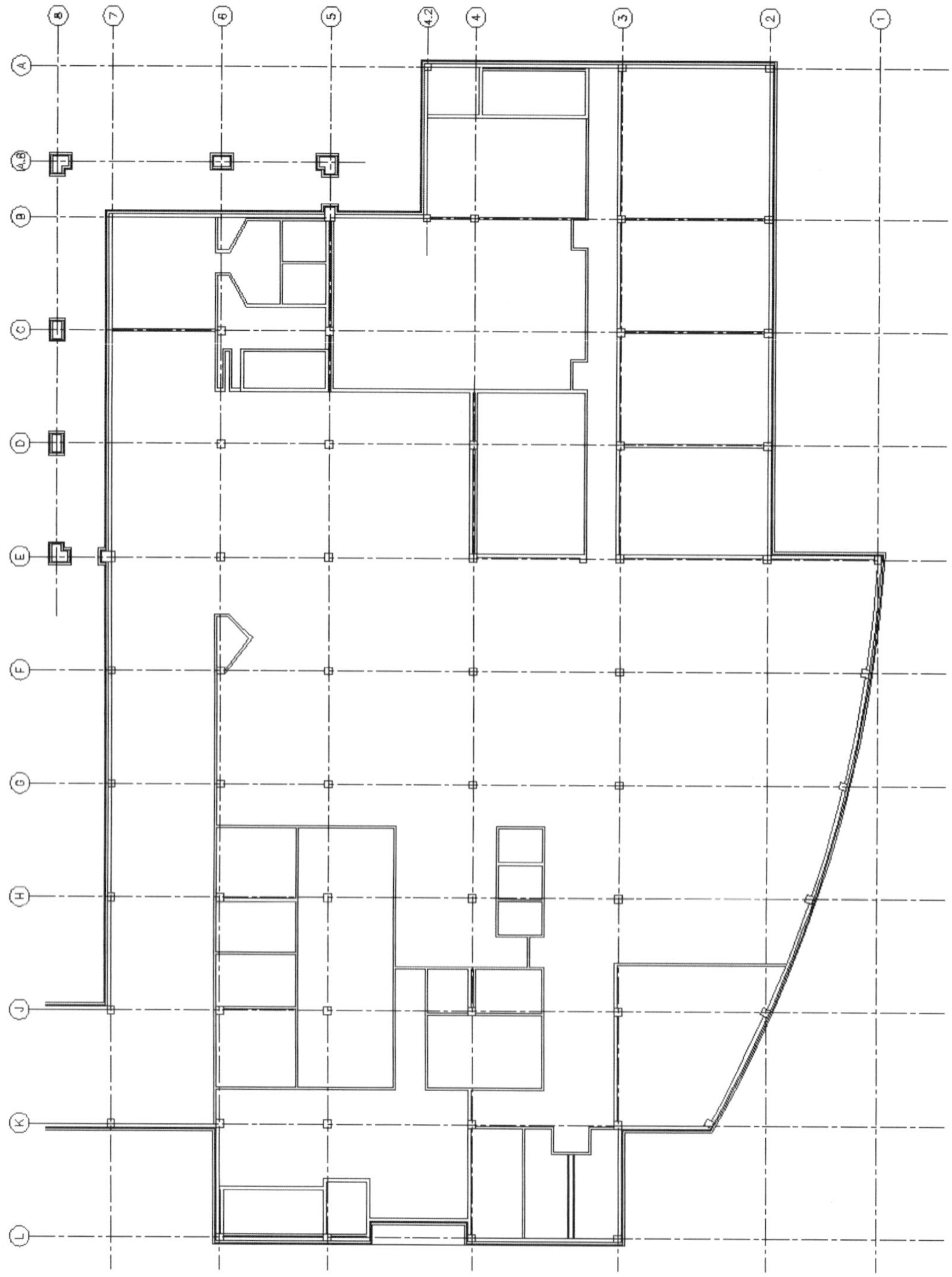

FIGURE 3-4.21 Overall view with all interior walls added; plan rotated to fit this page

Exercise 3-5:
Adding Doors and Windows

Now that you have drawn the walls, you will add the doors. This involves locating where the door opening will be in the wall and then trimming the wall lines to create the opening. Finally, you insert a door symbol that indicates which side the hinges are on and the direction the door opens.

New doors are typically shown open 90 degrees in floor plans, which helps to avoid conflicts such as the door hitting an adjacent base cabinet. Additionally, to make it clear graphically, existing doors are shown open only 45 degrees.

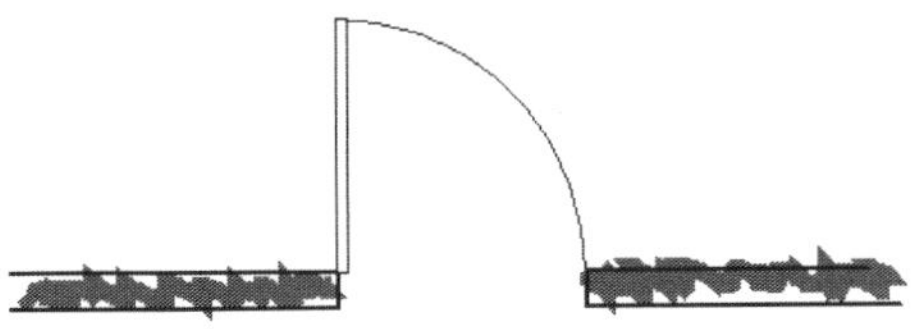

Door symbol Example – New Door drawn with 90 degree swing

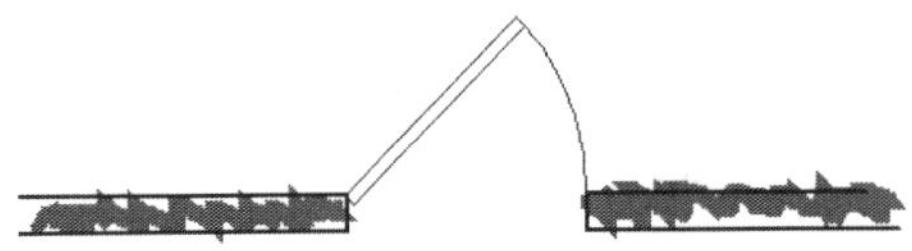

Door symbol Example – Existing Door shown with 45 degree swing

One of the most powerful features of any CAD program is its ability to reuse previously drawn content. With AutoCAD you can insert entire drawing files as symbols into your drawing. In this lesson you will use a *Dynamic Block* to represent the door symbol; you will investigate this feature in a moment.

For those new to drafting, you may find this comparison between CAD and hand-drafting interesting: When hand-drafting, one uses a straightedge or a plastic template that has doors and other often used symbols to trace.

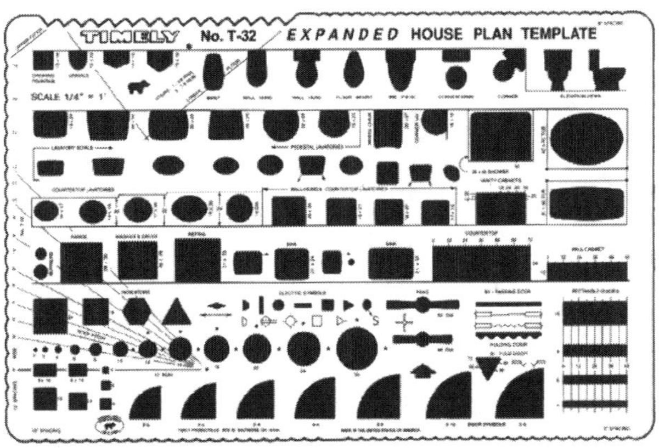

Hand Drafting Template – Plastic template with holes representing common residential shapes (at ¼″ – 1′-0″)
Image used by permission, Timely Templates www.timelytemplates.com

Placing a door usually involves the following commands: Offset, Extend, Trim, Move and Insert.

Getting Started with Doors:

First you will add six doors in the office area.

1. Open your floor plan drawing file.
2. **Zoom** into the [office] area shown in **Figure 3-5.1**.

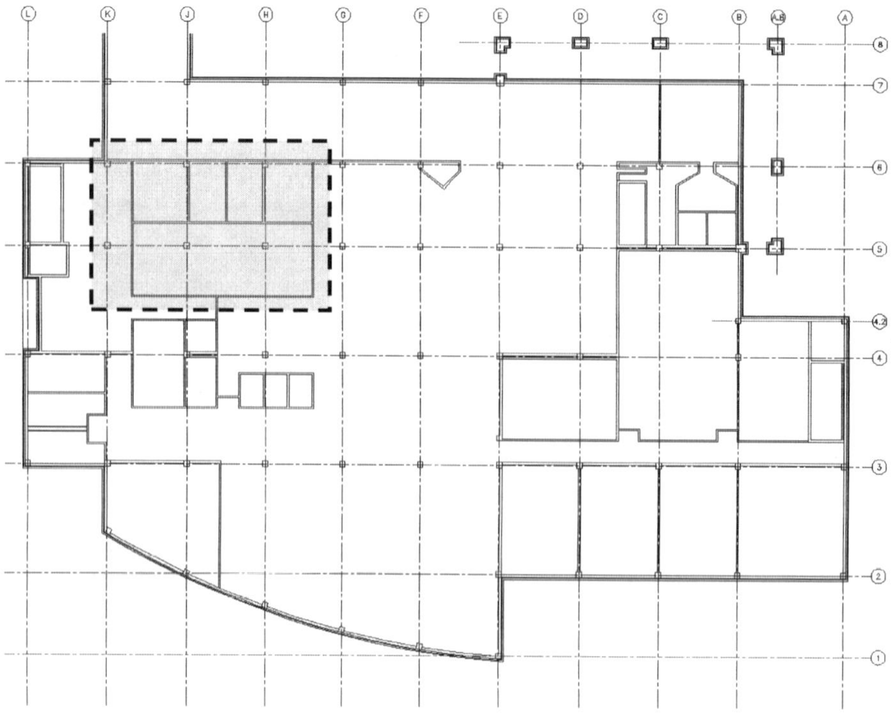

FIGURE 3-5.1 Zoom into area shown (this is the office area)

Accessible Doors:

All the doors, unless noted otherwise, will be 3′-0″ wide; there are a few doors in the service area that are wider to accommodate larger items coming to and leaving the building.

Most building codes in the US require that a door's clear opening to be a minimum of 32″ wide. If you look at a typical commercial door that is open 90 degrees you will notice that the "stops" on the door frame, the door thickness and the "throw" of the hinges all take space for the actual width of the door in the closed position (Figure 3-5.2); therefore 36″ wide (i.e., 3′-0″) doors are typically used.

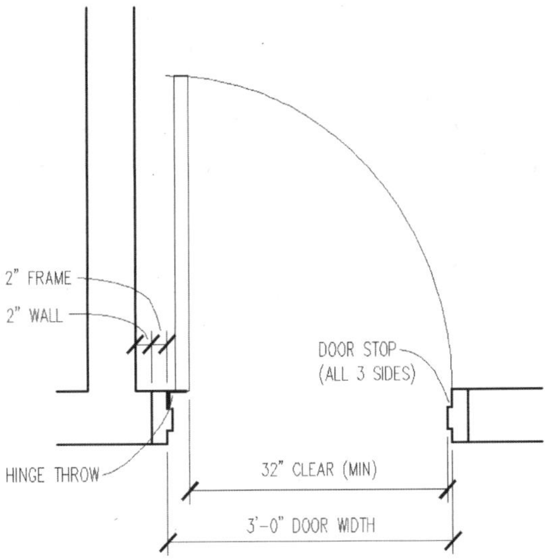

FIGURE 3-5.2
Details to know about accessible doors

Door Stops are usually in integral part of the hollow metal door frame. Its main function is to "stop" the door when being shut. However, it also provides visual privacy and can have sound or weather strips applied. Door stops are NOT typically drawn in floor plans.

Hinge Throw is the distance the door is projected out into the opening as the door is opened, which varies relative to the hinge specified.

The **2″ Wall** dimension is the amount of wall many designers provide between the frame and any adjacent wall. This helps to ensure that the door will open the full 90deg regardless of the doorknob/ lever/hinges selected.

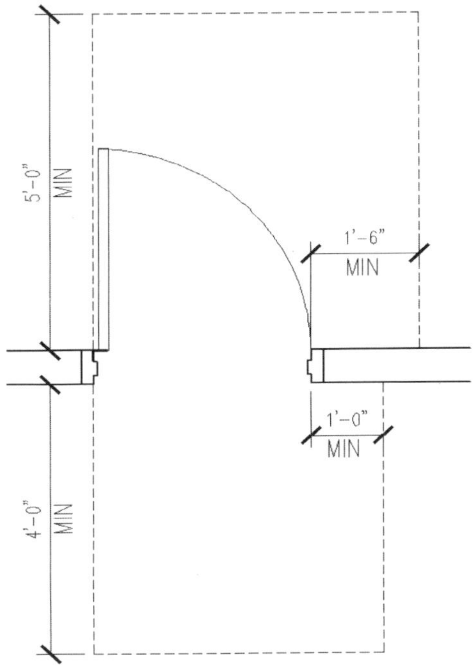

FIGURE 3-5.3
Clear floor space at accessible doors

Building codes can vary regarding clearances required at a door, but most are pretty similar. Typically, doors that have BOTH a closer and a latch must have sufficient space for a handicapped person to operate the door.

Pull Side of a door that is required to be accessible typically needs to have 18″ clear from the edge of the door (not the outside edge of the frame) to any obstruction. An obstruction could be a wall, a base cabinet or furniture.

Push Side of a door that is required to be accessible typically needs to have 12″ clear from the edge of the door to any obstruction.

Most building codes and ADA (Americans with Disabilities Act) require slightly different dimensions depending on approach (i.e., is the person approaching the door perpendicular or parallel to the wall/door?).

Dynamic Blocks:

You will use a pre-made *Dynamic Block* to represent the doors in the floor plan drawing. You should already be generally familiar with AutoCAD *Blocks*, which are symbols that can be placed in your drawings. *Dynamic Blocks* are relatively new in AutoCAD and take the concept of *Blocks* to the next level.

Here are a few quick examples of what Dynamic Blocks can do:

- One *Dynamic Block* can represent several symbols. For example, you can have a *Dynamic Block* simply named **Bed**. When you insert the Bed you can click on it, which then displays special icon-type symbols near the *Block*, you can then click the icon and choose which symbol to display (e.g., king, queen, twin, double, etc.).

- Another *Dynamic Block* might be a **Conference Room** table with four chairs around it. Clicking this Block reveals icons that allow you to stretch the table in pre-specified increments and maximums/minimums; stretching the table also causes chairs to be added or subtracted.

- In the case of the **Door** *Block* for this exercise, the symbol is adjustable for width, wall thickness and amount the door is open. *Flip* controls are also available to adjust the swing of the door.

An exhaustive study of *Dynamic Blocks* is beyond the scope of this book. You are, however, strongly encouraged to explore this powerful feature further on your own. You can start with the *New Features Workshop* and the *Help* system located under the **Help** pull-down menu. Also, Autodesk has made white papers available via their website, www.autodesk.com, which provide in-depth technical studies of how *Dynamic Blocks* work.

At this point you will explore the specific features associated with the door block you will be using.

3. Open the **Tool Palette** by pressing **Ctrl + 3** if it is not currently open (or via the *View* tab → *Palettes* panel).

4. Click on the **Architectural** tab to make it active (Figure 3-5.4).

   TIP: Click the "stack" of tabs at the bottom of the normal tabs to see a menu of all the available tabs, and select Architectural.

In Figure 3-5.4 you see that each symbol listed here is a *Dynamic Block* because they each have a lightning blot symbol superimposed on them. Next you will click on the *Door - Imperial* icon and then place an instance of it arbitrarily in the middle of a room so you can explore its features.

5. Click the **Door – Imperial** icon on the *Architectural* tab of the *Tool Palette* as shown in Figure 3-5.4.

Just like inserting a regular *Block*, the door symbol is attached to your cursor and ready for placement.

6. Arbitrarily click somewhere in the middle of a room to insert the symbol.

7. Position your cursor over the door symbol you just inserted, and click to select it.

With the door symbol selected, which is a *Dynamic Block*, you will take a few minutes and note a few things about it:

- First, looking at the *Layer* drop-down list on the toolbar, notice the door was placed on the current *Layer*. When you know you will be inserting several doors, for example, you should set that object types layer to be current; this will save a step.

- Second, look at Figure 3-5.5 for a description of each control grip that is currently visible. After reviewing the image, try clicking each control and "flex" the image to get a feel for how they work.

  FYI: *If the grips do not appear, the block is on a locked* Layer.

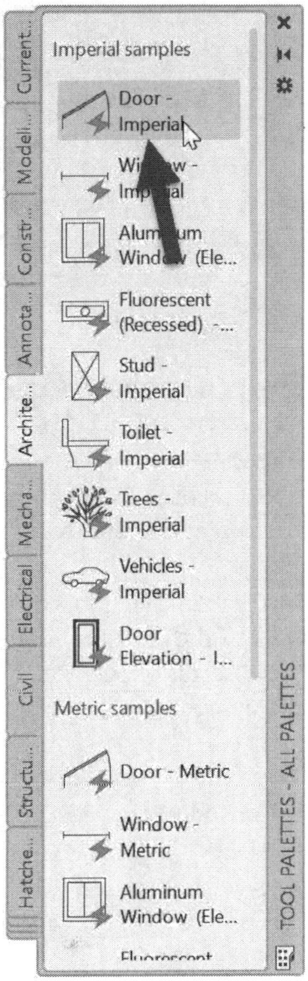

FIGURE 3-5.4 Tool Palettes

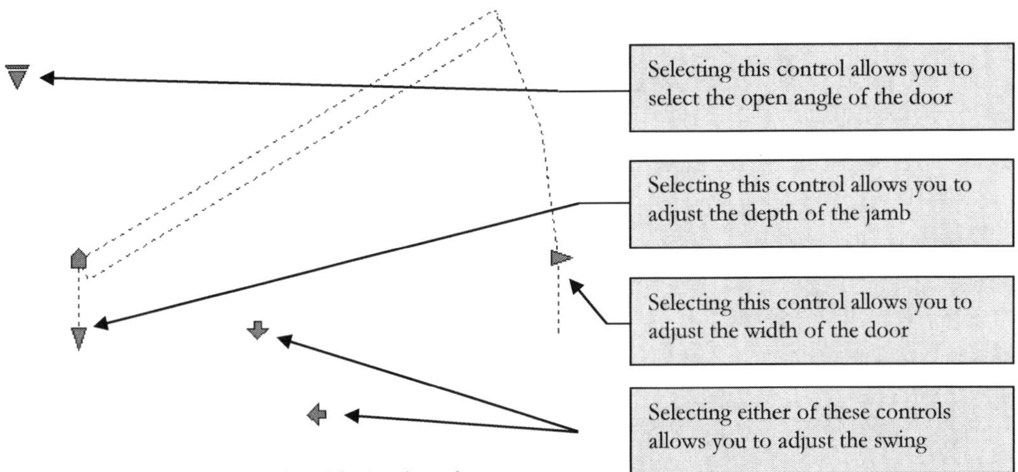

FIGURE 3-5.5 Dynamic door block selected

8. Place the *Block* on the correct *Layer*.

   ***TIP:** Select the Block and select the correct Layer from the Layer drop-down list (or via the floating Quick Properties, if turned on).*

9. Clicking the *Control Grip* allows you to adjust the Open Angle and select **Open 90°** item from the context menu (see image to the right).

Preparing the Opening for the Door Block:

The wall lines need to be trimmed at each door location; this can be done before or after the door has been located in the proper position. It is usually easier to trim the lines and add the frame first because this gives you and endpoint to snap to when inserting the door.

In this book, all doors adjacent to a wall will have a 2″ dimension between the wall and the edge of the door frame (Figure 3-5.2), and all other doors will be dimensioned. A note to this effect is usually found in a set of Construction Documents, which significantly reduces the number of doors that need to be dimensioned.

Your *Dynamic Block* does not have a door frame connected to it so you will use the Rectangle command to draw a 2″x6″ hollow metal frame on each side of the opening. As you can see in Figure 3-5.6, hollow metal frames typically have "stops" and project ½″ from the wall on each side. However, to simplify things graphically, a clean rectangle is used which ignores the "stops" and is flush with the wall thickness as shown in Figure 3-5.7.

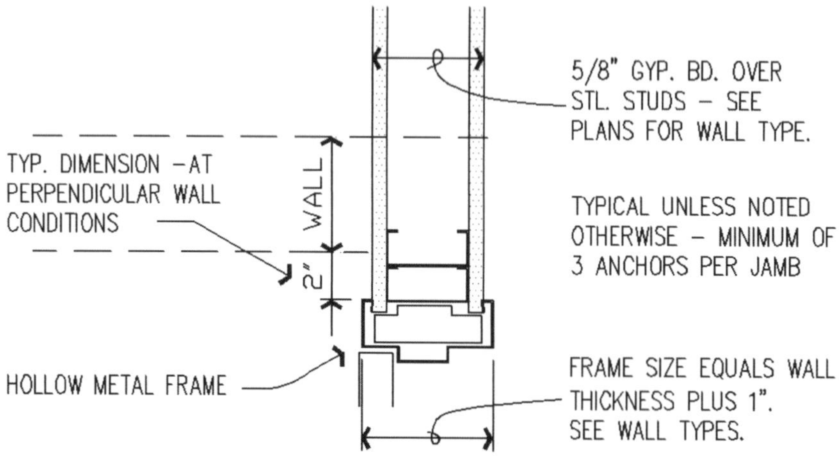

FIGURE 3-5.6 Typical hollow metal door jamb detail

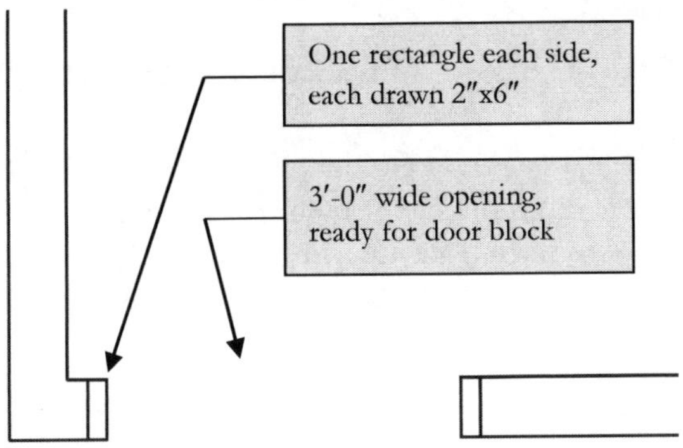

Using *Offset, Trim, Extend* and *Rectangle* you can easily prepare each opening to look like (or similar to) Figure 3-5.7.

FIGURE 3-5.7 Preparing a door opening for the door block

Adding Doors:

10. Add the 3′-0″ doors shown in Figure 3-5.8 using the Dynamic Door Block from the *Tool Palette*, plus:
    a. Prepare the opening per the previous paragraph *Preparing the Opening for the Door Block.*
    b. All door frames are to be 2″ away from the adjacent wall as discussed with Figure 3-5.2; place frame on A-Door-Fram *Layer.*

       ***FYI:** The word frame is abbreviated to comply with layer standards.*

    c. You can place each door by selecting the door icon from the Palette, or you can simply copy a previously inserted door around. (Remember to make sure it's on the correct Layer first.)

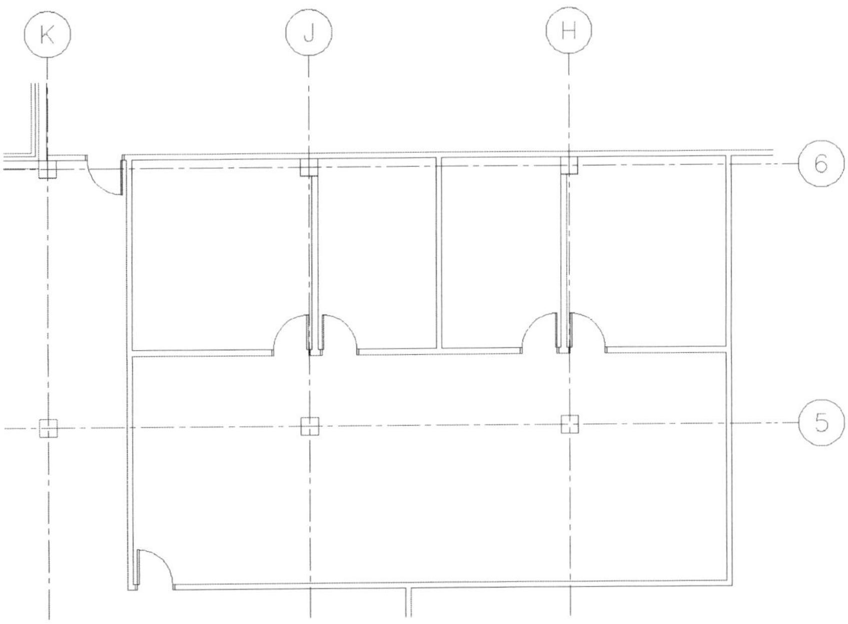

FIGURE 3-5.8 3′-0″ doors to be added in this step

11. Add the doors shown in Figure 3-5.9, plus:
    a. All doors are 3′-0″ EXCEPT the three doors with an asterisk (✱) which are 3′-4″ wide doors.
    b. Note that the door in the upper left was added in the previous step.
    c. An opening was added near the bottom middle of Figure 3-5.9; it shall be 4′-0″ wide centered on the room it opens into. Place the jamb lines on *Layer* A-Wall.
    d. The three doors in the lower right (the three equally spaced quiet rooms) are to be centered in the rooms.

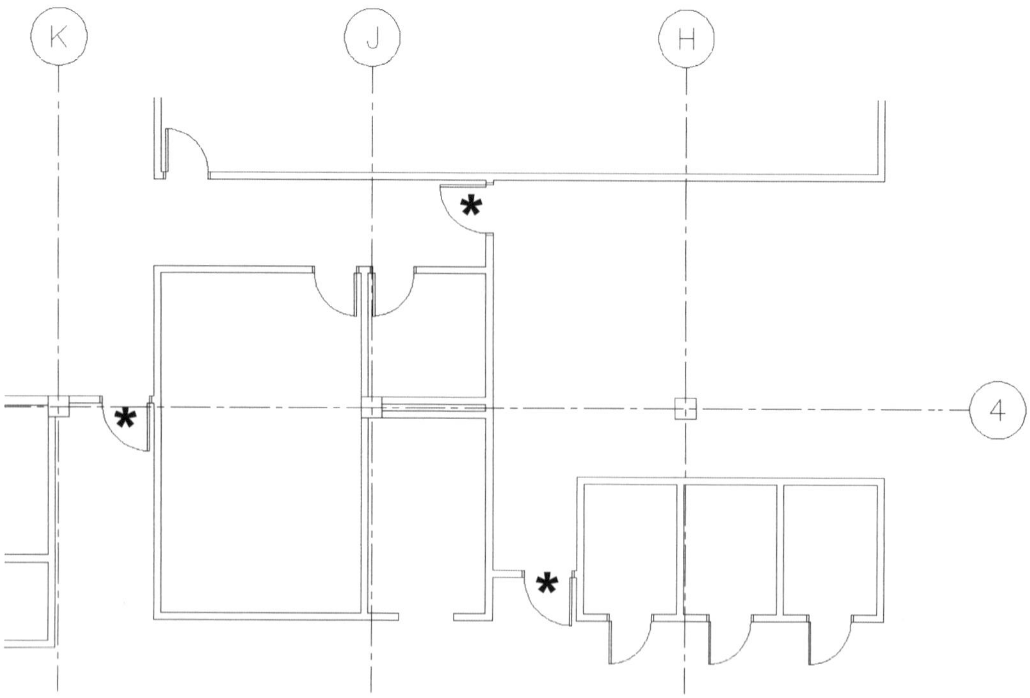

FIGURE 3-5.9 Doors and an opening to be added in this step

Adding Doors in Masonry Walls:

Next you will add interior and exterior doors to the west stair. In both cases, the doors are in masonry walls and in each you will draw the door frame the typical 2″x6″. Door frames are occasionally made to match the wall thickness of a masonry wall, but in this case, you will use a standard frame size of 6″ (actually 5-¾″ is the standard, 6″ is the nominal dimension). Drawing the frame the proper size helps to convey the desired position of the frame within the wall; sometimes the frame is centered in the wall, sometimes it is set back a certain distance, and other times it is flush with one side. The typical door size of 3′-0″ works well in masonry walls because the door width plus the two 2″ jamb frames equal 3′-4″ which matches coursing.

12. Add the 3′-0″ doors shown in Figure 3-5.10, plus:
    a. The interior door is flush with the right side of the wall.
    b. The exterior door is held back 3″ from the exterior face of the building.
    c. Draw the door frame on the A-Door-Fram *Layer.*
    d. Because the frame is not as wide as the wall, draw a line on the A-Wall layer to close the gap (a must for hatching later).
    e. See the ***FYI*** comments on the next page.

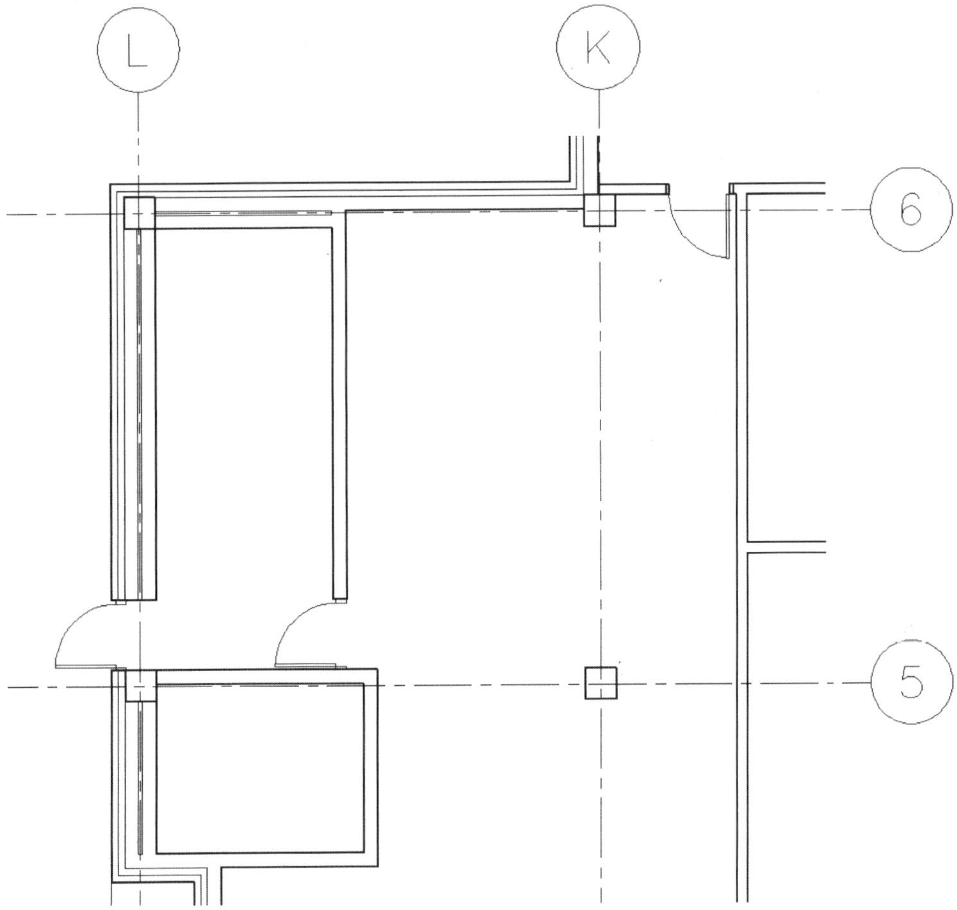

FIGURE 3-5.10 Doors added in masonry walls

Doors in the egress path must swing in the path of travel. This is why the exterior door in the stair shaft swings out (in cold climates, doors that swing out require a concrete stoop to prevent frost heave from blocking the door shut).

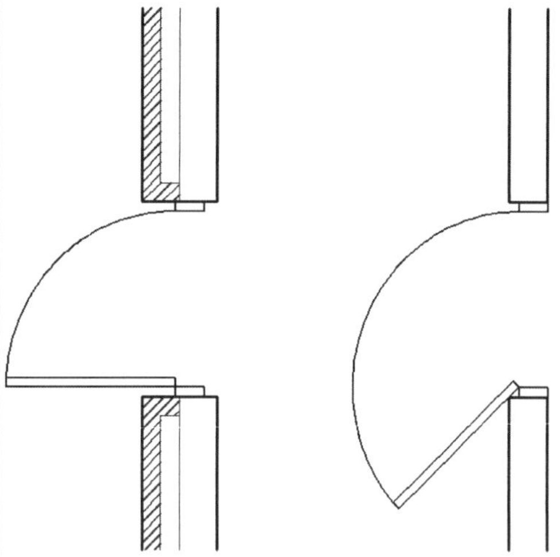

FYI:
Two things to think about related to the previous step:

1) *Sometimes the exterior doors are recessed more than 4" (which is the depth of the brick. To avoid having the air space and insulation be exposed, the brick is returned to the CMU at each jamb. This would be shown with the cavity lines.*
2) *The location of the door frame in an interior masonry wall can be important. The image to the left shows a potential problem with the door not opening fully because of an improperly positioned frame.*

Adding an Overhead Door:

Next you will add an Overhead Door (aka, O.H. Door). It is standard practice to show the O.H. Door dashed for the open position. This helps to avoid conflicts with lights, ductwork and adjacent walls and ceilings. The amount the door projects into the room varies; typically the projection equals the height of the door (e.g., a 9′-0″ OH door would project 9′-0′ into the room); however, in high-bay areas the jamb tracks can simply continue straight up the wall (which would result in virtually no projection into the room).

Similar to the previous ***FYI*** comments, you will show the brick returning at each jamb; again, so you don't see cavity insulation or concrete block from the exterior of the building.

> ***FYI:*** *When talking to a contractor or a person in the construction industry, the typical 3'-0" door is often referred to as a "man door" when it is adjacent to an O.H. door (i.e., "man" in the general sense; no gender bias intended here!).*

Loading Dock Example O.H. door on raised platform to load/unload trucks

13. Add the doors shown in Figure 3-5.11, plus:
    a. The "man" door is 3′-0″ wide; draw per previous step.
    b. Draw the O.H. door per the following:
        i. Use dimensions shown (do not add the dimensions).
        ii. Show the brick return as drawn below.
        iii. Draw the door in the "closed" position using a 2″x10′-0″ rectangle (drawn on the **A-Door** *Layer*).
        iv. Draw the door in the "open" position as shown below (drawn on **A-Door-Abov** setup per office standards).
            - Vertical dashed line is 9′-0″ from exterior wall.

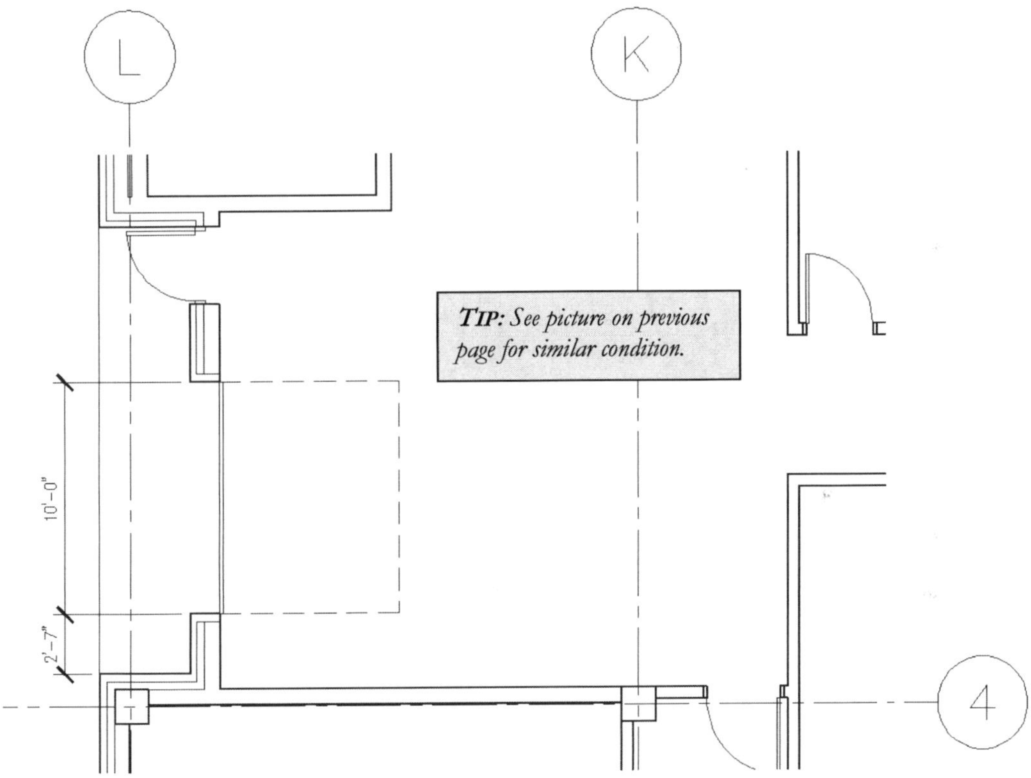

FIGURE 3-5.11 Adding a "man" door and an O.H. door

Adding More Doors

14. Add the 3′-0″ wide doors shown in Figure 3-5.12.

15. Add the 3′-0″ wide door shown in Figure 3-5.13.

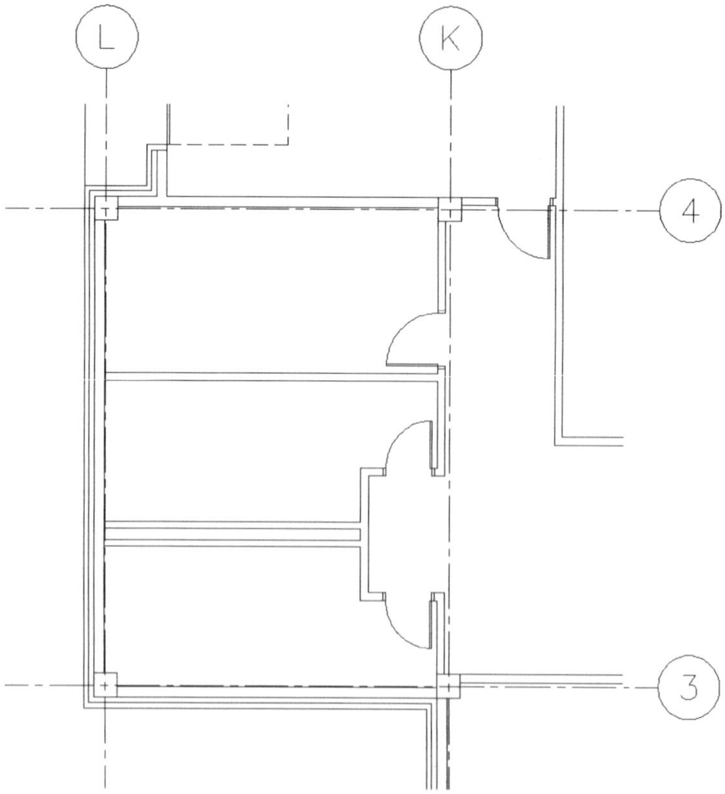

FIGURE 3-5.12 Adding doors to restrooms and janitor's closet

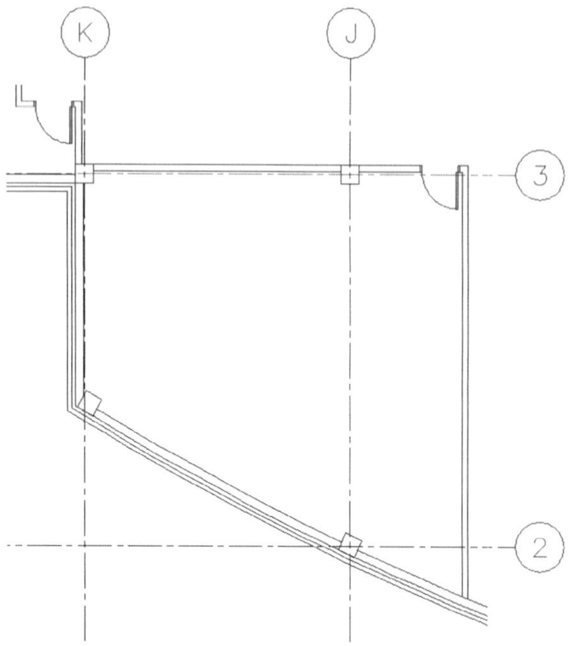

FIGURE 3-5.13 Adding a door to the group study room

16. Add the 3′-0″ wide doors shown in Figure 3-5.14.

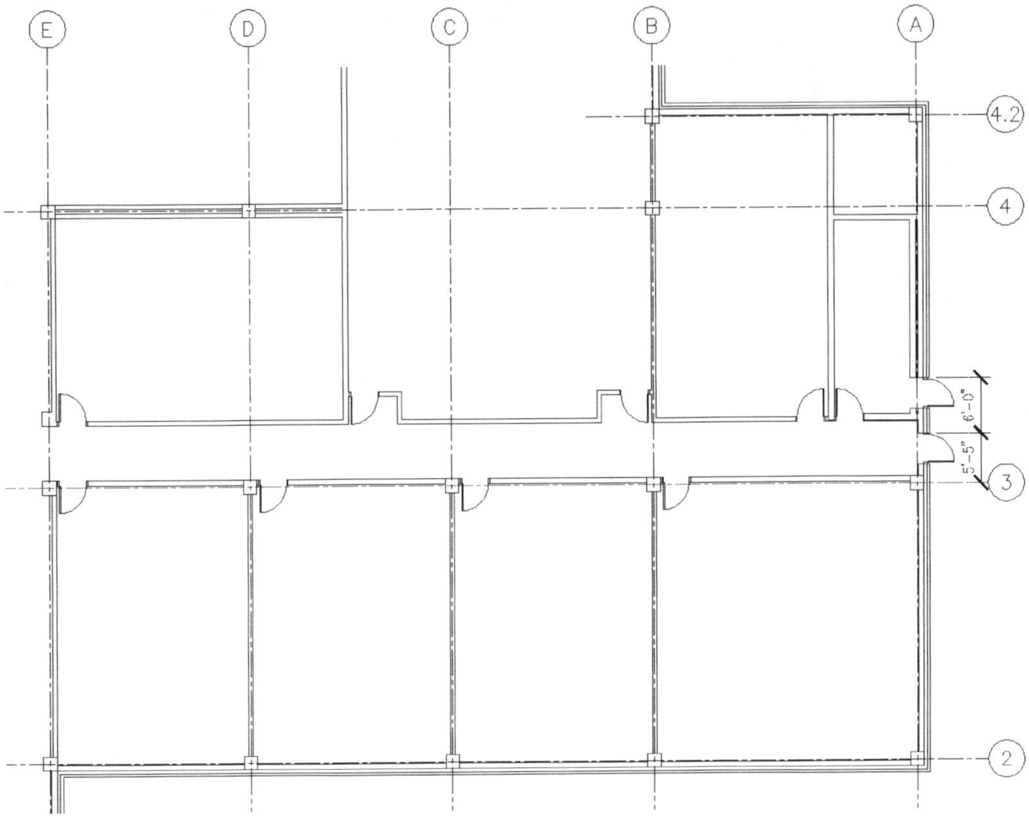

FIGURE 3-5.14 Adding doors to the floor plan

17. Add the 3′-0″ wide doors shown in Figure 3-5.16 (see next page).

NOTE: One door is centered on the wall.

18. Add the Horizontal Partition shown in Figure 3-5.15, per:
    a. Horizontal line goes on **A-Door-Abov** to get dashed line.
    b. Use *Pline* to draw arrow; set *Width* to 3″ (see Help System).

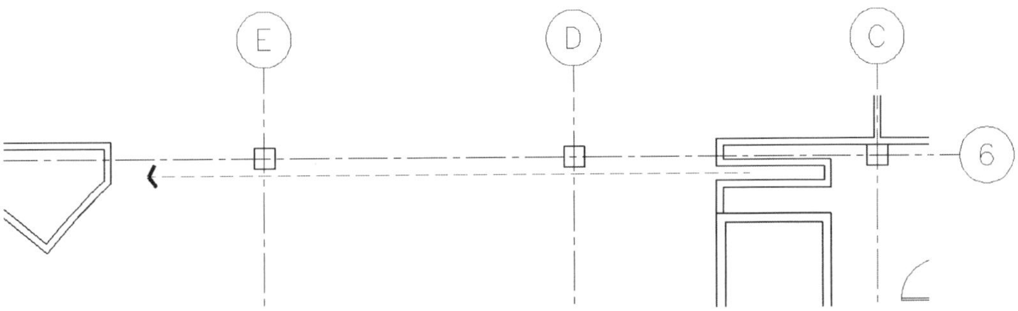

FIGURE 3-5.15 Adding doors to the floor plan

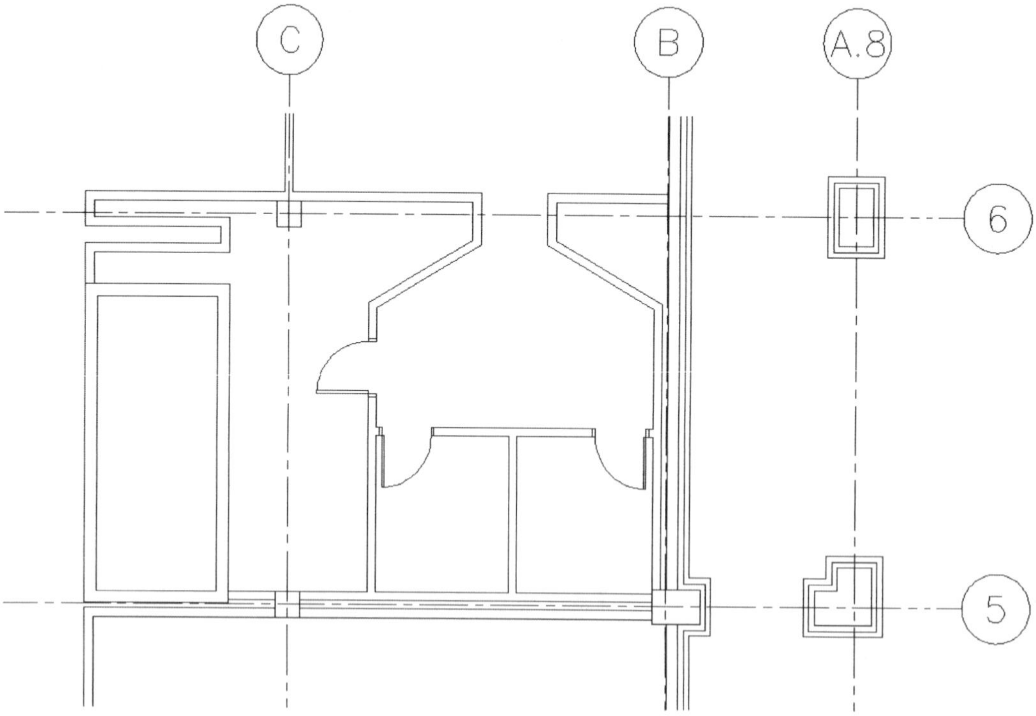

FIGURE 3-5.16 Adding doors to the floor plan

Drawing the Storefront System at the Main Entry:

The last step in this exercise is to draw the entrance system. In this project it will be an aluminum storefront system. These systems come in various shapes and sizes; however, they do come in sizes similar to the typical 2″x6″ frames previously drawn so that is what you will use.

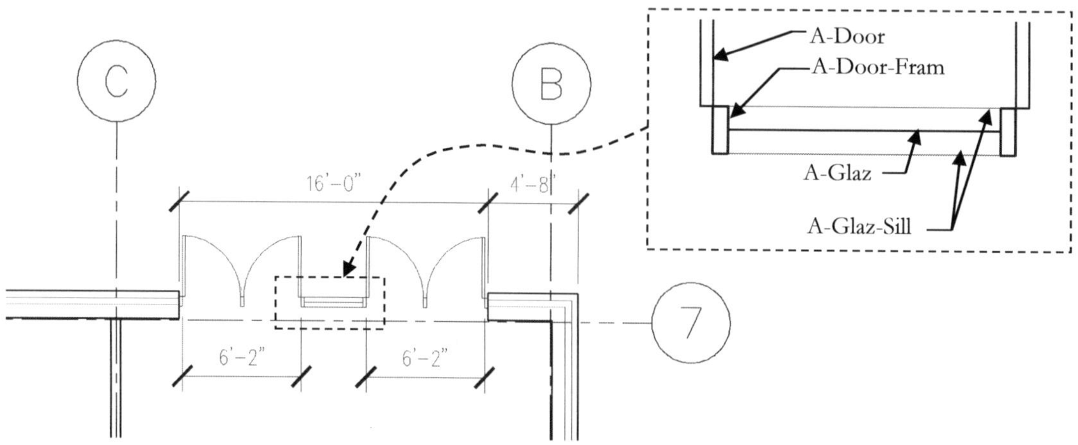

FIGURE 3-5.17 Drawing the entry system

19. Add the Storefront System shown in Figure 3-5.18, plus:
    a. Use the *Layer* and *Dimension* information given in Figure 3-5.17.
    b. All three have the same system.
    c. Do not add the dimensions.
    d. Use the rectangle command to draw the frames.
    e. Center storefront on corridor (between grids 6 and 7).

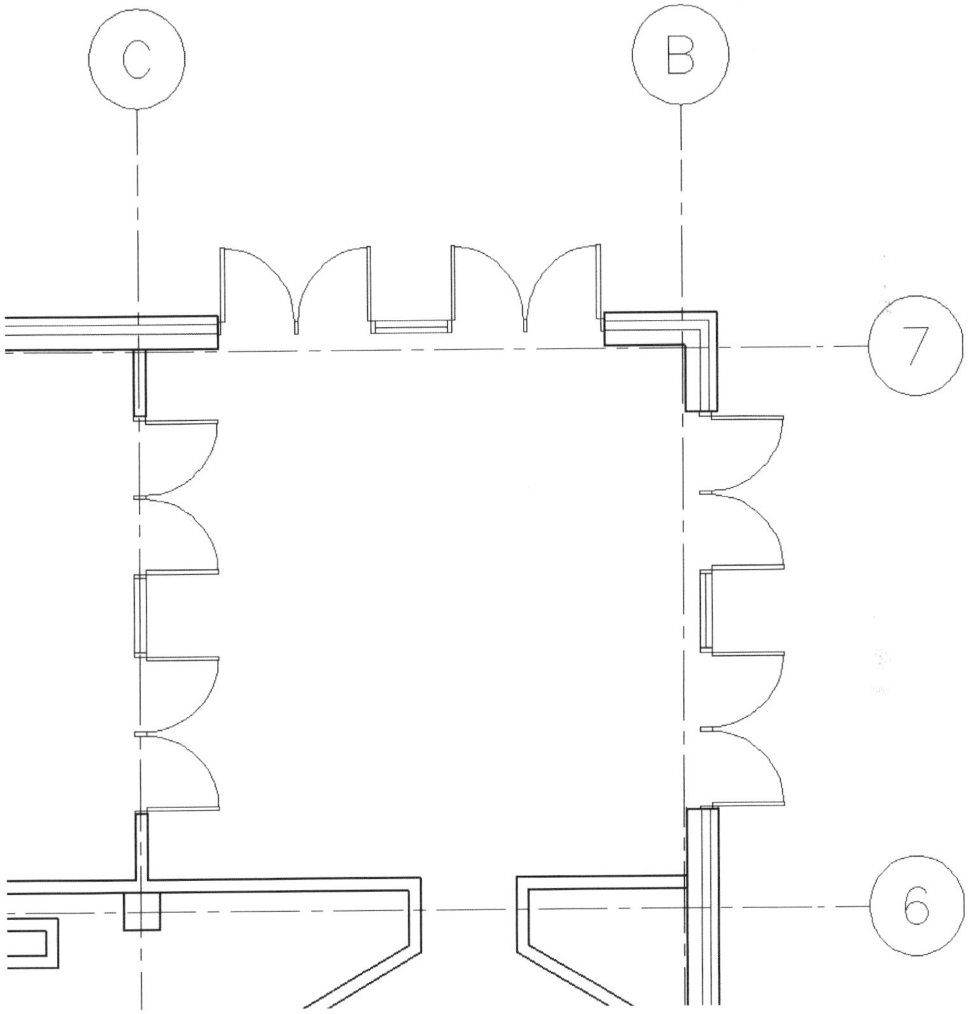

FIGURE 3-5.18 Adding the entry systems

That concludes the door portion of this exercise. Next you will add the windows.

Adding Windows:

Now you will add exterior windows to your plans. This is similar to placing doors, discussed in the previous exercise.

One difference between drawing doors and windows is that windows are drawn on three separate layers:

A-GLAZ	The glass (a.k.a., glazing) is drawn on this layer.
A-GLAZ-FRAM	The window frame (drawn with Rectangle tool).
A-GLAZ-SILL	The sill lines are drawn on this layer. (This represents the portion of wall that continues below the window).

Lineweights:

The primary reason that three *Layers* are used is to control lineweights. The thickness of a line (i.e., lineweight) is commonly controlled by which *Layer* it is on. One benefit to this is that you can adjust the lineweight setting in one location and all the lines on that *Layer* are updated.

When thinking about how lineweights relate to a window in plan, you need to consider whether the line is in section or not.

The diagram below shows the different components that make up a window in plan view.

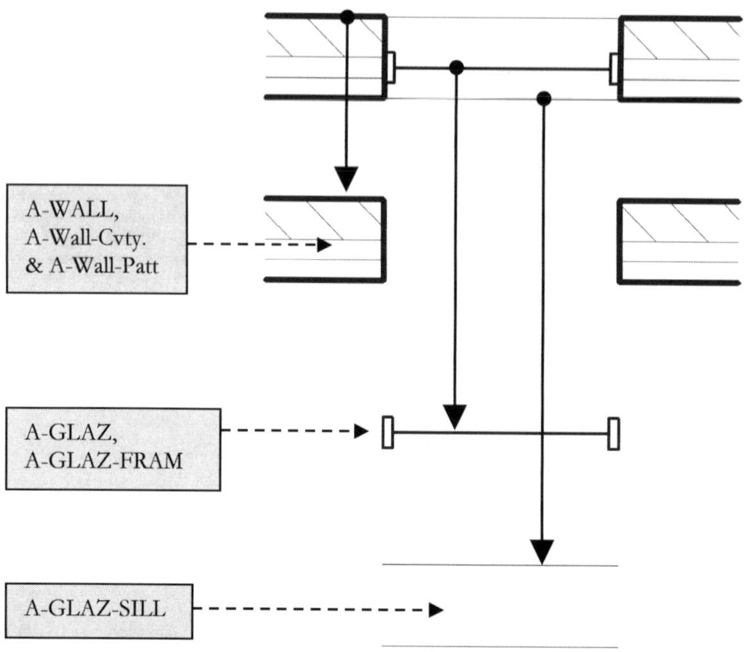

Window Opening Example Components/Layers for a window

Your project has three window sizes throughout. The typical window size is 4′-0″ wide. ***FYI:** The window frame is drawn within that dimension.* The windows surrounding the reading room are all 2′-0″ wide and the four large windows near the main entry are 7′-4″ wide. Notice that all these window widths are compatible with masonry coursing.

Seeing as the process to add windows is so similar to adding doors, you will be given minimal instruction in the remaining steps. Note that it is NOT necessary to add the dimensions at this time (the dimensions shown are strictly for you, the reader, to locate the windows and would not represent a complete dimensioning solution).

Adding the 4′-0″ Wide Windows:

20. Add the **4′-0″** wide windows shown in Figure 3-5.19a and 19b, plus:
    a. Make sure you remove the portion of the wall line (on layer A-Wall) below the new sill line (on layer A-Glaz-Sill).
    b. Do NOT draw the dimensions.
    c. Hold the window frames back 3″ from the exterior.
    d. Make the frames **2″x6″**.

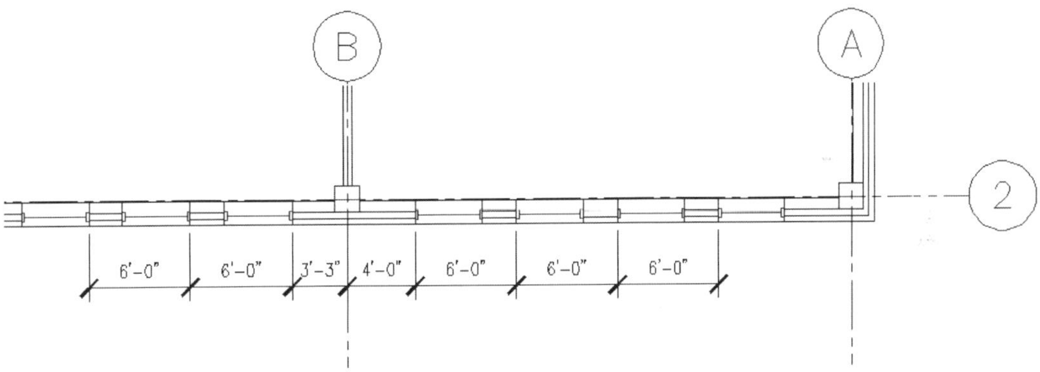

FIGURE 3-5.19A Adding 4′-0″ wide windows

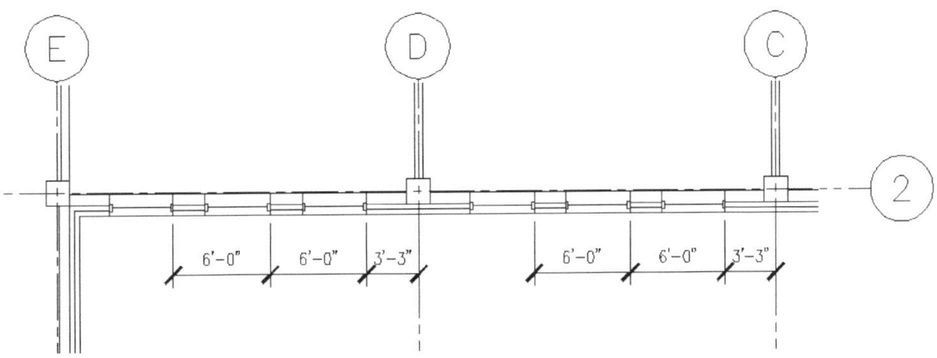

FIGURE 3-5.19B Adding 4′-0″ wide windows

21. Add the **4′-0″** wide windows shown in Figure 3-5.20.

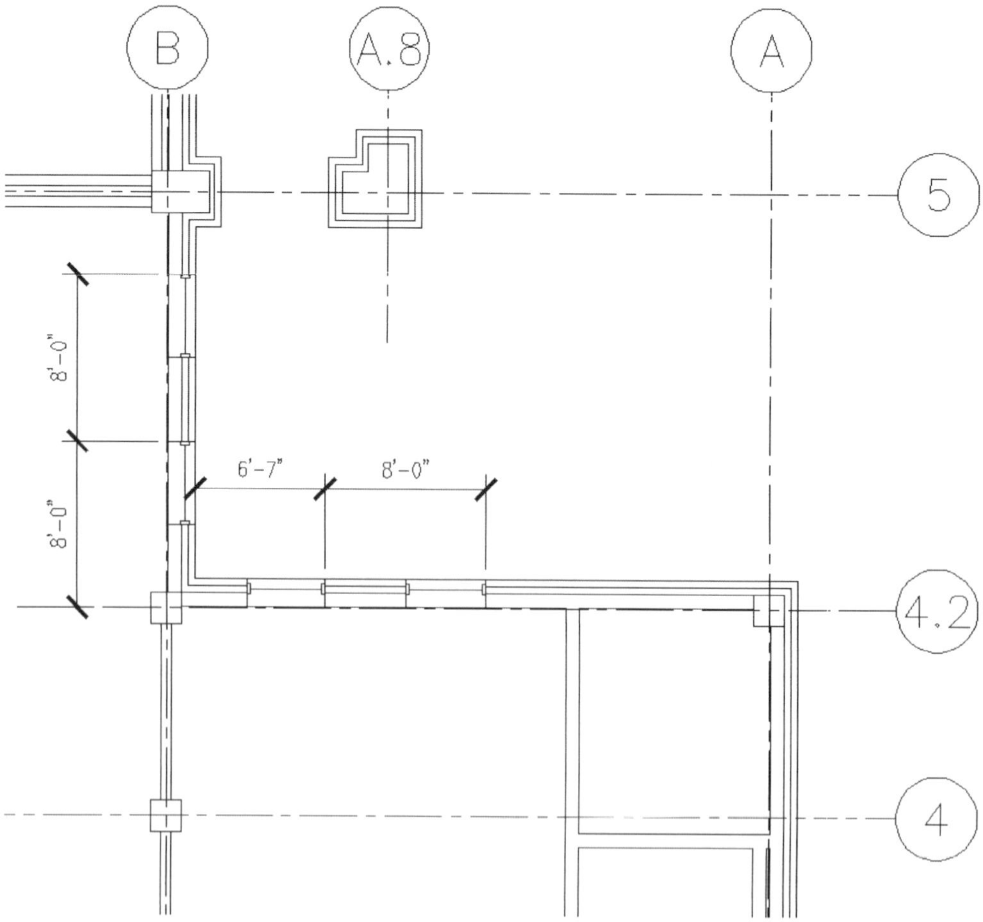

FIGURE 3-5.20 Adding 4′-0″ wide windows

Window locations often need to be coordinated with furniture, though this step is often overlooked. For example, when laying out systems furniture (cubical-like furniture) an Architect or Interior Designer would want to make sure any "upper" file cabinets did not block the window. The window locations are often derived from the aesthetic of the exterior views of the building, so changing the windows is not always an option. Sometimes the Interior Designer needs to develop unique solutions to solve such problems.

As mentioned previously, when the Interior Designer is heading up the **LEED** process on a building, it would behoove the Architect to work closely with the Interior Designer because certain rooms must receive natural light. This requirement is best implemented early in the design.

The next group of windows let light into the concourse. The area between two grids is referred to as a "bay"; often, the windows are placed in the same location in each "bay". Thus, in the next step you are given the dimensions for one "bay" and then instructed to place the windows in the same relative location in the other adjacent "bays".

22. Add the **4'-0"** wide windows shown in Figure 3-5.21a and 21b, plus:
    a. Use the typical dimensions in Figure 3-5.21a to draw the other windows shown in Figure 3-5.21b.

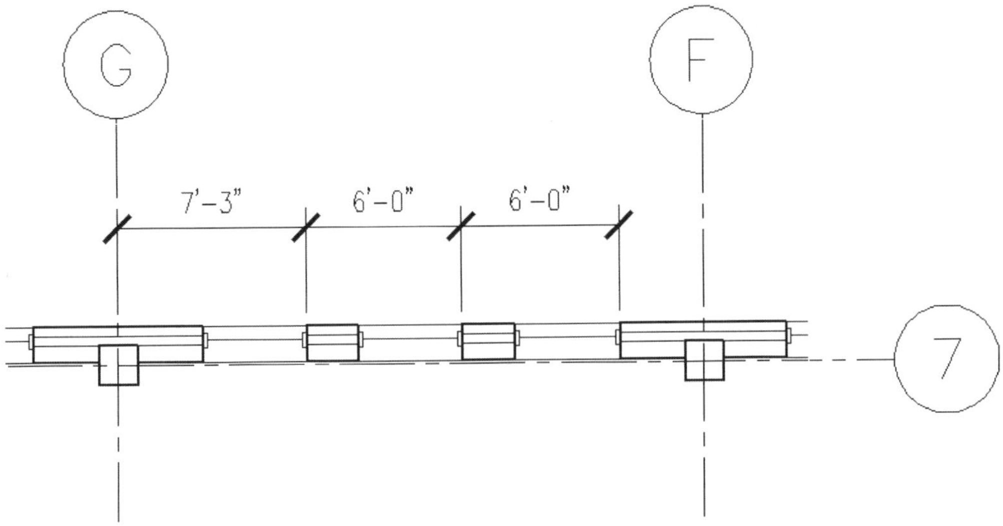

FIGURE 3-5.21A Adding 4'-0" wide windows

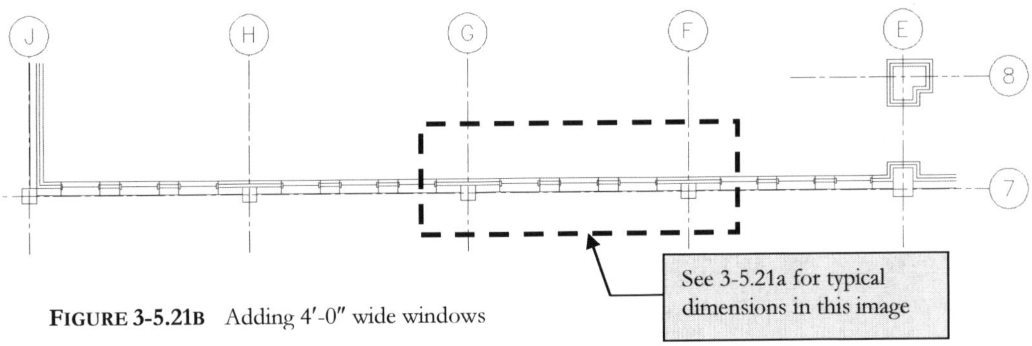

FIGURE 3-5.21B Adding 4'-0" wide windows

23. Add the **4'-0"** wide window shown in Figure 3-5.22.

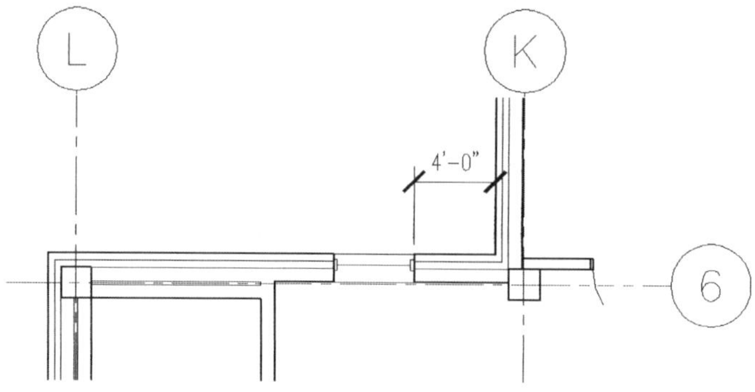

FIGURE 3-5.22 Adding a 4′-0″ wide window

Adding the 7′-4″ Wide Windows:

24. Add the **7′-4″** wide windows shown in Figure 3-5.23, plus:
    a. The two windows are equally spaced between [vertical] grids, with a 2′-0″ portion of wall between them.

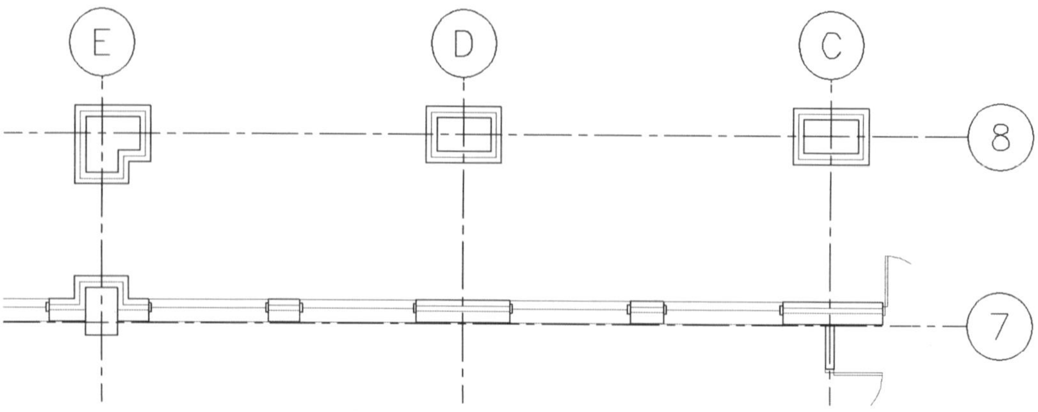

FIGURE 3-5.23 Adding 7′-4″ wide windows

Adding the 2′-0″ Wide Windows:

Next you will add the smaller 2′-0″ wide windows in the large reading room. The windows in the east and west walls are easy because they are orthogonal walls; the remaining windows are within the curved wall and are a little tricky to place.

25. Add the **2′-0″** wide windows shown in Figures 3-5.24 and 3-5.25.

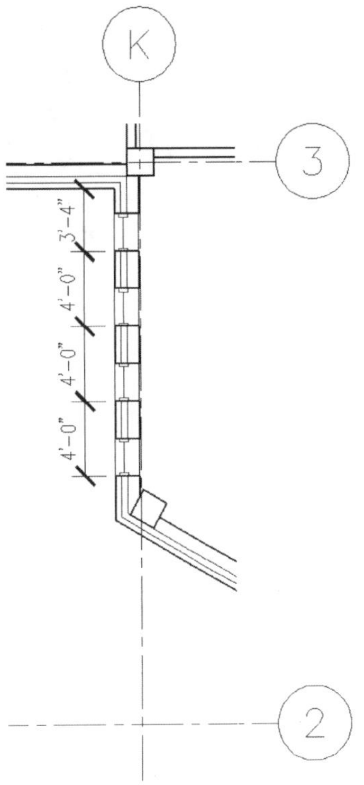

FIGURE 3-5.24
Adding 2′-0″ wide windows

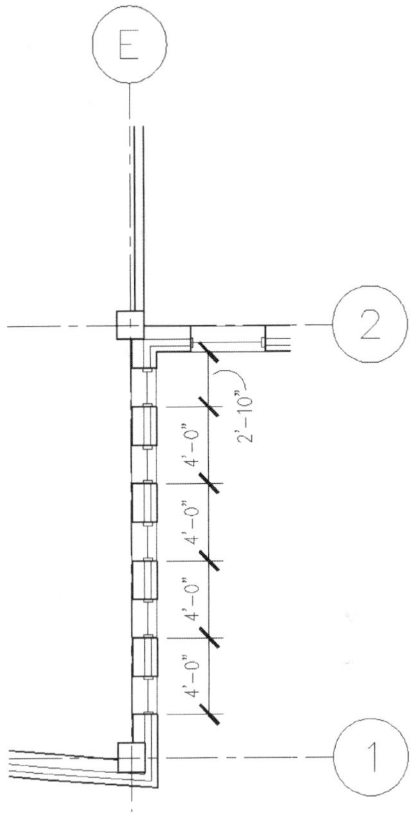

FIGURE 3-5.25
Adding 2′-0″ wide windows

26. Draw (or *Copy* and *Rotate*) a **2′-0″** window as shown in Figure 3-5.26. *Extend* the jamb lines (***FYI:** On layer A-Wall*) out past the sill lines 4″ in each direction. (This will make it easier to trim the jamb lines up to the curved wall lines.) The window is temporary, so its exact location is not important in this step.

27. Using the *Move* command and *Object Snaps*, move the window from the *Midpoint* of the top [horizontal] sill line, to the *Midpoint* of the interior-most curved line.

Next you will rotate the window to align with the curved wall. To do this you will use a sub-command of Rotate called Reference Angle which allows you to rotate the selected objects based on adjacent geometry.

28. Select **Rotate**, select all the window lines (using a selection window and picking from left to right), press **Enter** to finish selecting items to rotate, using the *Midpoint Snap* select the *Base Point* (Fig. 3-5.27), Press **R** and **Enter**, pick the *Reference Angle* (pick #2), pick the *Second Point* (pick #3), and then pick the *New Angle* (pick #4).

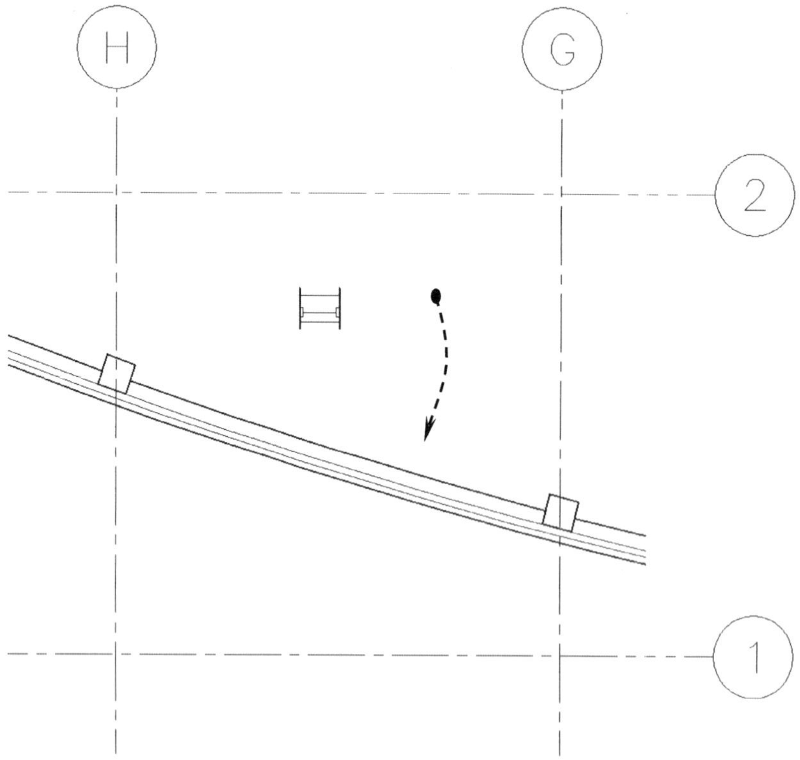

FIGURE 3-5.26
Adding 2′-0″ wide windows in curved wall

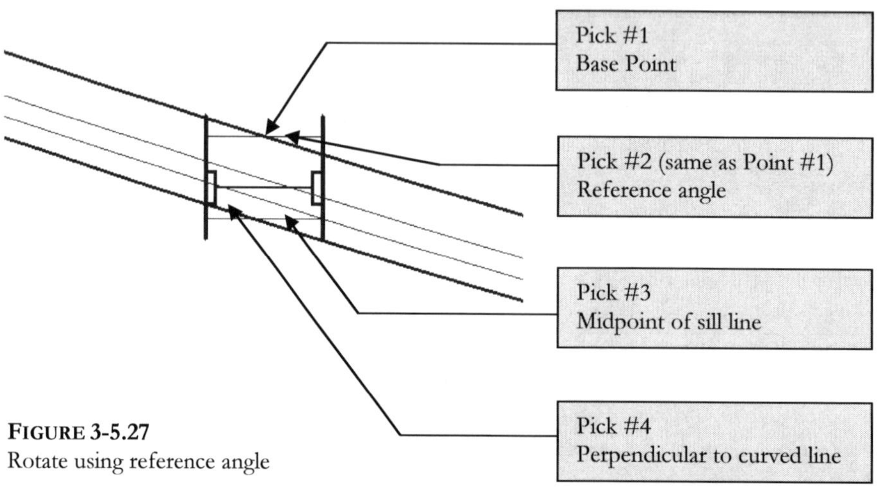

FIGURE 3-5.27
Rotate using reference angle

To finish the 2′-0″ wide window in the curved wall you need to trim the jamb lines and the wall lines; it may be helpful to *Freeze* the A-Glaz-Sill *Layer* in order to trim the wall lines that occur below the sill lines.

29. **Trim** the jamb lines and the wall lines (Figure 3-5.28).

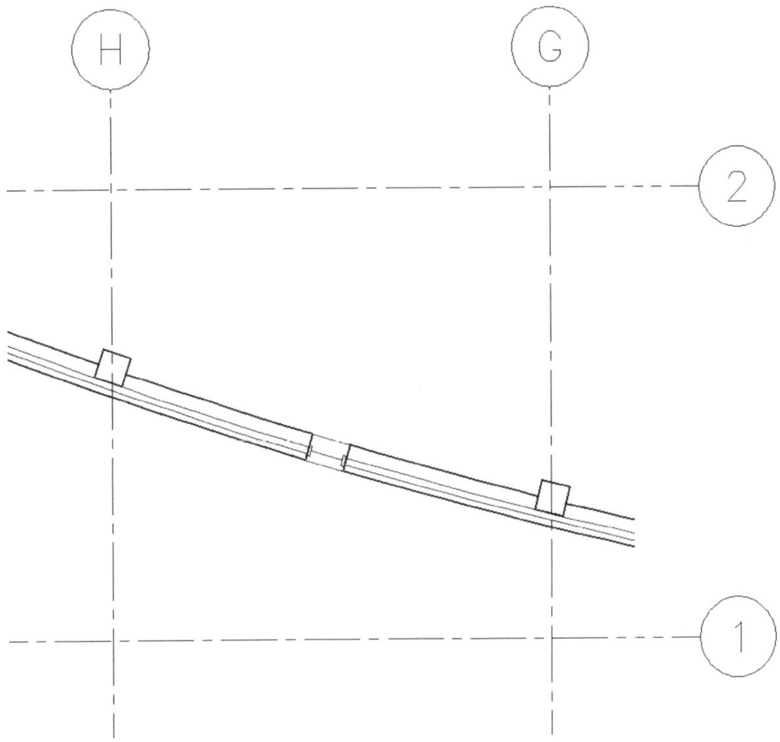

FIGURE 3-5.28 Windows added in curved wall

30. Using similar techniques to those just discussed, add the remaining windows in the curved wall; provide approximately 12″ of wall between each window (Figures 3-5.29 and 3-5.30).

This concludes this chapter on the essential components of drafting/designing a floor plan in AutoCAD. In the next chapter you will further develop several spaces.

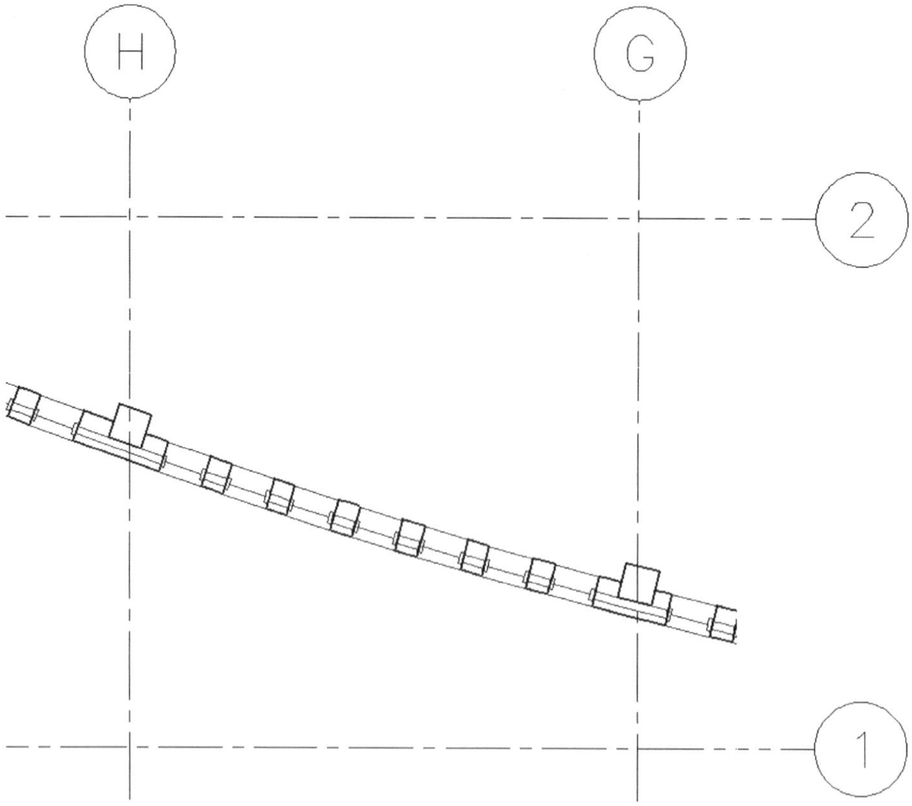

FIGURE 3-5.29 Windows added in curved wall

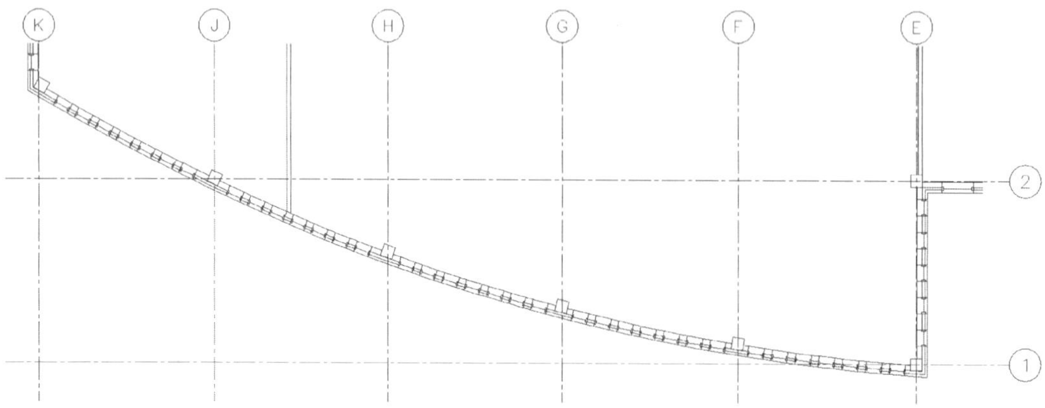

FIGURE 3-5.30 All windows added in curved wall

Self-Exam:

The following questions can be used as a way to check your knowledge of this lesson. The answers can be found at the bottom of this page.

1. It is important to place an Xref on the proper Layer. (T/F)

2. The Divide command splits the selected line into separate lines. (T/F)

3. Attach and Overlay are two ways to place an External Reference. (T/F)

4. The wall lines below a window opening go on _______________ layer.

5. You used a _________________ Block (the new multi-function blocks in AutoCAD) for the door symbol in the chapter.

Review Questions:

The following questions may be assigned by your instructor as a way to assess your knowledge of this section. Your instructor has the answers to the review questions.

1. A Block's name cannot be changed. (T/F)

2. It is important to keep track of a Block's base point when redefining it. (T/F)

3. "Middle" is the ideal justification for text in a grid bubble. (T/F)

4. When starting a "floor finish plan" you should copy the floor plan into your new drawing (T/F)

5. You can only draw within the *Drawing Limits.* (T/F)

6. All the Layers from an Xref'ed drawing have the Xref'ed drawings file name as a prefix to the *Layer* name in the "host" drawing (T/F).

7. For masonry coursing, what are the two options: 40′-____″ and 40′-____″

8. The keyboard shortcut for *Undo* is **Ctrl +** _____________ .

9. What *Layer* do the "inner" lines in a wall go on? ______________________.

10. When drawing stud walls that transition into CMU walls you need to know if the CMU will be exposed; if not, the stud wall is offset to align with the furring that covers the CMU wall. (T/F)

SELF-EXAM ANSWERS:
1 – T, **2** – F, **3** – T, **4** – A-Glaz-Sill, **5** – Dynamic

Notes:

Lesson 4
Library Project: FLOOR PLANS – Part 2

In this lesson you will continue to develop your floor plan for the Campus Library project; in the previous chapter you drew the walls, doors, windows and columns/grids. Throughout this lesson you will be introduced to a few new commands and design concepts. Specifically, you will add stairs, elevators, toilet room fixtures and casework.

The image below is another reminder of what your plan will look like when you finish Lesson 5. Notice, again, the classrooms in the lower-right, the office area in the upper-left, the main toilet rooms in the lower-left, the public concourse across the top, and the check-out area in the middle.

It is important to remember that your drawings are to comply with the “office standards” outlined in Appendix A; this includes layer naming conventions, lineweight standards (which are based on the lines color), dimension and text standards, dimscale and ltscale settings, and abbreviations. As previously mentioned, this is intended to simulate a real-world office environment.

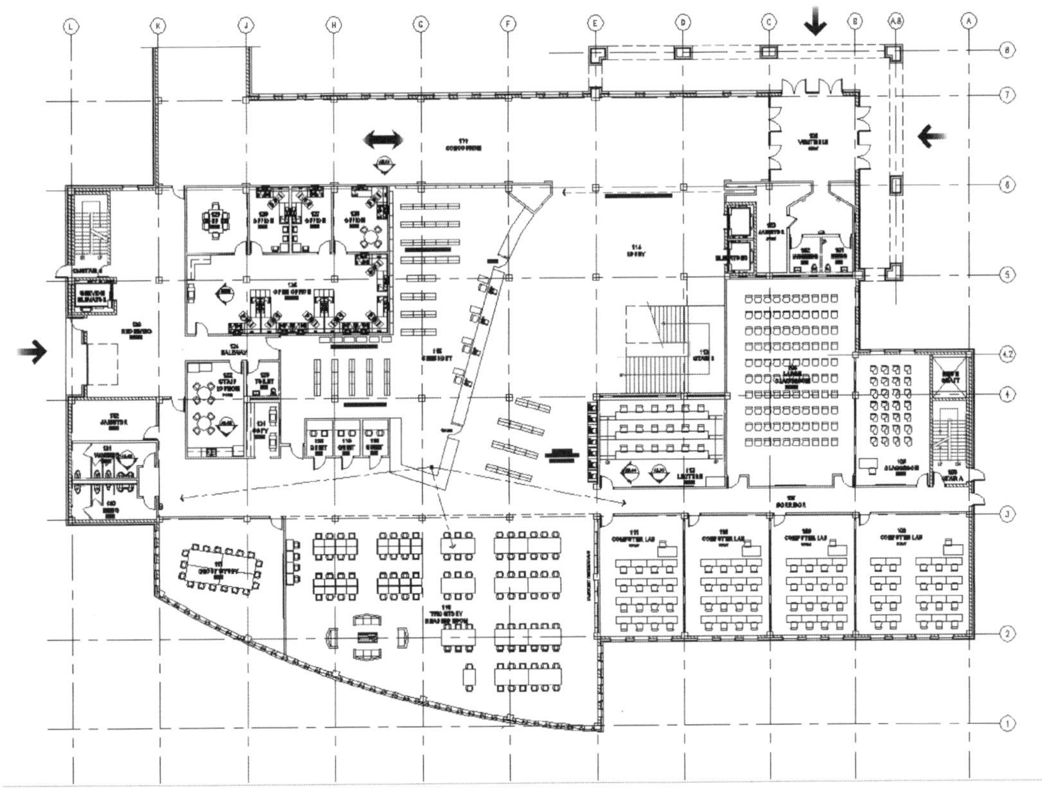

OVERVIEW: Example of what will be drawn in this book - First Floor Plan

Exercise 4-1:
Toilet Room Layout

Introduction

There are several important factors in laying out a toilet room. The primary consideration is typically accessibility; that is complying with local, state and federal accessibility codes so that people with various handicaps can easily access and use the toilet room facilities (or the entire building in general).

Other considerations include sight-lines. It is undesirable for a person in the hallway to see any of the toilet fixtures when the door is being opened by someone entering that space. It should be obvious that privacy (especially between males and females) should be expected in a toilet room design. Seeing the sinks (i.e., people washing their hands) is not too bad but the designer needs to make sure the sight-lines are not extended by the mirror above the sink. The design techniques employed to impede improper sight-lines often takes up a fair amount of floor space.

Another consideration has to do with the plumbing fixtures. It is important to have the correct type of fixture drawn and have it drawn the correct size. Some of the code requirements are based on the clear space in front of the fixture; thus, the fixture needs to be the correct size in order to verify compliance. Also, whether the fixture is wall-hung or a floor mounted tank-type fixture is important; the mechanical engineer needs to know (they specify the fixture in the Project Manual). If the toilet is wall-hung the wall needs to be thick enough to conceal the support bracket and the plumbing (the wall is even thicker when two toilets are back-to-back). From a Designer standpoint, wall-hung toilets are often desirable in commercial buildings because they are easy to clean under and can be equipped with automatic flushing to help ensure a better "space experience" for everyone!

Downloading Content from the Internet:

In the next several steps you will get a better understanding of how you can get CAD content from the Internet to use in your drawings.

> *A word of warning before proceeding:*
>
> Do not assume all CAD content found on the Internet is worthy of using in your drawings. There are many locations on the web where individuals have uploaded CAD drawings that are less than perfect, so use caution. On the other hand, if you are downloading content from a product manufacturer's website, you can be more confident that they have accurately drawn their own product and want you to have a successful project using both their product and CAD files!

In this exercise you will be instructed on how to download toilets, sinks and drinking fountains from a plumbing manufacturer's website. The AutoCAD drawing files you download will be saved to your hard drive and then inserted using the Insert [block] command.

In an office setting you might want to save the downloaded plumbing fixture drawings to a "Plumbing Fixtures" folder on your hard drive for convenient access in the future.

You will need to have access to the Internet for the next several steps…

1. Open your internet browser: Chrome, MS Edge, etc.

Next you will be instructed to browse to a major plumbing manufacturer's website.

2. Browse to the **Kohler** website (Figure 4-1.1) by entering the URL **https://www.us.kohler.com/us/** and then pressing **Enter**.

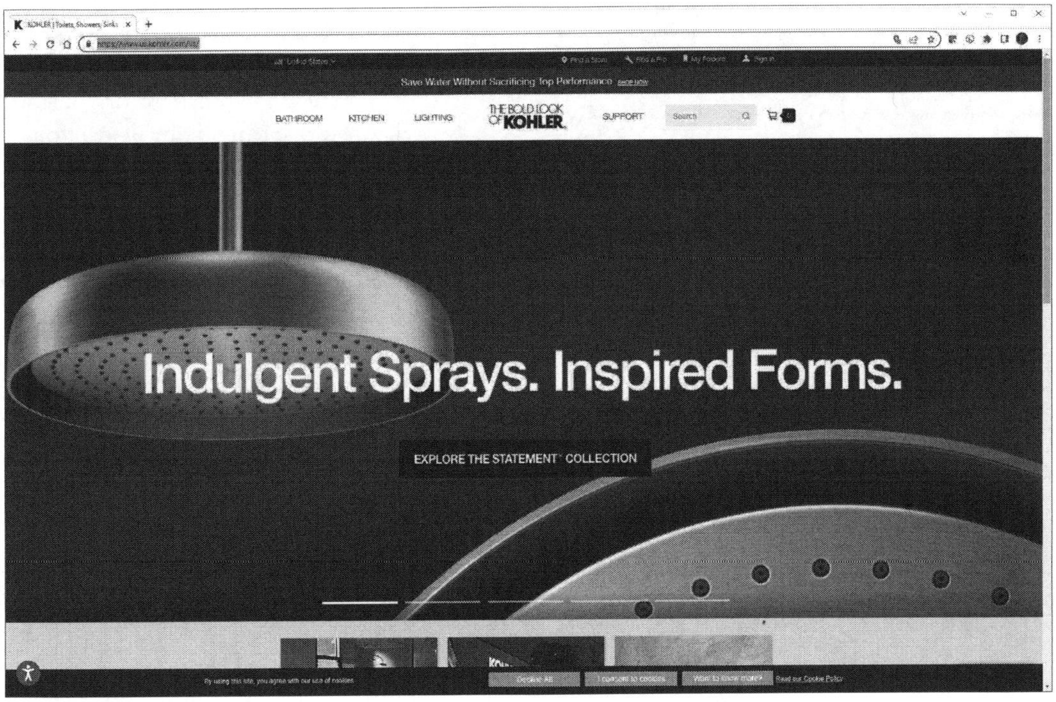

FIGURE 4-1.1 Plumbing manufacturer website

> *FYI: As you should be well aware, websites can change at any given moment. Companies often update their websites as new content becomes available or a fresh new look is desired. Even the model numbers change from time to time. So if the screen shots shown here are different than what you see on your screen you will have to interpret the steps based on what you see; you will likely still have access to the same content.*

3. Click in the textbox next to *Search* at the top of the webpage; type **kingston** and press **Enter**.

4. Click directly on the toilet image for model **K-4323-0** (Figure 4-1.2).

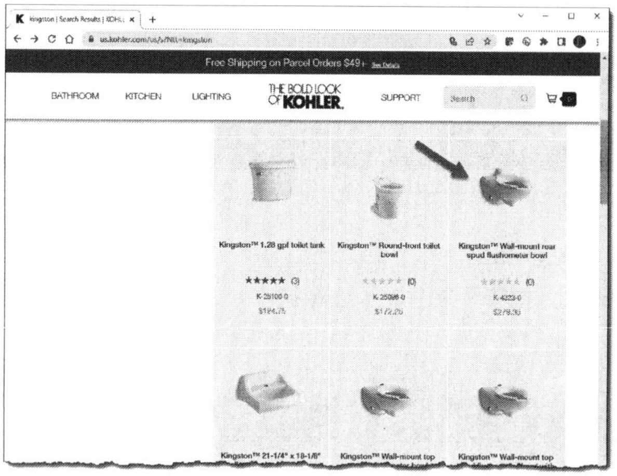

FIGURE 4-1.2 Website: www.kohler.com; search results

Take a minute to review the features of this toilet fixture.

5. Scroll down the page, click **Design Files**.

The previous step reveals specific design and installation information for the toilet (Figure 4-1.3).

The next link you are instructed to click will allow you to save a CAD file of this fixture to your hard drive. If in a classroom setting, your instructor may direct you to save these files to a different location.

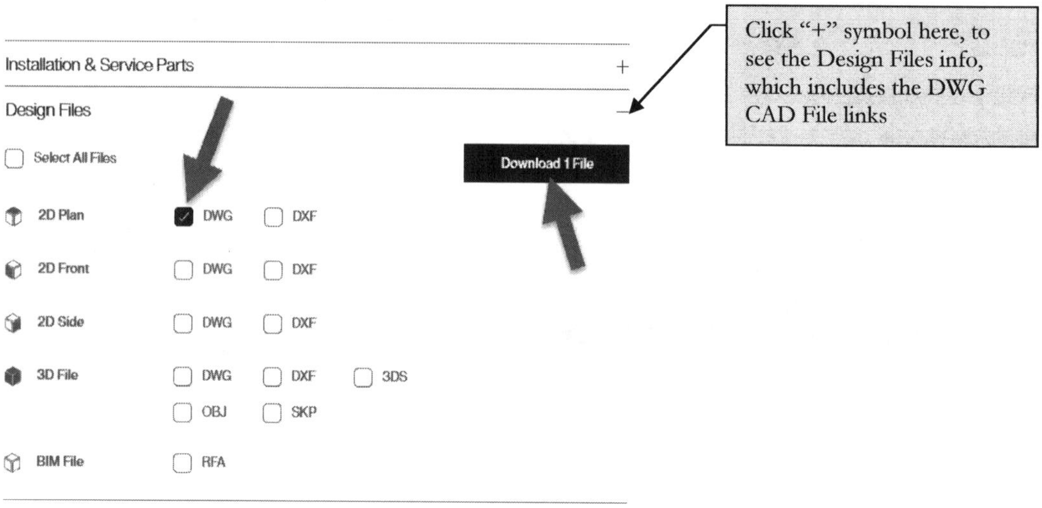

FIGURE 4-1.3 Website: www.kohler.com; downloading CAD Files

6. Click **DWG** next to *2D Plan View* and the download button to save the file to your *Downloads* folder.

Make sure you selected DWG CAD Files and not DXF CAD Files. The former is the native AutoCAD file format, and the latter is a file format conceived by Autodesk to allow designers to share CAD information between AutoCAD and other CAD programs not written by Autodesk. The DWG file format is more readily inserted into your current drawing than DXF (**D**rawing e**X**change **F**ormat).

You now have a copy of the toilet fixture on your hard drive, and it is ready to be placed in your floor plan! The file you just downloaded is named 4323pln.dwg and is saved in the

Windows *Downloads* folder; the name is the model number plus the view (pln for plan-view in this case). If you open the file directly you will notice the origin has been conveniently located at the back/ center of the fixture and all lines are on Layer zero. Having all lines on Layer zero is preferred; this way all lines in the *Block* will take on the properties of the *Layer* the *Block* is placed on.

Next you will be instructed to download the other fixtures required for your floor plan. Rather than giving you step-by-step instructions you will simply be given the model numbers; you can then find and download the other fixtures using similar techniques to those just covered.

7. Download the other two views (front and side) of the toilet.

8. Using techniques previously covered, download all three views (plan, front and side), from the Kohler website, for the plumbing fixtures listed below:
   - **K-2007 Kingston wall-mount lavatory**
   - **K-5024-T Dartfield Urinal**
   - **K-5250 Serra Drinking Fountain** (*discontinued, files provided with book*)

When finished you should have the following files listed in your **My Documents** folder:

- 5250sde.dwg
- 5250pln.dwg
- 5250frt.dwg
- 5024tsde.dwg
- 5024tpln.dwg
- 5024tfrt.dwg
- 4329sde.dwg
- 4329pln.dwg
- 4329frt.dwg
- 2007sde.dwg
- 2007pln.dwg
- 2007frt.dwg

Next you will draw a "lavatory system" from another major plumbing manufacturer called Bradley Corporation. You can also download this one from the Internet (and you will be given the URL), but the file is composed of multiple views and information, plus it is in a ZIP file, which makes for more work (as far as this tutorial is concerned).

9. *If you prefer to try the download*, browse to the following URL: https://www.bradleycorp.com/product/2-station-express-lavatory-system
   a. Click the link to download the CAD Files.
   b. You can also search for 2 Station Express Lavatory, Model **SS-2N**

10. In a new drawing, draw the *Lavatory System* shown in **Figure 4-1.4**; make sure the origin is at the back and centered.
    a. Approximate all dims and arcs not specified.
    b. Draw everything on *Layer* zero.

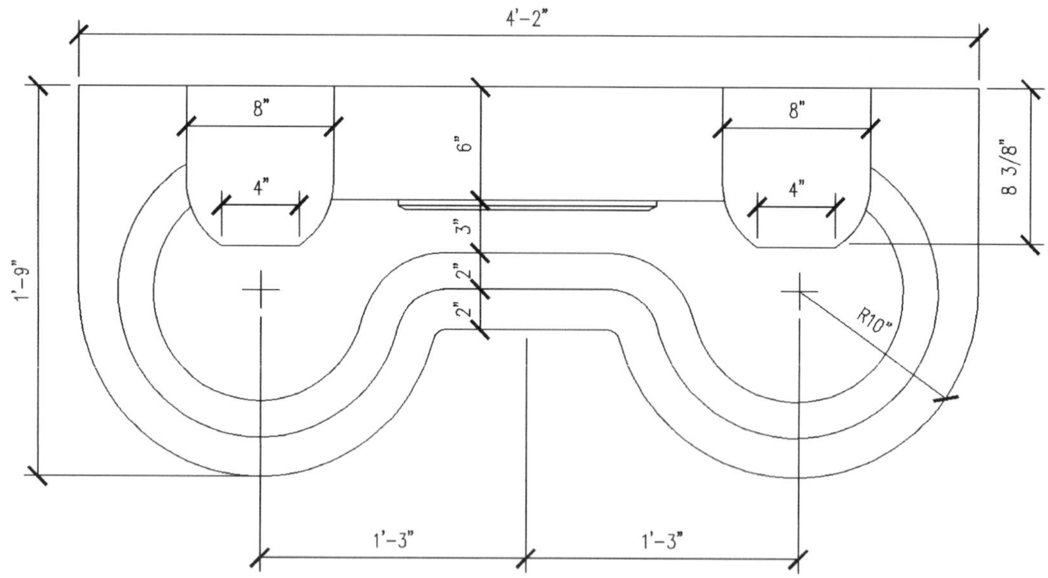

FIGURE 4-1.4 Draw this lavatory system in a new drawing file with origin centered on the back side

11. Save your drawing into your project folder; name the file **Lav_System_pln.dwg**.

Your new drawing file is now ready to be inserted into the floor plan drawing when needed!

12. **Close** the lavatory drawing.

You are now ready to add the plumbing fixtures to your floor plan. You will start with the small toilet rooms near the main entry.

13. Open your floor plan drawing, **DJS55803AGD01.dwg**.

14. Add the plumbing fixtures as shown in Figure 4-1.5, *plus*:
    a. Make sure the fixtures go on *Layer* **A-Mech-Pfix**.
    b. See **Figure 4-1.6a** for the grab bar dimensions.
    c. Draw the grab bars on Layer **A-Flor-Accs**.
    d. The room on the right has a toilet, sink and urinal.
    e. The room on the left has a toilet and a sink.
    f. Add a **drinking fountain** in the hallway.
    g. Do not draw the dimensions or the dashed lines.

TIP: *Select* ***Insert*** *from the* ***Insert*** *tab, and then click* ***Blocks from Library****. This will allow you to select AutoCAD drawing files from your hard drive to be inserted into the current drawing (onto the current Layer).*

The dashed lines shown in Figure 4-1.5 represent the clear floor space that must be considered when designing the layout of a toilet room. This tutorial will not get into the specifics related to the clear floor space at each fixture type; but you may want to consider creating a special layer to place this information on so it can be turned off when not needed.

Another technique you might consider related to clear floor space is to add these dashed lines to your *Blocks*. You can leave the fixture on *Layer* zero and add the dashed lines on a specific *Layer*. That way, when the "clear floor space" *Layer* is turned off, the fixture will still be visible (as long as the fixture was not inserted on the "clear floor space" *Layer*, or any other *Layer* that is turned off). You will employ this technique in Lesson 5 when you create furniture and fixture symbols (i.e., Blocks).

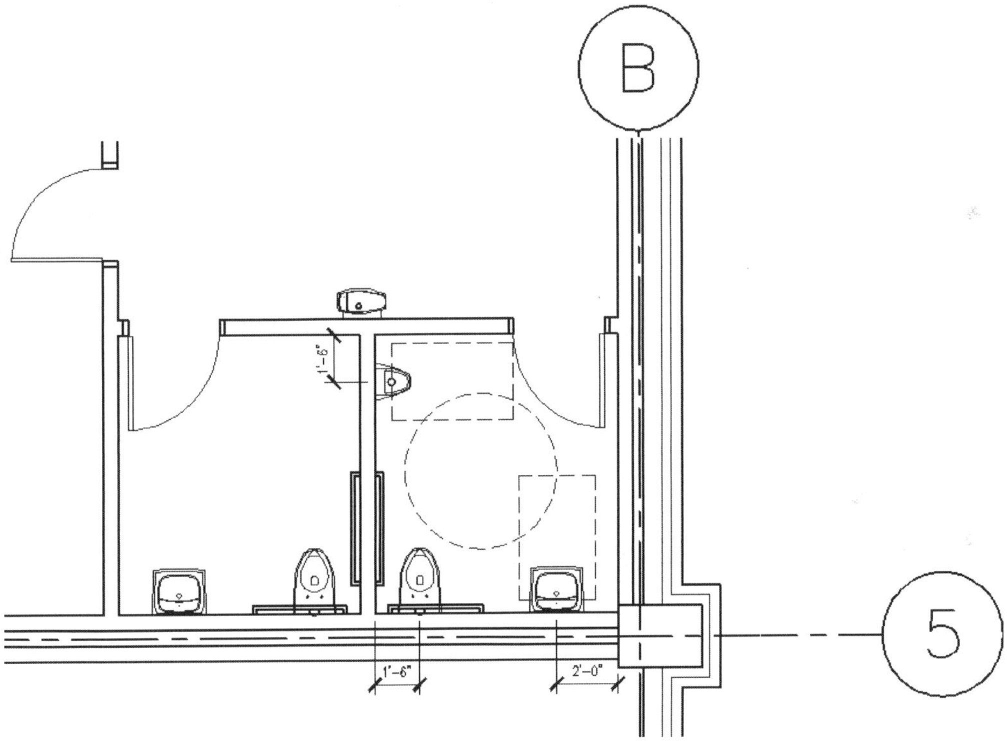

FIGURE 4-1.5 Place the fixtures shown (do not draw the dashed lines)

The sight-lines are not too bad here, considering the shape of the room outside the toilet rooms. However, the line of sight is not as critical in this situation because the toilet rooms are for single users. Most designers still prefer to ensure that plumbing fixtures are not visible from adjacent rooms, especially off of main entries and lobbies. In this case you created a small alcove-type space where a person needs to go out of their way to be in a position where the sight-lines matter; even a person walking straight towards the drinking fountain will not have any sort of vantage point towards the plumbing fixtures.

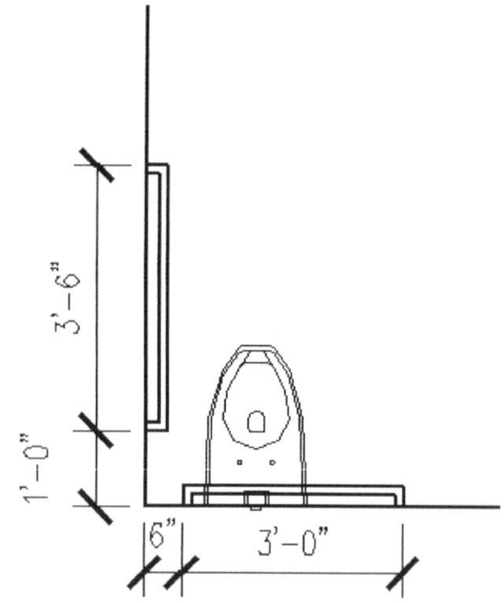

FIGURE 4-1.6A Grab bar dimensions; 1 ½" diameter pipe

FIGURE 4-1.6B Grab bar picture
Codes vary by location; some US states require a vertical bar as shown above.

Drawing the Large Multi-User Toilet Room:

You will jump right in and place the plumbing fixtures and then you will add the toilet partitions and review the sight-lines from the adjacent hallway. You will also review the requirements for wall thicknesses behind the wall-hung toilets.

15. Insert the plumbing fixtures as shown in Figure 4-1.7, *plus*:
    a. Make sure the fixtures go on Layer **A-Mech-Pfix**.
    b. See **Figure 4-1.6a** for the grab bar dimensions; see Figure 4-1.8 for grab bar locations.
    c. The northern room has (3) toilets and a Lavatory System.
    d. The southern room has (2) toilets, a urinal and a Lavatory System (obviously this is the Men's toilet room).

Sight-lines are typically explored by drawing a line from the adjacent hallway (or space), through the door opening, into the toilet room. Looking at Figure 4-1.7 you can see the sight-lines are quite acceptable. As previously mentioned, this design solution takes up a fair amount of floor space but is necessary.

An unacceptable design solution is shown in **Figure 4-1.8**. The toilet room is much larger and can even have another toilet fixture without the door modification for sight-lines; also, the door is right off the circulation path, which can be problematic. Notice two lines are shown to visualize the full visual range. Granted, some of this view is obstructed by a person's body as they pass through the door opening; it is still an undesirable design solution.

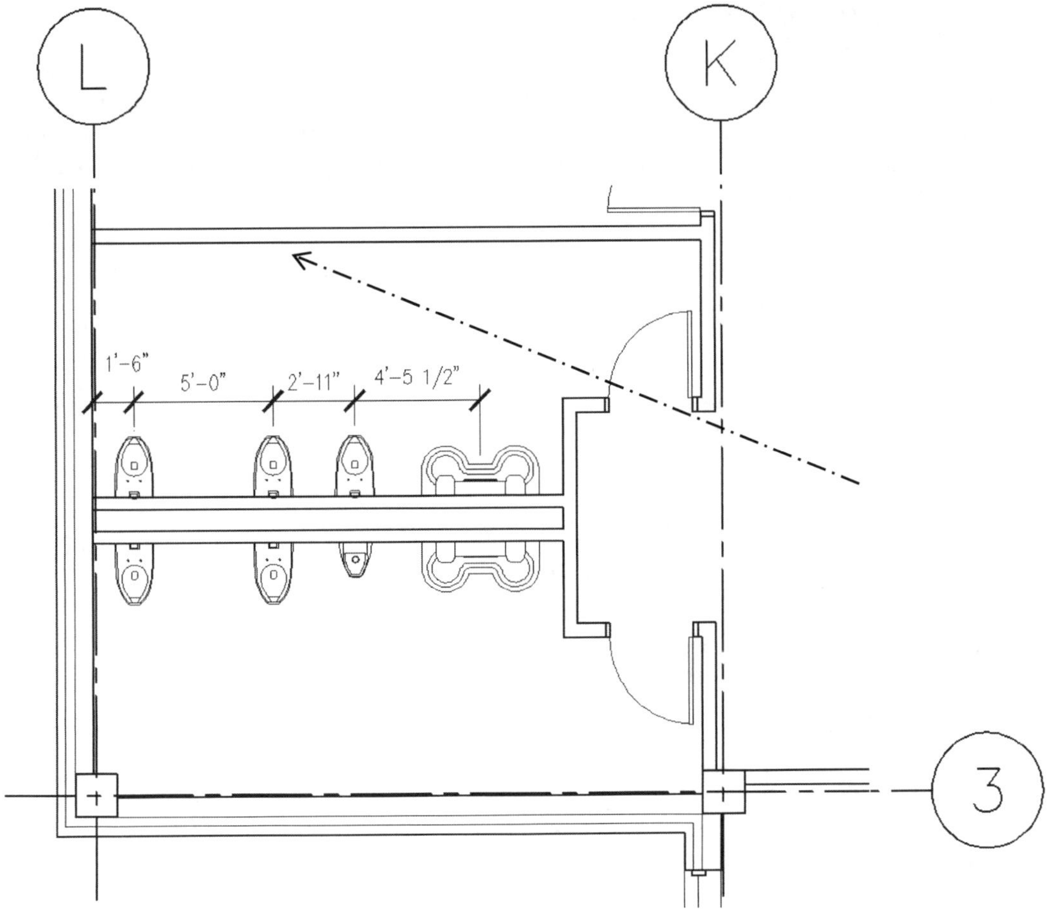

FIGURE 4-1.7 Place the fixtures shown; dashed line shows sightline

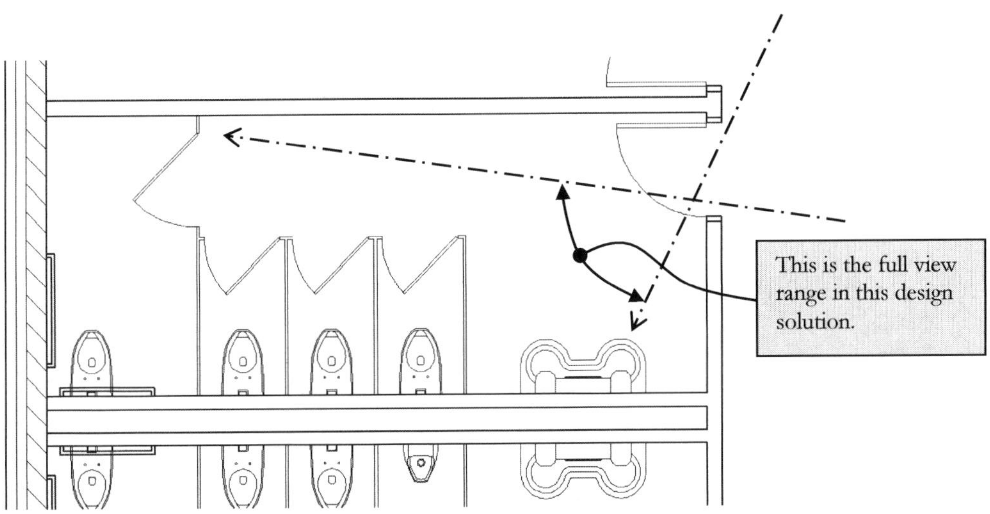

FIGURE 4-1.8 Dashed lines reveal unacceptable sightlines into the toilet room

Adding the Toilet Partitions:

The toilet partitions offer privacy for toilets and urinals. They come in a few styles and materials. Styles range from floor mounted to ceiling hung; the latter offers better access to cleaning the floors, like wall-hung toilets. Materials range from prefinished metal to Solid Phenolic Core (i.e., plastic) to stainless steel.

The divider panels, pilasters and doors come in various thicknesses. However, each is typically drawn 1″ thick and is dimensioned to the center of the panel so the thickness is not too important.

If you want to see images and more information on toilet partitions you can visit the Bradley Corporation website list below (select one of the Tech data sheet PDF links):
https://www.bradleycorp.com/product/bradmar-partitions

The example to the left shows a floor mounted, overhead-braced toilet partition system.

Also notice the urinal screen at the end of the countertop.

Floor drains are usually positioned beneath a toilet partition so users do not have to walk over the slightly uneven surface.

Notice the accent floor tile that also takes into consideration the location of the toilet partitions.

Accessibility codes offer several layout options for toilet partitions. For example, if the door swings into the stall, more room is required in the stall to maintain the required clear floor space for the toilet fixture. Having a cheat-sheet of several different layout options is a big help. Consult your local code for specifics.

The preceding image is very similar to the Men's toilet room you are currently working on.

16. Draw the toilet partitions as shown in Figure 4-1.9, *plus*:
    a. Make sure the partitions go on Layer **A-Flor-Tptn**.
    b. Use lines and arcs to draw the partitions; show all **1″ thick**.
    c. Do not draw the dimensions.
    d. Draw a **36″ wide door** into the end stall (i.e., Accessible Stall).
    e. Draw **30″ wide doors** centered on the remaining stalls.
    f. Draw the grab bars on *Layer* **A-Flor-Accs**.

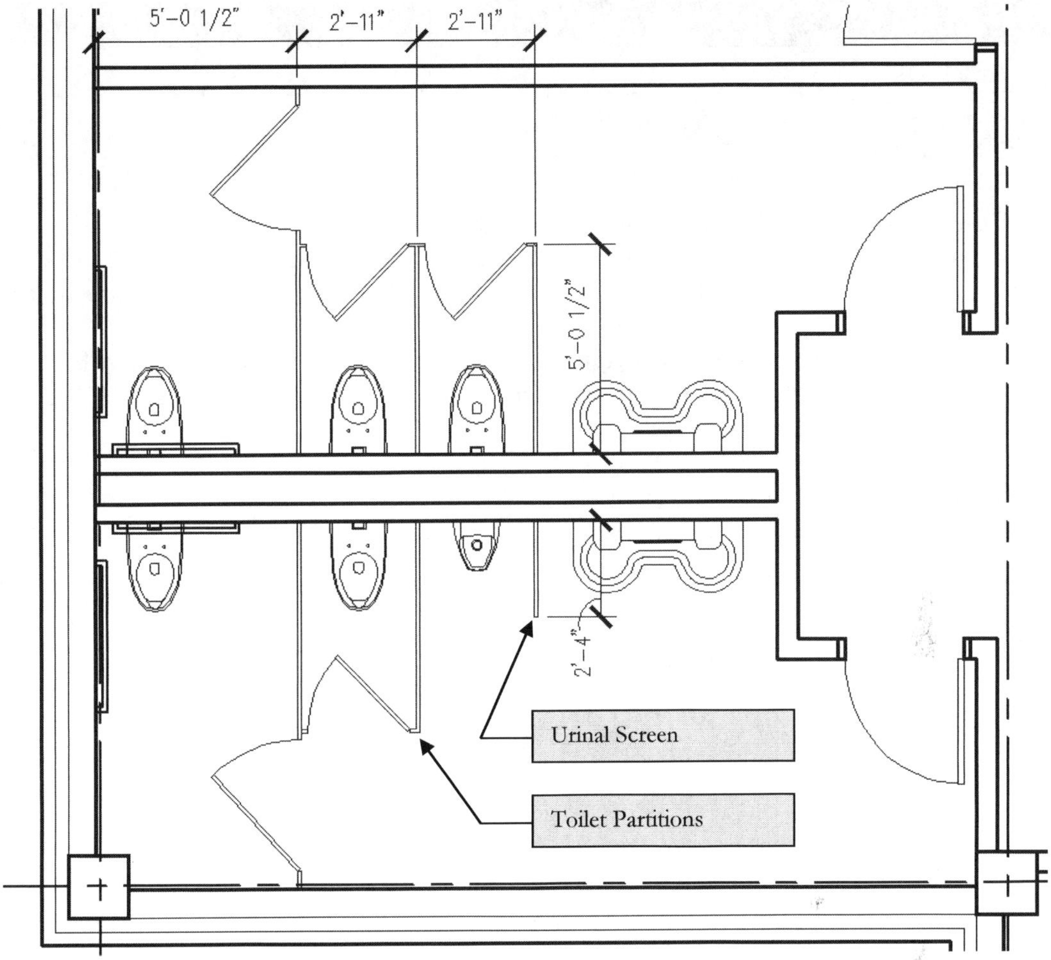

FIGURE 4-1.9 Drawing the toilet partitions and urinal screen

17. Add a **drinking fountain** just to the east (right) of the Men's toilet room, and centered on the wall, as shown in Figure 4-1.10.

For info on wall thicknesses behind double-hung toilets visit: **www.pdionline.org** and review the Publication: *Minimum Space Requirements for Enclosed Plumbing Fixture Supports.*

This concludes the toilet room floor plan exercise. You will study this a little more in the toilet room interior elevations tutorial later in this book.

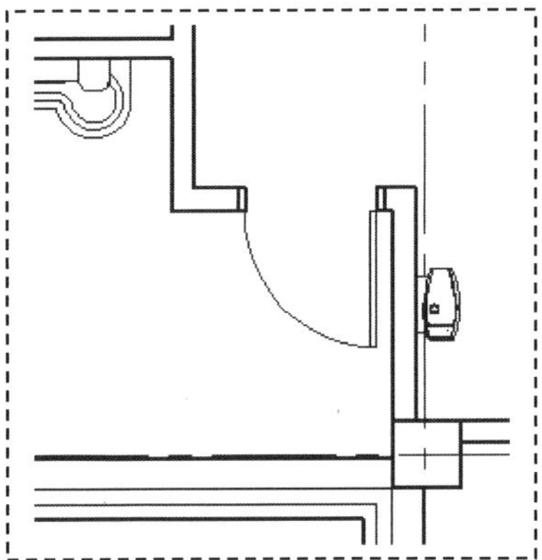

FIGURE 4-1.10 Drinking fountain centered on wall

Exercise 4-2:
Casework

Introduction

This exercise covers the basic techniques used to represent casework in plan. Casework is typically any built-in cabinets, countertops, desks, bars, etc. and is usually installed by a carpenter. This does not include systems furniture which is sometimes attached to the wall.

The architectural floor plans typically show the built-in items (i.e., casework) and the FFE Plan (furniture, fixtures and equipment) typically show the moveable items. The FFE Plans are covered in the next chapter.

The words "typical" and "usually" are used a lot because there is no exact science to how a set of drawings are put together. They can vary by country, state, city and even office.

First you will draw the casework in the open office area. These upper and lower cabinets represent the work area where copying and mailing occurs.

Work Area Cabinets:

Cabinets in a work area can vary quite a bit depending on the work being performed there. The picture below is similar to what you will be drawing next. The **base cabinets** are on the floor and are typically 24″ deep (but come in a variety of depths). The **wall cabinets** are attached to the wall and also come in various depths (12″ and 14″ being the most common).

As you can see the **electrical outlets** need to be coordinated with the electrical engineer; they need to be installed above the countertop and below the wall cabinets. When preparing the program, the designer (Architect or Interior Designer) should get a list of all the equipment required in each area. This will determine the number of outlets and locations. Often, items are overlooked or added later that can create an unsafe strain on the electrical system or require extension cords. For example, it is possible that the microwave shown in the image below was added by the users long after the design of the building; if the electrical system did not have enough capacity, it could make for an unsafe condition. If that were the case, a new outlet on another circuit would need to be added.

Notice two things about the wall cabinets: **1)** The cabinets have "**under-counter lights**" across the entire length. If this is desired by the client/designer, the electrical drawings need to be coordinated, and the bottom of the cabinet recessed so the light fixture is not directly seen. **2)** The space between the top of the cabinet and the ceiling is filled in with studs and gypsum board for a clean, dust-free finish (not always in the budget).

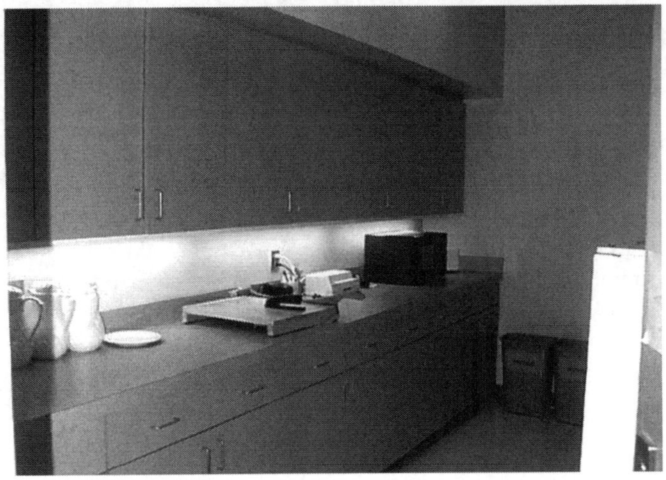

Example of typical work room cabinets; see comments on previous page

1. Draw the casework shown in Figure 4-2.1, *plus*:
    a. Base cabinet lines on Layer **A-Case**.
    b. Wall cabinet lines on Layer **A-Case-Abov**.
        i. Make sure you set the linetype correctly.
    c. Do not draw the dimensions.

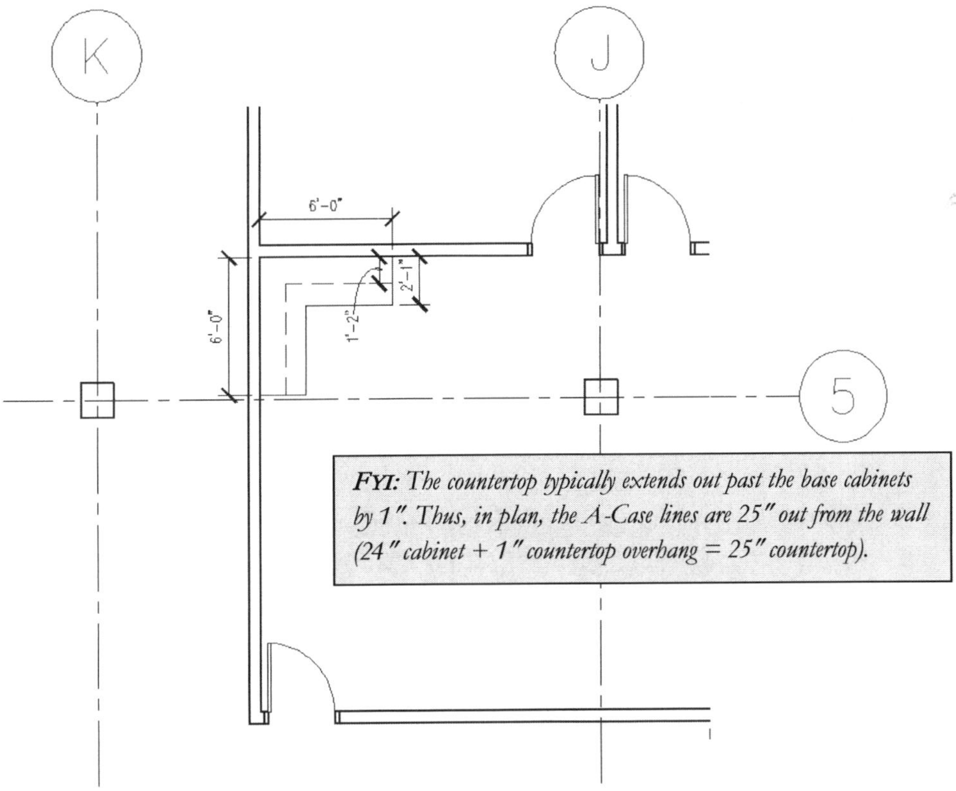

> ***FYI:** The countertop typically extends out past the base cabinets by 1". Thus, in plan, the A-Case lines are 25" out from the wall (24" cabinet + 1" countertop overhang = 25" countertop).*

FIGURE 4-2.1 Drawing the work area casework

Break Room Cabinets:

The cabinets in the break room have similar considerations as the work room cabinets. Additionally, you often have plumbing to coordinate as well (e.g., a sink or dishwasher). When drawing plans, these items are roughly placed and then more refined later with interior elevations, then the plans are updated.

The first thing you will do, to prepare for laying out the break room counter, is to draw a two-compartment sink.

2. In a new drawing, create the two-compartment sink as specified below (save to your project folder):

filename: **Sink-1.dwg**

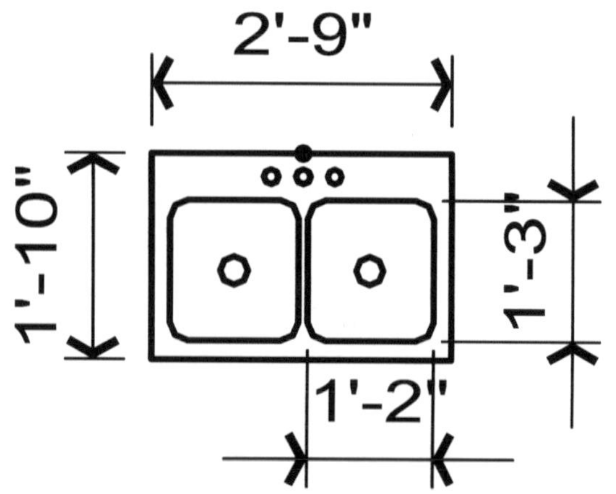

Draw this sink per the following specifications:

- 2″ space (i.e., offset) at sides and front.
- 3″ Dia. Circles centered in sinks.
- 2″ rad. for *Fillets*.
- 1½″ Dia. at faucet spaces; 3 ½″ apart.
- Black dot = *Origin*
- All on *Layer* zero.

3. Draw the cabinets shown in Figure 4-2.2, *plus*:
    a. The wall cabinets extend the full length of the room (14′-6″).
    b. The 3′-0″ space will accommodate a refrigerator.
    c. The countertop is at two heights; the sink area is lower for handicap accessibility (covered more with interior elevations).
    d. Add the two-compartment sink drawn in the previous step.
    e. Ensure the sink is placed on the correct *Layer (TIP: Plumbing)*.

***FYI:** The wall cabinets are shown with dashed line work in plan because they are assumed to occur above the floor plan cut plane. This also helps to differentiate between wall and base cabinets (the dashed line is controlled by the Layer).*

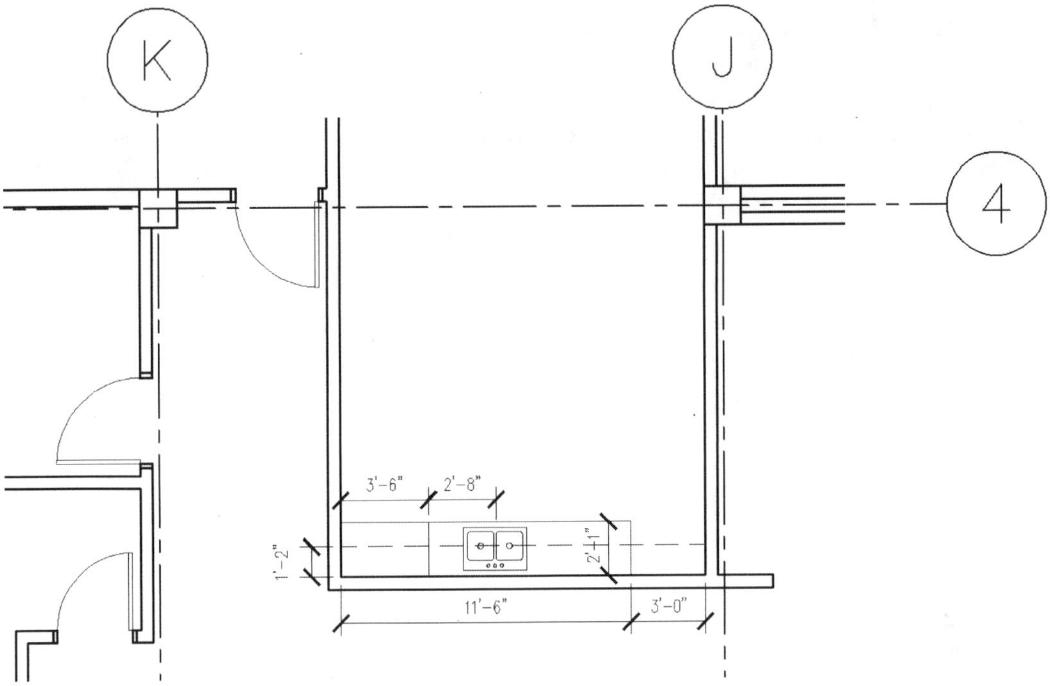

FIGURE 4-2.2 Drawing the break room casework

4. Draw the cabinets shown in Figure 4-2.3, *plus*:
   a. The wall cabinets are 14″ deep.
   b. The countertop is 25″ deep.

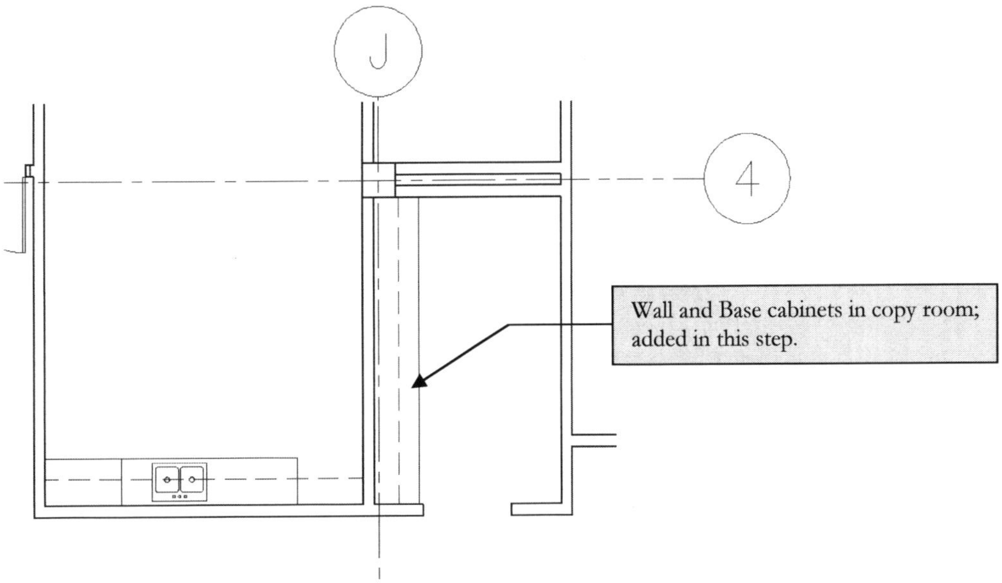

FIGURE 4-2.3 Drawing the copy room casework

Checkout Counter:

In the previous steps you placed base and wall cabinets, now you will design the checkout counter. The checkout counter is what is referred to as "custom casework." The base and wall cabinets can also be "custom casework" or they can be ordered from a catalog (the latter being the less expensive option).

Basically, "custom casework" is anything a local cabinet/woodworking shop would build, typically built in their shop and assembled on-site.

Custom casework gives the designer a wide range of functional and aesthetic opportunities. As you can see in the Figure on the next page (Figure 4-2.4), the angles and curves require a custom-built solution; these shaped cabinets are not found in a catalog of standard cabinets.

The cost associated with custom casework is, of course, higher than standard stock items. When the client can afford custom, they have the opportunity to get a more functional space in which to work. For example, a drawer can be located wherever it is needed, and a cubby can be made just the right size to hold the companies "odd" sized shopping bags (which make for better use of space and keeps the bags stacked neatly).

The checkout counter represents a drafting exercise where you have to draw various angles and curves per the given instructions. It is easy to draw linework in AutoCAD that kind of looks like what it should be, but it is the designer/drafter's responsibility to draw things accurately so things go smoothly during construction. This type of structured drafting, no matter if on your own time or in a classroom setting, will make you better prepared and more efficient in the workplace. Your instructor may have you print the checkout counter to scale and check it with an accurate drawing on transparence paper.

5. Draw the checkout counter shown in Figure 4-2.4a, *plus*:
    a. Draw all linework on **A-Case** layer.
    b. The countertop is **36"** deep.
    c. The doors (i.e., gates) are **36"** wide.
    d. The exact location of the gates does not matter (visually close).
    e. Do not draw the dimensions.
    f. Trim the curved line at grid 5 and then draw the longer angled line by "connecting-the-dots"; see Figure 4-2.4b.
        i. Select the line and use Properties to determine the length and angle (i.e., the "???" dimensions shown).
    g. Notice the radius for the curved portion of the counter matches the radius of the adjacent curved wall previously drawn; the casework line is held back slightly from the face of the wall.

***TIP:** Draw one side of the counter and then use **Offset** to create the other side.*

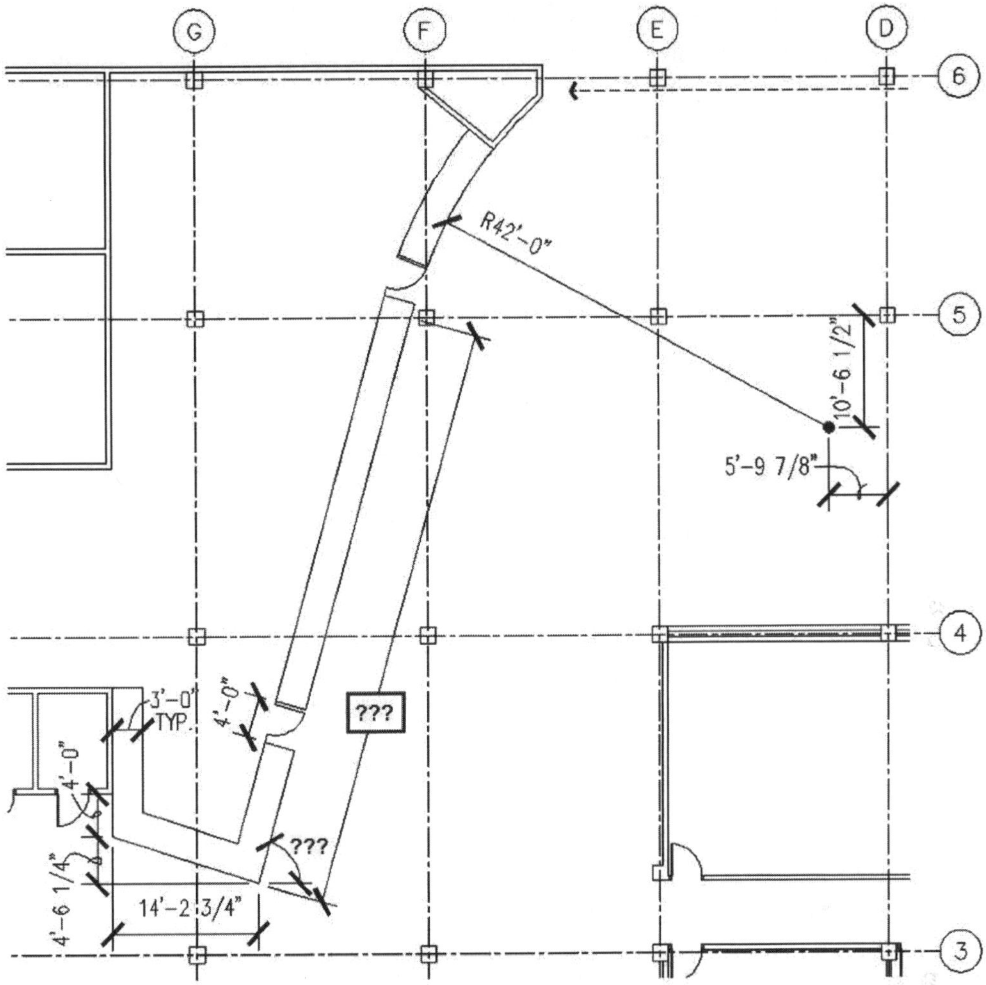

FIGURE 4-2.4A Drawing the checkout counter casework

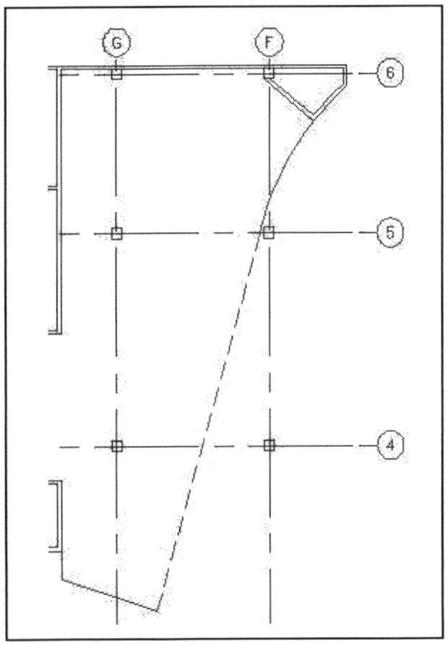

FIGURE 4-2.4B Drawing last main line

Thinking about sightlines again, looking at Figure 4-2.5, you can see the sightlines that have been added show how the design of the counter enhances the Librarian's ability to monitor the adjacent spaces.

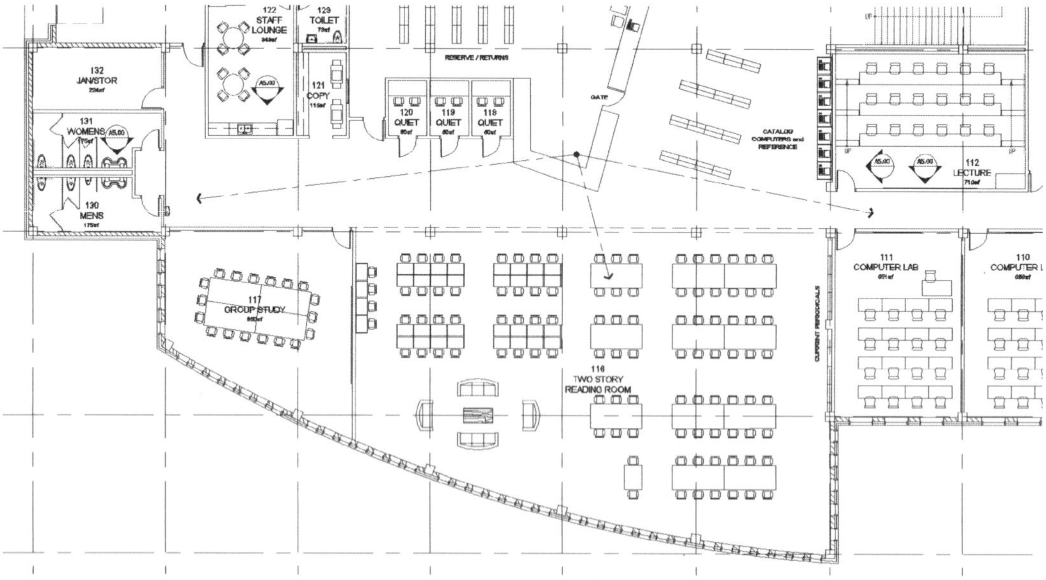

FIGURE 4-2.5 Reviewing sightlines associated with the checkout counter

CHECKOUT COUNTER EXAMPLE Second floor view showing gate and accessible checkout area with lower countertop.

Exercise 4-3:
Stairs and Elevators

Introduction

In this exercise you will add the stairs and elevators. There are several things to consider when drafting and designing these components within a building. Similar to the plumbing fixtures, you will download the elevator drawings from the internet.

Adding the Passenger Elevators:

Elevators come in several models and sizes. In this tutorial you will be adding two passenger elevators and a service elevator. Selecting the model and size depends on several factors such as: expected number of passengers in a given period of time, number of floors served, budget and speed to name a few.

In this made-up library project, the passenger elevators will have high quality finishes and are intended primarily for people (i.e., the public and staff) and book carts. The service elevator is only accessible by staff and has durable finishes to withstand large items being moved in and out on a regular basis.

The following steps could aid in determining the elevator shaft size. However, this information was previously given when you drew the walls.

Again, you will need access to the Internet before proceeding with this exercise.

1. Open your internet browser.

FIGURE 4-3.1 Elevator manufacturer's website

Next you will be instructed to browse to a major elevator manufacturer's website.

2. Browse to the **ThyssenKrupp Elevator** website by entering the URL **https://www.tkelevator.com/us-en/** and then press **Enter** (Figure 4-3.1).

3. Click the **Products → Elevators → All Elevators → All Elevators** (Fig 4-3.2).

4. Now select the **All Elevators** link (i.e., a link on the far left).

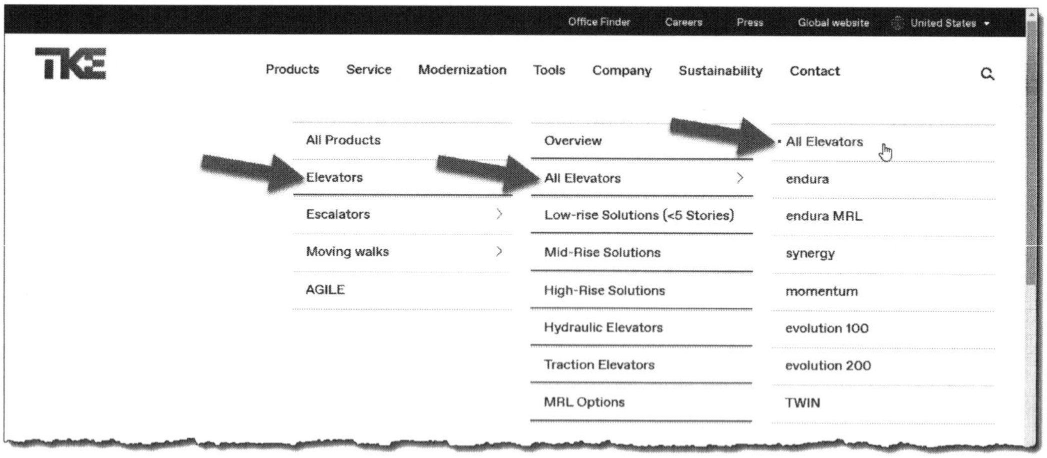

FIGURE 4-3.2 Select the 'All Elevators' option under Products

5. Click the **endura** product line option (Figure 4-3.3).

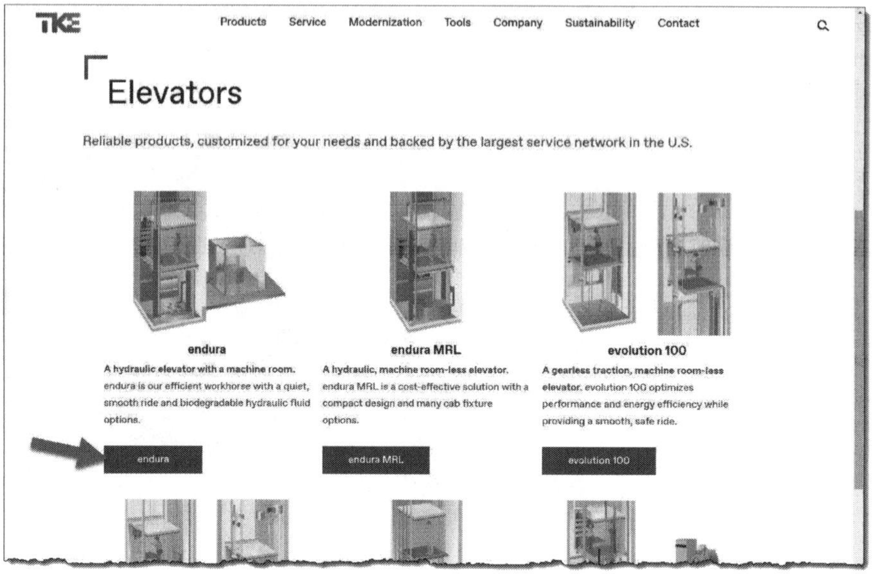

FIGURE 4-3.3 Elevator manufacturer's website

Next, you will use their wizard to configure an elevator.

6. Click the **Plan Your Elevator** button (Figure 4-3.4).

7. Select the following options (Figure 4-3.5):

   - Speed: **80** fpm
   - Capacity: **3500** lbs
   - Door Type: **Center**
   - Opening: **Front**

8. Click the **Access your drawings** button at the bottom of the view (Figure 4-3.5).

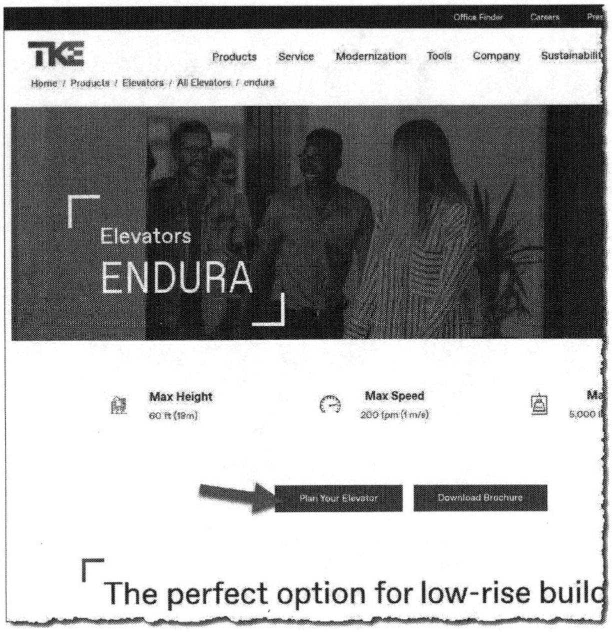

FIGURE 4-3.4 Elevator configuration wizard

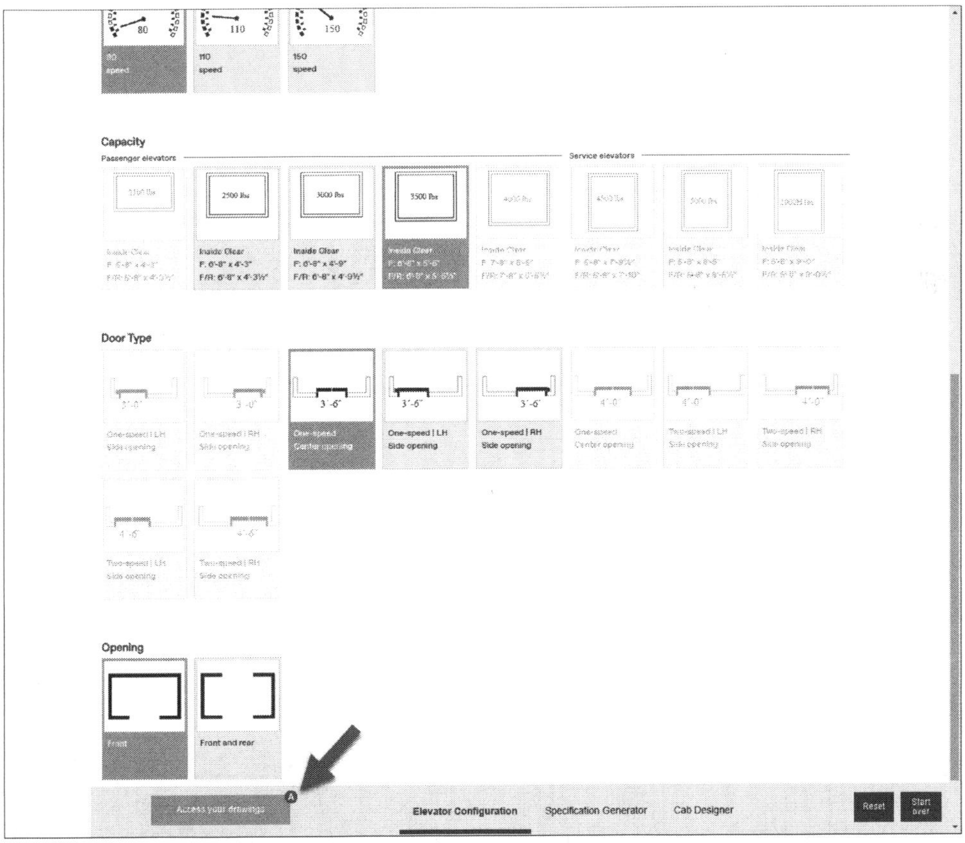

FIGURE 4-3.5 Elevator configuration wizard selections

9. Click the **DWG drawings** button in the Non-seismic section (Figure 4-3.6).

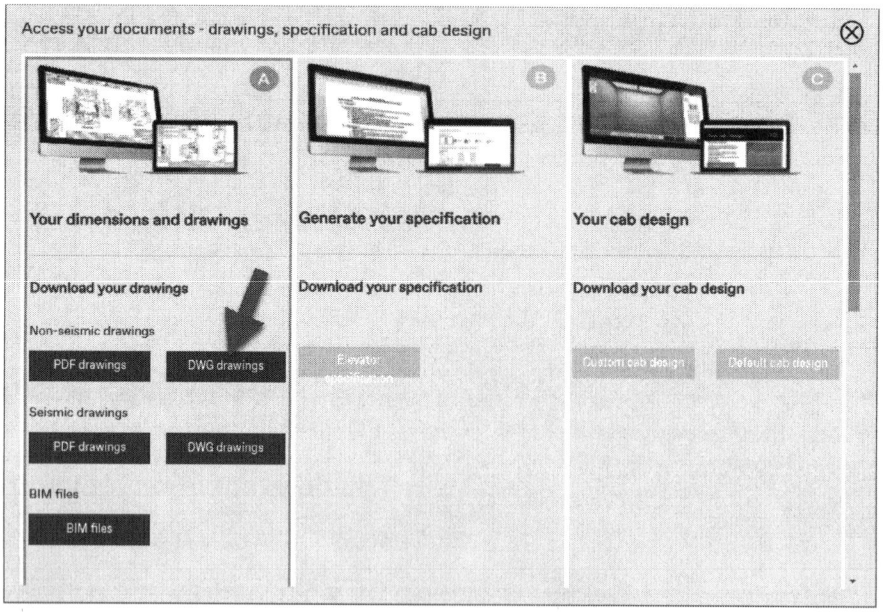

FIGURE 4-3.6 Download DWG CAD file

You now have an AutoCAD drawing file named **S35COTWIN1.DWG** saved on your computer's hard drive. This drawing is shown in Figure 4-3.7 and is packed with information. As you can see, details about the elevator shaft and the cab are given. In your case, this is more information than you need. So, you will open the drawing and Copy/Paste what you need into your floor plan.

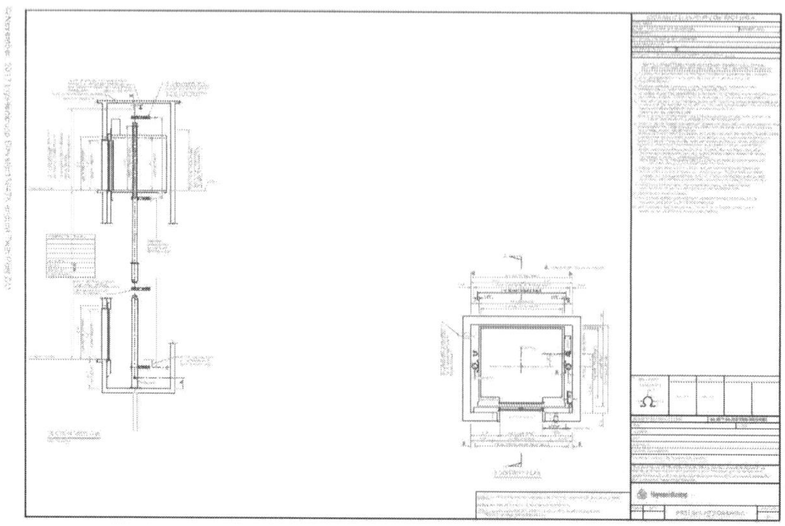

FIGURE 4-3.7 Contents of drawing file just downloade

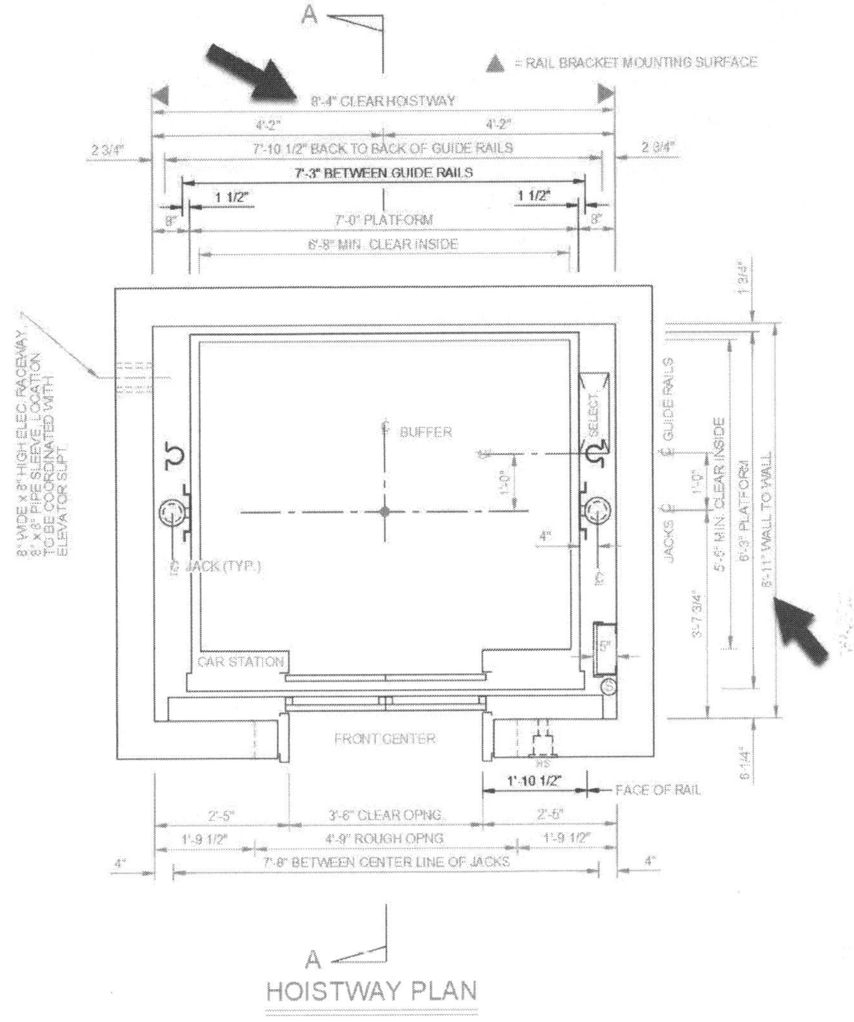

FIGURE 4-3.8 Enlargement of elevator drawing

10. Open **S35COTWIN1.dwg** (i.e., the elevator drawing just downloaded).

11. **Zoom** in to the elevator shaft plan view on the right.

Layer Freeze: a useful tool:

Next you will use a tool to freeze a *Layer* just by selecting objects on the screen. This will help you to select just the parts of the drawing you need.

12. Set the current *Layer* to **0** (i.e., zero). Delete layer filters if prompted.

TIP: Click the Layer drop-down list from the ***Home*** *tab and scroll up to Layer zero and click on it; as long as nothing in the drawing is selected, this will make the selected Layer current.*

13. From the **Layers** panel on the **Home** tab, select the **Freeze** icon (see image to right).

TIP: Explode (on the Modify *panel) any* Blocks *in this drawing so you can control the* Layer *color when it is loaded into the library floor plan.*

14. Click on all the text, dimensions, and centerlines until the drawing looks like Figure 4-3.9.

TIP: If you click on the wrong object and a Layer is frozen by mistake, type U and press ***Enter*** *on the keyboard. (This is not the main Undo command.)*

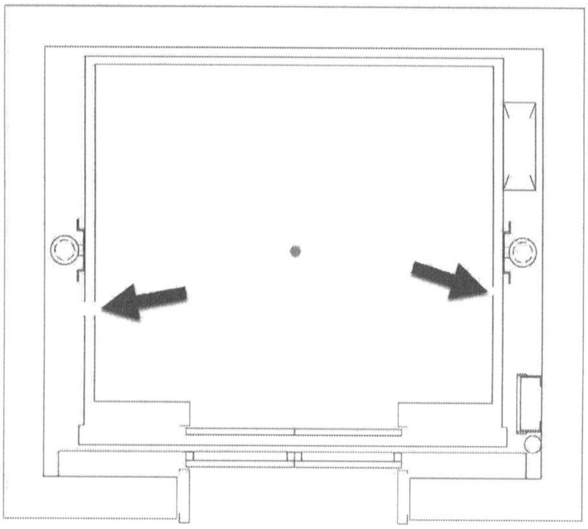

FIGURE 4-3.9 Gaps in linework to be adjusted

The elevator drawing is almost ready to be copied to the clipboard and pasted into your floor plan.

Before you copy the drawing to the clipboard, you will fix the broken lines (they were trimmed to accommodate notes and dimensions – which are now frozen).

Also, all the visible linework is currently on a *Layer* named "OBJECT" which does not conform to your office standards; you will fix this too.

Using the Join Command:

The join command allows you to select two or more aligned lines and turn them into a single line. You will try this next.

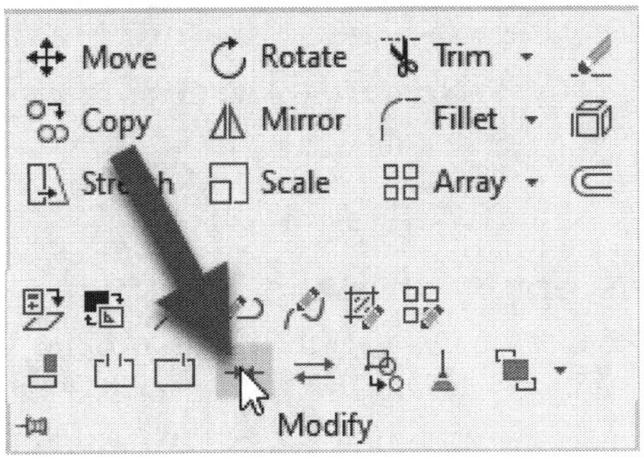

15. Select **Join** from the extended portion of the **Modify** panel, on the **Home** tab.

16. Select the **two** lines identified in **Figure 4-3.10** and then press **Enter**.

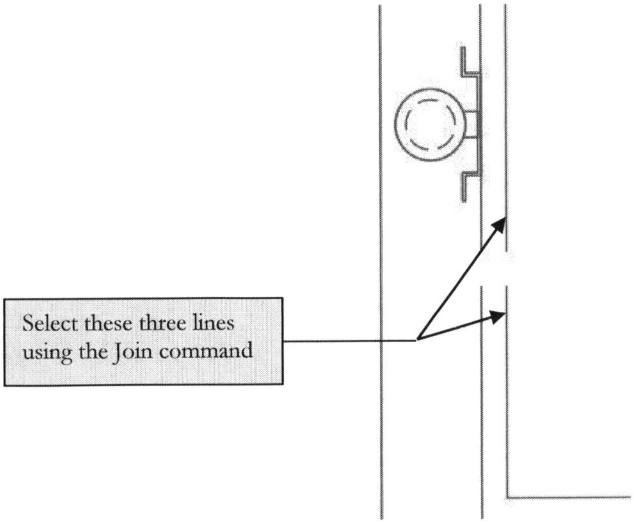

FIGURE 4-3.10 Elevator shaft drawing

17. Continue to use the **Join** command to clean up all sides of the elevator car as shown in Figure 4-3.11.

In the next step you will change all the linework to *Layer* zero before you copy/ paste into your floor plan. If you did not do this the *Layer* named "Object" would be created in your floor plan drawing. These types of extra *Layers* are not desirable.

18. Select everything visible in Figure 4-3.11 and change its *Layer* to **0** (i.e., zero).

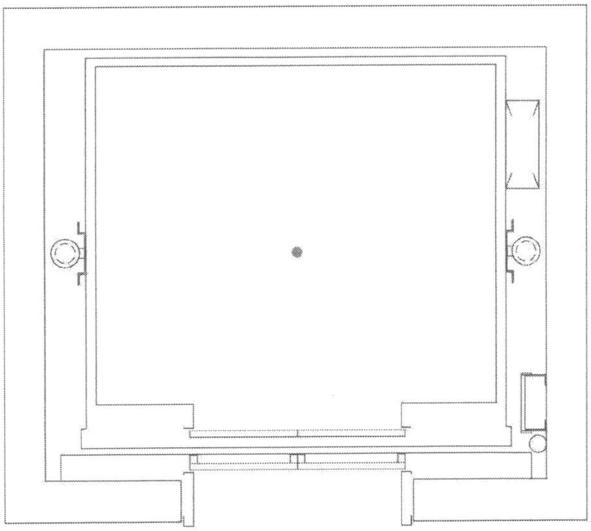

FIGURE 4-3.11 Elevator shaft drawing

Next you will rotate the elevator to align the orientation with your plan.

19. **Rotate** the elevator as shown in Figure 4-3.12. FYI: Dashed lines apply to subsequent step.

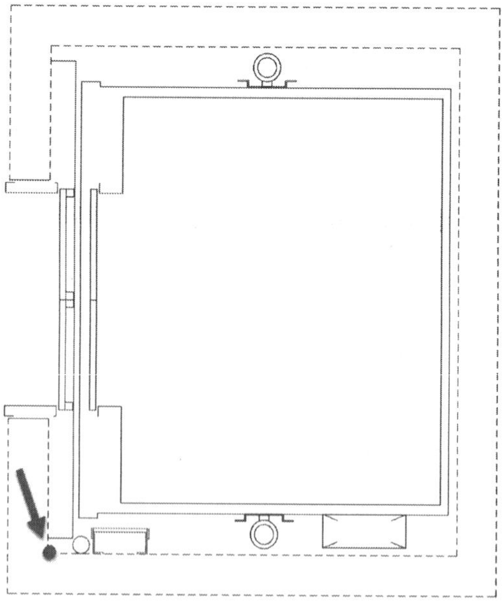

FIGURE 4-3.12 Elevator mirrored

Copy with Base Point:

Next you will *Copy* the elevator to the MS Windows Clipboard. This is a placeholder for information (it can be used within the same application or between programs, e.g., Copy from AutoCAD and Paste into MS Word).

AutoCAD offers the ability to specify a *Base Point* before placing the drawing information into the Clipboard. Thus, when you *Paste* the drawing information back into the same drawing or another drawing you can accurately place it.

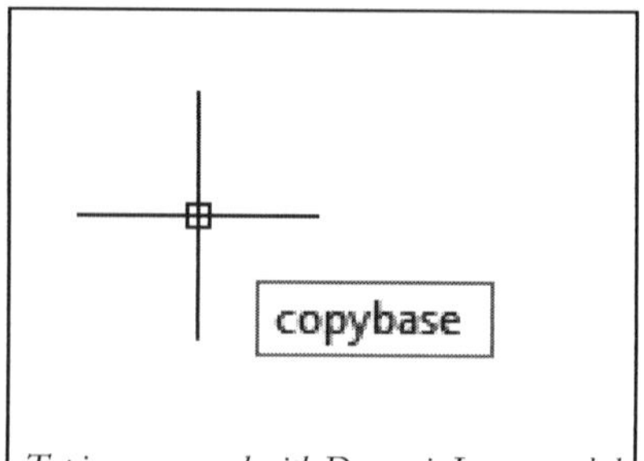

Typing command with Dynamic Input toggled on, near crosshairs.

20. Type **copybase** and then press Enter *(command not on the Ribbon)*.

You are now prompted to select a Base Point:

21. **Pick** the point identified by the **heavy dot** pointed out in Figure 4-3.12 using OSNAP's.

You are now prompted to select items to copy to the clipboard:

22. **Select** everything in Figure 4-3.9 except the walls which have been shown dashed for clarity (you already have walls in your plan).

TIP: You can use a crossing-window to select everything and then hold down the Shift key while selecting the wall lines (which will remove them from the selection set).

23. With everything but the wall lines selected, press **Enter**.

The elevator has now been copied to the clipboard. That information will remain there until the computer is turned off or AutoCAD (or any other program) copies new information to the clipboard.

Switch back to your library floor plan.

24. **Zoom** in on the elevator shaft near the main entry.

25. From the **Clipboard** panel, select the **Paste** icon (or Ctrl + V).

You should now see a ghost image of the elevator attached to your cursor. The *Base Point* previously selected is now the insertion point.

26. Select the same, relative, location as the insertion point (shown as a black dot in Figure 4-3.13).

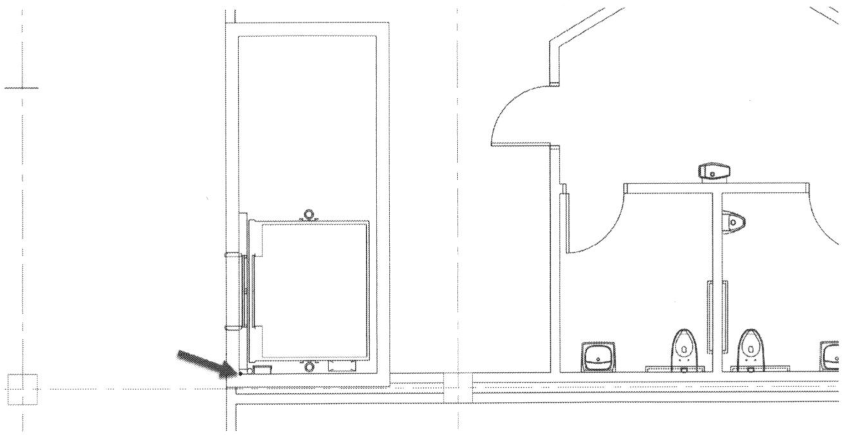

FIGURE 4-3.13 Elevator inserted into your floor plan (black dot in lower-left for reference only)

You now have one of the two elevator cars located within the shaft. In this plan you will have two elevators in the same shaft, separated only by a beam at each floor. So you still need to mirror the car and trim the wall lines at the elevator door opening.

27. Use the **Mirror** command to copy a mirror image of the elevator car to the opposite side of the shaft (Figure 4-3.14).

TIP: Use the midpoint of one of the vertical wall lines to establish the Mirror Line (with ORTHO on).

28. **Trim** the wall lines and place the jamb lines on **A-wall** layer (not the elevator frame, just the line that closes off the wall); see Figure 4-3.14.

29. Move all the elevator lines to the proper layer (see Appendix A).

> ***TRY THIS:***
> *While the drawing data is still in the clipboard, try opening a word processor like MS Word and select Paste from the Home tab on the Ribbon. Notice how the drawing looks in the document (also notice the down arrow and paste special).*

The Weight of Finishes?

Finishes are very important for several reasons when it comes to elevators. As previously mentioned, the use needs to be considered (passenger or service); this will dictate the durability and cost of the finishes.

Another consideration is the weight of the material. If the Interior Designer selects wood wall panels and tile flooring (which is perfectly acceptable) the elevator manufacturer needs to know how much these materials will weigh so they can properly size the motor for optimum performance.

So, similar to coordinating with the Electrical Engineer at casework locations, coordination must also occur with many other items in the building that the Architect or Interior Designer is directly responsible for.

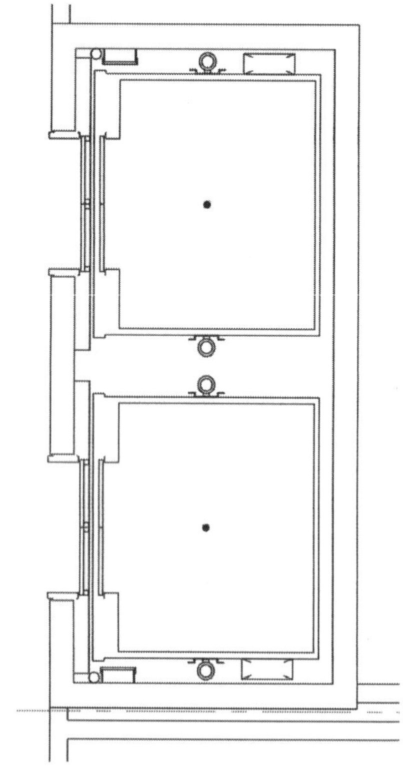

FIGURE 4-3.14
Elevator added to plan

30. **Add two lines**, 4" apart, between the elevators to represent a beam; place the lines on the same *Layer* as the elevator.

Your elevator should now look like Figure 4-3.14. Several details are drawn, such as the guide rail, the cab door, the floor level door and even the pit ladder.

Many architectural firms have a copy of the major elevator manufacturers' technical catalogs which provide enough information to manually draw everything in Figure 4-3.14. But it is not difficult to see how the Internet can save time when AutoCAD content is available; not all manufacturers provide AutoCAD drawings of their products.

Adding the Service Elevator:

This elevator is near the loading dock area (west side of the building) and is only accessible by the library staff. It is rated for a higher capacity than the passenger cars (3000lbs. vs. 5000lbs.). The cab size is also larger to make it easier to move objects in and out.

To save time, you can use the service elevator DWG file provided with this book.

31. Place the **service elevator.dwg** block per **Figure 4-3.15**, *plus*:
    a. Select **Insert → Blocks from library…**
    b. Browse to DWG files provided with book (see inside front cover for download instructions).
    c. For reference:
        i. Mfr: **ThyssenKrupp Elevator**
        ii. *Capacity:* **5000**
        iii. *Model:* **SPF 50**
        iv. Note the door orientation.

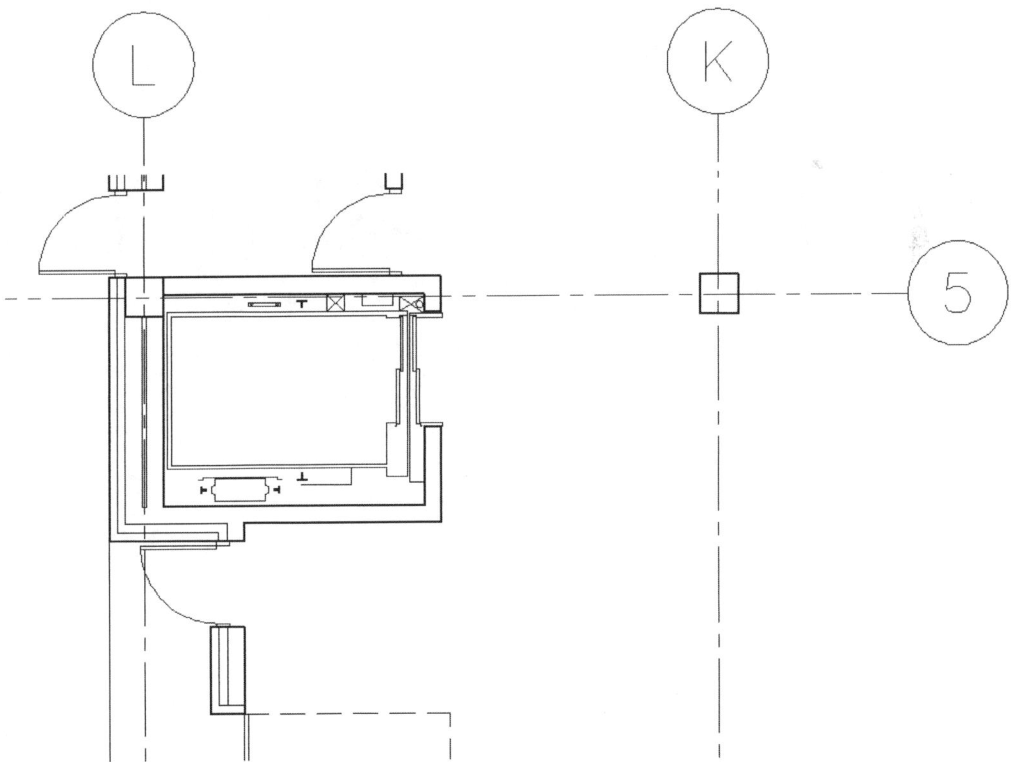

FIGURE 4-3.15 Service elevator added to plan

Adding the Open Stair:

The open stair is the primary stair used for vertical circulation in a building. This type of stair offers visual way-finding and can make an aesthetic statement for the building when located and designed well. Building codes often allow an open stair between two floors only; if one wishes to have a multi-story open stair it must have the ability to be closed off, which usually means overhead door-like fire shutters that will be lowered in the case of a fire.

Below is an example of a well designed multi-story open stair. The railings are glass with a wood cap, the treads and risers are high quality terrazzo, and the walls are lined with wood panels. The stair is located next to windows which help the users know where they are in the building relative to the outside (helps with way-finding). The photo was taken through a large piece of glass that makes the stair visible at each floor within the building; in the event of a fire the fire-shutters come down and close off this view!

OPEN STAIR EXAMPLE High quality stair with interesting design

32. Draw the open stair per **Figure 4-3.16**, *plus*:
    a. The tread lines are **13″** apart.
    b. Draw the treads on *Layer* **A-Flor-Strs**.
    c. The railings are to be drawn 2″ wide and 2″ out from the wall.
    d. The railings that are not continuous extend past the top/bottom riser by **12″** and return to the wall.
    e. Draw the railings on *Layer* **A-Flor-Hral**.
    f. The dashed lines represent the stairs and floor opening above the floor plan cut line.
    g. Draw the dashed lines on *Layer* **A-Flor-Strs-Abov**.
    h. Draw the arrow manually; you will learn a better way later.

       TIP: *Use lines and a solid hatch for this.*

    i. Use the **Donut** command to make the black dot (type the word "donut" in the *command window*).

       TIP: *Set the inside radius to 0″ and the outside to 4″.*

    j. Add the **text** (per standards for ⅛″ scale; 9″ high).
    k. Draw text and arrow on *Layer* **A-Flor-Strs**.
    l. Do not draw the dimensions.
    m. Draw the angled line shown on the stair *Layer*.

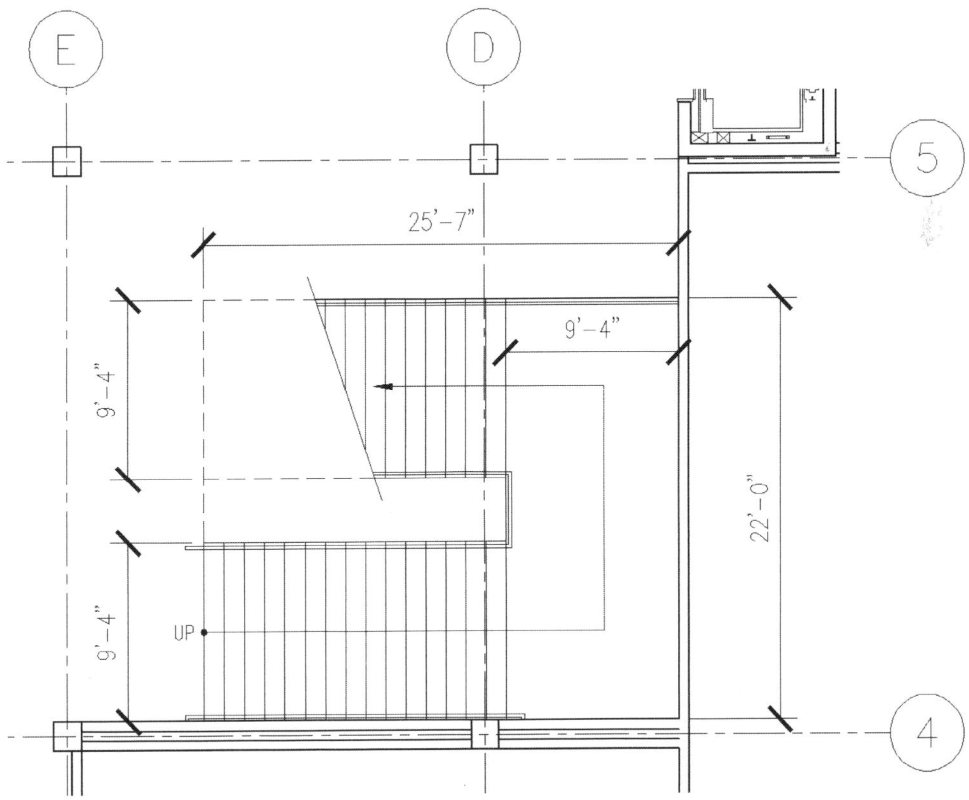

FIGURE 4-3.16 Open stair to be drawn

The angled line that trims the tread lines in Figure 4-3.13 represents the cut-line of the floor plan. The location of this line is not too critical; it is best to place it where the major features of the stair can still be shown. Depending on the distance between floor levels, you might have a significant space below the stair and need to show seating or flooring patterns. Codes require the lower portions of the stair (i.e., under the stair) to be enclosed so the visually impaired do not run into the stair. Sometimes it is desirable to enclose the underside of the stair completely to avoid hard-to-clean spaces; in this case you might see a wall pickup on the other side of the cut line. Even though the stair reached up past the cut line, the wall resting on the floor still continues for the length of the stair.

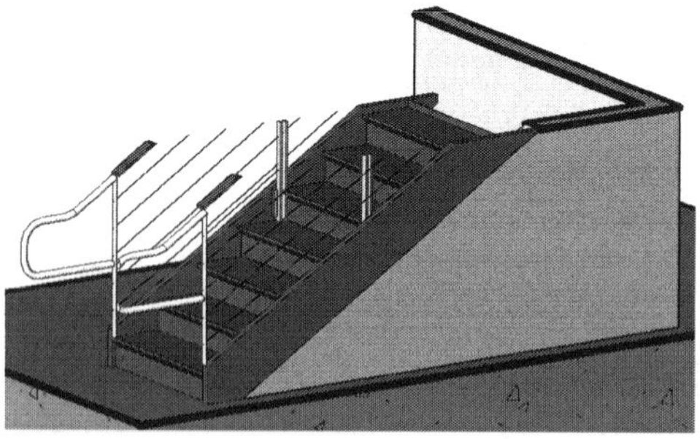

The image to the left is showing, three-dimensionally, how the floor plan cut plane impacts a stair which has a wall under it. In plan view, the break-line is added where the stair extends above the cut-plane; beyond the cut-plane you would show the wall below the stair because it is now passing through the cut-plane.

The handrail extension is dictated by the building code. The same is true with the handrails returning to the wall; this prevents people exiting the building (or fire fighters entering) from getting entangled with the handrails. The figure below (3.3.17) shows an elevation view of a wall mounted handrail to help you better understand what you are drawing.

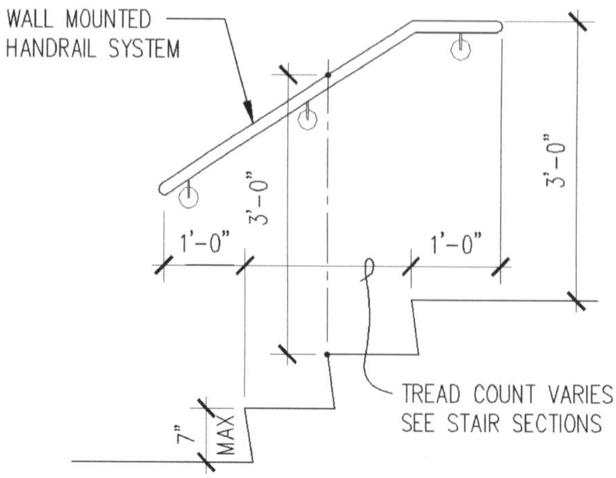

FIGURE 4-3.17 Handrail detail

In this floor plan, you would most likely add furring to the south wall to cover the structural concrete column (not required for this tutorial).

Adding the Utilitarian Stairs:

The two utilitarian stairs are almost identical; this is ideal whenever possible because it reduces the number of stair sections and details that are required in the construction documents.

As already discussed, the utilitarian stairs are not readily visible and primarily meant for emergency egress; their existence is primarily dictated by code. They are, however, often used as a means of vertical circulation within the building.

The finishes and light fixtures are simple – often painted CMU walls and surface mounted lights.

33. Following the same instructions as the previous step, draw the east stair per **Figure 4-3.18**, plus
    a. Draw the inside handrail 2″ in from the stair edge (see photo).
    b. Draw two angled break lines with void between.
    c. The tread lines are **11″** apart.

Notice in Figure 4-3.15 that the angled break lines help to delineate both the *up run* and the *down run*, which would otherwise overlap and be confusing.

34. Using *Copy* (not Copy to clipboard) and *Mirror*, copy the east stair into the west stair shaft (see **Figure 4-3.19**).

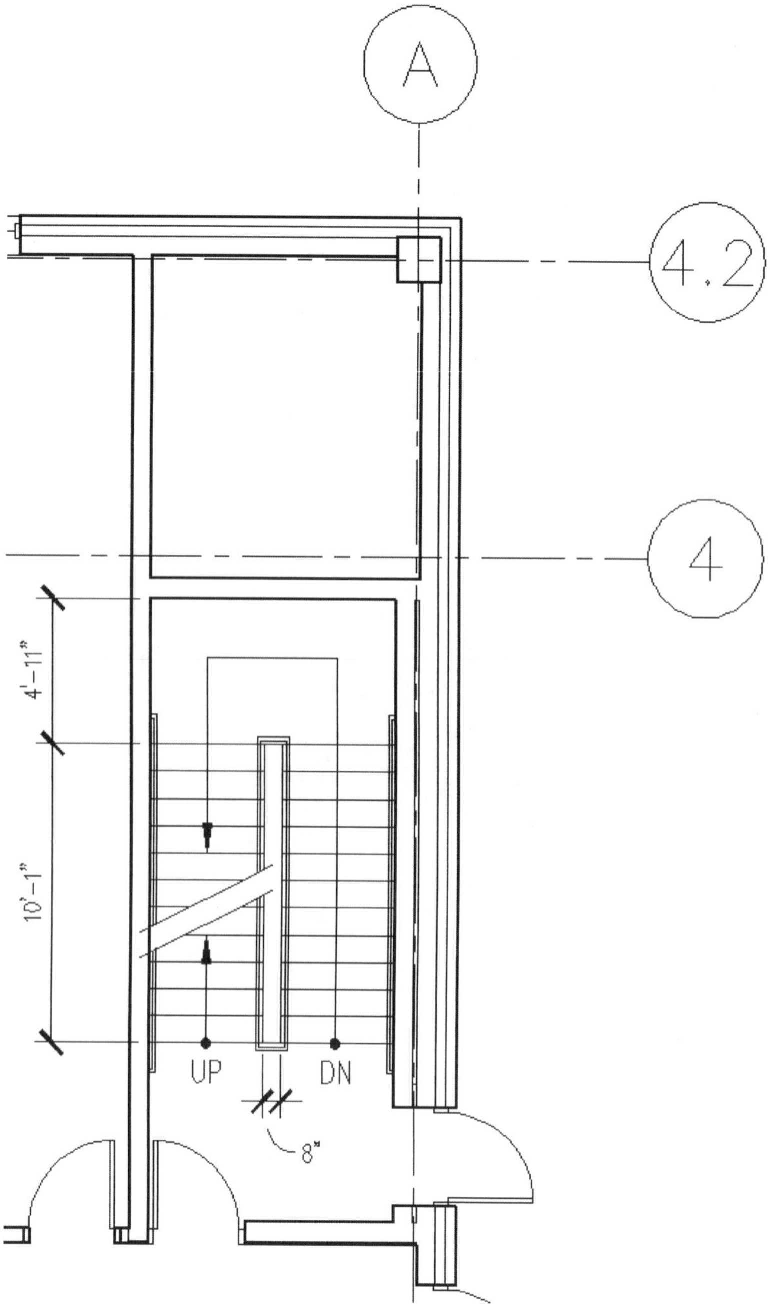

FIGURE 4-3.18 East utility stair shaft

Why two walls at the exterior walls in the stair shaft? This is a problem that requires the ability to think three-dimensionally. It should be obvious to you that a beam spans between two columns, typically at each floor level and at the roof. Well, the stair shaft is a tall room that passes multiple floors. Thus, the stair shaft needs to occur outside the beam line, which is centered on the column/grid lines.

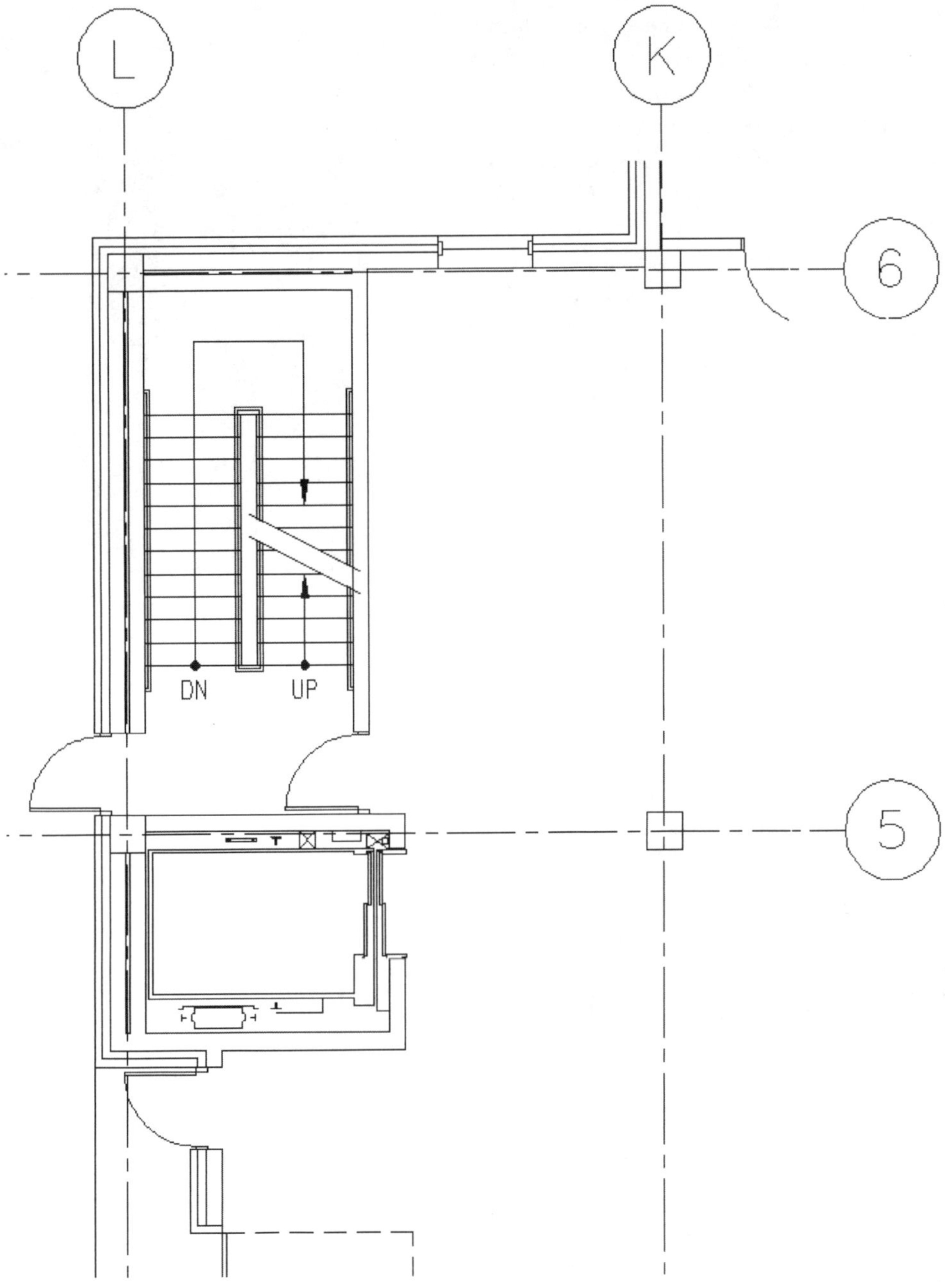

FIGURE 4-3.19 West utility stair shaft

If you were drawing the other floors in this building, you would Copy/Paste the stairs to the other drawings; the upper floor and basement would need to be modified.

In stairs, building codes often require a gate at the ground level and at the upper level (if the stair continues to the roof) as shown in the photo below. The reason for this is to help guide people in an emergency. Each floor in the utilitarian stair shaft looks the same, so it would be easy for a person (especially in a panicked state) to pass the ground level exit and continue down one or two more floors to the basement, extending their time in a dangerous situation. If the stair is used for normal, day-to-day, vertical circulation, some building officials will allow the gate to be placed on a magnetic hold-open which allows the gate to close in the event of a fire.

Most commercial codes also require that a sphere 4″ or larger not be able to pass through the guardrail. This has a large impact on design but creates a safe environment for the users; looking that the photo above it is not difficult to see how older codes allowed for unsafe designs!

Also notice, in the photo below, that the handrails return to the guardrail or the wall as previously discussed.

Exercise 4-4:
Annotations

Introduction

This exercise involves adding room names and numbers, as well as each room's square footage. The square footage will be added via an AutoCAD feature called *Fields*, which will update automatically when a room changes!

Room Numbering:

Room numbers typically start at the main entry and then proceed in a logical direction (e.g., clockwise). Sometimes the numbering is coordinated with the signage schedule (i.e., the rooms that are not numbered on a sign get skipped until the end numbers).

You will start the room numbering at the main entry and work in a clockwise direction. Later, you will use this information to generate a room finish schedule.

Room numbers will be three digits, with the first number corresponding to the floor that room is on. For example, the janitor's closet on the first floor might be **1**34 and the janitor's closet on the third floor might be **3**12.

Room Square Footage:

To get the square footage, one can draw a *Polyline* and use the *Area* command to list its square footage. Specifically, draw a continuous *Polyline* (pline) using *Object Snaps*, before picking the last point (i.e., the starting point) type C for close to create a Closed Polyline; and then type *Area* and select the polyline – the square inches and square foot will be listed. The polyline can be placed on *Layer* A-Area-Bdry and turned off for future reference (e.g., the room size changes and you need to update the area).

The text for the room names will be AutoCAD *Style* **Bold** per the "office standards" (see Appendix A). The room name and number will be 12″ high and the square footage text will be 9″ high. All the text (name, number, sf) shall all be in one Mtext object (i.e., typed all at once – not three separate commands). Just like working in a word processor, you can select a portion of text and edit its properties – this is how you have two text heights in one Mtext object.

1. Use the **Style** command to set up the "Bold" AutoCAD *Text Style* in your floor plan drawing. (See Appendix, page A-14, for more information.)

2. Create the *Layer* for your "area" polylines (see Appendix for *Layer* name and color).

3. Set the new area *Layer* to be current.

Next you will draw a *Polyline* to create an enclosed area for each room. A *Polyline* is a special line in AutoCAD that can contain several straight-line segments that are all connected together. When a *Polyline* is used, you can see how many square feet are contained with the enclosed area as well as the length of the perimeter. These values are very helpful for estimating quantities and project costs.

4. Using the **Polyline** command (see image to the right), draw an enclosed area in the Vestibule as shown in Figure 4-4.1.

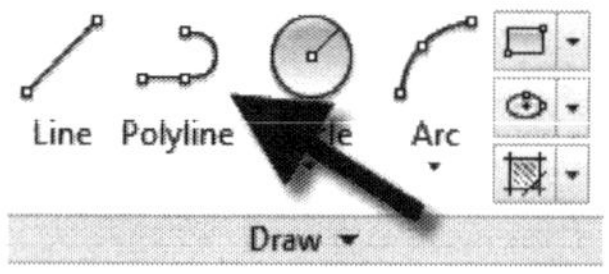

TIP: Start the Polyline command, and start picking points (all the inside and outside corners of the room, a.k.a., the finished face of the room).

TIP: Instead of clicking the last point directly (i.e., clicking on the first point), simply type C (for Close) and AutoCAD will finish the Polyline for you. This will make sure that the Polyline is truly closed, which is important for getting the square footage and hatching.

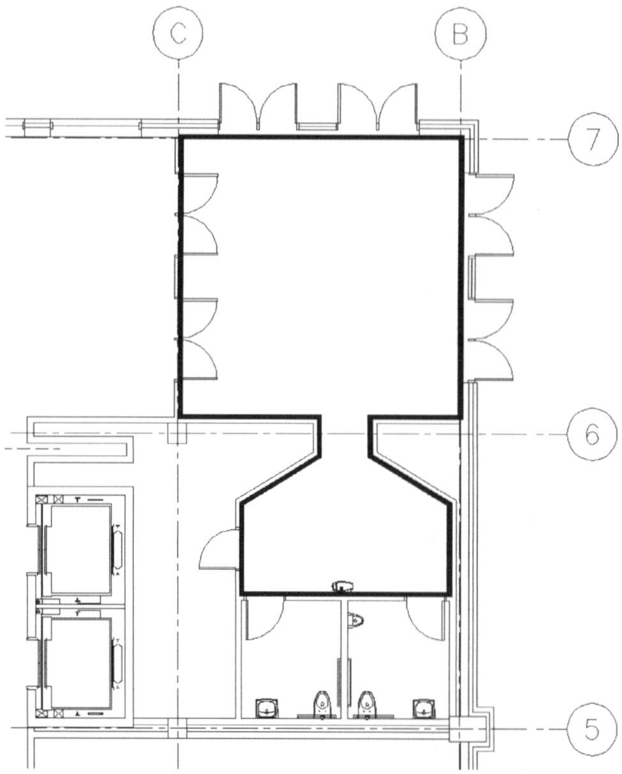

FIGURE 4-4.1 Adding a polyline at the vestibule

5. Select the *Polyline* created in the previous step.

6. Right-click and select **Properties** from the pop-up menu.

7. Notice the **Area** and **Length** (which is the Perimeter in this case) properties listed (Figure 4-4.2).

The *Area* property lists square inches and square feet; square inch is not very useful, but it is the default unit for architectural drawings.

Note that a *Polyline* does not have to be closed; it could be a curb for the length of a road or an irregular line representing the transition between two floor finishes.

8. Press **Escape** (i.e., the *Esc* key) to unselect the *Polyline*.

TIP: Be sure your cursor is not over the Properties Palette when you press the Esc key.

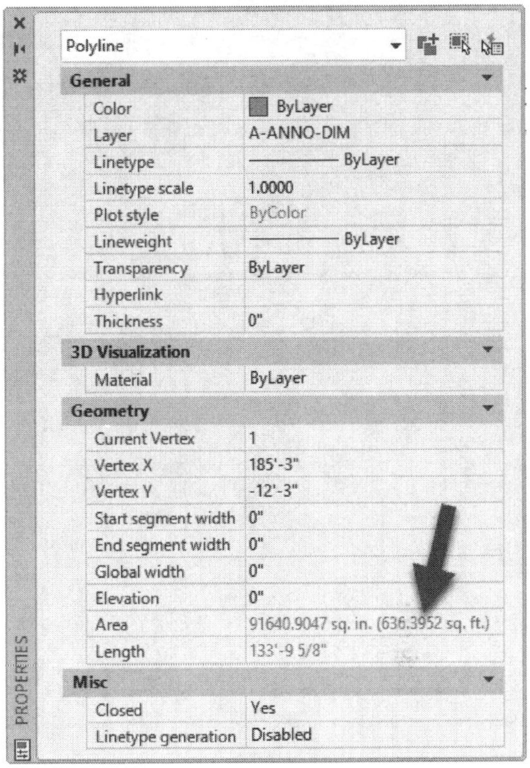

FIGURE 4-4.2 Polyline properties

Now you will use the *Mtext* command to add the room number, name and square footage. The square footage information will be added by placing a *Field* in the Mtext editor, which automatically gets the area from the *Polyline*.

9. Add the text to the Vestibule as shown (as Multiline Text) in Figure 4-4.3, *plus*:
   a. Place text on *Layer* **A-Area-Iden**.
   b. Style: **Bold**.
   c. Room name and number: **12" high**.
   d. All text in one *Mtext* object; proceed to the next step; do not exit the *Mtext* edit mode – see the note below.

*NOTE: You cannot have multiple text heights in one Mtext object. Therefore, to complete this section successfully you should not use the Annotative Scaling feature for text. Type **Style** and make sure the Bold style (see page A-14 in Appendix A) does not have Annotative checked and the Text Height field is set to 0'-0".*

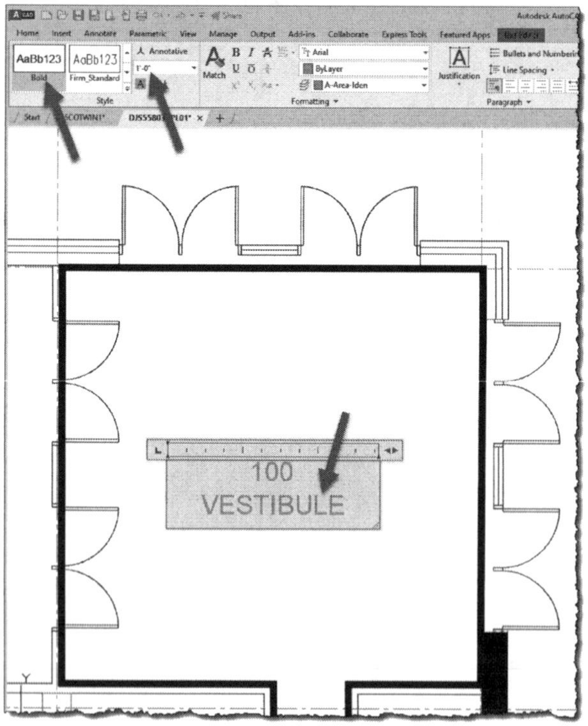

FIGURE 4-4.3 Adding vestibule number and name

Inserting Fields:

10. *While still in text edit mode,* press **Enter** to start a third line.

11. **Right-click** to access the pop-up menu.

12. Select **Insert field…** (Figure 4-4.4).

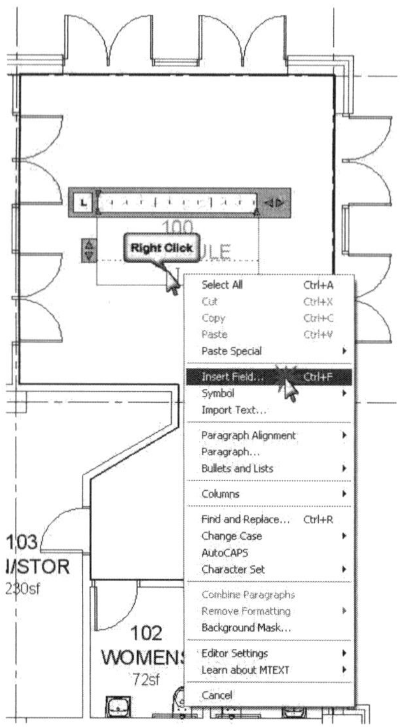

FIGURE 4-4.4 Adding a field

You are now in the *Field* dialog box (Figure 4-4.5) where you specify what type of information you want this specific *Field* to display. You can have things like the date, file name and much more, and they automatically update if they change.

> ***NOTE:** One* Field *object only holds one piece of information, but you can add as many* Fields *as required.*

13. Under *Field category*, select **Objects** (Figure 4-4.5).

14. Under *Field names*, click **Object** (Figure 4-4.5).

15. Under *Object type*, click the **Select object** button (Figure 4-4.5).

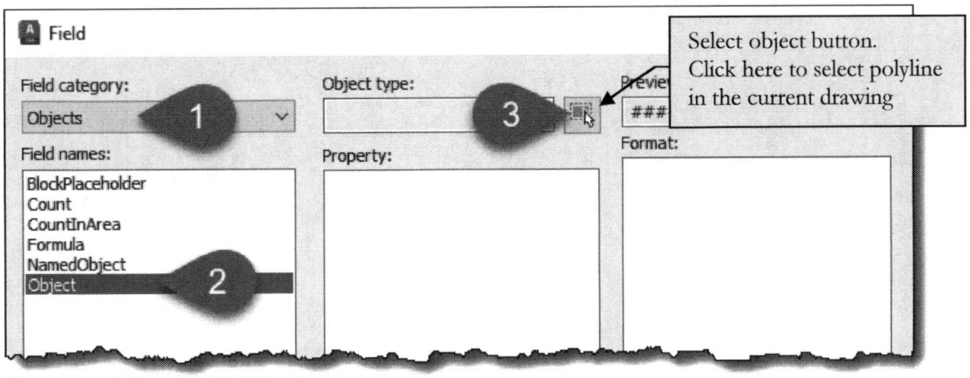

FIGURE 4-4.5 Field dialog box

16. **Select** the ***Polyline*** drawn at the perimeter of the vestibule; you can Zoom in/out using the scroll wheel on the mouse, if needed.

As soon as you select the *Polyline* you are returned to the *Field* dialog box. Notice that the *Object type* is listed as Polyline; this is a good way to make sure you selected the correct object. (If it listed Line rather than Polyline, that would mean you accidentally picked a wall or grid line.)

17. Select **Architectural** under *Format* and set the *Precision* to **0**. Notice the *Preview* changes (Figure 4-4.6).

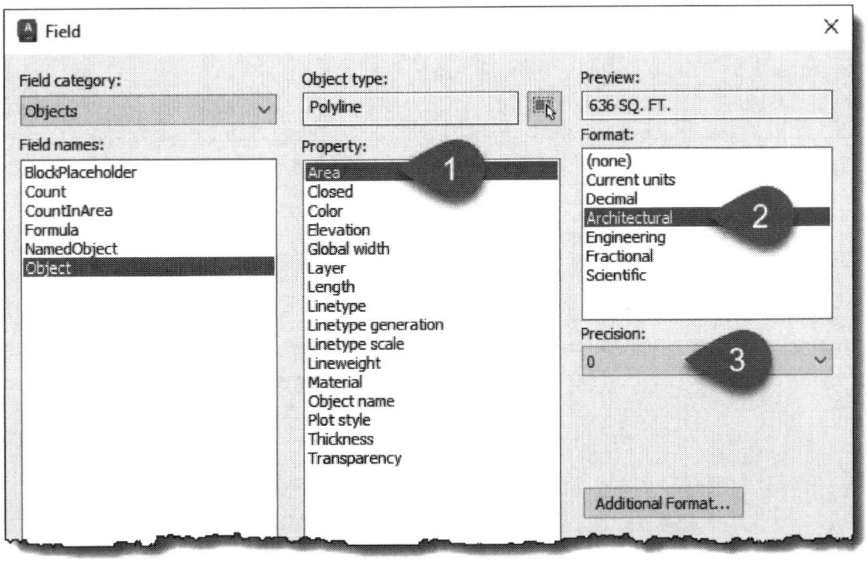

FIGURE 4-4.6 Field dialog box; polyline selected

18. Click **OK** to close the dialog and add the *Field* to the Mtext.

The area of the *Polyline* is now displayed in a shaded rectangle (Figure 4-4.7). The shaded rectangle does not print; it is displayed on the screen so you can easily tell the difference between regular text and *Fields*.

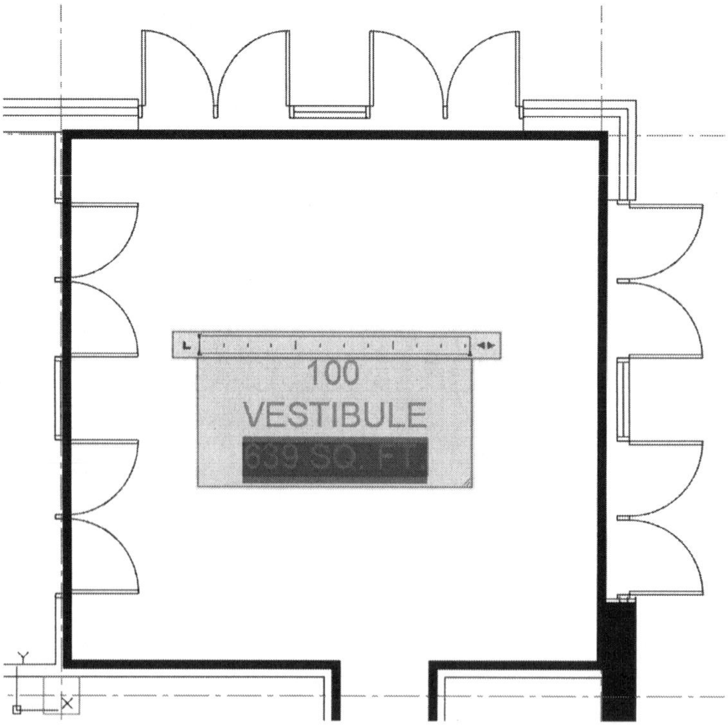

FIGURE 4-4.7 Field added to Mtext object

The last thing you need to do is adjust the size of the area text. It could be left as-is, but it will look better if it is a little smaller than the other text.

19. Click anywhere on the *Field* object and the entire *Field* will select. Set the text height: **9"** on the *Ribbon*.

20. Click **Close Text Editor** to finish the *Mtext* object.

As you can see, the Mtext object can contain various text heights and Fields. This is helpful when you want to move the text; you only have to select one thing to move rather than three (in this example).

Next you will take a quick look at how the *Field* information updates when the *Polyline* is modified. Before proceeding, you will undo these changes.

21. Stretch the interior wall and doors per the following tips:
    a. Make sure the **A-Area-Bdry** *Layer* is on and the *Polyline* is visible (you want the Polyline to be stretched).
    b. Select the **Stretch** icon from the **Modify** panel.
    c. Pick a ***Crossing Window*** (picking from right to left) as shown in Figure 4-4.8, being careful not to include the C/6 column's insertion point within the *Crossing Window*.
    d. *Select the two displacement points*: **First**, pick the lower left area of the selected objects, **and then** pick the outside corner (to the left) of the wall you are trying to align the doors with.

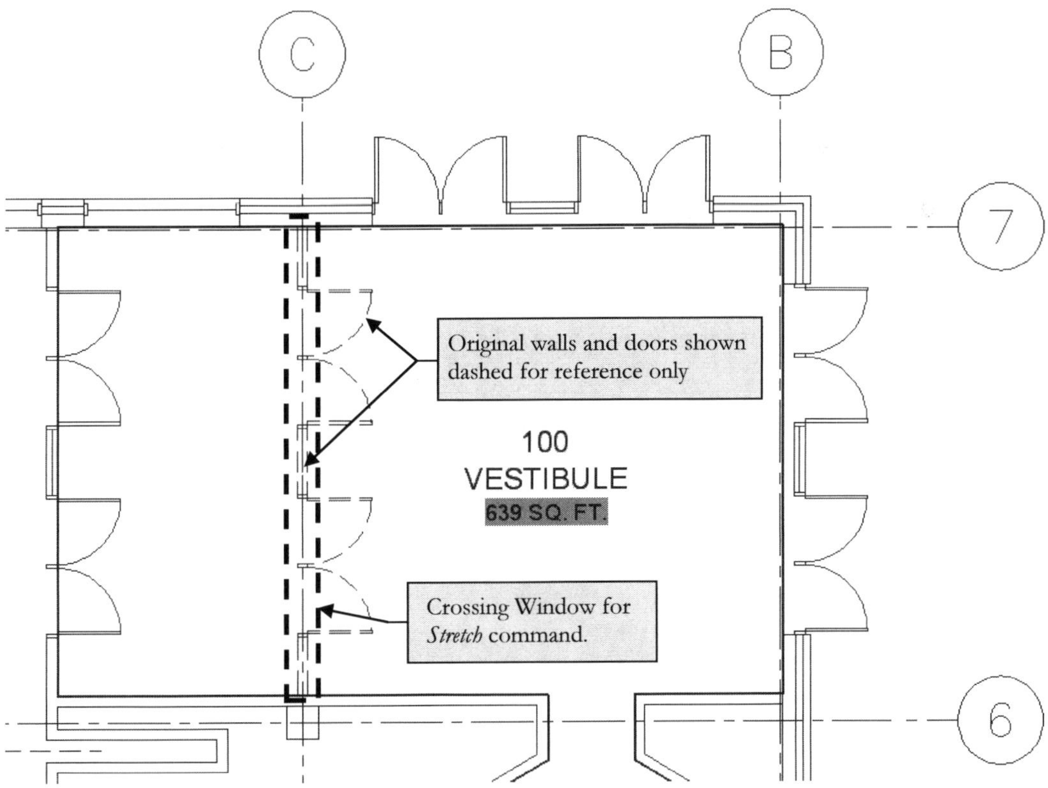

FIGURE 4-4.8 Stretching the vestibule wall

After stretching the Polyline you will notice the square footage did not update yet. The Field information is correct, but the graphic representation has not updated yet. The graphics are updated by a drawing regeneration, plotting and/or closing and reopening the drawing.

22. Type **Regen** in the *Command Window* and then press **Enter**.

Notice in Figure 4-4.9 that the *Field* is now updated!

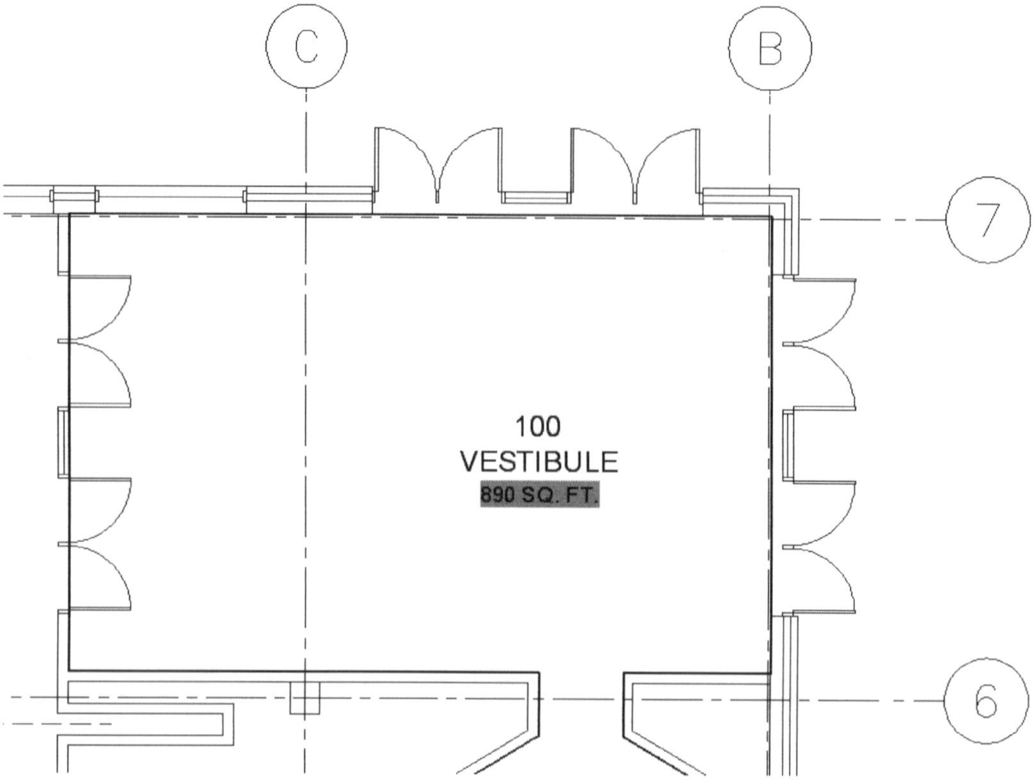

FIGURE 4-4.9 Field information updated automatically

23. Click the **Undo** icon twice (once for the Regen and once for the Stretch) to get your drawing back to its original state.

Practice Makes Perfect…

You will repeat the previous steps to add the room information to each space. The steps are pretty simple: (1) draw the *Polyline*, (2) create the *Mtext*, and (3) insert the *Field* before closing the *Mtext*.

Next, you will be given several plan views with all the room names, numbers and square footages (shaded rectangle for Fields is not visible in these views). If you have trouble reading the area numbers, don't worry as the field object will fill it in automatically; they do serve as a double-check to make sure you drew the rooms correctly.

24. Per the previous instruction: create a *Polyline* and add the room information (as *Mtext* + *Field*) for the remaining rooms, as shown in Figures 4-4.10 through 4-4.13; you may ignore the areas not labeled.

The text location can vary in each room, but the ideal location is centered in the room and aligned with adjacent room labels. These locations get moved as the plans develop, so the text does not overlap furniture/notes/ dimensions/etc.

25. Freeze the *Layer* **A-Area-Bdry** to make the *Polylines* disappear.

The *Fields* will still reference the *Polylines* even when they are on a frozen *Layer*. However, you need to remember to thaw this *Layer* before stretching or modifying any walls if you want the area to update automatically.

Once you get one room label set up with the properly formatted text (i.e., 12″ and 9″ high text) you can copy that one, with *ORTHO* on, into other rooms. Once copied, you can double-click on the text to open it in the *Mtext* editor. Then you can edit the regular text and right-click on the Field to select Edit Field, which will allow you to select another Polyline. (If you do not edit the Field, it will continue to list the area of the previous space.) Using *ORTHO* (toggle icon located on the *Status Bar*) helps to keep the text aligned horizontally or vertically.

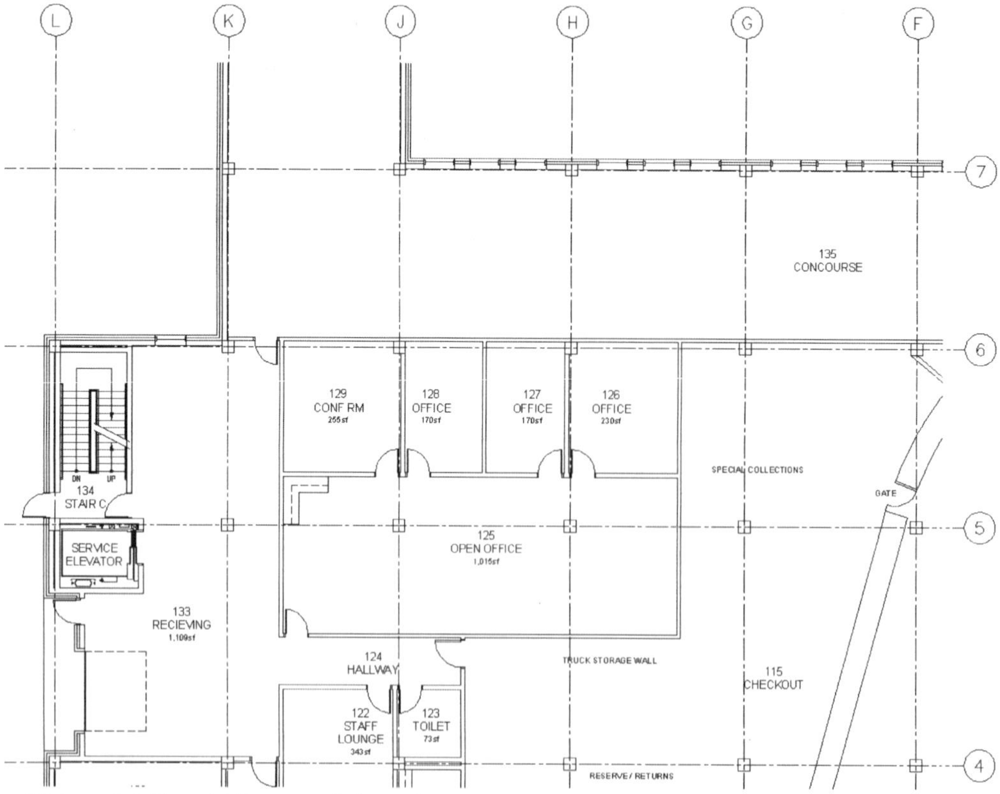

FIGURE 4-4.10 Adding room information

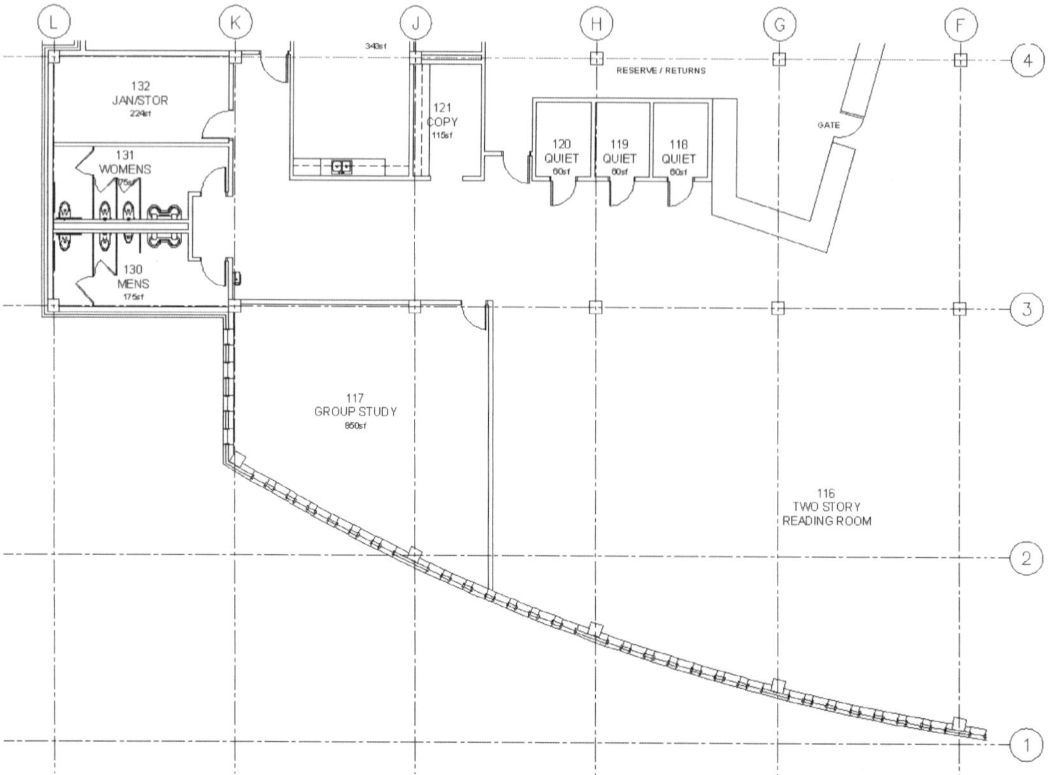

FIGURE 4-4.11 Adding room information

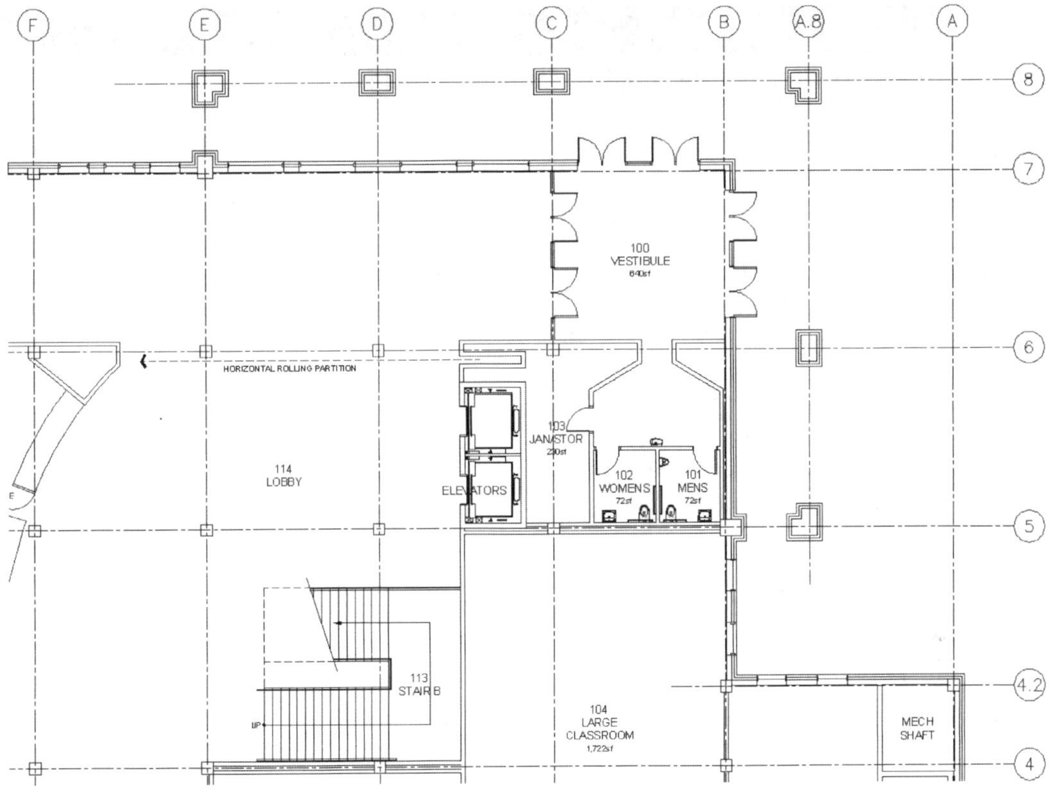

FIGURE 4-4.12 Adding room information

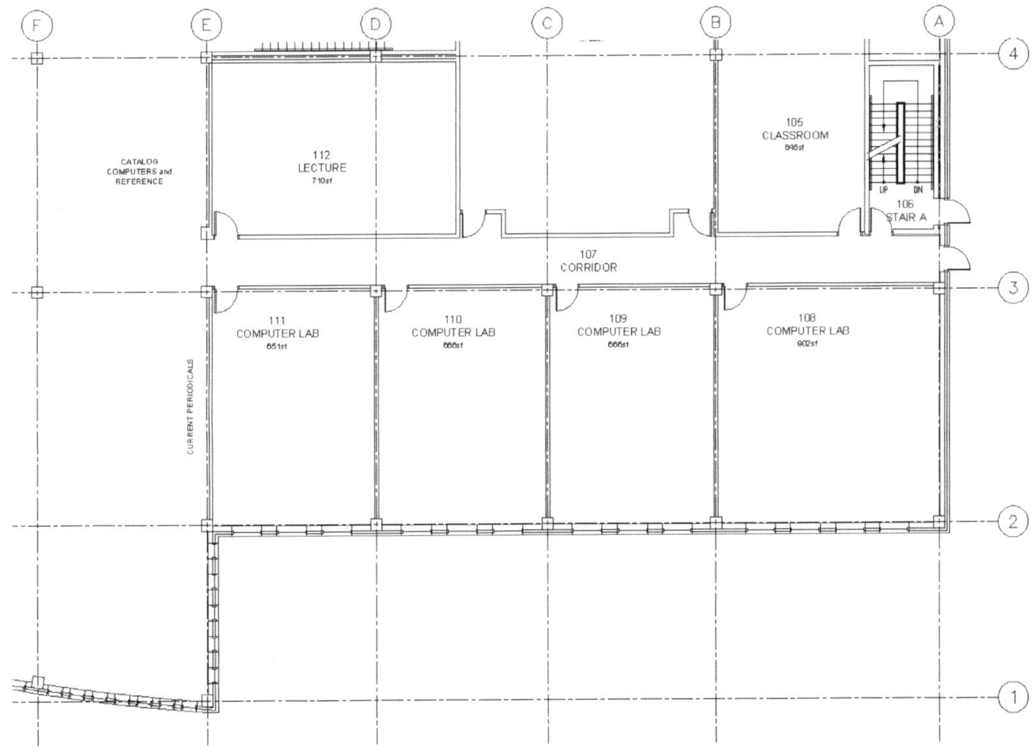

FIGURE 4-4.13 Adding room information

Exercise 4-5:
Presentation Graphics: Solid Filled Walls

Introduction

The walls are often filled solid during the Schematic Design and Design Development phases so the walls punch out better when presented to the client. This is done using the **Hatch** command and the hatching is placed on a special *Layer* that can be turned off as the plan develops (into the Construction Documents phase).

One of the many unspoken rules in many design firms is that hatching should be limited to only a few (or one large) areas. For example, when using the *Boundaries: Pick Points* feature of the *Hatch* command (a feature that automatically finds the boundary of an area by picking a point anywhere within the enclosed area) you need to limit how many points you pick at one time, or make sure you check the "make separate hatches" check box.

Otherwise, you might hatch half the plan which would be a single entity. If you need to change one little area (e.g., a wall moves 1″ to the west) you would have to erase the hatch and recreate the hatching for half the plan.

Another thing to be careful of is not to create too many "little" hatches in one area. For example, if you do check "make separate hatches", each click of the mouse creates a separate hatch. So if grid lines and break lines cross an area of wall it would be better if that hatch was one object rather than several small hatches that look like one.

Don't forget the power of the *Block*! If you had to add a solid fill to the structural columns, you could simply double-click on one of the columns to open it in the *Block Editor* (as instructed in Lesson 3), add the hatch and save/redefine the *Block*. All the columns will automatically be updated! Make sure the hatch is placed on a separate *Layer* so its visibility can be controlled independently from the column itself. Now you will hatch all the walls with a solid hatch, placing the hatch on a special *Layer*.

Looking at Figure 4-5.1 you can see it would take three picks just to *Hatch* the area between the two windows. Also, the grid lines bisect several walls which would require several extra picks as well. This is one of the main reasons for dividing things up onto separate *Layers*, so you can turn them off when they are not needed.

1. Using the *Layer* **Off** tool from the **Layers** panel (**Home** tab), turn off the grid lines and the wall cavity lines (Figure 4-5.1).

Notice how the *Layer Off* tool was able to turn off the grid line *Layer* even though it was part of an external reference!

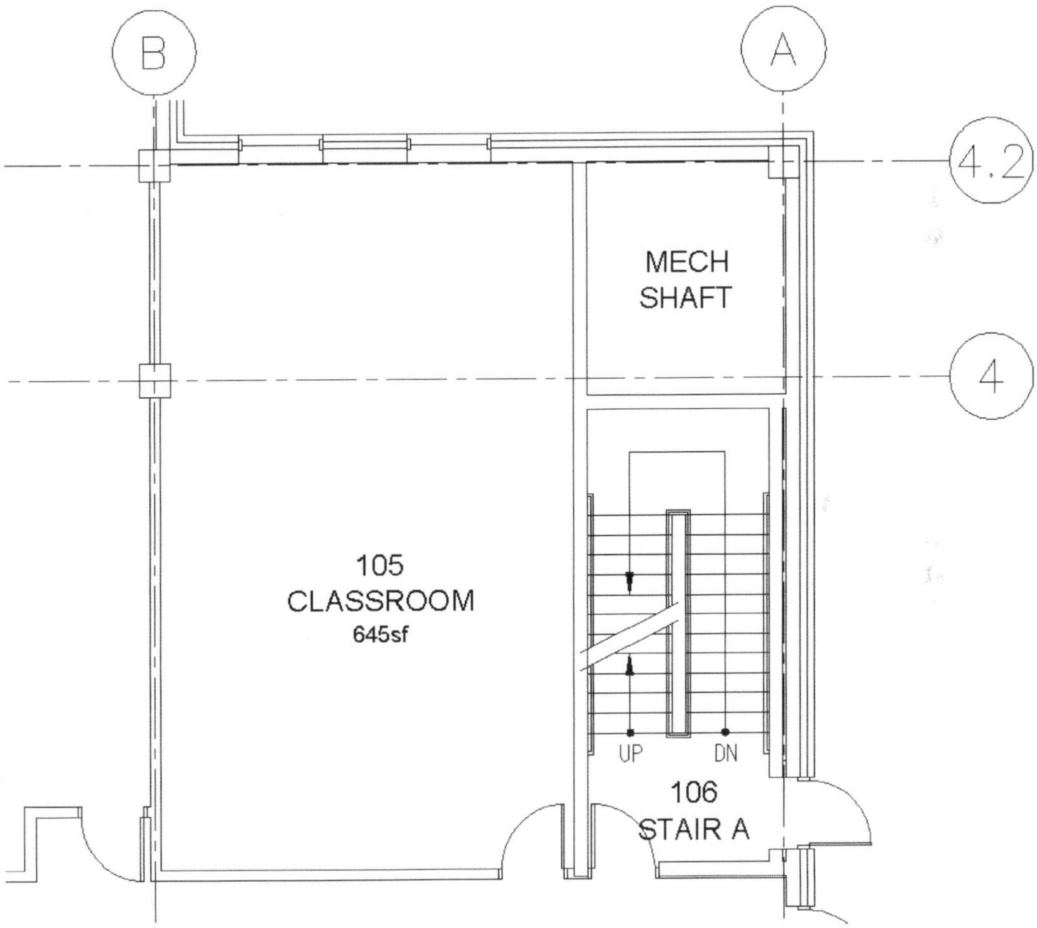

FIGURE 4-5.1 Plan view near east stair shaft

Notice the floor plan in Figure 4-5.2; the walls are now uninterrupted and ready to be hatched.

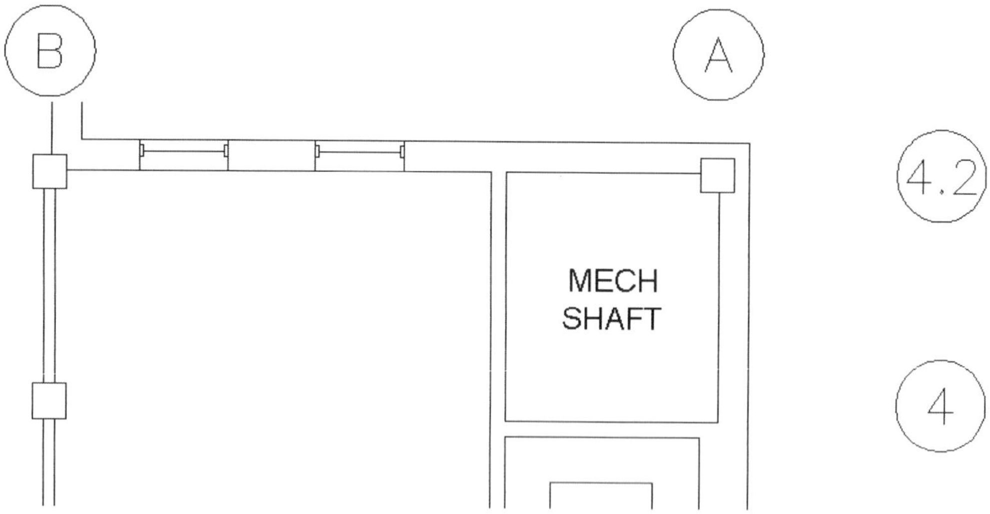

FIGURE 4-5.2 Plan view near east stair shaft – layers turned off

Next you will create a *Layer* to place the wall *Hatch* on.

2. Create *Layer* **A-Wall-Patt-Temp** (color red) and set it current.
   a. *If you want the hatch to be a shade rather than solid black, you can set the Layer color to 253 or 254.*

With the *Layer* set current, all *Hatching* will be placed on the proper *Layer* – avoiding the need to select the *Hatch* and switch its *Layer* after it has been drawn.

3. Select the **Hatch** icon on the **Draw** panel *or type H and Enter on the keyboard.*

4. Set the hatch *Pattern* to **Solid** (Figure 4-5.3).

5. In the *Options* panel (Figure 4-5.3):
   a. Select **Associative** *(should already be active).*
   b. Check **Create separate hatches** *(located in panel fly-out).*
   c. Set the *Draw Order* option to **Send behind boundary** *(located in panel fly-out).*

FYI: *The* ***Associative*** *feature of the* ***Hatch*** *command can be very handy. When it is selected, AutoCAD remembers the boundary that was used to create the hatch, and if the boundary changes that hatch is updated. So if you stretch a wall 12″ to the east the hatching will update automatically. If any part of the boundary gets erased the associativity will be lost.*

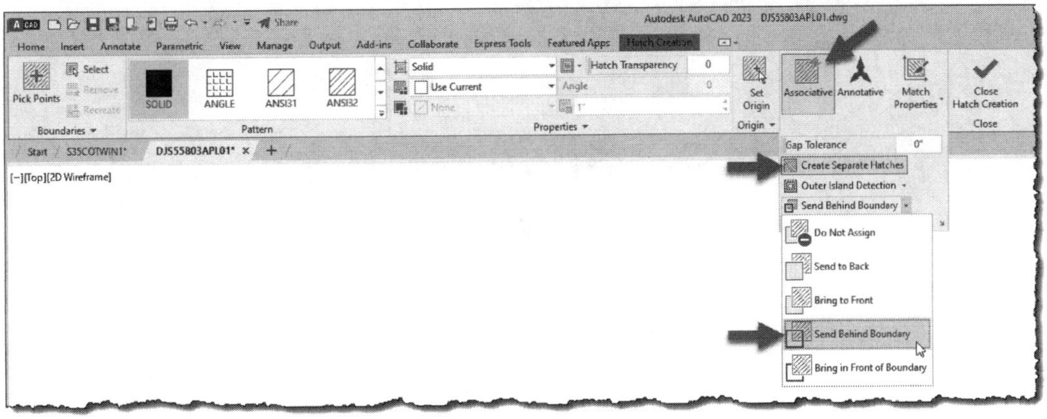

FIGURE 4-5.3 Hatch tab on the Ribbon (Options panel shown expanded)

6. With the *Ribbon* options selected, begin clicking within walls to select areas (they will highlight as you select them); click **Close Hatch Creation** to finish the *Hatch* command.

   TIP: *Even with "create separate hatches" checked you should still limit the number of areas you select at once to avoid messing up and having to start all over again.*

   a. Do not hatch the concrete columns at this time

7. Continue the hatching process until all walls are hatched.

   a. Again, do not hatch the concrete columns at this time

As you can see in Figure 4-5.4 the walls and window punch out very well compared to Figure 4-5.1. This is also true for items like casework and furniture; they read better!

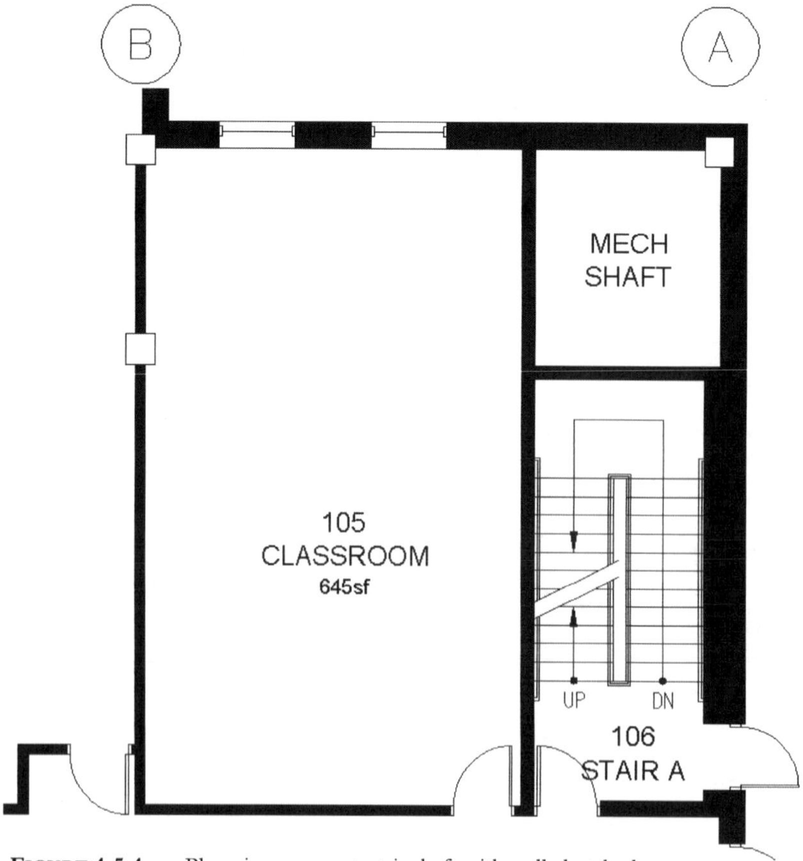

FIGURE 4-5.4 Plan view near east stair shaft with walls hatched

Once you get all the walls hatched you will want to turn the grid lines and wall cavity lines back on. There are two ways to do this quickly.

- If you have not made any other *Layer* manipulations or closed AutoCAD, you can simply click the **Layer Previous** icon.

- Another method is to open the *Layer Manager* and right-click on any *Layer* name and click "**Select All**" from the pop-up menu. Then you can click any *Layer* icon that is "off" and all *Layers* will be turned "on" (see Figure 4-5.5).

8. Using one of the methods just described, restore the visibility of the **A-Wall-Cvty** and ***DJS55803AGD01*| A-Grid** Layers.

Your drawing should now look like Figure 4-5.7.

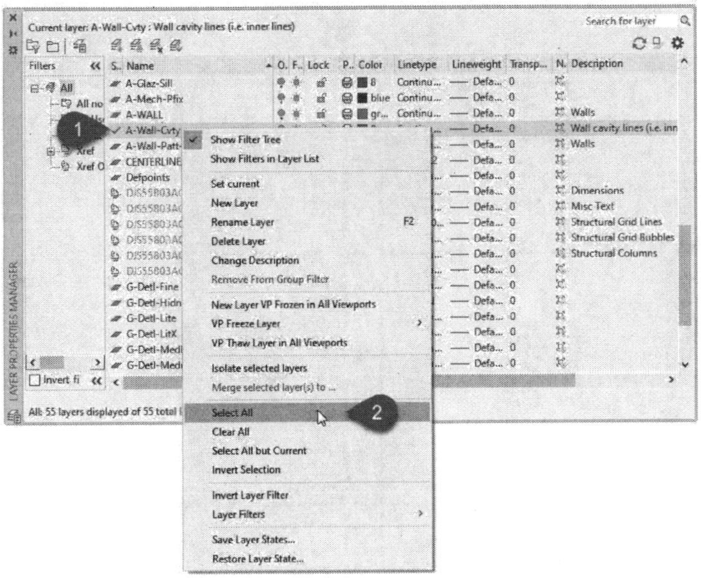

FIGURE 4-5.5 Layer Manager; right-click and pick "select all"

Take a moment and notice the other tools available in the right-click pop-up menu shown in Figure 4-5.5.

In the text box in the upper right of the *Layer Manager* (that has the light gray words "Search for layer"; see Figure 4-5.5) you can type something like ***grid*** and see only the *Layers* that have the letter/word "grid" in them (e.g., A-Grid, A-Grid-Iden, DJSAGD01|S-Grid, etc.). See Figure 4-5.6 below for an example where only the *Layers* with the word "**wall**" are listed.

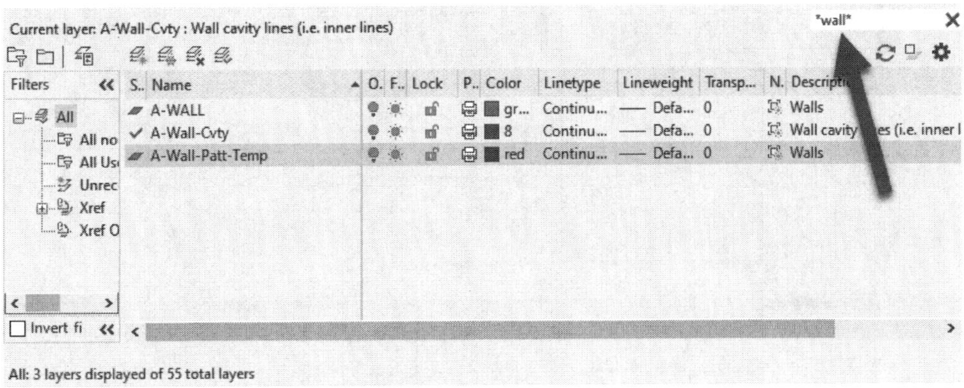

FIGURE 4-5.6 Layer Manager; search for "wall" layers

Later in this book you will learn about another feature called **Layer States**, which allows you to create "named" *Layer States* to control the visibility of *Layers*. Thus, you can quickly toggle between a presentation type drawing (i.e., minimal notes, dimensions and solid hatching in the walls) to construction documents (i.e., notes and dimensions visible, and solid wall hatching turned off).

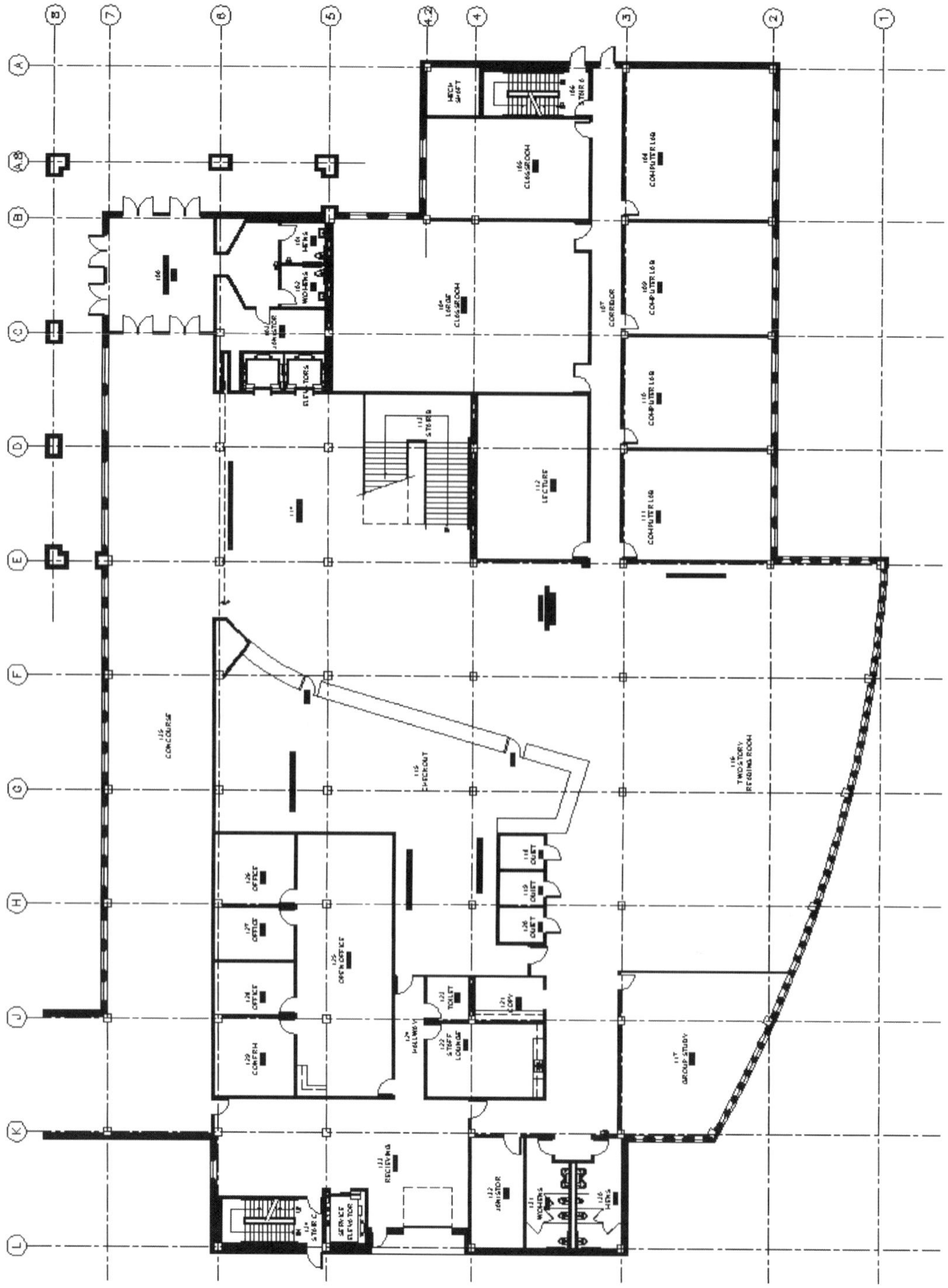

FIGURE 4-5.7 Overall floor plan with walls filled solid

Self-Exam:

The following questions can be used as a way to check your knowledge of this lesson. The answers can be found at the bottom of this page.

1. All drawing data downloaded from the Internet is perfect. (T/F)
2. Sightlines are important in toilet room designs. (T/F)
3. Right-click a Layer name to select all Layers in Layer Manager. (T/F)
4. The handrails for the stairs go on _______________ layer.
5. Which hatch feature saves you from having to re-hatch an area when you stretch a wall to a new location? _______________

Review Questions:

The following questions may be assigned by your instructor as a way to assess your knowledge of this section. Your instructor has the answers to the review questions.

1. Toilet partitions are typically drawn 1″ thick. (T/F)
2. Countertops are drawn 25″ for a 24″ deep base cabinet. (T/F)
3. Wall cabinets are shown with dashed lines in floor plans. (T/F)
4. The Layer Previous icon restores the condition of any Layers from the last time they were changed. (T/F)
5. You can Copy/Paste items between drawings. (T/F)
6. In the Layer Manager, you can modify the list of layers to just show the Layers that just have "door" in them? (T/F).
7. What did you draw in order to list a room's area? _______________
8. What command mends two lines together? _______________
9. What command lets you freeze a Layer by selecting an object on screen?

   ____
10. You can only have one text height within an Mtext object. (T/F) (assuming it is not an Annotative text style)

SELF-EXAM ANSWERS:
1 – F, **2** – T, **3** – T, **4** – A-Flor-Hral, **5** – Associative

Notes:

Lesson 5
Library Project: FLOOR PLANS: Furniture, Fixtures & Equipment (FFE)

In this lesson you will continue to develop your floor plan for the Campus Library project. Throughout the lesson you will be introduced to a few new commands, and you will add desks, tables, chairs, stacks, copiers, etc.

The image below is another reminder of what your plan will look like when you finish this chapter. Notice, again, the classrooms in the lower-right, the office area in the upper-left, the main toilet rooms in the lower-left, the public concourse across the top, and the check-out area in the middle.

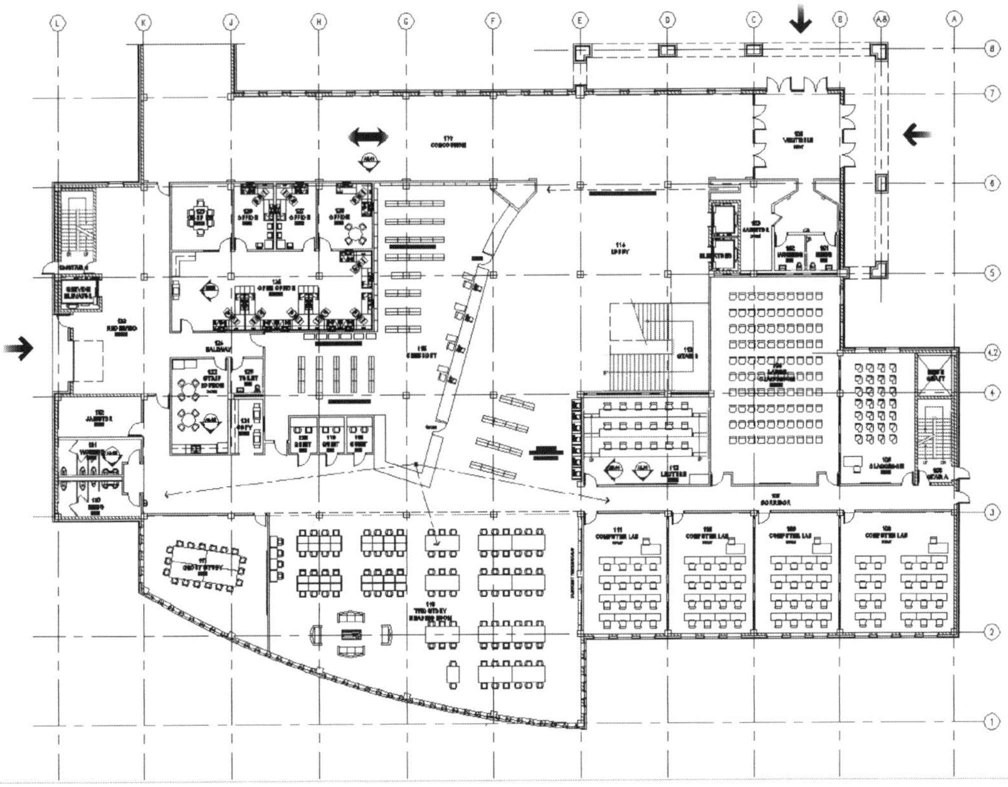

OVERVIEW: Example of what will be drawn in this book - First Floor Plan

Exercise 5-1:
Overview: Creating a Symbol Library

Introduction

All design firms have a collection of symbols that are available when needed as they are designing spaces. These symbols come from several sources, for example: internet, manufacturer, consultant, software, etc.

The collection of details obviously relates to the type of work performed by that firm. A firm that specializes in health care, for example, will have a symbol library that consists of exam tables, operating room equipment, etc.

These symbols can contain a wealth of embodied knowledge; that is, information to help the designer make better decisions. A symbol might have dashed lines that represent the clear floor area required near or around it (e.g., the space around the exam room table).

These symbols need to be stored in a logical location on a server for future access by all the members of a particular firm. This will increase the efficiency of the firm when set up properly.

There are several ways in which one might organize the content used by Architects and Interior Designers. Below is just one example that will be used to organize the symbols that you will draw in the next exercise.

In this book you will be instructed to draw the symbols in your *My Documents* folder as a default. However, if in a class setting you might want to create these folders on your personal network drive if you have one.

- 🗁 Documents (*My Documents* in Windows XP)
  - AutoCAD Symbols
    - Appliances — *Refrigerator, Microwave, Vending*
    - Chairs — *All Chairs (except lounge chairs)*
    - Tables — *All Tables*
    - Desks — *All Desks*
    - Equipment — *Copier, Computer, etc.*
    - Library — *Book truck, Stack, Carrel, etc.*
    - Fixtures — *Marker Boards,*
    - Lounge Furn — *Couch, Large chairs*
    - Misc — *Anything not listed above*

1. **Create** the folder structure outlined above via *My Computer* or *Window Explorer*; the *Documents* folder will already exist.

Adding a Hyperlink to the Symbols in Your Library:

AutoCAD gives you the ability to add a *Hyperlink* to the *Block*. Just like clicking a link (i.e., a hyperlink) on a webpage, you can click on a block (actually Ctrl + Click) to open your web browser and the specified web page.

This feature allows you to embed information about a symbol, at least indirectly, in that you or someone else using your drawing can open a web page that will provide more information about that item.

For example, you can add a *Hyperlink* to the conference room table. The *Hyperlink* can point to the manufacturer's website and, more specifically, to the product information page for that table.

The following steps will show you how to add a *Hyperlink* to your *Blocks*. Your instructor may require you to add a *Hyperlink* to each symbol created in this lesson. You may also add the *Hyperlink* on your own; simply do a search on the internet to find a manufacturer that makes the type of furniture you are drawing.

2. Open an empty, **new drawing** for the following steps (*template file*: Sheet Set\ Architectural Imperial).

3. Switch to **Model** space.

Next you will draw a rectangle that will represent a conference room table.

4. **Draw a Rectangle** (any size and location).

Creating a Block

A *Hyperlink* is added during the *Block* creation process and is available for each and every *Block* inserted into a drawing.

5. Click **Create Block** on the **Insert** tab.

6. Type **Conf-Table** for the *Block* name.

7. Under *Base Point*, click the **Pick point** button and select a point near the middle of the rectangle.

8. Under *Objects*, click the **Select objects** button, select the rectangle, and then press **Enter**.

9. Click the **Hyperlink** button (Figure 5-1.1).

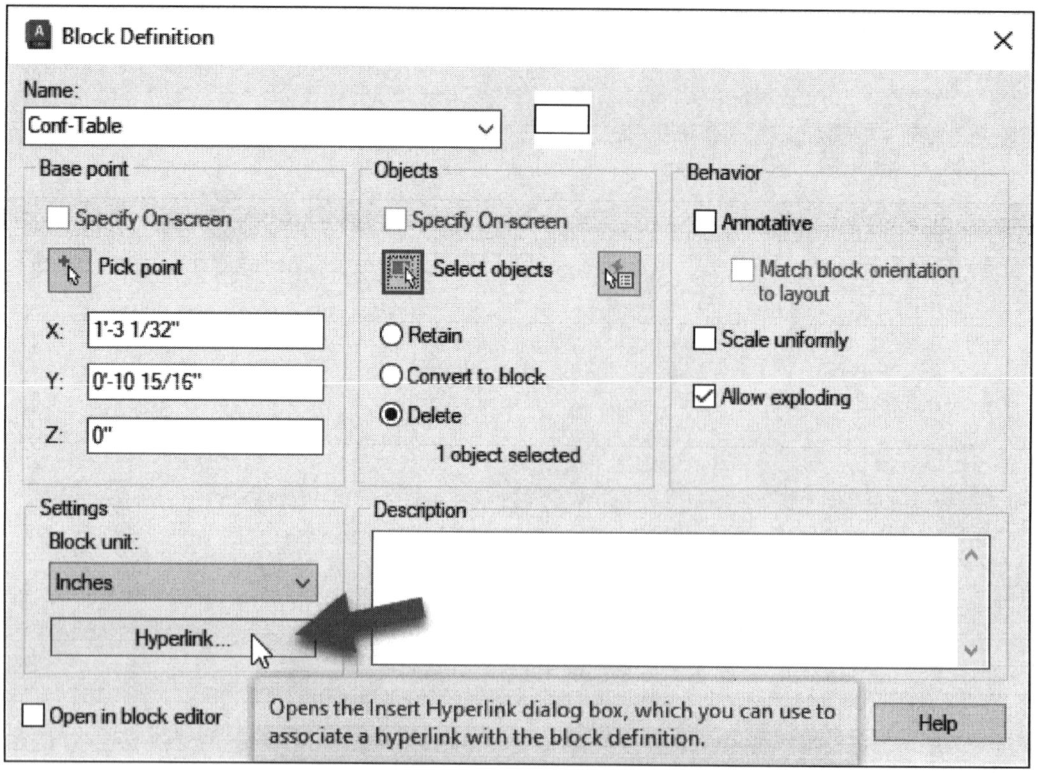

FIGURE 5-1.1 Block Definition dialog box

Adding a Hyperlink:

You are now in the *Insert Hyperlink* dialog box. Here you can type an internet address, browse for a file, or browse for a webpage (via your internet browser). You can also "copy – paste" an address from your internet browser (or other document) directly into this dialog box.

Some product web pages have rather complicated internet addresses (a.k.a., **URL** = Universal Resource Locator) because of the way the large number of products they carry are managed by the website. In the next step, the address listed was found by searching the **Herman Miller** website for a particular product type. Once the desired product was found, the current address listed in the internet browser was copied to the clipboard and pasted into the *Insert Hyperlink* dialog in AutoCAD (any URL will work for this exercise).

10. In the *Type the file or Web page name:* area type: **https://www.hermanmiller.com/products/tables/conference-tables/** (Figure 5-1.2).

11. Check the **Convert DWG hyperlinks to DWF** option.

    FYI: *This will create a hyperlink within DWF files. (DWF files are a lightweight version of your drawings that can be posted on the Internet or emailed.) Making DWF files is covered later in this book.*

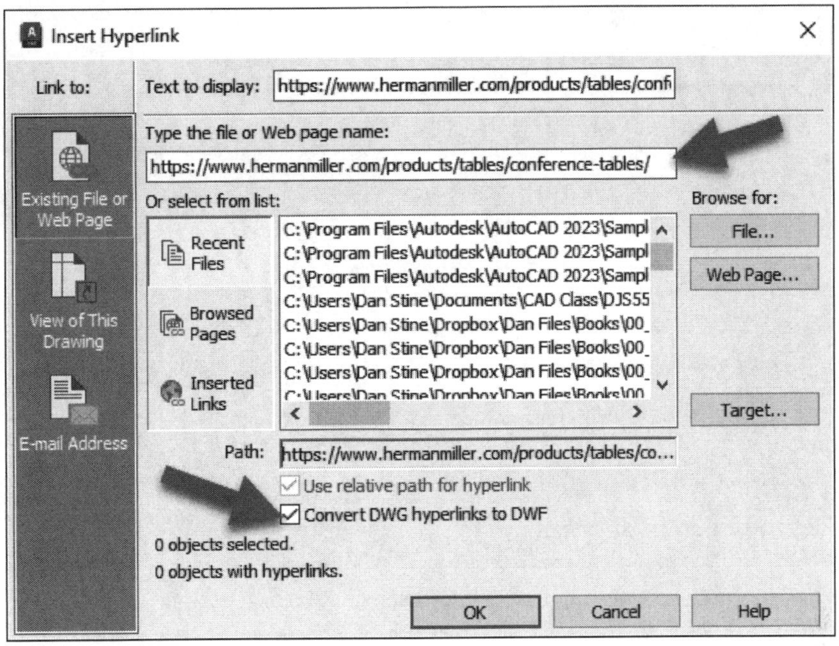

FIGURE 5-1.2 Insert Hyperlink dialog

12. Click **OK** twice to complete the *Block* creation process.

The value of adding *Hyperlinks* is that the most current product information can always be accessed. It is possible to add something called an *Attribute* to a *Block*, which can hold information such as model number, cost, etc. However, this information can quickly become obsolete so the ability to link to a website which can be updated at any time by the manufacturer is a big plus.

Testing the Block with the Hyperlink:

Now you will see how the *Block* with the *Hyperlink* works.

13. **Insert** the **Conf-Table** *Block* into the current drawing.

14. **Hover your cursor** over the *Block* to see the **tooltip** appear near the cursor (Figure 5-1.3).

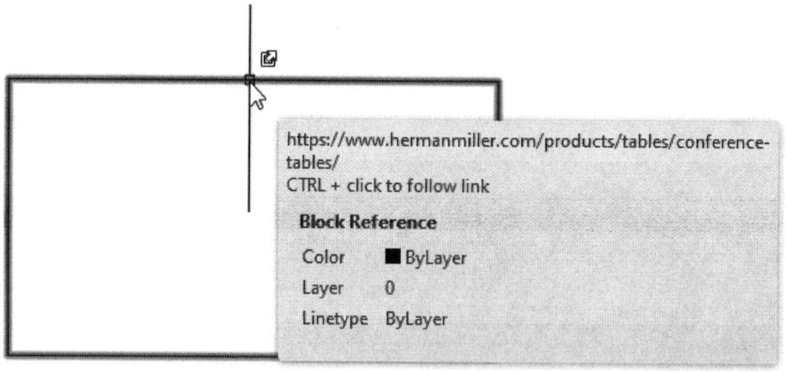

FIGURE 5-1.3 Conf-Table block: hover curser over block

15. Click to **select** the ***Block***.

16. With the *Block* selected, right-click and select *Hyperlink* → *click on the listed* URL (Figure 5-1.4). ***FYI:*** *The website can also be accessed by holding the* Ctrl *key and then clicking on the* Block *(as the tooltip in the image above states).*

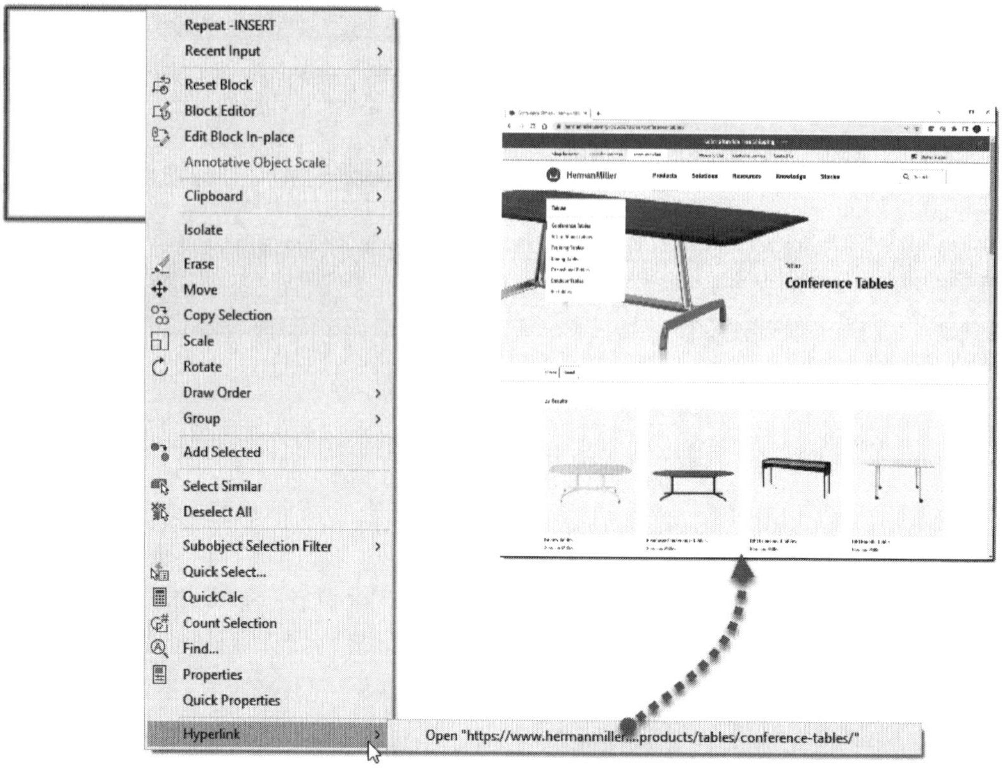

FIGURE 5-1.4 Conf-Table block: right-click to open webpage

Exercise 5-2:
Drawing Symbols

Introduction

Even though one can obtain symbols within your CAD program and from various sources on the internet, you will draw several symbols in this section. These symbols will sharpen your drafting skills and introduce you to a few new concepts.

You will not draw the dimensions as they are for reference only. Each drawing should be drawn in its own drawing file; save the drawing with the filename provided.

Finally, the black dot on each of the drawings below is for reference only. This dot represents the location of the *Drawing Origin* (0,0).

As previously mentioned, all the objects MUST BE drawn in SEPARATE drawing files. Each object will have a specific name provided, which is to be used to name the drawing file. All files should be saved in your personal folder created for this course.

Each new drawing created for this course should be done using the **Architectural Imperial.dwt** template file (*SheetSet* sub-folder).

Most dimensions are given; all other dimensions (not given) can be approximated so that your drawing looks as close to those shown as possible.

Office layout example: Notice the furniture in this university office. These pieces need to be laid out by an architect or interior designer that understands the function of the space and the related accessibility codes. Having pre-drawn symbols speeds this process.

Blocks and Layers:

Everything in this exercise should also be drawn on *Layer* zero (i.e., *Layer* 0); the only exception will be the "clear floor area" lines discussed momentarily.

As you may be aware, when a *Block* is inserted in a drawing it is placed on the current *Layer*; when that *Layer* is turned off the *Block* will disappear. Additionally, any lines within the Block that are on Layer zero will take on the properties of the *Layer* the *Block* was inserted on.

> ***For example***, if you created a Window *Block* (and all the lines within the *Block* were created on *Layer* zero) and inserted it on a *Layer* named A-Glaz (whose *Color* was set to red and *Linetype* was Hidden 2), the Window *Block* would be red and dashed. If you changed the A-Glaz *Layer* color, all the Window *Blocks* would change accordingly. This gives you the most control and also allows you to tell, visually, if the Window *Block* was inserted on the correct *Layer*. (If the lines in the Window *Block* were drawn on the A-Glaz *Layer* as opposed to *Layer* zero, the block would always look like it was on the correct *Layer* even when it was not.)

Even though most lines within a *Block* should be drawn on *Layer* zero, you may occasionally have a few lines within a *Block* that are on specific *Layers* to achieve maximum control over the *Block* (in terms of visibility and/or lineweight).

> ***For example***, in the Window *Block* mentioned above, you might have two lines within the *Block* on *Layer* A-Glaz-Sill and everything else on *Layer* zero. Thus, when the Window *Block* is inserted, the lines on *Layer* zero take on the properties of the *Layer* it was inserted on, but the sill lines are "hard-coded" to the properties of the A-Glaz-Sill *Layer*. If you accidentally placed the Window *Block* on the A-Door *Layer*, the "zero layer lines" will be the wrong color even though the sill lines look fine.

Now you will create a *Layer* called A-Flor-Nplt (*Nplt* stands for no-plot) which will be used to draw information on that is not intended to plot.

1. Create *Layer* **A-Flor-Nplt** and set the *Plot* column to not plot; see Figure 5-2.1.

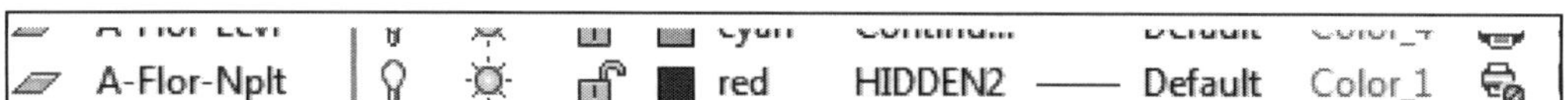

FIGURE 5-2.1 New layer created

filename: Bookcase.dwg

This is a simple rectangle that represents the size of a bookcase. The dimensions are not to be drawn, but the text "bookcase" will be added to the A-Flor-Nplt *Layer*. This text will help to keep the blocks orientated the same way in case you need to redefine this *Block*, so they all would get deeper (for example) in the same direction. This text will also help you distinguish this simple rectangle from others (desk, table, etc.).

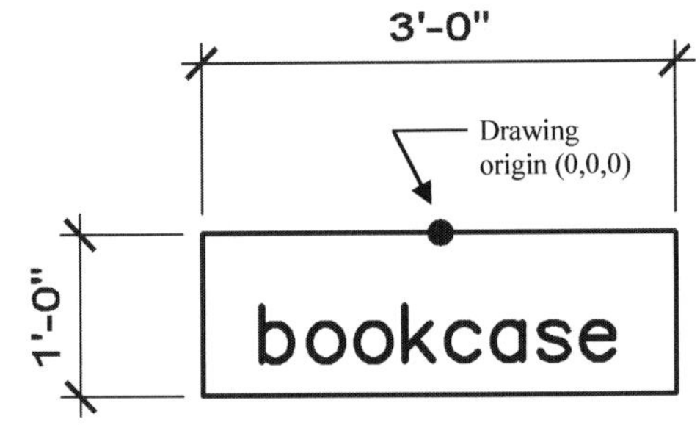

2. **Open** a new drawing.
3. Switch to **Model** space.
4. Use the **Rectangle** command to draw the bookcase.
5. Draw the **text**:
   a. *Style*: Roman
   b. *Height*: 4"
   c. *Layer*: A-Flor-Nplt
6. Verify the **Drawing Origin** is in the correct location.
7. **Save** your drawing per the name listed above.

---

filename: Coffee Table.dwg

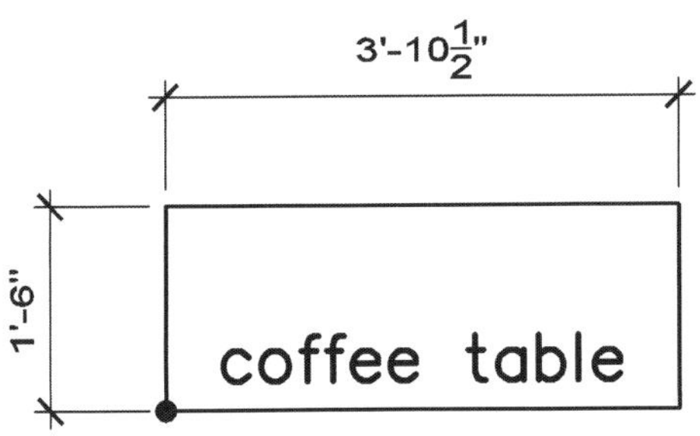

8. Similar to the steps listed above, plus the suggestions mentioned below, create the **coffee table** shown to the left.

REMEMBER: *This is another* <u>*new*</u> *drawing file.*

<u>Entering fractions</u>: the 3′-10½″ can be entered in one of three ways.

- 3′10.5 — *Notice there is no space between the feet and inches*
- 3′10-1/2 — *Note the dash location; it separates the inches: whole - fraction*
- 46.5 — *This is all in inches; that is 3′- 10½″ = 46.5″*

filename: **desk-1.dwg**

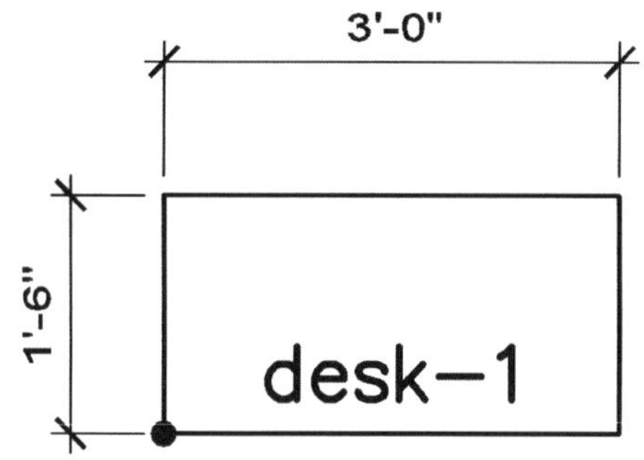

9. Draw the **Desk** in its own file, similar to the steps outlined above.

   FYI: *Again, the text is for use by the designer. However, if a designer wanted a technician to print the drawing with the A-Flor-Nplt Layer on to verify compliance, the No-Plot setting can be turned off in the Layer Manager palette.*

---

filename: **End Table.dwg**

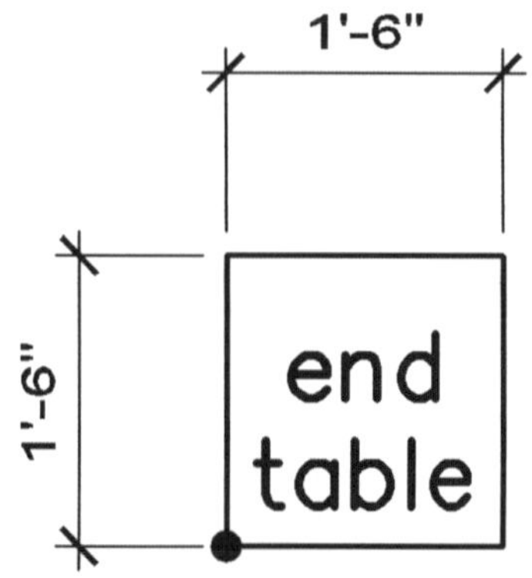

10. Draw this **Table**, similar to the steps outlined above.

---

filename: **Teacher Desk.dwg**

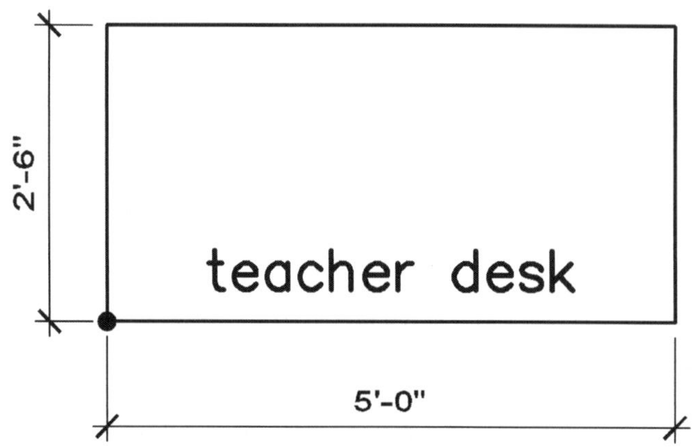

11. Draw this **Desk**, similar to the steps outlined above.

filename: **Stack.dwg**

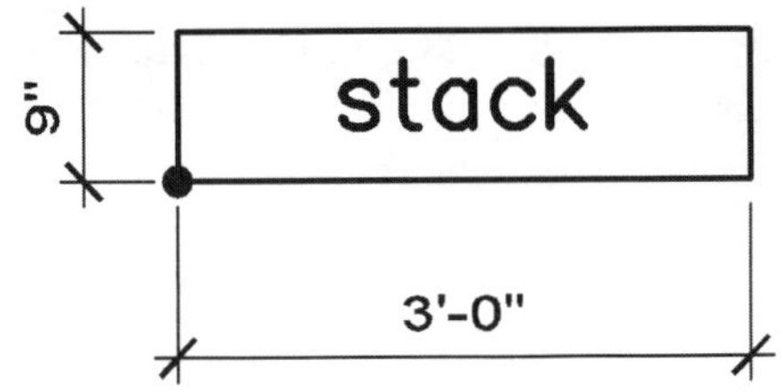

12. Draw this **stack**, similar to the steps outlined above.

    FYI: A stack is a library bookshelf.

filename: **Book Truck.dwg**

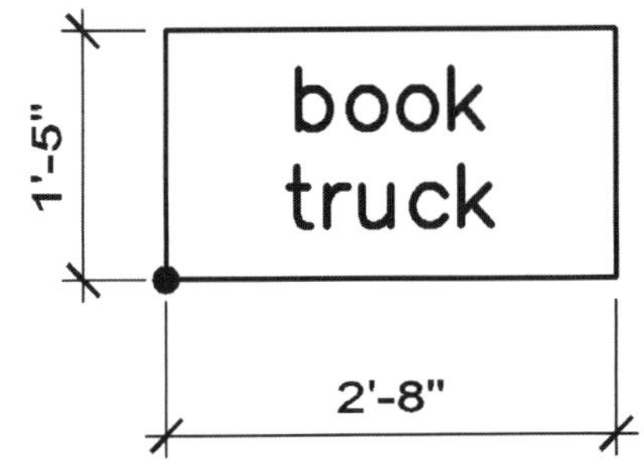

13. Draw this **book truck**, similar to the steps outlined above.

    FYI: A book truck is a four-wheeled cart used in a library.

filename: **Table (24x60).dwg**

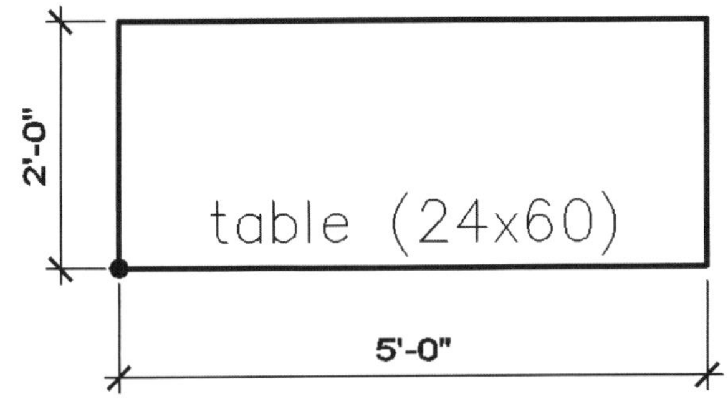

14. Draw this **table**, similar to the steps outlined above.

FYI: The dimensions were added to this table symbol because you may have several "table" blocks within the same drawing. If the Block name did not contain the size you would have to insert the various tables and measure them before you found the one you desired.

filename: **File Cabinet.dwg**

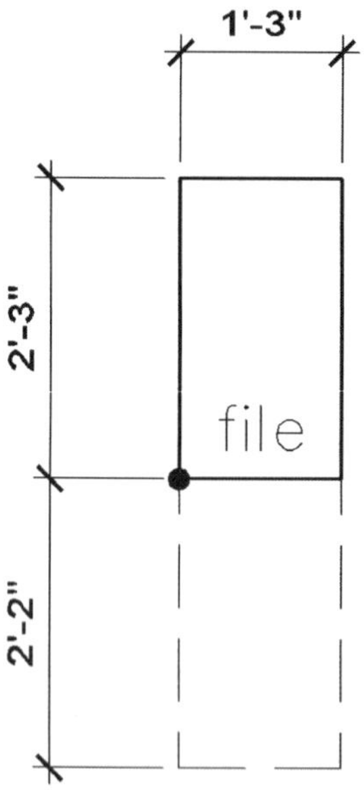

15. Draw the rectangle; see the next step for instruction on adding the dashed lines.

Next you will draw the dashed lines shown; these lines represent the space required in front of the file cabinet when a drawer is open.

A common mistake might be to place a row of file cabinets where one cabinet is in front of a column. Also, if you had a double-loaded aisle (i.e., file cabinets on each side), the dashed lines may overlap – provided the aisle is still wide enough – knowing that only one file cabinet drawer will likely be opened at a time.

16. **Draw** the dashed lines on *Layer* A-Flor-Nplt.

The examples below show how the file cabinet *Block* can be used to visually verify that the clear floor space required to open a drawer is available. The image on the left reveals a conflict with a column; the image on the right shows how the clear floor space can overlap when one can assume that only one drawer needs to be opened at a time.

Given that the dashed lines are on the no-plot Layer, the dashed lines will not actually print. If, at some point, you do not want to even see the dashed lines you can simply *Freeze* the A-Flor-Nplt *Layer* (only the file cabinet will be visible at that point).

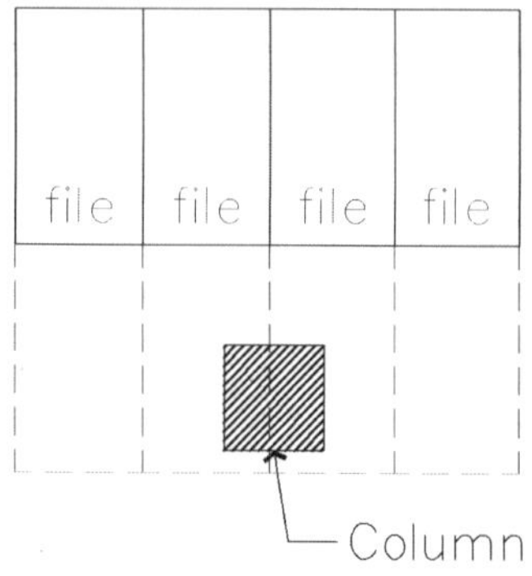

FIGURE 5-2.2 File cabinet conflict

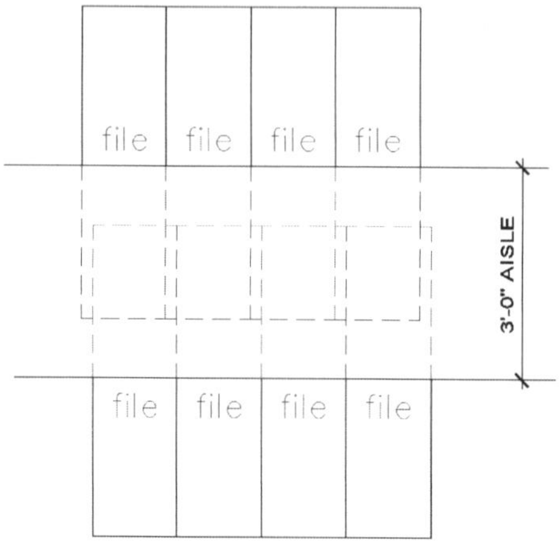

FIGURE 5-2.3 File cabinet conflict

filename: **Refrig.dwg**

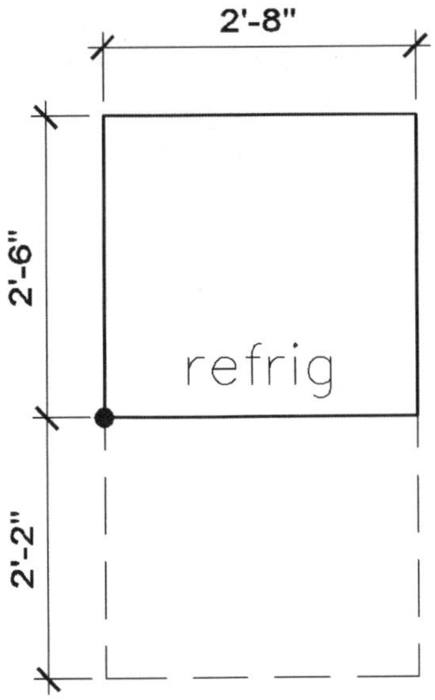

17. Draw this **refrigerator**, similar to the steps outlined above (drawing the dashed lines on *Layer* A-Flor-Nplt).

filename: **Vending-1.dwg**

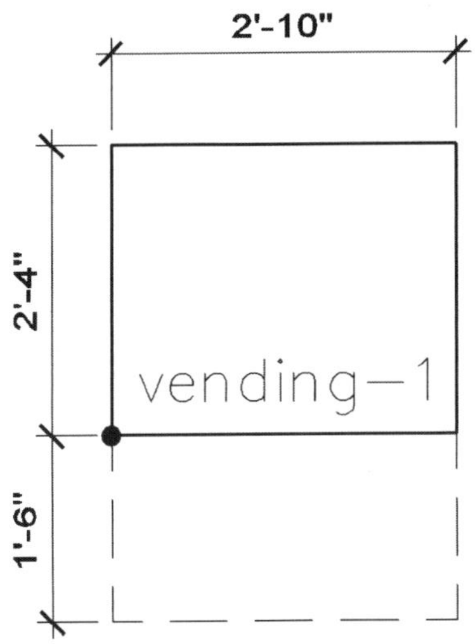

filename: **Vending-2.dwg**

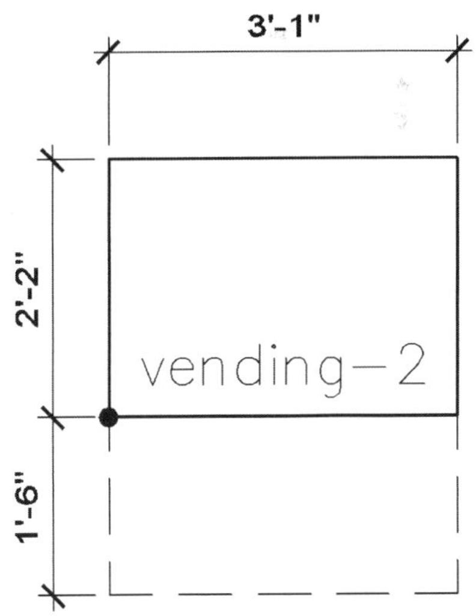

18. Draw these **vending machines**, similar to the steps outlined above.

filename: **desk-2.dwg**

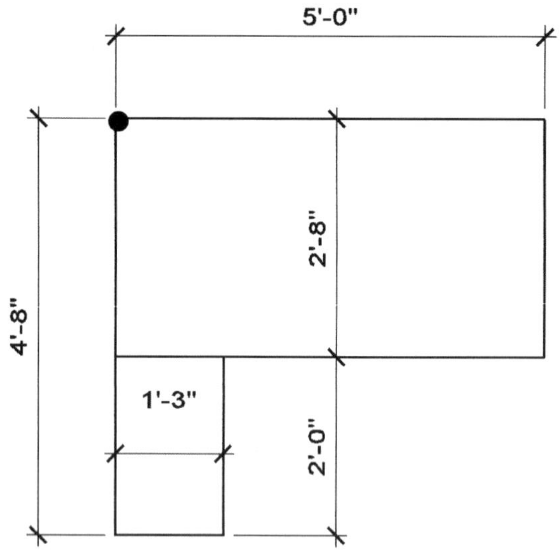

19. Draw this **desk,** similar to the steps outlined above.

filename: **Lounge Chair-1.dwg**

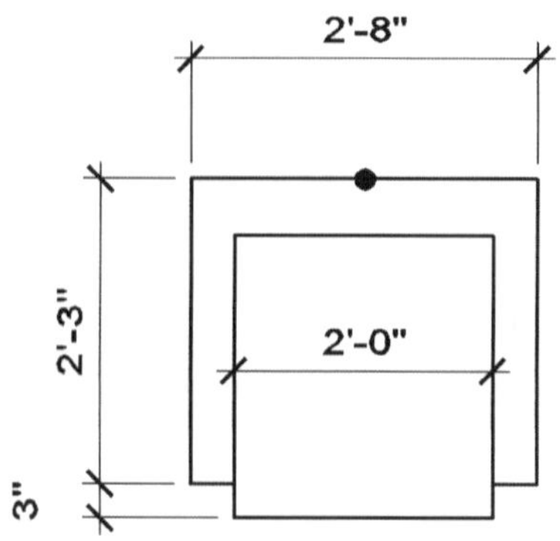

20. Draw this **lounge chair**.

filename: **sofa-1.dwg**

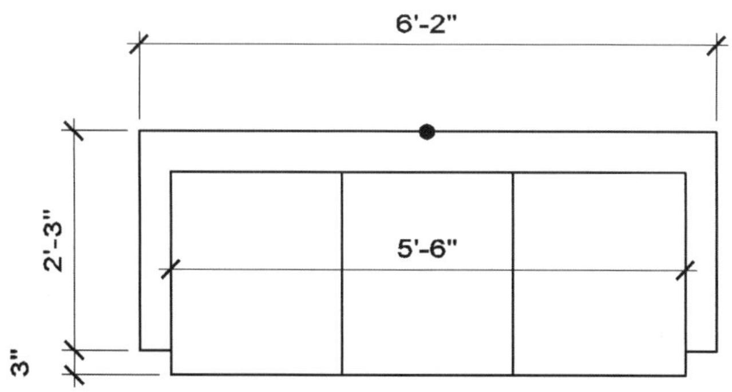

21. Draw this **sofa**.

filename: **Lounge Chair-2.dwg**

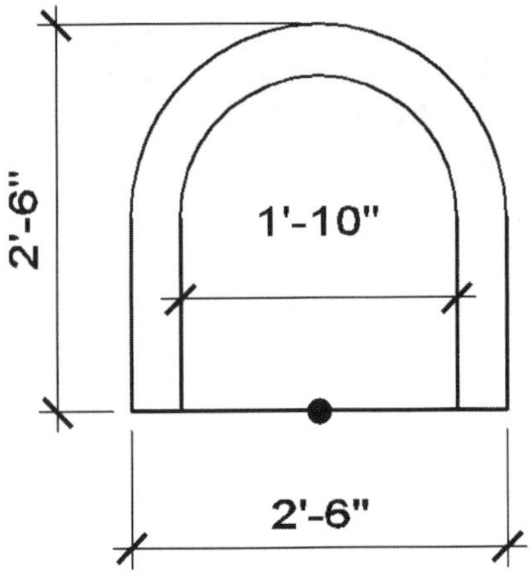

Now you will draw another chair. You can use the *Line* and *Offset* commands as well as the *Arc* command.

22. Draw this **chair**.

filename: **Love Seat.dwg**

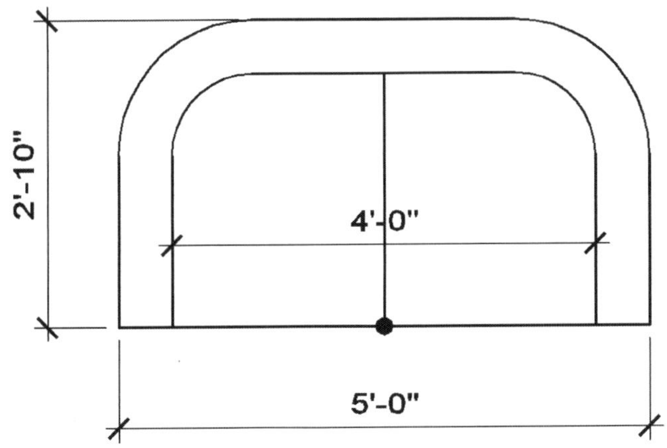

23. Draw this small **couch**.

filenames: **MB-8.dwg** and **MB-16.dwg**

24. Draw this **marker board**: 2″x8′-0″.

25. Draw another **marker board** (MB-16.dwg) at 2″x16′-0″ (make sure you change the text to read MB-16).

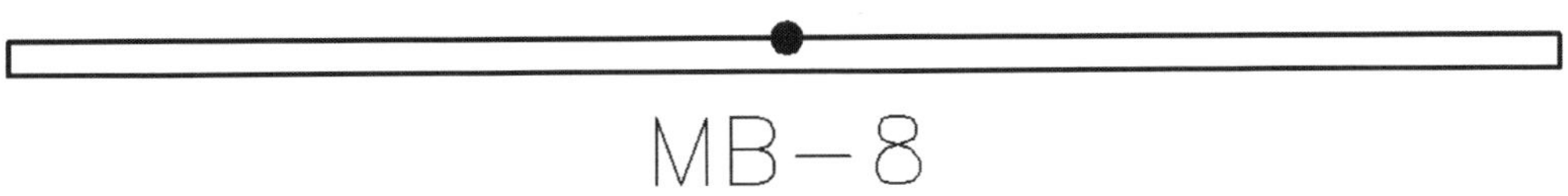

filename: **Chair-1.dwg**

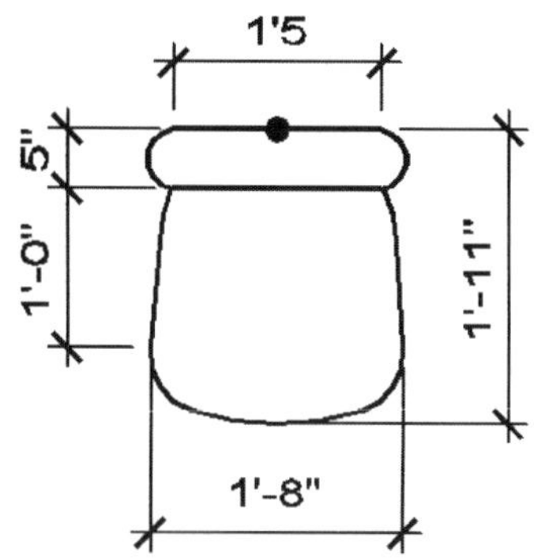

26. Draw the chair below per the following:
    a. Approximate radii of arcs so your drawing looks similar to drawing shown.
    b. As usual: do not draw dimensions or the black dot; they are for reference only.

You will not draw "clear floor area" lines due to the varied use of this symbol.

---

filename: **Chair-2.dwg**

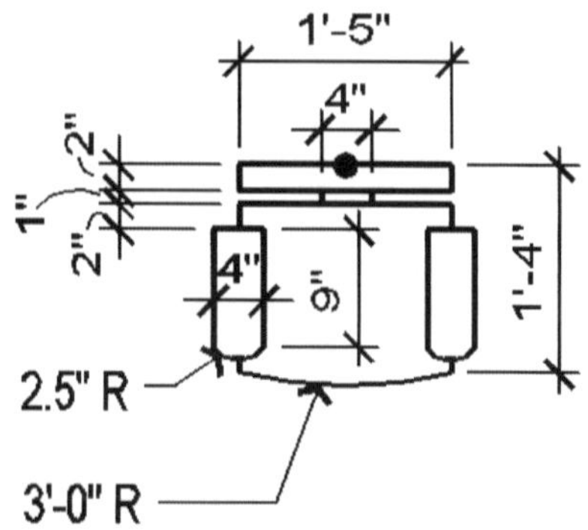

27. Draw the chair shown.

    TIP: Draw the left half of the chair and use the mirror command to quickly create the other half.

filename: **Chair-3.dwg**

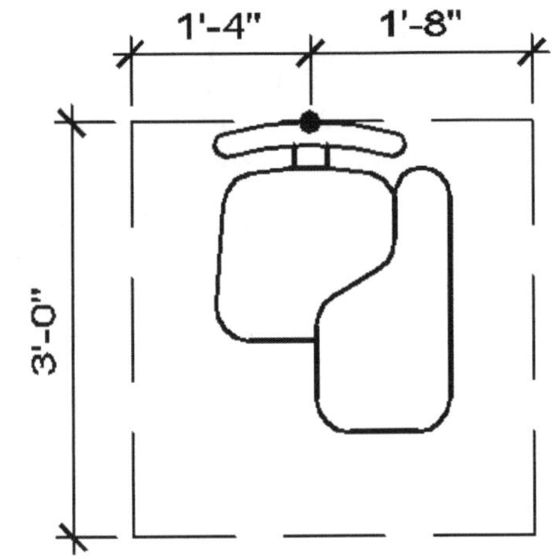

28. Draw this student chair with arm per the following:

TIP: Draw the chair in the order outlined below.

a. Draw the seat.

b. Draw the backrest.

c. Draw the side arm:
   i. Draw a closed **Polyline**.
   ii. Use the **Fillet** command with radius set to **2.5"** and type **P** for polyline to round off all six corners at once!

d. Remember to draw the dashed lines on *Layer* A-Flor-Nplt.

e. Approximate all dimensions not given.

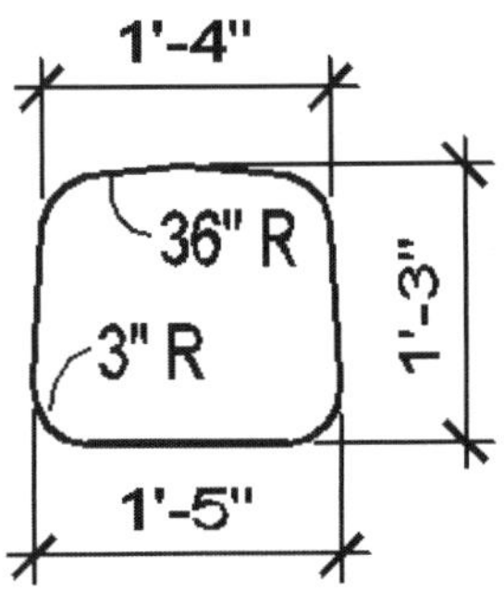

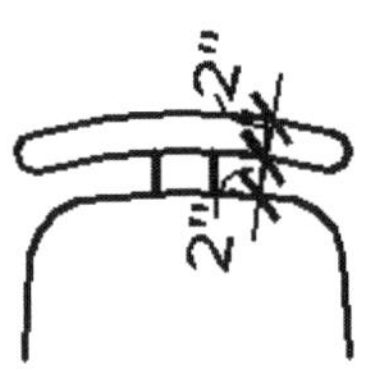

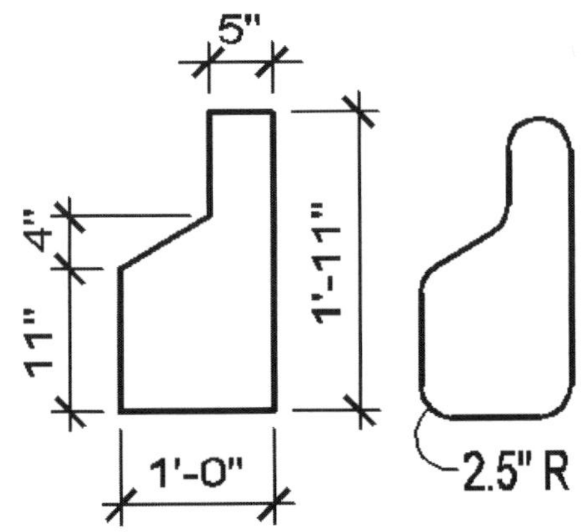

filename: **Copier.dwg**

29. Draw this copier:

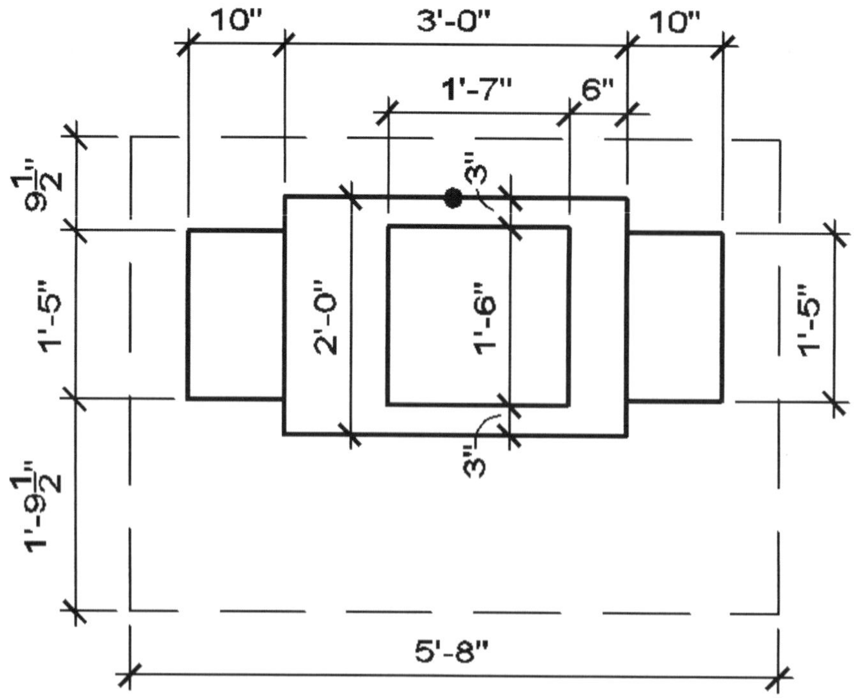

filename: **Computer.dwg**

30. Draw this computer:

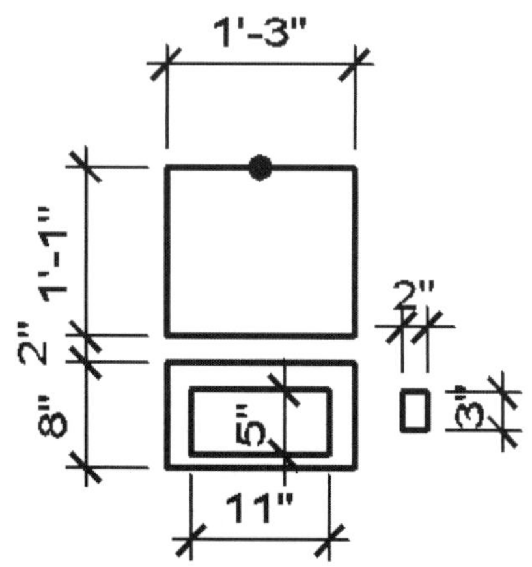

filename: **Systems Desk.dwg**

31. Draw this desk (see boxed note regarding chair; use the **Insert** icon):

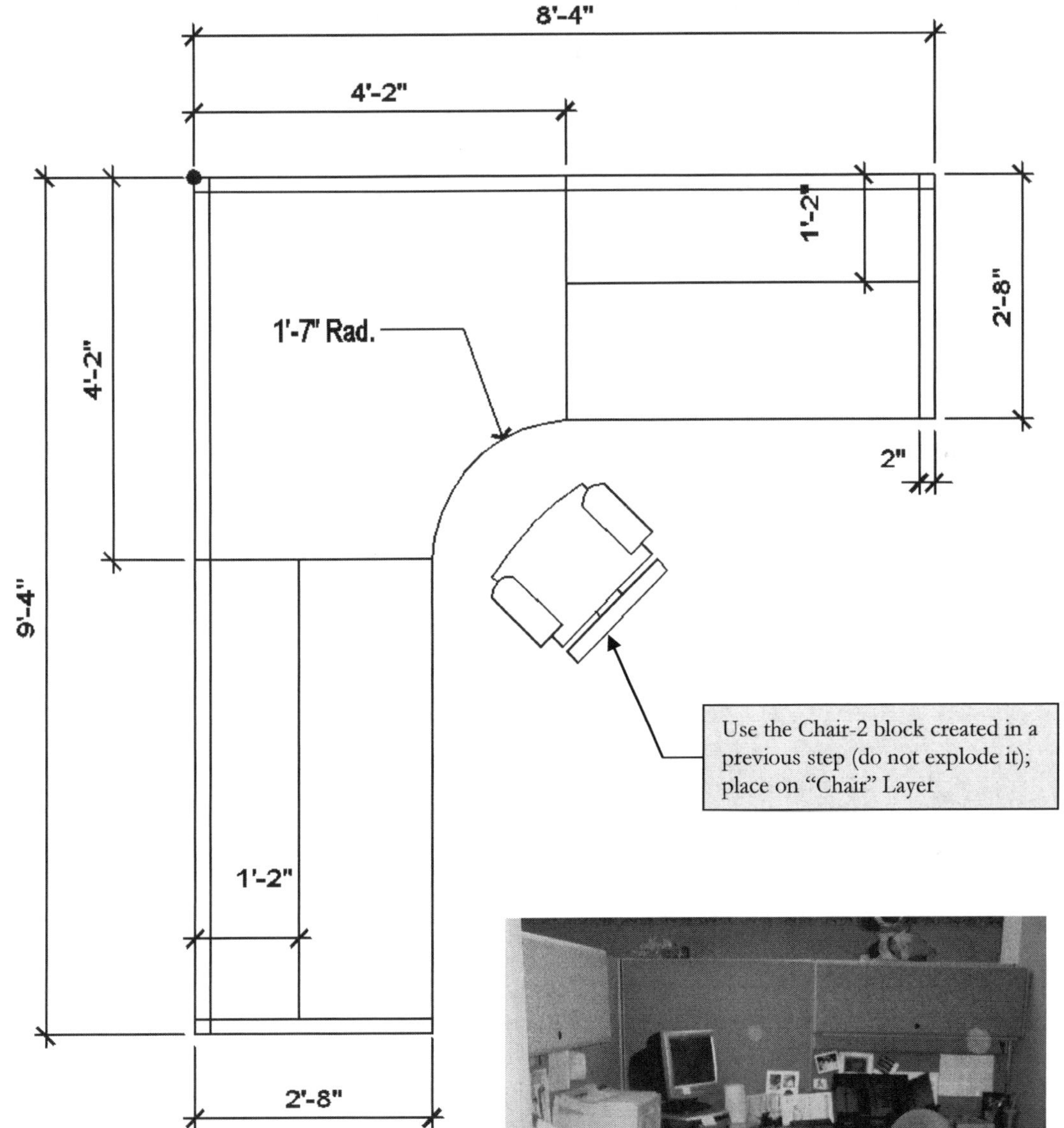

The 1′-2″ dimensions represent the upper cabinets (see photo to the right). The 2″ dimension is the privacy panels. Notice "extra" equipment: printer, file cabinet, items on the floor, etc.

EXAMPLE IMAGE Systems furniture

filename: **Round Table-4 Chairs.dwg**

32. Draw this table, per the following:
    a. Do not draw the angled reference lines.
    b. **Insert** the Chair 2 *Block* (do not explode); this will be what is called a *nested block*.
    c. Make sure the chairs are on the "chair" Layer.
    d. Draw the dashed lines on *Layer* A-Flor-Nplt.

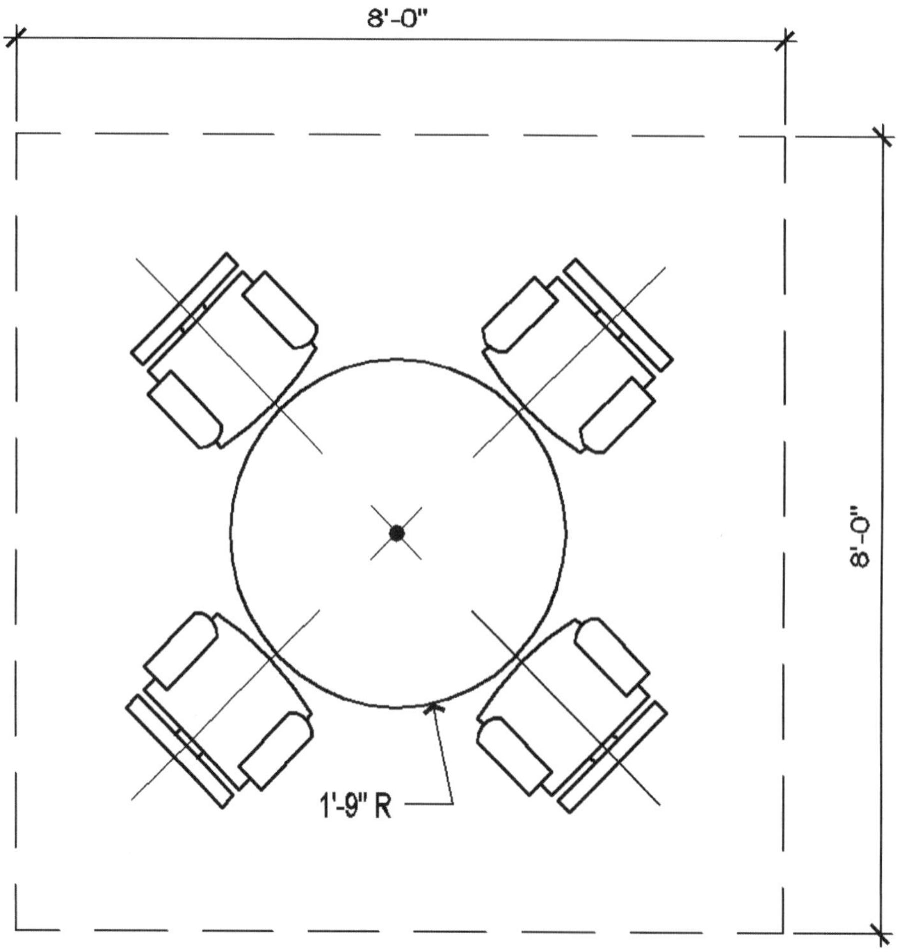

The dashed lines can be used to make sure you have the proper clear space around each table. Again, you would place the *Blocks* with the A-Flor-Nplt *Layer* on so you can SNAP the corners together. Then, when the design is mostly resolved you can turn the A-Flor-Nplt *Layer* off so only the table the chairs will be visible. Also, because the chairs are on their own *Layer* (within the *Block*) you can also control whether or not the chairs are visible as well.

filename: Study Carrel.dwg

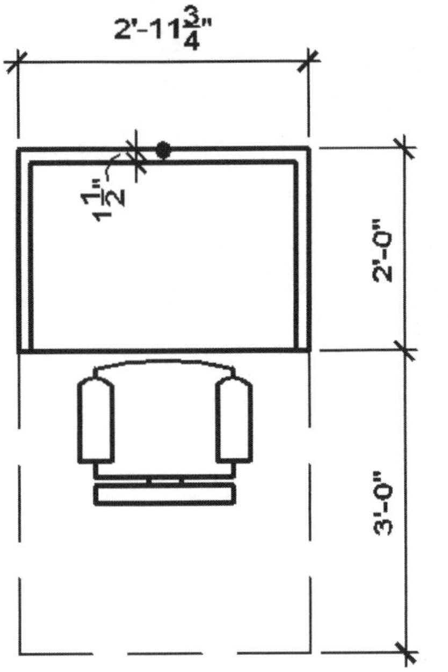

33. Draw this study carrel, per the following:
    a. Do not draw the dimensions.
    b. **Insert** the Chair 2 *Block* and make sure it is on the "chair" *Layer.*

STUDY CARRELS come in various shapes and sizes. Here is a more spacious, custom designed, library unit.

---

filename: Student Desk.dwg

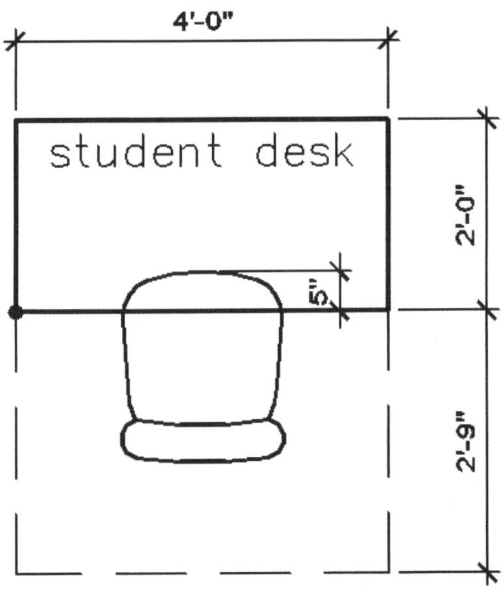

34. Draw this student desk, per the following:
    a. Do not draw the dimensions.
    b. **Insert** the Chair 1 *Block* and make sure it is on the "chair" *Layer.*
    c. Add the text on the "Nplt" Layer.

FYI: Student desks have minimal circulation space so the chair is shown "pushed in" so the circulation space can be visualized when several rows of desks are shown.

filename: **Reading Table-6 Chairs.dwg**

35. Draw this reading table (per the previous examples):

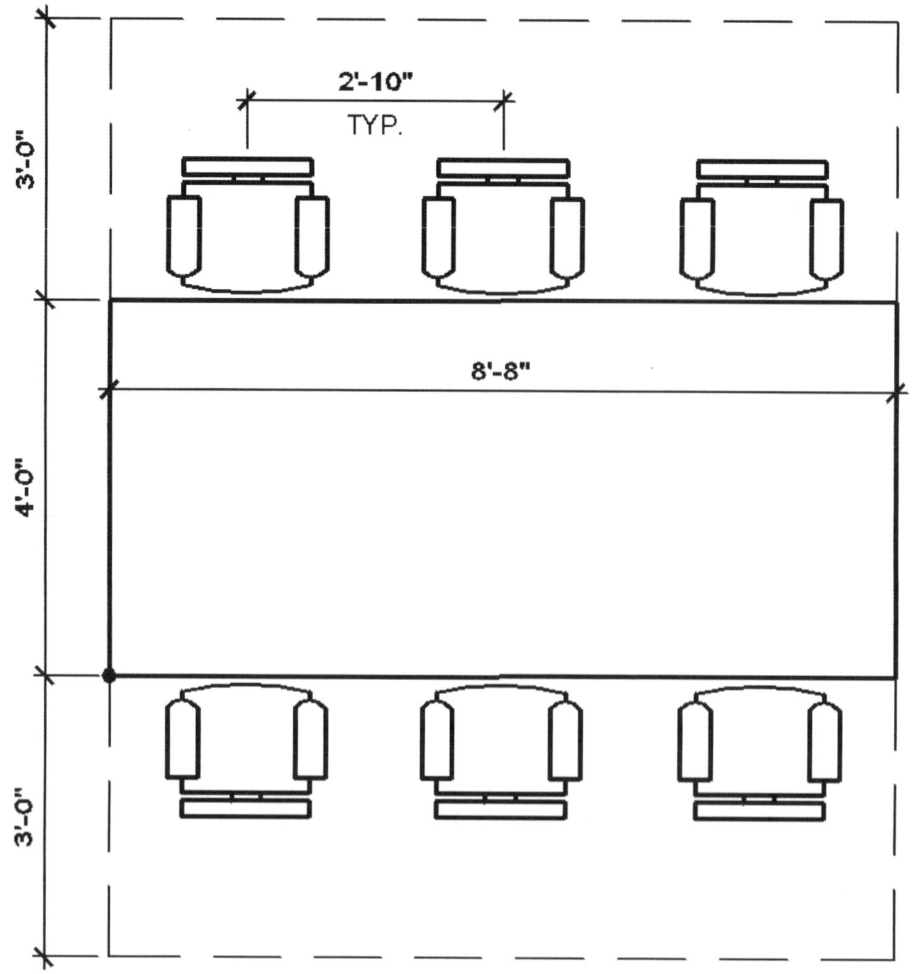

Given the various size and shaped rooms you will need to have more than one size reading table; you will draw two more sizes next. As your AutoCAD skills develop you might turn these three blocks into a *Dynamic Block* that stretches from the smallest table to the largest table (where the chairs are added and removed automatically).

STUDY CARRELS and **READING TABLES** example

filenames: **Reading Table-4 Chairs.dwg** and **Reading Table-2 Chairs.dwg**

36. Draw these reading tables (two separate drawings):

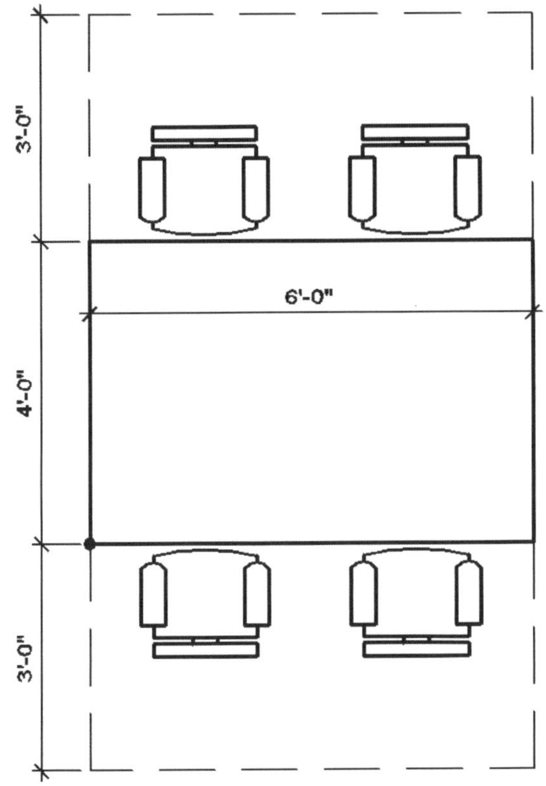

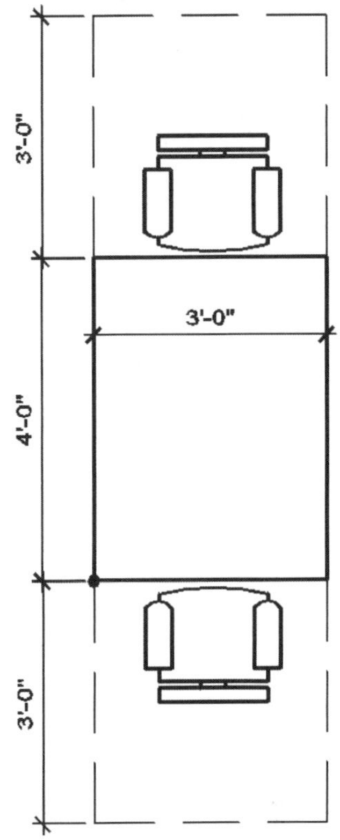

Reading Room
with various table sizes

filename: **Conf Table-6 Chairs.dwg**

37. Draw this conference room table (per the previous examples):

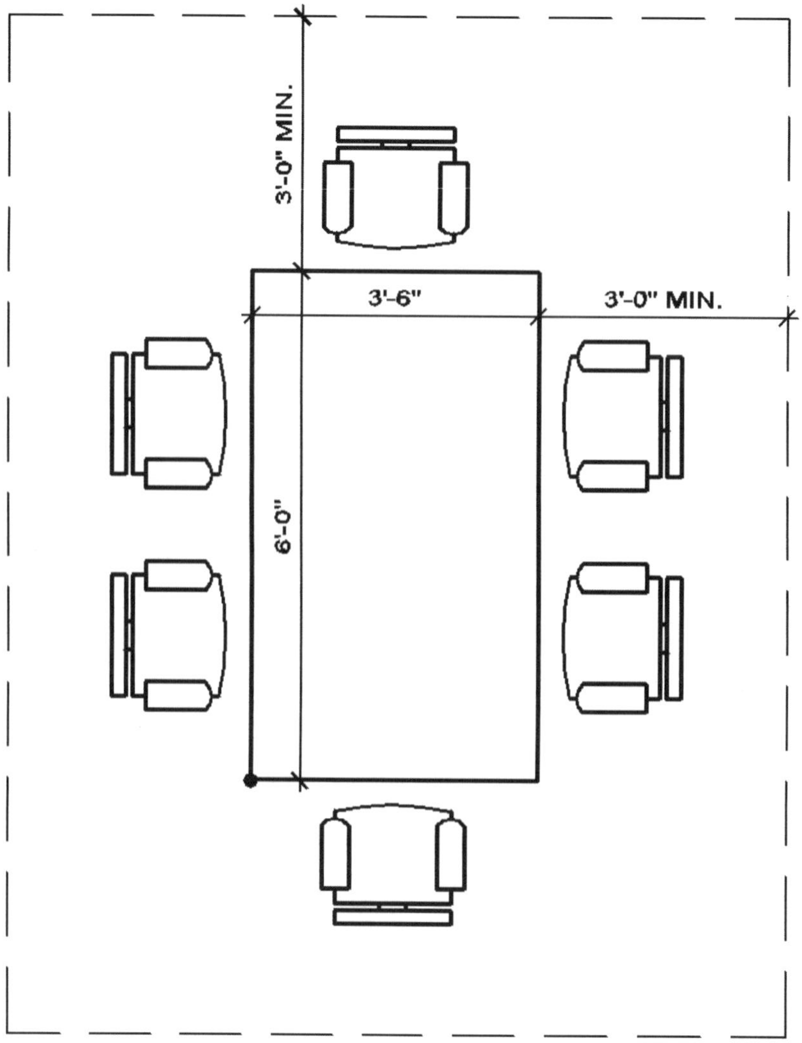

The room will typically be larger than the dashed lines. The dashed lines will help to ensure that nothing impedes the required clear floor space around the table. For example, you would not want any cabinets or walls to occur within the dashed lines. Given the room shape and size, the table may need to be a different size. In that case you could either *Explode* this *Block* and *Stretch/Scale* as required, or you might create a new *Block* and add it to your symbols library; however, extremely custom conditions only clutter a library.

Exercise 5-3:
Space Layout

Introduction

In this exercise you will use the symbols created in the previous exercise to populate the floor plan. You will lay out several types of rooms to give you exposure to various drafting techniques.

A Client benefits from an experienced Architect and/or Interior Designer. Many factors must be taken into consideration when designing a particular space. The following is just a few examples of design considerations related to space layout:

- Accessibility access and clearances
  - If furniture layouts are not done early enough, the room might need to grow in size to accommodate the program and accessibility codes – this type of revision can throw off estimates and create problems for adjacent spaces
- Sightlines (is tiered seating or privacy required)
- Furniture required (desk, tables or simply chairs)
  - An experienced designer will take the time to understand the program and the intended use of the space to make sure all needs are met, sometimes suggesting staffing or procedural ideas that may improve the client's efficiency.
- Light switch location (if room darkening is required often)
- Window treatment (again, if room darkening is required)
  - If unit is concealed in wall/ceiling, special details are required
  - Do exterior windows create excessive glare at certain times?
- Instructor desk location + wall jack location for ceiling mounted projector and internet (coordinated with electrical engineer)
- General circulation within the space
  - Are people coming and going at the same time?
  - Does the space require two exits due to its size?
- LEED© and Sustainable Design
  - Daylighting requirements / opportunities.
  - Functional materials with recycled content and low/no VOC's.
  - LEED© credit tracking (must be thought about continuously)

The list above is, again, just a sample of the thought process that a designer employs when designing a space.

Classroom Layout:

First, in this exercise, you will lay out a classroom with student chairs (the chairs with the reference arm).

1. Use the **Insert → Blocks from libraries…** command, from the **Insert** tab, and browse to the location where you saved the symbol **Chair-3.dwg**.

2. Adjust the *Block* location so it is in the lower right corner; this is in preparation for the array command (per dimensions given).

3. Use **Array** to quickly create all the chairs.
   a. Columns **4** *and* Rows **7**
   b. Row offset: **3'** *and* Column Offset: -**3'**
      NOTICE: *The minus will make the columns offset towards the west (left).*
      See Figure 5-3.2.

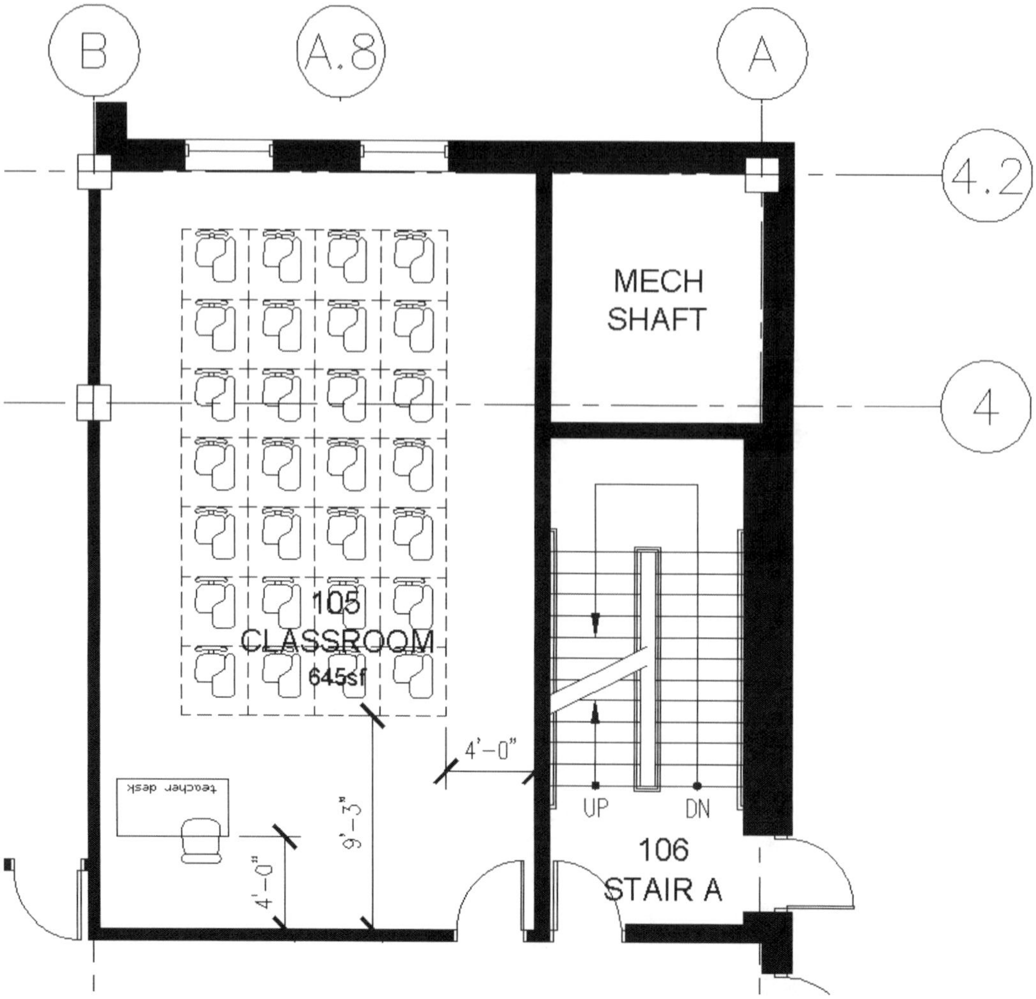

FIGURE 5-3.1 Classroom 105 with furniture added

The image to the right (Figure 5-3.2) shows the *Array* selected. Notice the highlighted grips. With the spacing set on the Ribbon, one can easily drag these grips and change the number of rows or columns. The other set of similar grips would change the spacing.

At least one aisle should be 4'-0" wide as shown in Figure 5-3.1; ideally this aisle would align with the door into the classroom for convenient wheelchair access.

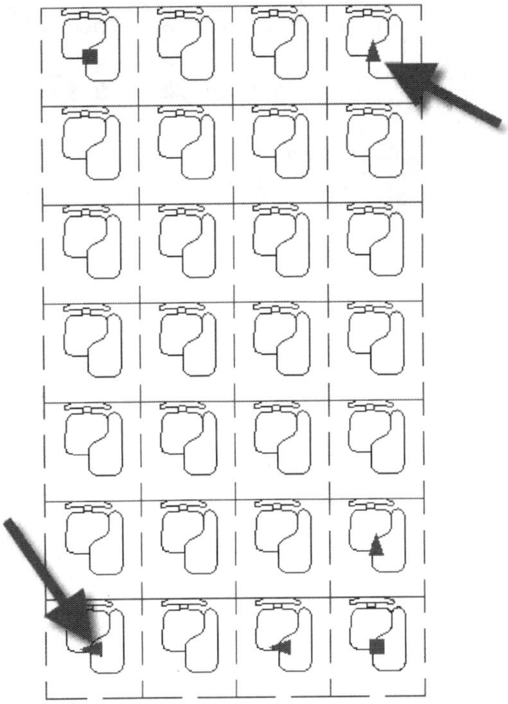

FIGURE 5-3.2 Array selected

4. Make sure the chairs (i.e., the *Block*) go on the **A-Furn-Char** *Layer.*

5. Insert the **Teacher Desk** as shown with Chair (Chair-1.dwg).
   a. Place desk on *Layer* **A-Furn.**
   b. Place the chairs on *Layer* **A-Furn-Char.**

You will notice in Figure 5-3.1 that the room text needs to move so it does not conflict with the furniture graphics. You should always try to avoid text overlapping lines so that readability does not become a problem.

6. Move the room name and number text down next to the teacher's desk (Figure 5-3.3).

Also, as you may recall, the dashed lines were created on their own *Layer* (A-Furn-Nplt). Whenever a *Block* in inserted, AutoCAD will create any *Layers* that exist in the *Block* but not in the current drawing. Even though the dashed lines are in the *Block*, their visibility can still be controlled via the *Layer Properties* palette. You will try this next…

7. From the *Layer Properties* palette (or type *LA* and *Enter*) **Freeze** *Layer* **A-Furn-Char.**

Both the task chair and the dashed lines have disappeared from the screen. Even though the dashed lines are on a different Layer (A-Flor-Nplt), they are first and foremost part of the chair *Block* (chair-3.dwg); and the *Block* is on *Layer* A-Furn-Char.

8. Select the *Layer* **Previous** icon on the **Layers** panel to undo the previous *Layer* command.

Now you will see what happens when you *Freeze* just the Nplt *Layer.*

9. From the *Layer Properties palette* **Freeze** *Layer* **A-Flor-Nplt**.

Your drawing should now look like Figure 5-3.3, showing just the chairs and desk. So here you have visibility control over linework contained within a *Block*.

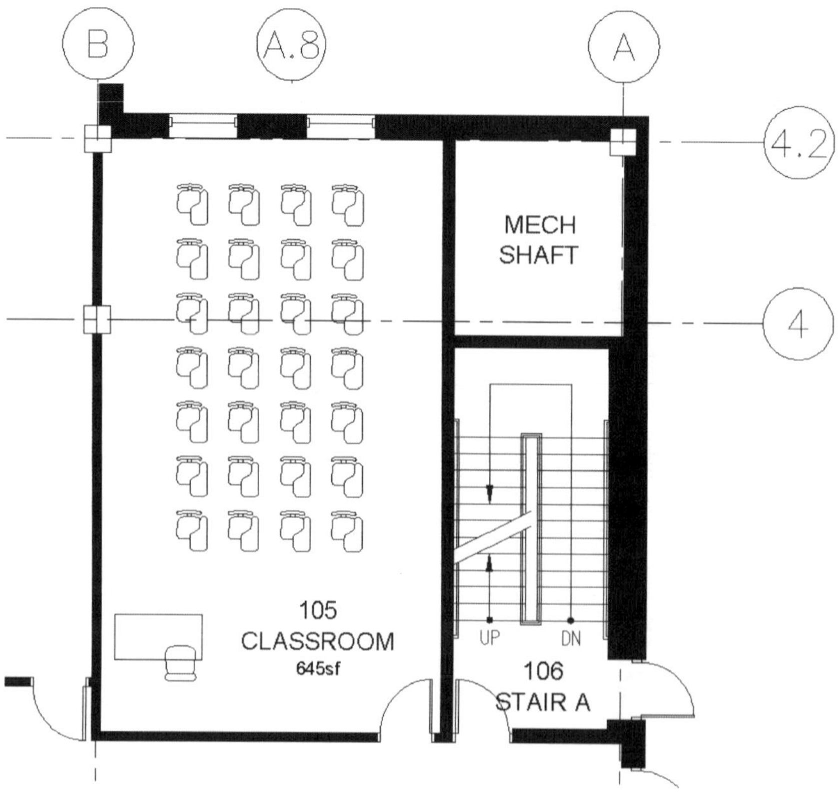

FIGURE 5-3.3 Classroom 105 with A-Flor-Nplt turned off

You will continue to lay out classrooms. The next few will have the "student desk" *Block* in addition to the "teacher desk".

10. Per steps previously outlined, use the **Insert → Blocks from libraries…** command, from the **Insert** tab, and browse to place the **Student Desk.dwg** as shown in Figure 5-3.4.

11. Place the Teacher's desk and chair as shown.

TIP: These can be copied from the previous room.

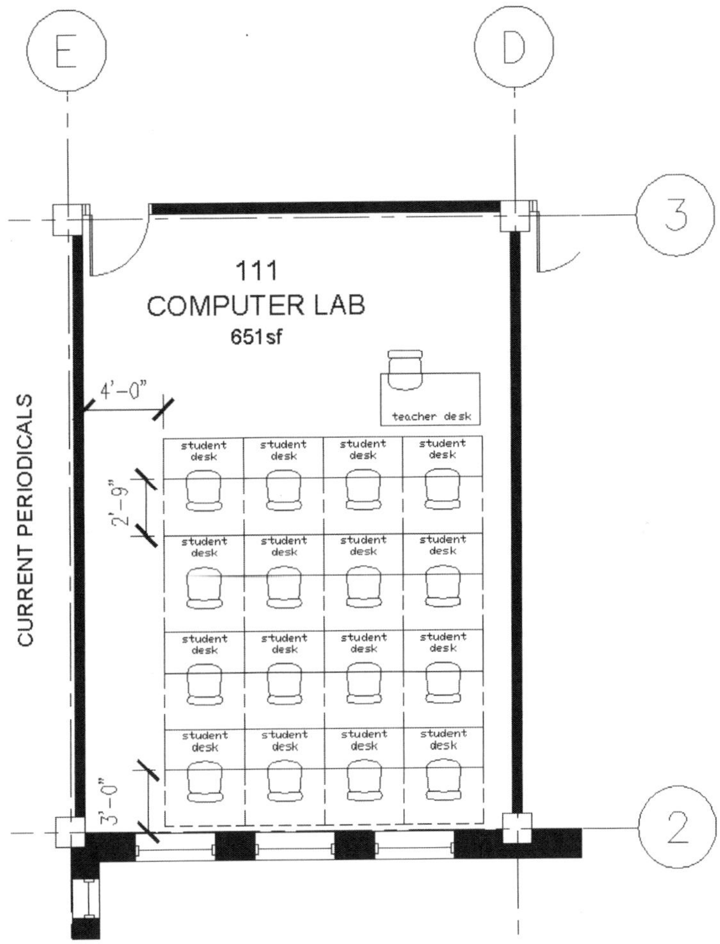

FIGURE 5-3.4 Computer Lab 111

12. Use AutoCAD's **Copy** command (not *Copy to Clipboard*) and copy the desk layout from classroom 111 to classrooms 109 and 110.

TIP: You should be able to accomplish this in one "copy" command: (1) select copy, (2) select objects, (3) pick common reference point – e.g., lower right corner, (4) pick lower right corner of rooms 109 and 110.

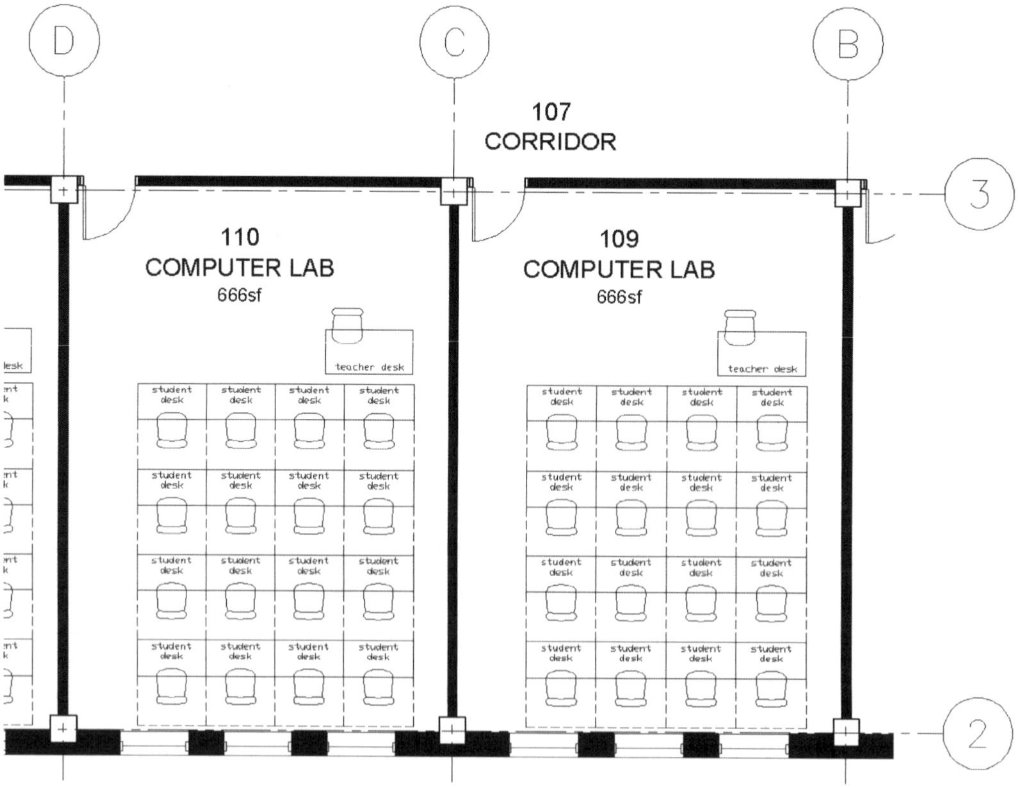

FIGURE 5-3.5 Computer Labs 109 and 110

13. Use the **Distance** command to verify the aisle on the left is at least 4'-0" wide (in rooms 109 and 110); adjust if necessary.

Once you understand the basics of laying out a certain type of space you can quickly design similar spaces. Next you will lay out a slightly wider space with an additional aisle.

14. Per the steps previously outlined, layout Computer Lab 108 as shown in Figure 5-3.6.

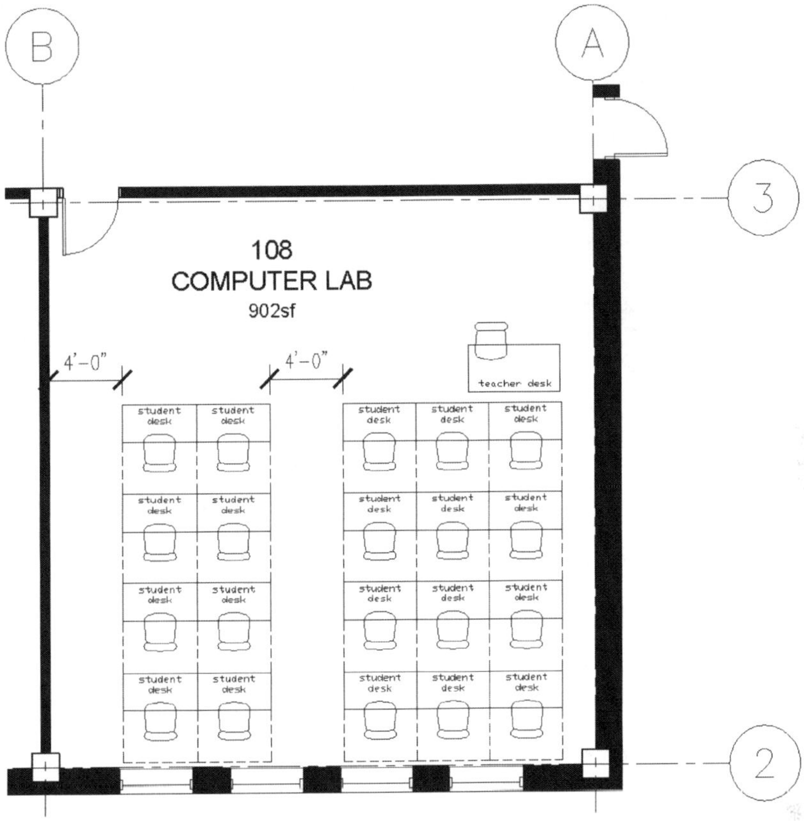

FIGURE 5-3.6 Computer Lab 108

Lecture room with raised-platform seating:

The next room you will lay out requires enhanced front-wall visibility; allowing the students to clearly see visually detailed presentations. The solution you will implement uses raised-platform (stadium-like) seating; thus, each row of desks and chairs is on a progressively higher surface.

To make the platform solid and long lasting, the platforms will be concrete (on metal decking or high-density insulation). Each raised surface will step up 14″. However, as you should recall, the maximum step allowed is typically 7″ so you will need to create (2) 7″ steps in the aisles for each platform.

15. Draw the platform/steps shown in Figure 5-3.7 per the following:
    a. Do not draw the dimensions.
    b. Draw the lines on A-Flor-Strs.
    c. Add handrails with typical 12″ extensions at top and bottom; place on the A-Flor-Hral layer.
    d. Add the arrows and Mtext per instructions in the previous chapter.
    e. See Figure 5-3.8 to help you better visualize what you are drawing.

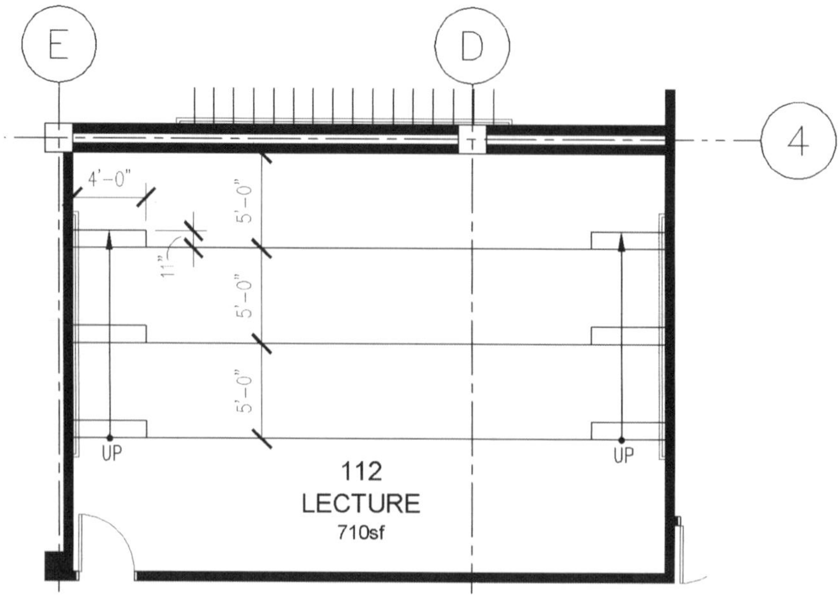

FIGURE 5-3.7 Lecture 112

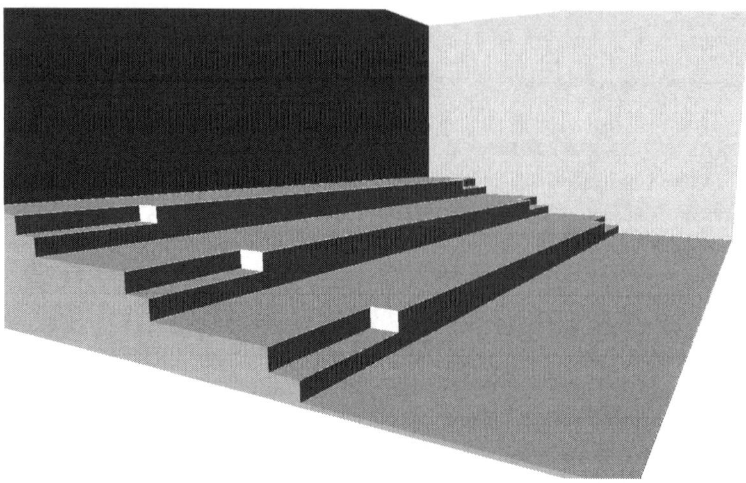

FIGURE 5-3.8 Lecture 112 – 3D view

Now that the "infrastructure" is drawn (and coordinated with the structural engineer in the real-world) you will draw the chairs and fixed tables.

16. Add (3) **2′-0″ x 24′-0″** tables as shown in Figure 5-3.9, plus:
    a. Draw the tables on the casework layer because they are built-in (i.e., not moveable); *Layer* **A-Case**.
    b. Align the front edge of the table with the 14″ step.
    c. Center the tables between the steps.

17. Add the chairs (chair-1 *Block*) as shown in Figure 5-3.9, plus:
    a. The chairs are "normal" furniture (not fixed), so they are to be drawn on *Layer* **A-Furn-Char**.
    b. Chairs are to be spaced **4′-0″** o.c. and centered on table.
    c. *Array option:* Draw the lower left chair and Array (6) columns and (3) rows with 4′ column spacing and 5′ row spacing.

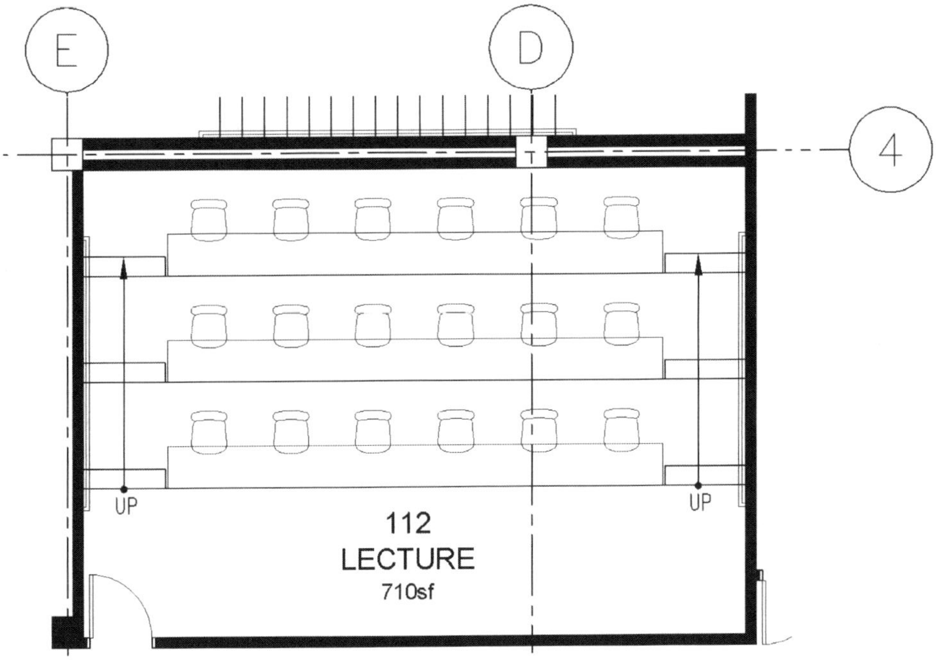

FIGURE 5-3.9 Lecture 112 – casework and chairs added

One additional note about this room layout before moving on: to accommodate handicapped accessibility, the first row might actually start at the main floor level and a section of tables might be movable to accommodate various situations. Some situations and codes require "equal access" to the various "quality" seats in the space. For example, in certain situations the top row might be the best place to sit, and therefore must be accessible. This would require a code compliant ramp.

Next you will look at a common design scenario where one space might accommodate several functions. Each function needs to be laid out independent of the others to verify program compliance. One way to achieve this is by creating additional *Layers*, which will allow you to control visibility such that only one layout is shown at a time. Lastly, you will study an AutoCAD feature that aids in toggling between several different *Layer* visibility configurations; the feature is called **Layer States**.

The Large Classroom (room 104) will be used as a classroom with various table/chair configurations. This room will also accommodate a gathering of the university's board members in a large conference room type layout.

Large Classroom 104: Layout Option A

18. Create *Layer* **A-Furn-LrgClass-OptA**.

    FYI: *You will occasionally need to create Layers like this that has not been defined by the "office standards". The name should be as close to the standard naming conventions as possible.*

19. Place the chair (**chair-1.dwg** *Block*) as shown in Figure 5-3.10, plus:
    a. 2′-6″ o.c. horizontally (columns)
    b. 4′-0″ o.c. vertically (rows)
    c. Refer to image for row with column count.

       TIP: *Place lower-left chair and then use the Array command.*

    d. Place on *Layer* just created.
    e. Do not draw the dimensions.

Next you will add text that will help to identify this option.

20. Add the text shown in Figure 5-3.10 per the following:
    a. Use the "office standard" style **Romans**; make sure the text style is set to be **Annotative** and 3/32″ *Paper Text Height.*
       i. See page 2-64 for a refresher on this.
    b. Set the Annotative scale to ⅛″ = 1′-0″.
    c. Place text on *Layer* just created.

You now have a layout showing how 100 students can fit in the large classroom. The chairs and text are on their own special *Layer* so visibility can be controlled for these items independently. In the next several steps, you will basically repeat this process: create new *Layer*, add space layout items, freeze previous layout *Layer*.

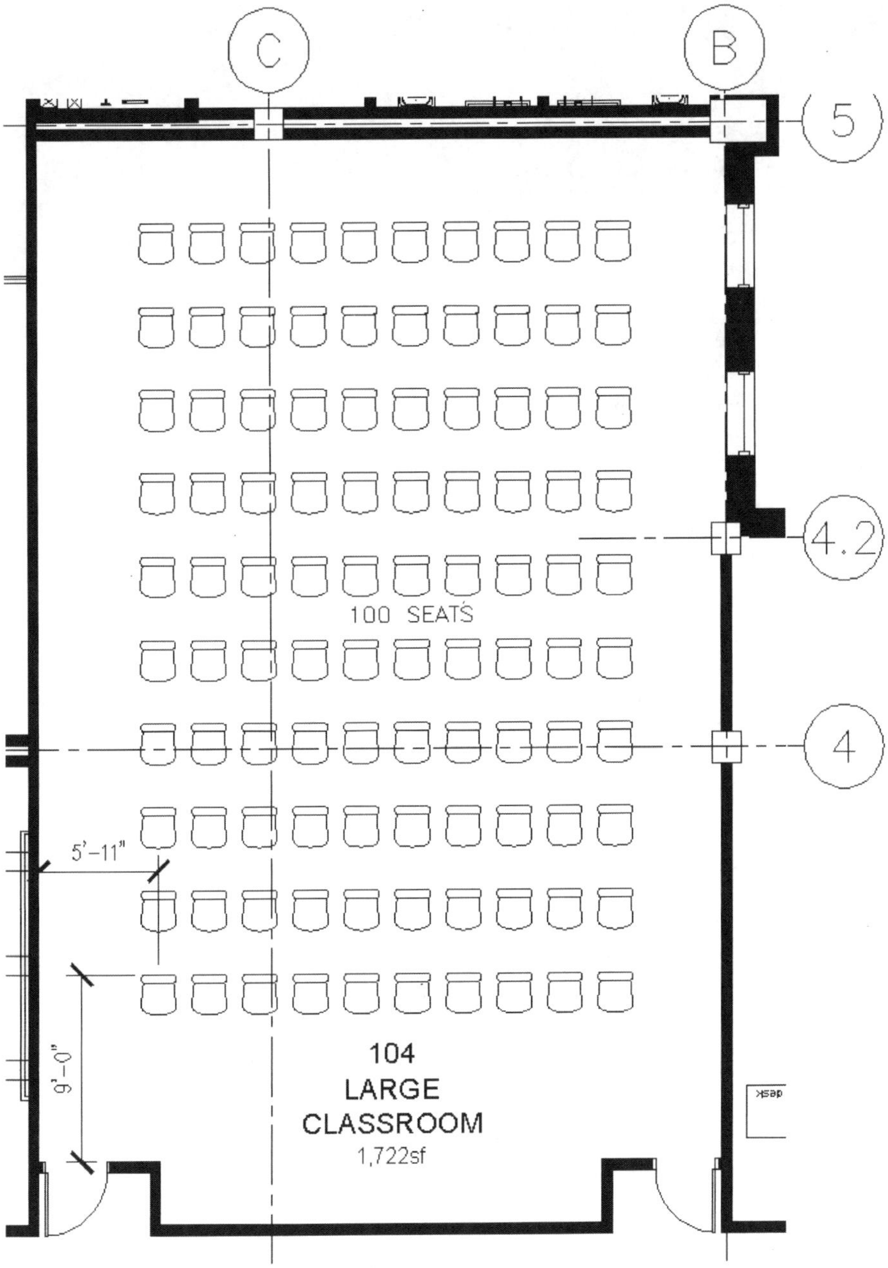

FIGURE 5-3.10 Large Classroom 104 – text & chairs added

TIP: In the next step you will be instructed to Freeze the Layer for Option B. One thing you need to be careful of is when you might need to move or copy/paste the plan into another drawing. You need to make sure all Layers are "on" and "thawed" first. Otherwise, you might "thaw" a Layer later and discover the items on that Layer are over in the toilet rooms (for example).

Large Classroom 104: Layout Option B

21. **Freeze** *Layer* A-Furn-LrgClass-OptA.

22. Create *Layer* **A-Furn-LrgClass-OptB**.

You now have a "clean slate" to begin the next layout in the Large Classroom. Next you will lay out student desks.

23. Create the layout shown in Figure 5-3.11 using the **Student Desk** *Block*.

24. Make sure the Student Desk has been placed on the proper *Layer* (the Option B *Layer*).

25. Add the **Teacher Desk** and **Chair** as shown (Figure 5-3.11).

    TIP: You can simply copy a teacher desk and chair from an adjacent room; you do not need to use Insert Block. Make sure you change the copied desk to the "Option B" layer.

    TIP: If using Array, you can place the student desk in the upper left corner per the dimensions given. Then, when entering Row spacing you can enter a negative distance (you cannot enter negative row/column quantity numbers).

26. Add the text "**48 SEATS**" as shown in Figure 5-3.11; place the text on the "Option B" *Layer*.

Large Classroom 104: Layout Option C

27. **Freeze** *Layer* A-Furn-LrgClass-OptB.

28. Create *Layer* **A-Furn-LrgClass-OptC**.

29. Create the layout shown in Figure 5-3.12 using the **Table (24x60)** and **Chair-1** blocks; center the layout in the east-west direction (as shown).

30. Make sure everything has been placed on the proper *Layer* (the option C layer), especially if you copied the chair from another room.

31. Add the text "**32 SEATS**" as shown in Figure 5-3.12; place the text on the "Option C" *Layer*.

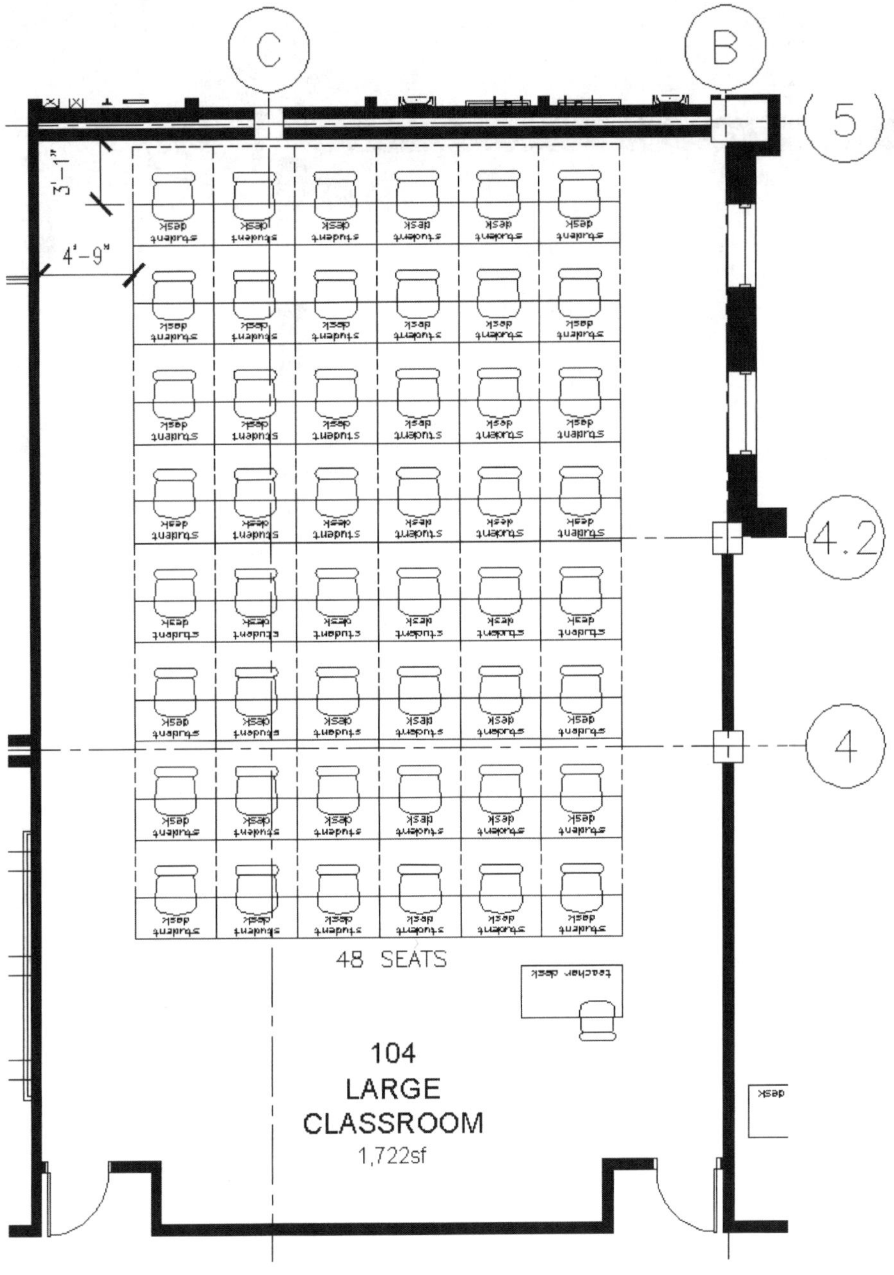

FIGURE 5-3.11 Large Classroom 104 – option B

Considering Figure 5-3.11, if the program required 56 student desks you would have to consider another option. One option might be to provide a single aisle (rather than two). The aisle might be down the center of the room with the desks pushed up against the wall. This option would restrict circulation and be more disruptive when students arrive late or need to leave early; this is yet another example of the many things that must be considered to achieve the best design solution.

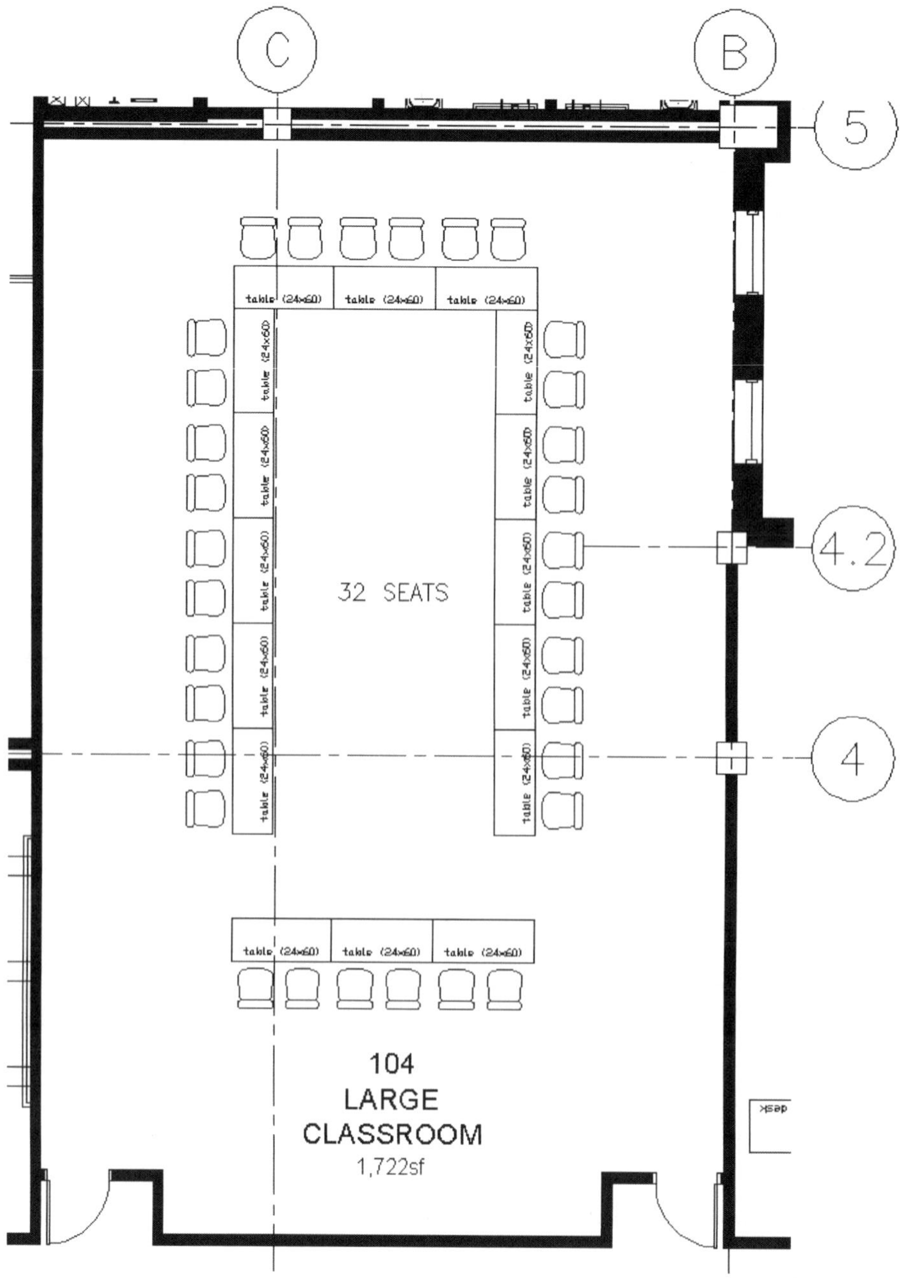

FIGURE 5-3.12 Large Classroom 104 – option C

One thing that would probably be required in a multi-function room like this is an adjacent storage room. This room would store the folded chairs and tables that are not needed. The most convenient design would have the door to the storage room open directly into the Large Classroom. It would be more difficult to add this room at this stage of the design because the adjacent rooms are nicely fit into place, so starting with a well developed "program" is worth more than words can describe!

Using Layer States:

Now that you have the three design options set up (i.e., *Layers* and drawings) you will now set up *Layer States* to quickly "toggle" between the visibility of the three options.

There are several uses for *Layer States*. One often used scenario is when the Floor Plan and Ceiling Plans are drawn in the same file. One might set up a *Layer State* that turns on all the *Layers* related to the Floor Plan and freezes all the *Layers* for the Ceiling Plan. Similarly, another *Layer State* is set up to make the Ceiling Plan visible.

Here are the *Layer States* that you will be creating:

Option A

Layers Thawed: A-Furn-LrgClass-OptA

Layers Frozen: A-Furn-LrgClass-OptB & A-Furn-LrgClass-OptC

Option B

Layers Thawed: A-Furn-LrgClass-OptB

Layers Frozen: A-Furn-LrgClass-OptA & A-Furn-LrgClass-OptC

Option C

Layers Thawed: A-Furn-LrgClass-OptC

Layers Frozen: A-Furn-LrgClass-OptA & A-Furn-LrgClass-OptB

In the next few steps you will adjust the *Layer* visibility so they are the way you want them just before creating a *Layer State*. Then, via *the Layer States Manager*, you will create a *Layer State* named "Option A".

32. The Current *Layer* does not come into play with *Layer States*, except in the fact that you cannot freeze the Current *Layer*, so **set Layer 0 to be current** for now so it does not hinder the next few steps.

33. **Thaw** (and/or turn on) Layer **A-Furn-LrgClass-OptA**.

34. **Freeze** Layers **A-Furn-LrgClass-OptB** and **A-Furn-LrgClass-OptC**.

Layer States Manager:

Now that the Layers are set the way you want them you capture these settings in a new *Layer State* called "Option A".

35. Click the **Manage Layer States** from the *Layer States* drop-down list; *Home* tab → *Layers* panel (see Figure 5-3.13).

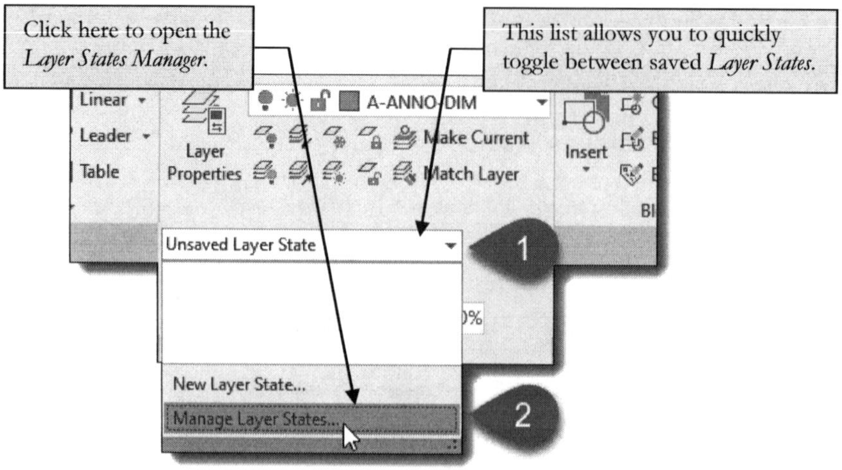

FIGURE 5-3.13 Layer panel on the Home tab; Layer State list expanded

36. Click the "arrow" icon in the lower right corner of the *Layer States Manger* dialog box to see additional options (Figure 5-3.14).

The image shown in Figure 5-3.14 shows the initial view of the *Layer States Manager* before any States have been saved. In addition to Saving and Deleting Layer States you can also Import and Export them. On a project like this, that has several floors, you could set up the *Layer States* for one floor, export them to a file and then import them into the other floor plan files. This, of course, requires each file to adhere to the same *Layer Standards.*

Two more things to notice before moving on: take a moment to look at the "Layer properties to restore" area. These are the various settings that the *Layer State* can remember; each of these can be turned on or off independently to give the user maximum control. Also, the "Turn off layers not found in layer state" check box at the bottom forces any new *Layers* created after the *Layer State* was created to be turned off. (You need to be careful here; this is not always what you want. It may be better to see the "offending" layer, freeze it and redefine the *Layer State.*)

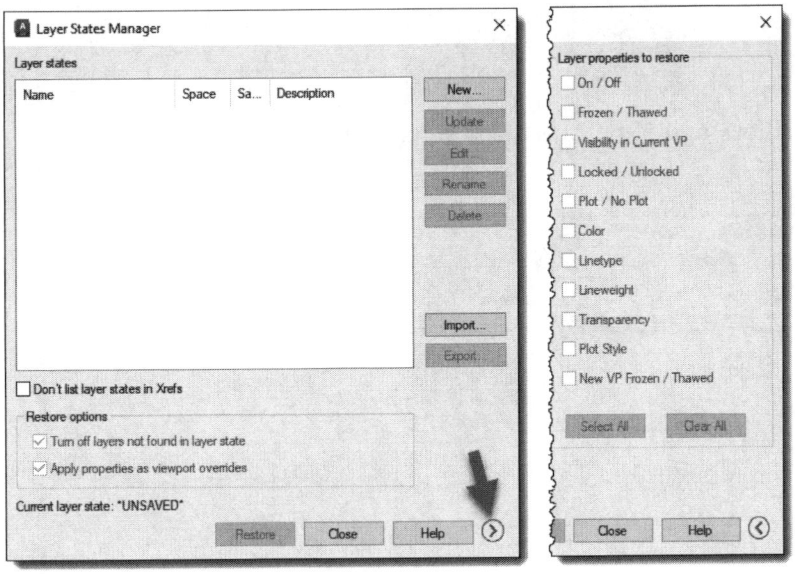

FIGURE 5-3.14 Layer States Manager, initial view – click arrow to expand

37. Click the **New** button (Figure 5-3.14).

You are now prompted to enter a name and description of the new layer state (the description is optional).

38. For the name, enter: **Option A** (Figure 5-3.15).

39. For the description, enter: **Large Classroom 104**.

40. Click **OK** to close the *New Layer State to Save* dialog box.

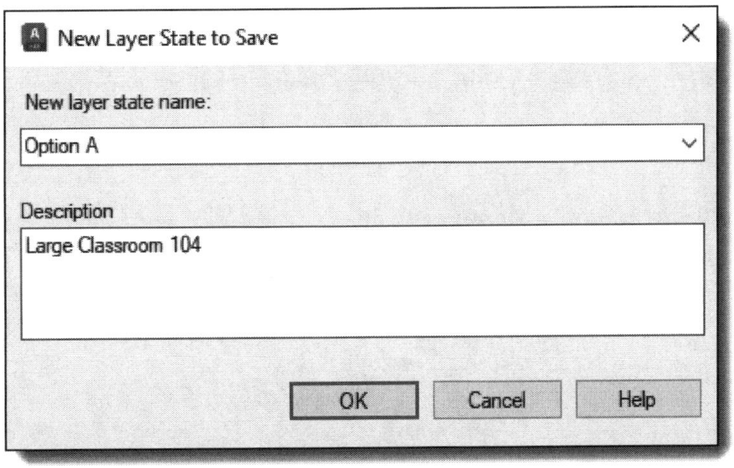

FIGURE 5-3.15 Naming a new Layer State

You are now back to the *Layer States Manager* (Figure 5-3.16). As you can see the new *Layer State* is now listed.

41. Click **Close** to exit the *Layer States Manager* dialog.

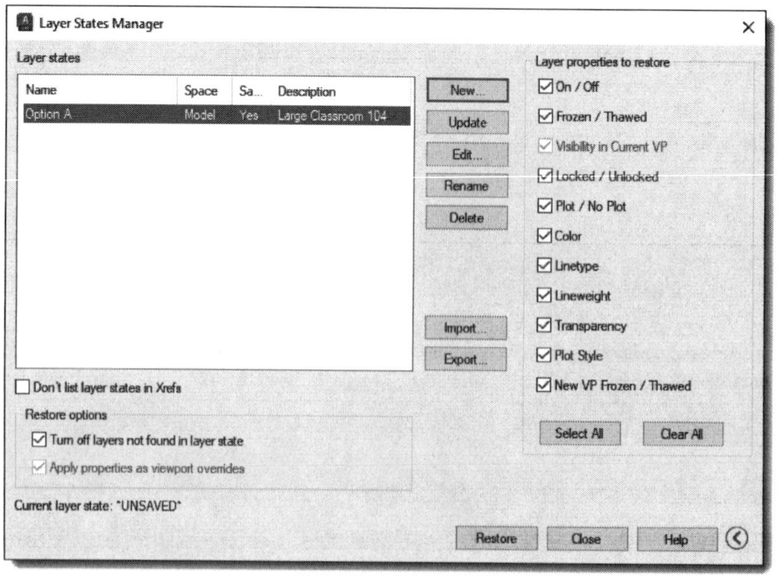

FIGURE 5-3.16 New Layer State added

Next you will set up the Option B "Layer State"; this process will be identical to the previous steps covered to set up Option A.

42. Open the *Layer Manager*, do the following:
    a. **Freeze** *Layer* **A-Furn-LrgClass-OptA**.
    b. **Thaw** *Layer* **A-Furn-LrgClass-OptB**.
    c. Verify that *Layer* A-Furn-LrgClass-OptC is still Frozen.

The Layers are now how you want them to be for the Option B layer state.

43. Open the **Layer States Manager** again.

TIP: The Layer States Manager icon is available within the Layer Properties palette. Also, the Layer Properties palette can stay open while you work.

44. Click **New**.

45. Enter the following information:
    a. Name: **Option B**
    b. Description: **Large Classroom 104**

46. Click **OK** and then **Close** to exit the Layer States Manager dialog.

47. Following the pattern for the process of creating the previous two Layer States, **create a third Layer State for Option C**.

48. **Close** the *Layer States Manager* dialog.

The *Layer States Manager* should now look like Figure 5-3.17, listing all three *Layer States*.

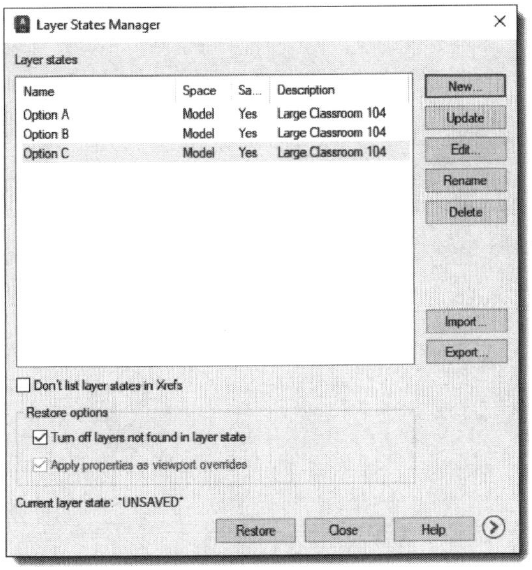

FIGURE 5-3.17 Layer State Manager

Obviously, on a large multi-million dollar project like this you could easily have one to two dozen *Layer States*, so you will want to take the time to provide descriptive names so you can tell them apart; for this exercise, you will leave them as named.

Now you will learn how to switch between the three *Layer States* just created.

49. On the **Home** tab, in the **Layers** panel, click the *Layer State* drop-down list (see image below and to the right).

50. Select **Option A** from the list of *Layer States*.

That's it! You can use this *Ribbon* feature to quickly toggle between various *Layer States*.

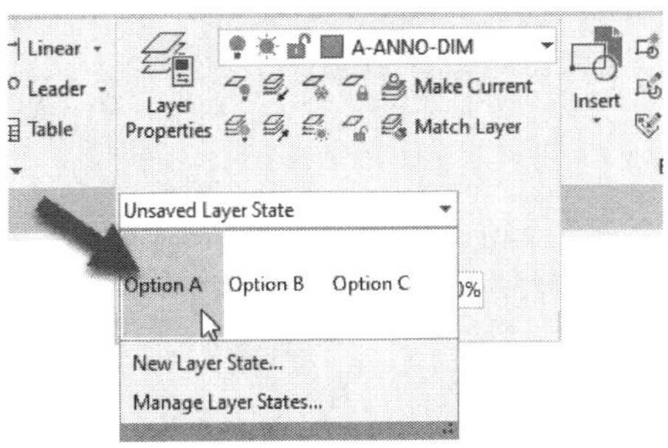

Also, notice you can gain convenient access to the New Layer State interface via this list.

You should now see the Option A layout on the screen (and not see any portion of Option B or Option C). Type **Regen** at the *Command Prompt* if the drawing does not look correct yet. See the tip below if the drawing still does not look correct.

> ***TIP:*** *If you do see a portion of Option B or Option C you should check one of two things: 1) select one of the visible items and verify what Layer that item is on; if it is on the wrong Layer, fix it; 2) if it is not on the wrong Layer you probably did not have that Layer turned off before you created the Layer State; repeat the steps again to create the Options and click "Yes" when prompted to redefine the existing Layer State.*

51. Follow the previous steps to view Options B and C.

Office Layout (rooms 125–129):

Next you will lay out the office spaces. This is pretty straightforward given the space layout.

52. Using the drawings previously drawn, add the office furniture as shown in Figure 5-3.18 (which includes):
    a. Chairs (block name varies)
    b. Tables (block name varies)
    c. Copier
    d. File cabinets
    e. Systems furniture (i.e., desks)

> ***FYI:*** *The desks in open office 125 share the same 1" cubical wall, so the two 1" thick cubical walls should overlap (the 1" thick cubical walls should be directly on top of each other).*

Looking at Figure 5-3.18, you can see the space has plenty of room for the required functions. The only conflict would be if a fourth cabinet were added near grid H/5, in which the column would prevent the file cabinet from opening (this is where the dashed lines help).

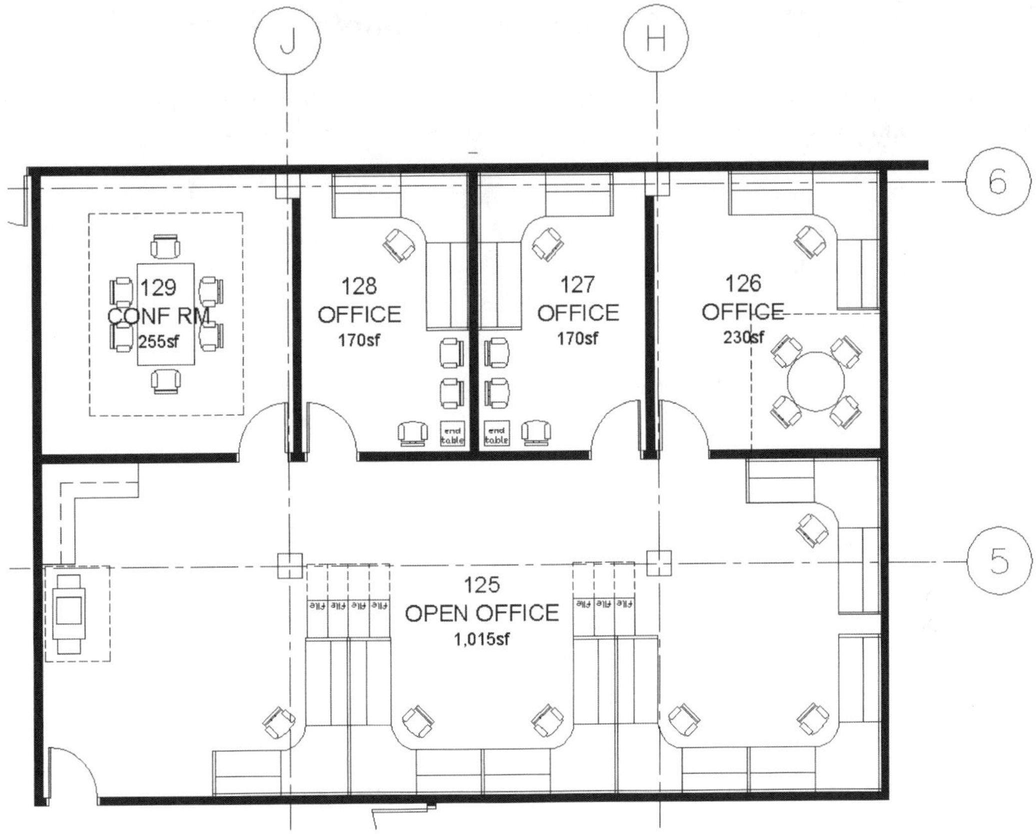

FIGURE 5-3.18 Office area

Notice in the image below, which shows "systems furniture," that the low wall (or cubical panel) is 1″ thick. If another desk were butting into the low wall from the foreground, another 1″ panel would not be required. Also notice the 1″ panel extends around the back.

Systems furniture example

Staff Lounge, Copy & Quiet Rooms (Rooms 118–123):

Next you will add tables, chairs and vending machines to the staff lounge, copiers in the copy room and chairs and built-in countertops in the quiet rooms.

53. Using the symbols previously drawn, add the furniture as shown in Figure 5-3.19 (which includes):
    a. **Staff Lounge 122**
        i. Round table with chairs
        ii. Refrigerator (*layer*: A-Eqpm-Appl)
        iii. Vending Machines (use both blocks) *layer*: A-Eqpm
    b. **Copy 121**
        i. Two Copiers (*layer*: A-Eqpm)
    c. **Quiet Rooms 118 - 120**
        i. Chairs
        ii. 25″ deep countertop in "Quiet" rooms (layer A-Case)

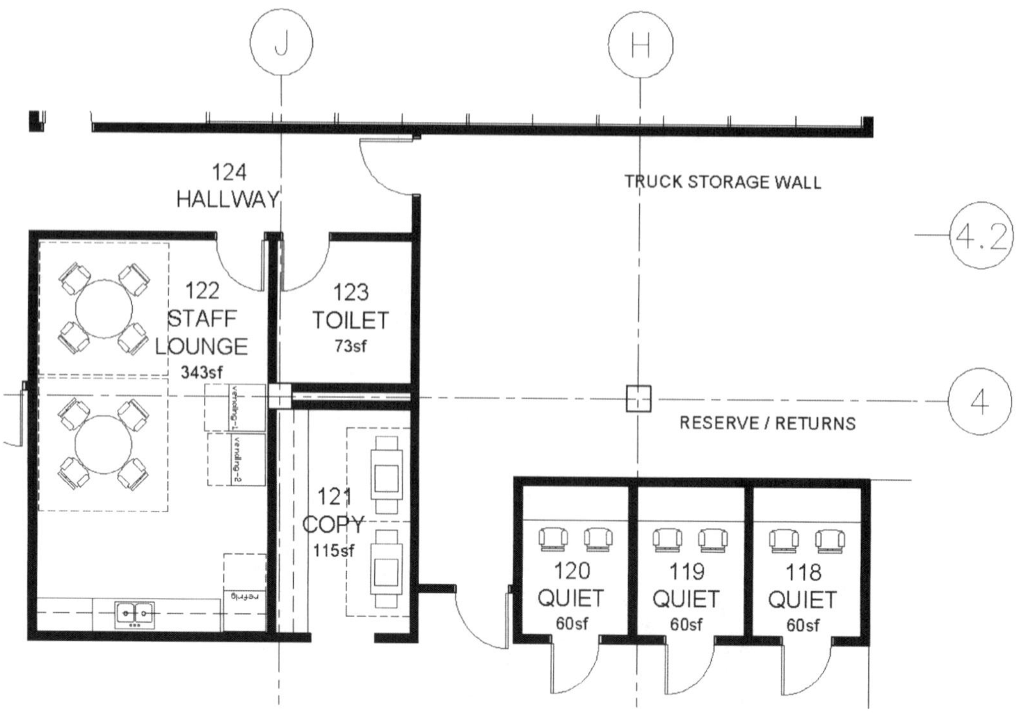

FIGURE 5-3.19 Break room, Copy room and Quiet rooms

In Figure 5-3.19 you will notice the space between the dashed lines, when walking from the door to the counter, is fairly tight. However, the dashed lines are not walls, so it would only be tight if people were both standing in front of the vending machines and sitting at the table, which is certainly possible. This is where the Architect or Interior Designer needs to make a professional judgment call. If the space is determined to be unacceptable, then the designer will first try laying out the room differently (moving everything around including the cabinets). If alternate layouts still do not achieve an acceptable solution, the space might need to become larger.

The tricky part about making the space larger at this point is that an adjacent space needs to get smaller. If one of the adjacent rooms is larger than the original program, then you can carve space from it. If the rooms are right at program or smaller, then the designer might need to review the situation with the owner to see if they want to make an adjacent room smaller than the programmed area or possibly even increase the overall size of the building (this would be a drastic measure for a break room but could happen for other more important spaces).

Below is an alternate design option for the break room which carves a space out of the adjacent copy room. In this revision, it would have to have been determined that the copy room could get smaller and did not require as much countertop area as was shown. This makes the break room more spacious and functional. If the space were revised (vending machines move, or cabinets relocated, you would need to inform the mechanical and electrical engineers so their drawings get updated (otherwise you will end up with outlets and plumbing in the wrong location); none of these revisions would affect the structural system so the structural engineer would have no need for this information.

FYI: You will not actually make this revision to your plan.

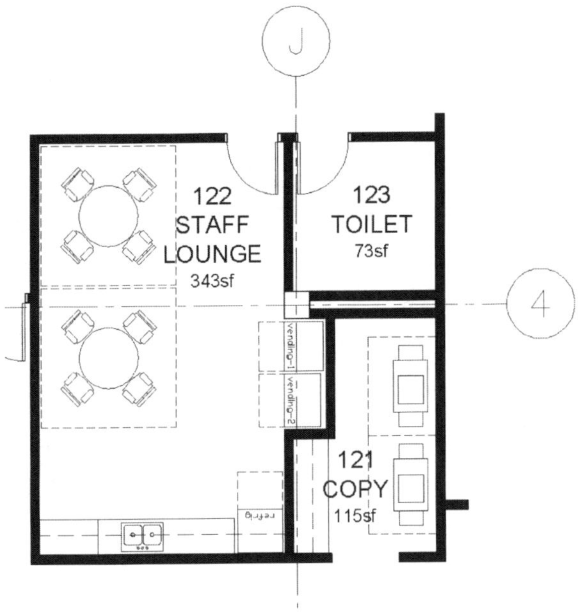

FIGURE 5-3.20 Alternate Copy room design

Reading Room Layout:

The main level reading room is meant to be spacious and comfortable. The entire area, from grid E to H.5 and from 1 to 3, is a two-story space. On the second floor, along grid line three is a railing (specifically, a 42″ high guardrail) which allows students on that floor to gaze down upon the reading room.

The layout shown on the next page shows some tables placed tight to the next tables "clear floor area" lines and others have a larger space between them to create circulation patterns within the reading room.

The photograph shown below is similar to what you will be drawing, a two-story space with reading tables and lounge furniture. Obviously furniture does not always stay where the designer intended. As you can see in the image below, one table is slightly out of alignment from the others and a lounge chair is positioned at a table (in place of a typical reading table chair). These types of modifications can sometimes encroach on accessibility codes and regulations (something the designer is rarely held accountable for). The designer would do well to consider a few of these potential deviations and how they might impact the space. A more extreme solution would be bolting the tables to the floor.

54. Using the symbols previously drawn, add the furniture as shown in Figure 5-3.21 (which includes):

    a. Reading tables with chairs
    b. Study Carrels
    c. Lounge furniture
    d. Stacks (along grid E, between grids 2 and 3)
    e. All on A-Furn layer

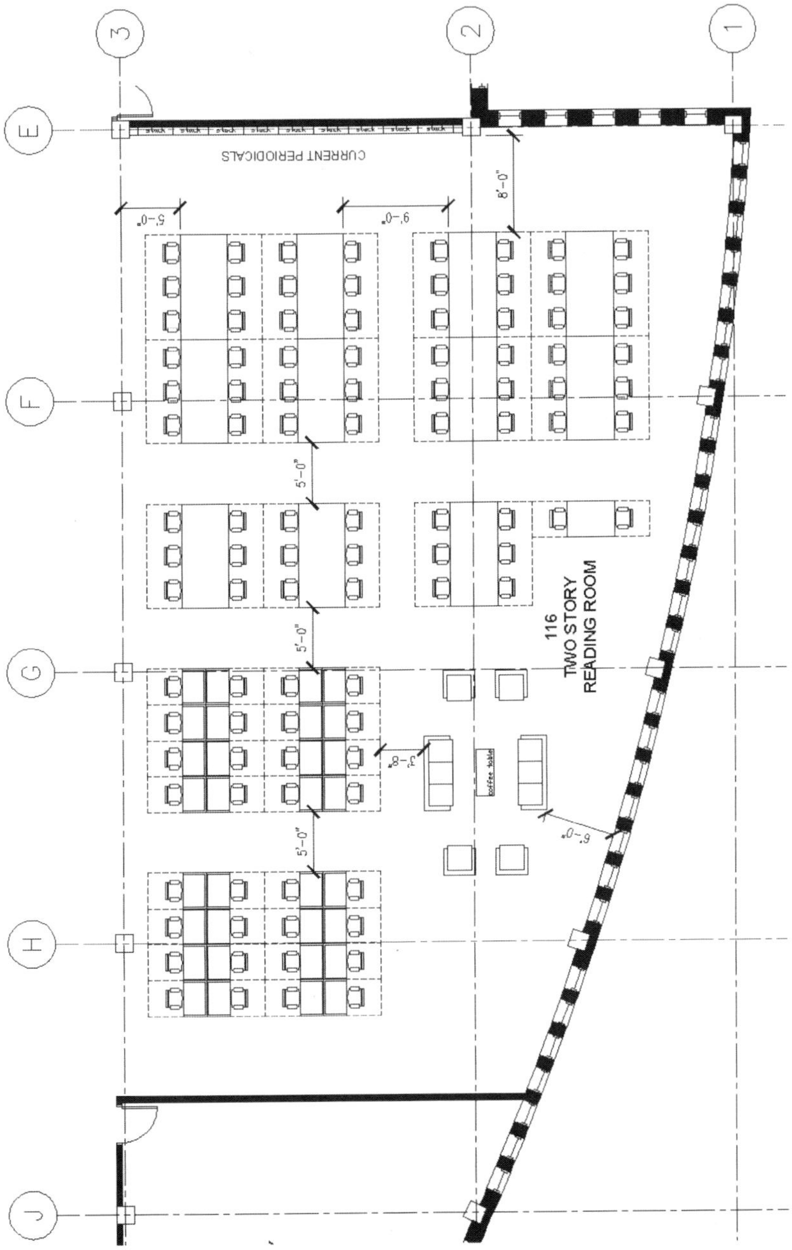

FIGURE 5-3.21 Reading room layout (image rotated to fit on page)

Catalog Computers and Reference Area:

In this section you will add a few more study carrels and stacks (i.e., library bookshelves). The first floor of the library actually has minimal stack areas; more concentrated areas would exist on the upper floors.

The stacks in this area are at an angle relative to the floor plan (and screen view). This is mostly an aesthetic decision where the stacks are perpendicular to the checkout counter and would also align with the ceiling orientation in this area (the ceilings are not covered in this book).

Having a group of furniture or equipment at an angle is fairly common. However, you have an added challenge of drawing and modifying entities that are not orthogonal to the current view. For example, when drawing a rectangle that is orthogonal to the current view you can turn on Ortho or Polar Tracking to quickly "point" the line in the correct direction and simply enter a length; when the rectangle is at an angle you need to provide the length and angle(s).

One solution to this is to adjust the UCS (user coordinate system) to temporarily align with the angle desired. This adjustment causes the cross-hairs to rotate to the desired angle. Also, Ortho mode is constrained to this angle which allows you to simply enter the length without the angle. This also makes stretch, copy, move, etc., much easier. The only thing that does not adjust is the selection window (which stays aligned with the drawing window).

> ***FYI:*** *Another option which also solves this selection window limitation is a feature called UCSfollow. This variable causes the entire screen to rotate when the UCS is adjusted.* ***You will not*** *explore this option in this tutorial, but you may want to explore it further on your own. This variable has one side-effect related to viewport scales changing in paperspace which is why it will not be covered.*

Finally, once the UCS has been adjusted you can save the current UCS settings to a Named UCS. This allows you to quickly toggle back and forth between various settings that are common to the current drawing. This is done via a UCS toolbar that you will turn on and make use of momentarily.

UCS Icon Visibility:

The first thing you will do is verify the UCS Icon is visible in the Drawing Window. This will help you know, visually, the current UCS orientation. As you will see shortly, when the UCS is rotated the UCS Icon rotates as well.

The UCS Icon not only indicates the current working angle but also the positive X and Y directions. As you should know, the default UCS settings (known as World UCS) has the positive X extending towards the right (or east) and the positive Y extending straight up (or north) in the Drawing Window. Looking at the UCS Icon identified in Figure 5-3.22, you can see the corresponding X and Y being identified as part of the UCS Icon.

55. Type **UCSICON** and press **Enter** to adjust this variable.

56. Select or type **ON** (if you type it you need to press enter).

If the UCS Icon was not previously on, it should be now. The next two steps will make sure the icon stays in the lower left corner rather than moving around on the screen when the drawings origin is visible in the Drawing Window.

57. Press **Enter** (or the spacebar); this causes AutoCAD to reactivate the previous command. (This assumes UCSICON was the last command used.)

58. Select or type **Noorigin**. (If you type it you need to press **Enter**.)

The UCS Icon should now be visible and in the lower-left corner of the Drawing Window (Figure 5-3.22).

> ***FYI:** Some AutoCAD variables only apply to the current drawing and others to the program in general. The UCSICON variable applies to the program in general, so any changes made will be visible in every drawing. Thus, you only have to make the change once and not in every drawing.*

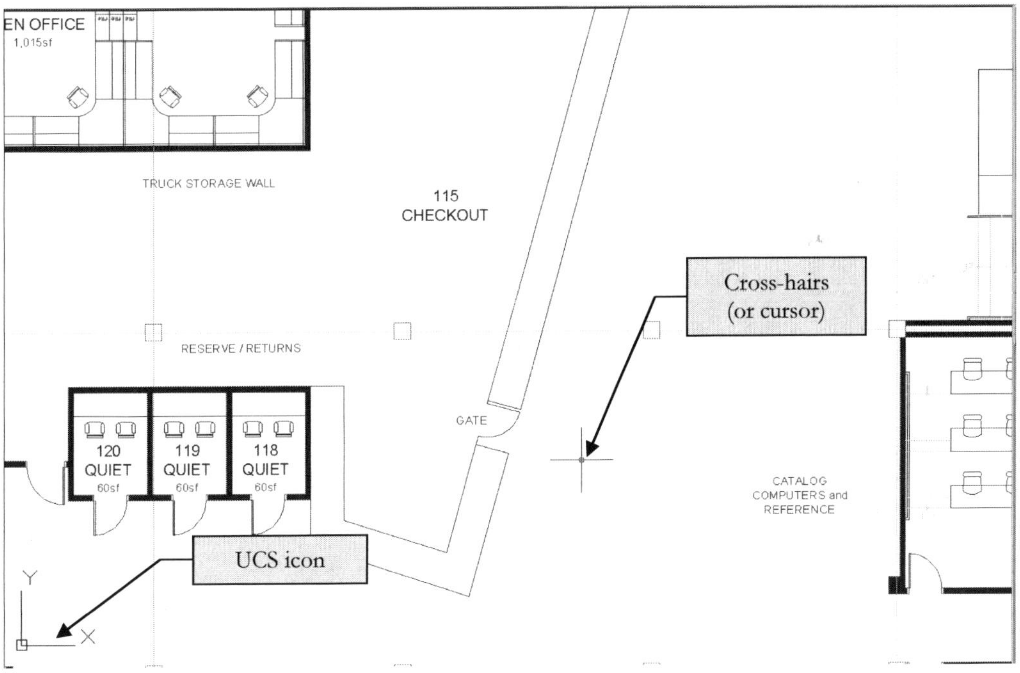

FIGURE 5-3.22 CATALOG COMPUTERS and REFERENCE area; UCS Icon shown in lower-left corner

Adjusting the UCS:

Now that the UCS Icon is visible you will adjust the UCS itself. When using the UCS command, you have several ways in which you can adjust the angle of the UCS.

One method of adjusting the angle of the UCS is to select an entity that is at the correct angle (this is an option while in the UCS command). This causes the UCS to rotate to the same angle as the entity selected. However, the resultant angle depends on the direction in which the entity selected was drawn; thus, the UCS will either be the angle you want or 180 degrees off.

Another method of adjusting the angle of the UCS, and the one you will use in this tutorial, involves entering the angle desired. The goal here is to adjust the UCS so it will align with the checkout counter which will aid in placing and laying out the nearby stacks. Looking back at page 4-18 you can see the "???" angle dimension for the checkout counter is actually a 74 degree angle (via properties); remember this number.

When you adjust the UCS you will be rotating it about the Z axis; this is the third axis of the typical three axis coordinate system (x,y,z). Because you are looking straight down on your drawing (i.e., plan view or top view), the Z axis is not visible on the UCS Icon; it is actually pointing straight at you. If you rotate the UCS 74 degrees the UCS Icon will appear as indicated in the center of Figure 5-3.23. If rotated -16 degrees (which is 90 – 74), the icon will appear as indicated to the right in Figure 5-3.23. The latter is preferred because it is closest to the World UCS, which helps when entering X and Y values for lengths and such.

Next you will be instructed on how to make the UCS adjustment.

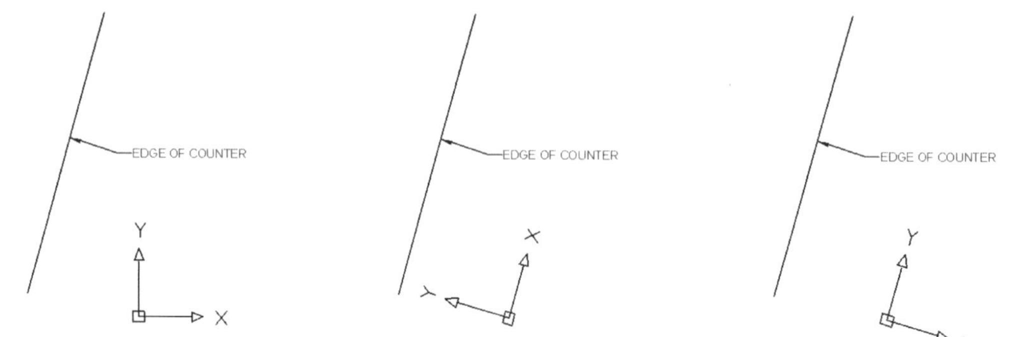

Initial condition:
UCS not adjusted (World)

UCS rotated about Z axis:
Angle entered: 74

UCS rotated about Z axis:
Angle entered: -16

FIGURE 5-3.23 Adjusting the UCS

59. Type **UCS** and then press **Enter**.

    Notice the current prompt:
    Specify origin of UCS or [Face/NAmed/OBject/Previous/View/World/X/Y/Z/ZAxis] <World>:

60. Type **Z** and press **Enter**.

    Notice the current prompt:
    Specify rotation angle about Z axis <90>:

61. Type **-16** and then press **Enter**.

TIP: Take a minute to notice a few points about the AutoCAD prompts shown above.

In addition to the program telling you what it expects from you next (i.e., pick a point or enter a distance) you may also have "sub-commands" available as with the UCS command above; the "sub-commands" appear in square brackets. To activate a "sub-command" you only have to type the uppercase letter(s), not the entire word. Not every command or prompt has "sub-commands".

Many prompts also indicate defaults or the previous value entered. The first time a command is used you will see a default; in the examples above you see <World> and <90>. If you use the offset command you have to enter a value the first time you use it, but then for each subsequent use you will see the previously entered value as the default – meaning you can just press enter and the value in the <> brackets will be used.

Saving the UCS settings:

Now you will save the current UCS settings to a Named UCS. This will allow you to access this angle again in the future.

62. Type **UCS** and then press **Enter**.

63. Type **NA** and press **Enter**.

FYI: NA is for the Named "sub-command."

    Notice the current prompt:
    Enter an option [Restore/Save/Delete/?]:

64. Type **S** and press **Enter**.

    Notice the current prompt:
    Enter name to save current UCS or [?]:

65. Type **Angled Stacks** for a name and press **Enter**.

FYI: This can be any name you choose as long as you can remember it.

The last thing you will do now, relative to learning about and setting up the UCS, is how to toggle between named views.

66. Right-click on the UCS icon on the screen (Figure 5-3.24).

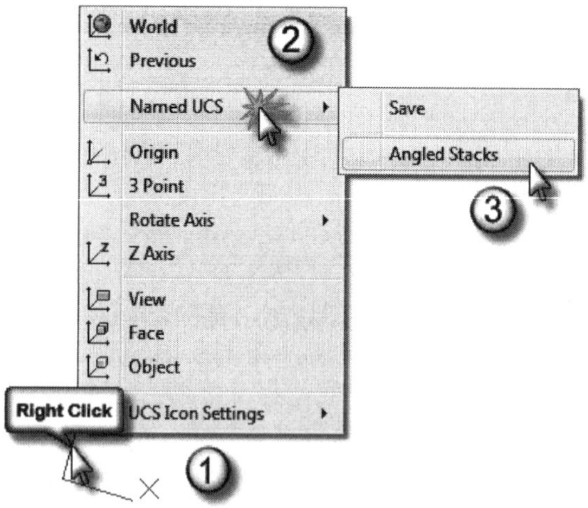

FIGURE 5-3.24 UCS right-click options

Now you can quickly switch between **Angled Stacks** and **World** by clicking the desired option from the pop-up menu (Figure 5-3.24). Try toggling between the two and observe the crosshairs change. When finished, make sure **Angled Stacks** is selected before moving on.

67. Select **Angled Stacks**. (Figure 5-3.24)

FYI: Notice the option to Save *a named UCS in the list as well. This could be used rather than typing the command as outlined in the previous steps.*

68. Insert the **Stack** blocks as shown in Figure 5-3.25.
    a. Place on *Layer*: A-Furn

FYI: Notice as they are inserted using the Block command that the symbol is rotated to match the current UCS.

If you try using the *Move* or *Copy* command and have *ORTHO* turned on, the selected item will move/copy along the current angle.

69. Switch back to **World UCS** (following the steps just outlined).

70. Insert the **study carrels** with a **computer** (two separate blocks: carrel and computer), as shown in Figure 5-3.25.

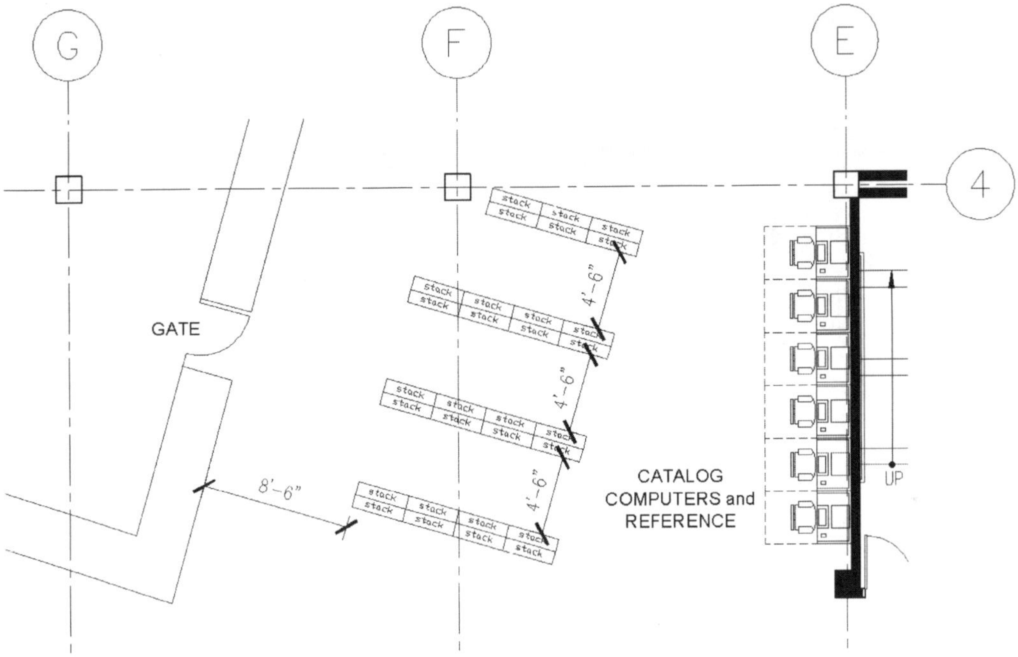

FIGURE 5-3.25 Stacks and carrels added

Checkout Area Stacks:

71. Insert the **Stack** blocks as shown in Figure 5-3.26.

    a. 3'-0" aisles typical (as dimensioned)

    FYI: *These aisles are tighter because they are only accessed by staff.*

    b. Place on *Layer*: A-Furn

    FYI: *All the stacks are positioned by column locations.*

    NOTE: *The columns have been specially sized (in conjunction with the structural engineer) so they align with the back-to-back stacks. This helps to avoid obstacles for the book trucks (if the columns protruded out) and dust collectors (if the columns were recessed in) – this becomes more obvious on the uppers floors which have vast areas filled with stacks. Even the grid spacing has taken the stacks row width into consideration.*

72. Add the **Book Trucks** on Layer **A-Eqpm** per Figure 5-3.26.

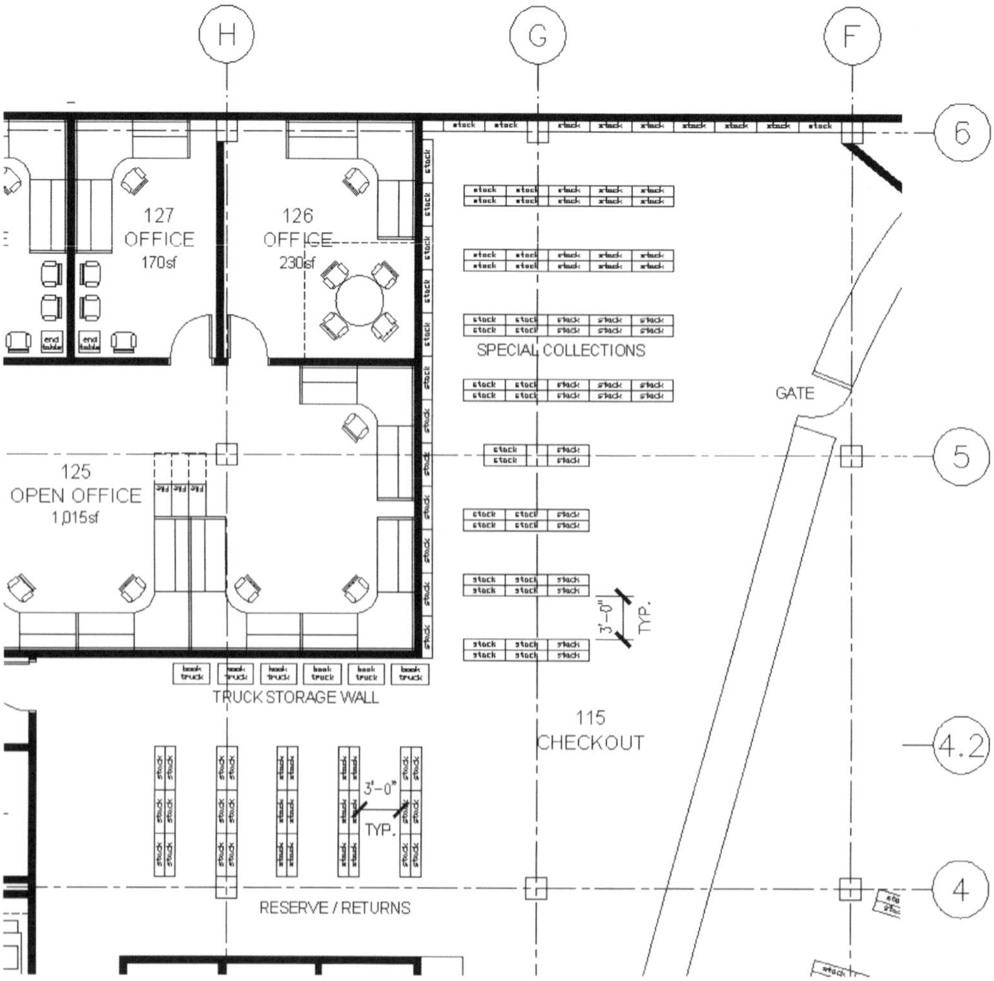

FIGRE 5-3.26 Stacks and book trucks added

73. Add the **Book Trucks**, **Chairs** and **Computers** per Figure 5-3.27; the Computers are to be 8′-0″ apart from each other.

TIP: Switch your UCS so the Blocks will insert at the correct angle.

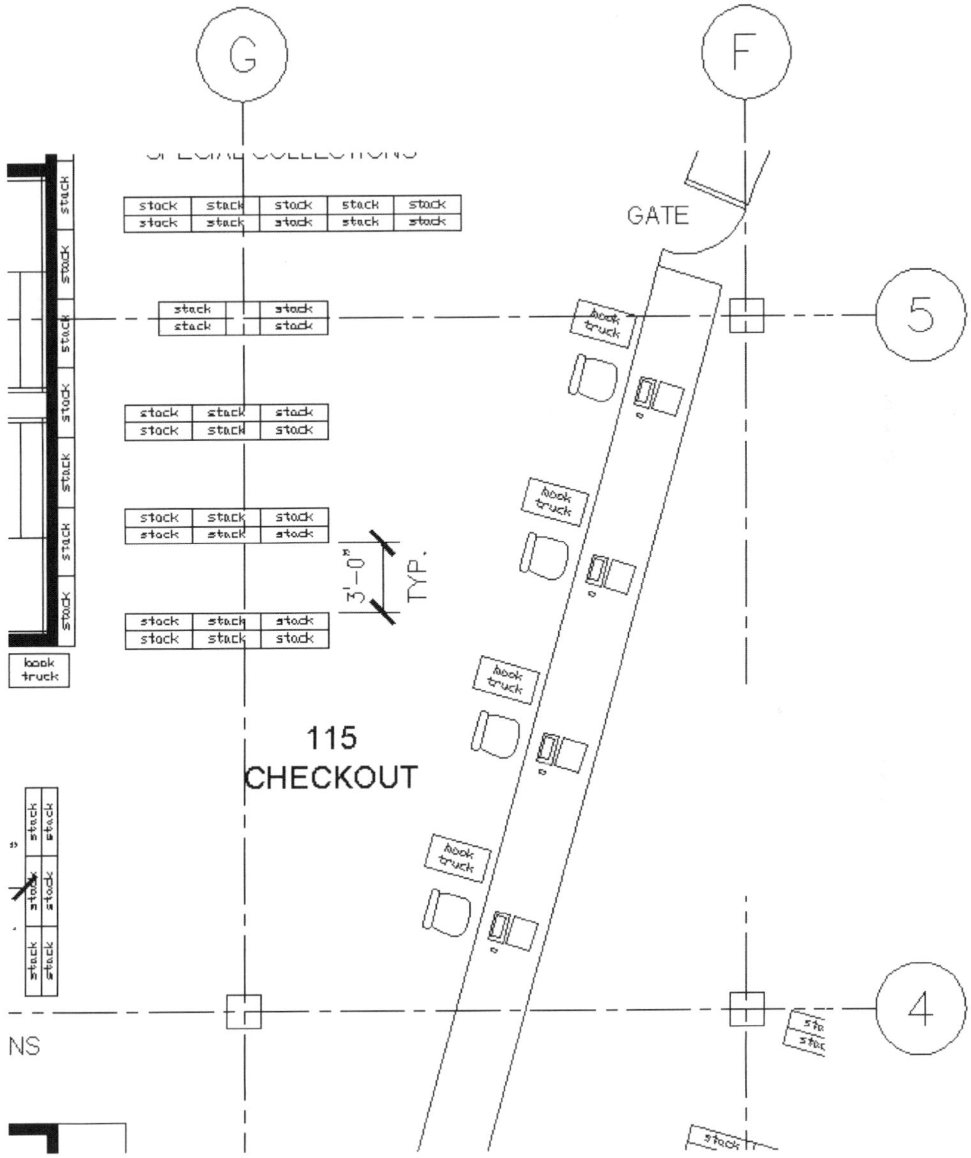

FIGURE 5-3.27 Checkout stations added

Exercise 5-4:
Annotation and Dimensions

Introduction

This short exercise will look at adding rotated notes and dimensions in the floor plan.

You will be instructed to add several dimensions and edit them to observe the various results; using different dimension tools and UCS settings.

1. In your first floor plan drawing, make sure the UCS is set to **World** (see previous exercise, page 5-54, for more information).

You have previously used the Linear Dimension tool; it is designed to draw vertical and horizontal dimension.

2. Draw the dimension using **Linear** from the *Annotate* tab on the *Dimension* panel (Figure 5-4.1).

This dimension is not very useful to the contractor in the field. It would be better to have the perpendicular dimension between the stacks.

3. **Delete** the dimensions just drawn.

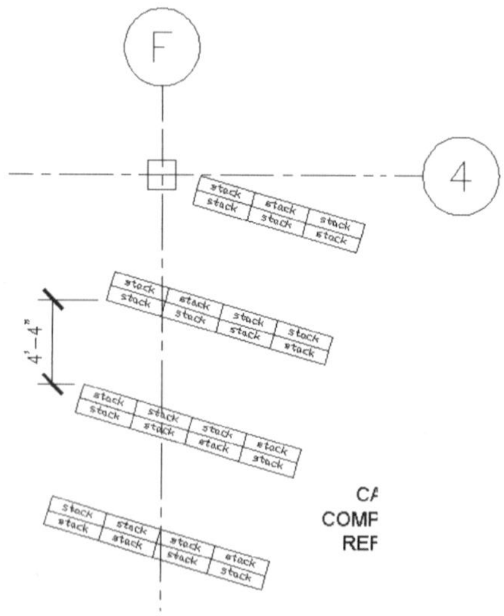

FIGURE 5-4.1
Linear dimension added (UCS set to World)

Using the Aligned Dimension Tool:

Next, you will add another dimension using another Dimension tool. This tool will make the dimension look correct but will offer limited editing opportunities once drawn. You will explore this now…

4. With the UCS still set to *World*, use the **Aligned** tool from the *Dimension* fly-out on the **Annotate** tab (Figure 5-4.2)

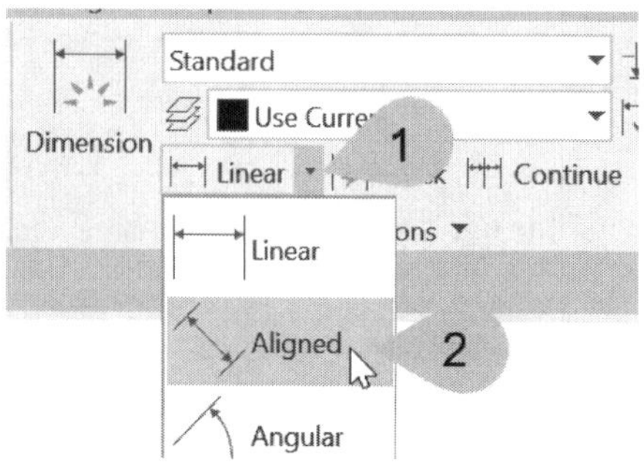

You should now have a dimension that lists the perpendicular distance between the stacks as shown in Figure 5-4.2. In the next step, you will see a limitation to using this particular dimension tool.

5. Click on the Dimension just drawn to select it.

6. Click to select the upper Grip touching the stacks (this process is called a Grip Edit).

   TIP: Do not "drag" the mouse button.

7. Click again to reposition the grip to the point shown in Figure 5-4.3 on the shorter row of stacks.

As you can see, the *Align* Dimension tool is meant to list the distance DIRECTLY between two points. So its use in angled floor plans is somewhat limited. Floor plans are always changing, even during the construction document phase, so it is not advised to use this type of dimension in a floor plan. Next, you will explore a better solution.

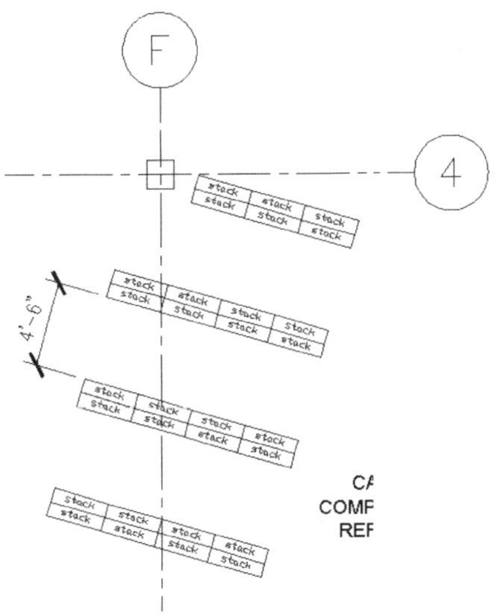

FIGURE 5-4.2
Aligned dimension added
(UCS set to World)

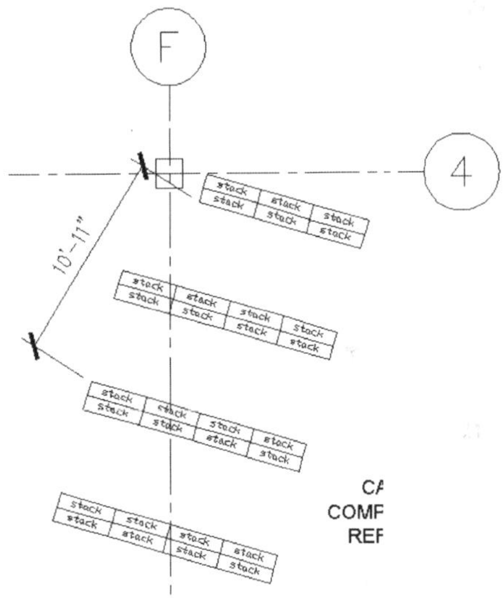

FIGURE 5-4.3
Aligned dimension edited
(UCS set to World)

TIP: If you were to Grip Edit the 4'-6" dimension, in Figure 5-4.2 above, so that the dimension extended to the southern-most row of stacks, the Align dimension would still look correct because the two points are still perpendicular to each other relative to the stacks (see image to right).

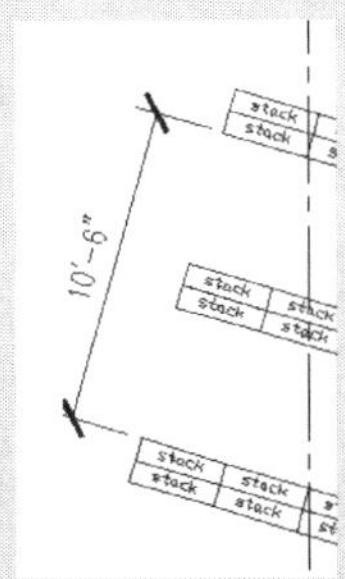

Using the Named UCS to Add Angled Dimensions:

Now you will look at adding the same 4′-6″ dimension previously drawn using the Named UCS (Angled Stacks) and the Linear dimension tool. When using this method you can edit the dimension (regardless of later UCS settings) and get the desired results for typical floor plan dimensioning.

8. **Delete** the previous dimension drawn (the 10′-11″ dimension shown in Figure 5-4.3).

9. Per previous instructions, switch to the **Angled Stacks** Named UCS.

10. Using the **Linear** Dimension tool, add the dimension shown in Figure 5-4.4.

    REMINDER: *Use Object Snaps for accurate pick points.*

11. Use the same steps to modify the dimension (Steps 5-7) which will result in the dimension shown in Figure 5-4.5.

Notice that the dimension did not change its alignment, only the Extension Line got longer on the modified end of the dimension. This is the main difference between Align and Linear.

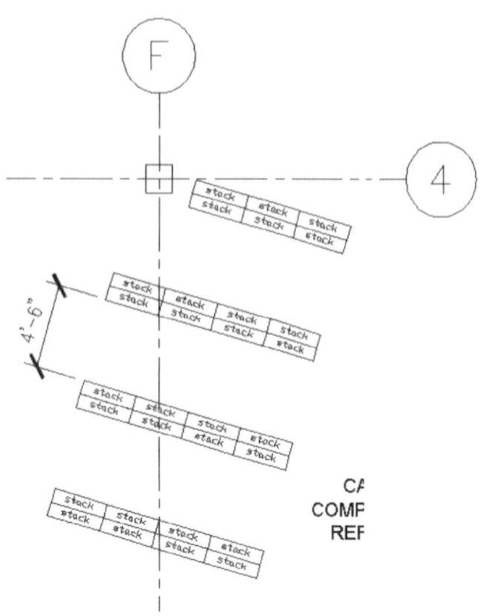

FIGURE 5-4.4
Linear dimension added
(UCS set to Angled Stacks)

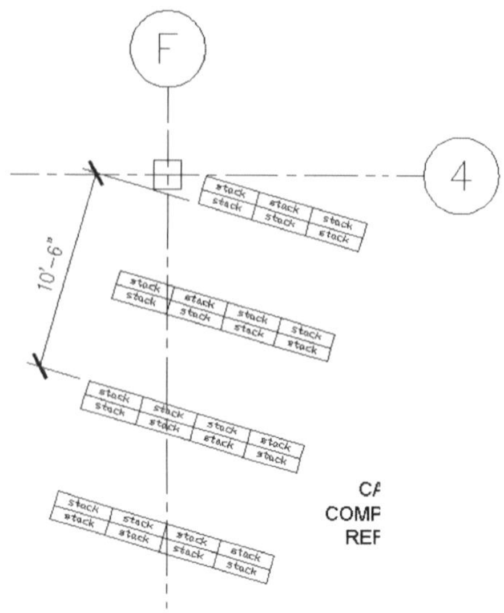

FIGURE 5-4.5
Linear dimension edited
(UCS set to Angled Stacks)

12. Before moving on, edit the dimension back to the **4′-6″** aisle dimension shown in **Figure 5-4.4**.

Modify Dimension Text:

When placing dimensions relating to furniture layout, it is sometimes necessary to modify the text shown in a dimension. You will take a minute to look at the various ways to add suffixes/prefixes and multiple lines to the dimension text object. This is better than "faking" a separate Mtext object next to the dimension to look like a suffix; this creates a problem when the dimension is stretched with a plan change or the dimension is moved because the Mtext object will not move with the dimension text.

Although the dimension length can be faked by editing the dimension text (e.g., changing 4′-0 27/64″ to 4′-0″), this should be avoided. It is a better practice to adjust the drawing so the dimension is correct. However, it is sometimes done on furniture plans to avoid fractions; on odd sized furniture adjacent to walls and columns that cannot be moved.

In the next several steps you will use the *Properties* palette to modify the selected dimensions text. The following are special entries that help to control dimension text (which you will try momentarily):

Value entered	Result
<>	Primary units are displayed
[]	Alternate units are displayed
\X	Moves subsequent text below dimension line
\P	Paragraph break (i.e., new line)

***NOTE:** The X and P need to be uppercase.*

All of the above values, or any combination, in addition to text can be added to any dimension string. You will study this next.

13. **Select** the 4′-6″ dimension at the angled stacks.

14. If the **Properties Palette** is not open, press **Ctrl + 1** to open it.

15. Click the down-arrows to the right of the "Text" category to expand and view that categories information.

You should now see the information shown in Figure 5-4.6. Many of these settings are being automatically set by the dimension style. The parameter you will be mostly interested in is *Text Override*; this is currently black which means there are no overrides. Also notice the previous parameter, *Measurement*, which will always indicate the dimension's actual measurement, even if the dimension has been manually changed to round off a fraction. (That is why the parameter value is grayed out, because it is not editable.)

Next you will add the suffix “TYP.” to the 4′-6″ dimension text. This is the abbreviation for the word typical. (See the standard abbreviations appendix.)

16. In the *Text Override* text box (on the *Properties* palette) type **TYP**. And press **Enter** (Figure 5-4.7a).

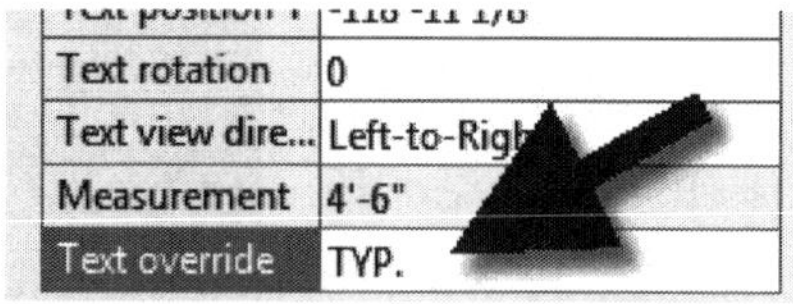

FIGURE 5-4.7A
Edited Text Override value

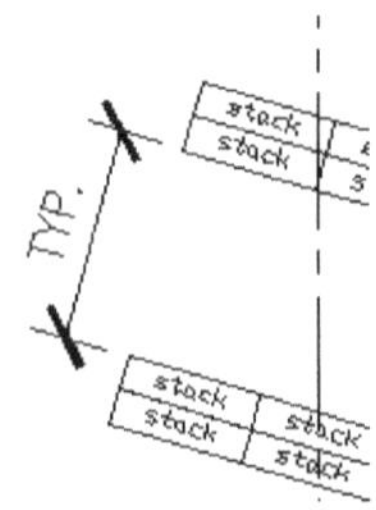

FIGURE 5-4.7B
Text Override results

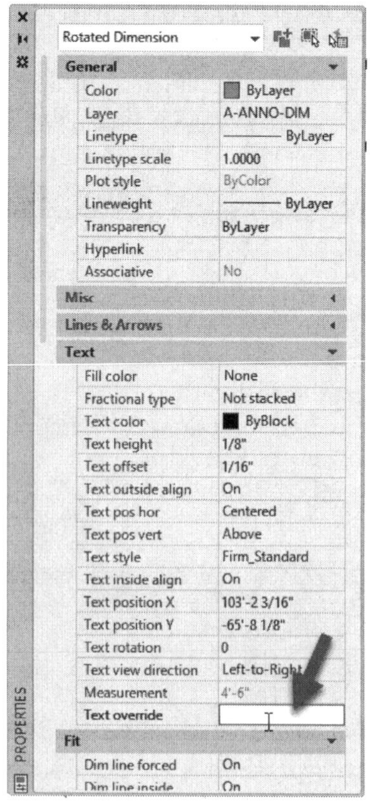

FIGURE 5-4.6
Properties for selected dimension

As you can see, the dimension text is completely replaced by the text typed in the Text Override field on the properties palette. Next you will add the placeholder that tells AutoCAD to insert the dimensions measurement when displayed on screen.

17. With the dimension still selected, edit the Text Override text box to read: **<> Typ.** and then press **Enter** (Figure 5-4.8a).

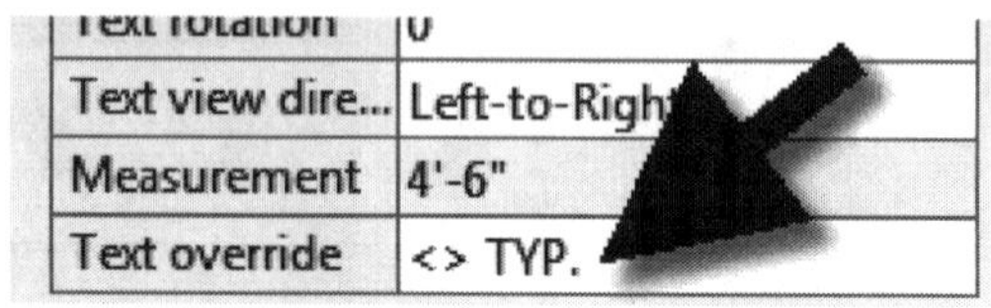

FIGURE 5-4.8A
Edited Text Override value

As you can see (Fig. 5-4.8b), the 4′-6″ dimension text has been added in place of the brackets. This will always display the actual dimension (based on units settings).

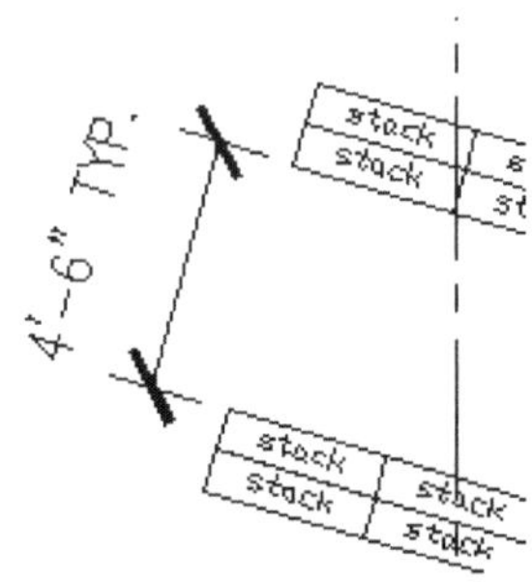

FIGURE 5-4.8B
Text Override results

18. Adjust the dimension (via Grip Edit) per the boxed ***TIP*** on the bottom of page 5-55.

As you can see (Figure 5-4.9), the modified dimension still shows the correct dimension and the suffix moved with the text dimensions. (If the suffix were Mtext, you would have to move that text object separately.)

The location of the brackets determines whether the text entered is a prefix, a suffix or both.

Suffix:	<> TYP.
Prefix:	TYP. <>
Both:	TYP. <> TYP.

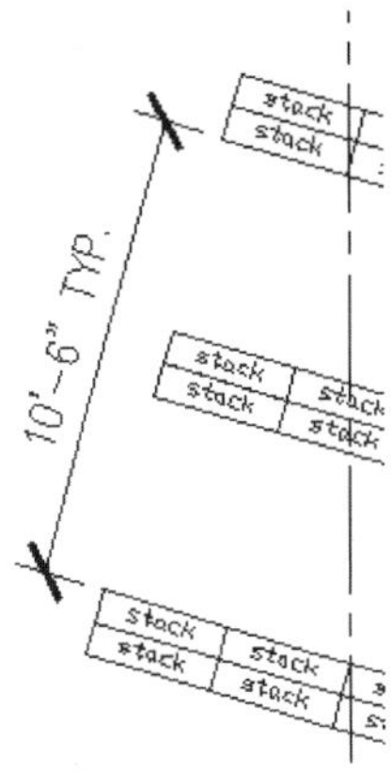

FIGURE 5-4.9
Modified dimension

19. With the dimension still selected, edit the Text Override text box to read: **<> Typ. \X REFERENCE STACKS**, and then press **Enter** (Figure 5-4.10a).

    TIP: The X must be uppercase.

As you can see (Figure 5-4.10b) the text after the "\X" is moved below the dimension line.

Text view direction	Left-to-Right
Measurement	4'-6"
Text override	<> TYP. \X REFERENCE STACK

FIGURE 5-4.10A
Edited Text Override value

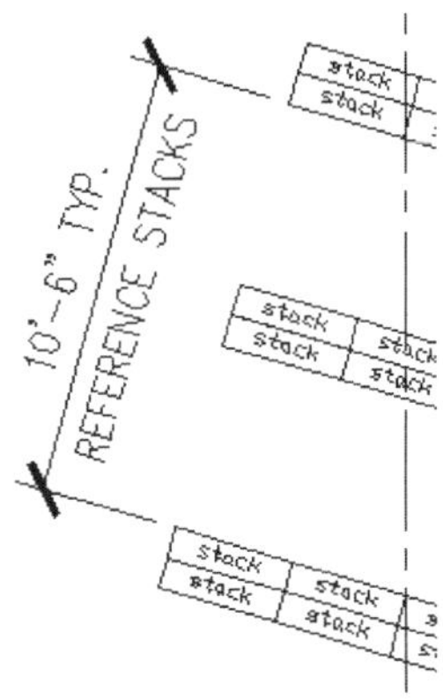

FIGURE 5-4.10B
Modified dimension

20. With the dimension still selected, edit the Text Override text box to read: **<> Typ. \X REFERENCE\PSTACKS** and then press **Enter** (Figure 5-4.11a).

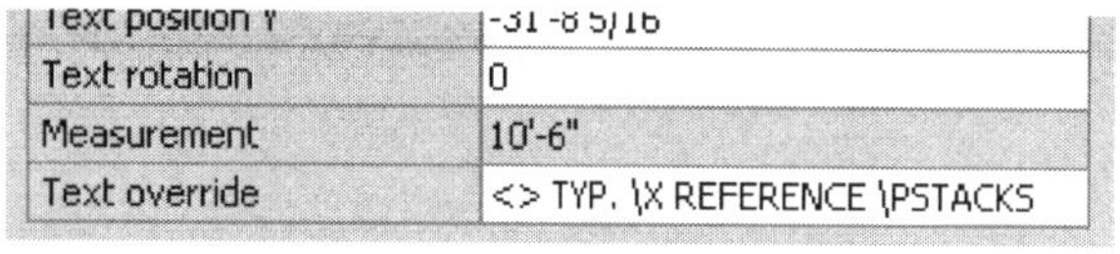

FIGURE 5-4.11A Edited Text Override value

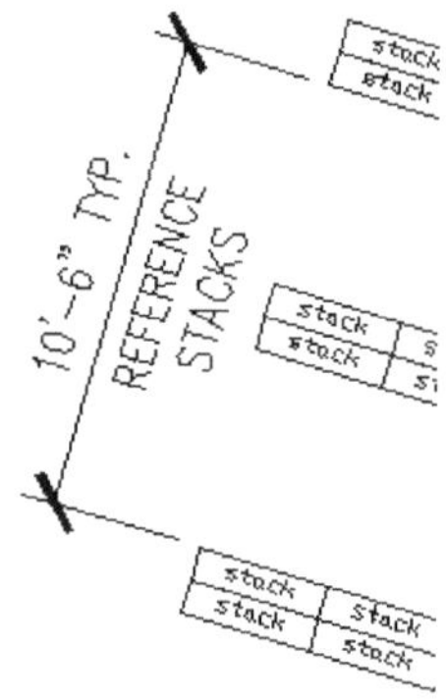

FIGURE 5-4.11B
Edited Text Override value

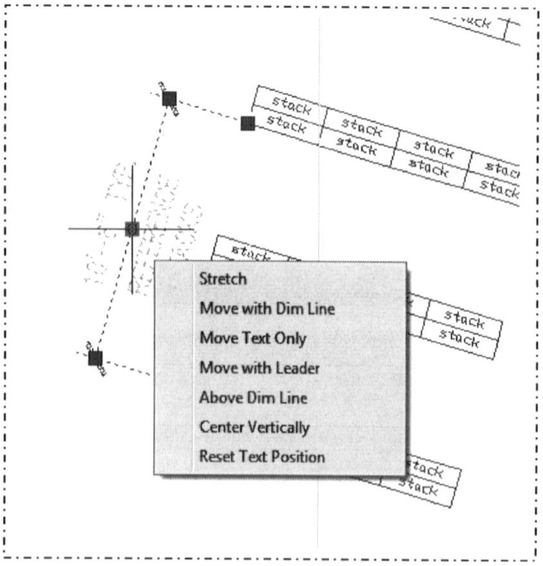

Now the text below the dimension line occurs on two lines (Figure 5-4.11b).

***TIP:** You can select multiple dimension objects and change them all at once via properties.*

A final note about dimensions in this exercise: select a dimension and hover your cursor over the text grip to see a few modify options available for the selected dimension(s) – see the image to the left. A few more options are available as well if you right-click.

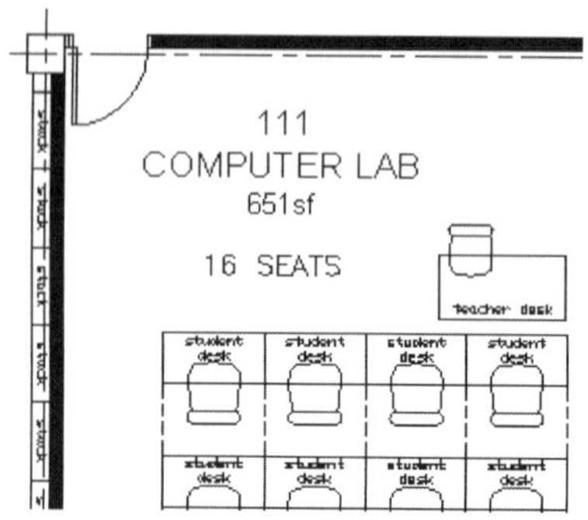

FIGURE 5-4.12 Text added

Adding Text:

The last step will be to add seating capacity text to the classrooms.

21. Similar to the Large Classroom, add the seating capacity text to each classroom and the reading room; place text on Layer A-Furn-Text, color 4 (Figure 5-4.12).

Self-Exam:

The following questions can be used as a way to check your knowledge of this lesson. The answers can be found at the bottom of this page.

1. The Base Point for a Block is important. (T/F)
2. You can use Grip Edit to modify dimensions. (T/F)
3. Use multiple Layers and Layer States for design options. (T/F)
4. The chairs go on ______________________ layer.
5. Name the icon used to access various UCS tools: ______________

Review Questions:

The following questions may be assigned by your instructor as a way to assess your knowledge of this section. Your instructor has the answers to the review questions.

1. Typically, all lines within a Block go on Layer zero. (T/F)
2. Use Copy (not copy to clipboard) to copy items around within the same drawing. (T/F)
3. When dimensioning angled items you should avoid using Aligned. (T/F)
4. It is ok for text to overlap other text and linework (T/F)
5. A Layer can be visible but not print by toggling the icon in the "plot" column of the Layer Properties palette. (T/F)
6. You can use the Array command to create several rows and columns of chairs in a classroom. (T/F).
7. Command to get measurement between two points:________________
8. Where do you add a suffix or prefix to a dimension? ________________
9. Command to turn on the UCS icon (make it visible) in the drawing window?

   ____
10. It pays to preplan and organize the folder structure for a drawing symbol library. (T/F)

SELF-EXAM ANSWERS:
1 – T, **2** – T, **3** – T, **4** – A-Furn-Char, **5** – Named

Notes:

Lesson 6
Library Project: INTERIOR ELEVATIONS

In this lesson, you will switch from drawing plan views to elevation views. This is where vertical relationships are explored and documented.

Exercise 6-1:
Overview: Non-plan Layers

Introduction

This section is an overview, in addition to Appendix A, which will help you to understand the *Layer* naming system you will be using for this Lesson (and all drawings in this book that are not plan views).

"**Non-plan**" drawings do not have to be as rigid as floor plan drawings because they are not typically shared with others (i.e., engineers), and the various *Layers* within a custom base cabinet detail (for example) would not typically need to be turned off as is often the case in a floor plan (e.g., turning off the dimensions in the reflected ceiling plan view). However, a standard is required for inter-office efficiency.

The best layering method for "**Non-Plan**" drawings deviates from the AIA Layer Standards. "Non-Plan" drawings like Elevations, Wall Sections, Details, Stair Sections, etc. can all use the same streamlined layering method. The only thing layers do in these drawings is indicate line weight.

The "office standard" layers for this section are shown on Page A-6. These names look a little odd at first, but they are descriptive and are displayed in order (lightest to heaviest).

Try to avoid the use of other *Layers*. If required, based on scope of project, you should coordinate with the Project Architect and/or CADD Manager prior to proceeding. Also, these *Layers* should NOT be used in floor plans as their names are too vague. Linetypes can be changed "*By Entity*" in "Non-Plan" drawings.

In an office environment you should have a command in a custom pull-down menu to create these *Layers* automatically. Below is an AutoLISP routine that can automatically load *Layers* into your current drawing whenever it is run.

AutoLISP is a custom programming language for AutoCAD which can be used to automate many aspects of the drawing environment and the drawing itself. This routine is meant to be an extremely limited introduction of this powerful feature. Below are the basic steps required to implement this routine:

- Enter the code shown on the next page using **MS Notepad**.
  (Be sure to change the file extension from .txt to .lsp when saving.)
- In AutoCAD, type **APPLOAD** and then **Browse** for and **Load** the file.
- At the AutoCAD command prompt, type **load_detlay** and press **Enter**.
- The new *Layers* should now be loaded into your drawing.
- This routine can also be added to a custom menu or icon.

Text file named ***LOAD_DETLAY.lsp***

```
(defun c:load_detlay ()
  (LoadLinetypes)
  (CreateLayers)
  (princ)
)

(defun LoadLinetypes ()
  (LtFunction "batting")
  (LtFunction "hidden")
  (LtFunction "hiddenx2")
  (LtFunction "hidden2")
  (LtFunction "center")
  (LtFunction "centerx2")
  (LtFunction "center2")
  (LtFunction "dot2")
)

(defun CreateLayers ()
  (LayerFunction "G-Detl-Thck" "continuous" "3")
  (LayerFunction "G-Detl-Lite" "continuous" "1")
  (LayerFunction "G-Detl-Medm" "continuous" "2")
  (LayerFunction "G-Detl-Xhvy" "continuous" "6")
  (LayerFunction "G-Detl-Xlit" "continuous" "5")
  (LayerFunction "G-Detl-Grid" "continuous" "7")
  (LayerFunction "G-Detl-Patt" "continuous" "8")
  (LayerFunction "G-Detl-Patt-Ex" "continuous" "252")

  (LayerFunction "G-Anno-Dims" "continuous" "4")
  (LayerFunction "G-Anno-Text" "continuous" "4")
  (LayerFunction "G-Anno-Ttlb" "continuous" "3")
  (LayerFunction "G-Anno-Ttlb-Text" "continuous" "4")

  (LayerFunction "G-Vprt" "continuous" "6")
  (LayerFunction "G-Xref" "continuous" "7")
)

(defun LtFunction (linetype)
  (if (= (tblsearch "ltype" linetype) nil)
    (command "linetype" "load" linetype "acad.lin" "" )
  )
)

(defun LayerFunction (lname ltype cname)
  (if (= (tblsearch "layer" lname) nil)
    (command "-layer" "new" lname "lt" ltype lname "c" cname lname "" )
  )
)
```

If in a class setting, your instructor may offer extra credit for this…

Exercise 6-2:
Drawing Symbols

Introduction

Even though one can obtain symbols within your CAD program and from various online sources, you will draw additional symbols to help you familiarize yourself with the sizes and proportions of various items in an interior elevation. You will draw a few symbols to be used in the next few exercises.

As before, the black dot represents the drawing origin and the dimensions are not to be drawn. Some of the linework within a symbol is more for "show" than anything else. For example, you will be drawing a microwave in this exercise – the microwave will have linework within the overall rectangle that is meant to represent the door and number-pad. The only thing that is really important here is the overall rectangle (if the microwave does not fit in the custom cabinet somebody is in trouble). However, the linework within the outer rectangle has no real significance other than trying to better convey what the symbol represents. Therefore, if the symbols to be drawn below are missing dimensions you are to draw the linework as close as possible.

---

filename: **Outlet-2.dwg**

This is a symbol that will represent a duplex receptacle (i.e., outlet). These are not always shown on interior elevations, but on more complex areas it can help coordinate everything.

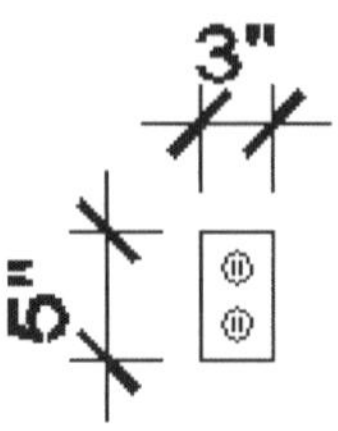

1. **Open** a new drawing.
2. Switch to **Model** space.
3. Draw everything on layer zero.
4. Use the **Rectangle** command to draw the outlet.
5. Draw two 1¼" circles with two vertical lines within each circle.
6. Locate the **Drawing Origin** in the lower left corner of the rectangle.
7. **Save** your drawing per the name listed above.

filename: Outlet-4.dwg

This is an outlet with four plugs rather than two.

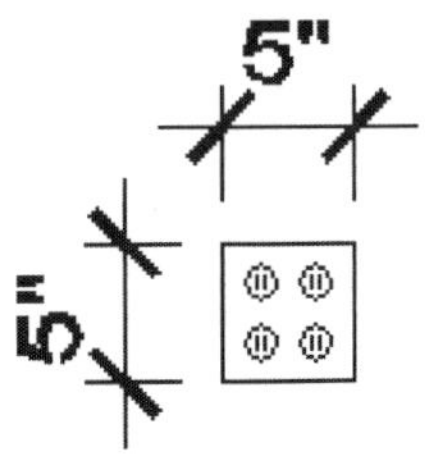

8. **Open** a new drawing.
9. Switch to **Model** space.
10. Draw the outlet shown using the information given for the previous symbol.
11. **Save** your drawing per the name listed above.

---

filename: Microwave.dwg

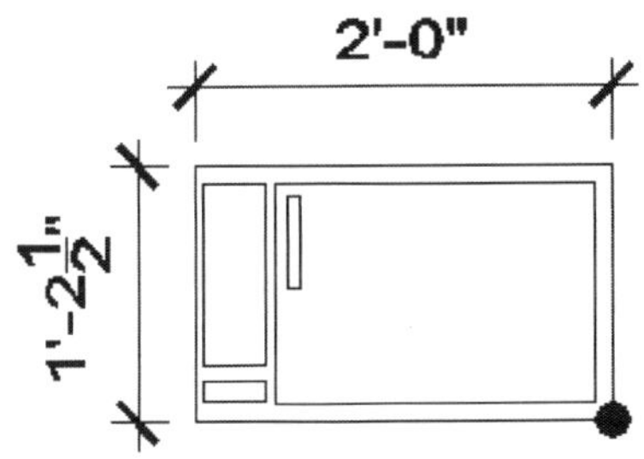

12. Draw the microwave shown; approximate the inner linework.

---

filename: Copier-Elev.dwg

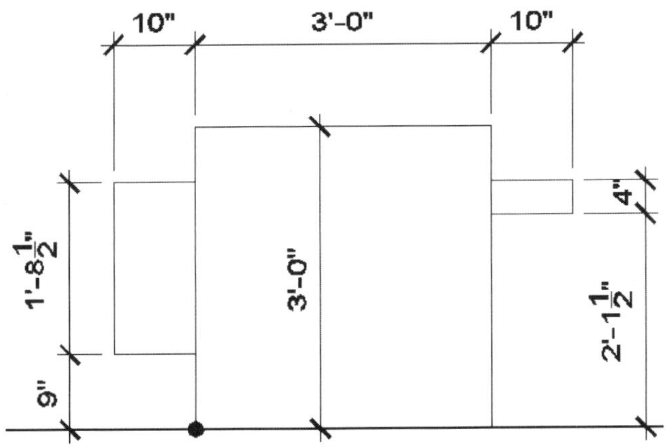

13. Draw the copier shown.

NOTE: The heavy line at the bottom represents the floor line but should NOT *be drawn in your symbol.*

filename: **Refrigerator.dwg**

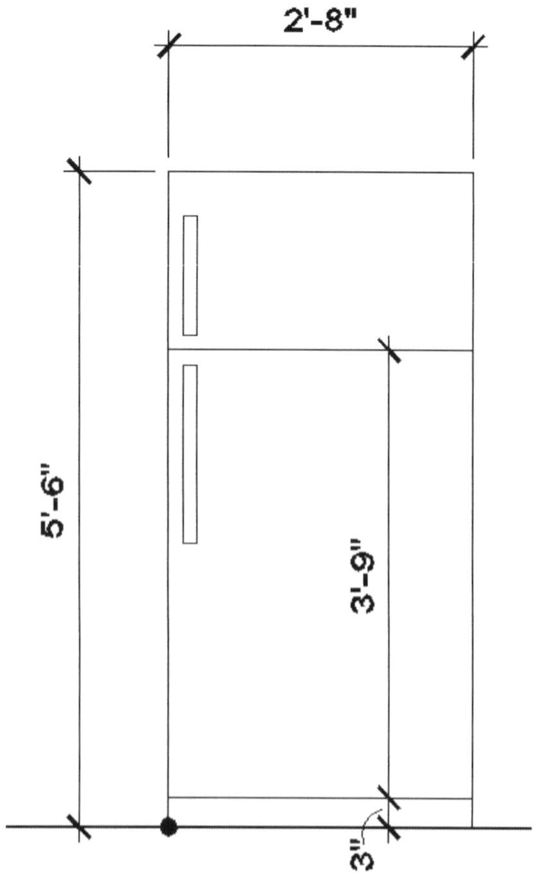

14. Draw the refrigerator shown; approximate the inner linework (i.e., the handles).

NOTE: *The heavy line at the bottom represents the floor line but should NOT be drawn in your symbol.*

filename: **Towel_Dispenser.dwg**

15. Draw the paper towel dispenser shown.

NOTE: *The heavy line at the bottom represents the floor line but should NOT be drawn in your symbol.*

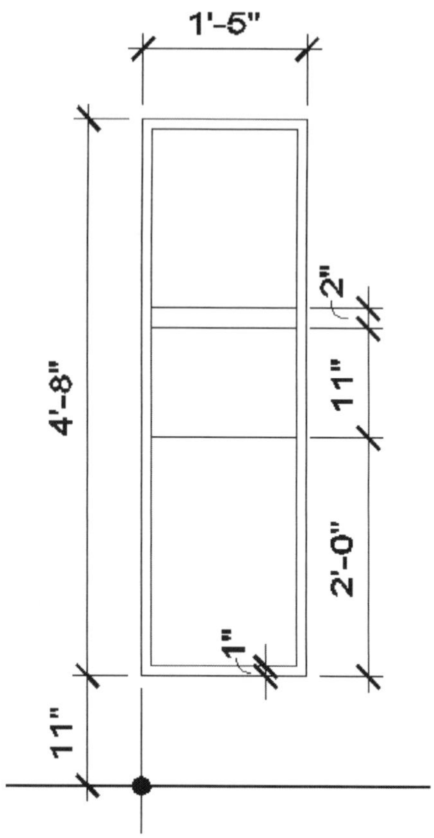

filename: FE_Cabinet.dwg

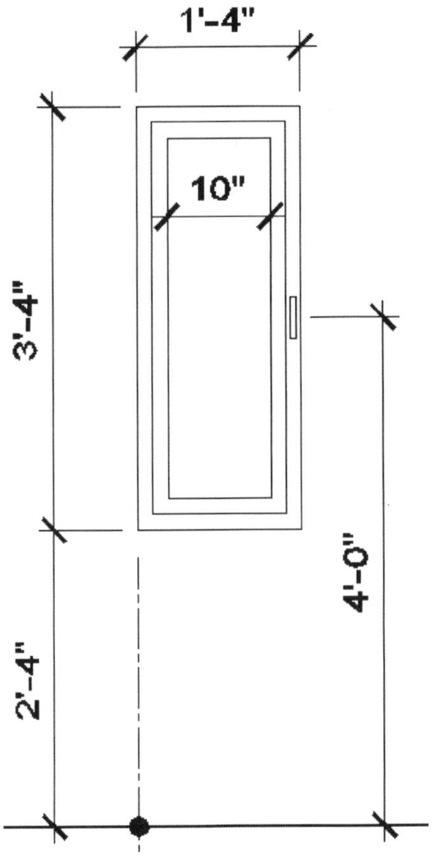

16. Draw the Fire Extinguisher Cabinet shown; approximate the inner linework.

***Note:** The heavy line at the bottom represents the floor line but should NOT be drawn in your symbol.*

filename: Pay_Phone.dwg

17. Draw the Pay Phone shown; approximate the inner linework.

***Note:** The heavy line at the bottom represents the floor line but should NOT be drawn in your symbol.*

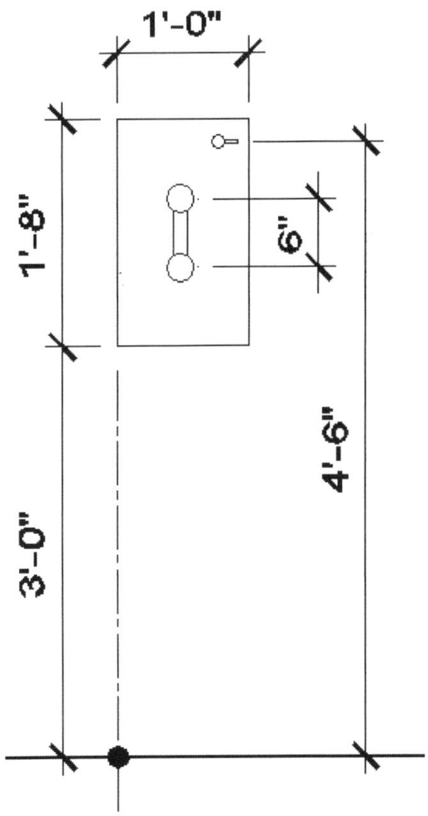

filename: **Hand_Dryer.dwg**

18. Draw the Hand Dryer shown; approximate the inner linework.

NOTE: *The heavy line at the bottom represents the floor line but should NOT be drawn in your symbol.*

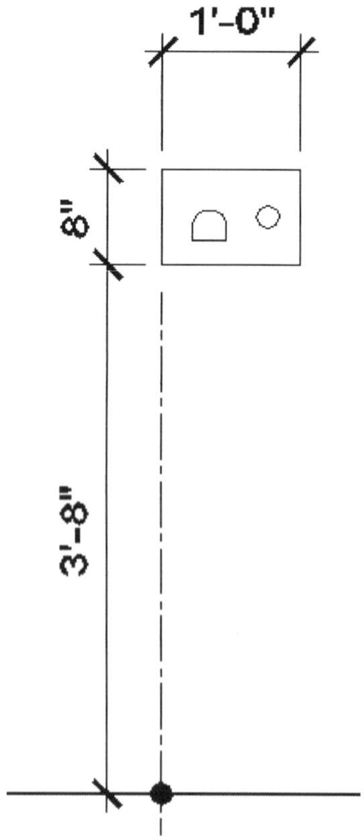

filename: **Soap_Disp.dwg**

19. Draw the Soap Dispenser shown; approximate the inner linework.

NOTE: *The heavy line at the bottom represents the floor line but should NOT be drawn in your symbol.*

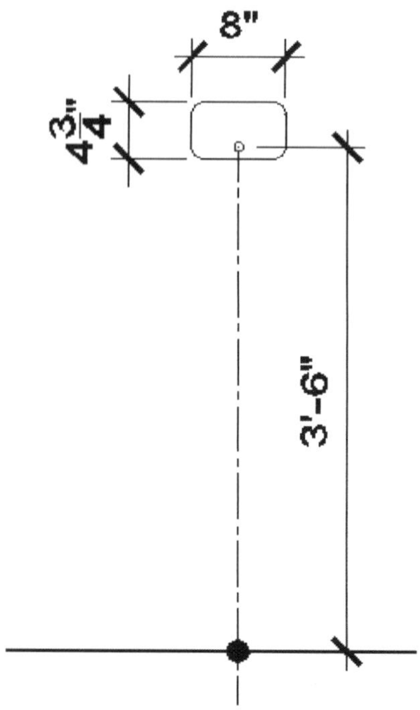

Exercise 6-3:
Creating a "Standard Mounting Height" Diagram

Introduction

In this exercise you will create a Standard Mounting Height Diagram; this is a drawing that lists all the mounting heights for fixtures and equipment. This helps to reduce the need to dimension every item in an interior elevation; instead, a note is added to the interior elevations sheet that refers to the mounting height diagram for more information.

Between the symbols you previously downloaded off the Internet and the symbols drawn in the previous exercise, you have almost everything needed to complete the diagram.

Most of the following steps simply refer to the overall (completed) mounting height diagram (Figure 6-3.1).

1. Draw the mounting height diagram per the following steps:
   a. Open a new drawing.
   b. Draw the floor (and wall) lines on *Layer* **G-Detl-Thck**.
   c. Draw all the dimensions shown using the "office standard" settings and place on *Layer* **G-Anno-Dims**.
   d. All inserted *Blocks* and additional linework to go on *Layer* **G-Detl-Lite**.
   e. The grab bars are 1 ½" thick in this drawing.
   f. Draw the flush-valve (for the toilet and urinals) per Figure 6-3.2.
   g. Draw the drinking fountain faucet per Figure 6-3.2.
   h. Use the symbols downloaded in Lesson 4 to place the toilets, urinals, drinking fountains and the lavatory.
   i. Add text as shown below each item.
   j. Use the "office standard" for the text and dimensions to be added.
   k. The **Mirror** should be 2′-0″ wide x 3′-0″ tall.
   l. Notice some items are dimensioned to that item's operable elements per many codes.
   m. Save the file as **M_Height_Diagram.dwg**.

The diagram you just created will be placed on a sheet in a future lesson.

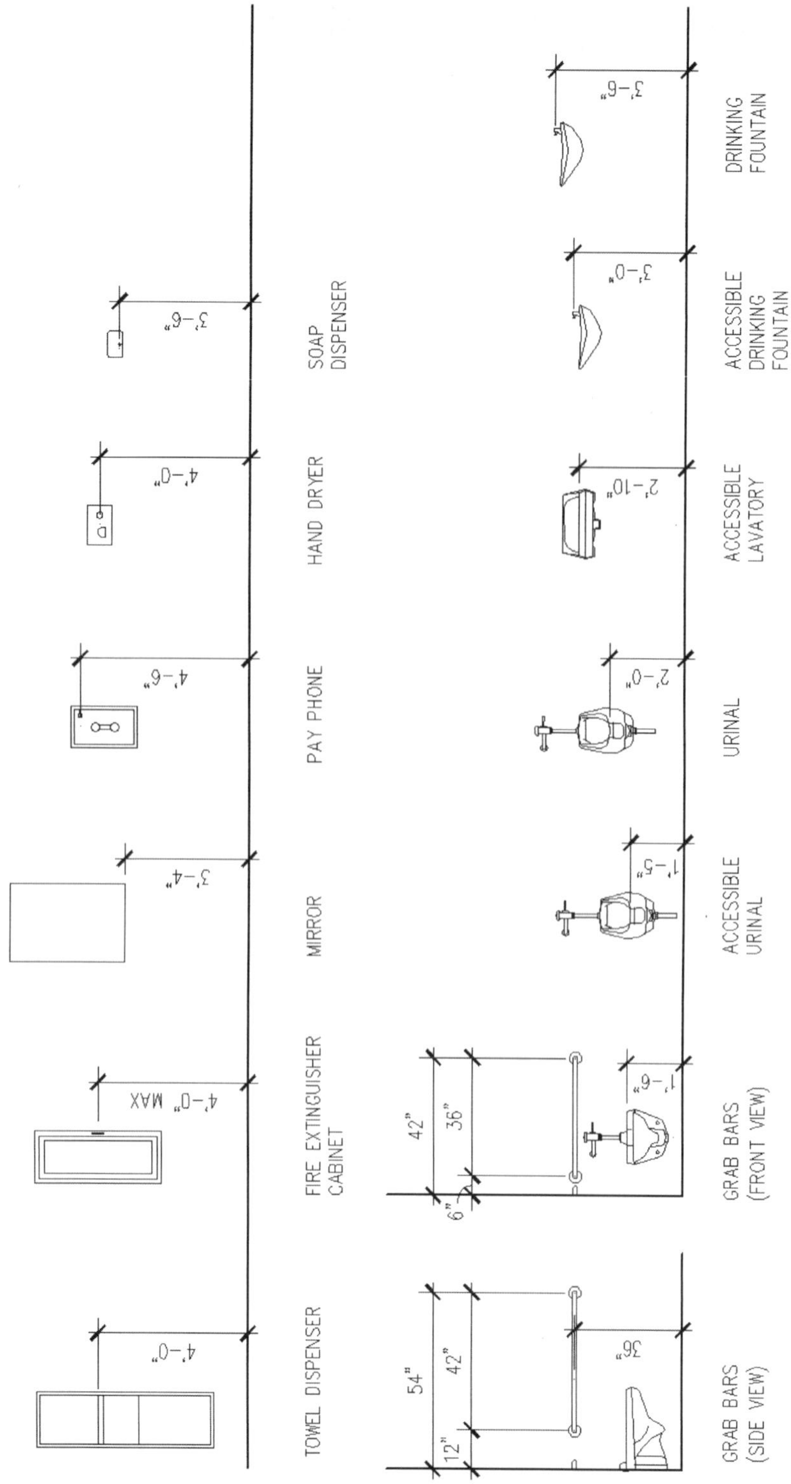

FIGURE 6-3.1 Mounting Height Diagram (rotated to fit on page)

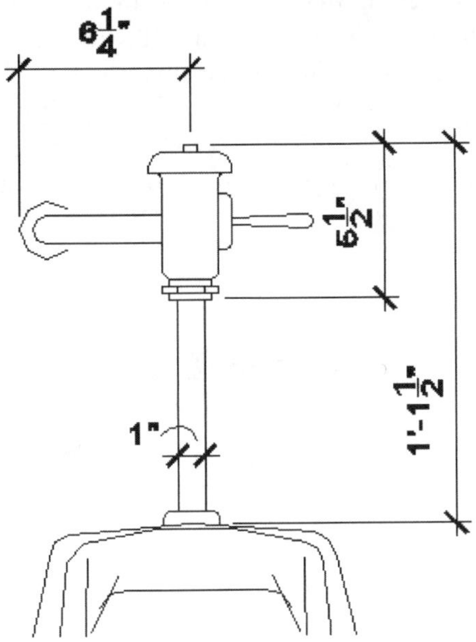

FYI: The flush value is helpful to show because it can conflict with the grab bars and other things if not properly coordinated.

This also lets the tile contractor know that they may have an extra obstacle when adding the tile (this may increase their bid).

Approximate the various items not dimensioned.

FIGURE 6-3.2 Flush value added to fixture

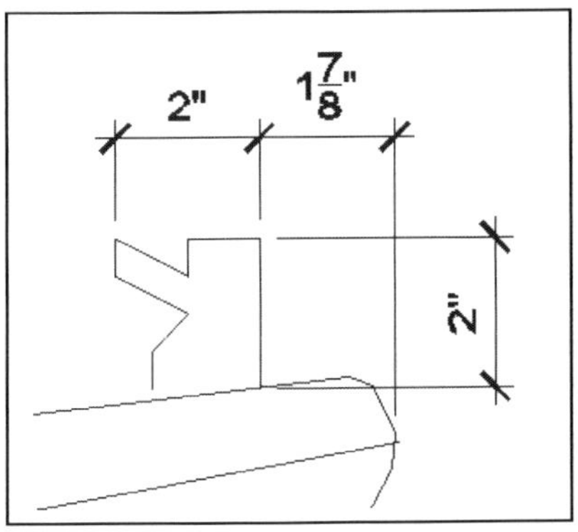

FYI: This is added so the correct dimension can be placed. Most codes require the operable part of various items be at certain heights; this is true for drinking fountains (you will need to verify code requirements in your area).

FIGURE 6-3.3 Drinking fountain faucet

Many of these symbols will be used again when you work through the next exercise.

Drawing Multileaders:

A *Multileader* is a line with an arrow on one end and text on the other end. *Multileaders* are very customizable and can have various symbols on the "arrow" end and a Block (e.g., a circle with a number in it) or nothing at all. You will need to use this feature in the next exercise (adding notes and pointing to various parts of the drawing) so you will take a moment to learn about it now.

The *Multileader* system is similar to the dimensioning system in that you first set up the style (of which you can have several, if needed) and then draw the leader and enter the text. If the style is modified, all instances of the *Multileader* that were created using that style will be modified.

First, you will set up the style; these steps could be done in a template file so you would not have to repeat them each time you create a new drawing.

2. Start a new drawing (SheetSets\Architectural Imperial) and then switch to **Model** space.

3. Set the *Roman* text style to be **Annotative** as described previously on Page 2-63, 64.

4. On the **Annotate** tab, in the **Leaders** panel, click the **Multileader Style** icon (Figure 6-3.4).

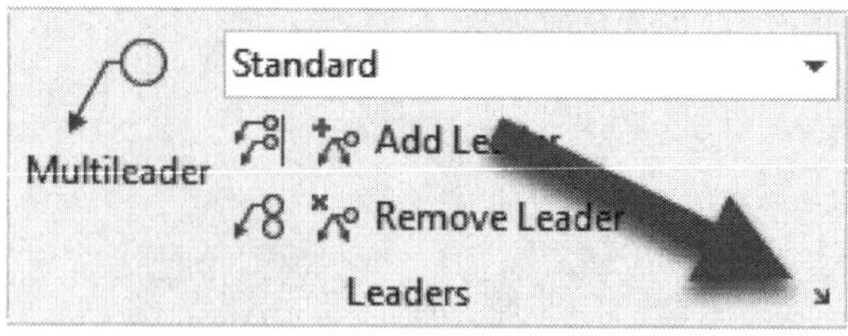

FIGURE 6-3.4
Found on the Annotate panel

5. In the *Multileader Style Manager*, with Standard style selected, click the **Modify…** button (Figure 6-3.5).

FYI: Notice how this looks just like the style manager for dimensions.

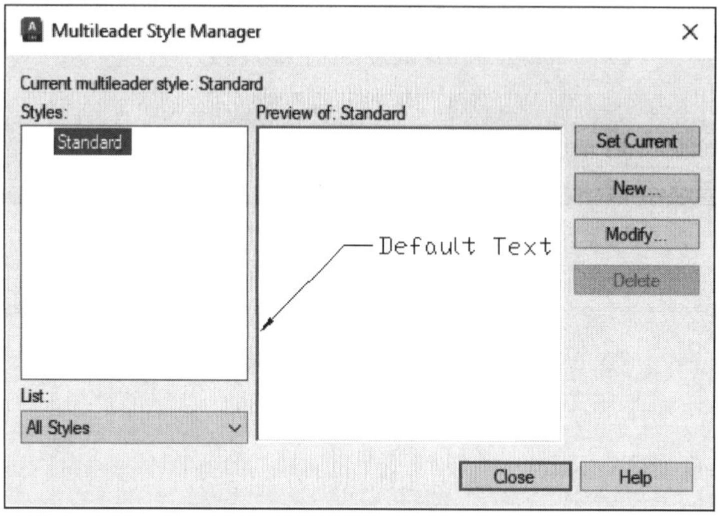

FIGURE 6-3.5 Multileader Style Manager dialog

6. Make the changes shown in the following three images (Figures 6-3.6a thru 6-3.6c).

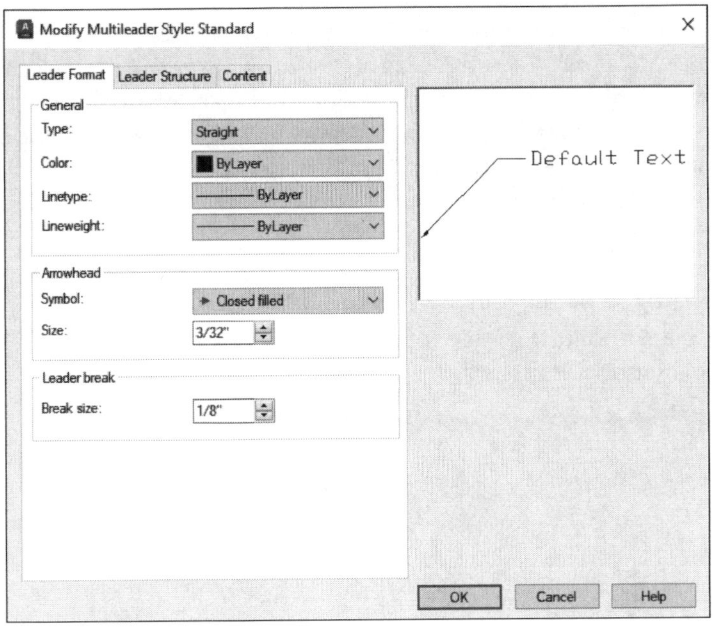

FIGURE 6-3.6A Leader Format tab: Modify Multileader Style dialog

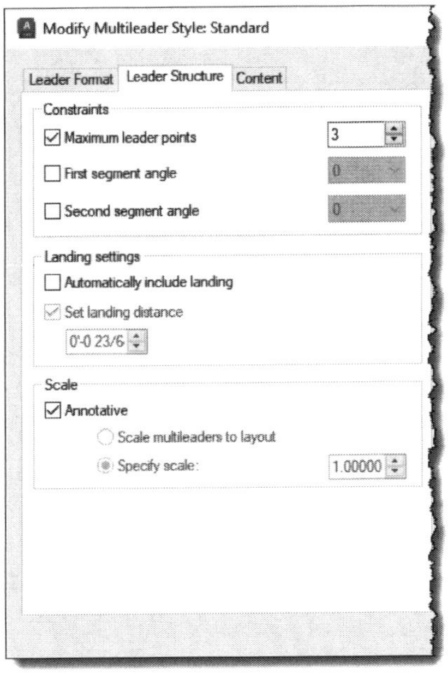

FIGURE 6-3.6B Leader Structure tab

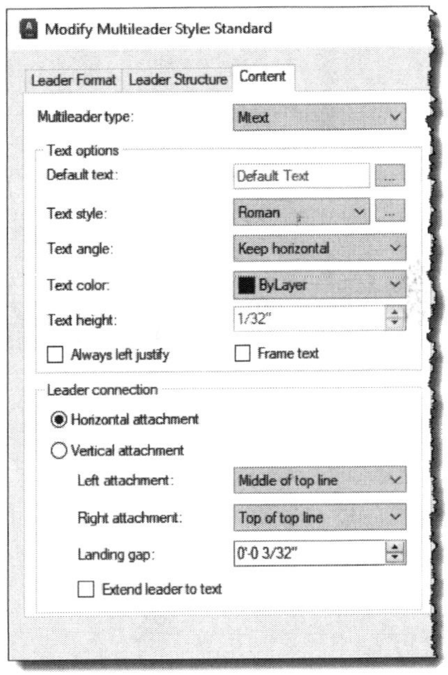

FIGURE 6-3.6C Content tab

7. When finished, click **OK** and then **Close** to exit these two dialog boxes.

You are almost ready to use your newly modified *Multileader* style, but first you need to set the *Annotation Scale* via the *Status Bar.* Over the next two chapters, you will need to change this on a drawing-by-drawing basis according to the required plot scale of the elevation or detail. Remember, in *Model Space* everything is always drawn real-world size; only the symbols and text are scaled up or down so that a sheet with multiple details of varying scale all have the same relative text height when the sheet is printed; this is where *Annotation Scale* comes in handy!

8. On the *Status Bar*, toggle on the option to **automatically add annotation scales** to objects, and set the **Annotation Scale** to ¼″ = 1′-0″ – this is the scale of the next exercise (i.e., the interior elevations).

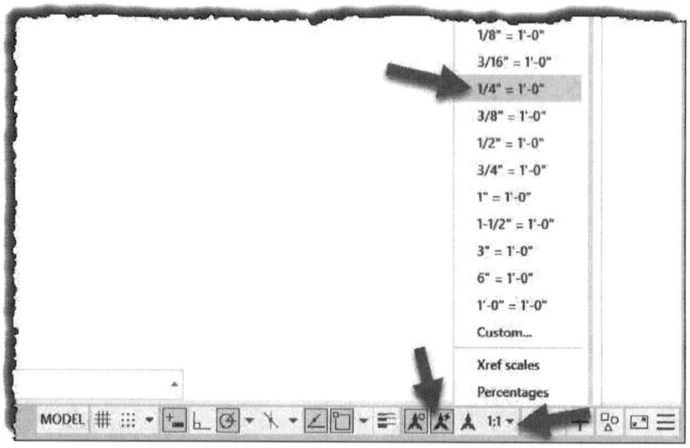

FIGURE 6-3.7 Setting the Annotative Scale via the Status Bar

9. Click the large **Multileader** icon (Figure 6-3.4).

10. Click three points similar to those shown below, type some text, and then click *Exit Text Editor* on the *Ribbon* when finished.

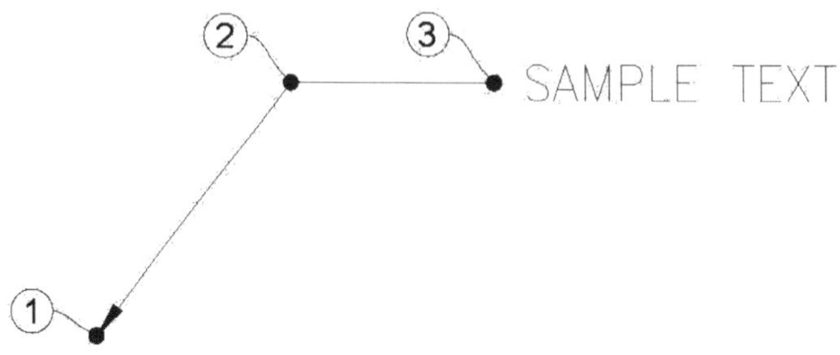

Try changing the *Annotation Scale* and notice the text and arrow size change automatically. You can now apply this technique throughout the remainder of this textbook.

FYI: *This could have been used on the stairs in your floor plans via a style set to never have Mtext.*

Exercise 6-4:
Drawing Elevations

Introduction

Interior elevations are an important part of a set of construction documents. Sometimes the Interior Designer actually draws the elevations and other times they, at the very least, review them. For example, if the Interior Designer specified wood base board in the room finish schedule, he or she will want to make sure that all the drawings, including the interior elevations, note/show wood base as opposed to vinyl or tile.

The interior elevations help to convey what the plan views cannot, namely, vertical relationships (i.e., heights above the floor) and accessories (mirrors, outlets, trim, etc.).

There are several ways to organize the drawing files within a project folder. Some firms draw all the elevations within one drawing file to maintain and coordinate vertical relationships. Another method often employed is to draw each elevation in a separate drawing file and Xref all the drawings into the "plot" sheet. You will use the latter method, which will allow you to take advantage of AutoCAD's Sheet Set feature in a subsequent lesson.

When drawing interior elevations, you use the floor plans to establish all the horizontal relationships. To accommodate this process, you will start a new drawing (for the interior elevation) and Xref the floor plan in at 0,0. Next, you will "crop" the Xref so that only the room you are working on is visible on the screen. At this point you can begin snapping lines to the Xref'ed floor plan and drawing reference lines to begin drawing your elevations. Finally, you will have learned more about how Xref's work which will allow you to leave the Xref in the drawing so you can monitor it for changes that might affect your elevation.

> *FYI: The floor plan will not show up in the "plot" sheet when the steps outlined in this exercise are used.*

Setting Up the Interior Elevation Drawing:

1. Start a **new drawing** file (SheetSets\ Architectural Imperial).

2. Switch to **Model** space.

Next, you will place the floor plan drawing as an external reference (Xref). You should understand that the file is not stored in your new drawing file in any way, nor is the file size increased by the Xref being added. Each time the elevation drawing is opened, the Xref is reloaded. Important: most firms have a well-established standard of always placing floor plan Xrefs at 0,0. This allows the Xref to be reattached more easily if necessary (if an arbitrary point is picked during placement, it would be difficult to re-attach the Xref in the exact same position, which is often required because drawing elements in the "host" drawing have been aligned with the Xref).

3. From the **Insert** tab select the **Attach** icon.

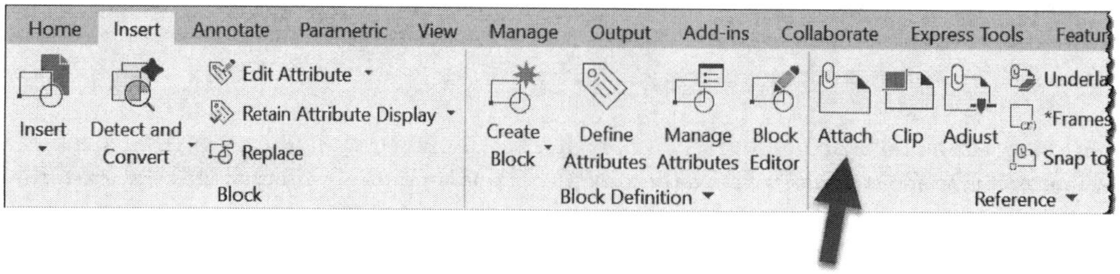

4. *Browse* to the location where you saved your **floor plan** drawing and **select it**. Make sure the *Files of type* is set to look for DWG files.

5. Click the **Open** button.

6. Click **Overlay**. (This is an important step; if "attachment" is selected, the floor plan will travel with the elevation when it is Xref'ed into the "plot" sheet). See Figure 6-4.1 below.

7. **Uncheck** "Specify On-screen" under *Insertion point* (Figure 6-4.1).

8. Click **OK** to place the Xref.

9. Per the *Layer* standard, move the Xref to layer **G-Xref**.

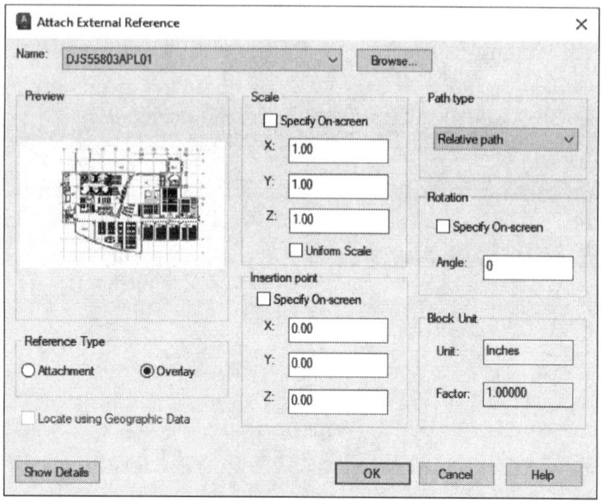

FIGURE 6-4.1 External Reference dialog box

> ***TIP:***
> *By default, AutoCAD fades any drawings that are linked in to make them stand out from the line work in the "host" drawing. This fading can be adjusted (or turned off) via the Options dialog box.*

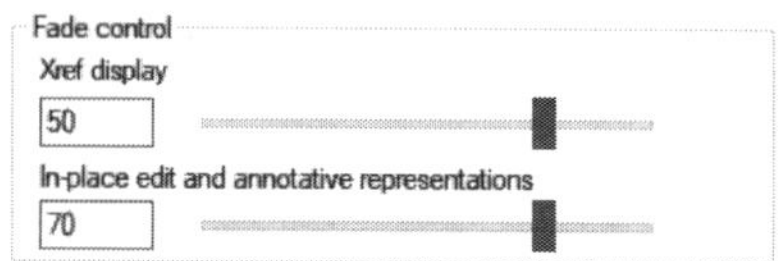

You now have the floor plan drawing Xref'ed into your elevation drawing. It could now be used as-is to aid in the creation of the interior elevation. However, it will be easier if you "crop" the plan so that only the room you are elevating is visible; this would also allow you to draw the elevation closer to the related floor plan line work. You will "crop" the plan next.

Using the Clip Command to Crop an Xref:

AutoCAD provides a command called *Clip* (aka Xclip), which allows you to "crop" an Xref. The "cropping" window is not a visible line, but the boundary can be deleted or reselected at any time using the *Clip* command.

10. **Zoom** into the primary toilet rooms as shown in Figure 6-4.2.

Notice in Figure 6-4.2 that the columns and grids are not visible because that drawing was Xref'ed as an Overlay so it does not follow the "host" drawing when it is Xref'ed. You do not need the columns for this drawing; if you did, you would need to Xref that file as well (at 0,0 so they align properly).

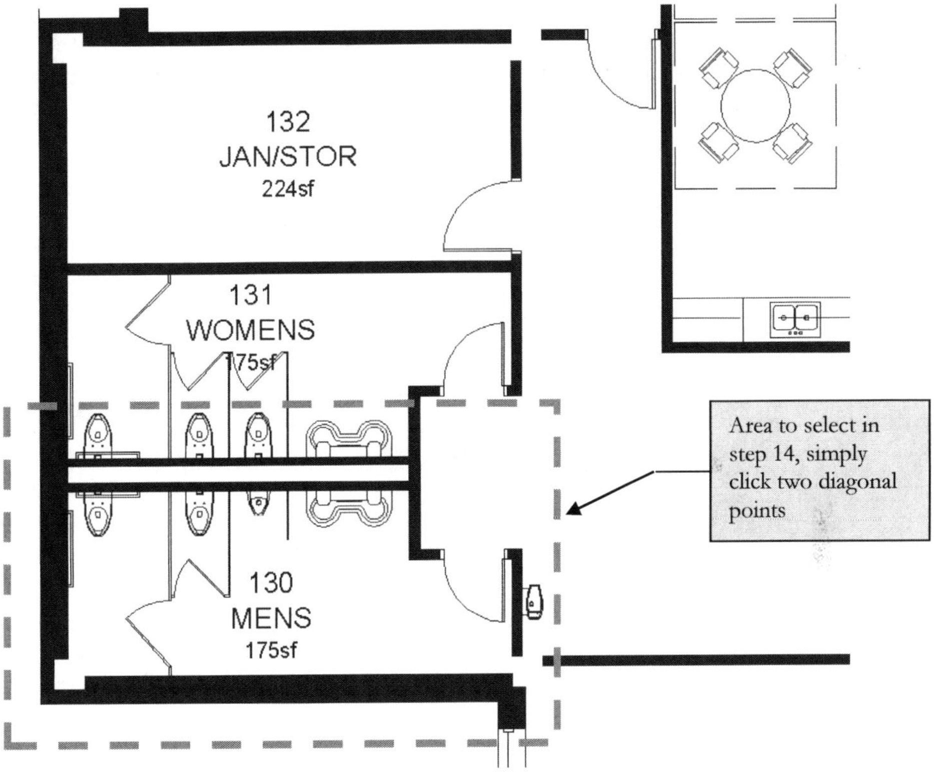

FIGURE 6-4.2 Portion of Xref to be Clipped

11. Select **Clip** from the **Reference** panel on the **Insert** tab. You are now prompted to select an object to be clipped.

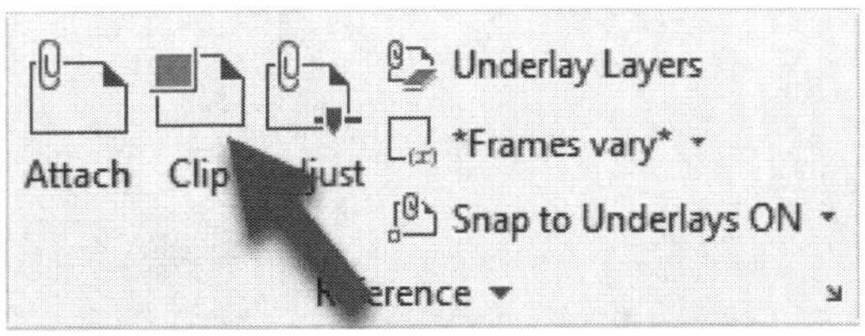

12. **Click** anywhere on the floor plan "Xref" to select it

13. Select **New Boundary** and then **Rectangular** from the on-screen menus.

14. Pick a rectangular area as shown in Figure 6-4.2.

    TIP: Be careful not to snap to anything when specifying the window.

You are now ready to begin drawing the interior elevation. You will begin by drawing a horizontal line to represent the floor line. Then you will draw vertical lines down from the Xref'ed plan, draw the ceiling line, trim the corners, and move on to the inner lines and symbols.

15. **Draw a horizontal line** (representing the floor line) approximately as shown in Figure 6-4.3; use *Layer* **G-Detl-Thck**.

16. On the same *Layer*, **draw three vertical lines** snapped from the floor plan to establish the wall lines (Figure 6-4.3). Ensure **Polar Tracking** (F10) is turned on, on the status bar, to make accurate vertical lines.

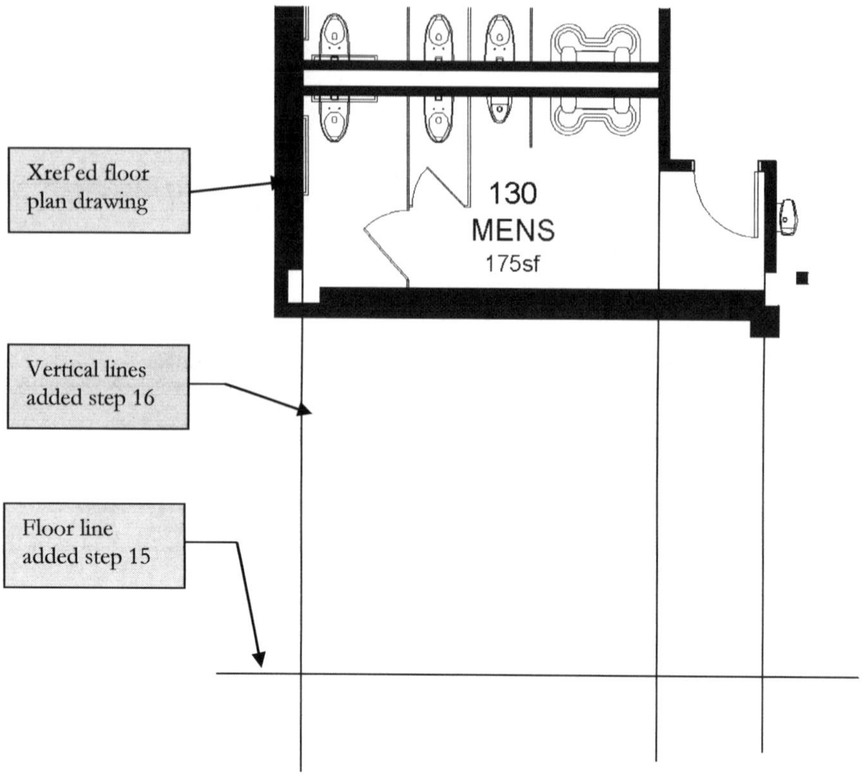

FIGURE 6-4.3 Portion of Xref to be Clipped

17. **Offset** the floor line up **8′-0″** to establish the ceiling line.

18. **Trim** and/or **Extend** all the lines to define the perimeter of the room.

19. Finish drawing the elevation as shown in Figure 6-4.4 following the following comments:

    a. Draw all the plumbing fixtures and the mirror on *Layer* **G-Detl-Medm**.

    b. Draw the toilet partitions on *Layer* **G-Detl-Thck**. (They are in section so they need to be heavy lines.)

    c. The **toilet partitions** are **4′-10″** tall and **1′-0″** above the floor (the urinal partition is 3′-6″ high).

    d. Draw the grab bars, TPD and door frame on *Layer* **G-Detl-Lite**.

    e. Draw the **6″x6″** tile base on *Layer* **G-Detl-Patt**.

    f. Refer to the mounting height drawing for applicable mounting heights (drawn in the previous exercise).

       FYI: The ACC. WC is 18″ high and the WC is 15″ high.

    g. Add the notes and dimensions on the proper *Layers*.

    h. See Figure 6-4.5 for **Wash Fountain** dimensions.

    i. Copy/Paste the **structural grids** from the floor plan; scale the bubble and text down 50%. (The plans will be printed at 1/8″ = 1′-0″ and the elevations will be printed at 1/4″ = 1′-0″.)

    j. The angled line within the door opening indicated the swing of the door (think of it as a large arrow pointing at the hinges). Draw this line on *Layer* G-Detl-Lite and change the lines type to Hidden2 via the *Properties* dialog (set the LTscale to 48).

    k. Your instructor may require you to add a hatch pattern to represent a tile pattern on the wall.

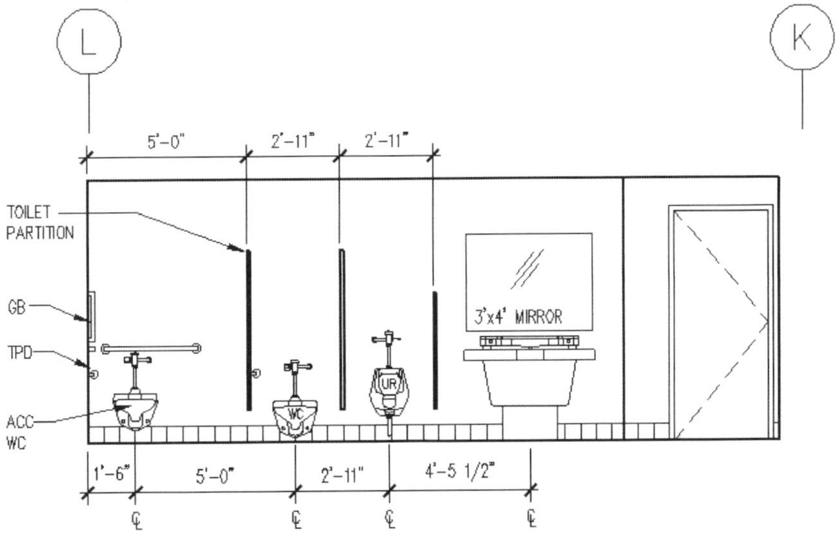

FIGURE 6-4.4 Interior elevation of Men's toilet room 130

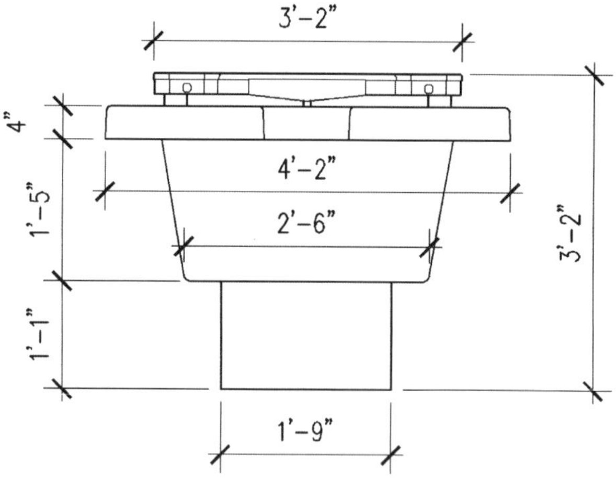

FIGURE 6-4.5
Wash fountain dimensions (do not draw dimensions)

That completes the toilet room elevation. The only thing left to do is save the file. As previously mentioned, all files are to have the "job number" as a prefix when naming files. Similar to the floor plan file name you will then have the letter "A" to represent architecture, "IE" for interior elevations, and then a two digit number that increments with each new elevation drawing created. A formal naming system is a must on large projects like this.

20. **Save** your elevation as **DJS55803AIE01**.dwg.

Interior Elevation with Cabinets:

Next you will draw an interior elevation with wall and base cabinets. To start this elevation you will do a Save As from the previous elevation (this will save time seeing as the Xref is set up and the layers created). You will learn how to modify a *Clip* as well.

21. **Open** the previous elevation DJS55803AIE01.dwg (if already open, make sure you save before moving on to the next steps).

22. **Save As** to **DJS55803AIE02**.dwg.

23. **Erase** the toilet room elevation.

Next you will delete the *Clip* to reveal the entire floor plan.

24. Select **Clip** again, select the floor plan "Xref", press **Enter** and then select **Delete** from the *On-screen* menu.

25. *Zoom* into **Open Office 125** and **Clip** the floor plan *Xref* and rotate (using the **Rotate** command after finishing the *Clip* command). See Figure 6-4.6.

    FYI: *This is one example where the Xref origin has to be changed (i.e., when the Xref was rotated) in order to easily draw the elevation.*

26. Draw the elevation shown in Figure 6-4.6 per the following:

    a. **9'-0"** high ceiling; **6"** high wall base.

    b. Determine *Layers* based on items being in section or elevation.

    c. Add notes and dimensions.

    d. Base cabinets are **24"** deep and wall cabinets are **14"** deep.

    e. Show open cabinet shelves **1"** thick.

    f. See Figure 6-4.7 for typical base cabinet dimensions.

    FYI: *The* ***3"f*** *text indicates a 3" wide filler panel; the other numbers (27", 18", etc.) indicate the width of each cabinet.*

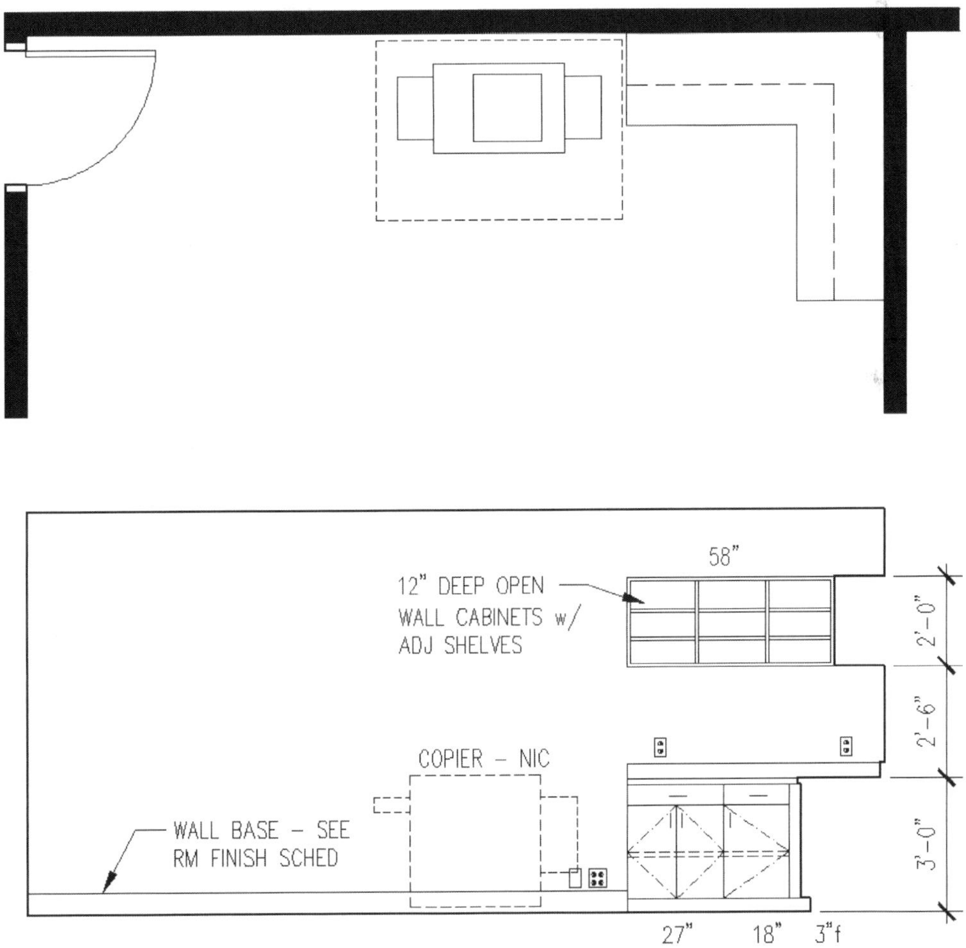

FIGURE 6-4.6 Work area (open office 125)

Notice in Figure 6-4.6 that the perimeter of the room has been modified to accentuate the cabinets in section. The cabinets in section are the ones that turn the corner. Also, the items dimensioned in Figure 6-4.7 are not actually dimensioned in the elevation (except the cabinet height) because this is typically a manufactured item, so the dimensions are what they are. They still need to be drawn correctly, but the dimensions do not need to be drawn because they would not help the contractor and would "muddy up" the drawings. The dashed lines represent shelving within the cabinets and door swing.

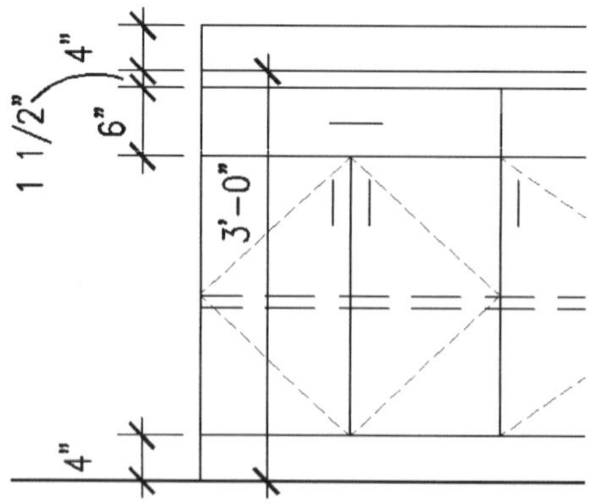

FIGURE 6-4.7 Typical base cabinet dimensions

Break Room Cabinets:

Next you will draw the interior elevation for the cabinets in the Break Room. This will mainly be more practice for what you just learned in the previous steps.

27. Set up a new drawing (do a Save As from the previous) and name it **DJS55803AIE03.dwg**.

    *TIP: Make sure you do a regular **Save** before doing a **Save As**. When you do a **Save As** the "current" drawing becomes the new drawing. So the "current" drawing only has changes in it up to the last time it was saved. Again, the **Save As** command essentially closes the "current" drawing without saving and creates a new drawing based on the "current" one.*

28. **Adjust the Clip** to view the cabinets in the Break Room.

29. Do NOT delete the Work Room elevation; you can use some of this linework for your next elevation.

30. Draw the interior elevation as shown in Figure 6-4.8 using the following information:
    a. Use all applicable information from step 26 above.
    b. Approximate the sink dimensions (use the plan view for the horizontal dimensions).
    c. Insert the Blocks (Refrig, Micro, etc.) and do not explode them – place them on a new layer based on lineweight and set the linetype to Hidden 2.
    d. Make the microwave shelf large enough to fit the microwave.
    e. Notice the following:
        i. The countertop steps down to make a portion accessible
        ii. The area below the sink is open to allow for accessibility
        iii. An area to the left is also open to accommodate a dish washer (this is sometimes shown dashed like the refrig).

31. **Erase** the work room elevation items to "clean up" and finish the drawing.

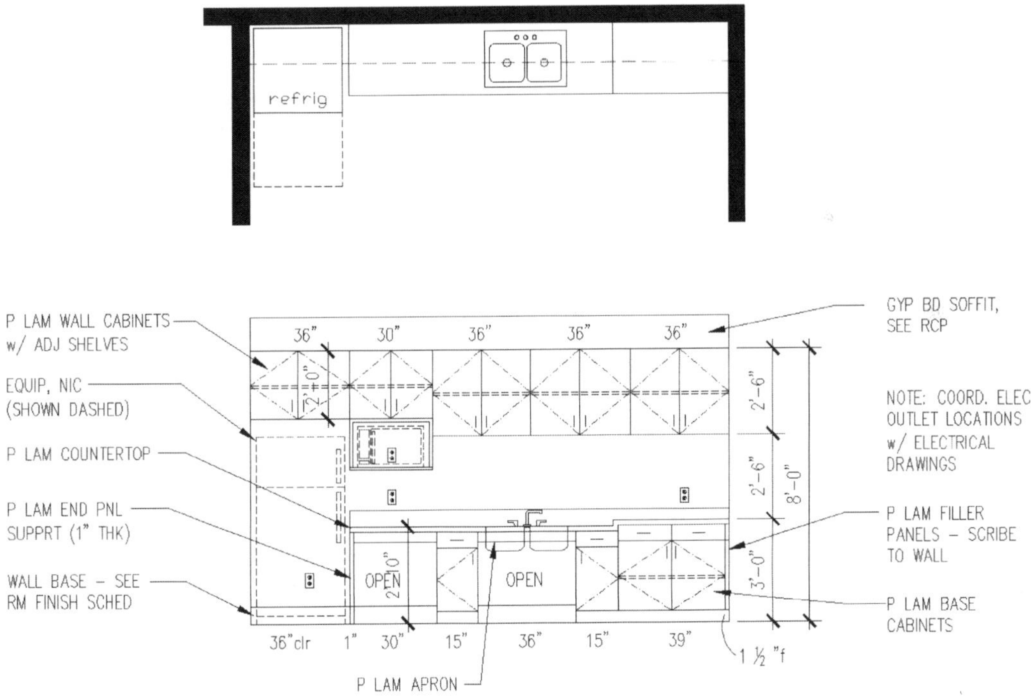

FIGURE 6-4.8 Interior elevations: break room cabinets

Lecture Room with Raised Seating Platforms:

32. Draw Lecture room (room 112) per the following (**DJS55803AIE04.dwg**):
    a. Use the steps/information previously provided.
    b. Draw everything shown in Figure 6-4.9.
    c. See Figure 6-4.10 for desk dimensions.

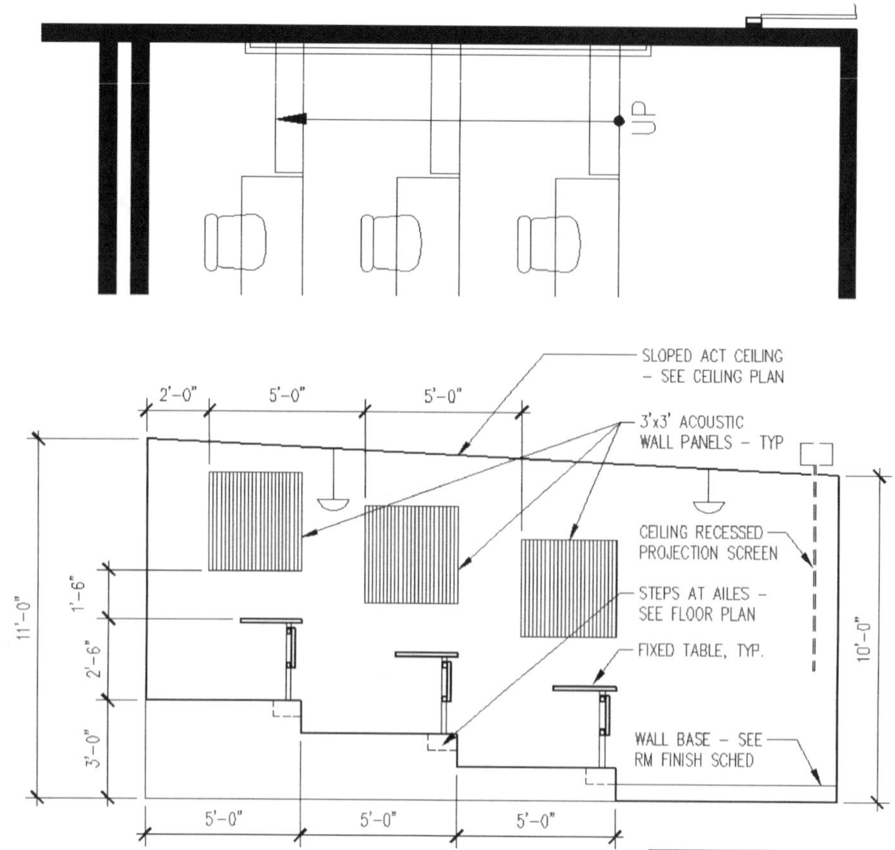

FIGURE 6-4.9 Interior elevations: lecture room 112

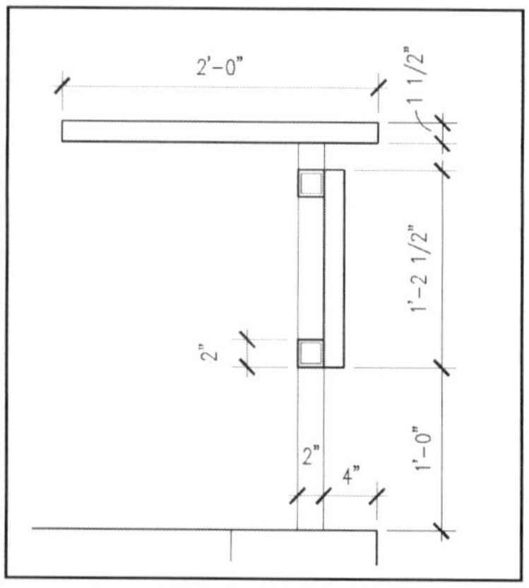

FIGURE 6-4.10 Desk dimensions

Public Concourse:

33. Draw the Concourse (room 135) per the following:
    a. Use the information previously covered.
    b. Draw everything shown in Figure 6-4.13 (including dimensions).
    c. See Figures 6-4.11 and 6-4.12, below, for wall additional dimensions (do not draw these dimensions).
    d. Virtually everything left that is not dimensioned should be equally spaced (windows, tiles, wall reveals).

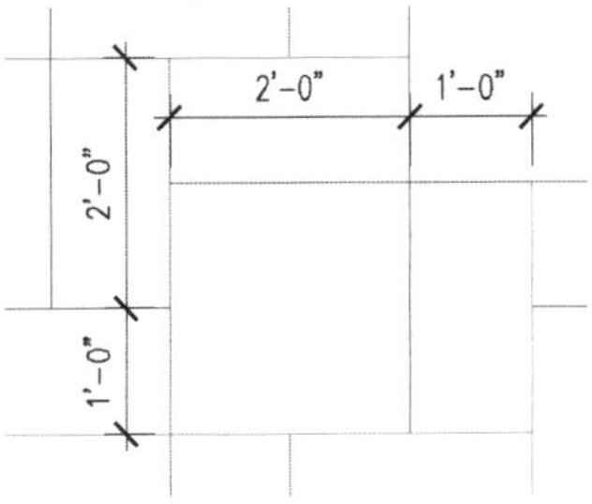

FIGURE 6-4.11 Tile dimensions

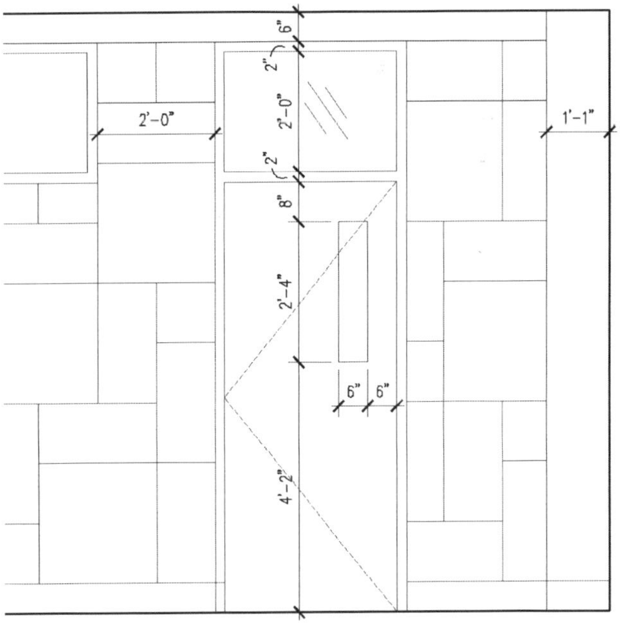

FIGURE 6-4.12 Door frame dimensions

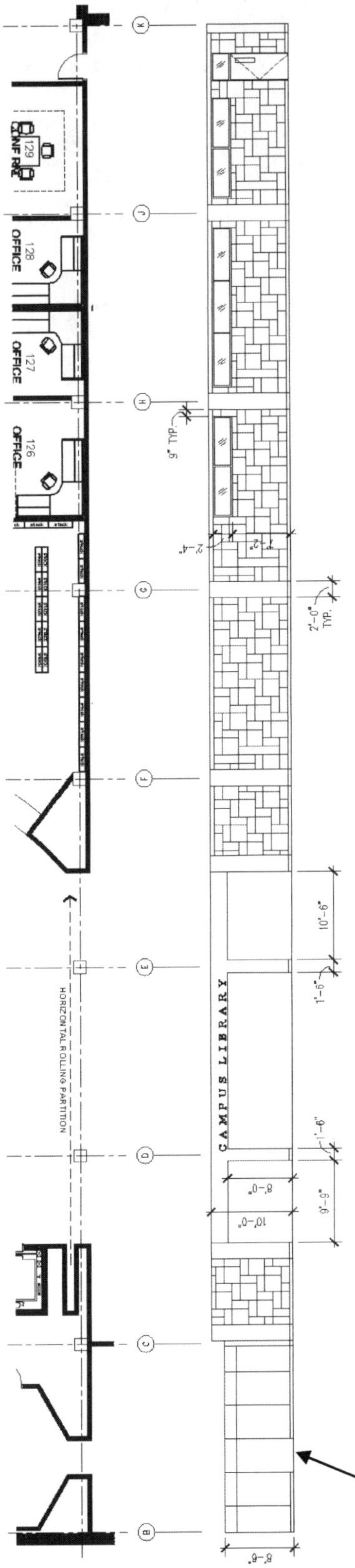

FIGURE 6-4.13 Concourse elevation

Self-Exam:

The following questions can be used as a way to check your knowledge of this lesson. The answers can be found at the bottom of this page.

1. Interior elevations use the same Layers as floor plan drawings. (T/F)
2. For interior elevations: items behind cabinet doors (e.g., shelving) are shown dashed. (T/F)
3. For interior elevations: Lines in elevation are heavier than lines in section. (T/F)
4. For interior elevations: text goes on the _______________ layer.
5. Which Layer should external references go on? _______________

Review Questions:

The following questions may be assigned by your instructor as a way to assess your knowledge of this section. Your instructor has the answers to the review questions.

1. Type APPLOAD to load an AutoLISP program into memory. (T/F)
2. Xref Overlays do not travel with the "host" drawing when the "host" drawing itself is Xref'ed into another drawing. (T/F)
3. You should use the floor plan to establish all the horizontal relationships in an interior elevation. (T/F)
4. What is the scale factor for a grid bubble when copied from an ⅛″ drawing into a ¼″ drawing? ____________
5. Layer representing the heaviest line used in this chapter is _____________.
6. A Clipped drawing cannot be rotated. (T/F)
7. What command allows you to "crop" an Xref? ________________
8. Why does the countertop step down in elevation 6-4.8? _______________
9. The height of the operable parts (on a phone or hand dryer for example) is what most codes are concerned about – not the top of the item itself. (T/F)
10. Each elevation in this chapter should have been drawn in separate drawing files. (T/F)

SELF-EXAM ANSWERS:
1 – F, **2** – T, **3** – F, **4** – G-Anno-Text, **5** – G-Xref

Lesson 7
Library Project: DETAILS

In this lesson, you will draw details, which is like cutting a building (or an object within the building) in half and looking at it from the cutaway side. In addition to elevations, this is where vertical relationships are explored and documented.

Many design firms have detail libraries containing many of the types of details drawn in this section. This allows the designer to spend more time designing the "big picture" portions of the project and less time on the "typical" details. A designer can flip through the three-ring binder or (better yet) an intranet for details that apply to the project currently being worked on. The marked details can then be placed on a "plot" sheet by the designer or a technician (i.e., drafter).

Not every detail is standard. In fact, many items that simply come out of a box do not usually need to be detailed unless you need to show how it connects or relates to the building. For example, windows are manufactured in a factory, but they are still detailed to show how they are to be attached and aligned within the wall opening. Many larger window manufacturers provide CAD files via their web sites.

Some details are very much custom and must be thoroughly detailed so the contractor knows how to build it. Sometimes these details can be started from a standard detail that is similar to the custom design and other times it will be started from scratch.

The key to detailing is to think smart: draw what needs to be drawn, make sure all necessary dimensions, grid lines and floor level references are given. You should also try to reuse as much accurate and previously drawn content as possible, whether from a detail library or a previous project.

Exercise 7-1:
Casework

Base Cabinet with Drawers:

This section will dive right into drawing cabinet details. These are often based on industry standard dimensions so many of the dimensions and material thickness can be omitted (assuming the project manual/specification covers this).

1. Using the non-plan layers in Appendix A, start a new drawing file and draw the cabinet detail shown below in Figure 7-1.1.

2. The materials in section are to be hatched with **ANSI36** hatch pattern with a scale factor of 3 (on *Layer* A-Detl-Patt).

3. Draw 2x4's on the floor, 1x4's on the wall, ½″ thick boards for drawer bottoms and backs and ¾″ drawer fronts and countertop and sub-top.

4. Add dimensions and text: detail to be plotted at 1″=1′-0″. (See Appendix for ltscale and text height settings.)

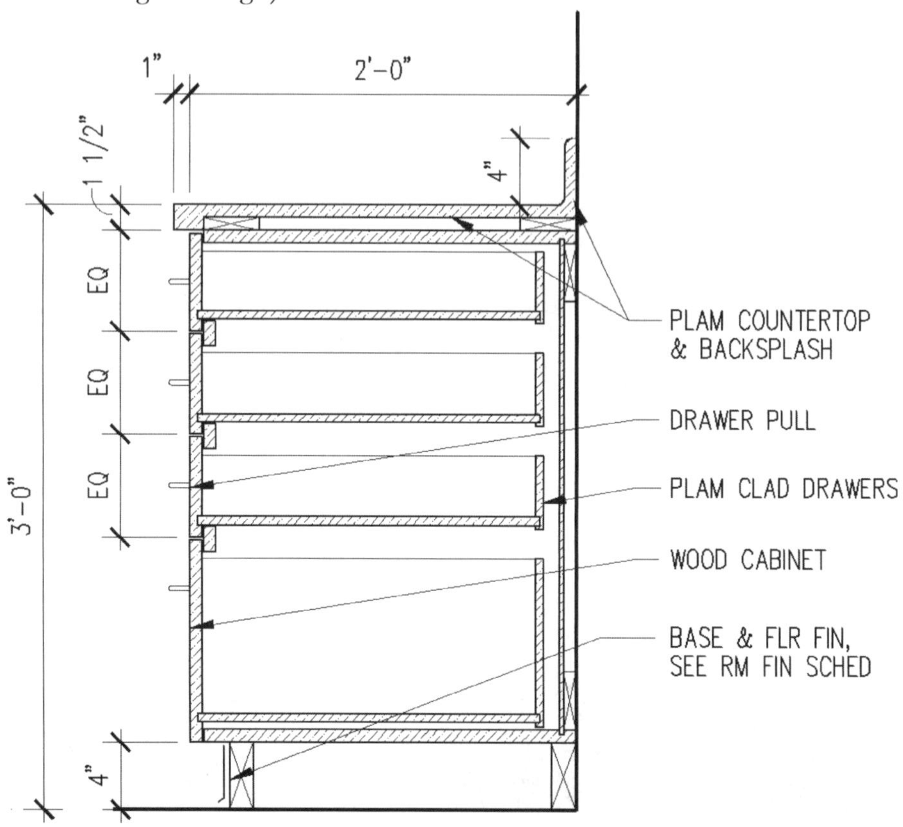

FIGURE 7-1.1 Cabinet section (with drawers)

5. Name your new detail: **DJS55803ADE01.dwg**.
    a. *A* = *Architecture* and *DE* = *Detail*
    b. Remember to use your initials as a prefix.

Some Things You Should Know About Detailing:

In the previous steps, you drew a typical detail showing a standard base cabinet with drawers. Interior designers occasionally draw these details, but more often, they simply review them for finishes.

The countertop material needs to match that which is specified in the **Project Manual** and intended for the project. A PLAM (i.e., Plastic Laminate, per the abbreviation standards in the Appendix) countertop would not be appropriate in a laboratory where chemicals would be used.

The base of the cabinet typically has the same wall base as the adjacent walls. For example, if the walls have a rubber base (also referred to as resilient base), the toe-kick area of the base cabinet would also receive rubber base; this is the type of base shown in Figure 7-1.1. If the project only had ceramic tile wall base, you would show that.

The **notes for details** (or any drawing) should be simple, generic and to the point. Notice in Figure 7-1.1 that the note for the base does not indicate whether the base is rubber, tile or wood. This helps avoid contradictions with the room finish schedule. The note simply says the cabinet and floor are to receive a finish and instructs the contractor to go to the Room Finish Schedule to see what the finish is. This is particularly important in buildings that have several variations of floor and base finishes.

Notes should not have any **proprietary or manufactures' names** in them either. For example, you should not say "Sheetrock" in a note because this is the brand name; rather, you should use the generic term "gypsum board". Similar, you use the term "solid plastic" rather than "Corian" when referring to countertops or toilet partitions. In any event, whatever term you use on the drawings should be the same term used in the project manual!

One last comment: the Construction Documents set should never have **abbreviations** within the drawings that are not covered in the Abbreviations list, usually located on the title sheet. Construction Documents are legal, binding documents, which the contractor must follow to a "T." They should not have to guess as to what the designers meant in various notes all over the set of drawings. It is better to spell out every word if possible, only abbreviating when space does not permit. You would not want a bunch of abbreviations in your bank loan or mortgage papers you were about to sign! Plus, non-documented abbreviations would probably not have much merit before a judge or arbitrator in the case of a legal dispute!

6. Use the same steps just covered, draw the base cabinet shown in Figure 7-1.2; name the file **DJS55803ADE02.dwg**.

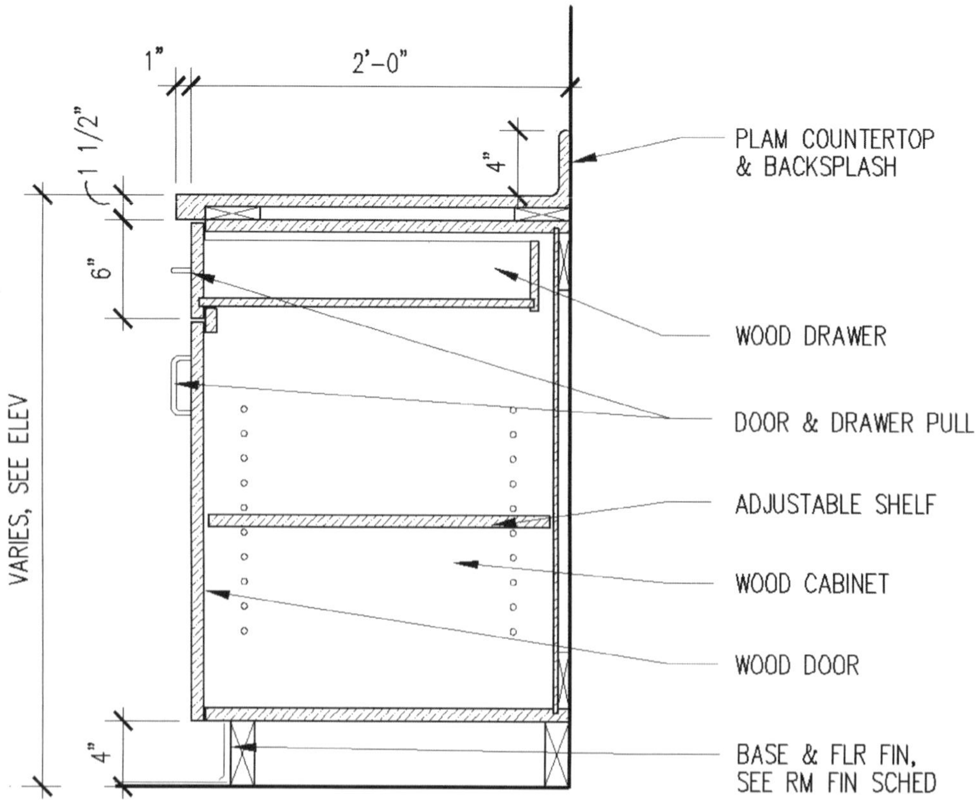

FIGURE 7-1.2 Cabinet section (door + drawer)

Cabinet details do not need to include every nook-and-cranny dimension because they are very much standard items in the construction industry. Furthermore, the Project Manual (specifications) usually references an industry standard for typical dimensions, thicknesses, and wood grades.

The vertical dimension shown in the cabinet detail above says "VARIES, SEE ELEV". This notation, rather than an actual number, allows the detail to represent more than one condition. The interior elevations are required to have these dimensions, which may be the standard 36″ or the lower handicap accessible height.

Exercise 7-2:
Flooring

Introduction

This section continues the use of the non-plan Layers which simply represent lineweights. The applied example here will be flooring details which are specified by the Interior Designer.

1. Open a new drawing and draw the floor transition detail shown below using the following information:
    a. The detail will be plotted at 3″=1′-0″ (this determines the text and leader size).
    b. Tile hatch is ANSI31 with a scale of 1.0.
    c. The grout (i.e., area under tile) is to be hatched with AR-SAND set to a scale or 0.15.
    d. Draw the tile ¼″ thick and 4″ wide.
    e. The grout is ¼″ thick.
    f. The resilient flooring is shown ⅛″ thick.
    g. The solid surface (i.e., Corian) threshold to 1⅞″ wide; draw an arc between the two floor thicknesses.
    h. Hatch the threshold with the solid hatch and set the hatch's color to 253.
    i. The bottom concrete floor line is to be the heaviest line.

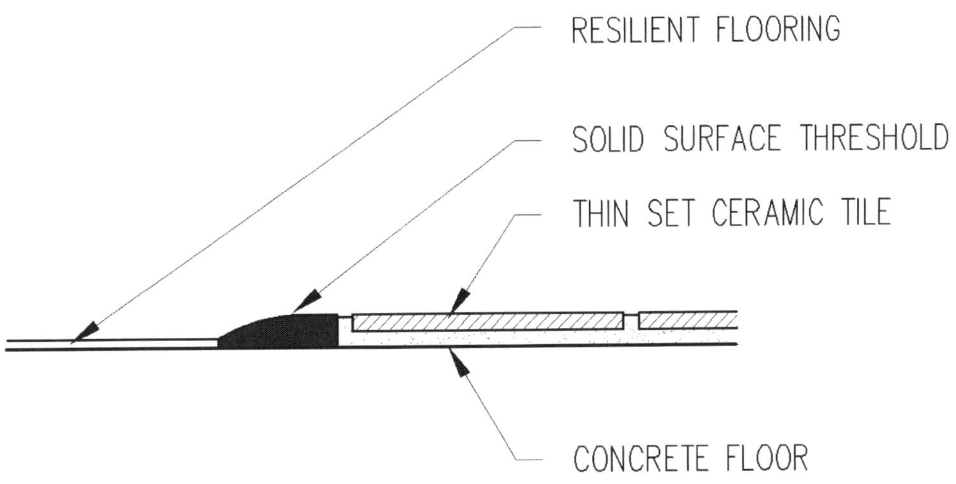

FIGURE 7-2.1 Floor transition detail: ceramic tile to resilient flooring

2. **Save** the detail drawing as **DJS55803ADE03.dwg**.

The previous drawing would typically occur in a door opening and the location of the door would also be shown in the detail. This lets the contractor know that the threshold is to occur directly below the door slab.

Next you will draw a high-end floor and wall base detail known as terrazzo. This finish is poured in a liquid state, allowed to dry and then polished to a smooth finish. The colors and aggregate options are virtually unlimited (for example, you could use a clear epoxy resin and place leaves within the flooring).

3. Draw the following flooring detail:
    a. *Plot scale:* 3"=1'-0"
    b. *Hatch:* AR-CONC
    c. Add notes and dimensions shown.
4. **Save** the detail drawing as **DJS55803ADE04.dwg**.

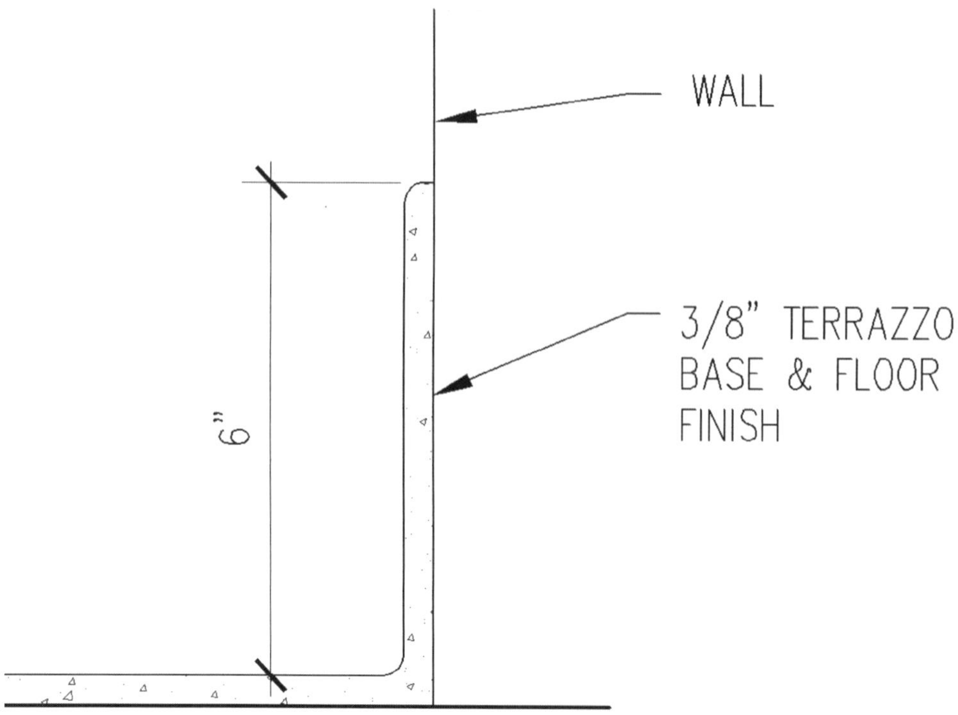

FIGURE 7-2.2 Terrazzo floor and wall base detail

Exercise 7-3:
Miscellaneous

Introduction

In this exercise you will draw more details.

Ceiling Detail:

The first detail you will draw in this section is a typical recessed light trough detail at the ceiling. This is typically used in toilet rooms.

1. In a new drawing, draw the following ceiling detail:
    a. *Plot scale:* 1 ½″ = 1′-0″
    b. *Gyp. Bd. Hatch:* AR-SAND
    c. Add notes and dimensions shown.
    d. *Studs in section:* 2 ½″ x 1¼″
2. **Save** the detail drawing as **DJS55803ADE05.dwg**.

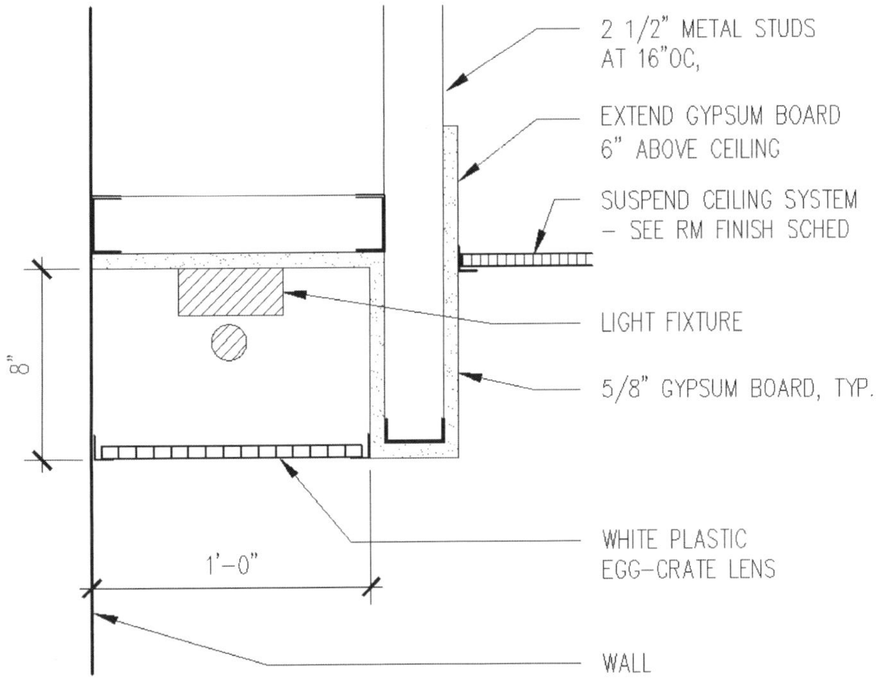

FIGURE 7-3.1 Ceiling detail

TIP: The notes in details should align on one edge as shown. Additionally, the leaders should not cross dimensions or other leaders unless it is totally unavoidable.

Fixed Student Desk at Raised Seating Classroom:

This detail would work nicely for the fixed desks in the Lecture Classroom. However, assuming this detail came from a standard detail library, you would have to coordinate with what you have previously drawn in the floor plan. For example, the overall depth shown in the detail below is about 1′-5″, and the depth drawn in plan is 2′-0″ (see page 6-21). They would need to match. (You do not have to make any plan changes at this time.)

3. In a new drawing, draw the following desk detail:
    a. *Plot scale:* 1½″ = 1′-0″
    b. Add notes and dimensions shown.
    c. *Studs in section:* 3⅝″ x 1¼″
4. **Save** the detail drawing as **DJS55803ADE06.dwg**.

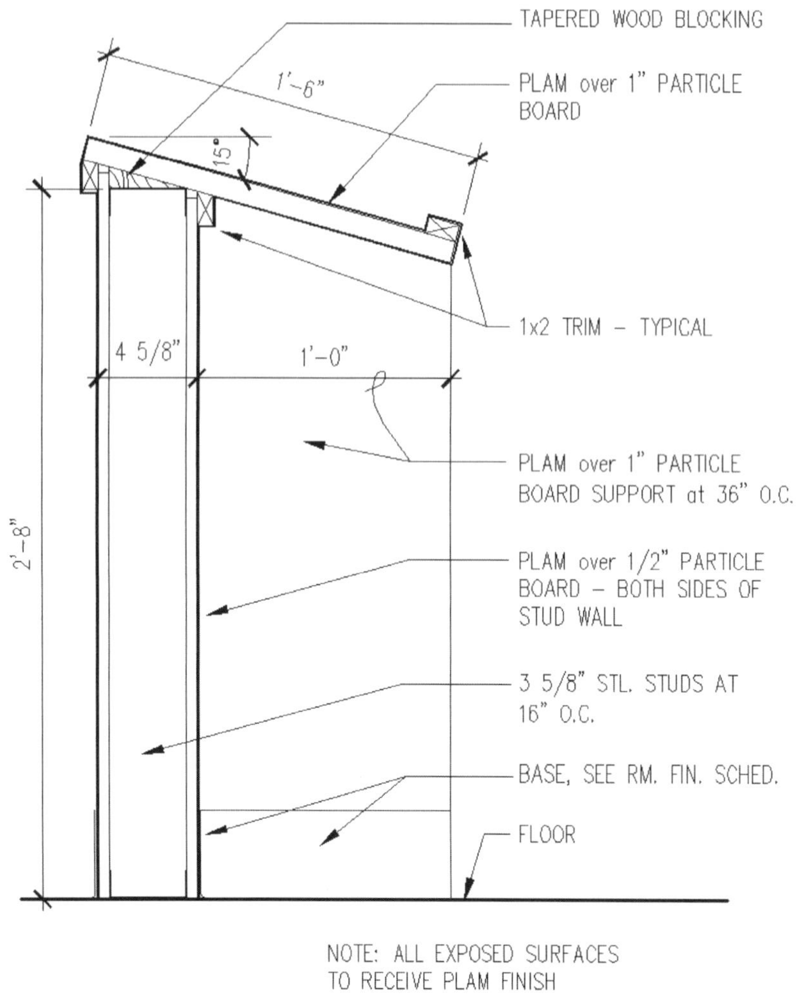

FIGURE 7-3.2 Fixed desk detail

Exercise 7-4:
Spell Check

Introduction

Given the fact that a significant amount of text is added to your drawings, to properly document your drawings it is nice to know that the program comes with a spell checker to verify the accuracy of your spelling. Even if you are an excellent speller, you may have typos or errors pasted in from another source.

AutoCAD's spell check is similar to other programs. Each word misspelled is displayed and you are given the opportunity to change the word to another (AutoCAD offers several possible options). You can also tell AutoCAD to ignore the word, and you can also add the word to the custom dictionary. Misspellings are also underlined in red in the text editor.

The custom dictionary is useful in an architectural and/or interior design office, as you can add industry-specific terms and abbreviations (see page A-15 for an example).

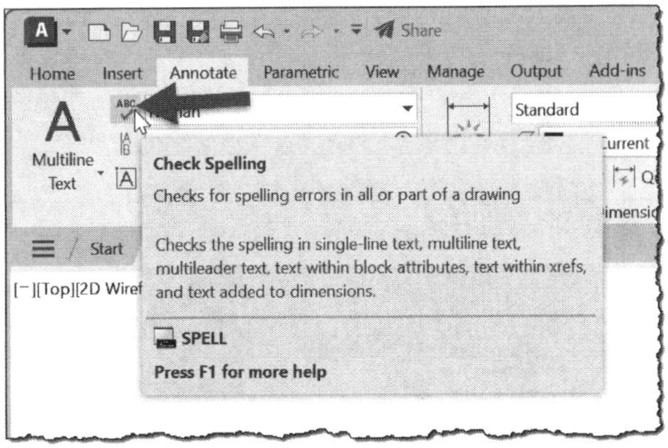

Check Spelling in a Drawing:

1. **Open** your **First Floor Plan** drawing file in AutoCAD.
2. From the **Annotate** tab, within the *Text* panel; select **Check Spelling**.

You are now in the *Check Spelling* dialog box (Figure 7-4.1).

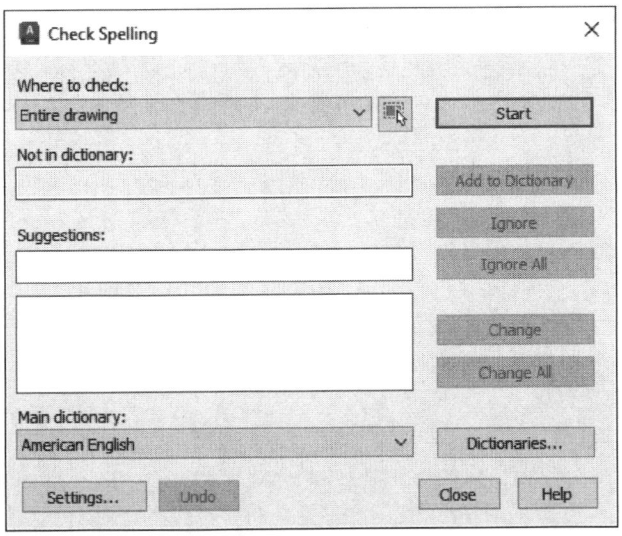

FIGURE 7-4.1
Check Spelling dialog box

3. Click the **Settings…** button (Figure 7-4.1).

As you can see in Figure 7-4.2, you can control how AutoCAD checks the drawing for spelling errors. Notice one of the options is to have AutoCAD check the spelling of any *External References* in the drawing.

You will uncheck Block attributes so the hidden information in the title block and plumbing fixtures from the internet do not confuse things for now.

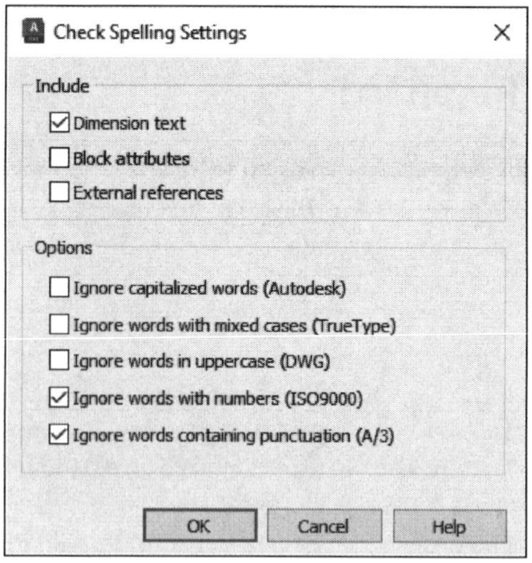

FIGURE 7-4.2 Check Spelling Settings dialog

4. Uncheck "**Block attributes**".

5. Click **OK** to close the *Check Spelling Settings* dialog.

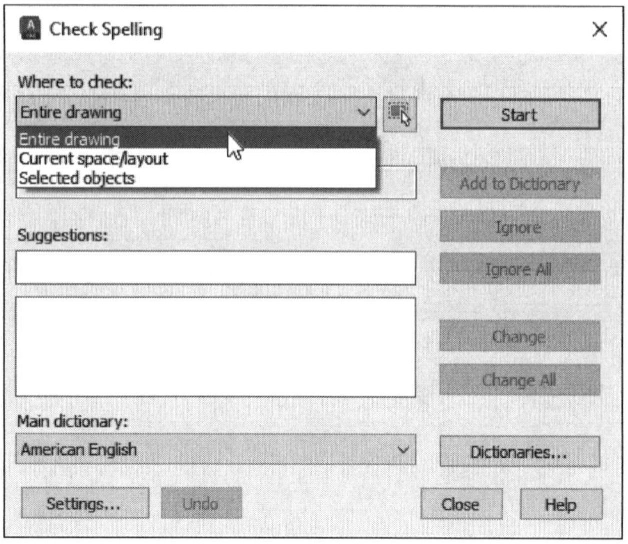

FIGURE 7-4.3 Check Spelling dialog

6. Click the down-arrow under "Where to check:" (Figure 7-4.3).

Notice you can tell AutoCAD to check the spelling of the **Entire drawing**, just the **current layout** you are on, or just the **Selected objects**.

The Selected objects option can save time if you have previously checked the drawing and only need to check the newly added content.

7. Select **Entire drawing**.

8. Click the **Start** button in the upper right.

Because you have text on locked layers, you get the prompt shown in Figure 7-4.4. You will want to check the text on any locked layers and leave the layers locked after Spell Check is complete.

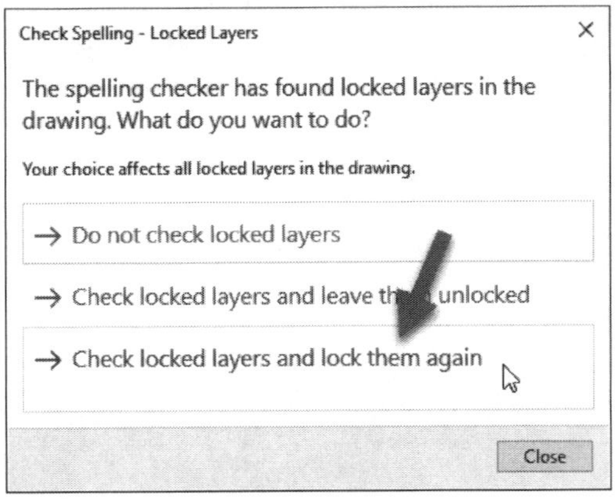

FIGURE 7-4.4
Check Spelling: Locked Layer prompt

9. Click the **Check locked layers and lock them again** "button" to proceed.

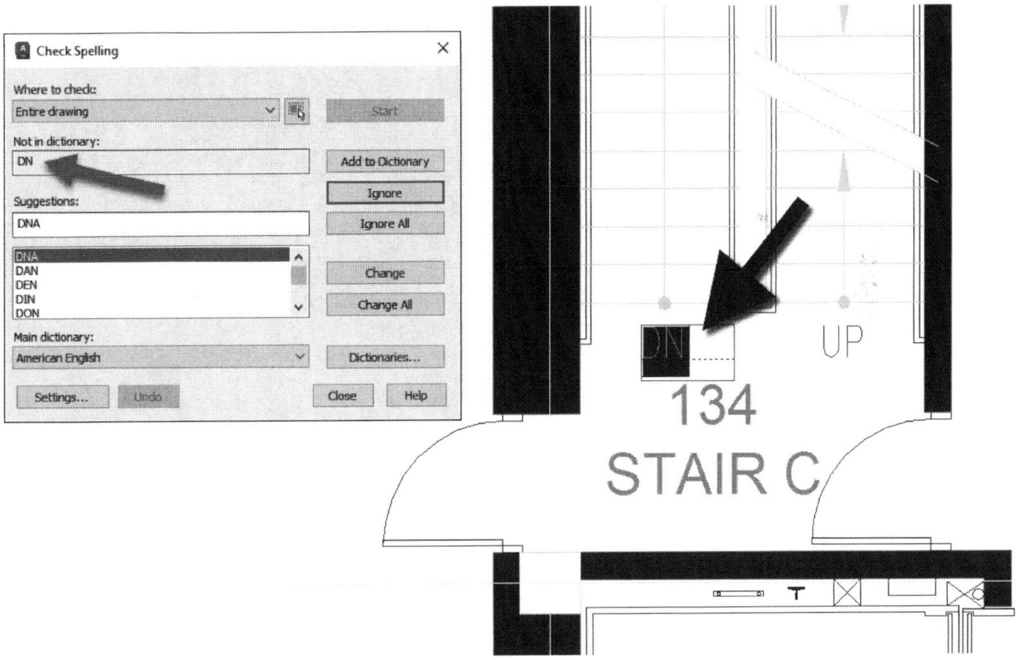

FIGURE 7-4.5 Check Spelling; showing first potential problem

AutoCAD zooms in on the first problem it finds, as shown in Figure 7-4.5. (Your first problem word may be different.)

10. **DN** is an abbreviation for **Down**, which occurs in this drawing more than once, and will be in future drawings, so click the **Add to Dictionary** button.

11. The example below shows a mistake that needs to be corrected; AutoCAD offered the correct spelling, so you simply need to click **Change** to fix the problem. (You may not have this same problem in your drawing.)

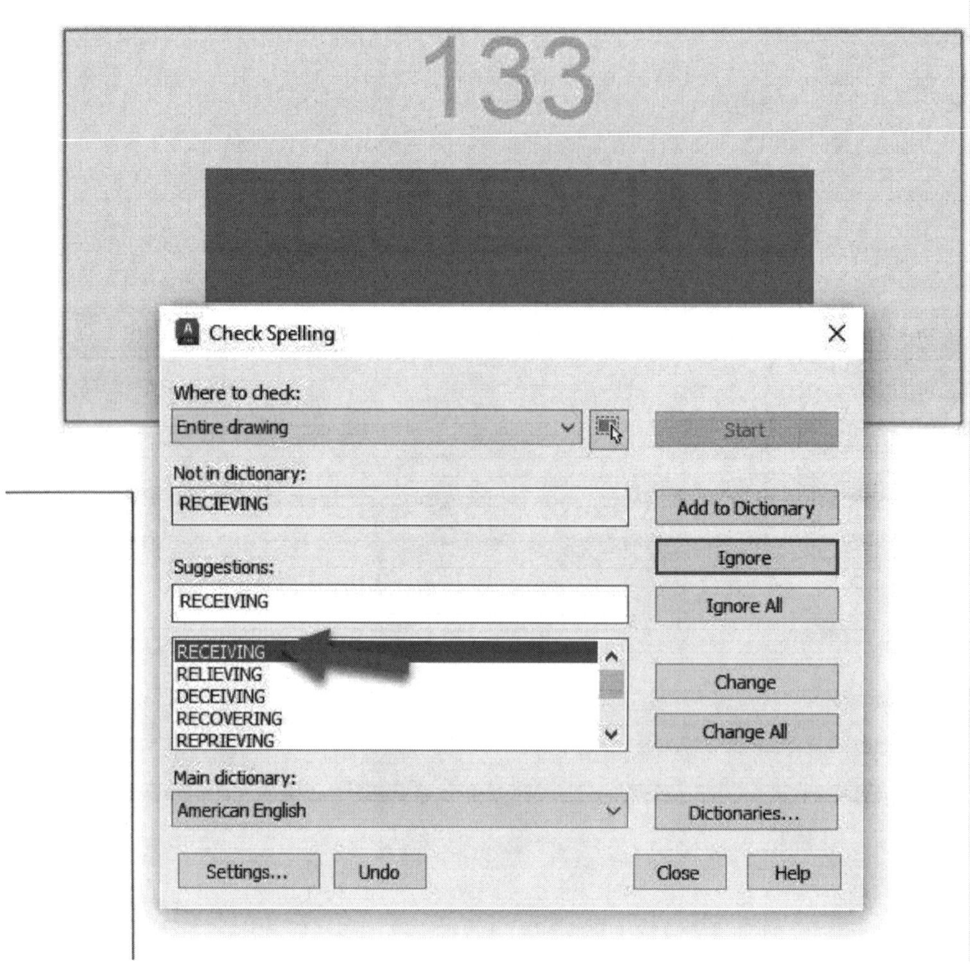

FIGURE 7-4.6 Check Spelling: Suggestions offered

Notice in Figure 7-4.6 that several "suggestions" are offered as possible solutions to the problem word. AutoCAD may not always offer the correct spelling as the default, so you have to select it from the list and then click **Change**.

The *Spell Check* function does not check grammar like some of the word processing programs do. This would be nice, but architectural notes on drawings are not really meant to be literary works, so it is not essential.

12. Continue through the remaining *Spell Check* prompts per the following:
    a. **Add to Dictionary**: the word is valid and you use it often.
    b. **Ignore**: the word is valid but not used very often or could be a typo for another more common word.
    c. **Ignore All**: the same word identified in the previous comment (i.e., Ignore), but occurs several times in the current drawing; this would avoid the need to review each one individually.
    d. **Change**: the word is wrong and you selected one of the suggestions or typed the correct word.
    e. **Change All**: the same word identified in the previous comment (i.e., Change), but occurs several times.

13. When you finish dealing with the last word you will get the following prompt; click **OK**.

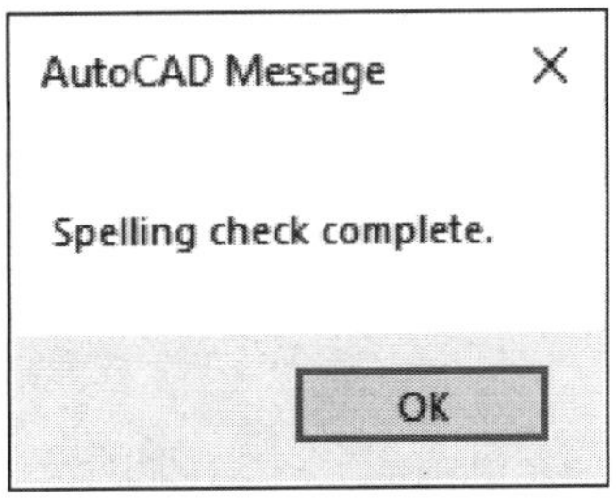

14. After clicking **OK**, then **Close** to finish the Spelling command.

15. **Save** your drawing to retain the spelling corrections.

TIP: You should review your drawing if any changes were required, because the change could have adjusted the size of the word causing an Mtext object to expand into another object. This can make a portion of the two objects illegible.

AutoCAD Checks Spelling as You Type:

AutoCAD also checks your spelling as you type. This is similar to the word processing programs in that any misspelled words are underlined with a red line to alert you to the fact that the program found a potential error.

The image on the next page shows several words underlined with a red line. Three of the four are indeed misspelled, but one is a technical term that simply is not in the program's spell check dictionary.

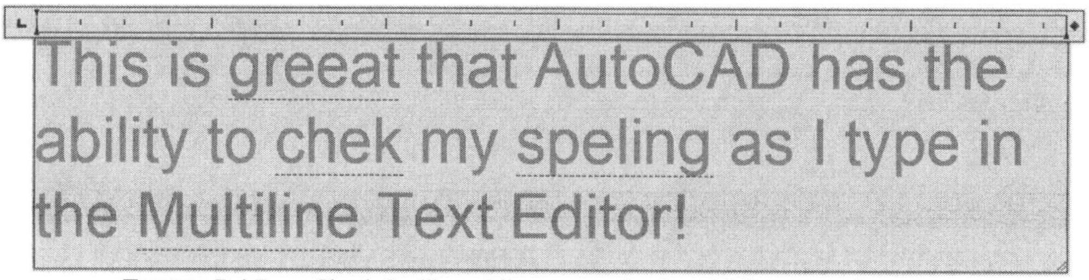

FIGURE 7-4.7 Check Spelling while you type in the Multiline text editor

When you right-click on an underlined word, the pop-up menu gives you several suggestions for the misspelled word. Also notice you can add the word to the dictionary so AutoCAD will not flag it as misspelled in the future (but you better triple-check that the word is indeed spelled correctly first); also, you have the option to simply ignore the flagged word and NOT add it to the dictionary.

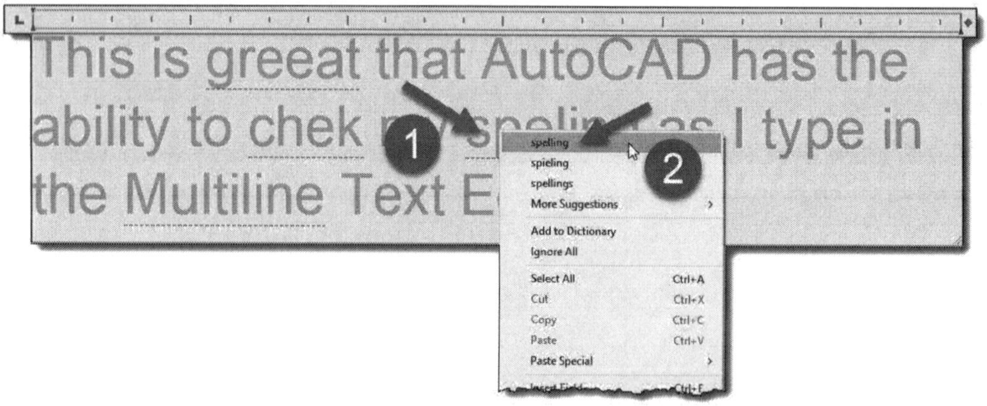

FIGURE 7-4.8 Right-clicking on a "flagged" word in the text editor

FYI: *This feature only works if the "Spell Check" option is toggled on while in text edit mode; this is found on the Ribbon as seen in this image.*

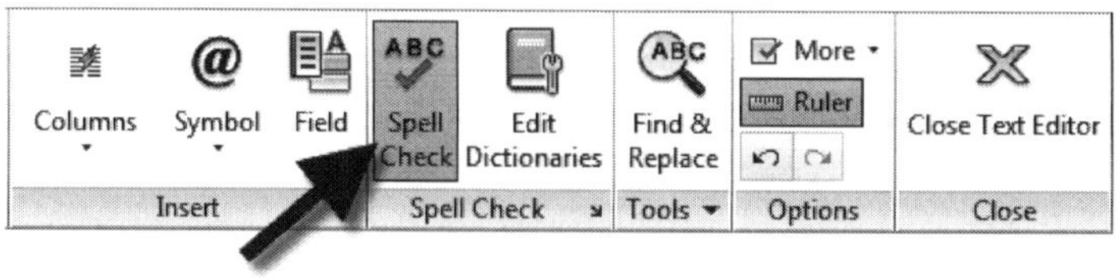

Self-Exam:

The following questions can be used as a way to check your knowledge of this lesson. The answers can be found at the bottom of this page.

1. The dimension style info is found in Appendix A. (T/F)
2. You cannot spell check words on locked layers. (T/F)
3. It is ok to use manufacturer names like "Corian" in your drawings. (T/F)
4. You should not use floor plan layers in a detail drawing. (T/F)
5. AutoCAD can check your spelling as you type in the text editor. (T/F)

Review Questions:

The following questions may be assigned by your instructor as a way to assess your knowledge of this section. Your instructor has the answers to the review questions.

1. All drawings are drawn real-world scale (i.e., 1:1), only the annotation changes in size. (T/F)
2. Items in section are heavier than items in elevation, for details. (T/F)
3. You should not use abbreviations not listed on the abbreviations list. (T/F)
4. Leaders should not cross dimension lines or other leaders when avoidable. (T/F)
5. Non-plan layer names relate directly to line weights. (T/F)
6. You can add words and abbreviations to Spell Check so it does not flag a specific word being misspelled. (T/F)
7. In the file name: DJS55803ADE01.dwg, what does the "A" and the "DE"

   stand for? A = ____________________ DE = ____________________.
8. Hatch pattern used for gypsum board in section? ________________
9. AutoCAD details can be stored in a library and reused on many projects. (T/F)
10. You should use generic terms like resilient base rather than specific terms like rubber base or vinyl base. (T/F)

SELF-EXAM ANSWERS:
1 – T, **2** – F, **3** – F, **4** – T, **5** – T

Notes:

Lesson 8
Library Project: SCHEDULES & SHEET SETUP

In this lesson you will learn to use the Table feature to create schedules in AutoCAD. You will also explore how drawings are set up on sheets so they can be plotted with a professional look and fashion.

Exercise 8-1:
Room Finish Schedule

Introduction:

A Room Finish Schedule indicates what finish the walls, ceiling and floors get in each room. This information is typically organized in a grid of rows and columns, where each row represents a room and each column represents a surface to be finished. AutoCAD has a feature, called *Tables*, that is designed to accommodate this type of data (i.e., schedules).

Most rooms have both a name and a number to facilitate accurate identification on plans and schedules. Using a number is necessary when you have multiple rooms with the same name. In your plan, for example, you have multiple classrooms and offices. On a large commercial project (similar to your library project), a floor plan might have 30-40 rooms all labeled "office," so it is easy to see how important numbers are.

1. **Open** your **DJS55803APL01** drawing.

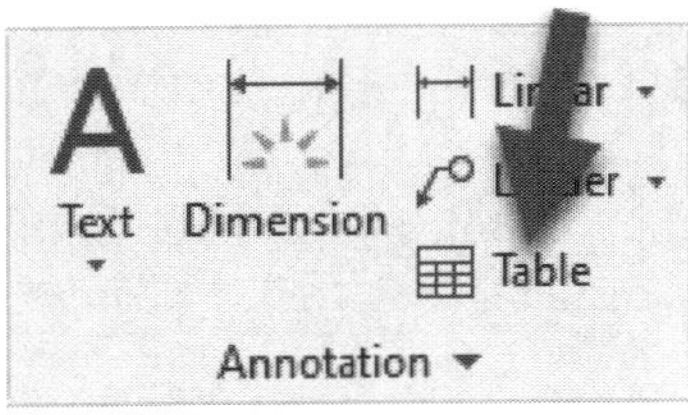

Creating a Table:

2. Create a **New** drawing, using **Architectural Imperial.dwt** as your template file *(located in the SheetSet sub-folder).*

3. Switch to **Model** space and then click the **Table** icon from the **Annotation** panel on the **Home** tab of the *Ribbon*; see the image above (or type *Table* and press *Enter*).

You are now in the *Insert Table* dialog box (Figure 8-1.1). At this point you could create a table using the Standard table style; if other styles existed, you could select one of them as well. You will create a Table using the Standard style.

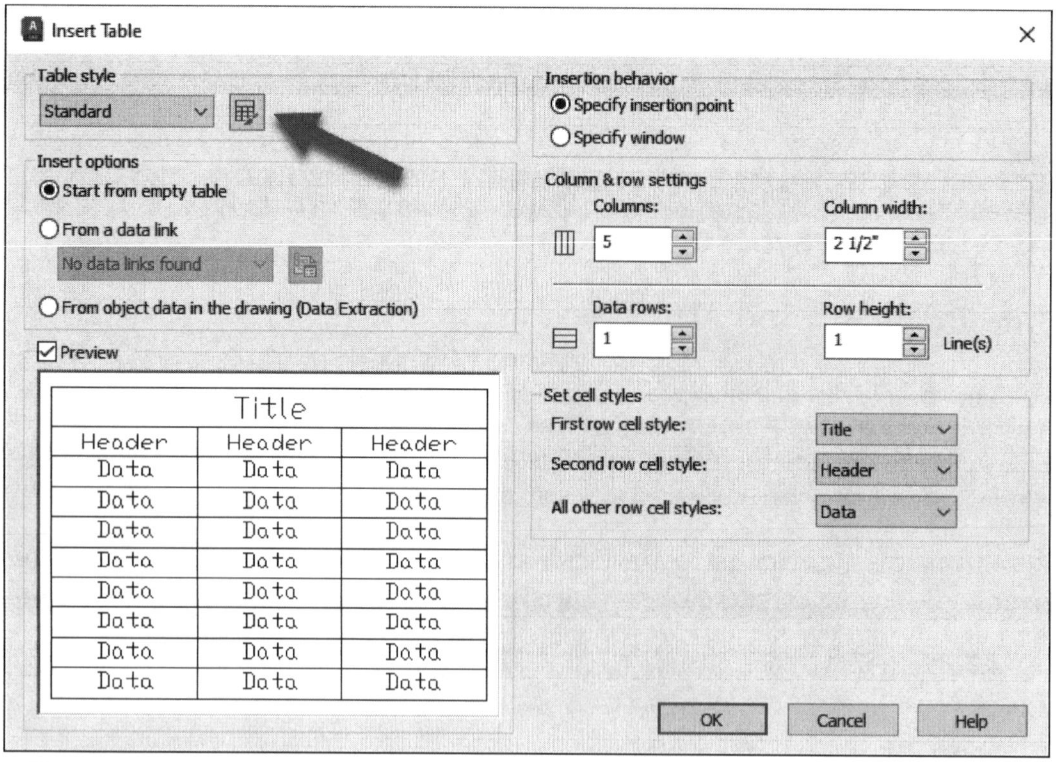

FIGURE 8-1.1 Insert Table dialog; initial view

Adjusting the Table Style Settings:

The first thing you will do is adjust the *Standard* Table Style. You will adjust the *Text Height* to a smaller size as well as change the *Text Style.*

4. Click on the *Table Style* settings button (Figure 8-1.1).

5. Click the **Modify…** button to Modify the Standard table style.

6. Make the changes shown in **Figure 8-1.2** to the **Data** Cell Styles.

7. Make the changes shown in **Figure 8-1.3** to the **Header** Cell Styles.

   FYI: Only the "text" tab has changes to it (typically).

8. Make the changes shown in **Figure 8-1.4** to the **Title** Cell Styles.

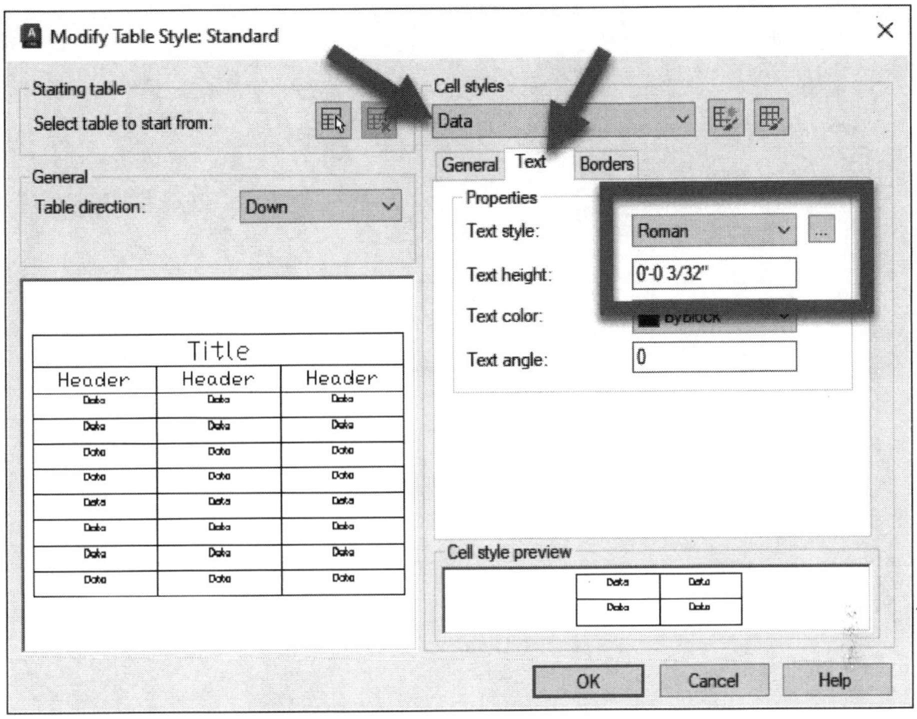

FIGURE 8-1.2 Modify Table Style dialog; Data tab

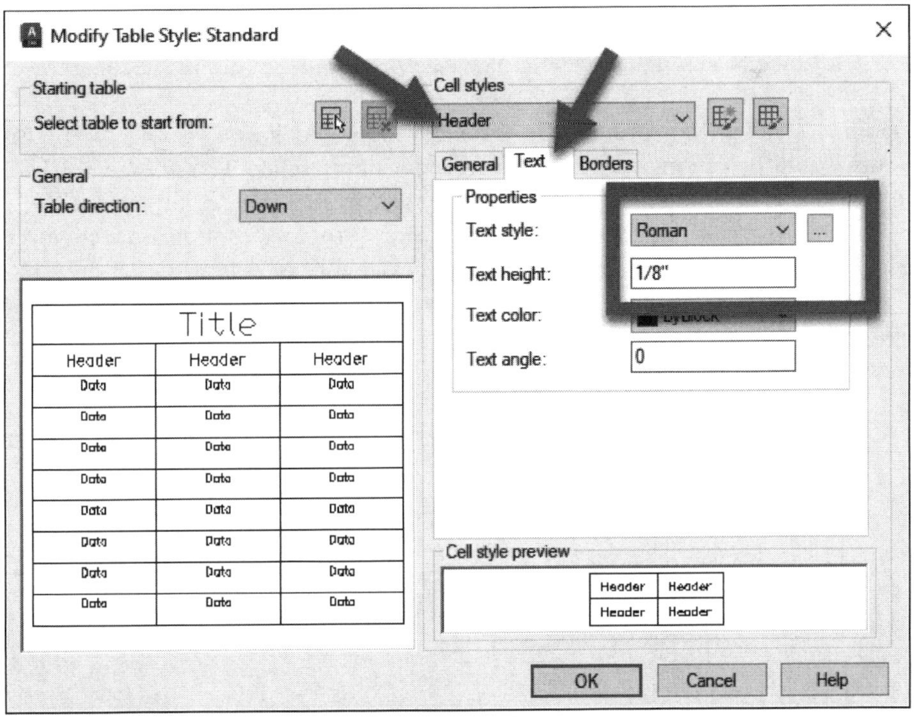

FIGURE 8-1.3 Modify Table Style dialog; Column Headers tab

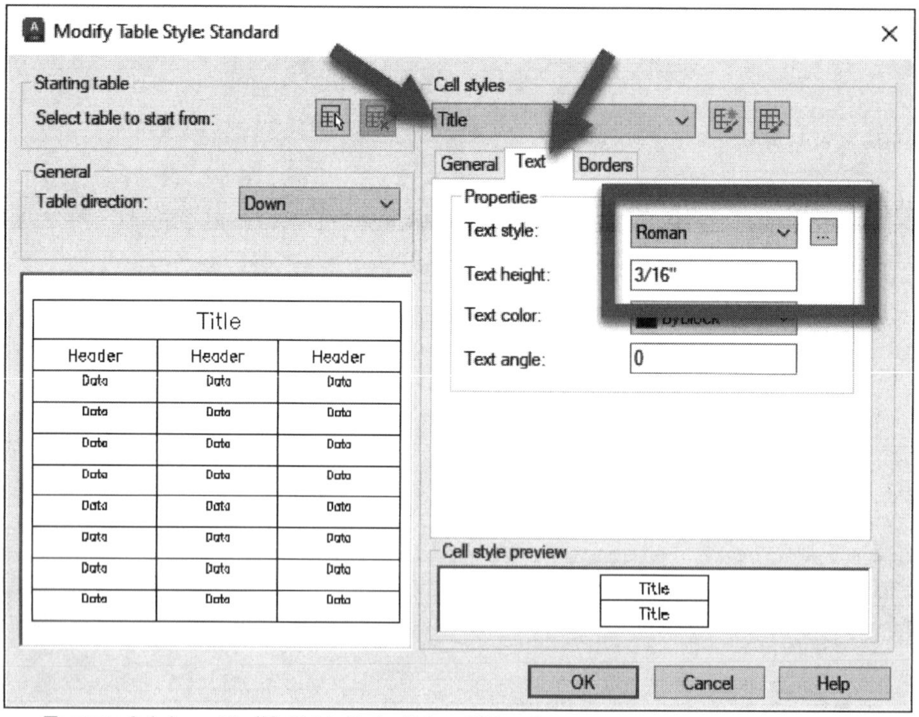

FIGURE 8-1.4 Modify Table Style dialog; Title tab

9. Click **OK** to close the *Modify Table Style* dialog.

10. Click **Close** to exit the *Table Style* manager and return to the *Insert Table* dialog.

At this point you need to have an idea how many rows and columns you need. You can sketch out what information you will need to display in the schedule (see Figure 8-1.5 for an example). You also need to specify the row height and the column width; this will be the size for the standard row/column. You will be able to adjust the size of individual columns/rows once the *Table* has been created. You can also add rows and/or columns after creating the *Table*. Therefore, you do not need to be too concerned about forgetting a row or column at this point as it can easily be added later.

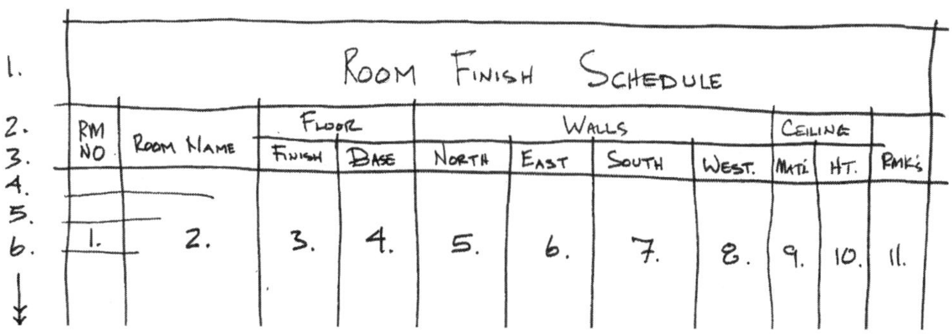

FIGURE 8-1.5 Preliminary Room Finish Schedule Sketch

Based on the sketch above, you will create a quick *Table* that has 11 columns and six rows. You will make additional adjustments later.

11. Make the following adjustments to the *Insert Table* dialog:
    a. *Columns:* **11**
    b. *Column Width:* **1"**
    c. *Data Rows:* **6**
    d. Leave everything else at the default (Figure 8-1.1).

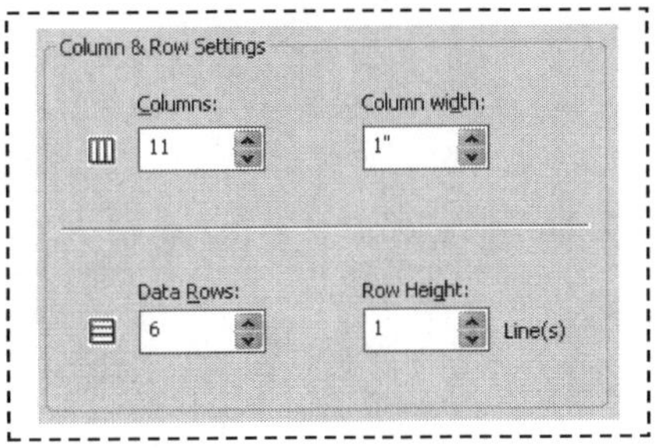

12. Click **OK** to insert the *Table.*

You should now see the specified *Table* attached to your cross-hairs so you can visually place it in the drawing.

13. Move your cursor so the entire *Table* is visible and centered on the screen and click the mouse to place it.

You are now automatically prompted for the title of the table.

14. For the *Table* title, type "**ROOM FINISH SCHEDULE**" (Figure 8-1.6).

TIP: Just start typing; no need to click anywhere.

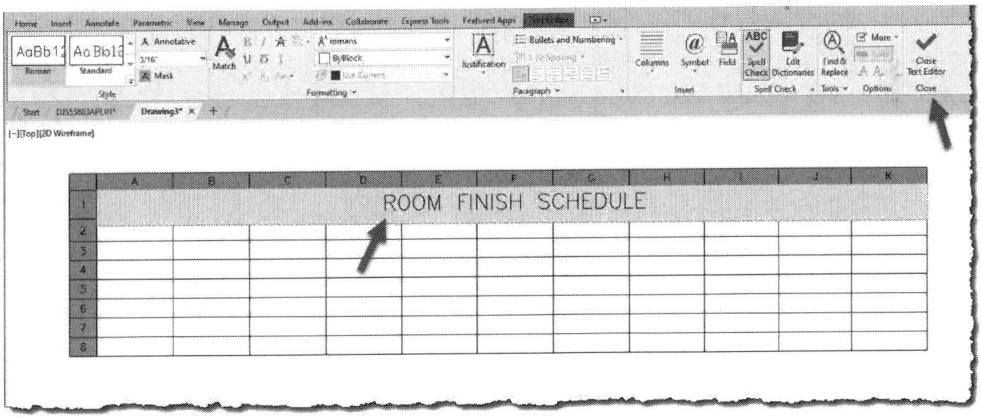

FIGURE 8-1.6 Inserted Table; entering table title text

15. Click **Close Text Editor** on the *Ribbon* to finish placing the table.

You now have a *Table* created in your drawing! Next you will adjust the width of the columns to match the sketch.

16. Select a column to adjust its width by doing the following:
    a. **Click and drag** the mouse from the lowest cell to the highest cell (or vice versa).
    b. See Figure 8-1.7.

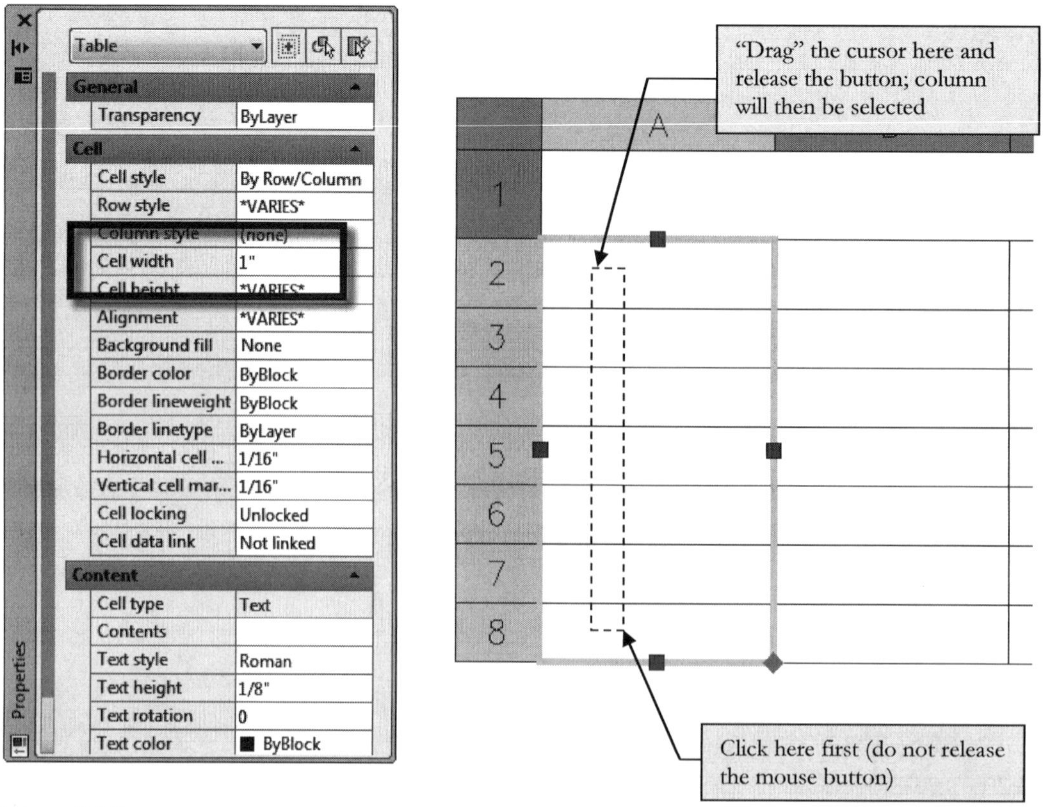

FIGURE 8-1.7
Table and its Properties;
Column selected (selected cells properties displayed)

17. In the *Properties* palette, change the *Cell width* to **.5"** and then press **Enter**.

The *Table* column has now been updated to display the *column width* per your specifications (Figure 8-1.8).

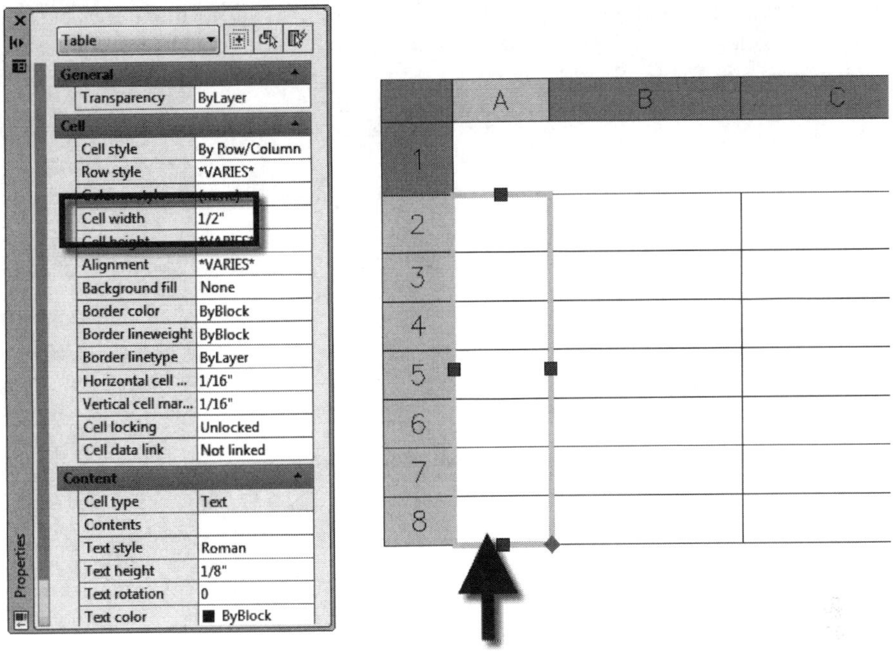

FIGURE 8-1.8 Table and its Properties; Column width adjusted

18. Press **Esc** to de-select the column.

19. Adjust the remaining column widths per the following information (Figure 8-1.9):

    a. *Column 2 (room name):* **2"**

    b. *Columns 3 – 10:* **1"**

    c. *Column 11 (remarks):* **2"**

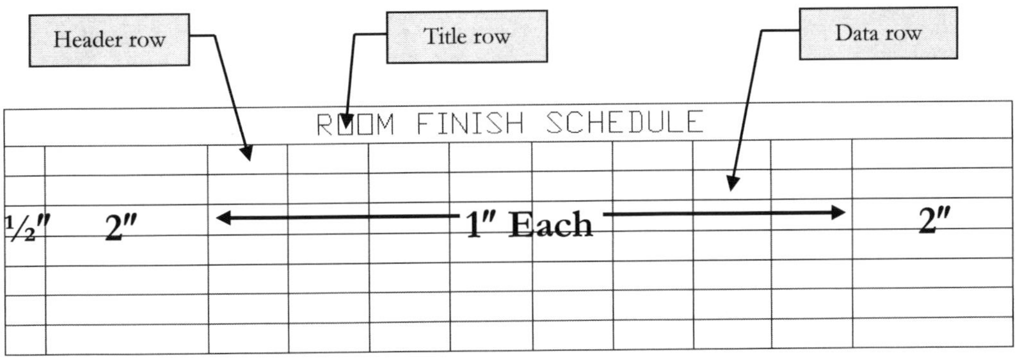

FIGURE 8-1.9 Table; all column widths adjusted

As you will recall, you specified 11 columns and six rows. In addition to that, a *Table* automatically has a *Title* row and a *Header* row. Compare the image above (Figure 8-1.9) with the preview image in Figure 8-1.4.

Merge Cells:

Next you will merge cells together to create larger cells within the *Table.*

20. Select the two cells identified in Figure 8-1.10.

    FYI: This is where the room number label goes.

21. Select the **Merge Cells → Merge All** icon from the *Ribbon* (Figure 8-1.11).

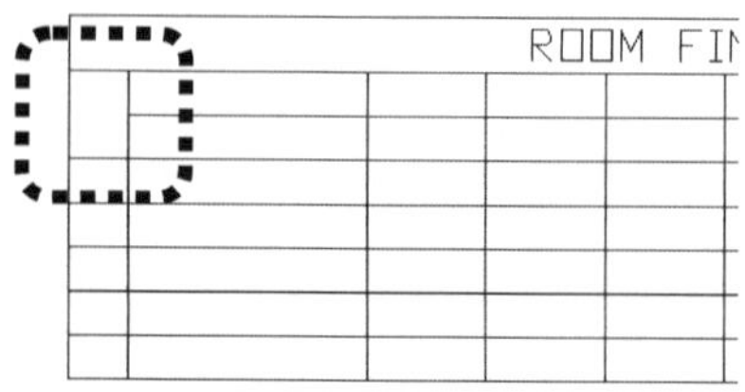

FIGURE 8-1.10
Table; two cells merged together

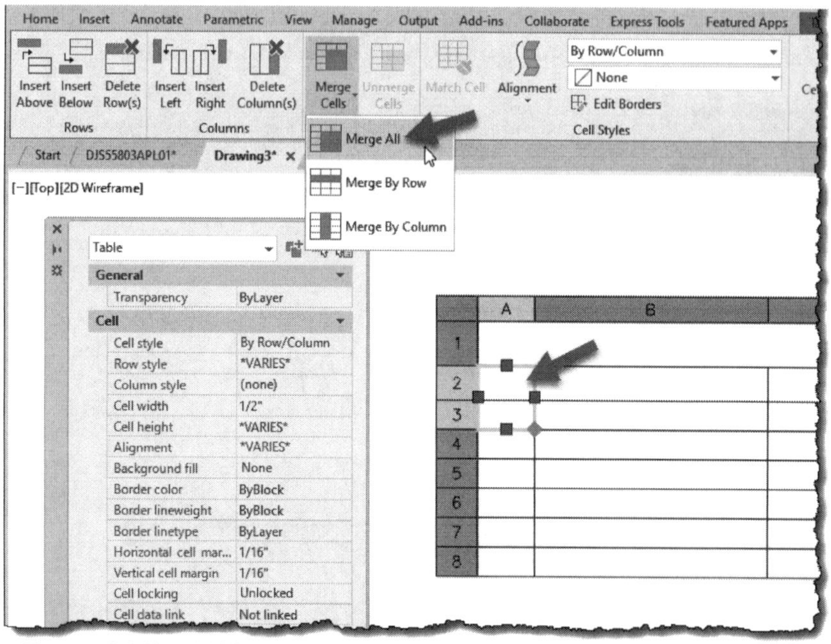

FIGURE 8-1.11 Table; merge two cells

You now have a merged cell in your *Table*! Take a moment to notice the other commands on the toolbar in Figure 8-1.11. (Hover cursor over each icon for tooltip of command name.)

Use the **Merge Cells** feature to make your table look like the one in Figure 8-1.12.

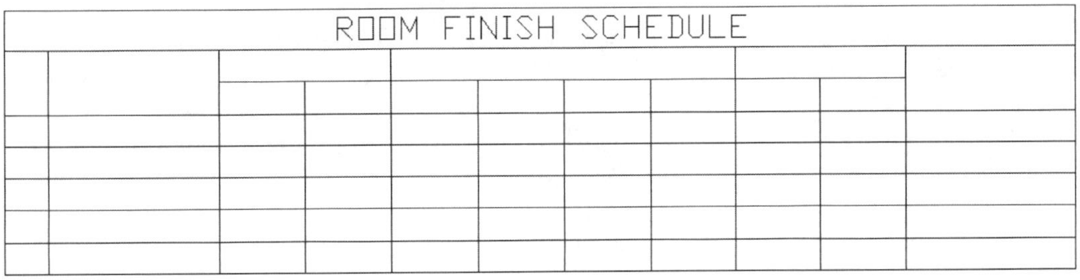

FIGURE 8-1.12 Merge Cells; several cells merged

Inserting Additional Rows:

Before adding data to the table, you will insert additional rows. A few too many will be added so you can learn to delete rows later.

22. Click in any *Data* cell and then click and select the **Insert Row Below** icon from the *Ribbon* (Figure 8-1.13).

23. Repeat the previous step until you have **20** *Data* rows.

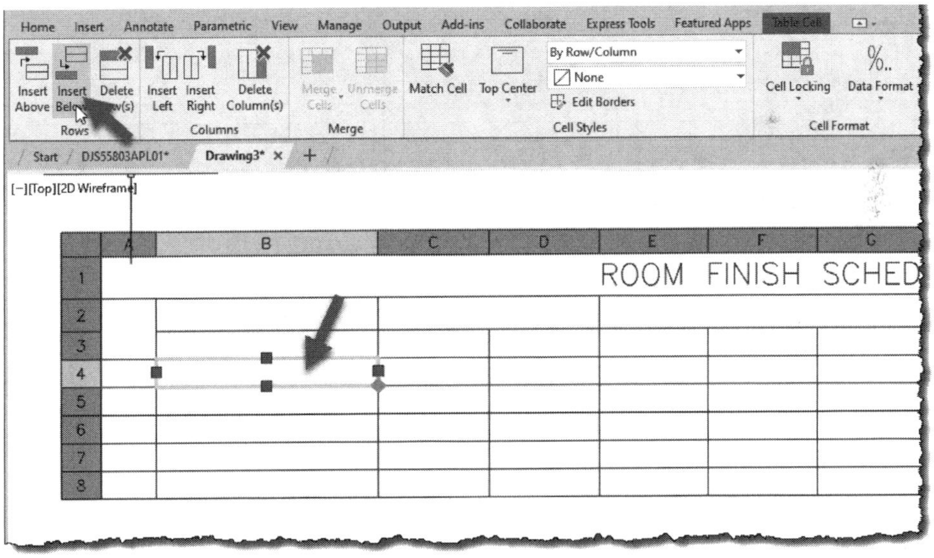

FIGURE 8-1.13 Insert rows; creates extra data lines

Now you can see why it is good to calculate the approximate number of rows you will need when creating the Table; you can type in the number of rows versus right-clicking for each row added later.

Adding Column Header Labels:

Now you will add the labels that indicate what information is in each column within the schedule (table).

24. Double-click within each *Header* cell and type the label per the sketch in Figure 8-1.5; see Figure 8-1.14 for the finished product.

    TIP: Once in "cell edit mode" you can arrow-key between cells.

Adding Data to Cells:

It is very easy to add data to your *Table*; you simply double-click in a cell and type. Next you will add the data to your table.

25. Looking at Figure 8-1.14, enter the data into your Table.

    TIP: After you double-click in a cell, you can use the Tab and Arrow keys to move between cells.

    TIP: You can Copy/Paste multiple cells; click and drag to select the Cells to Copy, then press Ctrl+C (copy to Windows Clipboard), then click and drag to select the Cells to Paste to, and then press Ctrl+V (paste from Windows Clipboard).

ROOM FINISH SCHEDULE										
RM NO	ROOM NAME	FLOOR		WALLS				CEILING		REMARKS
		FINISH	BASE	NORTH	EAST	SOUTH	WEST	MAT'L	HEIGHT	
100	VESTIBULE									
101	MENS TOILET									
102	WOMENS TOILET									
103	JANITOR / STORAGE									
104	LARGE CLASSROOM									
105	CLASSROOM									
106	STAIR "A"									
107	CORRIDOR									
108	COMPUTER LAB									
109	COMPUTER LAB									
110	COMPUTER LAB									
111	COMPUTER LAB									
112	LECTURE									
113	STAIR "B"									
114	LOBBY									
115	CHECKOUT									
116	TWO STORY READING RM									
117	GROUP STUDY									
118	QUIET									
119	QUIET									
120	QUIET									
121	COPY									
122	STAFF LOUNGE									
123	TOILET									
124	HALLWAY									
125	OPEN OFFICE									
126	OFFICE									
127	OFFICE									
128	OFFICE									
129	CONFERENCE ROOM									
130	MENS TOILET									
131	WOMENS TOILET									
132	JANITOR / STORAGE									
133	RECEIVING									
134	STAIR "C"									
135	CONCOURSE									

FIGURE 8-1.14 Room Finish Schedule; with data entered

Deleting Rows:

Next you will delete one of the extra rows. The following technique works the same way for columns as well.

26. Click within the Cell directly below **Concourse** (Rm. 135).

27. Select **Delete Rows** in *Ribbon* (Figure 8-1.15); delete any blank rows at the bottom.

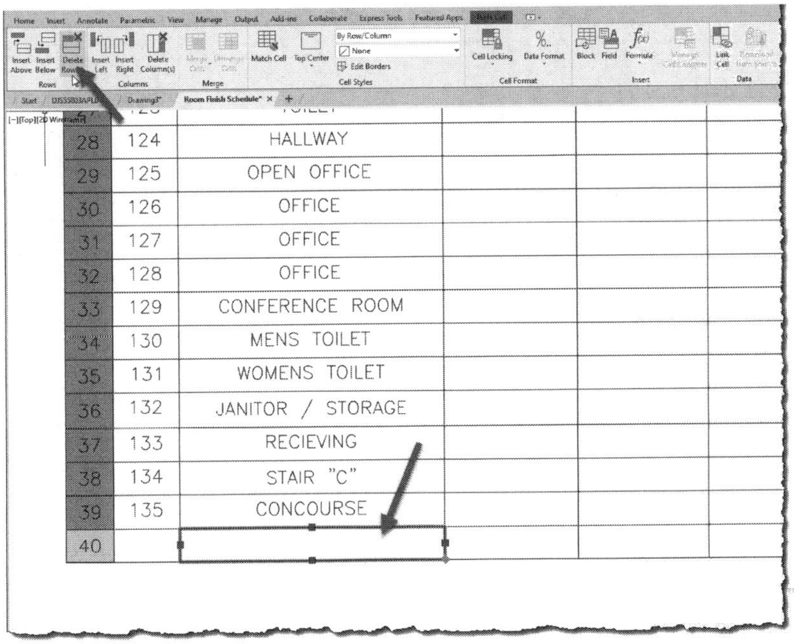

FIGURE 8-1.15 Room Finish Schedule; deleting a row

Making the Table Title Text Bold:

Finally, you will change the font for the *Table Title* (i.e., Room Finish Schedule) to Arial Black, which is a distinctive bold font. To do this you will need to create a new AutoCAD *Font Style* and then modify the *Table Style* to use the new *Text Style*.

28. Press the Esc key to unselect the table, and then click the **Text Style...** link, *Annotate* tab, *Text* panel.

You are now in the *Text Style* dialog where you manage AutoCAD Text Styles.

***FYI:** AutoCAD Text Styles allow you to predefine several settings for a particular type of note or label. Additionally, like other "styles" in AutoCAD, if you change a style setting (e.g., the Width Factor), all the text of that style will update automatically.*

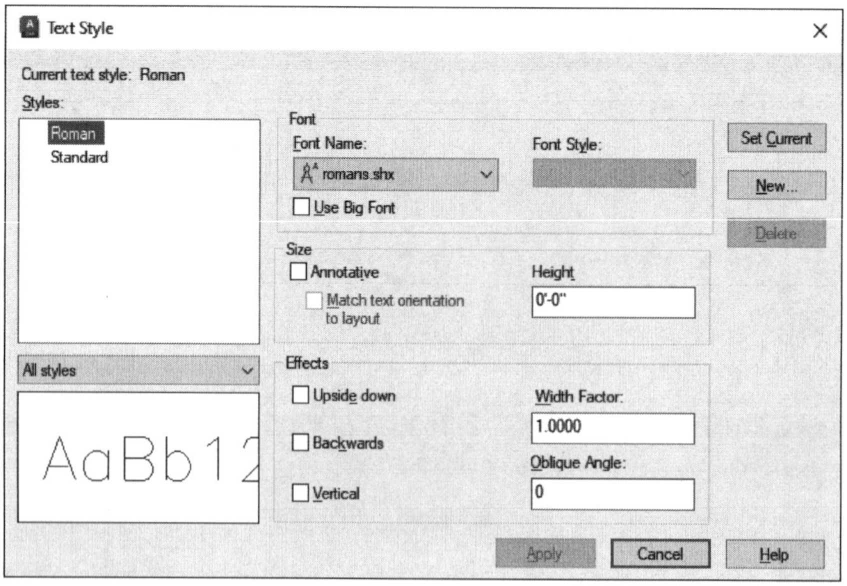

FIGURE 8-1.16 Text Style dialog; initial view

Notice, in the image above, the settings for the "Roman" *Text Style*. The *Font Name* is "romans.shx"; the *Style Name* is similar but can be anything. The *Height* is set to 0′-0″, which means you can adjust the height for each instance in your drawing.

29. Click the down-arrow, next to the *Style Name*, to see that only two Styles exist in the current drawing (Standard and Roman).

Now you will create a new *Style* named Bold.

30. Click the **New** button.

You are now prompted for a name (Figure 8-1.17).

31. Type the new *Style Name* **Bold** and then click **OK**.

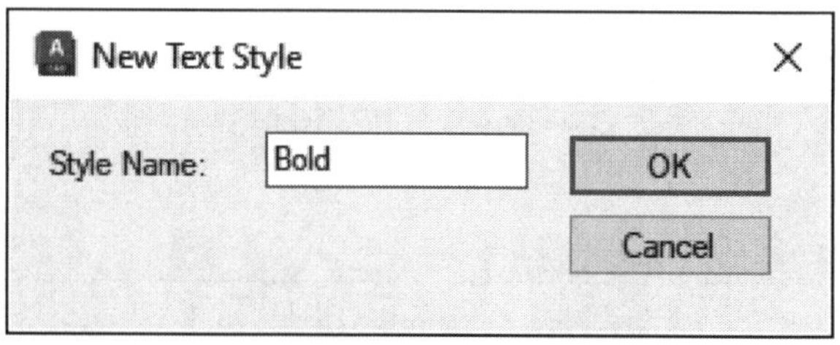

FIGURE 8-1.17 New Text Style dialog; style name "Bold" entered

32. Make the following adjustments (Figure 8-1.18):
    a. *Font Name:* **Arial Black**
    b. *Width Factor:* **.9**

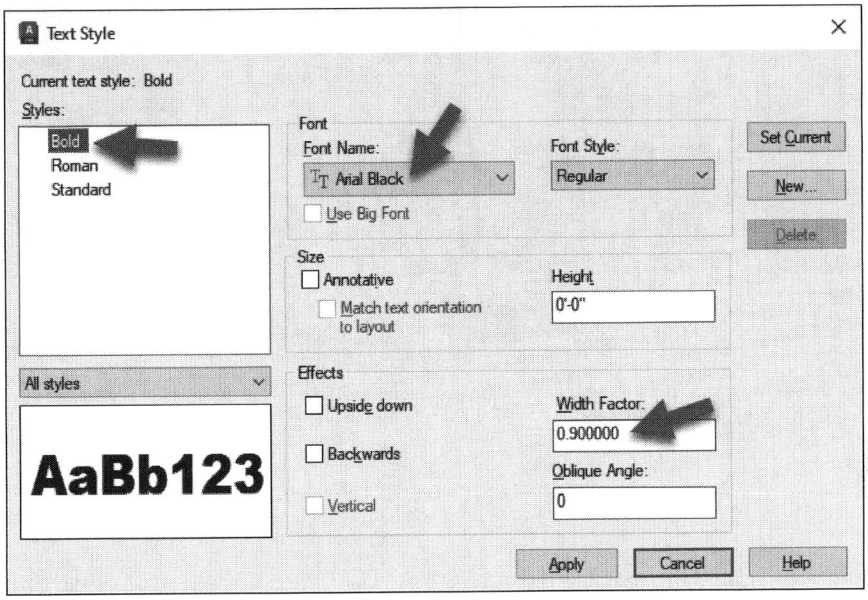

FIGURE 8-1.18 Text Style dialog; setting for text style named "Bold"

33. Click **Apply** to finalize your new *Text Style* settings.

34. Click **Close**.

The new text style is now available for use in the current drawing. If you want regular access to the Bold text style, you would add it to your Drawing Template file.

Now you will modify the *Table Style* title text.

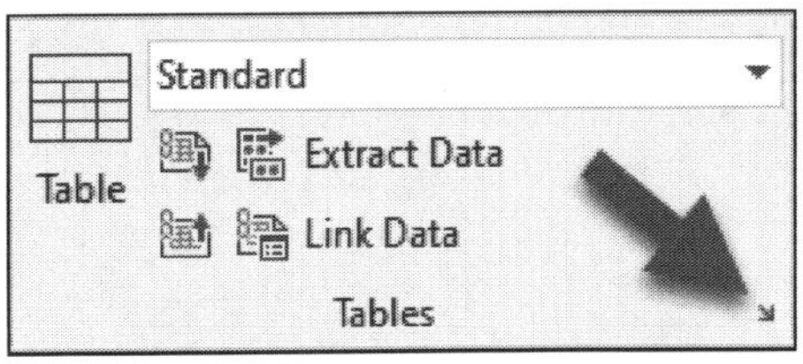

35. On the *Table* panel, in the *Annotate* tab, select the **Table Style** link *(see image to the right).*

36. Click the **Modify…** button *(to Modify the Standard table style).*

37. Under the **Title** *Cell Styles*, change the following (Figures 8-1.19a & b):
    a. *Text tab:* *Text style* to **Bold**
    b. *General tab:* *Fill color* to **Color 255**

***FYI:** Another option is to select the Title cell and adjust these settings in the Properties Palette.*

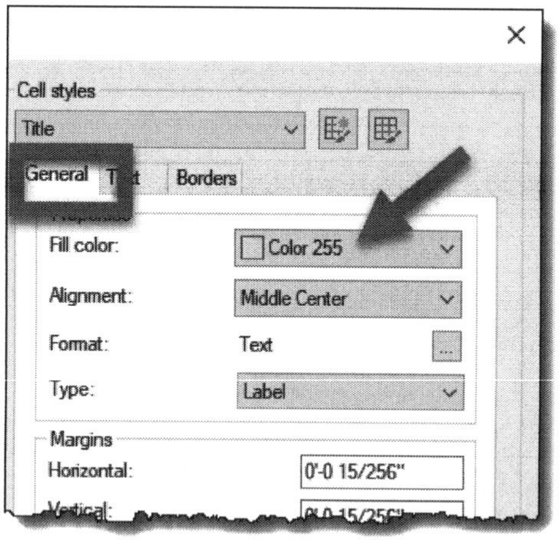

FIGURE 8-1.19A
Modify Table Style; Title – General tab

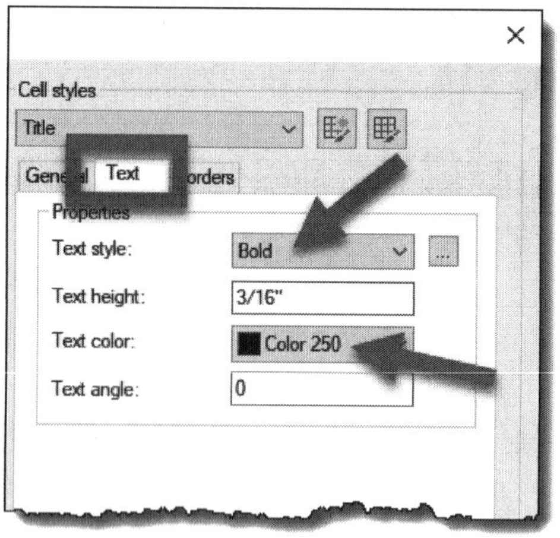

FIGURE 8-1.19B
Modify Table Style; Title – Text tab

38. Click **OK** and then **Close** to close the dialog boxes.

You should now notice the text for the title is now Bold and the cell is filled with color 255 (a grey shade) in your Room Finish Schedule (Figure 8-1.20). Similarly, if you had additional tables inserted into the current drawing (and using the standard style), they would all be updated to use the Bold font as well.

ROOM FINISH SCHEDULE										
RM NO	ROOM NAME	FLOOR		WALLS				CEILING		REMARKS
		FINISH	BASE	NORTH	EAST	SOUTH	WEST	MAT'L	HEGIHT	
100	VESTIBULE									
101	MENS TOILET									
102	WOMENS TOILET									
103	JANITOR / STORAGE									
104	LARGE CLASSROOM									
105	CLASSROOM									
106	STIAR "A"									
107	CORRIDOR									
108	COMPUTER LAB									
109	COMPUTER LAB									
110	COMPUTER LAB									
111	COMPUTER LAB									
112	LECTURE									
113	STAIR "B"									
114	LOBBY									
115	CHECKOUT									
116	TWO STORY READING RM									
117	GROUP STUDY									

FIGURE 8-1.20 Modify Table Style; Text style for title set to "Bold"

39. **Save** your drawing as **ROOM FINISH SCHEDULE.dwg**.

Exercise 8-2:
Sheet Setup and Management (Sheet Sets)

Introduction:

This exercise covers an AutoCAD feature called *Sheet Sets*, which represents a very powerful feature previously found only in more advanced, architecture specific programs like Revit Architecture.

The *Sheet Set* Manager allows one or more designers to see a list that represents all the sheets in the project set. Each sheet can be opened by double-clicking on the sheet label in the list. Once a sheet is open, you can place drawings on it. Reference bubbles can be placed on sheets which are automatically updated when the drawing numbers or sheet numbers are changed.

When you have completed this section, you will have created several sheets with title blocks (a.k.a., sheet borders) and placed your drawings on them using the *Sheet Set Manager*.

Procedural and Organizational Overview:

The following information outlines the basic procedure and organization of a *Sheet Set*. This will give you a good understanding of this feature before you actually try it.

Sheet Sets pivot around three types of files:

- ♦ Resource Drawings *(model views)*
- ♦ Sheet Files (Sheet Views)
- ♦ A Sheet Set Data File

In addition to the three types of files listed above, other files are used as well (e.g., callout blocks and template files). Next, you will take a closer look at the three file types listed above and what role they play in the *SheetSet* feature.

<u>Resource Drawings *(model views)*</u>:

- o Drawing files (DWG's)
  - Each floor plan, elevation, detail, etc., in a drawing file, has a *Named View* associated with it.
  - These files are the files you have created thus far in this book.
  - You will cover *Named Views* later in this exercise.
- o Any <u>text</u> or <u>dimensions</u> drawn in a *Resource Drawing* needs to be scaled appropriately based on the scale that drawing will ultimately be plotted at (recall the dimscale setting and annotation scaling).

<u>Sheet Files</u>:

- Drawing files (DWG's)
    - Each of these files represents a sheet in a set of drawings (e.g., 24″x36″ sheet)
- *Named Views*, from various *Resource Drawings*, are placed on these sheets.
- *Named Views* can be placed at various scales at the time of insertion. A drawing title tag is automatically inserted below the drawing view; the tag is even automatically filled out with the view's number (if/when one is provided in the *Sheet Set Manager*), and scale (i.e., the scale you selected when the view was placed on the sheet). The image below describes the default drawing tag:

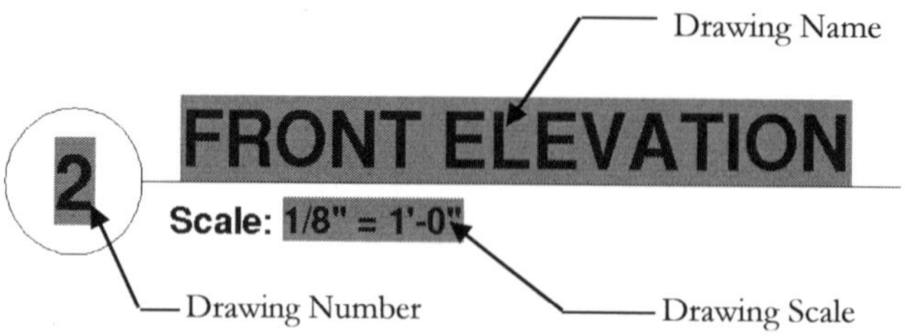

- Once a *View* has been placed on a sheet, you can specify a Drawing Number; you can also change the Drawing (view) Name. This must be done in the *Sheet Set Manager* to ensure all sheets and views are correctly cross-referenced.
- *Callout Bubbles* (elevation and detail) can be placed on sheets. The bubbles reference a *Named View* from a *Resource Drawing*. The reference bubble is automatically filled out with the View's number and the sheet number the view is placed on (all of which is stored in the Sheet Set Data file). The image below describes the basic components of a callout bubble:

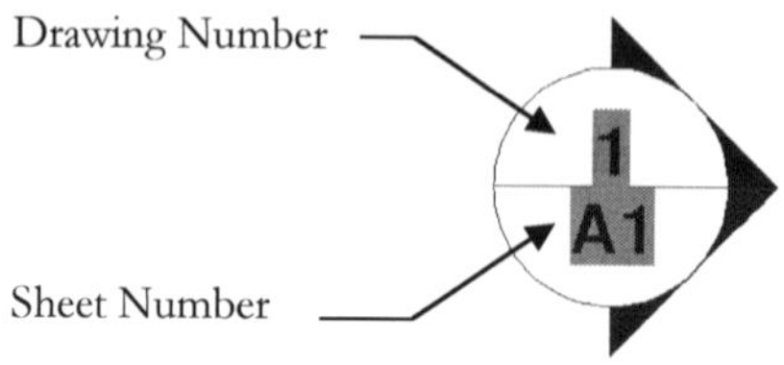

- The shaded rectangle behind the text lets you know that the text is updated automatically and should not be modified manually. Specifically, they are called *Fields*, and are updated at key points while working on a drawing (e.g., Open, Save, Plot, Regen). These are similar to the *Fields* in *MS Word*, the *Date Field* is shaded and automatically updated. You used fields to add the square footage to each room in the floor plans in Chapter 4.

A Sheet Set Data File:

- File name and extension: *filename*.dst.
- This file is a database that maintains information about the *Sheet Set* and detail/sheet numbering and cross-references.
- The file can be located anywhere on your system (including a network drive). This file should be stored in your project folder for easy backup.

Creating Named Views in Your Resource Drawings:

As mentioned above, the various plans, elevations, sections and details you wish to place on a sheet, each need to be identified by a *Named View*, which is simply defined by an imaginary rectangular area within a drawing file. If you move a door detail, for example, to another part of *Model Space*, the *Named View* does NOT move and would be "looking" at an empty portion of the drawing at that point. Named views allow you to have more than one detail in a drawing, but place them on different sheets in the set.

You will start with the floor plan.

1. Open your **DJS55803apl01** drawing previously created.

You will create one *Named View* of the floor plan drawing.

2. **Zoom** to view the entire floor plan.

3. Select **View Manager** from the *View* tab.

   ***TIP:** You can also type V and Enter to load View Manager.*

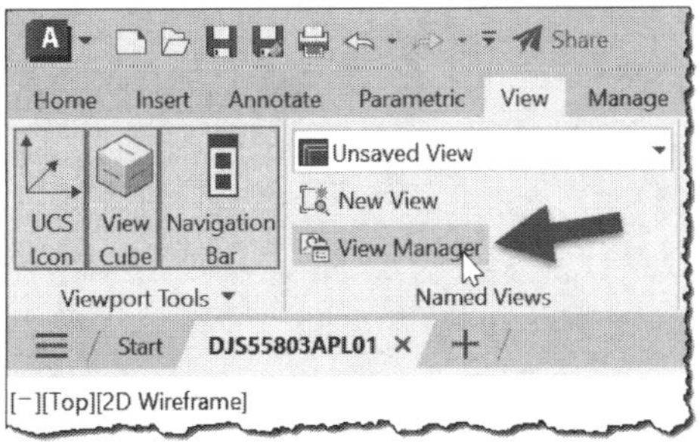

Views panel on View tab

You are now in the *View Manager* dialog (Figure 8-2.1).

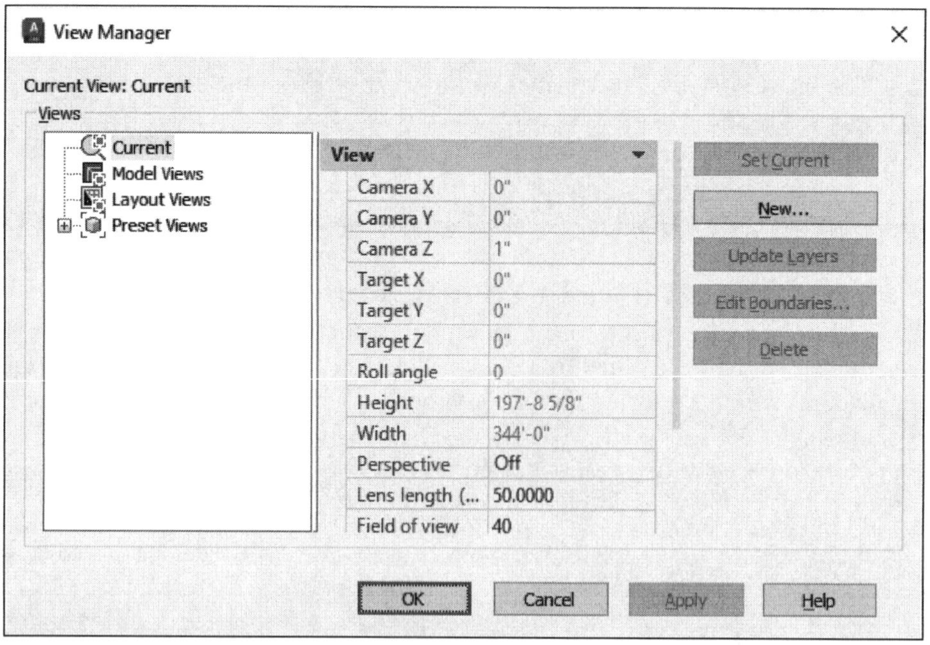

FIGURE 8-2.1 View Manager dialog box; click "New…" to create a named view

4. Click **New** to create a *Named View*.

You are now in the *New View / Shot Properties dialog* (Figure 8-2.2) where you can create a *Named View*.

5. Enter **First Floor Plan** for the *View* name (Figure 8-2.2).

   FYI: *The name entered here is the default name used in the drawing title tag, when the view is placed on a sheet.*

6. Click **Define window** in the *Boundary* area (Figure 8-2.2).

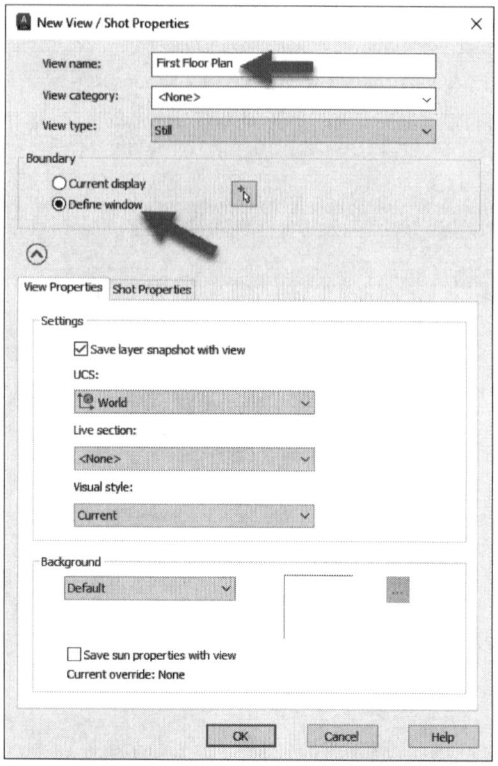

FIGURE 8-2.2
New View dialog; create a view named "First Floor Plan"

Immediately after clicking *Define window*, you are temporarily brought back to the drawing to select a boundary window around your floor plan.

7. Select a window (rectangular area) around your floor plan (Figure 8-2.3).

   TIP: *Note the following regarding your boundary window selection:*

   ****You should try to pick a window as tight to the drawing as possible, leaving room for any anticipated additions to the drawing (e.g., more building, dimensions or notes).*

   ****By default, the drawing title tag is placed just below the lower left corner of the view when it is placed on a sheet; so too much extra space to the left of the drawing would position the title tag so that it is not under any of the drawing.*

   ****If your drawing does grow larger than the Named View's specified boundary, you can use the Edit Boundaries feature (see Figure 8-2.1) to resize the boundary.*

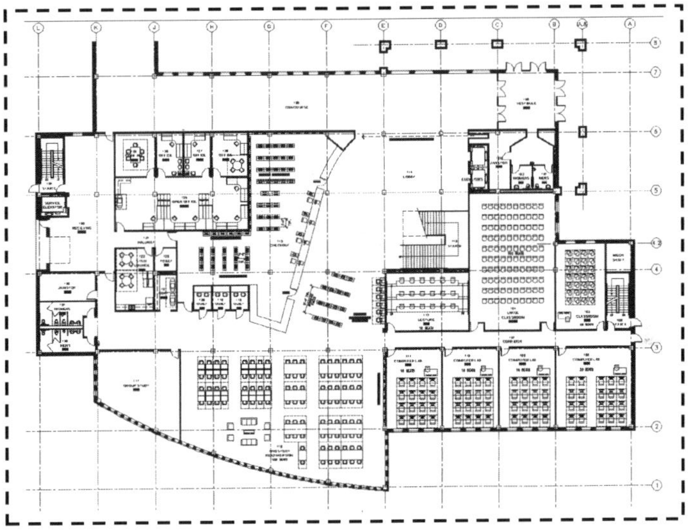

FIGURE 8-2.3
South Elevation; select window as shown to define view

8. Right-click to return to the *New View / Shot Properties* dialog box.

9. Click **OK** to close the dialog box and create the view.

10. Click **OK** to close the *View Manager* dialog box.

When finished, you will see a *Named View* listed in the *View Manager* dialog box in the label *Model Views* (Figure 8-2.4).

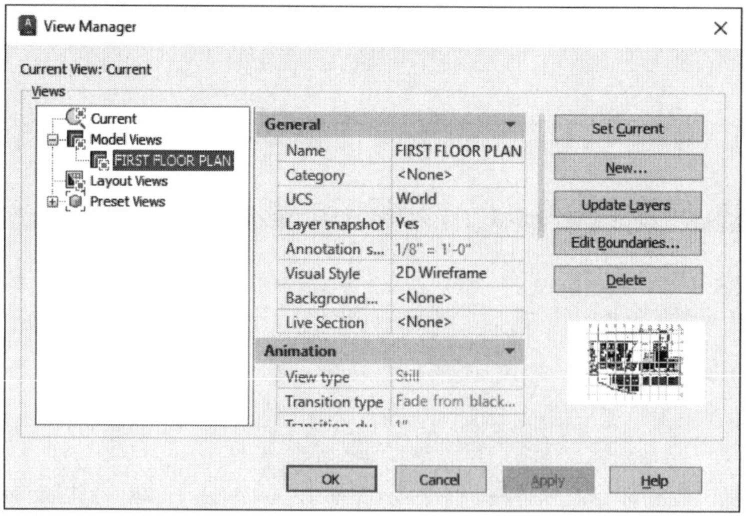

FIGURE 8-2.4
View Manager; a named view created for the floor plan drawing

11. **Open** your other drawings and create *Named Views* per the chart below. (All view names should be uppercase.)

Drawing name	Named View to create
Std-Mounting-Hgt.dwg	Standard Mounting Heights
DJS55803AIE01.dwg	North - Men's Toilet (130)
DJS55803AIE02.dwg	West – Open Office (125)
DJS55803AIE03.dwg	South – Staff Lounge (122)
DJS55803AIE04.dwg	East – Lecture (112)
DJS55803AIE05.dwg	South – Concourse (135)
Room Schedule.dwg	Room Finish Schedule
DJS55803ADE01.dwg	Drawer Base Cabinet Detail
DJS55803ADE02.dwg	Base Cabinet Detail
DJS55803ADE03.dwg	Floor Transition Detail
DJS55803ADE04.dwg	Terrazzo Base Detail
DJS55803ADE05.dwg	Ceiling Detail – Recessed Light
DJS55803ADE06.dwg	Fixed Student Desk Detail

FYI: These drawings will be referred to as the Model Views in the Sheet Set Manager.

12. **Save** your drawings; otherwise, your named views will be lost.

Next you will create the *Sheet Set Data* file via the *Sheet Set Manager.*

Setting Up a Sheet Set:

You will look at one of the methods provided to set up a Sheet Set. This involves using the Create Sheet Set Wizard.

FIGURE 8-2.5
Sheet Set Manager; click the Down-Arrow and select "New Sheet Set..." to start a new Sheet Set.

13. Make sure a drawing is open. You must have at least one drawing open to get started; it can be a blank drawing or one of your project files.

14. **Open** the **Sheet Set Manager** by clicking its icon on the **View** tab.

15. Now do the following:

    a. Right-click in the center and select the **Preview/Details** panel (optional step).

    b. At the top of the *Sheet Set Manager* palette, click the down-arrow and then select **New Sheet Set…** from the menu.

This starts the *Sheet Set Manager Wizard* (Figure 8-2.6).

16. Click **Next**.

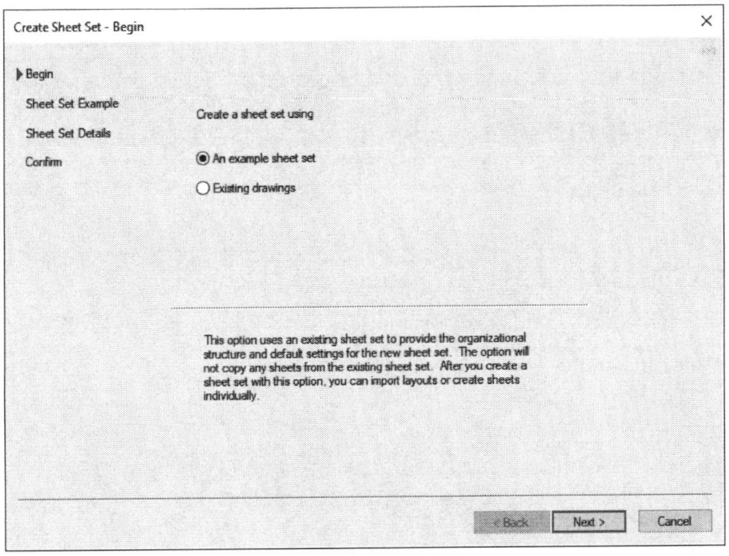

FIGURE 8-2.6 Create Sheet Set Wizard; Begin screen

17. Next, make sure **Architectural Imperial Sheet Set** is selected and then click **Next** (Figure 8-2.7).

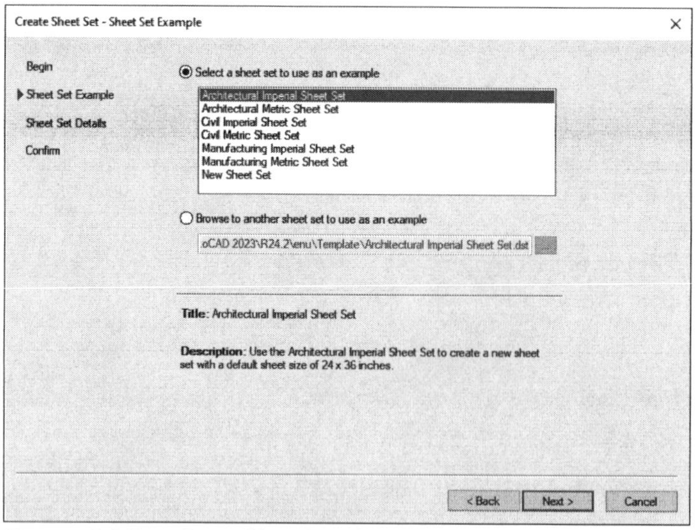

FIGURE 8-2.7 Create Sheet Set Wizard; Sheet Set Example screen

18. Enter the name of new *Sheet Set*, **Library Project**. See Figure 8-2.8 *(don't click* **Next** *yet)*.

19. Click the "" button to change the location where the *sheet set data file* will be stored: **a.**) Using *Windows Explorer*, create a subfolder named <u>Sheet Set Files</u> in the folder that contains the files created in this book; or **b.**) Select the new folder.

    ***FYI:** You are selecting a folder, not a file.*

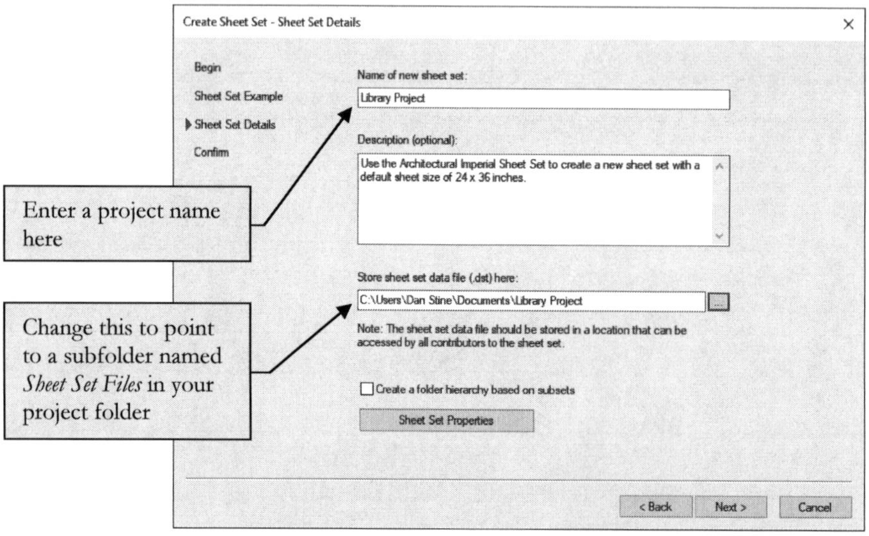

FIGURE 8-2.8 Create Sheet Set Wizard; Sheet Set Details screen

***TIP:** To ensure the remainder of this lesson proceeds smoothly, you should make sure all your project files are located in one folder. Only include the current files, not backup DWG (i.e., filename.BAK) files, or old copies. Do this via Windows Explorer (a.k.a., My Computer), not within AutoCAD.*

20. Click **Next**.

You are now at the final screen of the wizard. You are given detailed information on the "what and where" for the new *Sheet Set* about to be created.

21. Click **Finish** to create the new *Sheet Set* (Figure 8-2.9).

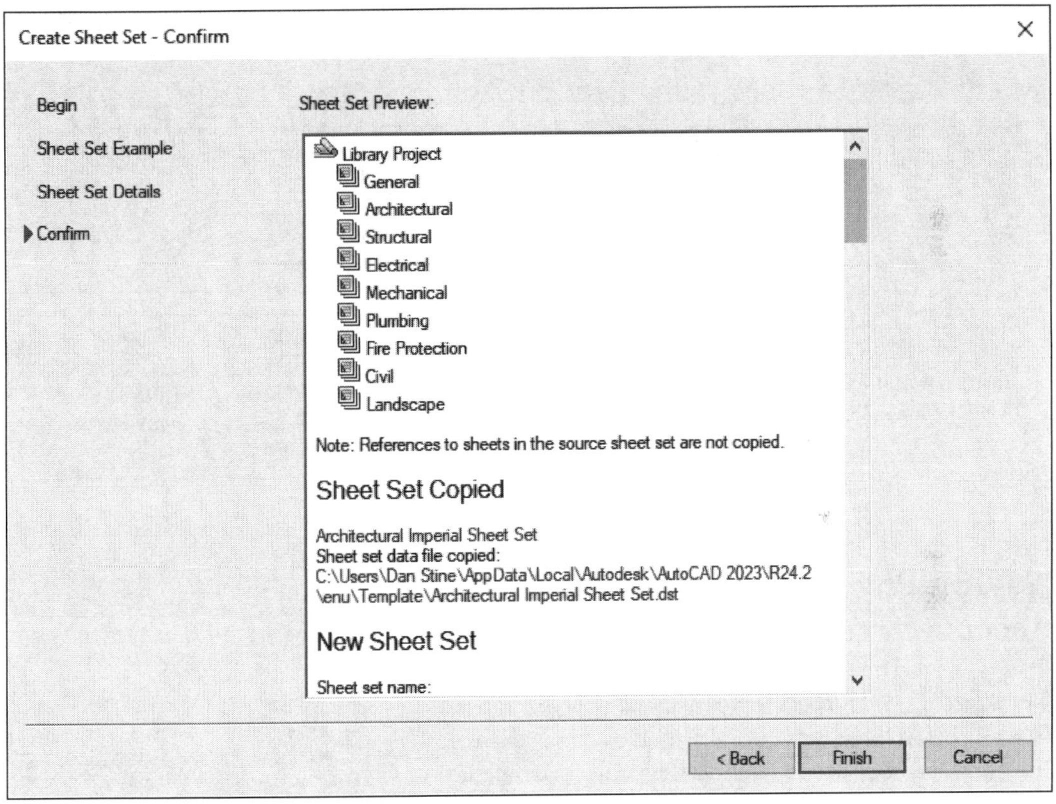

FIGURE 8-2.9 Create Sheet Set Wizard; Confirm screen

The wizard closes and the *Sheet Set Manager* is populated with the specified information. If you use *MS Windows Explorer* to browse to your *Sheet Set Files* folder, you will see a new file named "*Library Project.dst*"; this is the *Sheet Set Data* file previously discussed.

The *Sheet Set Example* file used contained several *Subsets* (e.g., Architectural, Structural, etc.), which are seen on the *Sheet List tab* (Figure 8-2.10). *Subsets* allow *Sheets* to be organized, by discipline in this example. The right-click menu allows you to easily add, rename or remove a *Subset* at anytime.

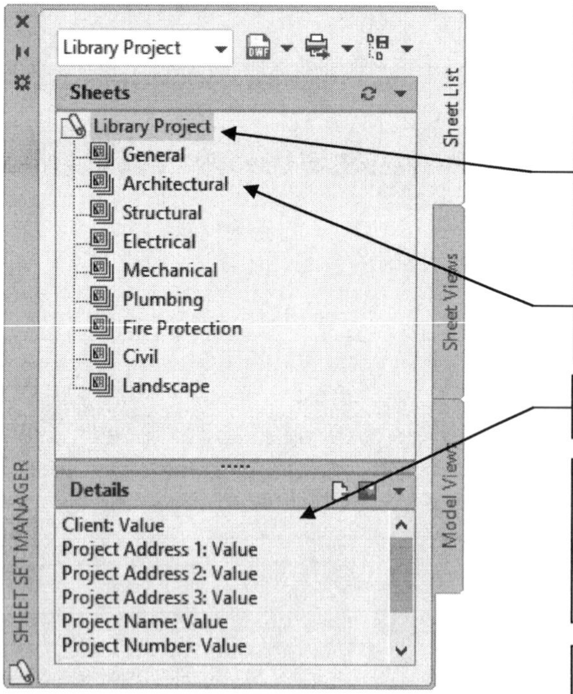

Sheet List tab: sheet files are added and managed here, including the ability to create and number sheets. You can also open sheet files by double-clicking them.

Sheet Set name, right-click for context sensitive menu which includes the option to Close the current Sheet Set.

Subsets: used to organize sheet files. All your sheets will be created in the Architectural subset.

Preview/Details Pane (see step 15a)

Sheet Views tab (currently empty): all views that have been placed on a sheet are listed here. This tab is where you number individual drawings and "link" callout bubbles to these views.

Model Views tab (currently empty): you can only place Drawing Views on Sheets from drawings that have been added to this tab. You select a folder and all the drawings in that folder are listed.

FIGURE 8-2.10
Sheet Set Manager; Sheet List tab

Adding Project Information to the Sheet Set Properties:

The *Sheet Set Properties* dialog contains key information that AutoCAD needs to properly manage and control the *Sheet Set*. Next you will enter the project name and address, which is automatically placed in the title block of each sheet in the set!

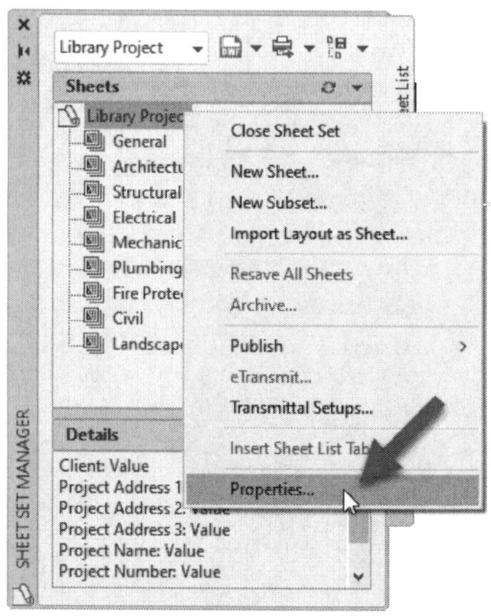

22. In the *Sheet Set Manager*, on the *Sheet List* tab, right click on the sheet set name (Library Project) at the top of the list – under the *Sheets* label – and select **Properties…** from the pop-up menu.

23. In the *Sheet Set Custom Properties* section, add information as shown in **Figure 8-2.11**.

    TIP: The scroll bar is on the left; you need to drag it down.

FIGURE 8-2.11 Create Sheet Set Properties; partial view of dialog

TIP: If you do not need one field, such as the "Project Address 3" line above, leave it blank, otherwise any text entered will show up on drawings.

24. Click **OK** to complete the changes.

Creating Sheets to Place Named Views on:

Creating a sheet with a title block, a number and client information has NEVER been easier in AutoCAD! In just minutes you will have all the empty sheets set up and ready for *Named Views* to be placed on them.

As you create sheets in the *Sheet Set Manager*, AutoCAD creates a drawing file in the specified folder (Sheet Set Files sub-folder in this example). This file IS the sheet. If the file is erased or corrupt, that sheet will no longer be available. Therefore, you should back up the files in the Sheet Set Files sub-folder, just as you would your Resource Drawings (or Model Views) or any important files on your computer.

Next you will set up the entire set of sheets, starting with the project Title Sheet.

25. On the *Sheet List* tab, in the *Sheet Set Manager*, right-click on the *General* Subset, and then click **New Sheet…** from the pop-up menu (Figure 8-2.12).

You are now in the *New Sheet* dialog box where you enter the sheet title and number, as well as specify the name of the drawing file that will be created.

26. Enter the following:
    a. *Number:* **G0.01**
    b. *Sheet title:* **Title Sheet**
    c. *File Name:* *default*
    d. See **Figure 8-2.13**.

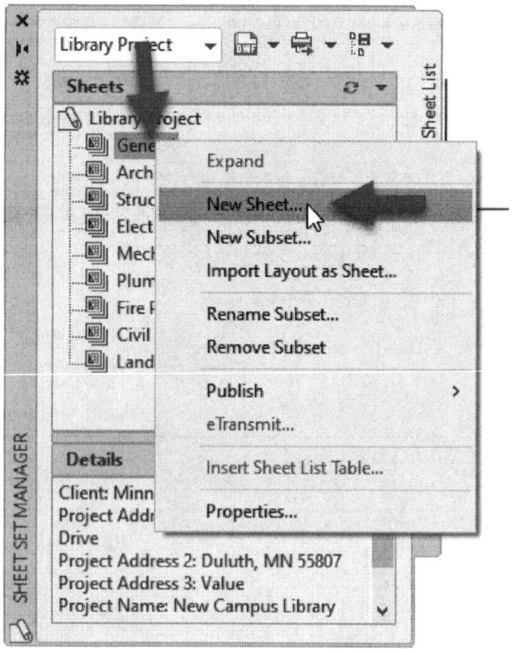

FIGURE 8-2.12
Sheet Set Manager; create new sheet

27. Click **OK** to create the sheet.

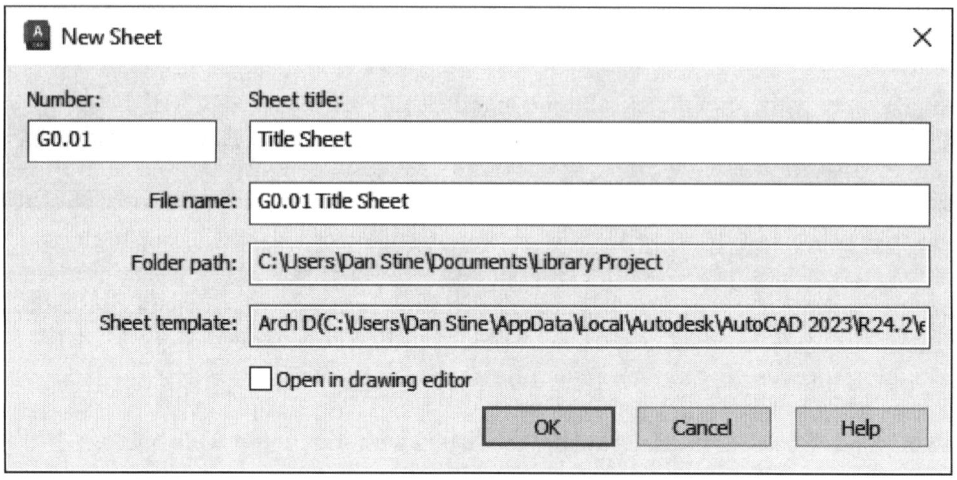

FIGURE 8-2.13 New Sheet dialog; enter sheet number, title and file name

You have just created your first sheet! You now see the sheet listed under the *General Subset* in the *Sheet Set Manager* (Figure 8-2.14).

28. Per the steps above, create new sheets (under Architectural) so that you have all the sheets listed in the table below.

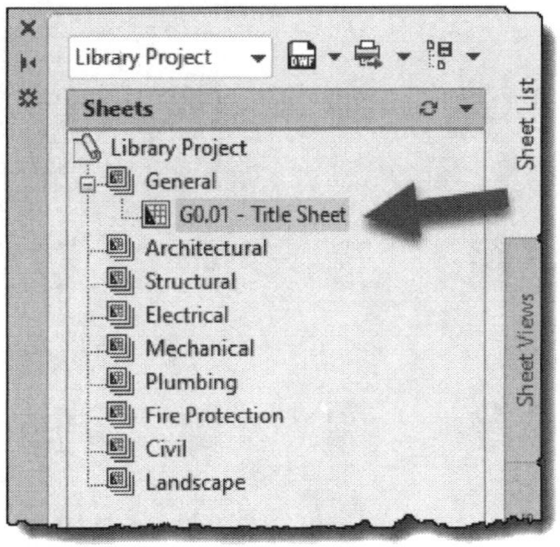

FIGURE 8-2.14
New Sheet Manager

Sheet name	Sheet number
Title Sheet	G0.01
Basement Floor Plan	A2.00
First Floor Plan	A2.01
Second Floor Plan	A2.02
Third Floor Plan	A2.03
Exterior Elevations	A3.00
Building Sections	A3.01
Wall Sections	A4.00
Interior Elevations	A5.00
Details	A6.00
Schedules	A7.00
First Floor Furniture Plans	A8.00

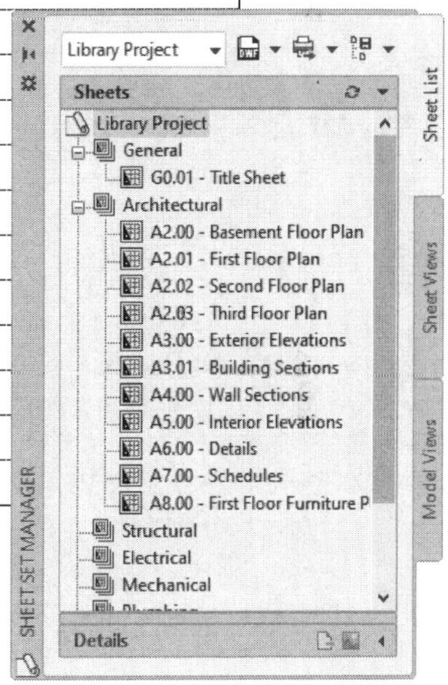

Once finished, all the sheets will be listed in the *Sheet Set Manager* as shown in Figure 8-2.15.

FIGURE 8-2.15
New Sheet Manager – sheets created

FYI: In the previous step you created a few more sheets than you actually have drawings for. However, this will set things up to look more like a real project. Also note that this sheet numbering system allows additional sheets to be added without the need to renumber the subsequent sheets.

Take a minute to browse to the *Sheet Set files* folder you previously created and notice an AutoCAD file has been created for each sheet (Figure 8-2.16).

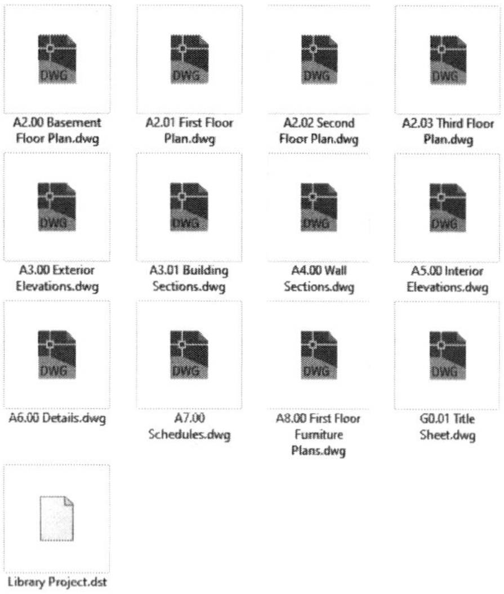

These files can be opened here, by double-clicking, or from *Menu Browser* → *File* → *Open* within AutoCAD.

Next you will see how the *Sheet Set Manager* allows you to do this.

FIGURE 8-2.16
Windows Explorer view of your *Sheet Set Files* sub-folder you created in your project folder (step 19); files automatically created with the Sheet Set Manager

Opening Sheets from the Sheet Set Manager:

In the *Sheet Set Manager* you can double-click on a sheet title (on the *Sheet List* tab) to open the drawing file that represents that sheet. Once the drawing is open you can save and close it just like any other drawing file.

Next you will open the first floor plan sheet A2.01 to place one of your drawings on it.

29. On the *Sheet List* tab, in *Sheet Set Manager*, double-click on the sheet title **A2.01 – First Floor Plan**.

The drawing **A2.01 – First Floor Plan** (located in your *SheetSet Files* sub-folder) is now open.

30. **Zoom** in to the lower right corner of the sheet to see the information that was automatically entered in the title block (Figure 8-2.17).

31. Notice that the sheet number, project name and date have been automatically added to the title block.

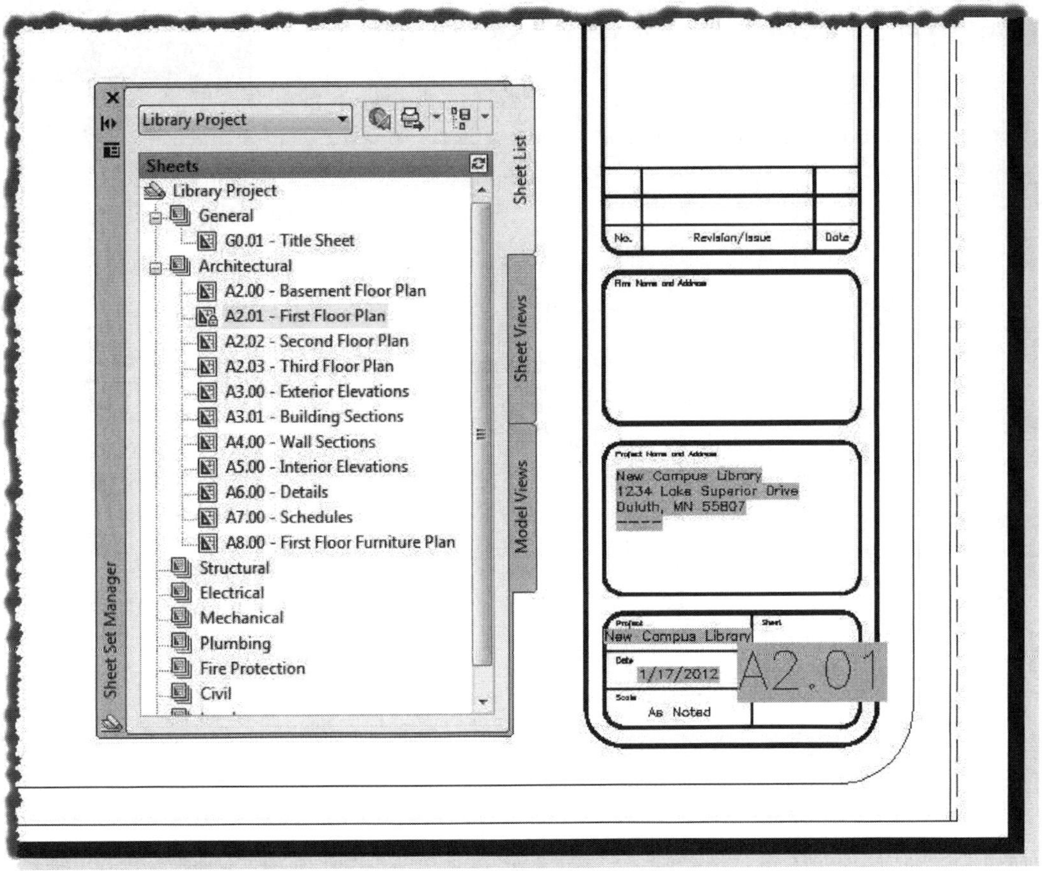

FIGURE 8-2.17 Sheet A4 – Exterior Elevations;
Shaded text are fields, which are modified/updated using the Sheet Set Manager

32. **Zoom Previous** so you see the entire sheet.

Notice that the sheet number does not fit in the title block. This can be corrected but is beyond the scope of this book. In an office setting, the *Sheet Set Manager* would use a custom template to create a sheet file, which would be set up for the sheet number to work and have the company's logo in the title block.

> *TIP: If you hover your cursor over a sheet name in the Sheet Set Manager, a pop-up preview pane will appear!*

Specifying Resource Drawing Locations:

You are just about ready to start placing drawings on sheets. But first you need to tell the *Sheet Set Manager* where to look for your drawing files that contain the *Named Views*. You will do this next.

33. Click on the **Model Views** tab in the *Sheet Set Manager.*

34. Double-click the **Add New Location…** icon (Figure 8-2.18).

35. Browse to the location where all your drawings created in the book are stored, and then click **OK** *(see TIP below).*

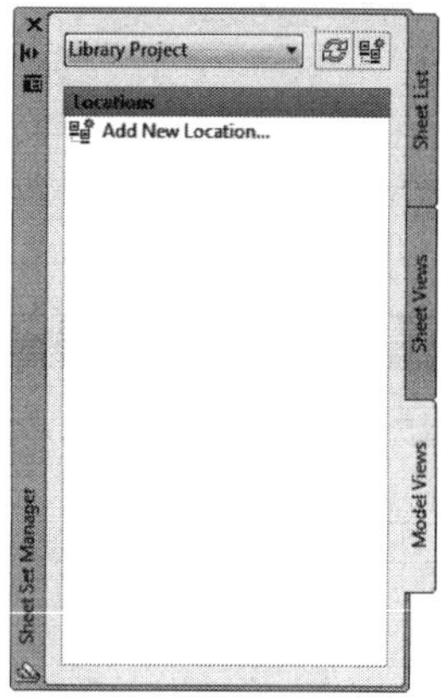

FIGURE 8-2.18 Model Views tab; no folder listed yet

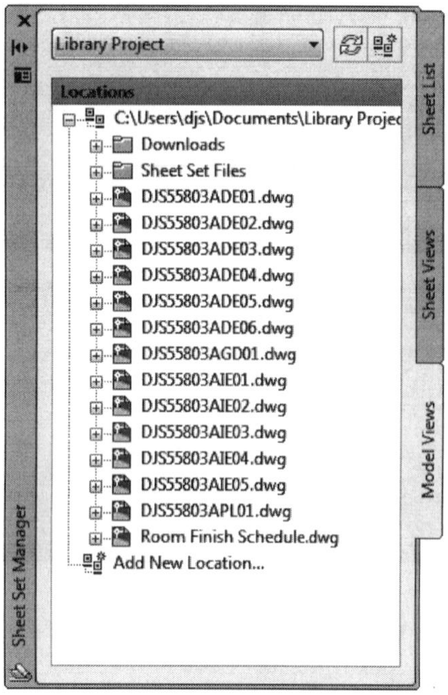

FIGURE 8-2.19 Model Views tab; Library Project folder now selected

TIP: In step 35, you are selecting a folder, not a file. You will not see your AutoCAD DWG files while browsing for the folder.

Also, you are not selecting the Sheet Set Files folder either – but the one above it that contains your floor plan and other drawing files.

Notice in Figure 8-2.19 that the folder you selected is now listed in the *Locations* panel (on the *Model Views* tab). Additionally, all the drawings in that folder are listed.

FYI: You can right-click on the folder "location" and remove it from the list if you picked the wrong folder. You can also add additional folders, if one needs to.

Adding Named Views to Sheets:

You are now to the point where you can start placing drawings (*Named Views*) on your *Sheets*. Basically, you drag on a *Named View* from the *Model Views* tab onto your *Sheet.*

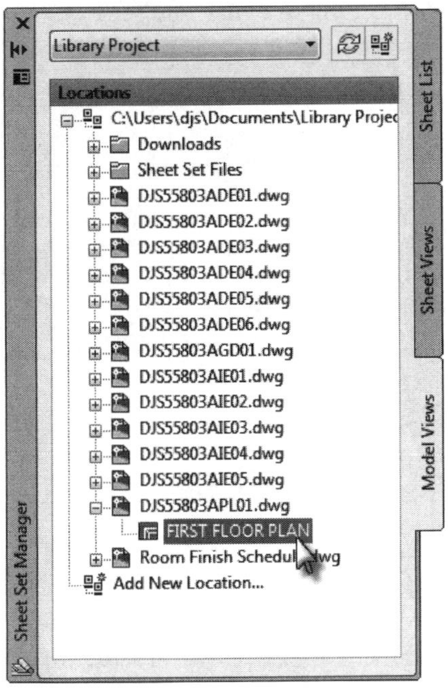

FIGURE 8-2.20 Model Views tab;
Named Views in *exterior elevations.dwg*

FYI: *The "plus" symbol next to the drawings (listed in the Model Views folder) expands that drawing's view to display its Named Views.*

First you will open a sheet to place a drawing (i.e., Named View) on.

36. On the *Sheet List* tab, double-click the **A2.01 – First Floor Plan** sheet to open it (if not already open).

37. Click the **Model Views** Tab to make it current.

38. Click the "**plus**" symbol next to the **DJS55803APL01** drawing to view that drawing's *Named Views.*

FYI: *These are the Named Views you created back on page 8-20.*

You can now see the *Named Views* you created in the "DJS55803APL01" drawing (Figure 8-2.20).

39. Click and drag the **First Floor Plan** *Named View* from the *Sheet Set Manager* onto your **A2.01 – First Floor Plan** sheet (Figure 8-2.21).

Move your cursor about the screen to see how the View is attached to your cursor and AutoCAD is prompting for the location in which to place the drawing. Before you click to place the drawing you need to specify the scale you want the drawing printed at; you will do that in the next step.

40. **Right-click** to display the *Insertion Scale* pop-up menu (Figure 8-2.21).

41. Select **3/32" = 1'-0"** from the list.

Notice how the size of the drawing changes to correspond to the selected scale. Displaying the drawing at the correct scale helps you to correctly position the drawing on the sheet. You should also notice that a drawing title tag is positioned below and to the left of your view which you will look at closer after the view is placed.

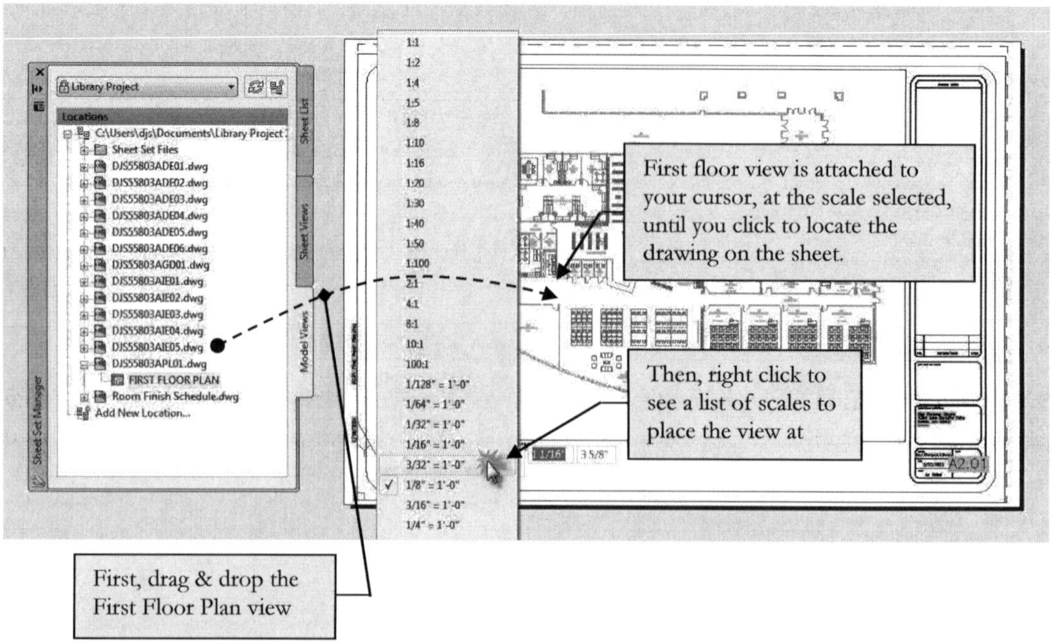

FIGURE 8-2.21
A2.01 – First Floor Plan; placing the floor plan view and right-clicking to see scale options

42. Position your mouse so the floor plan is centered on the sheet and then click to place the view on the sheet.

You have placed your first drawing on a sheet! (See Figure 8-2.22.) In just minutes you could have all the *Named Views* placed, but first you will explore a few other options and see how they are affected when you change a few sheet numbers.

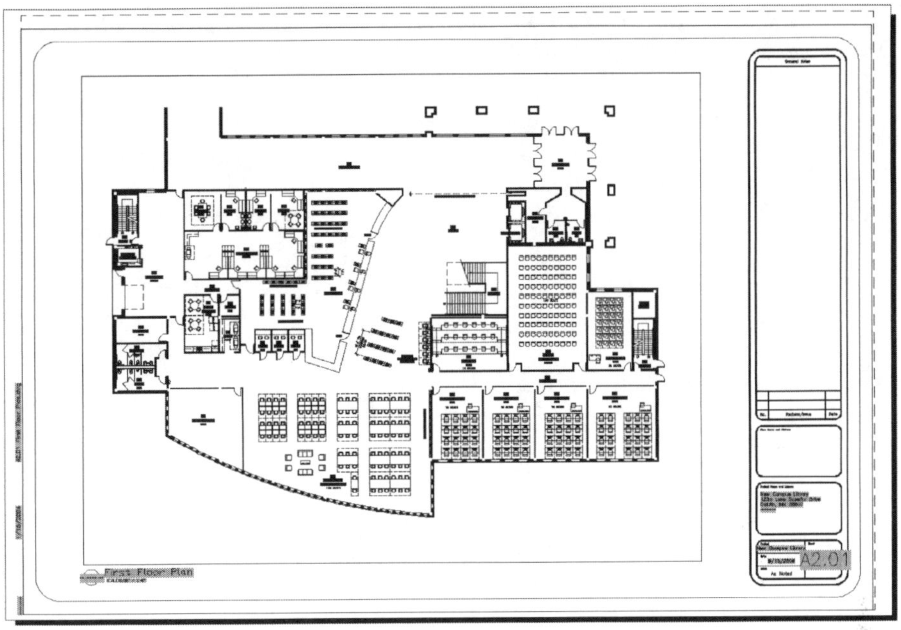

FIGURE 8-2.22 A2.01 – First Floor Plan; floor plan placed at 3/32"=1'-0"

NOTE: *The grids and columns are not showing up? That is because the Xref type was set to Overlay rather than attachment.*

43. **Zoom In** on the *Drawing Title* tag (Figure 8-2.23).

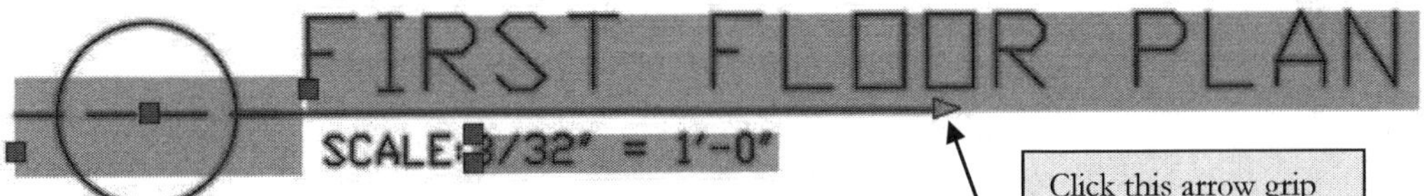

FIGURE 8-2.23
A2.01 – First Floor Plan; zoomed in on drawing title tag

Notice that the drawing name has been automatically filled in using the name you provided when you created the *Named View* in the *Resource Drawing* (DJS55803APL01.dwg).

Also notice that the drawing scale has been added and, of course, corresponds to the scale you selected when you placed the view.

The only field not filled out yet is the drawing number. You enter the drawing number for a view, once it is placed on a sheet, in the *Sheet Set Manager.* Next you will provide the sheet number via the Sheet Set Manager.

TIP: If the fields are not visible, delete the symbol. Then right click on the view name in Figure 8-2.24 and select "place view label block."

WARNING: Do not change the number in the drawing as it will be overwritten by the Sheet Set Manager.

44. Select the **Sheet Views** tab and then click the "+" next to sheet A2.01 to view the *Named Views* placed on that sheet.

Notice that the First Floor Plan view is listed. Eventually all your *Named Views* will be listed here, once they are all placed on sheets (Figure 8-2.24).

45. Right-click on the *First Floor Plan* view and select **Rename & Renumber…** from the pop-up menu.

46. Enter number **1** in the Number text box (Figure 8-2.25).

47. Click **OK** to apply the change.

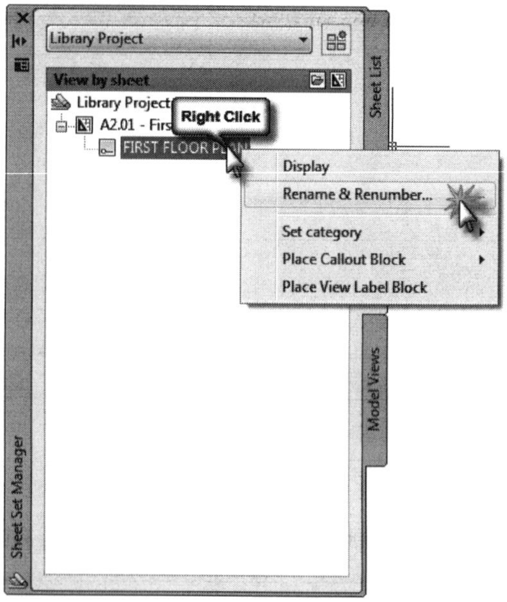

FIGURE 8-2.24
Sheet Set Manager; Sheet Views tab

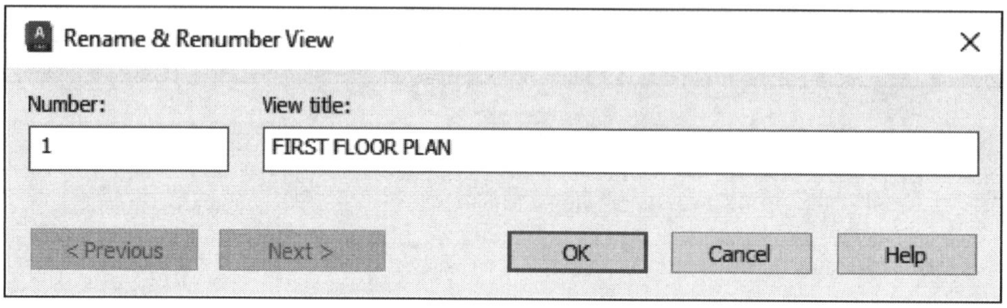

FIGURE 8-2.25 Rename and Renumber View; enter number 1

You will notice that your drawing has not updated yet. The following step will cause the drawing title tag to update.

48. Type **Regen** (or just "re") and then press **Enter**.

The drawing title tag now has the number 1 in the circle (Figure 8-2.26). A few other key events cause AutoCAD to update the tags. A few examples are opening and plotting a drawing.

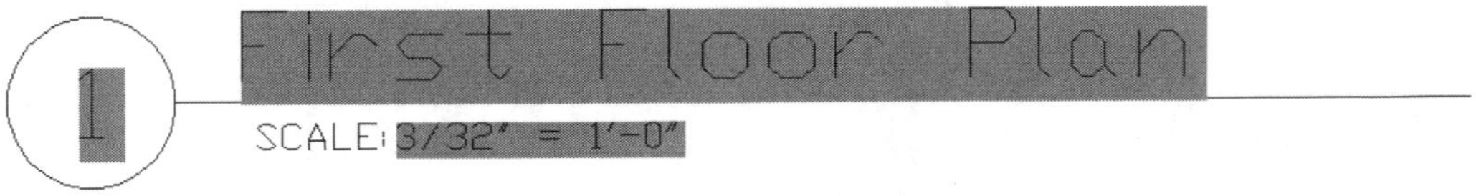

FIGURE 8-2.26 A2.01 – First Floor Plan; field updated automatically

Placing Callout Tags:

Another powerful feature related to *Sheet Sets* is the ability to place *Callout* tags that are automatically cross-referenced with a sheet and drawing number. Next you will place an elevation Callout tag (that references the toilet room elevation) on the floor plan.

First, though, you will place the interior elevation on the sheet.

49. Per the steps previously outlined, place **DJS55803AIE01 →** (NORTH – MEN'S TOILET (113) view at **¼" = 1'-0"** onto sheet **A5.00 – Interior Elevations**; *Rename & Renumber* to **1 – Typ. Toilet Elev** (Figure 8-2.27).

TIP: Open the sheet from the Sheet List tab and then drag the view from The Model Views tab. Also, every sheet starts with detail #1.

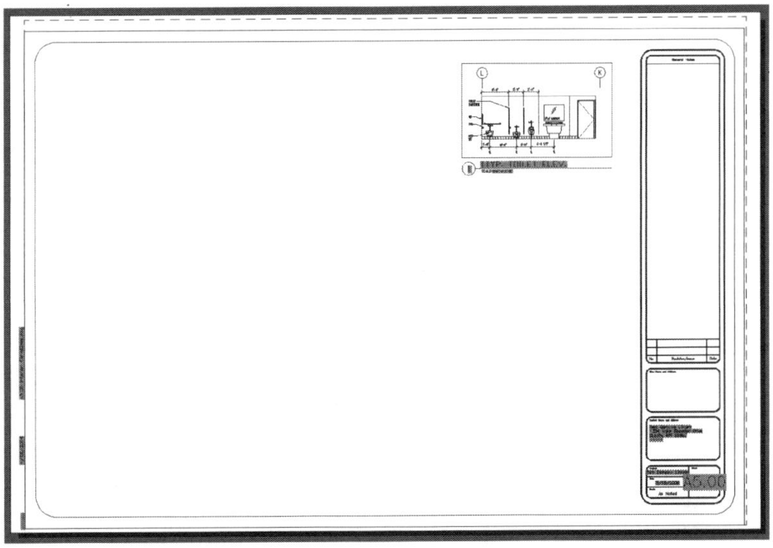

FIGURE 8-2.27 A5.00 – Interior Elevations; toilet view placed on sheet at ¼"

50. Now open sheet **A2.01 – First Floor Plan** and **Zoom** into the toilet room area of the sheet (not the floor plan drawing itself).

51. On the *Sheet Views* tab, right-click on the **1 – Typ. Toilet Elev** view, and then select **Place Callout Block → Callout** (Figure 8-2.28).

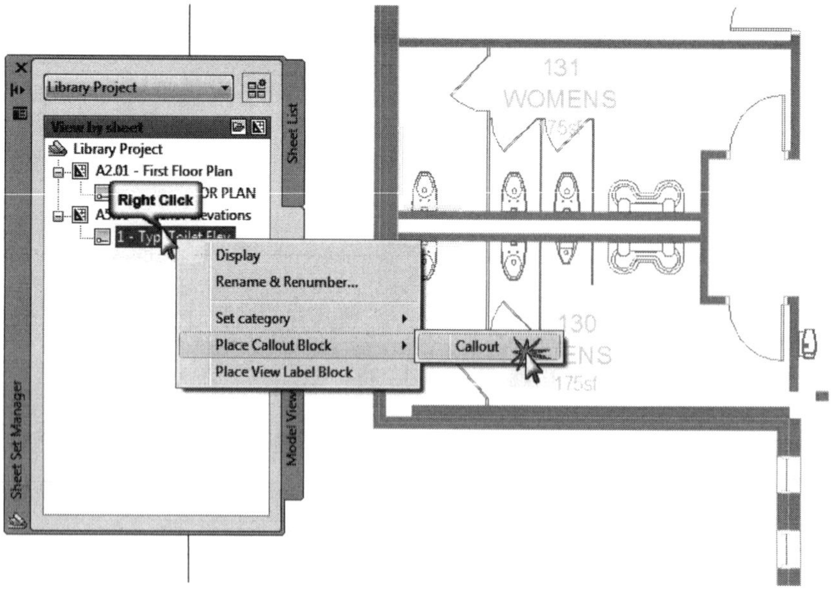

FIGURE 8-2.28 View List tab; right click on "1 – South Elevation"

52. Click to place the elevation tag approximately as shown in Figure 8-2.29 (it will be pointing to the right).

Notice that the drawing and sheet number has been automatically filled out. It referenced the sheet number where the elevation (i.e., the elevation the tag is pointing at) can be found.

The *Callout* symbol is a *Dynamic Block* that is set up to allow easy rotation of the pointer arrow (without rotating the text). The default orientation is pointing to the right, so you will adjust the arrow so it points north. Also, the arrow type defaulted to "Exterior Elevations"; you will change this to "Interior Elevations." The next numbered steps will walk you through this process. As you recall, selecting a *Dynamic Block* causes its special control grips to display. One of these controls the rotation of the arrow (which has been set up to snap to certain angles).

53. Click to select the symbol; Click the round grip; move the cursor so the arrow is pointing north and click.

54. Click the "down arrow" grip; select **Interior Elevation** from the list.

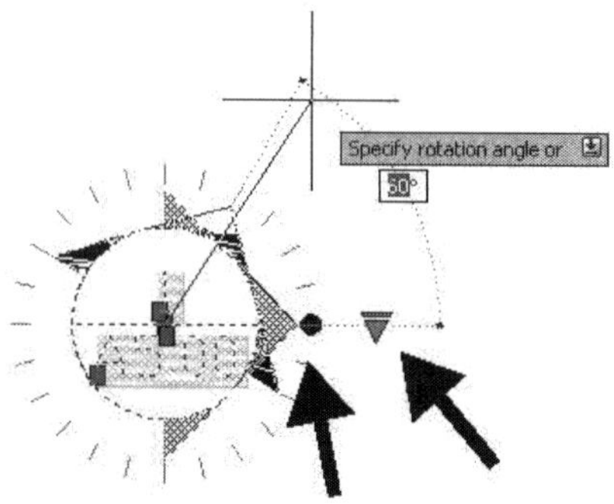

55. Use the **Scale** command to decrease the callout size by **.75**.

That's it, the callout has been modified.

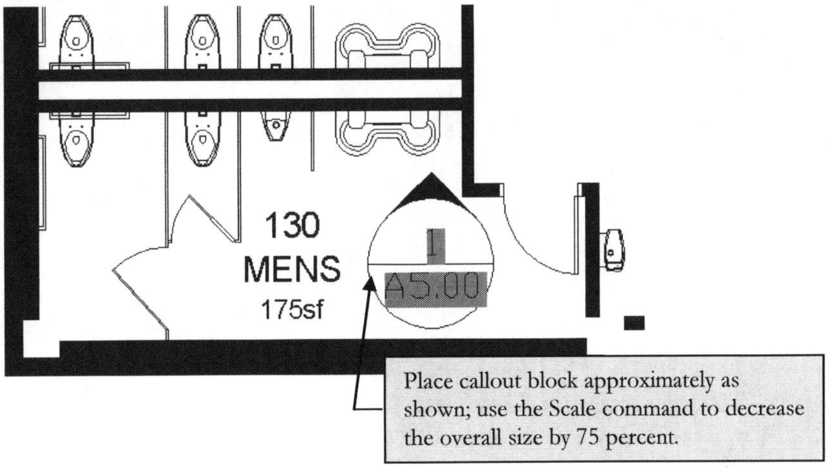

FIGURE 8-2.29 First Floor Plan sheet; elevation callout placed

56. **Save** and **Close** both your elevation and plan sheet. (Select the **Save** icon on the *Quick Access* toolbar or press *Ctrl + S*; don't forget to save often so you don't lose any work.)

Changing Sheet Numbers:

You decide you need another interior elevation sheet and would prefer it came before the one previously set up. Next you will renumber sheet A5.00 to A5.01 and insert a new sheet A5.00 into the mix; all this is done in the *Sheet Set Manager*. (Sheet A5.00 MUST be closed for these next steps to work!)

57. On the *Sheet List* tab, right click on sheet **A5.00 – Interior Elevations** and select **Rename & Renumber**.

58. Make the following changes in the dialog box:
    a. Change the Number to **A5.01**.
    b. Check all boxes under **Rename options**.
    c. Click **OK** (Figure 8-2.30).

TIP: Sheet A5.01 must be closed first.

This is similar to renumbering and renaming a view on the *View List* tab (look back at Figure 8-2.24).

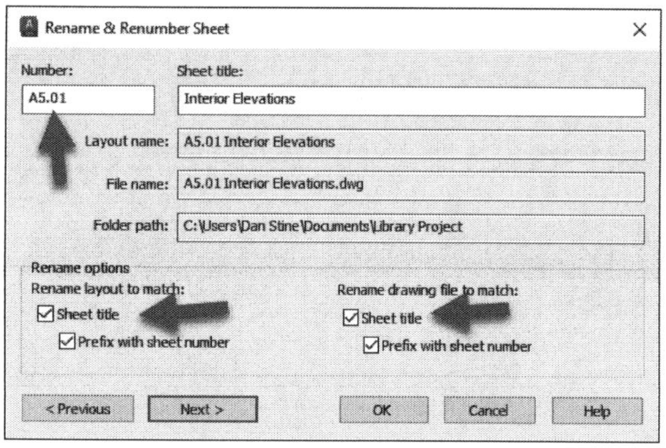

FIGURE 8-2.30
Rename & Renumber Sheet; change sheet A5.00 to A5.01

TIP: When renumbering several sheets, use the Previous button (see Figure 8-2.30 above) to step back through the sheets.

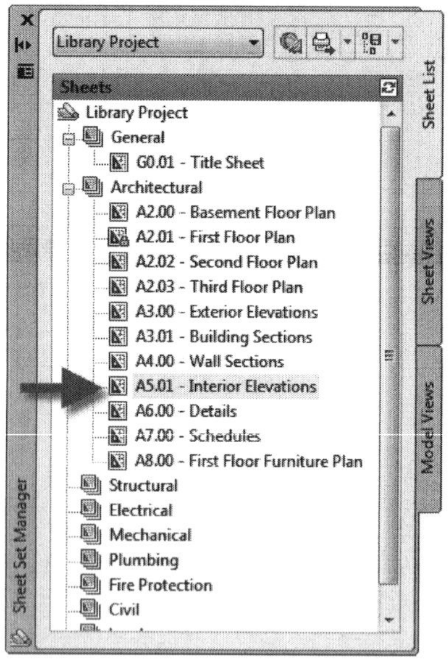

FIGURE 8-2.31
Sheet View tab; sheet renumbered, making room to insert new sheet

Notice, in Figure 8-2.31, the sheet A5.01 has a small **padlock** associated with its icon. This means that the file is open by you or someone else on the project team (in an office setting). If sheet A5.01 were open during the previous step, the "rename file" options would have been grayed out because the *Sheet Set* manager cannot edit a file when it is open.

Normally, changing sheet numbers is not a good idea because, no matter how hard you look, you will usually miss one reference bubble, leaving the bubble pointing to the wrong sheet. This leads to confusion and possible loss of time and money.

AutoCAD has provided a solution to this problem. The callout bubbles, drawing titles and sheet borders are all linked to the information in the *Sheet Set Manager*. So once you changed the sheet numbers in the *Sheet Set Manager*, all the sheets were (or will be) updated automatically. You will verify this next.

59. In the **A5.01 – Interior Elevations** sheet, zoom into the lower right corner to see the sheet number (Figure 8-2.32).

TIP: You may need to Regen the drawing to see the change.

FIGURE 8-2.32
A5.01 – Interior Elevations sheet; sheet number in title block has been updated automatically

As you can see the sheet number has been updated automatically!

What about the elevation tag you placed on the floor plan sheet?

60. On the **A2.01 – First Floor Plan** sheet, zoom in on the callout bubble (elev indicator). See Figure 8-2.33.

    TIP: You may need to Regen the drawing to see the change.

As you can see, the elevation callout tag has been updated automatically thus, eliminating the possibility of cross-reference errors when this system is used.

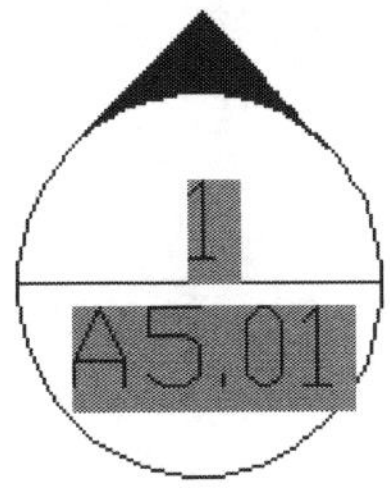

FIGURE 8-2.33
A2.01 – First Floor Plan sheet; sheet number in callout block has been updated automatically.

61. Add the following sheets to complete the set:

    TIP: You can drag the sheet labels (on the Sheet List tab) to change the listed order.

Sheet name	Sheet number
Interior Elevations	A5.00
Interior Elevations	A5.02

62. Place the remaining *Named Views* (see step 11 – page 8-20) on the appropriate sheets.

    FYI: Place the standard mounting height drawing on sheet A5.00 and the room schedule view should be placed at a scale of 1:1 on sheet A7.00. Refer back to chapter 7 for the drawing scales of the detail drawings.

63. On the *Sheet Views* tab, give each view a number (see ***TIP*** on next page).

TIP:

Drawings are typically numbered in the direction indicated below. The first drawings are placed in the upper right, and fill in the sheet toward the left. The main reason for starting on the right is this: if a sheet is only half full (for example), you would not have to open the set all the way to see the drawings on that sheet.

Also, it is usually a good idea to wait until the sheet is mostly full before numbering drawings. That way you can organize the drawings neatly on the sheet and avoid a situation where the drawing numbers are not in sequence.

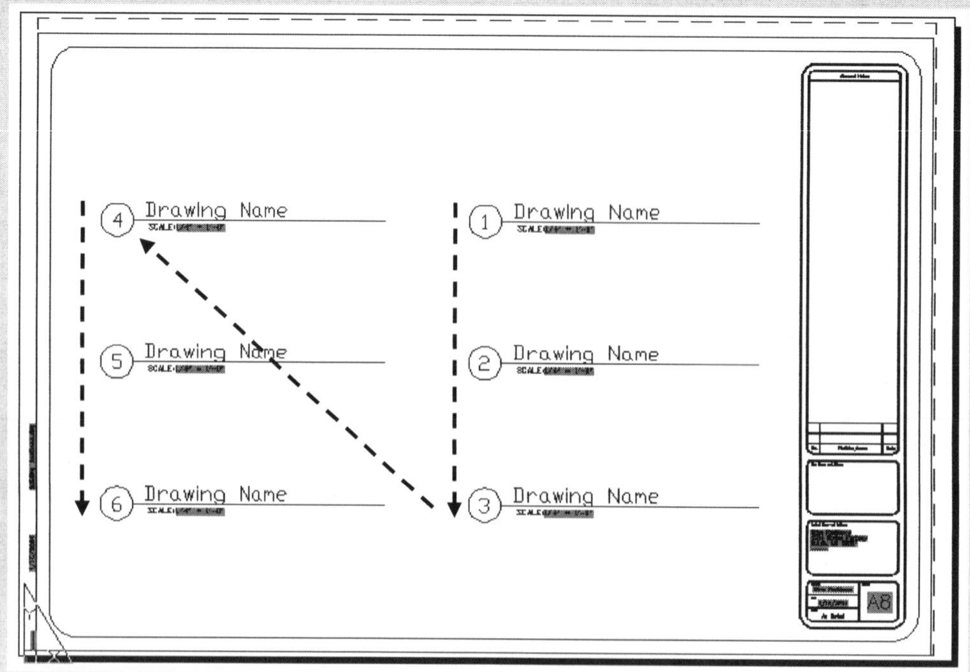

64. Place **Callout** blocks on your floor plan sheets to reference all your elevations. See Figure 8-2.34.

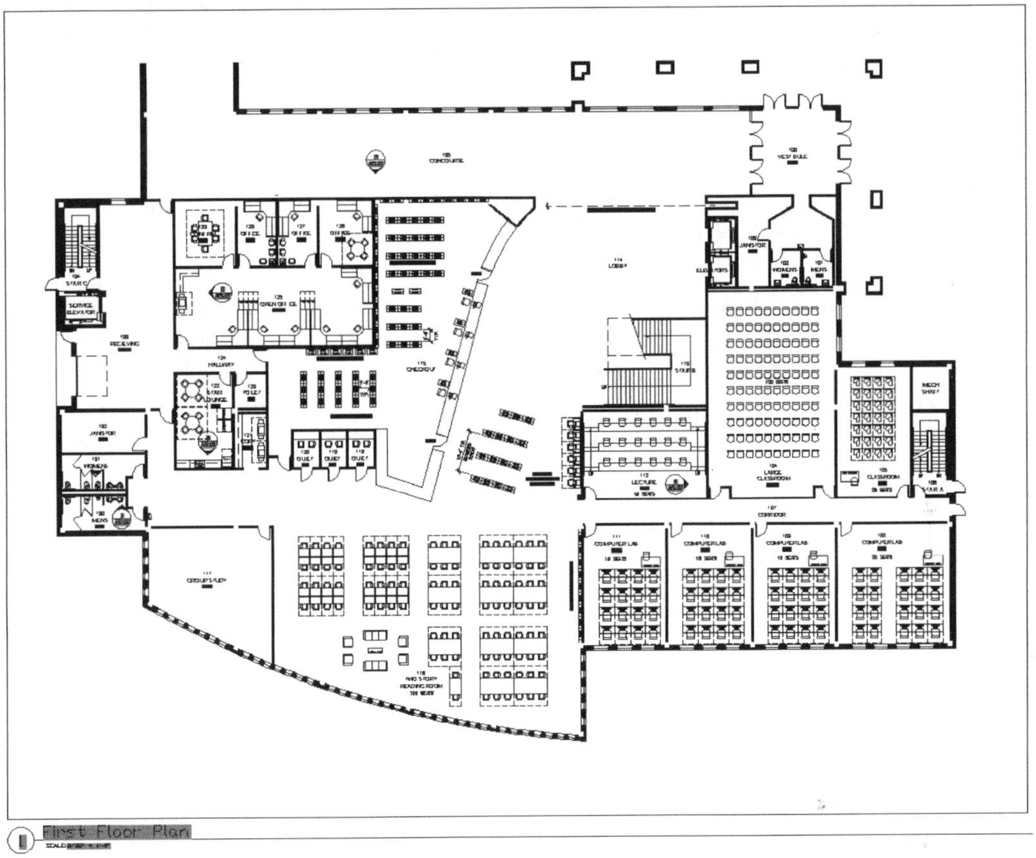

FIGURE 8-2.34
A2.01 – First Floor Plan sheet; callout bubbles added

> ***TIP:*** *The rectangle surrounding your drawings when placed on a sheet (cf. Figure 8-2.34) is called a viewport. This line cannot be erased, but it can be moved to its own layer (e.g., viewport) and then that layer can be Frozen; the drawing will still be visible, but the rectangle (viewport) will not.*

65. **Save** and close all your open drawing files.

66. **Close** the Sheet Set data file via the *Sheet Set Manager;* right-click on the *Sheet Set* project name (i.e., Library Project) and select **Close Sheet Set**.

This concludes the study on *Sheet Sets.*

Manually Setting Up a Sheet:

On occasion you will want to know how to set up a sheet without using the *SheetSet Manager*. This will help you better understand what the *SheetSet Manager* is automatically doing for you every time you add a view to a sheet.

You will use the *Layout View* existing in your Flr-1 drawing. This tab came from the template you started from. Every drawing must have a *Model Space* tab and at least one *Layout View* (paper space) tab. If you recall, after creating each new drawing you had to switch to *Model Space* because the *Layout View* tab was current.

As previously stated, *Model Space* is where all the drawing is done, and *Layout View* is where the plot sheet is set up. On the plot sheet you draw a special rectangle, called a *Viewport*, that looks into *Model Space*. You can set the scale for the *Viewport*. Also, you can have several *Viewports* in the *Layout View*. They can each have a different scale if you need it, and they can look at the same drawing. That is, you can have one Viewport looking at the overall floor plan at 3/32″ = 1′-0″ and another looking at the toilet rooms only, at ¼″ = 1′-0″.

1. Open your **DJS55803apl01** drawing file. You do not need to have the *SheetSet Manager* open for this.

2. Switch to the **Arch D** *Layout View* tab (a.k.a., *Paper Space*).

3. Type **MV** to activate the *Make Viewport* command.

4. Pick two points on the screen to define the extents of the *Viewport* (Figure 8-2.35).

   You now see everything in *Model Space*, which is zoomed to fit the *Viewport*.

FIGURE 8-2.35
Manually adding a viewport

5. Select the *Viewport*, and set the scale to 3/32″ = 1′-0″ via the *Status Bar* (Figure 8-2.36)

The scale is now set correctly. Sometimes it is necessary to pan the drawing within the *Viewport*. This can be done by double-clicking within the *Viewport* and using the *Pan* command. Be careful not to zoom as this will mess up the scale. When finished, double-click outside of the *Viewport* or select the Model button on the Status Bar (which says Paper when you are not in the Viewport).

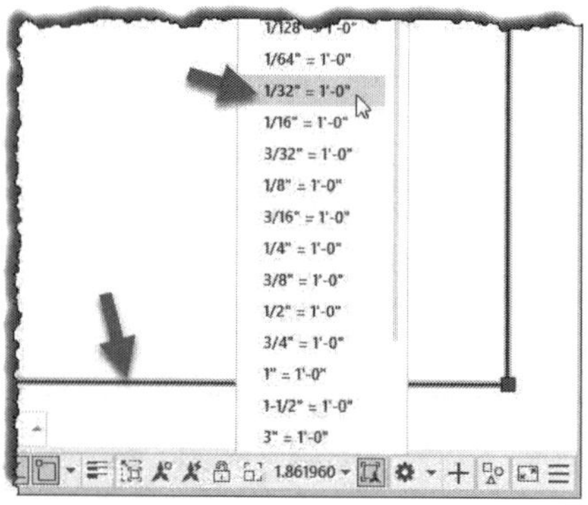

FIGURE 8-2.36
Setting the scale for the selected viewport

When the *Viewport* is selected you may also click the **Lock** icon on the Status Bar to lock the scale for the selected *Viewport* so it does not accidentally change (see image below).

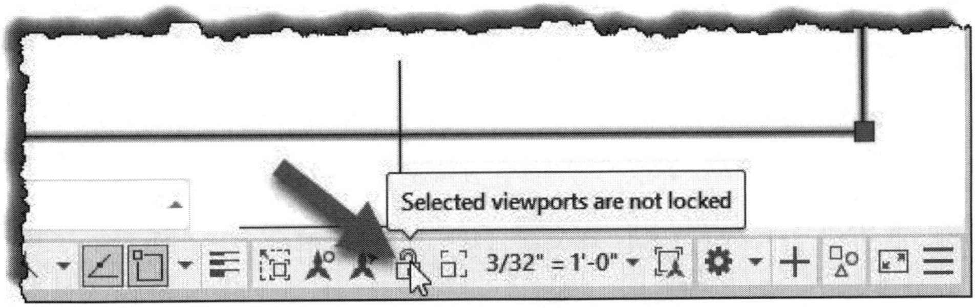

FIGURE 8-2.37 Locking the scale of a manually created viewport

6. Create another *Viewport* as shown in the image below (a smaller rectangle within the larger one), zoom in on the toilet room and set the scale to **¼″ = 1′-0″**.

   TIP: *Press* Ctrl+R *to toggle between* Viewports *once one is active.*

7. Create a *Layer* called **Viewport**, move the two *Viewports* to this *Layer* and turn its visibility off.

8. **Save** your Flr-1 drawing file.

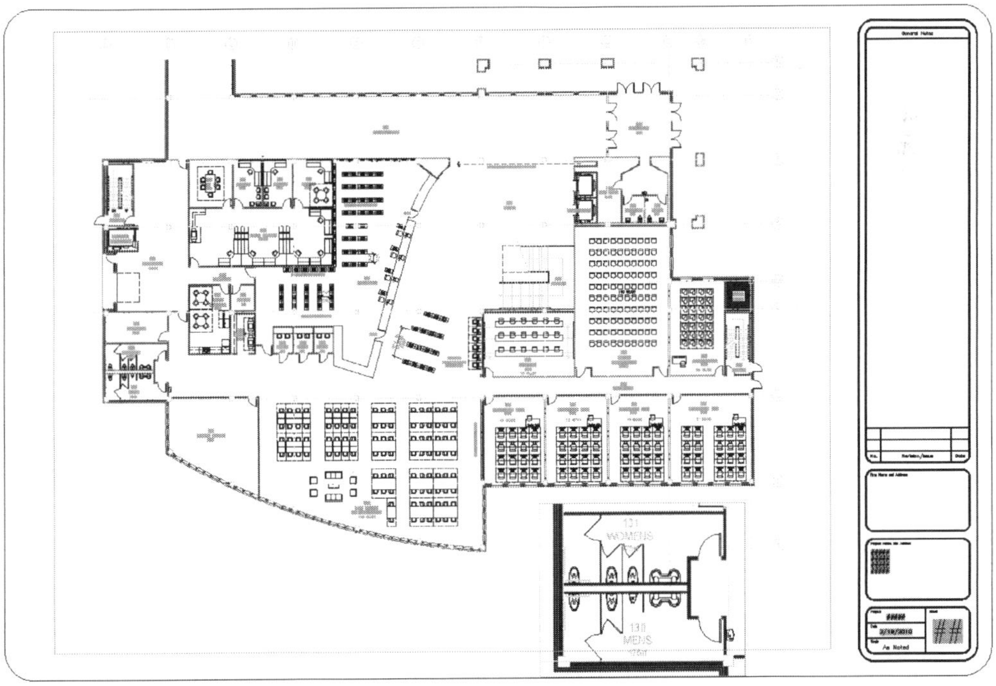

FIGURE 8-2.38 Two viewports created

Exercise 8-3:
Sheet Index

Introduction:

In this exercise you will take a look at the *Sheet Index* feature that takes advantage of both *Sheet Sets* and *Tables*. The *Sheet Index* feature extracts information stored in the *Sheet Set Data* file (sheet name and number) and then generates a *Table* to be placed on one of your sheets in the *Sheet Set.*

The *Sheet Index* also has hyperlinks embedded in each listing; thus, you can "Ctrl + click" on a sheet name or number to open that sheet. As you will see in the next Lesson, these hyperlinks transfer to the electronic set (DWF file) which allows a client or consultant to easily navigate the set of drawings.

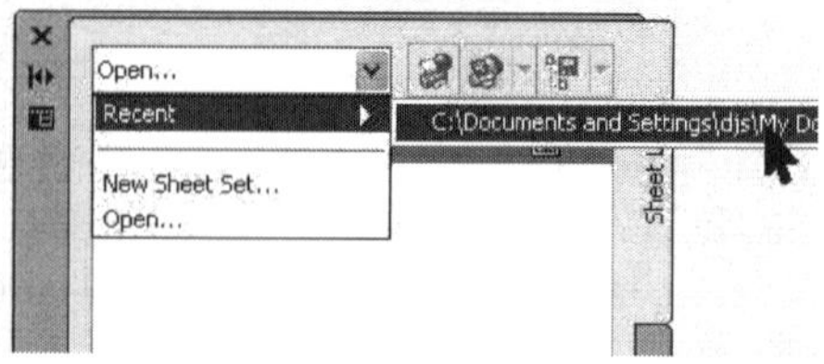

Opening an existing Sheet Set; via *Recent* flyout or *Open...* and browse

1. **Open** your *Sheet Set Data* file (*Library Project*.dst).

2. Open **G0.01 – Title Sheet** from the *Sheet List* tab.

3. Using *Mtext*, add large, bold text as shown in **Figure 8-3.1**.

   TIP: Use the Bold text style throughout.

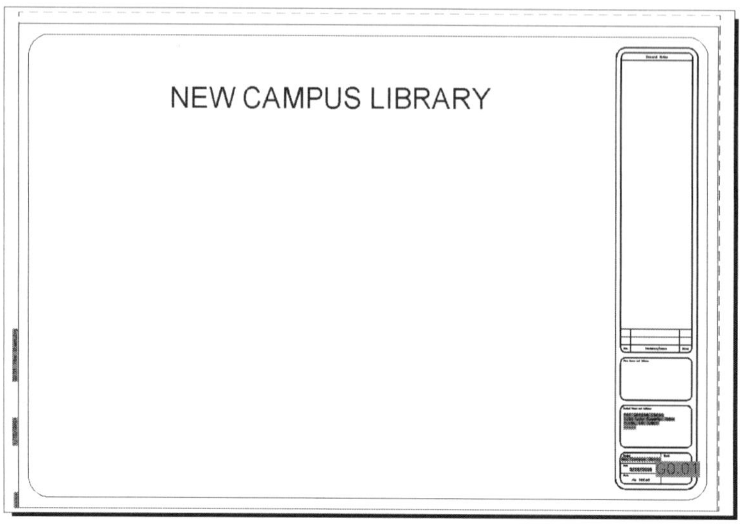

FIGURE 8-3.1 G0.01 – Title Sheet; text added to sheet

FYI: *A title sheet usually has the project title as its focal point. Additionally, you will typically find the following information:*

- *Rendering or picture of a model of the project*
- *Sheet Index*
- *Abbreviation Legend (e.g., TYP. means TYPICAL)*
- *Symbol Legend (e.g., show a swatch of AR-CONC hatch pattern and identify it as the symbol for concrete)*
- *Building Code/Zoning Summary*
- *Site Plan (typically on smaller projects)*

The Legends, which are used over and over, without modification, can be created in a separate drawing and inserted as a block on the Title Sheet.

Next you will insert a sheet index.

4. Right click on the *Sheet Set* project title (at the top of the list on the **Sheet List** tab).

5. Select **Insert Sheet List Table…** from the pop-up menu (Figure 8-3.2).

You are now in the *Insert Sheet List Table* dialog (Figure 8-3.3).

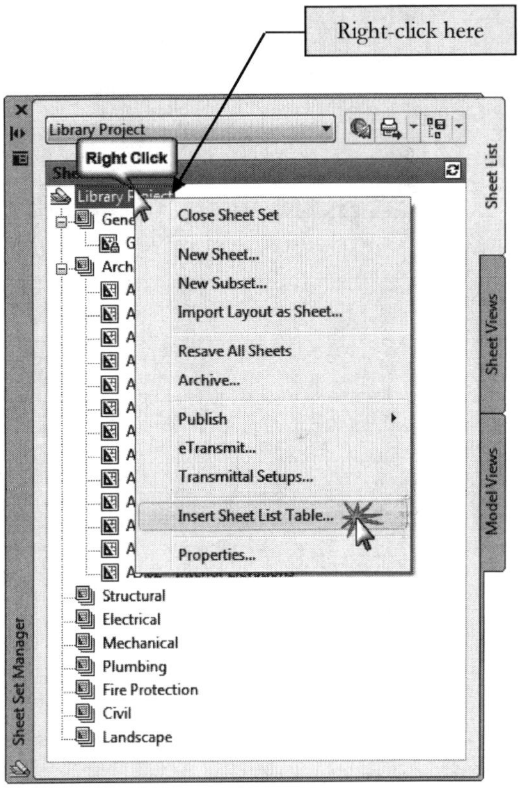

FIGURE 8-3.2
Sheet Set Manager; right click on project title (Library Project in this example)

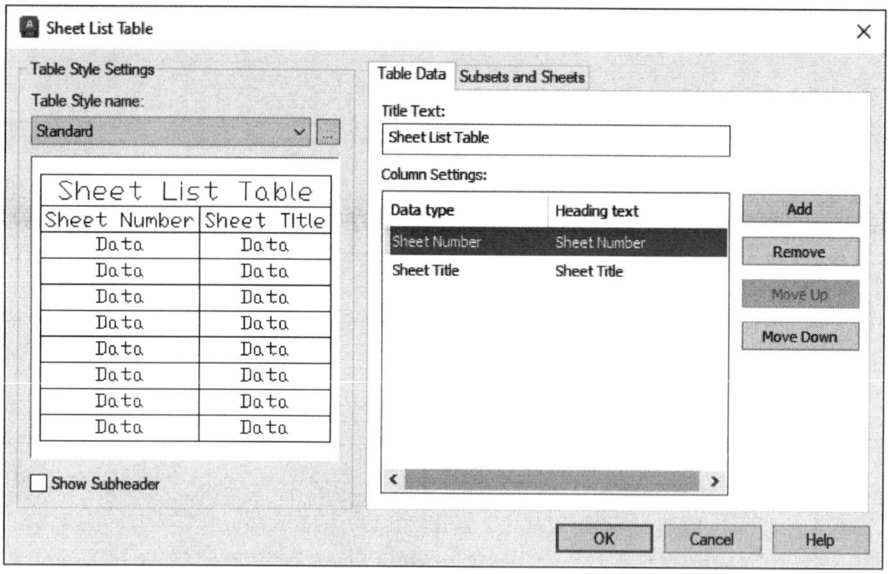

FIGURE 8-3.3 Insert Sheet List Table dialog

6. Click **OK** to close the dialog.
7. The sheet index is now ready to be placed on your title sheet.
8. Click anywhere on your *C0.01 - Title Sheet* to place the *Sheet List* table.

The table is now placed on your Title Sheet (Figure 8-3.4).

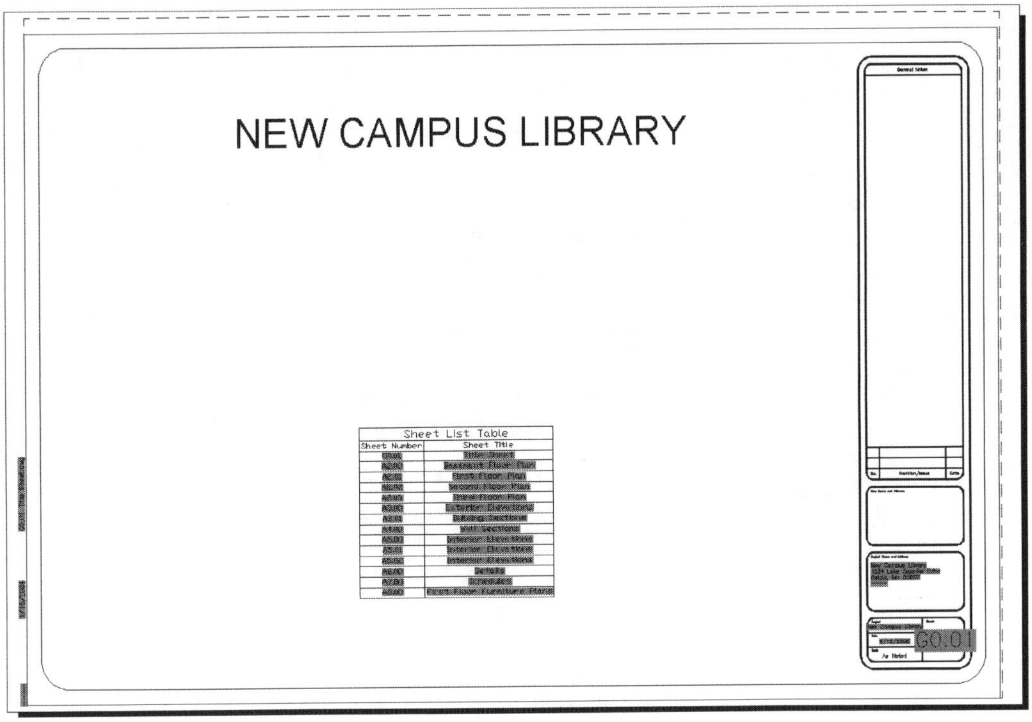

FIGURE 8-3.4 G0.01 – Title Sheet; inserted sheet list table

After inserting the *Sheet List*, you decide to change the justification of the data cell so that everything is left justified. You will make this change now…

9. Click on the table to select it.

10. From the *Annotate tab*, select **Table Style** link (small arrow in lower-right of the *Table* panel).

11. Select the **Standard** style and click the **Modify** button in the *Table Style Manager.*

12. Set *Cell Style* to **Data**.

13. Set the *Alignment* to **Top Left** on the *General* tab.

14. Click **OK** to close all the open dialog boxes.

As you can see, this is the same process previously described in the Room Finish Schedule exercise, because the Sheet List is a table!

Sheet List Table	
Sheet Number	Sheet Title
G0.01	Title Sheet
A2.00	Basement Floor Plan
A2.01	First Floor Plan
A2.02	Second Floor Plan
A2.03	Third Floor Plan
A3.00	Exterior Elevations
A3.01	Building Sections
A4.00	Wall Sections
A5.00	Interior Elevations
A5.01	Interior Elevations
A5.02	Interior Elevations
A6.00	Details
A7.00	Schedules
A8.00	First Floor Furniture Plans

FIGURE 8-3.5 G0.01 – Title Sheet; modified sheet list table

If you change a sheet number via the *Sheet Set Manager*, the *Sheet List* will be automatically updated (you need to *Regen* to see the changes on any open sheets).

Inserting Raster Images into a Drawing:

While you still have your title sheet open, you will take a quick look at inserting a raster image in a drawing. This can be done in any drawing file. The process is similar to Xrefing a drawing.

This example will involve adding a raster image to the title sheet. Ideally, you would be adding a raster image that contains a rendering of the exterior of your building. However, because you do not have one at the moment, you will insert an image that is installed with AutoCAD 2027.

15. From the *Insert* tab, select the **Attach** icon. 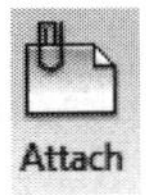

16. Browse to: **C:\Program Files\Autodesk\AutoCAD 2027 \Sample\VBA**.

17. Select the file **WorldMap.TIF** and click **OPEN** (Figure 8-3.6).

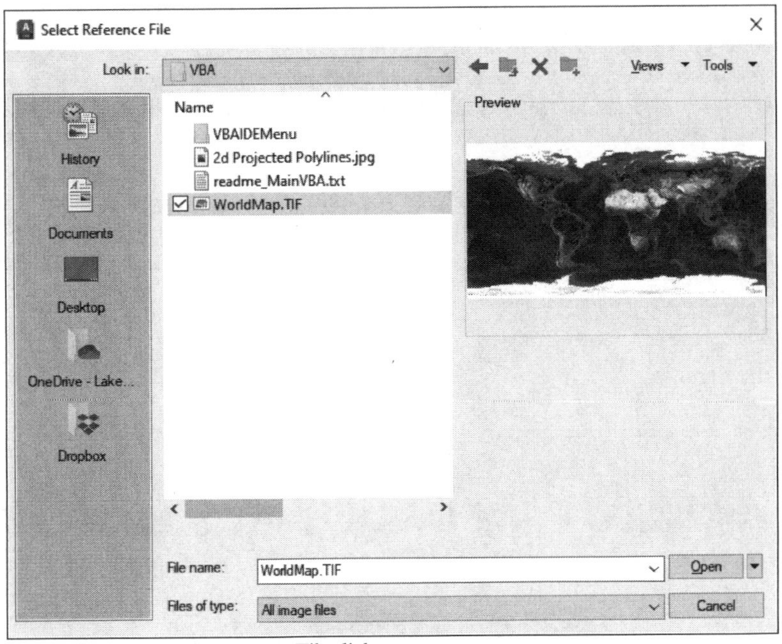

FIGURE 8-3.6 Select Image File dialog

You are now in a dialog which is similar to inserting external references (Xref's).

> ***FYI:*** *If you click the drop-down list next to* Files of type, *you can see the* *<u>many</u>* *file formats AutoCAD is able to work with (i.e., TIFF, JPG, etc.).*

18. Accept the default settings and click **OK** (Figure 8-3.7).

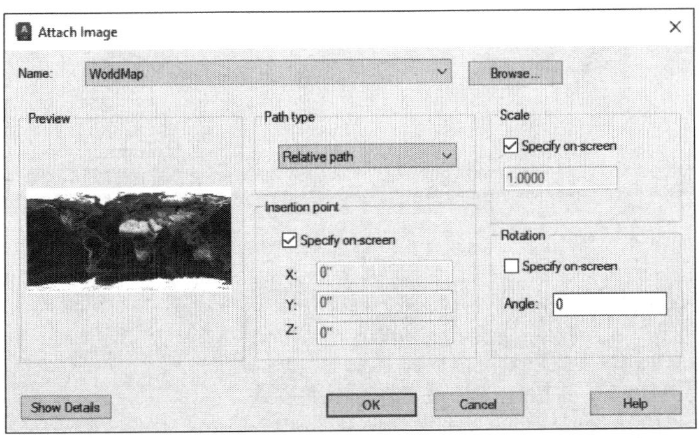

FIGURE 8-3.7 Image dialog

> ***TIP:*** *Click the Details button to view size and resolution information for the selected image file.*

You now see the image outline near your cursor for insertion. Click to place the image approximately centered below your large text. At this point, you can visually move the mouse to adjust the image size or type a value (you will accept the default value of 1).

19. Press **Enter** to accept the default scale of 1.

    FYI: *The image can be moved, rotated, scaled, erased at any time (after insertion) using the standard AutoCAD commands.*

    TIP: *If you don't want the rectangle around the image, you can turn it off using the* ***imageframe*** *variable. The default value is* ***1****, which makes the outline show and plot;* ***0*** *makes the outline invisible and the image is not selectable (i.e., you cannot move, scale, etc.);* ***2*** *makes the outline show but not plot.*

20. **Move** the *Sheet Index* to center it under the image.

The title sheet should now look like Figure 8-3.8.

FYI: *You can detach or unload images via the External References Palette… (See the next page.)*

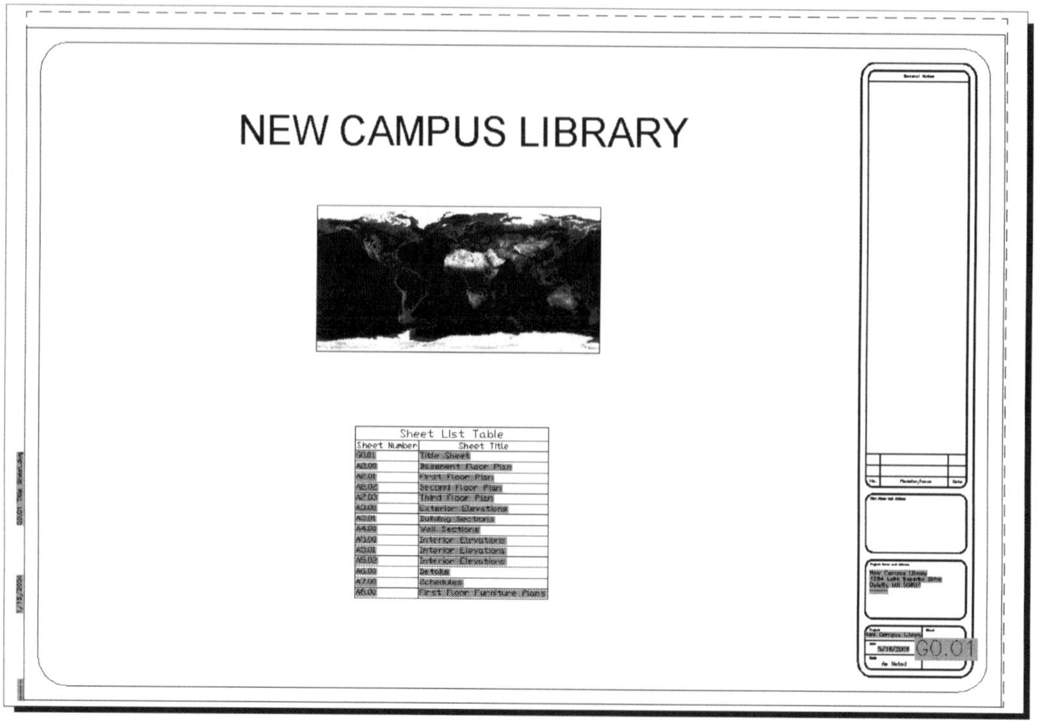

FIGURE 8-3.8

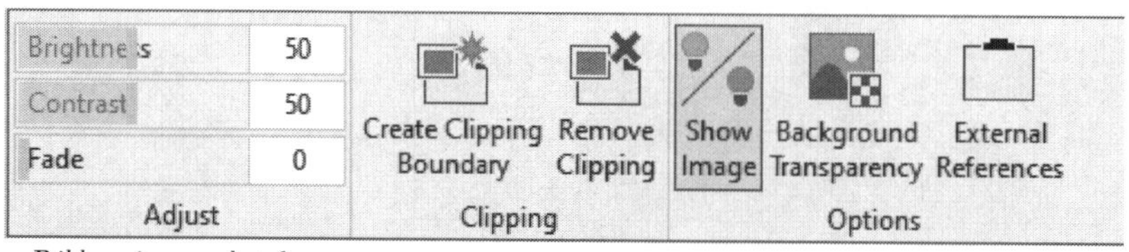

Ribbon; image selected

If you select the image and then right-click, you will see a few options for editing the selected image. Selecting **External References…** from the *Insert* tab loads a palette that shows all referenced files. Notice the *Ribbon* has several settings related to the image when it is selected (see images at the top of the next page).

You can also scan a blueprint of a floor plan (or anything else) and use the scanned file to trace over with AutoCAD lines. You need to use *Scale* and its subcommand *Reference* to accurately adjust the size of the image before tracing.

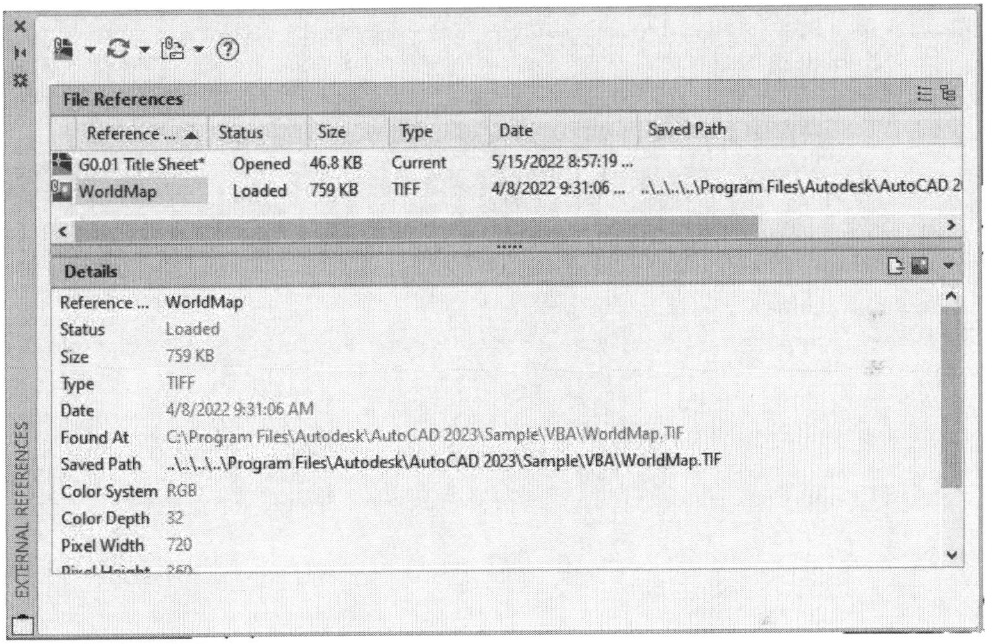

External Reference Palette

You can also place photos of existing conditions on a sheet and add (AutoCAD) notes and leaders on top of the photo. For example, point out an entry roof to be removed on the front of a building (see example image to left from an AutoCAD drawing).

21. **Save** your **G0.01 – Title Sheet** drawing.

This completes the introduction to sheet list tables and raster images.

Self-Exam:

The following questions can be used as a way to check your knowledge of this lesson. The answers can be found at the bottom of this page.

1. The Table Style Manager is where you change a table's text height. (T/F)

2. You need to create Named Views for each drawing/detail that you want to place on a sheet. (T/F)

3. Once a Sheet List table is placed you have to manually update it if you add or remove any sheets. (T/F)

4. When dragging a view from the Sheet Set Manager onto a sheet, you _______________ to get a listing of scales to insert the view at.

5. In the Named Views dialog, you can change the view's boundary. (T/F)

Review Questions:

The following questions may be assigned by your instructor as a way to assess your knowledge of this section. Your instructor has the answers to the review questions.

1. Once a Table is created, you cannot add rows or columns. (T/F)

2. It is not possible to combine two or more table cells into one. (T/F)

3. AutoCAD creates a drawing file each time you create a new sheet in the Sheet Set Manager. (T/F)

4. Views are placed on sheets by dragging the view name from the _______________ tab; views are numbered (and renamed) on the _________________ tab in the Sheet Set Manager.

5. You cannot specify where the Sheet Set Data file is stored. (T/F)

6. The bottom number, in an elevation callout bubble, indicates the _________________ number the elevation is located on.

7. This icon () allows you to insert a ____________________________.

8. AutoCAD can only insert TIFF format raster images. (T/F)

9. You should not move or rename the files created by the Sheet Set Manager (except what you are able to do in the Manager itself). (T/F)

10. You right-click on the ____________ to see the insert Sheet List option.

SELF-EXAM ANSWERS:
1 – T, **2** – T, **3** – F, **4** – right-click, **5** – T

Lesson 9
Library Project: PLOTTING

In this final lesson you will look at how lineweights work in AutoCAD. Finally, you will take another look at plotting; this time plotting to scale from the Sheet Set Manager.

Exercise 9-1:
Plotting: Digital Set

Introduction:

In this exercise, you will learn how to quickly and easily publish your entire set of drawings to a single file that can be viewed and printed by downloading a free viewer from Autodesk (allowing clients to view drawings without the need to own AutoCAD).

The file is referred to as a Design Web Format (DWF). A DWF is smaller than the drawing file because it is only for viewing and printing, not editing. They can even be password protected. In fact, one of the best things about DWFs is that they cannot be edited. Thus, you can share the DWF set with a client or contractor and not have to worry about them accidentally (or purposefully) changing the drawings.

The first thing you need to do is adjust the Page Setup in each "sheet" drawing, so the "sheets" are ready to plot.

1. **Open** your sheet **A2.00 – Basement Floor Plan** from the *Sheet Set Manager* (See Exercise 8-1 for instruction on this).

2. Right-click the A2.00 Basement Floor Plan *Layout view* tab and then Click **Page Setup Manager**.

FYI: When in a sheet opened via the Sheet Set Manager, you are in a Layout View by default. This is where "sheets" are plotted from.

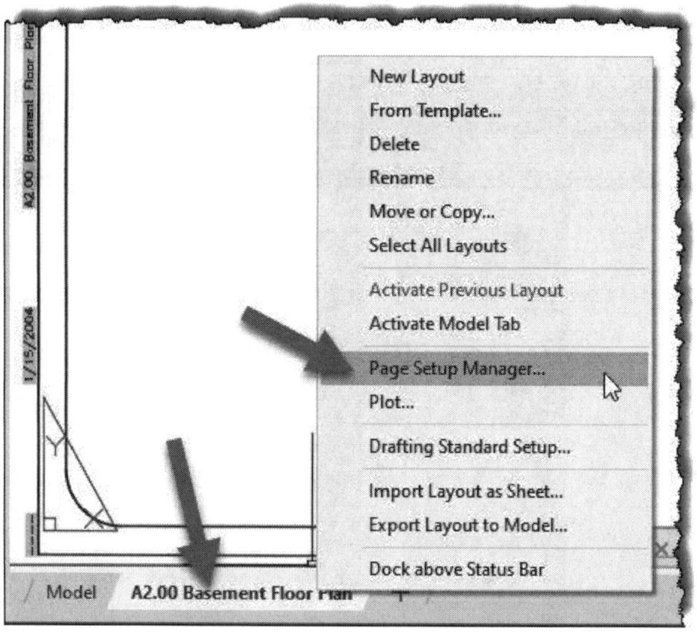

FIGURE 9-1.1 A2.00 – Basement Floor Plan; notice the Layout tab is active

You are now in the *Page Setup Manager* dialog for the current drawing.

3. With ***A2.00Basement Floor Plan*** selected, click the **Modify…** button (Figure 9-1.2).

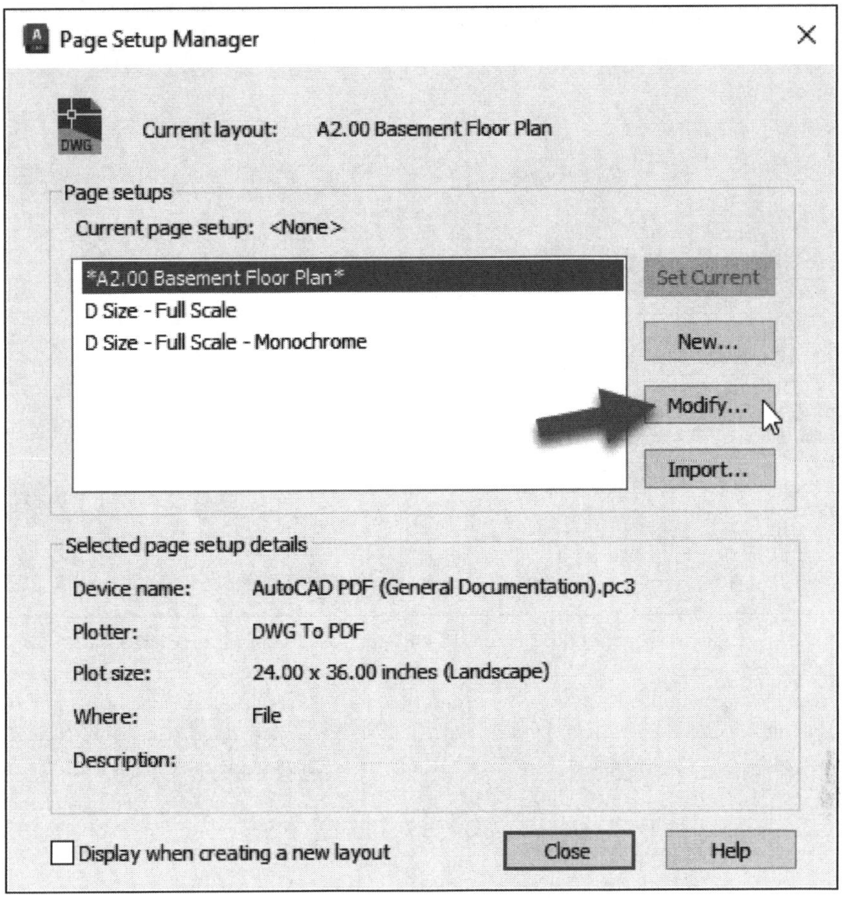

FIGURE 9-1.2 Page Setup Manager; modify the default layout settings

4. Select your *Plot Style Table* (created in Appendix A), named: *yourname*-Full.ctb (Figure 9-1.3).

5. **Check** the "*Display Plot Styles*" option just below the selected *Plot Style Table* (Figure 9-1.3).

Notice how this dialog box is similar to the *Plot* dialog box? Well this makes sense when you consider the settings in the *Page Setup* dialog are the defaults for plotting.

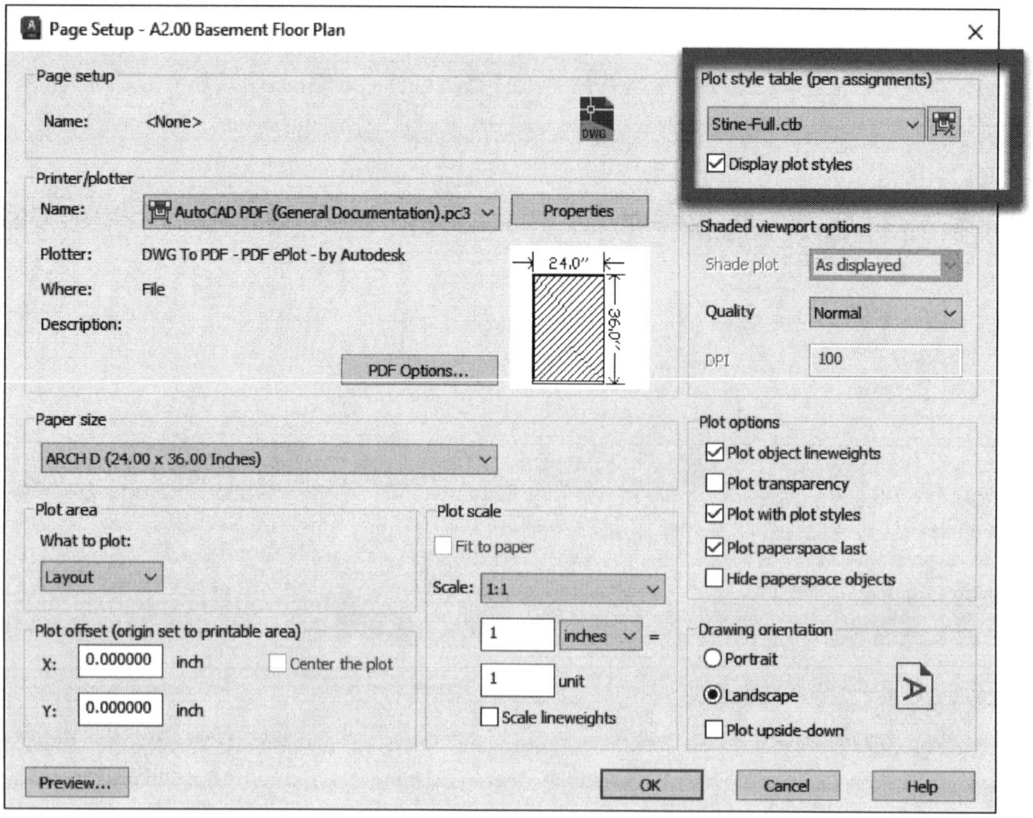

FIGURE 9-1.3 Page Setup – A2.00 Basement Floor Plan; select your plot style table

FYI: Checking the Display plot style box tells AutoCAD to display the drawing in the Layout View more like the way it will plot (e.g. black and white rather than color).

6. Click **OK** and then **Close** to exit the open dialog boxes.

7. **Save** and **Close** the *Basement Floor Plan* sheet drawing.

8. Now open each sheet in your *Sheet Set* and make the same modification; **Save** and **Close** each drawing when done.

Now you will look at the *Options* related to *Publishing* "sheets" from the *Sheet Set Managers.*

9. If not open, **Open** your *Sheet Set Data* file (see Exercise 8-2).

10. Right-click on the *Sheet Set* project title (*Library Project* in this example). See Figure 9-1.4.

11. Select **Publish → Sheet Set DWF Publish Options…** (Figure 9-1.4).

TIP: At least one drawing must be open to access this feature.

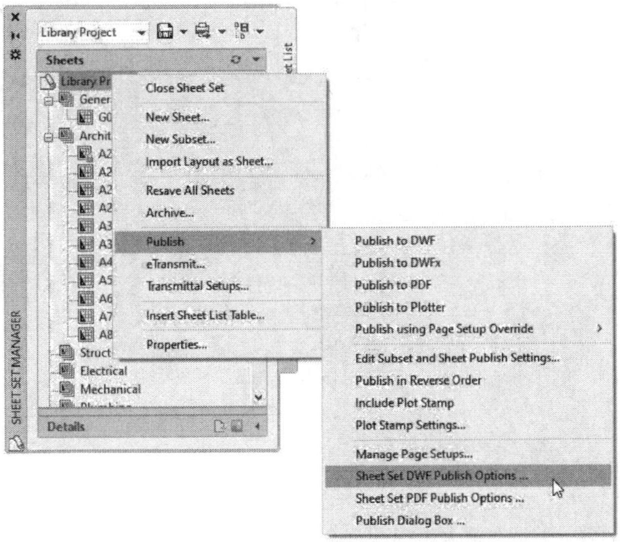

FIGURE 9-1.4
Sheet Set Manager – right-click menu for sheet set label (Library Project in this example)

Take a minute to notice the various options available for publishing sheets from the *Sheet Set Manager*; see Figure 9-1.5.

- **Default output directory (plot-to-file)**
  Here you can specify a default location to save a file to.

- **File type**
  When **Single-sheet** is selected, each sheet is created as a separate **DWFx** file. When **Multi-sheet** is selected, all sheets are published into one DWFx file. You can also create **PDF** files and the older **DWF** file (without the "x").

- **DWF naming**
  Here you can specify the file name or have AutoCAD prompt you for the name each time you publish; this option is only available if **Multi-sheet** is selected above.

- **Password Protect**
  Allows you to assign a password to the DWF file. When a password is assigned, you, and anyone you send the file to, will need to know the password to view the DWF file.

- **Layer information**
  Allows you to include the AutoCAD layers in the DWF file. With this option selected, you can control *Layer* visibility in the DWF file viewer; for example, turn off dimensions and notes to print a clean plan.

- **3D DWF**
  Controls settings related to 3D drawing information.

  FYI: You are only drawing 2D information in this book.

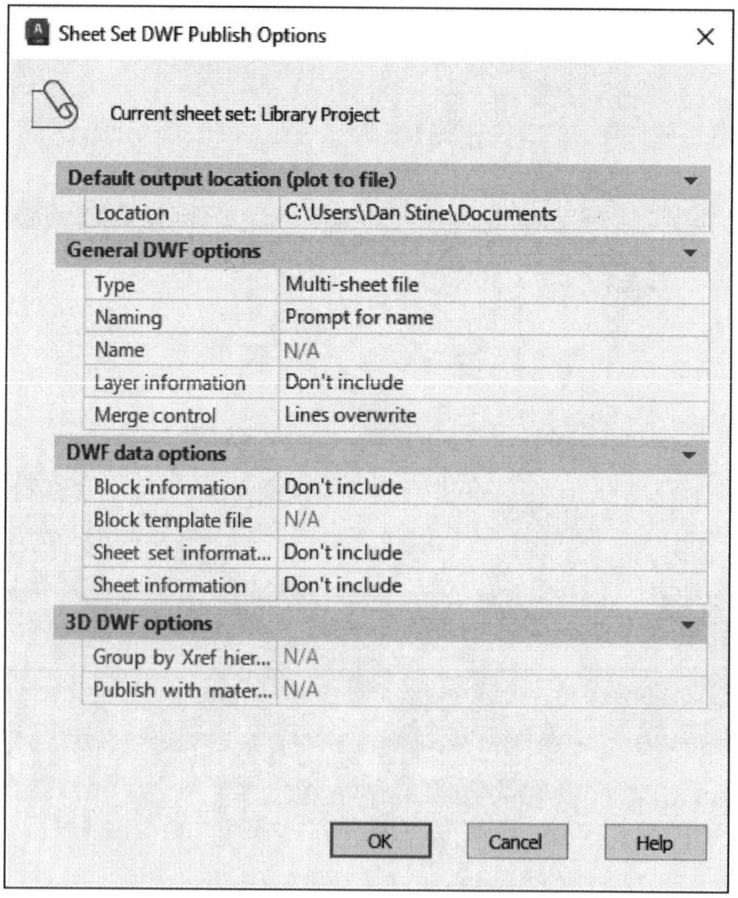

FIGURE 9-1.5 Sheet Set Publish Options – default settings shown

12. Accept the default options and click **OK**.

13. Right-click on the *Sheet Set* project title (*Library Project* in this example). See Figure 9-1.4.

14. **Publish → Publish to DWFx** (Figure 9-1.4).

You are now prompted to specify the name and location for the DWFx file. Notice, though, that the default location is "My Documents", which is the specified folder in the *Publish Options* dialog. AutoCAD suggests the *Sheet Set* project name for the file name; you will accept that name next.

15. Browse to your project folder, accept the suggested file name and then click **Select** to start the Publishing process; also, click **OK** if you get the prompt at the bottom of this page (Figure 9-1.6).

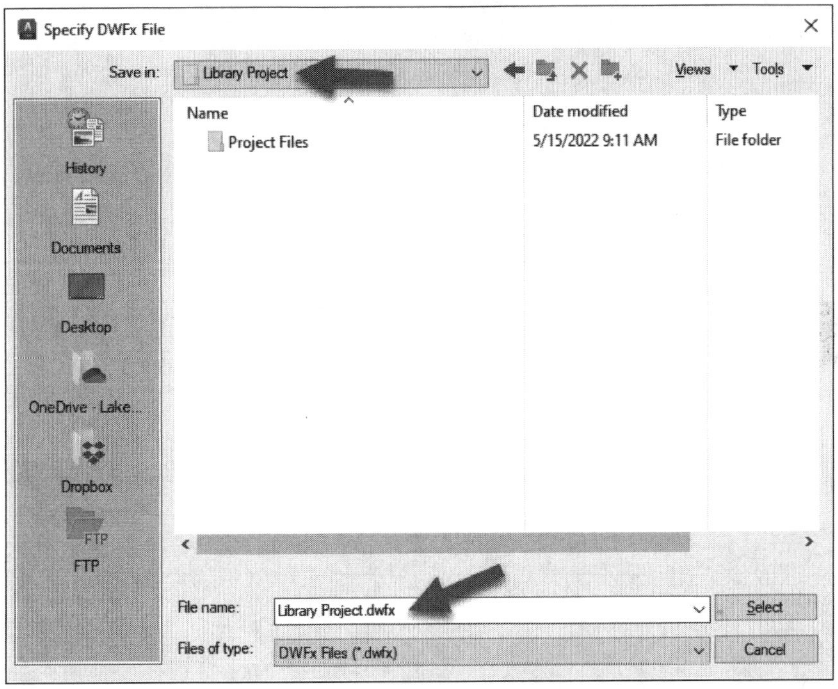

FIGURE 9-1.6 Select DWF File dialog– specify DWF file name and location

AutoCAD now begins to publish each drawing to the DWFx file you specified. The *Publish* routine runs in the background so you can continue to work. Depending on your computer speed, a set this size might take five to 15 minutes. AutoCAD has to open each file and plot it.

AutoCAD provides a small "plotter" icon on the right-hand side of the status bar. You can hover your cursor over this icon to see a tooltip that displays the status of the background Publish project (Figure 9-1.7).

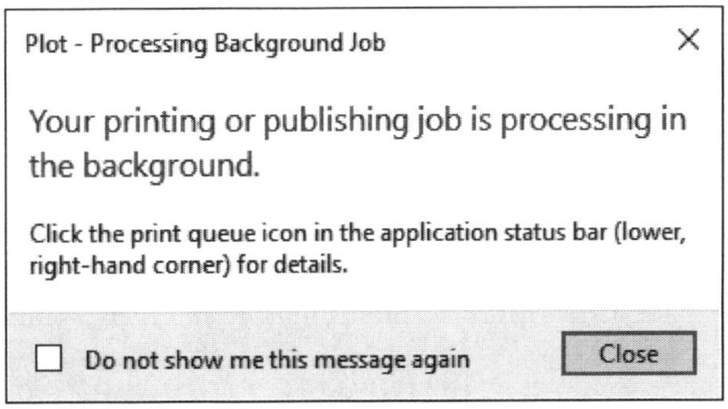

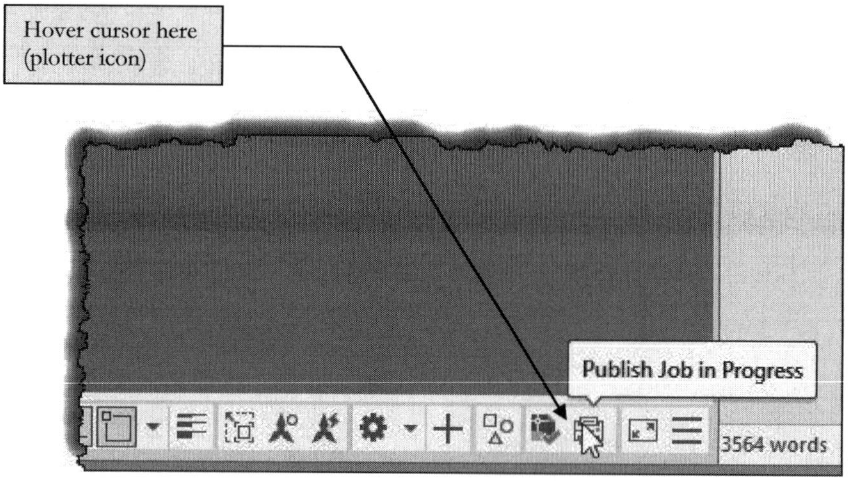

FIGURE 9-1.7 Plot and Publish Status Icon: hover cursor over icon to display status tooltip

When the publishing process is complete, a balloon message will be displayed (Figure 9-1.8) indicating such, and also provides a link to a report. You will take a quick peek at the report before viewing the DWFx file.

FIGURE 9-1.8
Plot and Publish Status Icon: balloon notification that job is complete

16. Click on the link "*Click to view plot and publish details…*" in the *Plot and Publish* balloon notification message (Figure 9-1.8).

Notice the report lists the date, number of sheets, the location of each plotted file and the location of the DWFx file (Figure 9-1.9).

17. Click **Close** to close the *Plot and Publish* window.

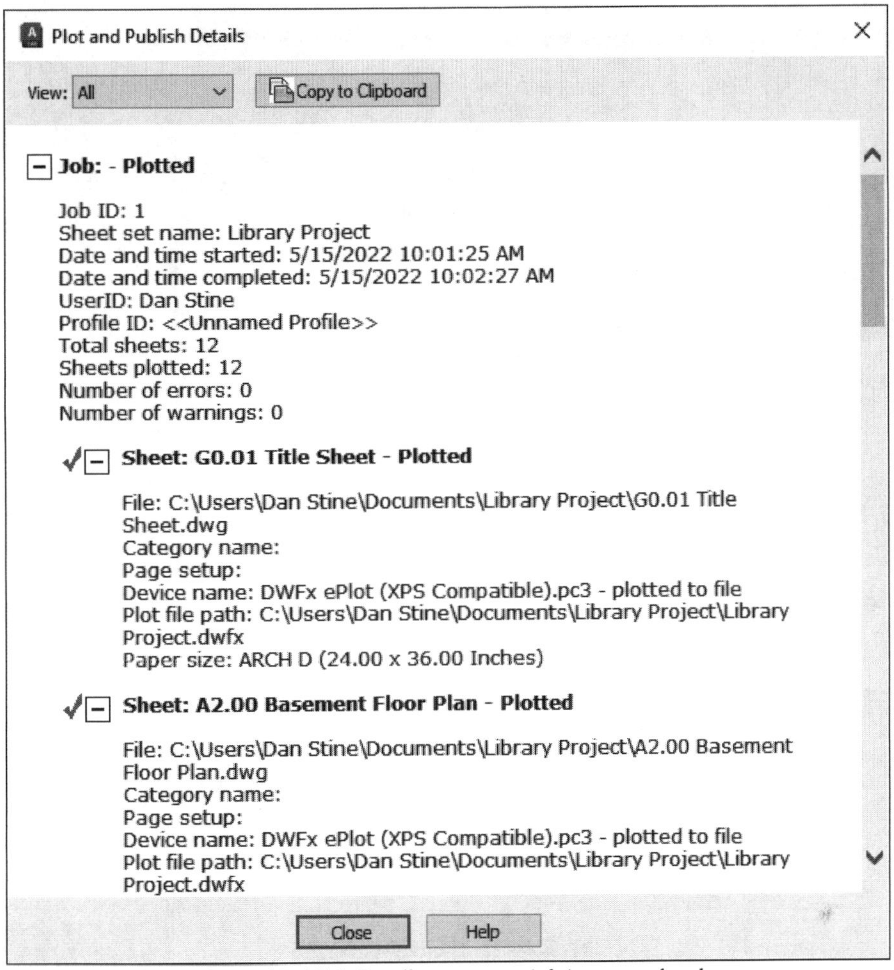

FIGURE 9-1.9 Plot and Publish Details: report on job just completed

Viewing the DWFx File:

Next you will view the DWF file using the *Autodesk Design Review* – which needs to be installed first. You can view this file by double-clicking the file in *Windows Explorer*, or you can access the file from the *Plot and Publish Icon.*

Download here: https://www.autodesk.com/products/design-review/overview

18. Right-click on the *Plot and Publish Icon* on the right side of the *Status Bar.*

19. Select **View Plotted File…** from the pop-up menu (Figure 9-1.10).

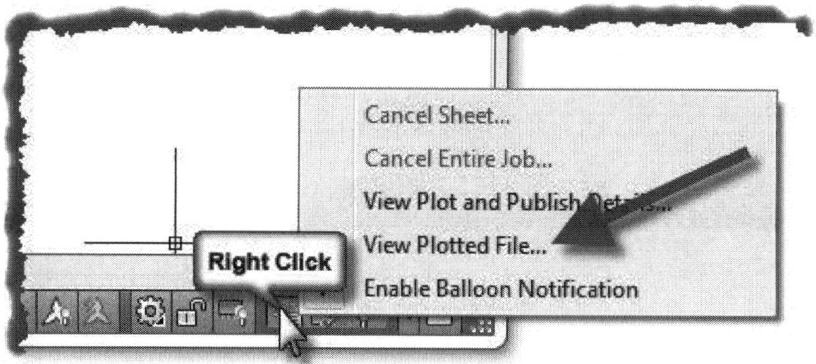

FIGURE 9-1.10 Plot and Publish Icon Menu; right-click on icon to see menu

A totally separate program (*Autodesk Design Review*) now opens with the DWF project you just created (Figure 9-1.11).

The Viewer allows you (or a client) to zoom, pan, redline and print the sheets in the multi-sheet DWF file.

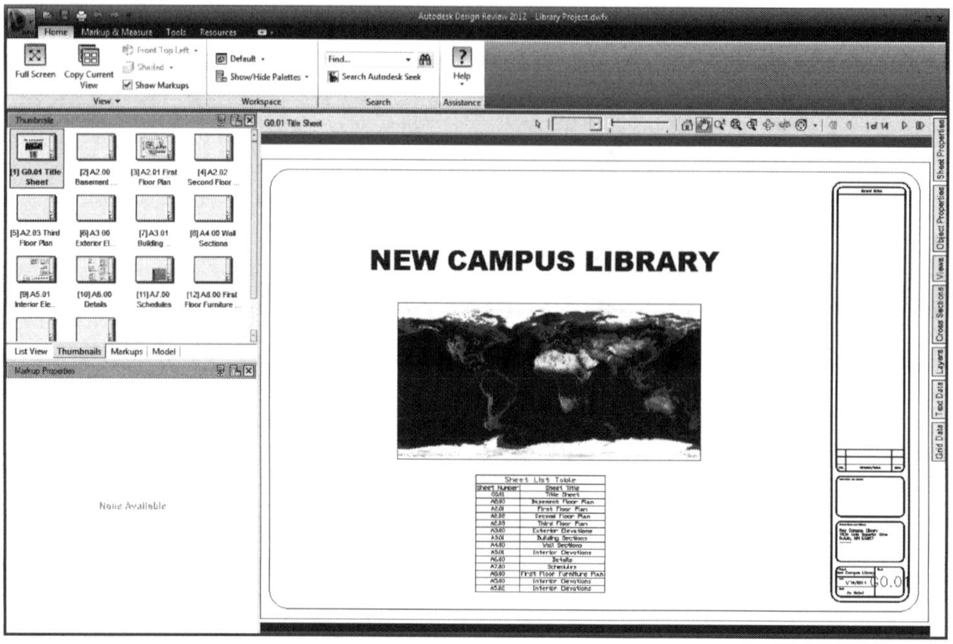

FIGURE 9-1.11 Autodesk Design Review (DWF file viewer); your residential project loaded

You can view the various sheets in the DWF file by either clicking on one of the *Thumbnail* images on the left or by clicking the right/left arrows on the toolbar (in the upper right).

A DWF file is still a vector-based file, so, like the DWG file, you can zoom in really far and not see any pixelating of the image. These drawings also have all your line weights assigned in them so your drawings will print accurately.

Next you will navigate to another sheet and zoom in to see the drawing's lineweights.

20. Scroll down in the *Thumbnails* pane until you see your **A5.01 Interior Elevations** sheet.

21. Click on the Thumbnail image to select it.

22. Using your wheel mouse (or the zoom icon), zoom in on the elevation as shown in **Figure 9-1.12.**

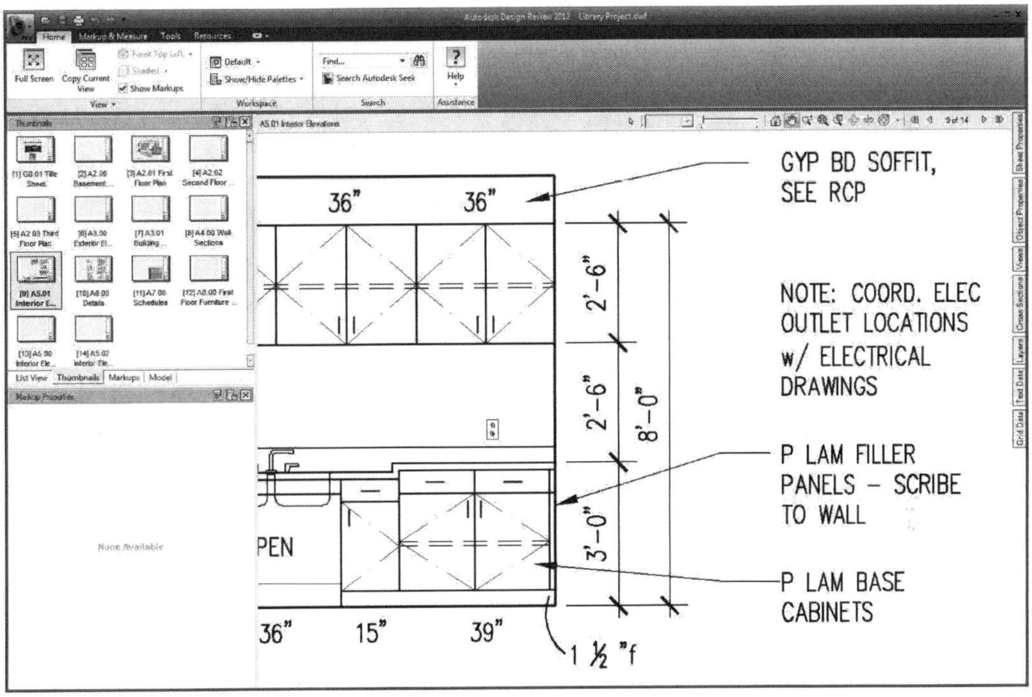

FIGURE 9-1.12 Autodesk Design Review; sheet A5.01 – Interior Elevations displayed

NOTE: In Figure 9-1.12, various lineweights can be seen in the elevation drawing.

Autodesk Design Review should have been automatically installed with AutoCAD 2027. If not you can download it for free at *www.autodesk.com/DWF*. As mentioned, you can instruct contractors and clients to download this program by giving them this web address; once they download and install the software, you can email them project files. They can actually redline and comment on the DWF and then you can link that file back in and see their comments superimposed on your drawing right in AutoCAD. DWFs can be referenced in just like the Xref command!

Hyperlink Feature in the Multi-Sheet DWF File:

Another great feature associated with *Sheet Sets* and multi-sheet DWF files is the hyper linking embedded in the sheet list and callout bubbles.

23. In your DWF file, switch back to the *Title Sheet* and zoom in on the *Sheet List.*

24. Hover your cursor over the "A2.01 – First Floor Plan" text to see the pop-up tooltip (Figure 9-1.13).

The pop-up tooltip displayed in Figure 9-1.13 indicates you can follow a link by clicking the text. You will try this next.

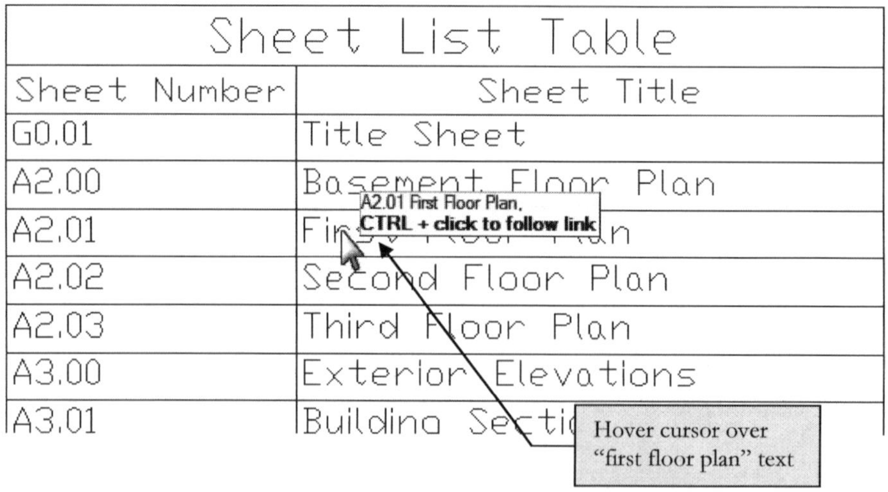

FIGURE 9-1.13 Multi-sheet DWF file; hyper linked text in Sheet List

25. Click the "**First Floor Plan**" text in the *Sheet List Table* location on the title sheet.

If you want the elevation tags to be linked to the sheets, you can select the tags back in AutoCAD and, via Properties, set the Hyperlink parameter as follows: **.\A5.01 Interior Elevations.dwg** (everything in bold including the preceding period must be entered).

As you can see this is an easy way for you or a client to navigate a set of drawings.

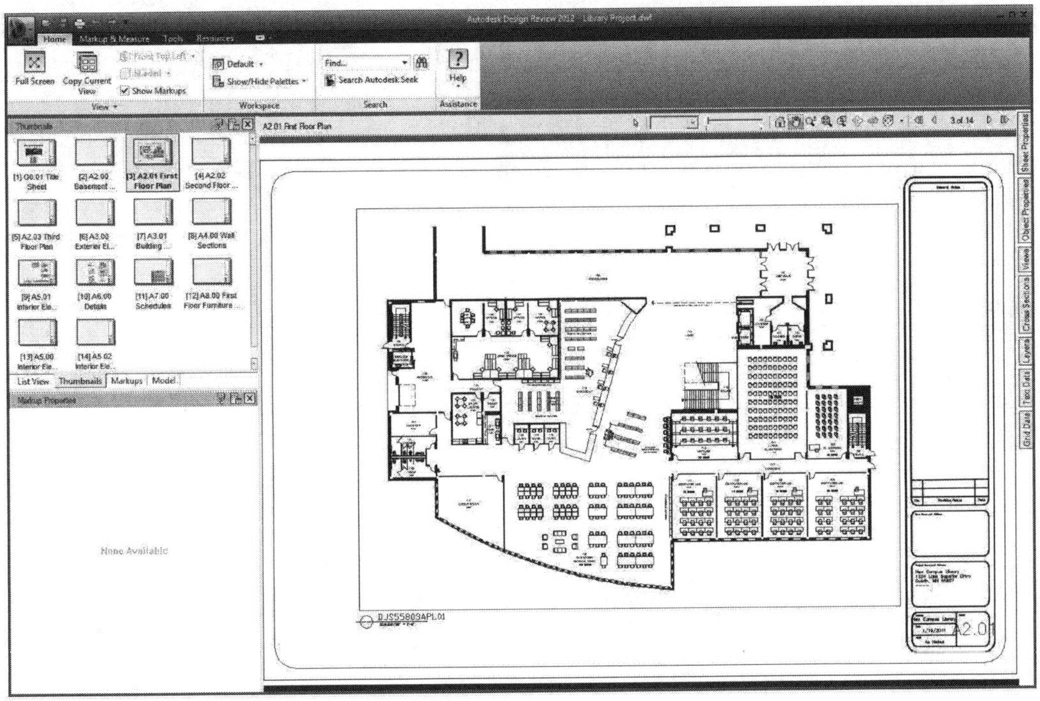

FIGURE 9-1.14 Multi-sheet DWF file; view displayed by clicking hyper-linked sheet index on title sheet

DWF files do not typically take up a lot of disk space. The DWF file just created should only be about 600kb; you can verify this with Window Explorer. Given the files small size, it can easily be emailed or loaded on a web site.

The Viewer's print dialog (Figure 9-1.15) allows you to print one sheet of the entire set to-scale on 24″x36″ paper <u>or</u> "Fit to page" on 8½″ x 11″ as you can see in Figure 9-1.15.

FYI: If you plan to create a DWFx file on a project, you can print your hard copy set(s) from this DWF file, eliminating the need to complete the steps outlined in the next section (9-2); which shows how to print directly to the plotter rather than to a DWF file.

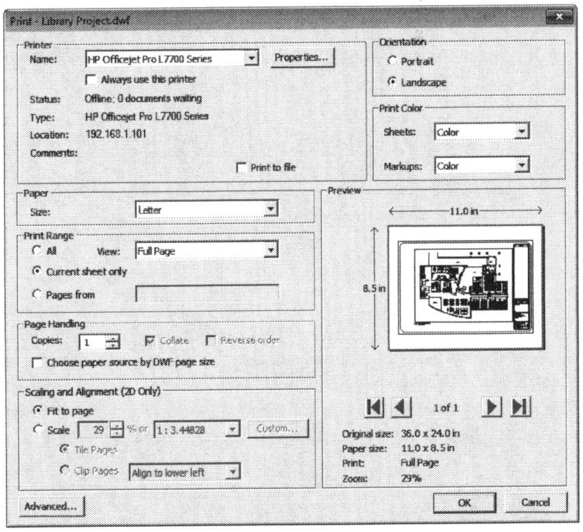

FIGURE 9-1.15 Autodesk DWF Viewer; print dialog box

Downloading the Autodesk Design Review:

If you will be sharing your DWFx files with someone that does not have a *DWFx Viewer* (***NOTE:*** *AutoCAD cannot open DWFx files directly - but you can xref them in)* installed on his or her computer, you can give them instructions on downloading the free program from Autodesk's website.

Using an internet browser, such as *Microsoft Edge*, go to https://www.autodesk.com/products/design-review/overview . Next, click to download *Autodesk Design Review.*

From the product's page (Figure 9-1.16), one can follow the onscreen directions to download and install the program.

26. **Save** and **Close** all files and programs to complete this exercise.

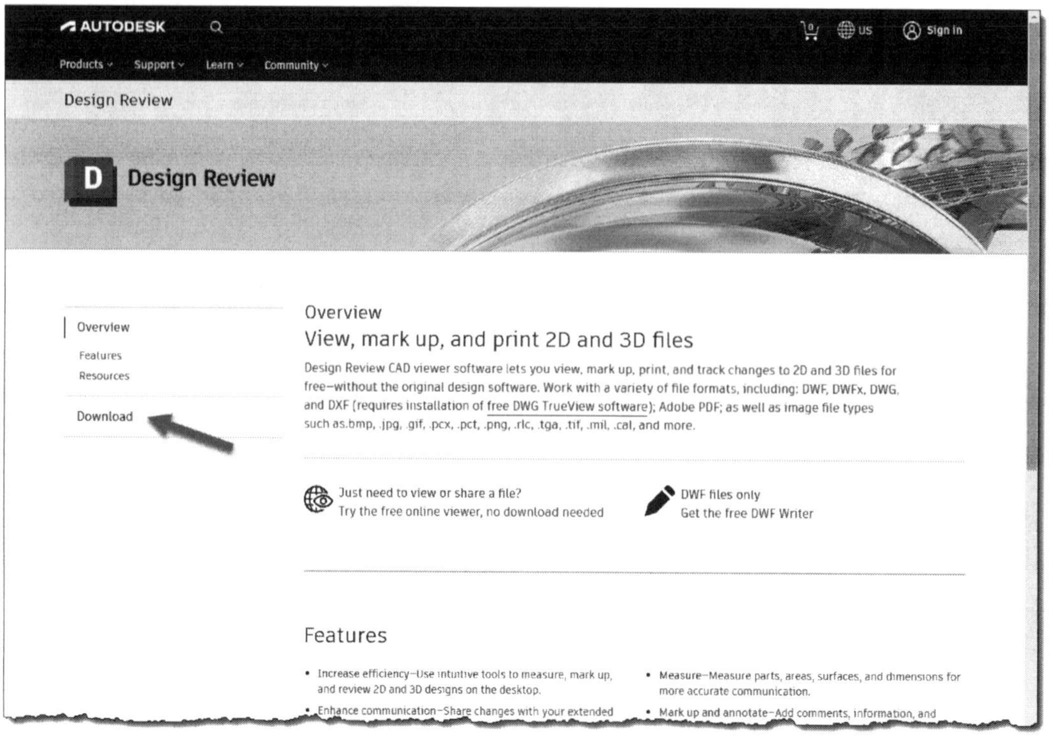

FIGURE 9-1.16 Autodesk website; DWF Community product page

Exercise 9-2:
Plotting: Hardcopy Set

Introduction:

In this final exercise you will look at a few settings that you should be aware of to create high-quality printouts (i.e., plots). You will look at plotting both from an individual sheet and from the Sheet Set Manager.

Xerox 510 Digital Solution
High speed B/W plotter + scanner

HP Designjet 1000 series
High quality color and B/W plotter

Page Setup Settings for your Layout View:

Page Setup allows you to pre-set things like scale and paper size. Each *Layout* view has its own *Page Setup* settings. The *Page Setup* dialog looks almost exactly like the *Plot* dialog. In fact, the *Plot* dialog box gets its initial settings from the current *Page Setup* settings. Again, each drawing file has its own *Page Setup* settings for each *Layout View* tab; this saves time when plotting because each drawing/*Layout View* can be pre-set and ready to plot.

1. **Open** your **A2.01 – First Floor Plan** "sheet" from the *Sheet Set Manager. (This can be opened directly from the Open command as well.)*

2. Right-click on the *Layout View* Tab and select **Page Setup Manager...** (See similar Figure 9-1.1)

You are now in the *Page Setup Manager.* Here you can create/modify named *Page Setups*, apply one to the current Layout and Import Page Setups from other drawings. You will modify an existing Page Setup.

3. Select **D Size – Full Scale** from the list and then select **Modify…** (Figure 9-2.1).

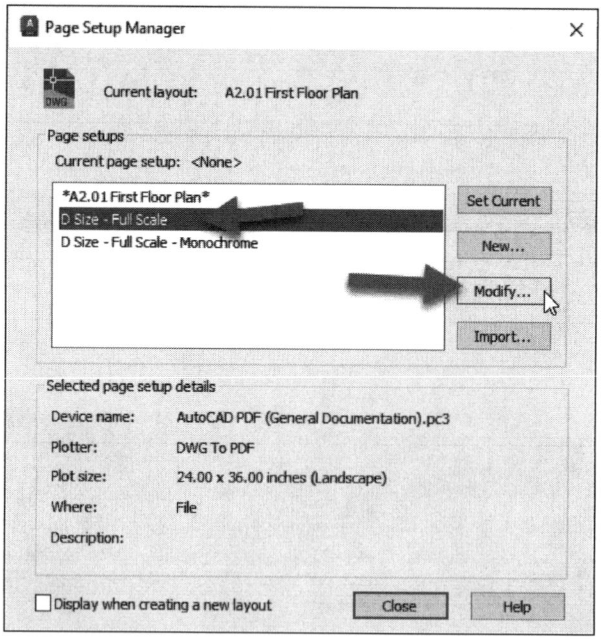

FIGURE 9-2.1
Page Setup Manager; Page Setup "D Size – Full Scale" selected

You are now in the Page Setup for "D Size – Full Scale".

4. Note and adjust the following settings (**Figure 9-2.2**):
   a. *Select your plotter*, in this case, one that is capable of printing a 24″x36″ sheet.
   b. Make sure your *Plot Style Table* is selected, **Stine-Full.ctb** in this example (per Appendix A).
   c. Check the box next to "Display plot styles".

      FYI: *This setting will make the on-screen display look more like the plotted version of your drawing. (You can also click the LWT toggle on the status bar to see the lineweights on-screen as well.)*

   d. Check the box next to "Scale Lineweights:"

      FYI: *If the drawing is printed half-scale, for example, the lineweights are adjusted.*

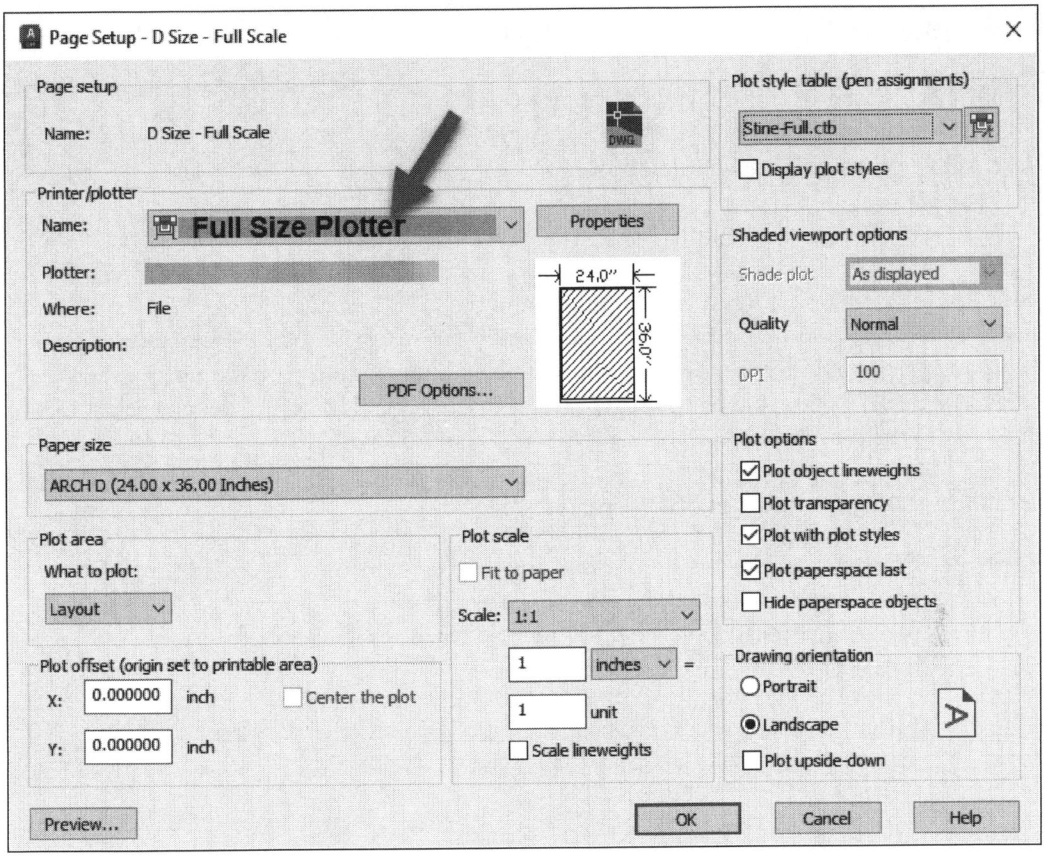

FIGURE 9-2.2 Page Setup; "D Size – Full Scale" modifications to be made

e. Note these settings as well; they should be set already as they are the default (Figure 9-2.2).

  i. The paper size is set to **24"x36"**.

  FYI: *This setting controls the size of paper you see on the screen in each Layout View.*

  ii. The *Plot Area* is set to **Layout.**

    1. *Layout* = *the paper size selected*
    2. *Extents* = *all lines selected to print*
    3. *Display* = *only lines displayed on screen*
    4. *Window* = *user selected area to be plotted*

  iii. The *Plot Scale* is set to **1:1**.

  FYI: *The 1:1 scale means the 24"x36" sheet will print 24"x36".*

  iv. **Plot with plot styles** is checked.

5. Select **OK** to close the *Page Setup* dialog box.

6. Click **Close** to exit the Page Setup Manager.

Next you will explore the *Plot* dialog box.

7. Select **Plot** icon from the *Quick Access Toolbar.*

Notice the similarities between the *Plot* dialog and the *Page Setup* dialog (Figure 9-2.3). You should also notice that the settings previously set in *Page Setup* are NOT the defaults in the *Plot* dialog. Your modifications are not the default settings because you did not set the "D Size – Full Scale" page setup to be current (see Figure 9-2.1). However, you can select this on the fly in the plot dialog.

Additional settings on the Plot dialog box (vs. Page Setup):

- **Plot to File**: Creates a "plot file" that can be copied to disk and brought to a print shop (if you don't have a large format printer or color). You need to call the print shop and ask which printer driver to use because the "plot file" is printer specific.

- **Number of copies**: You can specify the number of prints here.

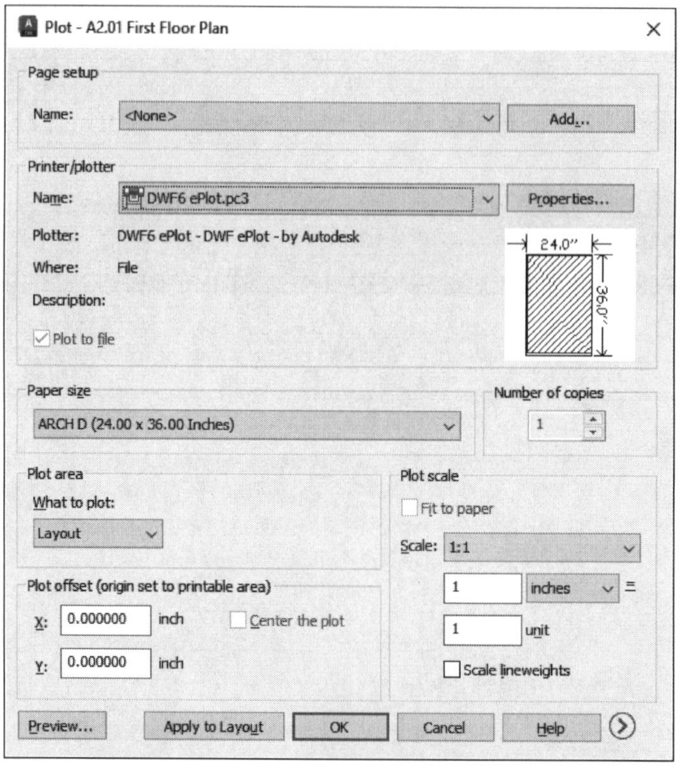

FIGURE 9-2.3 Plot dialog; initial settings; no page setup selected

8. Select **D Size – Full Scale** from the *Page Setup* drop-down list near the top of the dialog (Figure 9-2.3).

Notice how all your settings change to correspond with the selected *Named Page Setup* (Figure 9-2.4 – fully expanded dialog view).

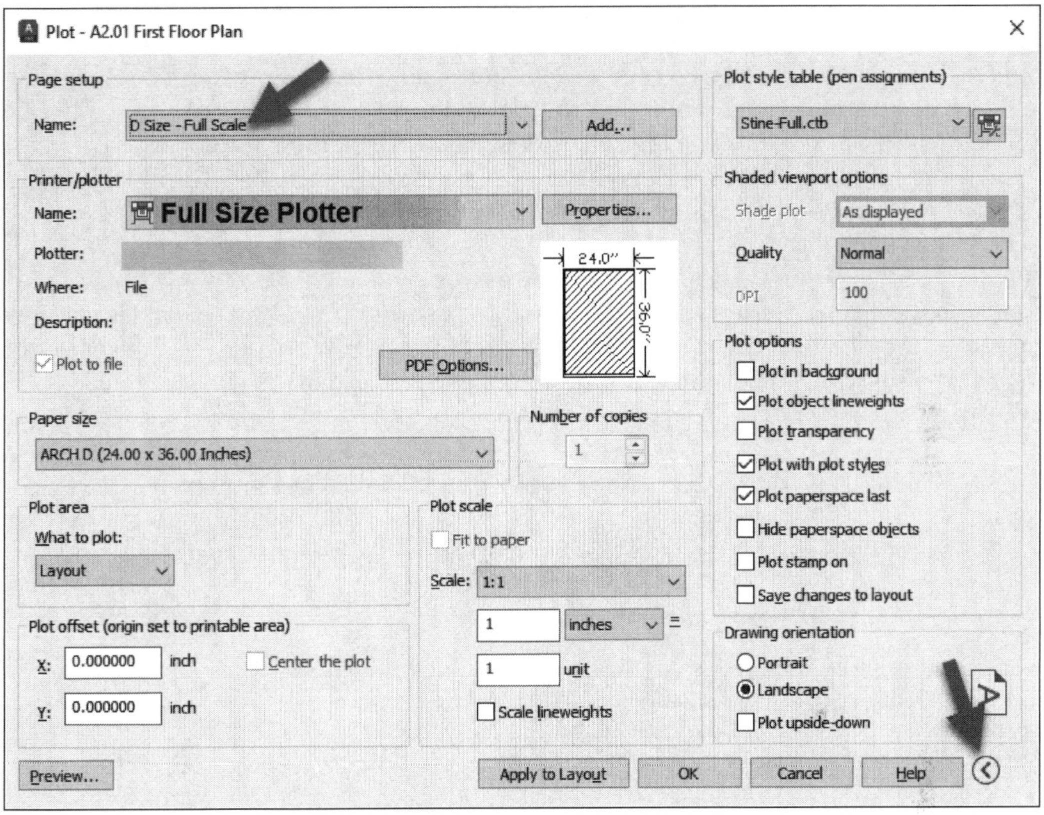

FIGURE 9-2.4 Plot dialog; page setup applied

If you click the arrow pointing to the right (Figure 9-2.3), in the lower right corner, you will see additional plot settings. These settings are less used, so they are hidden so the user is not bothered by too much information (compare Figure 9-2.4).

Next you will print your floor plan sheet. If you do not have access to a large format plotter you can skip ahead to the discussion on how to print sets via the *Sheet Set Manager.*

9. Click **OK** to plot the floor plan drawing (if you have access to a large format plotter).

You should now have a 24″x36″ plotted sheet. You should also be able to see lineweights in your drawing and all the lines are black, not gray.

10. Plot the interior elevations sheets per the previous steps.

Plotting Sets Using the Sheet Set Manager:

The previous steps are useful when printing one or two sheets. However, on large projects with 20-30 sheets it would take a lot of your time to open and plot each sheet. Large commercial projects can have hundreds of sheets.

The *Sheet Set Manager* allows you to print the entire set of drawings at one time. When printing large sets, it can still take quite a while. But anytime the computer can do the work and save the user time is well worth the effort. Also, the plotting occurs in the "background", which means you can still work in AutoCAD during this process.

11. Open your *Sheet Set* via the *Sheet Set Manager.* (See Exercise 7-2 for information on how to do this.)

Similar to the first part of this exercise, the *Sheet Set* has a *Page Setup Manager.* Here you can prepare a *Page Setup* that can be used for all "sheets" in your *Sheet Set*; this is called a *Page Setup Override.* The Override option ensures consistency and eliminates the need to open every drawing if a *Page Setup* change is required.

12. Right-click on the Sheet Set title (Library Project in the book example).

13. Select **Publish → Manage Page Setups…** from the pop-up menu (Figure 9-2.5).

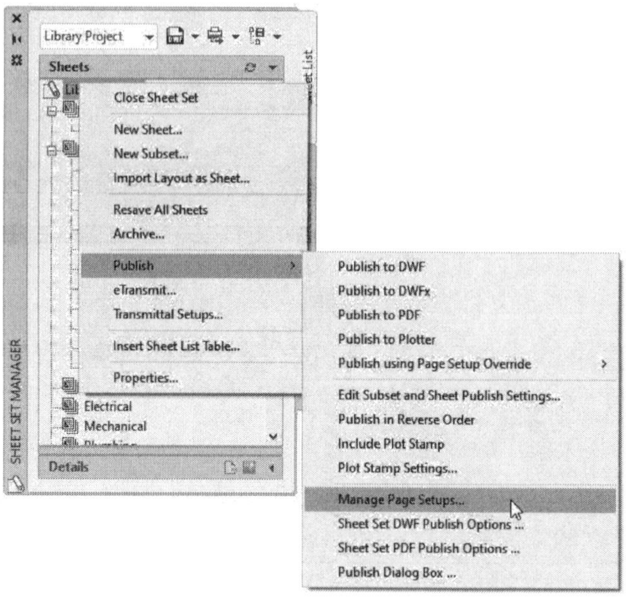

FIGURE 9-2.5 Sheet Set Manager; Select Manage Page Setups…

You are now in the *Page Setup Manager* (Figure 9-2.6). This is almost identical to the one previously discussed (see Figure 9-2.1). The difference is this *Page Setup Manager* applies to the current *Sheet Set* (Library Project) whereas the previous one applied to the *Layout View* (paper space) in that drawing. Notice one reads "current sheet set" and the other "current layout" at the top of the dialog box.

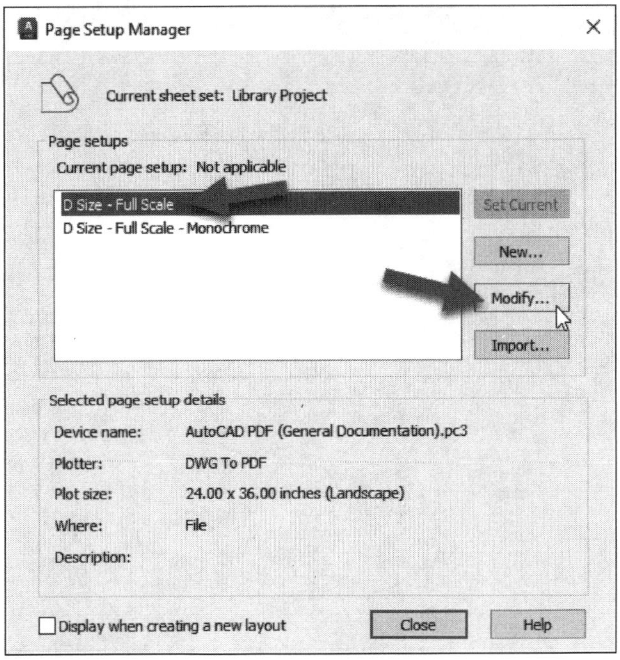

FIGURE 9-2.6
Page Setup Manager; D Size – Full Scale selected

14. Select the *Page Setup* named "**D Size – Full Scale**".
15. Click the **Modify…** button.

You are now able to adjust the settings for the named page setup. Again, this is identical to what you just did a few pages ago (the difference is the icon next to the page setup name).

16. Make the changes shown in **Figure 9-2.7**.
17. Click **OK** and **Close** to save the changes and exit the *Page Setup Manager*.

TIP: Select a plotter you have access to.

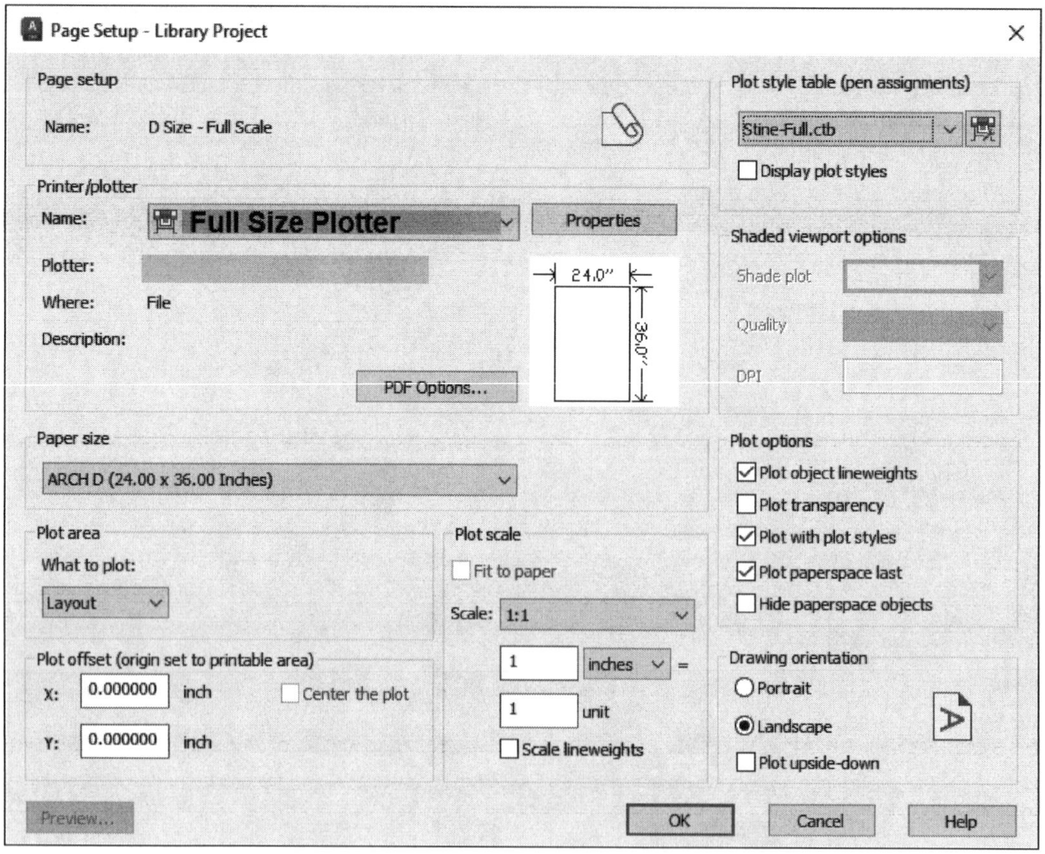

FIGURE 9-2.7 Page Setup; adjust settings for the selected named page setup

Publishing the Sheet Set:

Looking back at Figure 9-2.5, notice two things: under the Publish fly-out menu, you have "Publish to Plotter" and "Publish using Page Setup Override". The former uses the current page setup settings in the "sheet" file, whereas the later uses the specified Page Setup from the sheet set manager. You will try the override option next.

18. Right-click on the sheet set title and select: **Publish → Publish using Page Setup Override** (Figure 9-2.5).

    *FYI: This step will actually print sheets, if you have a plotter. From the Override fly-out, select **D Size – Full Scale**.*

The plotting process now begins in the background. You will notice the Plot and Publish icon on the right side of the status bar. ***FYI:** You can right-click on it to cancel the current print job at any time.*

Drawings should start printing shortly after the process begins!

Publishing a small review set:

The last variation on plotting will be to print out a small, not to scale, review set; this is better on the environment and takes less space on your desk! This time you will create a new page setup for use in the *Page Setup Manager*.

19. From the Sheet Set's *Page Setup Manager* select **New…** (Figure 9-2.6).

20. Enter "**A Size – Scaled to Fit**" for the name and select "*D Size – Full Scale*" from the *Start with* area (Figure 9-2.8).

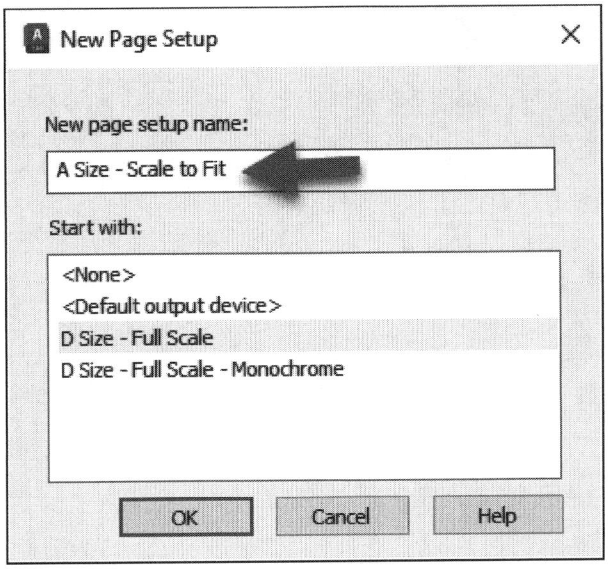

FIGURE 9-2.8 New Page Setup; creating a new page setup

21. Select **OK** to continue.

22. Make the changes shown in **Figure 9-2.9**.

FYI: Notice the "what to plot" is set to Extents; this is a work-around necessary to plot a layout setup for 24x36 onto an 8½ x 11 piece of paper.

TIP: If you have access to a printer that has 11"x17" paper, you can select that paper size; sets are a little larger and easier to read. Also, one nice thing about using 22"x34" sheets (rather than 24"x36") is that 11"x17" sets are half-scale, which is better than scaled to fit.

23. Select **Save** and then **Close** to complete the open dialog boxes.

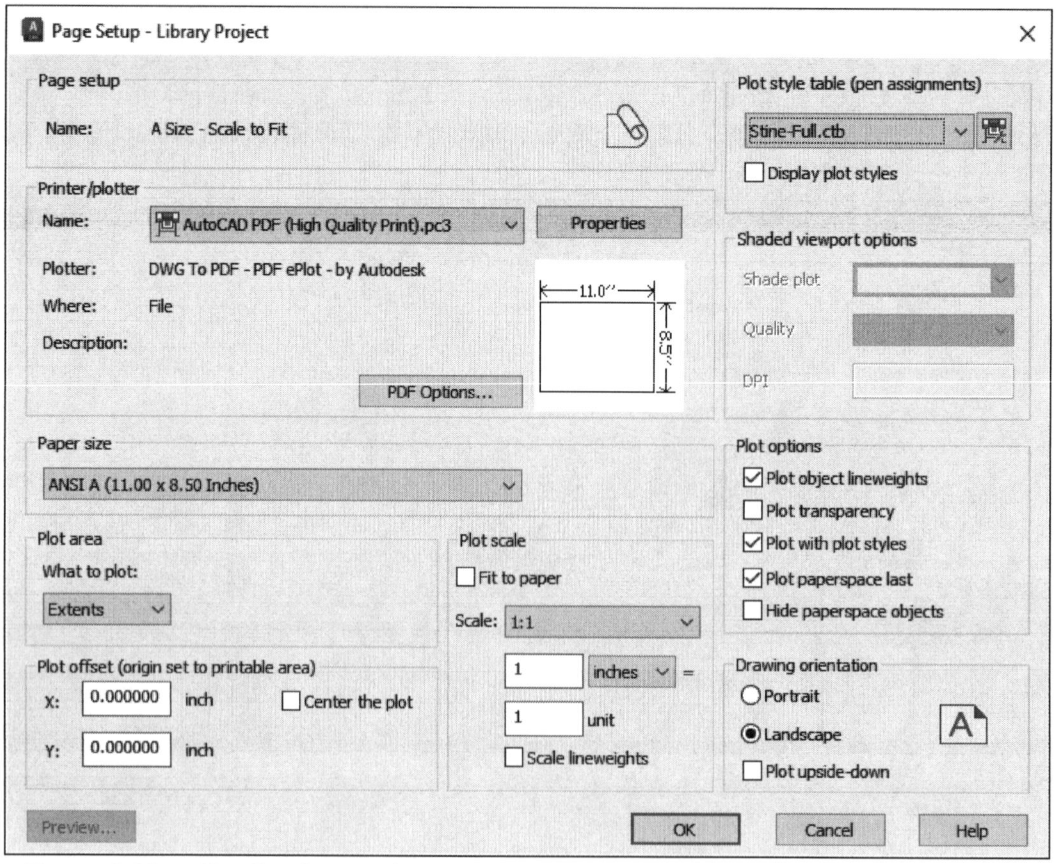

FIGURE 9-2.9 New Page Setup; make changes shown

24. Now, simply *Publish* using a *Page Setup Override* as previously reviewed, selecting the new page setup: "A Size – Scaled to Fit".

Your drawing will begin to print in a moment.

25. **Save** your drawings and close your sheet set.

You have now completed this book!

With the solid foundation you have built using this book you should be able to explore and develop additional commands and techniques on your own. Using the Help system, News Groups and a little "trial and error", you can draw just about anything. **Good luck with your CAD drafting and design endeavors!**

Self-Exam:

The following questions can be used as a way to check your knowledge of this lesson. The answers can be found at the bottom of this page.

1. You can print a full set on 11"x17" paper via the Sheet Set Manager. (T/F)
2. You can specify "number of copies" via Page Setup. (T/F)
3. You access page setups via the page setup manager. (T/F)
4. The DWF view *Autodesk Design Review* is somewhat cost prohibitive. (T/F)
5. The Layout view is real-word scale for the paper. (T/F)

Review Questions:

The following questions may be assigned by your instructor as a way to assess your knowledge of this section. Your instructor has the answers to the review questions.

1. The callout bubbles are placed in the "Model View" Drawings. (T/F)
2. Plot setting "Display" only prints what is on the screen. (T/F)
3. The lines in the Sheet Index in a multi-sheet DWF file are ________________ so you can "jump" to the referenced drawing.
4. You specify which Plot Style Table to use in the Page Setup dialog. (T/F)
5. In a Layout view's Page Setup, the plot scale should be set to __________.
6. What controls the application of lineweights? ______________________
7. You can plot an entire set of drawings from a multi-sheet DWF file. (T/F)
8. You can organize "sheets" in subsets within the sheet set manager. (T/F)

SELF-EXAM ANSWERS:
1 – T, **2** – F, **3** – T, **4** – F, **5** – T

Notes:

Appendix A
Office CAD Standards

This appendix offers a brief description about "Office CAD Standards" and then defines the standards that are to be used throughout this book. This aspect of the book is intended to expose the student to the real-world scenario of adapting to a particular standard as a new hire in a design firm. As a new-hire you would be expected to follow the firm standards and not deviate from them to "save time" or because you know a "better way".

The "Standards" Concept:

The main reasons standards are implemented are to save **time** and **money**. When members of a firm work in a consistent manner (e.g., layers, filenames, file folders, etc.), the result is increased productivity.

Many design firms have adopted the U.S. National CAD Standard (NCS) (www.nationalcadstandard.org). The NCS is a comprehensive standard, which can be purchased from the site listed above. Due to the cost, the NCS documentation is typically something a firm or university would buy rather than an individual. Many firms will make slight adjustments to this standard to meet their specific needs.

The client may have standards which the design team may be required to follow. Many large institutions implement CAD standards to streamline electronic document storage and reuse (including facilities management). This author has worked on projects for universities, technical colleges, U.S. Military and on collaborative projects with other design firms, all of which require the use of their specific standard. This requirement is often spelled out in the contract, which makes it legally biding on the design team. Some design firms will work on a project using their own standards and then run a custom program that will convert their files over to the client's standards, thus not losing efficiency in document production (this requires a high-level CAD tech/manager to implement).

Design firms often automate many aspects of their standards to make them easier to comply with; for example, clicking on an icon that automatically loads all the floor plan layers or references in the title block (because the title block always has the same name and is stored in the same relative location within each project folder). Drawing template files are also used to this end. The architectural programs produced by Autodesk, such as AutoCAD Architecture (ACA) and Revit Architecture, have many of the standards integrated into the program; for example, ACA always draws its "smart" walls on the proper layer: A-Wall.

Reference A-1:
Layer & Lineweight Standards

Layer Name Format:

The layer naming format used by most design firms is similar to the layer standards outlined in this appendix. The format is as follows:

x-xxxx-xxxx-xx *example*: A-Glaz-Sill-Ex

The first position represents the **Discipline Designator**, second is the **Major Group**, third is the **Minor group** and finally a **Status** indicator; the Minor group and Status indicator being optional.

Here is a breakdown of the example above:

A	Architectural
Glaz	Glazing (i.e., glass)
Sill	Window sill
Ex	Existing

Other examples:

S	Structural
Anno	Annotation
Text	Notes
DM	Demolition

Thus, all the *existing window sills* (or lines representing the wall below the opening) are drawn on this layer. The "other examples", A-Anno-Text-Dm, would contain all the demolition notes on a structural engineer's drawing.

As mentioned, the *Minor* group and *Status* indicator are optional. For example, you may have a layer simply named **A-Door**. This is the layer all the new doors go on (new is assumed in the absence of the status indicator). However, in addition to the A-Door layer you may also have additional door information that requires separate layers, for example: **A-Door-Ex** (an existing door); **A-Door-Iden** (door number tag).

The majority of companies include all architecture and interior design under the **A**rchitecture *Discipline Designator*, even though **I** is a reserved designator for interiors.

A company will have Template files which have the standard layers created and ready to go; this helps with naming consistency and format. You can create a template file (if you know how), add the standard layers to your existing template file or simply create each layer as you need it.

Most of the layer names in the "office standard" below are self-explanatory. Some of the abbreviations take some time to get used to (for the major and minor groups, four characters are required – no more and no less!). To help make the intent clear a description has been provided with each layer name.

Floor Plan Layers:

The following layers are to be used as the "office standard" for the project in this book. The layering scheme is very important in an architectural floor plan as they are referenced by several different disciplines.

Architecturally, the base plans are used in several ways: floor plans, ceiling plans, enlarged detail plans (toilet rooms, stair shafts, etc), furniture plans and floor finish plans.

The Mechanical and Electrical engineers will typically reference the architectural base plan into their sheets and draw the Piping, HVAC and Electrical components on top of the referenced base plan. Any changes made to the architectural base plan will then automatically propagate to all sheets (when properly set up).

The base plan layers can be controlled separately in each sheet. The ceiling plans will have layers like the doors, dimensions and wall tags turned off. On the other hand, the HVAC drawings would have the door layers on and adjust the layer color (which controls lineweight) of all the architectural layers, making them lighter and allowing their items to read better.

This brief description should make it easy to understand why floor plan layers need to be managed carefully. Each item needs to go on the proper layer, and all linetypes and colors need to be controlled "by layer" and not changed manually (via Properties or the toolbars), in order to achieve maximum flexibility in visibility control.

Layer Name	Layer Description	Line Type	Color
A-Anno-Dims	Dimensions	Continuous	4
A-Anno-Legn	Legend	Continuous	2
A-Anno-Revs	Revison text	Continuous	4
A-Anno-Symb	Symbols - Bldg section tags	Continuous	2
A-Anno-Text	Misc text	Continuous	4
A-Area-Bdry	Area Calculations (Pline)	Continuous	6
A-Area-Iden	Room tags (i.e., room name and number)	Continuous	4
A-Case	Casework - base cabinets	Continuous	1
A-Case-Abov	Casework - upper cabinets	HIDDEN2	1
A-CLNG	Soffit lines	Continuous	2
A-Clng-Abov	Major ceiling features above (floor plans)	HIDDEN2	1
A-Clng-Elec	Electrical Light Fixtures	Continuous	3
A-Clng-Eqpm	Equipment on the ceiling (projectors/etc)	Continuous	2
A-Clng-Grid	Ceiling Grid	Continuous	1
A-Clng-Mech	Mechanical Diffusers and Sprinkler heads	Continuous	3
A-Clng-Patt	Ceiling Hatch Patterns (poché)	Continuous	8
A-DEMO	Demolition items (Remodel Projects)	HIDDEN2	2
A-DOOR	Man Doors, Garage Doors, Folding Doors	Continuous	1

A-Door-Abov	Doors completely above floor plan cut line	HIDDEN2	1
A-Door-Blow	Doors completely below floor plan cut line	Continuous	8
A-Door-Fram	Door frames	Continuous	2
A-Door-Iden	Door tags (i.e., door number)	Continuous	4
A-EQPM	Equipment (e.g., Ice Maker, Copier, Etc.)	Continuous	7
A-Eqpm-Appl	Appliances (e.g., Stove, Refrig., Dish Washer, etc.)	Continuous	7
A-Eqpm-Fire	Fire extinguishers and Cabinets	Continuous	1
A-Eqpm-Iden	Equipment tags and text	Continuous	4
A-Flor-Accs	Misc accessories (toilet accessories)	Continuous	1
A-Flor-Evtr	Elevator (lines within the shaft – cab/rails)	Continuous	4
A-Flor-Hral	Handrails (for stairs, ramps and guardrails)	Continuous	1
A-Flor-Levl	Changes in levels (ramps, flr drain area slopes)	Continuous	1
A-Flor-Ovhd	Overhead items	HIDDEN2	7
A-Flor-Nplt	No plot layer: clear floor areas, etc.	HIDDEN2	1
A-Flor-Patt	Hatch patterns (poches)	Continuous	8
A-Flor-Strs-Abov	Stairs above floor plan cut line	HIDDEN2	8
A-Flor-Strs-Blow	Stairs below floor plan cut line	HIDDEN2	8
A-Flor-Strs	Stairs (does not include the handrails)	Continuous	1
A-Flor-Tptn	Toilet partitions	Continuous	2
A-FURN	Furniture	Continuous	7
A-Furn-Char	Chairs	Continuous	7
A-Furn-File	File Cabinets	Continuous	1
A-Furn-Free	Free standing furniture	Continuous	7
A-Furn-Iden	Furniture tags and Text	Continuous	4
A-Furn-Pnls	Panels – office systems furniture	Continuous	2
A-Furn-Stor	Storage units	Continuous	7
A-Furn-Wksf	Worksurfaces – office systems furniture	Continuous	2
A-GLAZ	Glazing (i.e., glass)	Continuous	1
A-Glaz-Abov	Glazing above	HIDDEN2	8
A-Glaz-Blow	Glazing below	Continuous	8
A-Glaz-Fram	Window frame	Continuous	2
A-Glaz-Iden	Window tags (i.e., Window Numbers)	Continuous	4
A-Glaz-Sill	Window sill (wall below the window)	Continuous	8
A-GRID	Structural grid lines	CENTER2	2
A-Grid-Iden	Grid bubbles	Continuous	3
A-Mech-Pfix	Mechanical Items (toilets, sinks, floor drains, etc.)	Continuous	1
A-ROOF	Roof overhangs	HIDDEN2	7
A-Roof-Patt	Hatch patterns (poches)	Continuous	8
A-Sign	Signage	Continuous	1
A-Sign-Iden	Signage tags	Continuous	4

A-SITE	Sitework	Continuous	3
A-Site-Misc	Cars, people, etc.	Continuous	5
A-Site-Util	Utilities	Continuous	7
A-Stru-Cols	Structural columns	Continuous	3
A-Wall	Walls	Continuous	4
A-Wall-Abov	Walls completely above floor plan cut line	HIDDEN 2	1
A-Wall-Blow	Walls completely below floor plan cut line	HIDDEN2	1
A-Wall-Cvty	Wall cavity lines (i.e., inner lines)	Continuous	8
A-Wall-Head	Wall opening heads @ doors and windows (for ceiling plans)	Continuous	7
A-Wall-Iden	Wall tags	Continuous	4
A-Wall-Move	Moveable wall partitions	HIDDEN2	250
A-Wall-Patt	Wall hatches patterns (poches)	Continuous	8
A-Wall-Prht	Partial height walls	Continuous	1
A-Wall-Rtng	Wall fire ratings (special lines and text)	Continuous	6

After creating the layers you should fill in the *Description* column, in the *Layer Properties Manager*, for each layer in the list. This will help you to quickly determine which layers things should go on.

In this book you only draw one floor plan so you can create the layers right in the floor plan drawing file. However, in an office setting you would want to do all the layer set up in a template file, thus eliminating excessive drawing set up time.

Below is an example of the Layer Descriptions typed into the *Layer Properties Manager*.

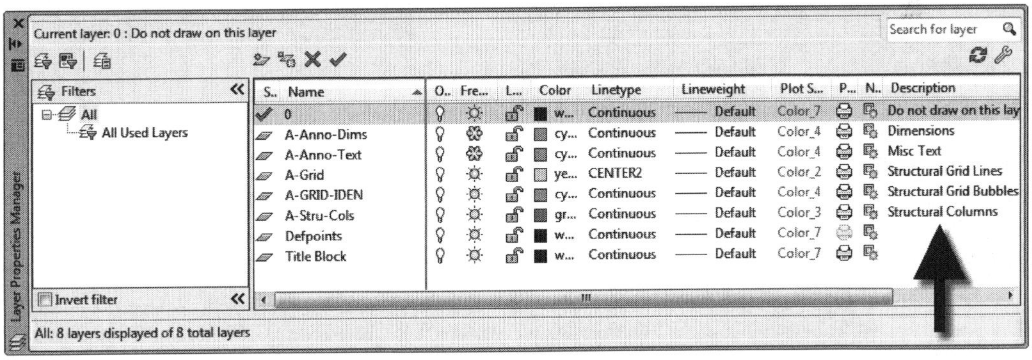

FIGURE A-1.1 Layer descriptions added

> *TIP: The area on the left, in the Layer Properties Manager, allows you to set up filters. You could create a filter that only looked for Layers that ended in DM. Thus, clicking on this saved filter would quickly reduce the list of Layers in the current drawing to just the demolition Layers.*

Non-Plan Layers:

The Non-Plan layers are to be used for all drawings that are NOT plans. A few examples of the type of drawings under consideration are Elevations, Sections, Details, Schedules, Legends, etc.

These layers should not be used in floor plan drawings as the names are too vague and would cause confusion and reduce flexibility.

In Non-Plan drawings, the primary concern is lineweight. It is not usually necessary to draw all the bolts on a "bolt" layer or all the base cabinets on a "cabinets" layer. The main reason this is done in floor plans is to control visibility. With rare exception, the layers in a detail or elevation never need to be turned off. Therefore, the Non-Plan layer names have been formulated to conform to the standard format and describe the line thickness for items on each layer and allow the layers to appear in order (from lightest to thickest).

Layer Name	Layer Definition	Line Type	Color
G-Anno-Text	Text and Notes	Continuous	4
G-Anno-Dims	Dimensions	Continuous	4
G-Anno-Symb	Annotation Symbols	Continuous	4
G-Anno-Legn	Legends	Continuous	4
G-Anno-Mtch	Match Lines	Phantom2	252
G-Xref	External References	Continuous	7
G-Detl-Fine	Extra Fine Linework	Continuous	5
G-Detl-Lite	Light Weight Linework	Continuous	1
G-Detl-Medm	Medium Weight Linework	Continuous	2
G-Detl-Thck	Thick Weight Linework	Continuous	3
G-Detl-XBld	Extra Bold Linework	Continuous	6
G-Detl-Patt	Hatch Patterns	Continuous	8
G-Detl-Shde-Lite	Shades Areas (light)	Continuous	254
G-Detl-Shde-Medm	Shaded Areas (medium)	Continuous	252

When you need a Medium line to be dashed, you change that line's properties; that is, select the line and change the *Linetype* parameter to Hidden 2 (for example). ***FYI:*** *You should never make this type of "By Entity" change in a floor plan drawing.*

<u>Top image</u>: line selected is on Layer G-Detl-Medm and its linetype is ByLayer (i.e., the layer settings control the linetype. <u>Bottom image</u>: line selected is on the same layer but its linetype has been manually set to Hidden2 (layer setting overridden).

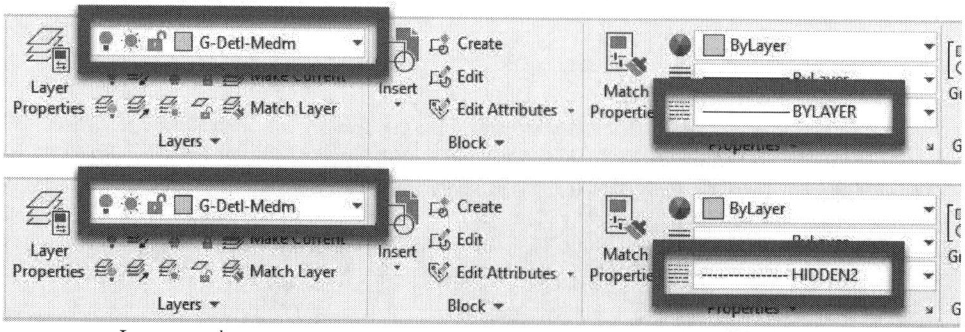

Layers panel *Properties panel*

Lineweight Standards:

The following chart indicates the required lineweight settings for a custom *Plot Style Table.* Color Dependent *Plot Style Tables* (CTB) allow you to associate a lineweight with each of AutoCAD's 255 colors. Once this file has been created, you can select it in the *Page Setup* dialog and the *Plot* dialog. Once the *Plot Style Table* is properly selected it controls how lines are printed, which is ultimately based on entity color. When a line needs to be thicker than the thickest setting in your *Plot Style Table* you would use a *Polyline* and adjust its *Width* using the *Pedit* command; this makes the line have an actual thickness.

Index Color	Full	Half	Quarter
1 (Red)	0.2000 mm	0.1000 mm	0.0500 mm
2 (Yellow)	0.3000 mm	0.1500 mm	0.0750 mm
3 (Green)	0.4000 mm	0.2000 mm	0.1000 mm
4 (Cyan)	0.3000 mm	0.1500 mm	0.0750 mm
5 (Blue)	0.0900 mm	0.0450 mm	0.0225 mm
6 (Magenta)	0.6000 mm	0.3000 mm	0.1500 mm
7 (White/Black)	0.2000 mm	0.1000 mm	0.0500 mm
8	0.0900 mm	0.0450 mm	0.0225 mm
250 (Gray Scale)	0.2500 mm	0.1250 mm	0.0625 mm
251 (Gray Scale)	0.2500 mm	0.1250 mm	0.0625 mm
252 (Gray Scale)	0.2500 mm	0.1250 mm	0.0625 mm
253 (Gray Scale)	0.2500 mm	0.1250 mm	0.0625 mm
254 (Gray Scale)	0.2500 mm	0.1250 mm	0.0625 mm
255 (Gray Scale)	0.2500 mm	0.1250 mm	0.0625 mm

FYI: Color 7 is white on a black background and black on a white background. This color will print black by default – regardless of the background color.

Creating a Plot Style Table:

1. Open a new drawing using the correct template file. (See Exercise 1-4 for the correct template file.)

2. On the *Output* tab, click **Page Setup Manage** from the *Plot* panel.

3. Click the **Modify…** button.

4. From the *Plot Style Table* drop-down list, select **New…** (Figure A-1.2).

TIP: If you only see tables that end with .STB you started your drawing with the wrong template.

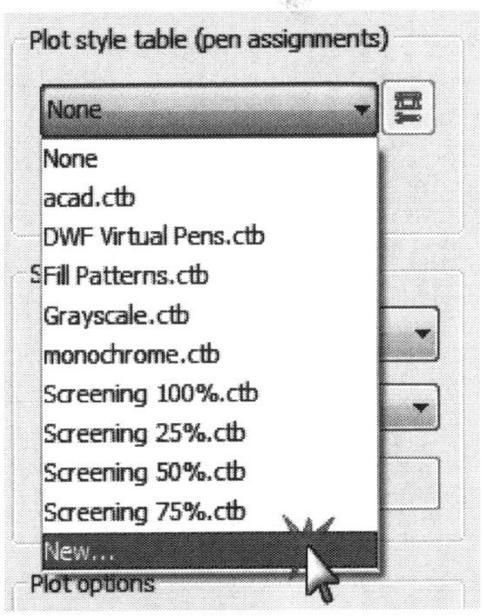

FIGURE A-1.2
Page Setup; creating a new Plot Style Table

You are now in the *Add Color-Dependent Plot Style Table* Wizard, which will walk you through the steps and information necessary to create a *Plot Style Table.*

5. Select **Start from scratch** and then click **Next >**.

6. Type ***your last name*-FULL** (e.g., Stine-FULL) for the *Plot Style Table* file name and then click **Next >**.

7. Accept the default settings and click **Finish**.

Your new *Plot Style Table* is now selected as current in *Page Setup*. Next you will modify your new table so that certain AutoCAD colors equal a particular lineweight.

8. Click the *Edit Plot Style Table* icon. 

9. Click on the **Form View** tab.

10. Click **Edit Lineweights…** Do not make any changes; **OK**.

11. Modify each of the first eight *Plot Styles* (i.e., Color 1 thru Color 8) so the *Color Property* is set to **Black**.

12. Assign the first eight colors a lineweight (see the table on the previous page, looking at the *Full* column).

13. Assign each of the last six colors (250-255) the lineweight **0.25mm**; leave the *Color* property set to **Use Object Color**.

TIP: *When you set a Layer's color to 250-255, the objects on those Layers will print in five shades of gray (depending on which of the five colors are used). This is used for building lines that are very far back in the elevation/or existing. Another use would be for a hatch pattern that represents brick coursing (which are lines that are close together and can be overpowering if not printed with grayscale lines). One more use might be for a solid hatch that might indicate circulation (i.e., hallways) or sidewalks and driveways.*

14. Click **Save and Close** to apply these changes to your *Plot Style Table* (Figure A-1.3).

15. Click **OK** to close *Page Setup* and then **Close** to exit the *Page Setup Manager*.

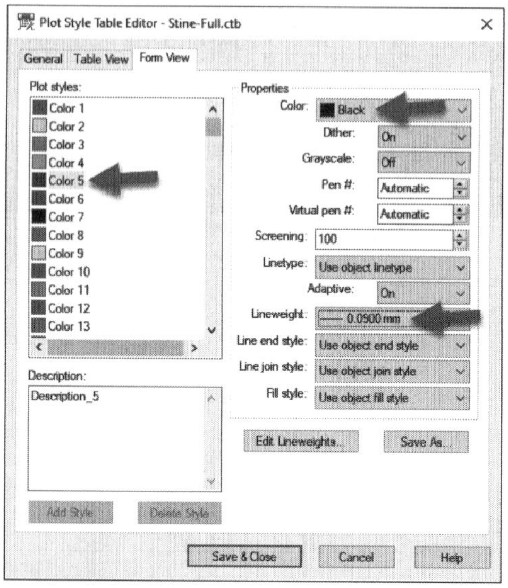

FIGURE A-1.3
Plot Style Table Editor; Color 5 selected

> ***FYI:** Now, in any drawing file, when your Plot Style Table is selected in Page Setup, any entity that is Color 5 (Blue) will print as a fairly light line (0.09 mm).*

Once you adopt a standard, and use it for a while, you will instinctively know what color equals what lineweight.

The following chart can be used as a reference to help you remember which color is the heaviest line and which color is the lighter grayscale, for example. This chart has not been calibrated with the printers so be informed that the lines in the chart are not indicating the actually lineweight; it is meant to a relative indicator.

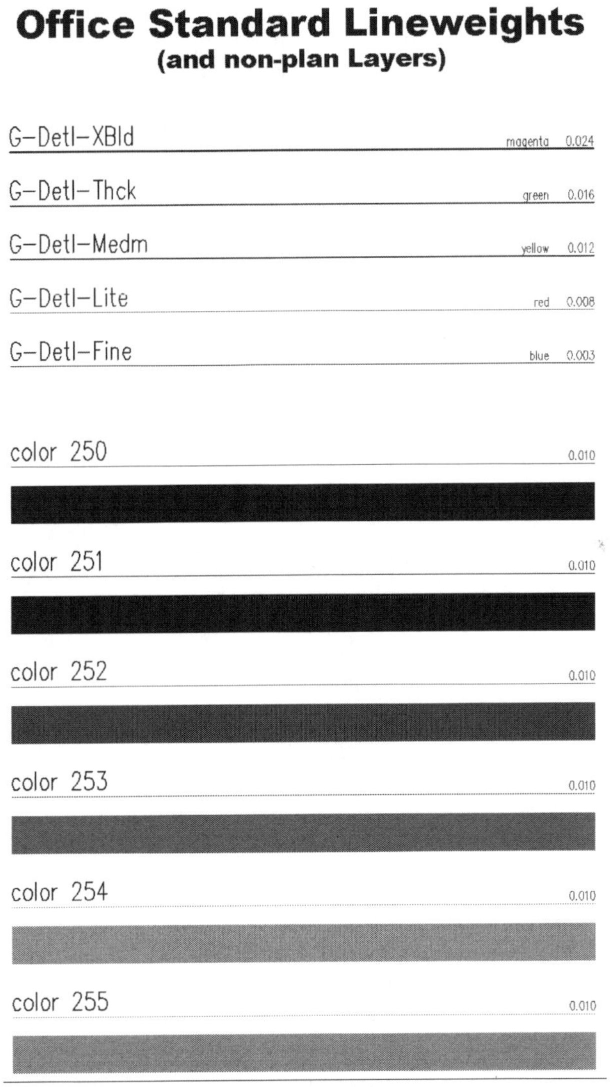

Reference A-2: Text and Dimensions

Dimensions:

A floor plan has all the major elements dimensioned on them. It is not desirable to leave the location of these major components to be scaled off the blueprints; in fact, with most commercial projects, the contract prohibits the contractor from scaling the drawings. (They are instructed to request the information from the Architect/Designer.)

The following describes how to set up the dimension style in your drawing. Once again, applying these settings to a template file would save much time.

1. Create the Layer **A-ANNO-DIMS** (Color 4) and set it *Current.*

2. On the **Annotate** tab, click the **Dimension Style** link (see image to right).

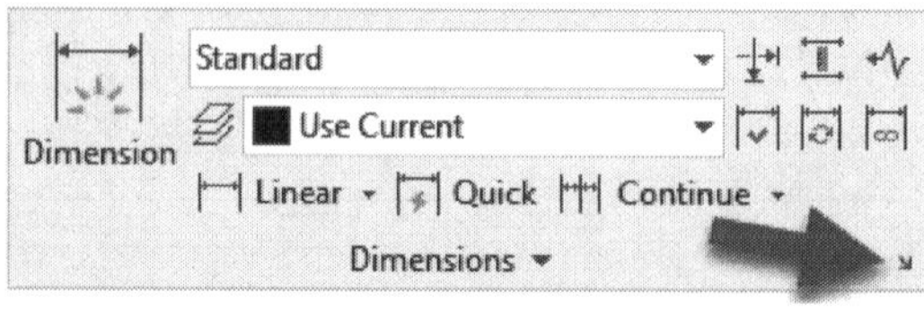

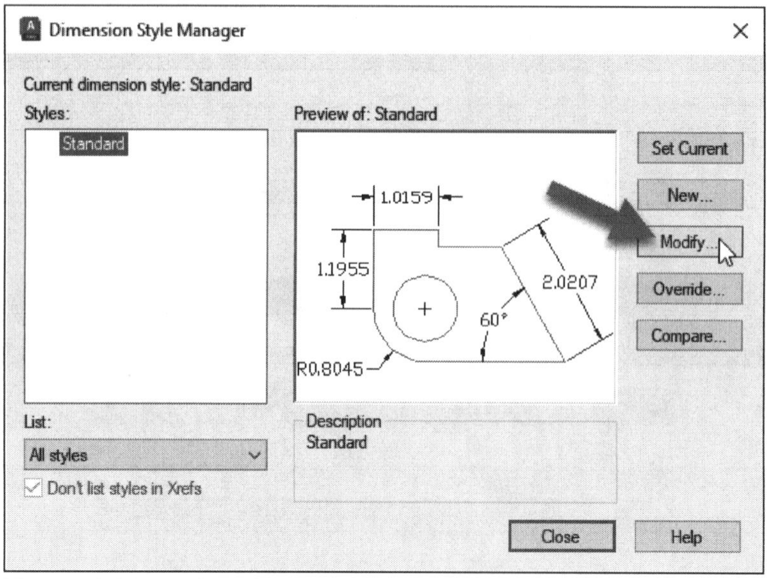

FIGURE A-2.1 Dimension Style Manager; Standard style selected

3. Click the style **Standard** (on left), and then click **Modify...**

You are now in the dialog box that allows you to control how the dimensions look when you draw them. You will adjust a few of these settings (Figure A-2.2).

4. Make the changes identified with a star (★) in Figures A-2.2, A-2.3, A-2.4, A-2.5, and A-2.6.

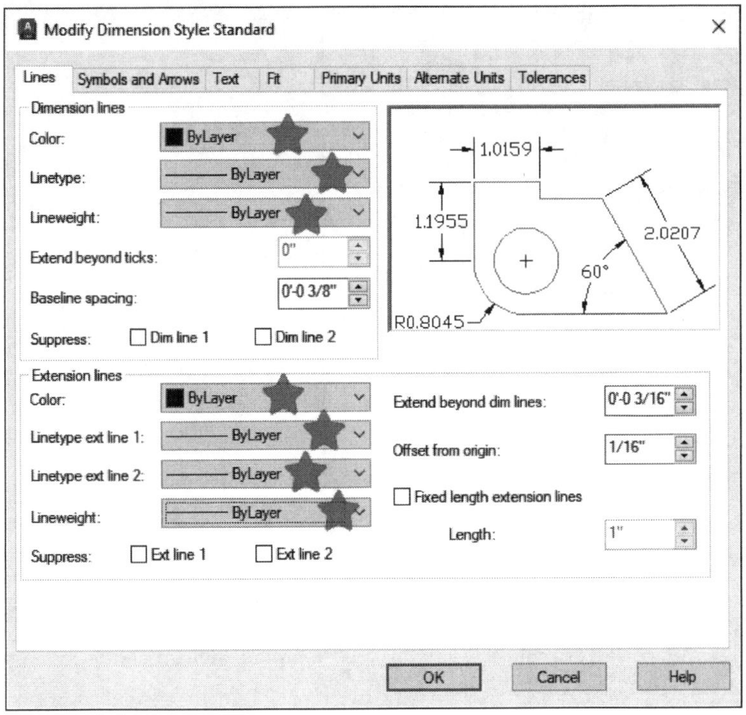

FIGURE A-2.2
Modify Dimension Style; *Lines* tab

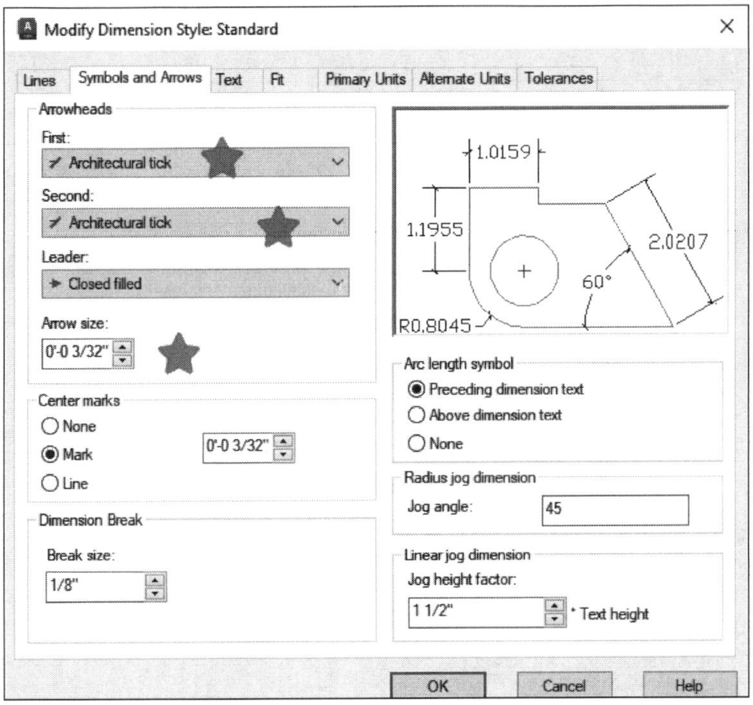

FIGURE A-2.3
Modify Dimension Style; *Symbols and Arrows* tab

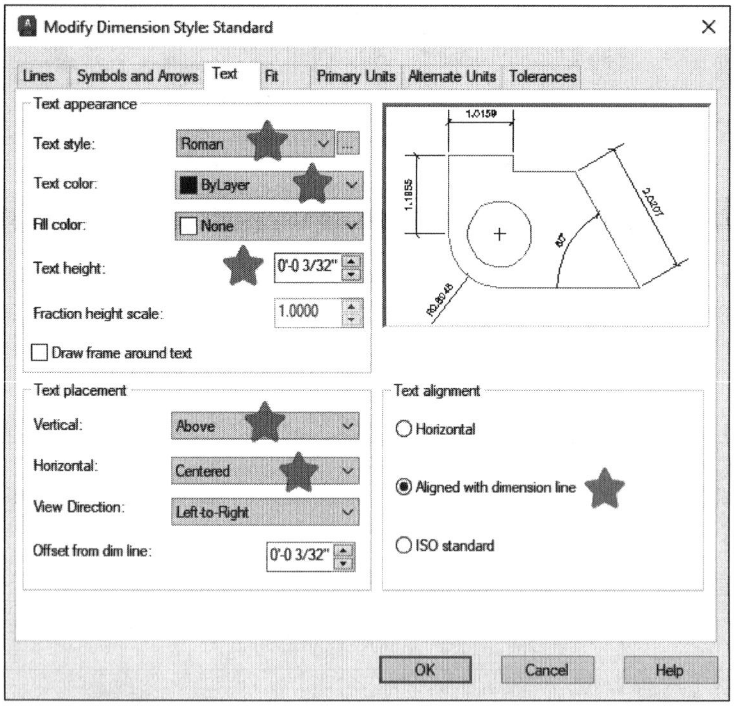

FIGURE A-2.4
Modify Dimension Style;
Text tab

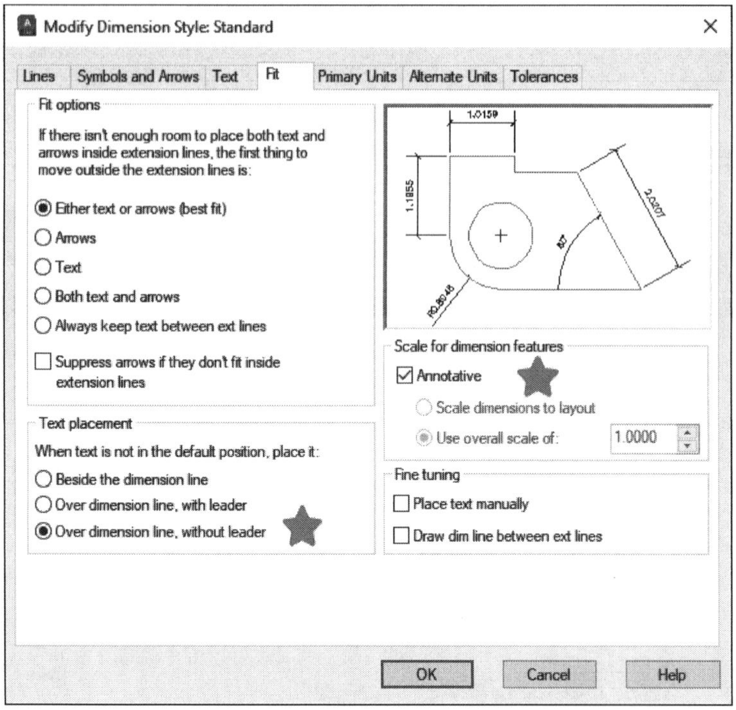

FIGURE A-2.5
Modify Dimension Style;
Fit tab

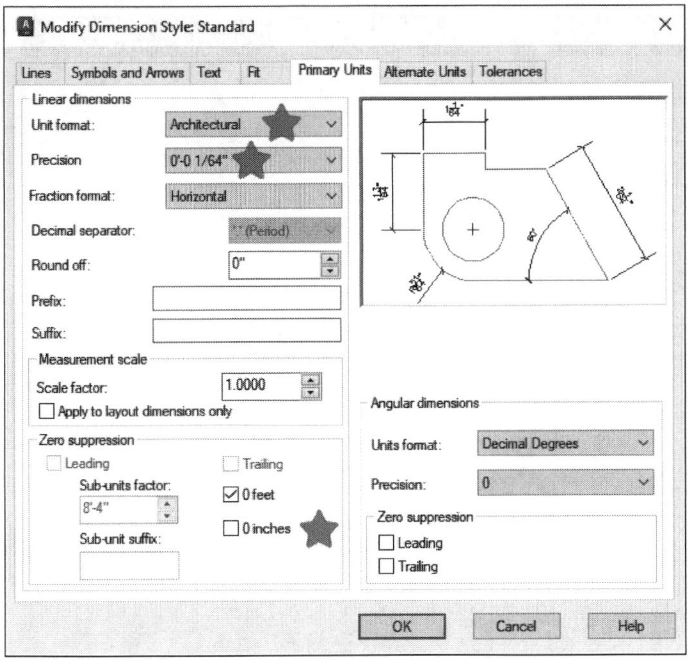

FIGURE A-2.6
Modify Dimension Style; *Primary Units* tab

5. Click the **OK** button.

6. Click **Close** to exit the *Dimension Style Manager.*

Many of the changes you just made are self-explanatory by the description and the preview images which change as you adjust the settings.

Additional information about annotative scaling can be found in Lesson 2 as it relates to both text and dimensions.

The table on the next page talks about a DIMSCALE variable; this controls the size of dimensions when NOT using annotative scaling. The information is still useful as the same numeric value is also used to control the size of the dashes in dashed lines – also when not using annotative scaling.

SCALE	DIMSCALE	TEXT		SCALE	DIMSCALE	TEXT
Full	1	3/32"		1″ = 10′-0″	120	11.25"
1/16″ = 1′-0″	192	18"		1″ = 20′-0″	240	22.5"
3/32″ = 1′-0″	128	12"		1″ = 30′-0″	360	33.75"
1/8″ = 1′-0″	96	9"		1″ = 40′-0″	480	45"
3/16″ = 1′-0″	64	6"		1″ = 50′-0″	600	56.25"
1/4″ = 1′-0″	**48**	**4.5"**		1″ = 60′-0″	720	67.5"
3/8″ = 1′-0″	32	3"		1″ = 100′-0″	1200	112.5"
1/2″ = 1′-0″	24	2.25"				
3/4″ = 1′-0″	16	1.5"				
1″ = 1′-0″	12	1.125"				
1 ½″ = 1′-0″	8	.75"				
3″ = 1′-0″	4	.375"				

FIGURE A-2.7 DIMscale, LTscale and Text Height settings

The *DIMSCALE* variable multiplies many of the settings in your dimension style by 48. Thus, for the text and arrows, 48 x 3/32″ = 4.5″.

Linetype Scale:

To make dashed lines look correct in your drawing do the following:

- Set LTSCALE = 1
- Set MSLTSCALE = 1
- Set PSLTSCALE = 1
- Set the **Annotation Scale** to the indented plot scale

Text:

This applies to annotation as well. All your notes typed with Mtext should be 4.5″ high (for a ¼″ print out). The chart above also lists the standard text height for each scale.

Use the **Style** command to create the following text styles. Note that the height is set to zero, which allows for various heights. Also, the *Width Factor* set to 0.8 makes the text tighter horizontally, thus taking up less space.

Standard Text: *Style*: Roman *Height* 0.0″ *Width* Factor 0.8 *Font*: Romans.shx Height of Standard text when plotted should be 3/32″.
Bold Text: *Style*: Bold *Height* 0.0″ *Width* Factor 1.0 *Font*: Arial Black Height of Bold text should equal 2 times Standard text height (3/16″).

Reference A-3: Abbreviations

Most companies have a standard abbreviations list. This helps with space, consistency and efficiency, but most importantly it helps to make sure the contractor does not get confused and understands exactly what he is supposed to do. The drawings become legal documents when the contract with the owner is signed, so undocumented abbreviations can lead to liability problems. Do not make new abbreviations; type them out.

A

AB	Absolute
AC	Acoustic
ACBD	Acoustic Board
ACT	Acoustical CeilingTile
ADDM	Addendum
ADJ	Adjacent
ADJ	Adjoining
ADJ	Adjustable
AFF	Above Finished Floor
AHU	Air Handling Unit
ALT	Alternate
ALUM	Aluminum
AP	Access Panel
APPROX	Approximate
ARCH	Architect
AWT	Acoustic Wall Treatment

B

BB	Bulletin Board
BD	Board
BITUM	Bituminous
BLDG	Building
BLK	Block
BLKG	Blocking
BM	Bench Mark, Beam
BMU	Burnished Masonry Unit
BOT	Bottom
BRG	Bearing
BUR	Built-Up Roofing

C

CAB	Cabinet
CB	Catch Basin
CI	Cast Iron
CJ	Control Joint
CT	Ceramic Tile
CEM	Cement
CEMPLAS	Cement Plaster
CHBD	Chalk Board
CG	Corner Guard
CL	Center Line
CLG	Ceiling
CLR	Clear
CMU	Concrete Masonry Unit
CO/COR	Contracting Officer (Rep)
COL	Column
COMP	Composition
CONC	Concrete
CONF	Conference
CONT	Continuous
CONTR	Contractor
CPT	Carpet
CSG	Casing
CUH	Cabinet Unit Heater

D

D	Depth
DBL	Double
DEMO	Demolition
DET	Detail
DF	Drinking Fountain
DIA	Diameter
DIM	Dimension
DISP	Dispenser
DN	Down
DR	Door
DR	Drain
DS	Down Spout
DT	Drain Tile
DW	Dishwasher
DWG	Drawing

E

E	East
EA	Each
EF	Each Face
EFIS	Exterior Finish Insulation System
EJ	Expansion Joint
EL	Elevation
ELEC	Electrical
ELEV	Elevator
ENCL	Enclosure
EQ	Equal
EW	Each Way
EWC	Elec. Water Cooler
EXP	Expansion, Exposed
EXPMATL	Expansion Material
EXT	Exterior
EXIST	Existing

F

FD	Floor Drain
FDTN	Foundation
FE	Fire Extinguisher
FEC	Fire Extinguisher Cabinet
FIN	Finish
FLR	Floor
FP	Fireproofing
FR	Frame
FT	Foot
FTG	Footing
FWC	Fabric Wall Covering

G

GA	Gage
GALV	Galvanized
GB	Grab Bar
GEN	General
GI	Galvanized Iron
GL	Glass
GLU LAM	Glued Laminated Wood
GYP	Gypsum

H

HC	Hollow Core
HD	Hand Dryer
HDBD	Hardboard
HDW	Hardware
HDWD	Hardwood
HNDRL	Handrail
HM	Hollow Metal
HORIZ	Horizontal
HT	Height

I, J, K

ID	Inside Diameter
INSUL	Insulation
INT	Interior
JAN	Janitor
JST	Joist
JT	Joint

L

LAV	Lavatory
LF	Linear Feet (Foot)
LINO	Linoleum
LKR	Locker
LOC	Location, Locate

M

MATL	Material
MAX	Maximum
MECH	Mechanical
MET/MTL	Metal MEZZ Mezzanine
MFR	Manufacturer
MH	Manhole
MK BD	Marker Board
MIN	Minimum, Minute
MIRR	Mirror
MISC	Miscellaneous
MO	Masonry Opening
MR	Moisture Resistant
MTG	Mounting

N

N	North
NA	Not Applicable
NIC	Not In Contract
NTS	Not To Scale
NO	Number

O

OC	On Center
OD	Outside Diameter
OFF	Office
OPNG	Opening
OPP	Opposite
OH	Overhead
ORIG	Original

P

PC	Portland Cement
PBD	Particleboard
PERF	Perforated
PL	Plate
PLAS	Plaster
PLAM	Plastic Laminate
PLYWD	Plywood
PREFIN	Prefinished
PTD	Paper Towel Dispenser
PTH	Paper Towel Holder
PT	Paint

Q

QT	Quarry Tile

R

R	Riser, Radius, Range
RAD	Radiator
RB	Resilient Base
RD	Roof Drain
REC	Recessed
REF	Refrigerator
REINF	Reinforce
REQD	Required
RESIL	Resilient
RM	Room
RO	Rough Opening
RS	Rough Sawn
RTF	Rubber Tile Flooring

S

S	South
SAT	Suspended Acoustical Tile
SC	Solid Core
SCHED	Schedule
SECT	Section
SD	Soap Dispenser
SGD	Sliding Glass Door
SGT	Structural Glazed Tile
SHTHG	Sheathing
SIM	Similar
SND	Sanitary Napkin Dispenser
SPEC	Specification
SQ FT	Square Foot
SS	Stainless Steel
STL	Steel
STOR	Storage
STRUCT	Structural
SUSP	Suspended
SV	Sheet Vinyl

T

T	Tread, Toilet
TB	Towel Bar
TD	Towel Dispenser
TEL	Telephone
TEMP	Tempered
TER	Terrazo
TKBD	Tack Board
T&G	Tongue and Groove
TPD	Toilet Paper Dispenser
TYP	Typical

U

UNEX	Unexcavated
UNFIN	Unfinished
UNO	Unless Noted Otherwise
UR	Urinal

V

VB	Vinyl Base
VCT	Vinyl Composition Tile
VERT	Vertical
VIF	Verify In Field
VWC	Vinyl Wall Covering

W, X, Y, Z

W	West
W/	With
W/O	Without
WC	Water Closet
WD	Wood
WDW	Window
WGL	Wire Glass
WH	Water Heater
WWM	Welded Wire Mesh
WI	Wrought Iron

Notes:

Index

R

S

T

U

W

X

Z